D1131053

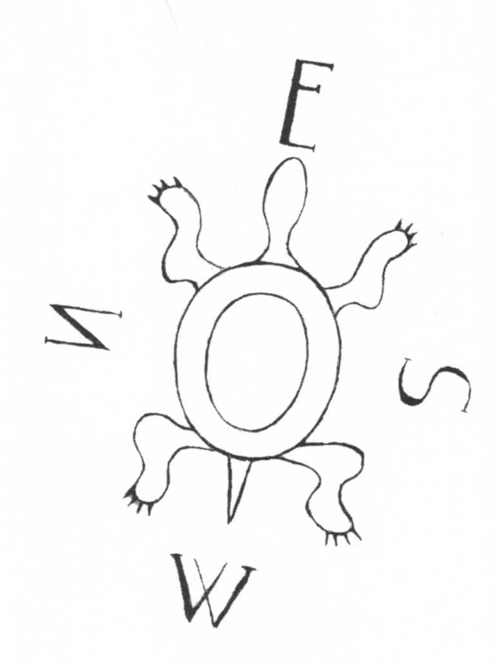
E
S
W
N

WOODSTOCK

HISTORY AND HEARSAY

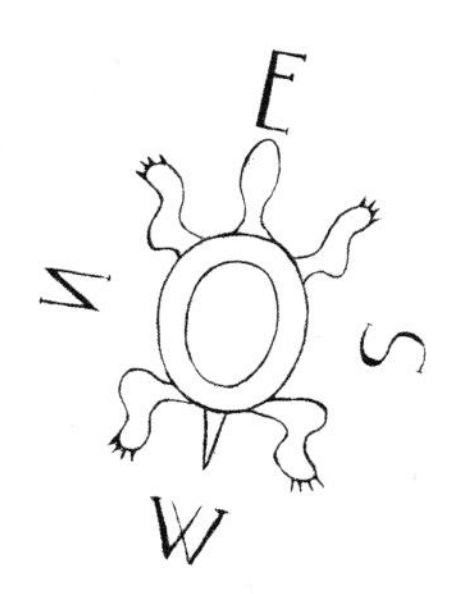

WOODSTOCK
History and Hearsay

Anita M. Smith

WoodstockArts
Woodstock, New York

Books by Anita M. Smith

As True as the Barnacle Tree
It Happened in Woodstock (with the Blelocks)

1st Printing: 1959
2nd Printing: 1970

10 9 8 7 6 5 4 3 2

WoodstockArts
P.O. Box 1342
Woodstock, New York 12498
T: 845-679-8111
F: 845-679-8999
Info@WoodstockArts.com
www.WoodstockArts.com
Telephone orders: 800-431-1579

Cataloging-in-Publication Data
Woodstock : history and hearsay / Anita M. Smith. - 2nd ed.
336 p. : ill. ; 21 cm.
ISBN 0-96792684-X
1. Woodstock (NY) - History. I. Smith, A.M. (Anita M.), 1893-1968.
II. Title.

F129 .W85 S5 2006 974.734
LCCN: 2006923991

Book design by Abigail Sturges

ISBN 13: 978-0-9679268-4-1
ISBN 10: 0-9679268-4-X

Printed in the United States of America

END PAGES: *According to a creation story of local Native Americans, their god Manitou sent down from the sky the first woman in the shape of a tortoise. To honor the indigenous peoples, Anita M. Smith etched a tortoise compass into a flagstone on the back terrace of Stonecrop, her home in Woodstock.*

TITLE PAGE: *A line drawing of Overlook Mountain by Anita M. Smith. Overlook was regarded as the home of Manitou, and is considered sacred ground. AMS Collection.*

CONTENTS

LIST OF MAPS

PREFACE

Weston Blelock writes:
Anita M. Smith, painter, herbalist and writer, was a direct and formative influence in our lives. In 1954 Nelle Jones Blelock, an aspiring writer married to William W. Blelock Jr., should have been content. Her husband's company had recently built a house for the couple and their two small children (my sister, Julia, and me) according to her design. But she heard voices and had visions. In a recurring dream she saw herself meeting a wise woman who lived in a house made of books. At Nelle's urging, the family left Bedford, Quebec, and made their way back to the United States. In the fall of 1956 Bill Blelock accepted an offer from Rotron Inc. to join the company as one of its early employees.

A year later Nelle was introduced (by Sally Carlson, daughter-in-law of John F. Carlson) to Anita Smith. Anita was seeking new tenants for Stonecrop, her bluestone house in Woodstock. The Blelock family moved into Stonecrop, and Nelle visited Anita for the first time in her cottage next door—formerly her herb shop, now converted. The living space had built-in shelves, cabinets and tables piled with books. It seemed to Nelle that if she were to move a single volume the house would come tumbling down. Our mother had met the woman in her dream.

Miss Smith was diminutive in height but packed a formidable personality. Her family had been pillars of Quaker society in Philadelphia since the nation's founding. As a result of numerous journeys to Europe she regarded France as a second home and was fluent in French. She had turned her back on Philadelphia in 1912 to pursue her art and seek fulfillment as a painter in the fledgling art colony in Woodstock. Once, in her native city, while waiting in line for a theater engagement, she had become aware of her privileged status when she saw that others were forced to queue on the opposite side of the velvet rope. She resolved to seek out experiences beyond that velvet safety barrier and to devote herself to the deeper meaning of life. One way of doing so was to dedicate herself to her painting, instead of to the traditional role of wife and mother. Consequently Anita never married nor had children.

She braved Woodstock winters—just as the men folk did—in an uninsulated barn with only a woodstove for heat, a kerosene lamp for illumination and a stream as a natural dishwasher. It was a trying yet exciting time. She believed it was necessary for her to learn about the people who lived in the Catskill Mountains before she could successfully paint the landscape. Anita became acquainted with the local residents by helping the women to preserve their summer produce, by participating in quilting bees and by assisting at apple pressings. In turn, the women and then their husbands shared with her their generational stories about the supernatural doings and heroic actions of their ancestors. In this way she rooted her canvases in the local landscape—and began keeping extensive files for this history of Woodstock.

Among Anita's favorite writers were Marcus Aurelius, Virginia Woolf, Rabindranath Tagore and Madame de Sévigné. By the time she moved into her herb cottage in the 1950s, she had in her collection over a thousand cookbooks and her cabinets contained many ancient herbals such as Gerard's *The Herball or General Historie of Plantes* (1633) and

Culpeper's *English Physician and Complete Herbal* (1813). Anita set high standards for herself, and she had a sign posted on her door warning that casual visitors were not welcome before four in the afternoon because she was writing until then and did not wish to be disturbed.

Julia Blelock continues:
To my brother, Weston, and me, Anita Smith was "Nietsie" (an affectionate soubriquet used by her nephews). We first met her as children in 1957. Nietsie proved to be very supportive of our mother's creativity and lent her an old studio so she could write her plays in peace, away from family interference. In turn, our mother became like a daughter to Anita, and assisted her in the final stages of writing the first edition of this book.

Miss Smith did not suffer fools—or children—gladly. I well remember as a five-year-old riding in the back seat of her car, with Anita and our mother chatting in the front. When I interrupted their conversation once too often, Nietsie turned around with eyes narrowed and handed me a rubber band. "What's that for?" I piped. "It's for your mouth," replied Anita. But that same year Nietsie arranged for me to take art and pottery lessons at the Woodstock (Byrdcliffe) Guild, and she was often willing to include Weston and me as dinner guests for her delicious meals of coq au vin or coquilles Saint-Jacques. Our parents chose not to have a television set in our home when we were growing up, so it was a great treat to visit Nietsie in her cottage next door and see the young Clint Eastwood as Rowdy Yates in *Rawhide* or Leonard Bernstein conducting a Young People's Concert. On those happy occasions Kami, her ancient Siamese cat, dozed away on top of the TV set, and Susie, a wire-haired terrier, nuzzled our hands for surreptitious treats.

In the summer of 1964 Nietsie invited our family to join her for the month of August in Céreste, a village in the south of France, where she had rented a villa with two wings joined by a bridge over a narrow street. Every day we set out by car to explore the Roman ruins of Arles and Nîmes, Van Gogh's cell near Saint-Rémy, the castle at Aigue-Mort or the cowboy country of the Camargue. By then Susie had passed away and Anita's canine companion was Mais Oui, a French poodle who joined us on our travels that summer.

A couple of years later Anita went to one of her friends for a letter of recommendation, and this helped me matriculate at Miss Porter's School in the fall of 1967. That winter was a particularly cold one, and Nietsie wasn't well. My father drove over to MPS in late May 1968 to fetch me for a terribly sad occasion. Nietsie had passed away. She was to be buried in the Artists Cemetery in Woodstock.

When our mother passed on in 1999, Weston and I returned to Woodstock—to the house she had inherited from Anita. After much thought and discussion, we resolved to honor Anita and our mother through a program of restoration—including the Stonecrop buildings and gardens and a collection of intellectual property. Further, we determined to embrace and celebrate a mindset and way of living that had been handed down to us from Anita. This was the genesis of our company, WoodstockArts.

One of our first major projects was to develop and publish a second edition of Anita's 1959 classic, *Woodstock History and Hearsay*. It was our aim to gently polish the original but to retain Anita's voice. Weston took on the task of developing a complete set of endnotes, guided by Anita's musings, notebooks and various artifacts. We greatly augmented the original set of eighteen illustrations, always taking care to select images that would be compatible with Anita's own visual palate and sensibilities. We also decided to include in the new edition a number of AMS's own Woodstock canvases from 1920 to 1928. We believe they contribute significantly to a documentation of Woodstock's ambience when viewed in conjunction with the text.

The reader will note that the voice and perspective of this book are those of 1959. Where Anita used words such as Negro or squaw, we have not changed them to terms that would be more conventional or deemed more acceptable today. As a Quaker who revered all of life—including the human, animal, plant and mineral realms—she certainly meant no disrespect. Additionally, the section near the end of the book devoted to Woodstockers in Service has not been researched or updated; it appears as it did in the first edition.

The turtle icon was a powerful symbol for AMS. In the first lines of this book she recounts how the indigenous god Manitou sent down from the sky the first woman in the shape of a tortoise. Much later, the Esopus Indian chief Nanisinos signed important documents with the mark of a turtle. Anita felt so strongly about this animal as a totem that she chiseled a tortoise compass into a flagstone on the terrace of her home in Woodstock. She also included a turtle image on the cover of the first edition of this book. We have continued that tradition in this second edition, adding a copy of Anita's tortoise compass to the end papers, and using it throughout the text.

Weston adds this note:
It is utterly peaceful when a great snowstorm has mantled Overlook and the surrounding countryside in a blanket of white. At a time like this the magic of Woodstock emerges. This can also happen in the throes of spring when the flowers burst out in wave after wave with the rising heat. Anita's paintings and writings capture these moments. She admitted late in life that there was, still, a lot of her Quaker heritage in her makeup. It was as though she threaded her art through the eye of the needle that was her still, small voice.

Her personality was inextricably intertwined with her role as observer and gentle translator of Mother Nature's moods and beauty on canvas and in prose. These moods allow one to drift—as into the sanctuary created by the bend in a stream—and to be at peace. There are great lessons to be learned through a partnership with nature, and we feel that Anita Smith's stories guide us toward a better understanding and appreciation of our wild selves.

Anita's Stonecrop has proven to be our haven, and since 1999 we have been gradually restoring the various buildings and gardens. The soil is now full of earthworms and is once again able to support a rich variety of herbs and flowers. Two years ago we restored an arbor and replanted a pink rose bush on a back terrace. In the same way we have brought to fruition the second edition of this book.

Julia finishes with these words:
We have purposely not updated Anita's story to continue the arc through to the twenty-first century. We feel strongly that the book serves well as a prequel to the Woodstock Festival of 1969, which took place just a year after her death. Many of us today are looking for wise and comforting voices redolent of an earlier time, and we feel that Anita's story resonates in that way. We believe that Woodstock—known internationally because of its art heritage and the 1969 festival—represents a special blend of imagination, creativity and commitment to an alternative way of life.

More than once Nietsie pointed out to Weston and me ancient farms in the south of France with their tier upon tier of cultivation up steep hillsides. Each generation contributed as much as it could. Like the waves of an incoming tide, those who follow carry the efforts of their forebears further up the shore. It is in this spirit that we put the finishing touches on the second edition of Anita Smith's *Woodstock History and Hearsay*.

—Weston Blelock and Julia Blelock
Stonecrop, 2006

ABOVE: *The mark of a turtle by the Esopus Indian Chief Nanisinos can be seen at the center of this detail from a 1707 deed, which was also signed by the early landowner Johannis Hardenbergh.* Courtesy of the New York State Library, Manuscripts and Special Collections.

ABOVE RIGHT: *Anita M. Smith etched a tortoise compass into the bluestone terrace of her home in Woodstock—symbolizing her respect for the Native American spirit and her own great love of nature. A stone rubbing was made of the etching, and the image is used as a motif throughout this book.*

ACKNOWLEDGMENTS

We wish to thank the people of Woodstock and in particular the librarians at the Woodstock Library—notably D. J. Stern and Amy Raff—for their patient help with our innumerable inquiries. The Historical Society of Woodstock was another source of assistance: our thanks to co-presidents Joanne Anthony and Kathy Longyear. Richard Heppner, the town historian, was very helpful, as were Linda Freaney of the Woodstock Artists Association and Carla Smith of the Woodstock Byrdcliffe Guild.

The Kingston Library was a great source of information. L. J. Cormier was particularly helpful. The librarians at Ulster County Community College, the State University of New York at New Paltz, the Catskill Library, the Saugerties Library, the New York State Library and the New York Public Library were unstinting in giving us their time. Thanks go to Karen LaRocca-Fels of the Kent Public Library as well. Deana Preston and Amanda Ciardi at the Kingston Senate House State Historic Site provided background material and documents on the down-rent war.

We would like to thank the former and current Woodstock town clerks, Katherine Anderson and Jacquelyn Earley, for their assistance in locating town records. The town clerk of Shandaken, Laurilyn J. Frasier, was similarly helpful. Florence M. Prehn, the Esopus town historian, and Karlyn Knaust-Elia, the Ulster County historian, also lent their assistance.

Others to whom we are grateful include Robert Eric (Bob) Carlson, Roy Wood Jr. (art dealer and AMS scholar) and Philip Rosenfeld of the Pennsylvania Art Conservatory. Edwin M. Ford, City of Kingston historian, and Frank Warren also deserve mention for their help. We are indebted to Jency Elliot, Barbara and Dinah Carlson, Louise Allen, William Pierpoint, Charles Howland, Emma Baccarellia, Lawrence Todd, Penny Carlson, Ann Braun, Tad Richards and Christopher Evers for graciously granting us image permissions. A great debt of gratitude is owed to our project editor, Jane Broderick, whose steadfast and expert assistance made this second edition possible. We also thank our marvelous book designer, Abigail Sturges.

Finally, we express heartfelt gratitude to our parents, Nelle Jones Blelock and William W. Blelock Jr., for their unwavering support of our vision.

Any errors or omissions in this book are our own. We would like to apologize in advance for any inconsistencies or mistakes in this second edition.

—Weston Blelock and Julia Blelock

ANITA M. SMITH

BIOGRAPHICAL TIMELINE

1893 Anita Miller Smith is born at Wyndlawn, the Smith family estate in Torresdale, Pennsylvania. She is the fifth child of Henry Cavalier Smith and Lucy Pancoast Smith, both descendants of early Quaker settlers.

Her paternal ancestor Giles Knight sailed with William Penn in 1682, settling at final landfall in the Byberry section of Philadelphia. Her mother was a descendant of Richard Ridgway, who arrived in what is now known as Bucks County, Pennsylvania, in 1679.

1904 In an August 11th letter to her son Ridgway, Mrs. Smith writes that she expects to go abroad with her daughters Frederico Lucy (Frieda) and Anita, to educate them well in Europe and to avoid the expense of running a large home.

AMS arriving in Woodstock with her painting paraphernalia. Photo: AMS Collection.

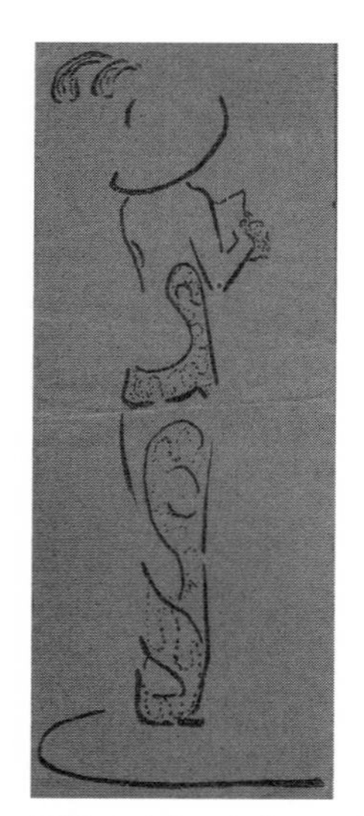

AMS in a beaded suit. This sketch was published in the Philadelphia Evening Bulletin *in 1911.* AMS Collection.

The travelers pass through England and sail to Brittany, where they visit St. Malo, Carnac and Quimper. They also spend a few days at the popular artists' summer retreat at Concarneau, before proceeding to Vevey, in Switzerland, where Frieda and Anita are enrolled in the Villa St. Martine School.

1909 AMS's diary records that she is a student of the Philadelphia artist Benedict Osnis.

1910 In the company of her mother, Anita embarks on a study journey through Europe, Asia Minor and North Africa, visiting museums, galleries and archeological sites to observe classical and contemporary styles of art. In April she enters the Académie Julian under Jean-Paul Laurens in Paris. In June she and her mother proceed to Venice by way of Vevey, Milan and Verona. After arriving in Venice, AMS enrolls in the Atelier Scattola. In September the two depart for Constantinople and arrive via Vienna and Budapest. The following month they journey to Egypt, where AMS attends classes at the Atelier Forcello in Cairo. In November they return to Europe and AMS attends the British Academy of Fine Arts in Rome.

AMS dressed as peasant at a Maverick festival. Photo: AMS Collection.

1911 AMS is introduced as a debutante into Philadelphia's Inner Assembly. She continues to take art instruction from Benedict Osnis.

1912 AMS travels to Woodstock, New York, and joins the village's fledgling artists' colony for an entire summer—with money that had been intended for a ball gown. In the fall she returns to Philadelphia and begins taking lessons and criticism from William Merritt Chase.

1913 She registers with the Art Students League and studies with Frank DuMond and John F. Carlson. Her Rock City contemporaries include Andrew Dasburg, Marion Bullard, Frank Chase, Henry L. McFee and Eugene Speicher.

1916 AMS exhibits *House in the Dunes* and *The Harbor* at the National Academy of Design in New York City.

1917 She exhibits work at the Art Institute of Chicago and at the Maverick in Woodstock.

1918 AMS exhibits *Summer Clouds* at the National Academy of Design and begins exhibiting with the National Association of Women Painters and Sculptors (NAWPS).

1919 AMS is residing in New Hope, Pennsylvania. She exhibits *House in the Dunes* at the Pennsylvania Academy of the Fine Arts in Philadelphia. She also exhibits work with the NAWPS in New York and with the Newport Art Association in Newport, Rhode Island. Other exhibition venues include the Peru Academy in Indiana; Brooks M. S. in Memphis, Tennessee; Hollins College in Virginia; and in Provincetown, Massachusetts (probably at the Provincetown Art Association).

1920 AMS exhibits *New Hope Roofs* at the Art Institute of Chicago, both *New Hope Roofs* and *Dunesville* at the Pennsylvania Academy of the Fine Arts, and *Magee's Farm* at the National Academy. She also exhibits in Northhampton, Massachusetts, at the Peru Academy, and with the NAWPS in New York, the Wilmington Society of Fine Arts in Delaware and the Woodstock Artists Association. *New Hope Roofs* is shown at the Art Gallery of Toronto (later renamed Art Gallery of Ontario) in Canada.

1921 AMS exhibits with the Art Club of Philadelphia, the NAWPS, the New Haven Paint and Clay Club in Connecticut, the Newport Art Association in Rhode Island, the Wilmington Society of Fine Arts and the Woodstock Artists Association, as well as at the Carnegie Institute in Pittsburgh, the Connecticut Academy in Hartford and the Memorial Gallery in Rochester, New York.

1922 She exhibits *Shady Village* at the National Academy. AMS also exhibits at the Connecticut Academy

Anita M. Smith Self-Portrait. Courtesy of Anita M. Smith Estate.

in Hartford, the Hillyer Gallery in Northampton, Massachusetts, the Manchester Institute of Art and Sciences in New Hampshire, the Maryland Institute in Baltimore and the Philadelphia School of Design, as well as with the NAWPS, the Philadelphia Art Alliance and the Woodstock Artists Association.

1923 *House in the Dunes* is acquired by the Pennsylvania Academy of the Fine Arts as winner of the Lambert Prize. AMS's fellow honorees are Paulette Van Roekens and Lilian Westcott Hale.

1924 AMS exhibits with the Newport Art Association and the Woodstock Artists Association and at the Ralston Gallery in New York City.

AMS circa 1925. Photo: AMS Collection.

1925 She exhibits *Shady Barns* at the National Academy and *The Gossips* as part of the Arts Students League Retrospective. Additional paintings are shown by the NAWPS and the Philadelphia Art Alliance.

1926–27 AMS travels to the south of France. She resides and paints landscapes in Arles, Avignon, Cagnes, Les Baux and St. Paul du Var. In 1926 her works are shown by the Louisville Art Association in Kentucky and at Macy's Art Gallery in New York City. She exhibits *Fig Trees* and *Olive Pickers* with the Springfield Art Association in Illinois. She also exhibits with the Artists' Co-op in Ocean City, New Jersey.

1928 She exhibits *Saint Paul du Var* at the J. B. Speed Museum in Louisville.

1929 She exhibits *Saint Paul du Var* with the NAWPS and *Shady Village* with the Philadelphia Art Alliance.

North wing of Stonecrop before the walls were erected. Alice Henderson is seated. Of those standing, Clark Neher is third from right. Photo: AMS Collection.

1930 A family tragedy engages her entire attention. AMS takes over the care of three small nephews.

1931 As a result of her interest in the local people and their lore, AMS compiles and presents the first in a series of papers to the Historical Society of Woodstock. This paper, "Hearsay and History," would later become *Woodstock History and Hearsay*, the first published history of the town.

1934 AMS opens the Stonecrop Gardens and Shop on her property in Woodstock.

1937 She builds a greenhouse at Stonecrop, her home in Woodstock.

1938–39 AMS has more than sixty herbs under cultivation. Her clients include private citizens from all forty-eight states as well as large companies such as H. J. Heinz. She writes and illustrates *As True as the Barnacle*

AMS in her "show-off" herb garden. This block print by Maud and Miska Petersham first appeared in AMS's As True as the Barnacle Tree *(1939).* AMS Collection.

Tree, a book of herbal lore, and has it printed at Woodstock's Maverick Press.

1940 AMS travels over nine thousand miles through Mexico, visiting Aztec and Mayan archeological sites. In addition to working on several landscapes, she collects native herb seedlings and artifacts for her herb shop. On September 1, 1940, the *New York Herald Tribune* publishes an account of her business, dubbing AMS "The Herb Lady of the Catskills."

1942 During the Second World War an observation post is erected on her property and AMS becomes Chief Observer under the U.S. Army Air Force Fighter Command. Medals are awarded to those spotters logging more than two hundred and fifty hours. AMS sets the record, with over twelve hundred hours of faithful service.

In the 1950s AMS converted her herb shop into a living space that she called "the cottage." Here she wrote Woodstock History and Hearsay, *among other works.* Photo: AMS Collection.

Terrace at Stonecrop in front of completed north wing. Photo by Jesse Tarbox Beals. AMS Collection.

1945 At the request of Dr. James T. Shotwell, AMS compiles, for the Town of Woodstock and the Historical Society, the service records of all Woodstockers who fought in the Second World War.

1946–47 AMS lives in postwar France and writes "The Travels of Miss S," a first-person account of the effects of war on her adopted homeland.

1956–59 She researches, writes and publishes the first history of Woodstock, titling it *Woodstock History and Hearsay*. It is favorably reviewed and reaches a wide audience. Its first print run is quickly exhausted.

1961–62 and **1964** AMS journeys to Europe, traveling through France, Switzerland, Italy and Spain. She begins research for a proposed book, *The Landscape of History*.

1967 AMS travels to Turkey to carry out the final research for *The Landscape of History*. Her canvas is breathtaking as she moves from the megaliths at Carnac—and the famous cave paintings of Lascaux in France and Altamira in Spain—to the ancient capitol of the Hittites in Turkey.

During this period she writes a book about her ancestors, titling it *The Quest of Abel Knight: The Quakers and Shakers*. She documents the story of the Knight family in America during the seventeenth, eighteenth and nineteenth centuries, and their search for a utopian community, first as Quakers and then as Shakers.

1968 In May AMS passes away and is buried in the Artists Cemetery in Woodstock.

Nelle, Julia and Weston Blelock summered with AMS in Céreste, France, in 1964. Mais Oui, Miss Smith's poodle, is in the foreground. It is late August and the Blelocks are leaving for Paris. Photo by Anita M. Smith. AMS Collection.

Alf Evers (1905–2004). Courtesy of Historical Society of Woodstock.

INTRODUCTION

There are certain important days in the life of every community—the day the first settler arrives, the day when a church or town hall is completed, when a good highway first links the place to the outside world, when a fine doctor or a dedicated minister comes to town to stay. Perhaps equally important is another day—the one on which a community acquires its own published volume of local history. This book becomes a mirror of the community's little world—a magic mirror that reflects and ties together past and present and supplies inspiration for the future. A local history is as truly an asset of a community as are its bank deposits or its real estate. But while our visible assets merely show what we are worth, a good local history reflects what we are. Now at last Woodstock has such a history.

Why, until now, have all who tried to tell Woodstock's story met with failure? The answer may lie in the unusual character of the place. Even in the eighteenth century Woodstock people were cosmopolitan and polyglot. Dutch, French, Walloon, German, English and a bit of Welsh was the basic mixture. To this were added, in the nineteenth century, a shrewd dash of New England Yankee and a lively jigger of Irish. Geography had placed Woodstock on the route to the back settlements and made her people tavern keepers for hopeful settlers; trappers with beaver skins for John Jacob Astor; land speculators with their bags of papers and their heads full of schemes; drovers with their cattle and turkeys; and teamsters with loads of hay and apples and tubs of sweet Delaware butter. It was geographical chance, too, that endowed Woodstock with her lovely scenery of mountains and valleys, forests, cliffs and streams, which was to attract so many summer boarders as the town shared in the aura of glamour and romance so skillfully woven about the blue Catskills by Washington Irving, Joseph Jefferson and Thomas Cole. Artists, poets and stage people settled down here and there in the mountains singly or in groups—Woodstock could boast of the famous actor Dan Sully and visits from eminent persons in the world of art. Industries had come to Woodstock—glass making, bluestone quarrying and woodworking—and each had brought new people and new ideas. At the same time, in the shady and mysterious hollows that stretch from the town's sunny valleys like long bony fingers, old ways of thinking and doing lingered on and an occasional witch remained in business. This was the Woodstock of 1902—a pleasant community that could hold its head high among its neighbors. Its own Phillip Rick had long ago originated that world-famous aristocrat of apples—the juicy, aromatic Jonathan. Every afternoon thousands and thousands of New York City children played "London Bridge" on sidewalks made of Woodstock bluestone. Woodstock farmers had long before earned a niche in the history of their state by their activity in the down-rent war. The guidebook to the United States of Karl Baedeker of Leipzig gave the view from Overlook Mountain the accolade of a star, and even had a kind word for Aaron Riseley's boardinghouse. It didn't matter much that the bluestone business was slow, or that the hymns of Woodstock's two Lewis Edsons—so popular in my grandfather's time—were being dropped from the hymnbooks. The town still had plenty to feel proud of.

It was to this community that intellectual and idealistic Ralph Radcliffe Whitehead came with an idea born at Oxford's Balliol College and matured through years of thought in France, Italy, Austria and California. Farmers, boarders and quarrymen rubbed their eyes as Whitehead swiftly built Byrdcliffe to show the world that some of the evils resulting from the Industrial Revolution could be banished by men and women making cloth, pottery, furniture and metalwork with their own hands. The colony soon burst out of Byrdcliffe and spilled over much of Woodstock, losing its original social objective and taking on a lustier, sometimes even rowdy, character as it spread. Finally, while the art colony was at its peak of productivity, a different human element was introduced. Workers, technicians, engineers and junior executives in the Hudson Valley's new industries came to live in Woodstock in large numbers. The early log cabins of the town had been followed by well-kept white farmhouses and capacious red barns. Rows of quarrymen's shanties had appeared on the mountainsides. The buildings at Byrdcliffe, which anticipated much of the spirit of modern architecture in their handsome simplicity, had been followed by barns converted to studios and corncribs adapted to the needs of poets and musicians. Housing developments and neat suburban lawns made their entrance.

Is it any wonder that would-be local historians faced with this rich and varied complex of human activity threw up their hands and turned to less difficult tasks? Then, too, most of the early town records had vanished; months of weary pursuing of faint clues among the mountainous record books in the County Clerk's office in Kingston and elsewhere would have to be faced. The same event would differ as related by a pioneer artist, an old quarryman, a retired farmer. Certain hard questions would have to be answered. Was it true, as some said, that the central fact of Woodstock was its art colony and all that had happened before was of little interest? Or was the art colony, as others claimed, but a single brilliant scene in the town's long history?

It is fortunate that when Woodstock's history came into being it was written by one who not only had the courage to overcome all obstacles but loved both the old farming, summer boarding, glass-making town and the newer one of painters, sculptors, musicians, assorted intellectuals, engineers and businessmen. In 1912 Anita Smith came to Woodstock as a talented young painter. In 1931 she presented her first paper to the fledgling Historical Society of Woodstock. This "Hearsay and History" of Shady and Willow was a model of what such a paper should be in its judicious handling of both history based on documentary evidence and folklore collected on the spot. In 1945, at the suggestion of Dr. James T. Shotwell, our Historical Society asked Anita Smith to undertake the task of compiling for publication the war record of Woodstock and those of its men who had served in the armed forces. The result of this assignment forms part of this volume.

The writing of *Woodstock History and Hearsay* was a natural development of Anita Smith's love of Woodstock and her work for the Historical Society. She has collected and presented the facts and lore of early Woodstock with objectivity and painstaking care. Her account of the beginnings and growth of the art colony is no less valuable for having been written by an active participant in events. It is full of color and vitality and fascinating personal reminiscences.

One afternoon when I was visiting Anita Smith in her low-ceilinged living room, filled with old Woodstock furniture and mementos and rich with the fragrance of herbs from her garden hanging on the beams to dry, I saw an interesting photograph. It showed Anita Smith's brother as a baby, sitting on the knee of his great grandfather—who in his youth had known George Washington. I think this can serve as a symbol of Anita Smith's approach to the history of our town. For she recognizes the flow of history through generation after generation, sometimes slow, sometimes tumultuous, but forever moving in a continuous and unending stream.

— Alf Evers
President,
Historical Society of Woodstock, 1959

WOODSTOCK

HISTORY AND HEARSAY

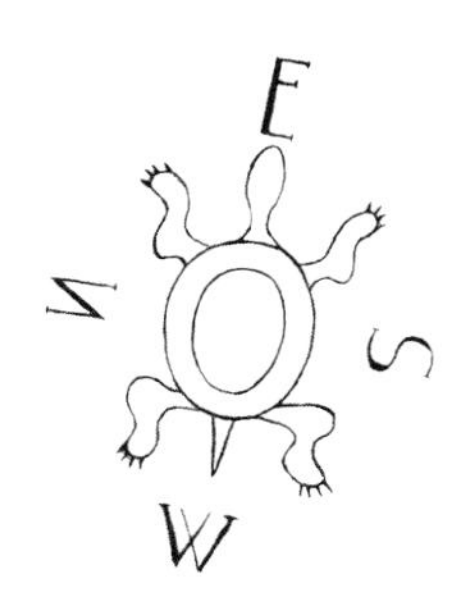

To ye Honble John Nanfan Esqr Lieutenant Governour & Comander in Chief of his Majties Province of New York in America & ye Territories thereunto belonging & to ye Honble Councill of ye said Province

The Humble Petition of Albert Rosa of ye County of Ulster

Sheweth

That there is a parcell of unimproved Land containing about Three Hundred Acres called by ye Indians by ye Name of [illegible] Lying to ye Northwest of Kingstown in Ulster County upon a certain Creek called Sawkill Westerly above a certain Saw Mill of Wm Legg & near ye High Mountains wch Lands are in ye Hands of ye Native Indian Proprietors who are willing to sell to ye Petitioner

Yr Petitioner therefore humbly prays yr Honours Licence to purchase ye said Land of ye Indians in order to ye obtaining a Grant & Confirmation of ye same

And yr Petitioner as in Duty bound shall ever pray &c

[illegible signature]

OPPOSITE: *This work was found in a home in Old Katskill (now known as Leeds), Greene County, and is thought to have been painted circa 1733 by John Heaten. Peak at left is earliest known depiction of Overlook.* Courtesy of Fenimore Art Museum.

Page from land petition of Albert Rosa, March 12, 1701. The Rosa farm is considered to have been the first in what is now known as Woodstock Township. Courtesy of New York State Library, Manuscripts and Special Collections.

Chapter 1

EARLY SETTLEMENT

HISTORY, INDIAN LEGENDS AND SETTLERS' TALES

When the great sea subsided and the Catskill Mountains emerged, the Indian god Manitou sent down from the sky the first woman in the form of a tortoise—and she became the ancestor of the Mohicans, who were part of the Algonquin tribe. The Esopus Indians, so called because they lived along the valley of that stream whose headwaters rise upon Slide Mountain, were a small sub-tribe of the Mohicans. The Mohicans lived behind the ramparts of the Wall of Manitou, which for many miles stands two thousand feet above the valley. If they had not been lured to the banks of the Hudson River they might not have lost their last battle with their traditional enemies, the Mohawks. In 1614 the first map of the Hudson River Valley was made, to be sent to Holland, and on this map the name Esopus is marked. The Indian name for river is *sepu*, and *es* means small. The Dutch referred to this region as the Esopus and to the aborigines of this locality as the Esopus Indians, but it is not known whether the Indians had previously used that name.[1] The Indians called the mountains the Onteoras, which means "mountains of the sky."[2] They also referred to them as the Blue Mountains because the forests of enormous hemlock trees colored the hills, casting shadows along the trails and gloom upon the thickets of balsam and laurel that harbored the wolves, bears and lynx.

This community was called Woodstock as far back as 1778 when Robert R. Livingston Jr. (known as Chancellor Livingston) mentioned it in a letter as an established settlement.[3] It was probably named after the town in Oxfordshire, England. Adolphus Ballard, a historian from Oxfordshire, says the word is Saxon, meaning "a woody place"; another historian says it means "a stockaded settlement in a wood." R. B. Ramsbotham, in a guide to Woodstock, England, says the roots of the name go back to Saxon times; it is derived from *wudu*, meaning wood, and *stoc*, meaning place, and it was originally "a base for the English court when the King was hunting in the nearby Wychwood Forest."[4]

Neil Stevens, in a paper on the geological history of Woodstock, tells of the hard rock substance of the Catskills, which withstood the erosion of the last ice age several thousand years ago. There was a period of uplift but the hard stone neither crumpled nor folded, and when the soft shale was washed away it left the flat tops and terraced sides of bluestone that

Historical Society of Woodstock field trip to an Indian shelter on lower Overlook, 1933. Society members are (l to r): Eno Compton Jr., Winifred Haile, Carl Schleicher, Irwin Arlt, Agnes Schleicher and Frieda Milne. Image at right shows the group from a distance. Photos: AMS Collection.

characterize these mountains. He also said the glacier, which at one time dammed the wide clove below Mead's as well as the Shady gorge, pushed the familiar boulders ahead of it and eventually brought most of the soil to the Woodstock valley.[5]

In 1700 Woodstock was a wilderness inhabited by a few Indians and an occasional trapper, but the settlers were soon to come. Among papers filed in Albany is the record of a man named Albert Rosa who requested a license in 1701 to purchase from the Indians three hundred acres of land that they called Anguagekink (and that we now know as Zena) "Northwest of Kingstown in Ulster County upon a certain Creek called Sawkill Westerly above a certain Saw Mill of Wm Legg & near ye High Mountains."[6] Rosa's farm may have been the first in what is now Woodstock Township. The mill was probably the same one over which, a number of years later, a dispute arose between Johannis Hardenbergh and the Kingston Corporation as to its ownership, because Kingston claimed its Commons extended as far as the mountains. In 1755 Hardenbergh requested a license to purchase from the Indians two hundred and fifty acres on the Sawkill. This was added to that vast tract known as the Hardenbergh Patent. He and several others had bought that land for sixty pounds from an Esopus chief named Nanisinos, who signed the deed with his mark of a turtle. After the provincial government had confirmed the deal it was presented in a petition to Queen Anne, who in 1708 granted the patent in return for an annual quitrent of three pounds payable at or on the Feast of the Annunciation.[7]

Although Hardenbergh and his partners described their claim as a small "tract of Vacant unappropriated Land Scituate in the Countys of Ulster & Albany,"[8] the site was found to encompass a million and a half acres, consisting of large parts of Sullivan, Delaware and Ulster, in addition to a strip of Greene County.[9] Although Robert Livingston (often called Robert of Clermont, and grandfather of Chancellor Livingston)[10] was not among the original petitioners, he owned some thirteen thousand acres of land across the Hudson River known as Clermont. Within a few years he acquired the largest share of the Hardenbergh Patent.

Little is known regarding the Indians who are said to have camped on our Village Green. However, this site was on the route taken by the ambassadors of the Five Nations to extract tribute from the Indian tribes along the river.[11] There is an overhanging shelter above Rock City where broken pottery and arrowheads have been found. This place is not far from my home and one of the thrills of my life was finding an arrowhead under a basil bush in my own backyard. It is a link between the Rock City of the artists and the aborigines. The Dutch did not often venture this far into the wilderness but the pass we now know as Mead's they named the Wyje, or Wide

Clove, to distinguish it from the more precipitous clefts in the Wall of Manitou such as the Kaaterskill and Plattekill cloves. In deeds filed a hundred years later there is mention of the Wide Clove Kill, which runs through Rock City and provides the water for two little falls before it reaches the village. Sometimes this stream becomes a torrent and ravages the countryside along its banks, as if the squaw who the Indians believed controlled the weather from atop the mountains has grown angry watching us destroy the trees and sends the storms to wash us off the hills and valleys.[12]

Some historians have said the first settler was Philip Bonesteel, who established an inn at Woodstock in 1770, but there is reason to believe Bonesteel found other settlers nearby.[13] The earliest date in my files is 1737, although it refers to land a few miles east of the Woodstock line. In that year the trustees of the Kingston Corporation issued a grant to "Jan Wolvin [of] that Land Lying on the Platte Kill where the Indians lived and [he] is to give three Sciple of Wheat Yearly, the first Year Excepted."[14] This spot has been identified as the place where the Plattekill crosses what is now the road between Woodstock and Saugerties. Near the present dwelling is a little cemetery where many members of the Wolven family are buried. In those days it required courage to live that far from other habitations and to be surrounded by Indians.

On the other end of town, a girl named Maria Dorothea Graft was recorded as living in Schindaking (Shandaken)[15] when she married Jan Crispel in 1753.[16] The census of 1790 lists a Jan Crispel as head of a family living in Woodstock.[17] In 1774 John Carl took out a mortgage for land in the southeast half of Great Lot 24 in the Hardenbergh Patent.[18] This was land in what we now call Willow. Twenty-two years later Robert R. Livingston Jr. gave Carl a deed for this property, which was probably held previously on a lease. There are still descendants of the Carl family living in the town today.

The French and Indian wars did not end until 1763 and it has been suggested that the unsettled conditions of that era retarded settlement of the Hardenbergh Patent. There exists today a deed from the Crown made out to one Newkirk for his services in the French and Indian wars, for land along what was later called the Glasco Turnpike in Woodstock.[19] This property came into the possession of a Newkirk descendant named Ricks, who sold it to Mr. Whitehead of Byrdcliffe, reserving the privilege of living on it during his lifetime. Not interested in keeping the house and barn in good repair, old man Ricks allowed them to decay around him, keeping pace with his own disintegration; consequently he was always known to the art students as "Rickety Ricks."

It is reasonable to suppose that Philip Bonesteel would not have opened his tavern at the big bend of the Sawkill a mile east of the present village if he had not expected customers from the neighborhood as well as the few travelers who went on into the mountains.[20] The first road from Kingston went through Awaghkonk (Zena) and over Chestnut Hill, and every wagoner or rider would pass his door.

Bide Snyder, who died in the 1920s, told the story of a peddler who had stopped there on a spring afternoon many years before. The peddler had an old horse-drawn cart full of tinware with extra pails and kettles hanging about to make a clatter to announce his approach to the farmhouses. For a long time they were stilled before the tavern while the peddler refreshed himself with glass after glass of rum. The refreshment state was long since passed and he was thoroughly benumbed with liquor when the stableman pushed him back upon the cart and set the pails to jingling as the nag was started for the village. By now it was dark and they had gone less than half a mile when the decrepit rig became bogged in a bottomless slough. The horse must have floundered about unable to extract himself from the mud, being held by the loaded cart, and the driver was too insensible to direct his

Indigenous tools and flints collected by AMS. Note the stone ax at left. Photo: AMS Collection.

Margaret Beekman Livingston (1725–1800) managed the estate of her son Robert (Chancellor Livingston), collecting the rents from Woodstock farmers. She was the wife of Robert R. "Judge" Livingston and daughter-in-law of Robert of Clermont. The portrait on the left was painted circa 1750, that on the right in 1795. Courtesy of New York State Office of Parks, Recreation and Historic Preservation, Clermont State Historic Site.

efforts. There were no travelers passing that way throughout the night, and by morning the whole rig was gone. The only evidence was a few pieces of tinware that might have been thrown aside when the cart was tipped over. Nothing was ever learned about the peddler, but when the frost comes out of the ground in the early spring, those who have listened by the old mud hole have heard the sound of tinkling pails.[21]

There were few roads in Woodstock that were not boggy in wet weather, yet the settlers traveled them to take up their abodes along the creeks in the valleys, gradually spreading into the even less accessible hollows. One of the early farms was that of Frederick Rowe in Little Shandaken (present-day Lake Hill); he received a deed in 1787 from Margaret Livingston, who for years managed the estate of her son, Chancellor Robert R. Livingston. However, it is known that Rowe lived there before the Revolution and in the deed there is mention of "the road that leads to the Dwelling House of John Carrol" as well as the farms of one Haniger and the leased lands of Hendrick and Thomas Chadewick—proving there were already homes in that area.[22] In addition, there was Isaac Davis, who wrote from that locale to Governor Clinton during the Revolution. Closer to Woodstock village, a number of families arrived whose names would always be associated with Woodstock's history. To name but a few of the householders, there were Peter Short, Peter Miller, Henry Shultis Sr., Jacobus Du Bois and Edward Short—who settled in Yankeetown at an early date. That Woodstock was a growing community is shown in a letter, dated March 1778, from Chancellor Livingston to the Trustees of the Kingston Corporation offering land in the Hardenbergh Patent to those who had lost their homes when the British destroyed that town.[23] He stipulated that the land offered was not to be in Woodstock or Shandaken because those places were already settled.

The houses were far apart and it took a brave spirit to travel after dark, for those were eerie times when certain spots were haunted, if only by goblins who danced in the meadows by lantern light and whom we now designate as glow worms. Folks caught out late in Kingston clutched staves as they hurried home through the great swamp at Mutton Hollow to ward off the wolves that were known to abound thereabouts.[24]

There was a dreaded place on a hill above Bearsville that was said to be haunted because there a Tory hid his treasure, and to ensure its safety buried a live pickaninny with it. The Tory did not return but nobody dared attempt to locate the treasure. One night a rider, returning home late, saw a dog lurking around the spot. He tried to lash the dog with his whip but the thong went right through the strange dog without harming it, and the man raced his horse away from the accursed place. Nothing more was heard of the treasure until modern times when Wilna Hervey and Nan Mason bought the farm on the old Lake Hill road said to have been where the Tory treasure was buried. They had a foundation dug for a new room and the workmen unearthed an ancient snuffbox, a silver spoon and a handmade pair of scissors, but no bones or additional treasure could be found. This house is said to have been the original Lasher homestead, which makes it old in terms of Woodstock's dates. When telling of this find, Wilna Hervey added to the history of the place by saying it was the farm where the mules had been wintered during the life of the Delaware and Hudson Canal.[25]

It is hard for us now to imagine the density of the forests that covered the Catskills before the 1800s. The hemlocks, beeches, chestnuts and oaks were enormous and rose rank upon rank up the ravines, to lesser heights on the ridges. Here the windswept ledges gave scant foothold to the spruce and scrub oaks, which were dwarfed by the sun-baked soil and buffeted by the winds that distorted their natural symmetry until they seemed to stretch their arms to leeward. No wonder the primitive Natives believed an occasional tree was a witch chained to the ledge. When fires made openings in the forest, the pines and birches and soft maples would fill them in with their faster growth. Along the watercourses and beside the innumerable springs grew ferns, violets, lady's slippers, marsh marigolds and dozens of other wildflowers. Under the canopy of trees the laurel and pinxter would bloom, and on the edges of the wood the shadblow and dogwood would flower in turn as the spring advanced. When pastures were opened they were quickly filled with daisies, devil's paintbrush and bluegloss. The woods were full of game for the hunter, and there are still deer, bears and foxes, although the wild turkeys have disappeared[26] and few beavers remain. In 1827 an advertisement by F. C. Vorhees & Co. in the *Ulster Sentinel* offered gloves made of Woodstock beaver.[27]

James MacDaniel, long since dead, told me of the last wild Indians around here. His father saw them, dressed in skins and walking in single file through the woods on the way to Echo Lake.[28] Although the Indians are no longer here, there is Indian blood in several well-known families of the town. One such descendant is a handsome man, swarthy, with gentle eyes and a soft voice and the posture and tread of a man of the woods. He is proud of his ancestry and has inherited those extrasensory feelings for weather and directions that are typical of a free soul. A strain of Indian tradition may account for the many supernatural stories told and retold in our mountains.

There is a legend that when the Indians were on long marches they avoided passing through the Wide Clove because Overlook exerted a drag upon their footsteps. It would be necessary for them to camp for a while before they could muster enough strength to overcome the backward pull and continue their journey. It is not unusual to hear of people coming to Woodstock for a day or a week and being unable to tear themselves away until they have completed what may have been their most creative work—a home.

It takes more than one person or even one generation to produce a climate suitable for original work. It is more than can be defined in any history, and it is greater than the physical aspect of the landscape, though these may be contributory elements. From our valley emanates this creative spirit that may have lain dormant for years—but when the first artists were brought by horse-drawn stages around the turn at West Hurley and faced the Woodstock valley with Overlook Mountain beyond, they breathed deeply and realized this was where they belonged. Here they have sung their poetry, painted their canvases and made great music; they have woven fine fabrics and turned their potters' wheels to form the right bowls for the right uses. It does not matter whether the village is full of hangers-on and charlatans, for their output will wither, and only those works will persist that have substance and beauty.

Detail of advertisements in the Ulster Sentinel, *February 14, 1827. The last item mentions Woodstock beaver.* Courtesy of Kingston Area Library.

Black, white, straw, blue and green bow CORD.
Black and white BRAID.
Black and coloured Nankin and Canton CRAPES.
Super black BOMBAZINE, green and black GAUZE.
Black and green SINCHEW, SARCENET, black and white plain and figured LEVANTINE SILKS.
Black, blue, crimson, brown and green SILK.
TABBY VELVET.
Ladies' kid and beaver GLOVES,
do. black and white French and English GLOVES.
[illegible] white kid GLOVES.
Gentlemen's French, buck, Woodstock beaver and dog skin GLOVES.

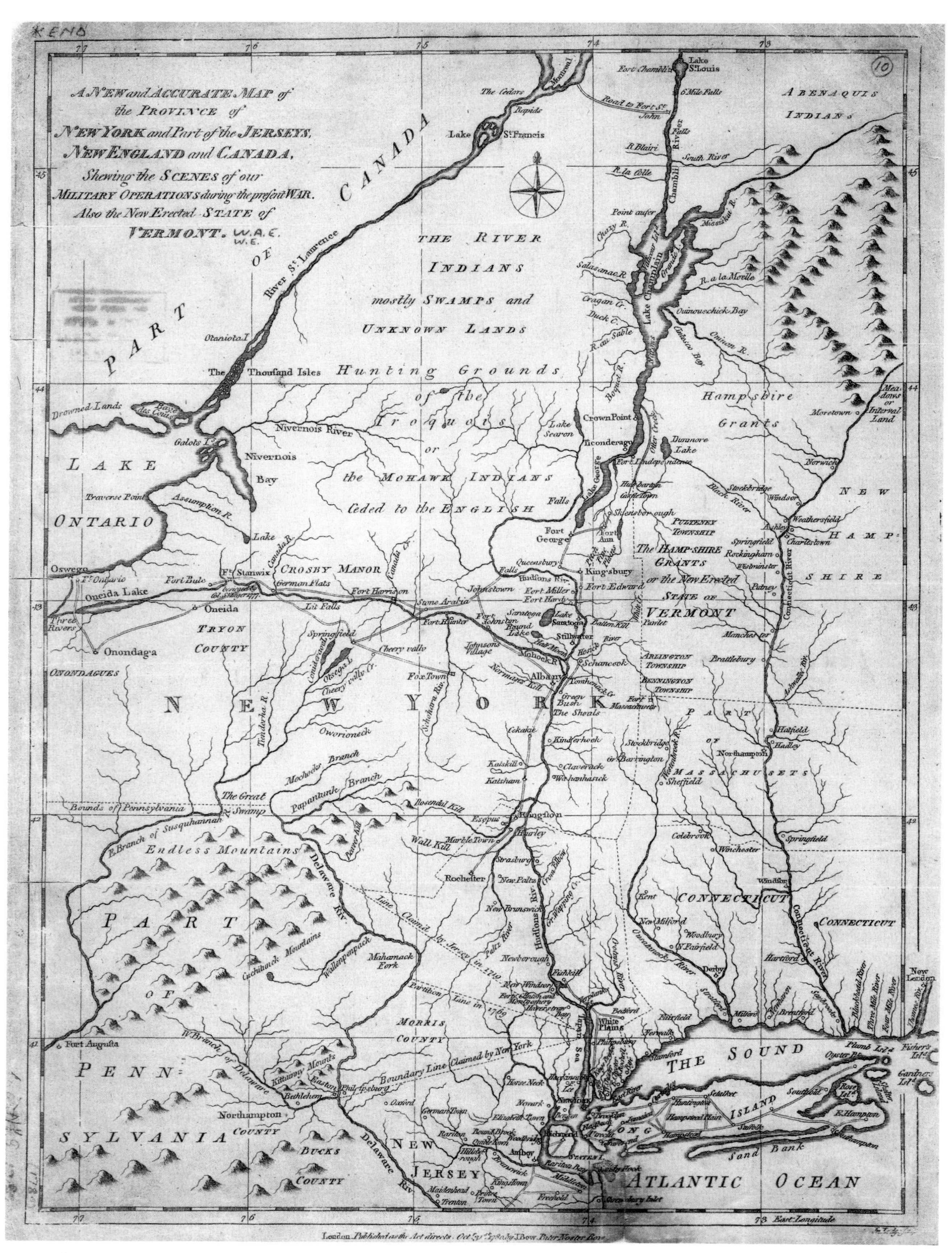

A map of the Province of New York and part of the Jerseys, New England and Canada showing the military battle theater during the Revolutionary war. Drawn by John Lodge in 1780.

Courtesy of The Lionel Pincus and Princess Firyal Map Division, The New York Public Library, Astor, Lenox and Tilden Foundations.

Chapter 2

FRONTIER DAYS

INDIAN FORAYS, REVOLUTION AND LIBERTY

Soon after the battle of Lexington most of the residents of Ulster County signed the Articles of Association to join the Revolutionary cause. It has been stated that there were but one hundred and eighty persons in the county who refused to sign. There is no question that the signers were brave to have themselves registered on the side of the fighters for freedom—when by doing so they might lose all they had, including their lives. But those who would not sign could truthfully call the others rebels. Further, they might well have taken pride in remaining devoted to their king, provided this was not merely an attempt to conserve their own fortunes. Before 1775 the majority of Americans believed it right to be loyal to their Sovereign Lord and King, but a few years later such loyalty was considered traitorous.[1]

Woodstock was divided, although far the greater number fought for liberty. There ensued tragic quarrels among neighbors and even within families. The British sympathizers, or Tories as they were called, were augmented by men fleeing from the river settlements to take refuge in the foothills of the mountains. As the Revolution progressed and the issues were clarified, those who chose the path of freedom were even more convinced of the justice of their cause. The others, being in the minority, became embittered and ended by fighting as guerrillas without standards of decency.

Woodstock represented an important part of the western frontier, and two of the four Ulster County outposts were located here. One of them was at Little Shandaken (now known as the Lake Hill–Willow Valley), the other at Great Shandaken (near Mount Tremper, later separated from Woodstock Township). The post at Willow was probably located on a hill discernible in the upper end of the valley, where it could have commanded the route leading to the four corners (at Mount Tremper). Here, long ago on the Eighmey farm, a British saber was plowed up. The post at Great Shandaken has been definitely located about a mile south of the corners on a low moraine to the north of what is now the Onteora Trail. Here the stones used in the construction and the general outline are visible although the logs have long since decayed. The latter post was the more important because it dominated the main Indian trail from the upper Delaware to the settlements along the Hudson River. Route 28 was laid out along this trail.

So many of the able-bodied men from Ulster County had been recruited for the First Line Army, in particular to serve under General Sullivan, that the forces of the Militia under the command of General George Clinton were seriously depleted. General Clinton was expected to protect the mid-Hudson towns as well as the outlying settlements with only a few troops, but it was impossible to cover all this territory. His forces were engaged down the river and he was unable to come to the help of Kingston before it was burned by the British General Vaughan in October 1777.

The year following was one of terror for the inhabitants of Ulster County. The battle of Oriskany had just been waged, with more than a hundred

Major General John Sullivan (1740–95), who, together with General James Clinton, the governor's brother, helped to end the Indian raids in western New York. Artist unknown. Published in 1776. Courtesy of Emmet Collection, Miriam and Ira D. Wallach Division of Art, Prints and Photographs. The New York Public Library, Astor, Lenox and Tilden Foundations.

Indians killed, and the Indians were eager for revenge. They planned forays to collect the scalps of women, children and even infants in addition to those of the menfolk, and in this work they were encouraged by the British army as well as by Tory sympathizers. Joseph Brant, a Mohawk chief who had been educated among the whites, and the cruel Butlers, both father and son, led the attacks in Ulster County. At the beginning of the hostilities the Esopus Indians declared their friendship for the Americans fighting for liberty, but Brant persuaded them to join the main Iroquois federation, which sided with the British. Farms were burned, their owners scalped, and not a family along the frontier was safe as raid after raid occurred. Meanwhile in Kingston a committee had been empowered to take legal action against "the disaffected [persons] and the Tories." Brought before this body was a member of the well-known Newkerk family of Ulster County. Some members of this family were staunch patriots, just as members of the Rowe family were divided in their allegiance. What is sad, though true, is that these Tories were frequently the most zealous and cruel in their treatment of their former neighbors, whom they called rebels and outlaws.[2]

The following story is hearsay. It was told to me over a quarter of a century ago by a very old man in Mink Hollow. He said he had heard it in his youth from an ancient fellow named Simms of Rock City. During the Revolution the Indians had been instigated by Tories to massacre a whole family near Woodstock. For a while a tiny baby was overlooked until an Indian caught sight of the infant smiling up at him from its crib. He refused to put it to death, but a Tory named Newkerk ran his bayonet through the infant and carried it out upon the tip of the weapon. A couple of years after the war this man returned but his neighbors refused to shake his hand. Then my informant went on with the moral of the tale. For, he said, when it came time for this Newkerk to die he was not allowed to go in peace because the devil threw him from his bed and he had to die alone out in the barnyard! Fortunately we are not told what became of him after he was dead.[3]

It is a matter of record that a Cornelius Newkerk and a William McDarmoth, both of Wagh Konk, now called Zena, were brought before the Committee of Safety and Observation of the Town of Kingston on the 9th day of April 1777, accused of "Treasonable Discourses." The charges against Newkerk resulted from a story told by two informers, James Atwater and Daniel Wilson. On the previous Saturday Atwater and Wilson had met a man named Doud on the Kingston–Woodstock road and led him to think they were king's men in need of a place to hide. Thereupon Doud told them he was of like mind and wished to join the British Regulars.

Further, Doud told them to beware of Philip Miller, Peter Short, Jeremiah Snyder, Tobias Wyncoop and Christian Meyer, for they were staunch Whigs (named after the political party in England and designating those fighting for their freedom in America). He went on to say they could go to John Rowe or Helmer Rowe under the Blue Mountain, or to Zachariah Snyder for he had "carried" Tories one night in February, or they would be safe at Gysbert Vanatte's. The informers thereupon proceeded to the home of Vanatte, who, as expected, admitted he was friendly to the king's forces and gave them the names of several other Tories. They visited some of those homes and when they reached

Cornelius Newkerk he said he and his sons were also for the king and had guns and supplies in readiness to join the Regulars.

When Newkerk and McDarmoth (also implicated by the informers) were caught and brought before the committee for questioning they denied the accusations. They took an oath "to be good and true Subjects of the State of New York," and upon paying fines they were allowed to go. It was late when they left Kingston to return home to Woodstock, and instead of attempting the ford after dark they stopped for the night four miles out of town at Joseph Osterhoudt's on Lake Katrine. After they were in bed they conversed about the day's proceedings and were overheard by a Mrs. Yeomans to tell each other that, although they had taken the oath, they remained true and loyal to the king. The eavesdropper also heard them declare that someone would hang. The next day Newkerk and McDarmoth were rearrested on the woman's testimony and confined to prison.[4]

One of the persons mentioned at the hearing was Frederick Rowe of Shandaken. His name is to be found among those confined the previous year at the Manor of Livingston in Columbia County. He was later ordered to be sent under proper guard to Fort Montgomery in the Hudson Highlands—and there to remain, subject to the pleasure of the committee and not to be discharged until a fine of five pounds had

George Clinton (1739–1812) was the first governor of New York and a general who helped the colonists prevail against the British. Detail of a portrait by Exra Ames. Courtesy of The New-York Historical Society.

BELOW LEFT AND RIGHT: *Clinton's grave in the Old Dutch Church cemetery on Main Street in Kingston, New York.* Photos by Weston Blelock.

The Tragical Death of Miss McCrea *depicts the hazards of frontier life in 1777. This incident occurred near Fort Edward, north of Albany. Engraving by William B. Annin after a work by Robert Smirke.* Courtesy of Emmet Collection, Miriam and Ira D. Wallach Division of Art, Prints and Photographs, The New York Public Library, Astor, Lenox and Tilden Foundations.

been paid and sufficient security established.[5] These conditions must have been met, or perhaps he was released when Fort Montgomery fell to the British army, because Frederick Rowe was next reported three years later with the British army in Canada.

Merritt Staples, who lived until a few years ago on part of this land, now called Lake Hill, told me a story that had become a legend in his family. Before the Revolution, Frederick Rowe had acted as a kind of agent for the Livingstons, who owned about half of Woodstock. To encourage settlement the Livingstons offered land to farmers who had no money, for which they were required to pay a yearly quitrent. The worst feature of these transactions was that they could never become free holdings because the Livingstons (like other proprietors of that time) gave title on what were called "three-life leases." The settlers could put the names of two living heirs upon these leases, besides their own, but when all three of the people designated were dead the land was to revert to the heirs of the proprietor. Rowe had been particularly diligent in collecting these quitrents and he expected to receive payment in land, but to his chagrin it was a three-life lease he was offered. Rowe wrote his name and that of his son, using a large part of the bottom of the sheet. After leaving just enough space for Livingston's signature, he added for the third name that of the devil, who he said would never die. The aristocrat Livingston is alleged to have refused to put his signature above the name of Satan, and gave a regular deed to Frederick Rowe. "That is why," said my friend Staples, "this piece of land has always been owned outright!"[6]

In his history of Kingston, Marius Schoonmaker tells of about twenty Tory deserters who lived in a log cabin in the vicinity of Little Shandaken. They came forth only at night, and when there was snow they wore their boots hind-side-forward to confuse searchers. A slave belonging to the Rowe family was known to have carried supplies for them.[7]

The settlers were as much in fear of the Tories as they were of the Indians. The former might be harbored in the homes of their neighbors, or hidden among the deep hemlocks of the mountains where they could stab like lightning and disappear as quickly, after their forays.

About ten miles from the Hudson River on the eastern face of Overlook Mountain is a cave reputed to have been used by Indians and Tories during the Revolution as a place to cache arms and provisions. For years the location of the cave was forgotten by the good people of the valley, until a hunter named Yawger (probably an ancestor of the Yeager family) and his dog were pursuing a bear along dangerous ledges and rocky slides when the dog suddenly disappeared into a deep hole. It was too precipitous for the hunter to reach his dog or for the animal to climb out. After vain efforts to rescue him, the man was obliged to leave, though he feared the bear would kill his pet before morning. Every day he returned with food, which he lowered in a basket, but he could not hoist the dog to the surface. At the end of a week a friend was persuaded to accompany the hunter, and with ropes and torches they descended and carried the dog to safety. As far as we know, Yawger's cave, although revisited in 1871, has never been thoroughly explored. I asked the much-respected Woodstock blacksmith, Mr. Peper, who had lived near West Saugerties, if he knew about this cave. He had visited it himself many years before but was not sure of the dimensions of the interior chambers. When I inquired about the exact location of the cave, with the intention of exploring it myself, old Mr. Peper looked me over and, with a twinkle in his eye, told me the entrance was very narrow and he didn't believe I could make it!

In 1778 General Clinton ordered the settlers and their families from the outlying districts to be withdrawn to the vicinity of the posts. But before they were assembled Cobleskill was attacked, with nineteen persons killed and the frontier set ablaze. The general issued orders to keep Ulster County patrolled, placing Colonel Cantine in command of the southern section and Colonel Johannis Snyder the northern area—which included Woodstock. Johannis Snyder was a distinguished patriot originally from Saugerties. He was a member of the First Assembly of New York and had already served with the Clinton brothers in the French and Indian wars, and therefore was experienced in frontier warfare.[8] Keeping the peace in this vicinity was difficult because under the Catskills and on up the valley of the Esopus were a number of loyalist families.

Captain Jeremiah Snyder from Blue Mountain was in command of the post at Little Shandaken. He appealed to General Clinton (who was also the governor) for ammunition:

> Little Schondeacon, Octbr. 15, 1778.
>
> Sir, I think proper to let you know that upon my taking the Command at this Place I found that the Company was in a bad posture of Defence in Regard to Ammunition. I, therefore, would be glad you would endeavour to send a fresh Supply as soon as possible, that we may be able to make some Resistance in case the enemy should make an excursion upon this Settlement; but we have at Present no Intelligence of there being near this Place.
>
> The Company now Consists of Forty one Private, besides Serjeants & Corporals, and these I can not Suply with three Cartirages a peice; from this you may Judge what Defence we can make. My Request is, therefore, you will Send a Supply as soon as Possible and you'll oblidge, Sir,
>
> Your Most Hble Serv't
> Jeremiah Snyder, Capt.
>
> To Gov. George Clinton.[9]

That winter while Captain Snyder was leading a patrol under the mountains he and his soldiers were attacked by a band of Indians and Tories, who were warded off after many shots were fired. Evidently the captain had received the needed ammunition.

Colonel Cantine, in command of the post at Great Shandaken, soon made a like request for supplies. There were but twenty-five men and two officers there at that time, but this post was soon to become more important. On May 11th a man named Isaac Davis wrote to General Clinton that a few Indians had been scouting at Shandaken and were now on their way to fetch Brant and his marauders and would come down the banks of the Esopus. He wrote that the information was secret, having been told him by his wife; she was the daughter of Frederick Rowe, the Tory.[10]

This Isaac Davis lived then at Little Shandaken but subsequently bought a large tract in Woodstock village. The governor deemed Davis's letter of such importance that he issued orders that two of the posts be made into forts. He sent the letter on to his brother, General James Clinton, saying he was en route to Kingston, called there by the appearance of one hundred Indians and Tories at Great Shandaken. About twenty-seven loyalists, including Hessians, were piloted through the mountains by local Tories and joined the enemy at Great Shandaken. The Indian and Hessian party evidently found the settlements in this neighborhood too well protected by the outposts to permit a successful attack and therefore veered off toward Wawarsing.

Majors Pawling and Wyncoop were directed to take charge of the erection of the fort at Great Shandaken while Colonel Cantine went to superintend the building of another at "Leghweck" on the upper Rondout Creek. According to this order of General George Clinton:

> Block Houses are immediately to be erected at each of those places inclosed by a Breastwork proof against Musquetry with an Abettis round it. These works are each to be . . . Defensible with one hundred Men, [and] at the same Time capable of containing one hundred & fifty or two hundred [men] . . . The troops stationed at these Posts are constantly to Keep out patrolling Parties and Scouts, those at Shandeken to go as far Northward as the Albany County Line [Palenville], and Westward to Paghkatacken [Arkville] . . . The one fourth of Colo Snyders Regiment is immediately to repair to the Posts at Shandeken . . . These Detachments are to draw Provision from the Commissary.
>
> Signed George Clinton
>
> General Orders of May 12th, 1779[11]

On May 24th Colonel Levi Pawling wrote, "The fort at [Great] Shendeken is done."[12] The fort was then placed under the command of Colonel Johannis Snyder, who retained command of the Ulster frontier defenses until the end of the war. In an application for a pension after the war a Lieutenant Van Hoevenberg, whose company was stationed for eight months at Great Shandaken, describes that place as a "picket-fort, round the dwelling of one Longyear." They went scouring the frontier to the north along the Blue Mountain as far as the south boundary of Albany County and westward to a place called Poghkatocking, a settlement on the east branch of the Delaware River. Nothing befell Van Hoevenberg, but one of his companions, John Rider, was killed and scalped. There is no mention of patrolling to the south, probably because another outpost covered that territory. For an additional term of service in 1781 Van Hoevenberg was ordered to take his "station at a place called Shokan, where we built a picket-fort and log house for our protection."[13] Here their scouting extended to the north. The site of that fort is now covered by the Ashokan Reservoir.[14]

During the summer preparations were made for an expedition under the direction of General Sullivan. He and General James Clinton were moving their armies to a rendezvous at the headwaters of the Delaware and Susquehanna rivers. To augment these forces, Colonel Pawling began a march toward Tioga with six hundred of the Ulster Militia. They encamped for a while beside the fort at Shandaken and then marched westward but were detained by floods and arrived too late to meet up with General Sullivan. They had to return by the route they had come, which brought them back to Shandaken.[15] The little fort must have assumed a truly military aspect with all these troops encamped about it, and no doubt the settlers in Woodstock were temporarily relieved of their fears. When these soldiers had gone, the Indian raids resumed. Probably the bloodiest was led by Brant at Minisink.[16] General Washington wrote General Clinton that he was greatly concerned about these raids. He was determined to put a stop to the massacres in Ulster County, and he committed the task to General Sullivan. This general swung his forces eastward, trying to engage Brant—who, with a hundred and fifty Indians, was marauding and killing at a place called Fantinekill, west of Napanoch. Brant himself escaped by running into the hills, but Sullivan's men subdued most of the hostile Indians, scattering them into small bands. The latter, however, caused plenty of trouble in our district for the next two or three years.[17]

The following August two of Brant's spies named Huff and Cool were captured while scouting along the Esopus Creek. Benjamin Brink in his magazine *Olde Ulster* asserts that Brant may not have been quite as bad as he was depicted; after all, he was faithful to his pledges. Brink quotes the following letter as indicative of the better side of Brant's character. It was sent to Colonel Vroman, who passed it on to Governor Clinton:

> Sir, I understand that my friend Hendrick Huff & Cool is taken Prisoners near at Esopus, I wou'd be glad if you wou'd be so kind as to let those people know that took them, not to use my friends too hard, for if they

PORTFOLIO I

ANITA M. SMITH'S PAINTINGS OF WOODSTOCK, 1920–28

Church Hill, *1921, Shady, New York.*

Woodstock Landscape, *n.d.*

Woodstock Farm, *n.d.*

White Guineas, *n.d.*

Lake Hill Bridge, *n.d., Lake Hill, New York.*

Village Trees, *n.d.*

Herc Davis, *n.d., Lake Hill, New York.*

Willow Post Office, *n.d., Willow, New York.*

will use [them] hard or hurt them, I will certainly pay for it, for we have several Rebels in our hands makes me mention this for it would be disagreeable to me, to hurt any Prisoner; there fore, I hope they will not force me. I am, your Hu'ble S't

Jos. Brant August 11th 1780[18]

Many of the Indians took refuge in the Catskills with their Tory allies. One of their strongholds was located between Roundtop and Highpeak mountains near the Plattekill Clove at a place later designated as Tory Swamp. It was built of stones and logs and the ruins were discernible a hundred and thirty years later when a group of mountain climbers from Twilight Park visited it. Here in the late 1770s and for several years thereafter the enemy foregathered under Brant, who was known to assemble various Indian chiefs for council meetings.[19] In an old Indian history Samuel Gardner Drake states that Brant had—in addition to the fort described above—an encampment west of the Plattekill Clove that overlooked a wide territory and from which he could descend to prey upon local settlers. If one studies a map of the region it is apparent that the best spot from which to see the valley must have been our own Overlook Mountain. Here the highest ridge faces east and south and would have permitted any raiding party to descend either through the Plattekill Clove or by way of the Wide Clove (Mead's) to Woodstock.[20] The word clove comes from the Dutch *kloof*, meaning cleft or split. No doubt it was from one of these strongholds that the raiders came in May of 1780 to snatch Captain Jeremiah Snyder and his son Elias away from their farm at Blue Mountain, to take them on a cruel march to Canada, where the British paid the Indians for the delivery of American prisoners. It was the policy for the Militia to allow as many soldiers as practical to return to their farms to plant and harvest the crops so necessary for the preservation of Washington's army; this accounts for Captain Snyder being found planting a field of grain on that spring day in 1780.

It was rewarding, after many hours of searching through old newspapers in the Kingston Library, to find, in an *Ulster Sentinel* from January 1827, an account of this dramatic incident written while Snyder was still alive, at the age of eighty-nine. The writer (it was unsigned) said he had one of the sons of the old soldier looking over his shoulder to corroborate the facts as they were set down, which makes this the most authentic story anyone is likely to find. The Jeremiah Snyder farm at Blue Mountain close under the Catskills is two or three miles outside our present township line, but since the captain had served Woodstock well during the Revolution, and since the fort he commanded was located in what is now called Willow, his history is most interesting. Also, several of his descendants are living amongst us.

That the Indians and Tories feared young Captain Snyder and had marked him for death or capture is evident from the amount of effort focused on him during the year prior to his being taken prisoner. At one time he was scouting with a group of men along the foot of the mountain when most of his companions ran off in pursuit of wild turkeys. (The sound of turkeys gobbling might have come from the Indians, meant to lure the men into the deep forest.) Snyder and one man were left alone and although they proceeded with caution they were ambushed from a high ledge. They were within deadly range of their assailants' guns, and the enemy probably recognized them since all their shots were concentrated upon the officer. The Tories shouted for him to surrender but he preferred to run, and succeeded in escaping along with his companion.

The next year on that fateful May day while Snyder was peacefully working in his field, the plowhorses suddenly bucked in terror as a band of Indians and Tories leaped from the woods and closed in upon him and two of his sons. Seeing himself entirely surrounded, Snyder surrendered to an Indian chief whom he subsequently learned was the famous John Runnip. It was a rule of the frontier that a prisoner belonged to the one who first laid hands on him or took his scalp; at that moment another brave struck at Snyder's head with his tomahawk. Although he inflicted a wound, Runnip managed to parry the blow and save the captain's life. When the subject of capture had been settled, all proceeded to the house—from which the women and children had managed to flee into the underbrush. The Indians raided the place of all money, took as much meat, clothing and maple sugar as they could carry, and set the house afire. Snyder pleaded with them to leave enough food to keep his family from immediate starvation and this request was granted. The Indians allowed the younger son, Ephraim—who was lame—to go free, and they made no attempt to capture the women and little children. Only Snyder and his eldest son, Elias, were marched off to the Kaaterskill Clove, where they all climbed the steep cleft, pulling themselves up from ledge to ledge until they came to two lakes where they camped for the night. The next day they proceeded to the Schoharie, through which they waded breast high, and by a roundabout route made the journey to Fort Niagara. Snyder told of meeting Frederick Rowe at the Genesee Flats but Rowe would not speak to him. He also related an incident about Runnip, who was taken with fever and ague along the march: the other Indians caught a rattlesnake, which they cut up and boiled, and when Runnip had eaten the flesh and drunk the snake soup he was cured.[21]

At Fort Niagara the prisoners were handed over to Colonel Guy Johnson for the usual reward and then confined in the guardhouse. On the third day a man named Rowe visited them. He was not the Rowe they had met at Genesee but rather a neighbor of the Snyders who had come to inquire about his relatives.[22] They were also visited by Brant, whom Snyder described as being of fierce aspect. Within a week they were removed to a vessel on Lake Ontario and taken to the fortress of La Chine not far from Montreal. Later they were imprisoned at the Bevot, where a sordid existence began. After six prisoners escaped, those who remained were very cruelly treated by a Hessian guard until he learned that the Snyders were of German descent and thereafter favored them. Two years passed before Captain Snyder and his son Elias escaped in boats along with three others, and crossed the St. Lawrence River ten miles below Montreal. They had a perilous journey through the wilderness and almost starved until Elias found the thigh of a moose stripped of flesh; the sinew and the marrow sustained them for two days. Eventually they reached New Hampshire where the inhabitants received them with kindness. When they had been fed and re-outfitted, they proceeded to the Hudson River and thence to their homes.

Within a month the Indians and Tories set upon another Woodstock family. This is the story as told to

The Mohawk Chief Joseph Brant (1742–1807) led many forays throughout Ulster County, keeping the Americans on high alert. Painting by George Romney (1734–1802). Photo © National Gallery of Canada, Ottawa, transfer from the Canadian War Memorials, 1921.

Marker located 2.2 miles east of Woodstock on Route 212, placed by the New York State Education Department in 1935. Photo by Weston Blelock.

me by one of the descendants of Petrus Short. The Short family had settled before the Revolution along the Wittenberg road in the town of Woodstock. Some years before, when there were numerous Indians throughout the Catskills, a half-starved and ill savage came to their door and asked for help. The Indian was fed and allowed to spend the night with the family. He told them his name was Joe Dewitt. (After a century of contact with the white people the Indians frequently assumed their names.) The next day this Indian was given a bottle of whiskey and sent on his way, and soon he disappeared from the mountains. It was several years later on a pleasant June afternoon in 1780 when Petrus Short and Annaatje, his wife, along with their daughter and her husband, Petrus Miller, drove to the Dutch Church at Kaatsban for the baptism of their grandson, another Petrus. Dominie De Ronde performed the ceremony without incident other than that a suspected Tory was seen to leave the church before the service was over. It was believed he went to apprise his friends of the situation, because when the family party was on its way home and had reached Wolven Hill, a short distance from Woodstock along the Saugerties road, they were ambushed by a band of Indians and Tories. The women and children were set free after a terrifying interval in which an Indian took the Sunday hat of one of the men and waved it while he danced and grimaced. Short and Miller were taken prisoner and sent along that torturous trail to Canada, but, though they were mistreated and half-starved, they finally arrived in Quebec to be confined with many other Americans. Short and Miller were both marked with a black streak on their heads, which a friendly Indian explained was a sign they were meant to be killed. To their amazement this Indian asked Short if he came from Woodstock, and then revealed himself to be Joe Dewitt, whom Short had once befriended. It was through the help of this Indian that Short and Miller were able to escape and, after many adventures, return to their families.[23]

The Mohawk chief, Joseph Brant, led many of the raids in Ulster County. His tribesmen were responsible for scalping, the burning of farms and the torturing of prisoners. Yet Brant was known on some occasions to have dissuaded his people from abusing their captured enemies—instead giving them an ox to torment and feast upon, and thus appease their lust. However, he was the dread of the frontier and

Joseph Brant studied under Dr. Eleazar Wheelock at Moor's Indian Charity School in Lebanon, Connecticut, forerunner to Dartmouth College in New Hampshire. Painting by Joseph Steward (1753–1822), The Reverend Eleazar Wheelock (1711–79), 1st President of Dartmouth College (1769–79). *Oil on canvas, 79⅛ x 69⅞ in.* Courtesy of Hood Museum of Art, Dartmouth College, Hanover, New Hampshire; commissioned by the Trustees of Dartmouth College.

women and children shuddered at the mention of his name. The white Tories also were cruel, and other settlers were known, under the provocation of enemy excesses, to have done some scalping themselves. One such recorded incident was committed by a Lieutenant Boyd of Sullivan's army, but the same fate soon befell him. No act of cruelty was proved against Brant personally. Actually, to him,

> the civilized custom of imprisoning men was the worst of cruelty. A man's liberty, he held, was worth more than his life. Of the Indian custom to torture he did not approve, but when a man must die for a crime, he thought it better to give him some chance to make atonement in a courageous and warrior-like death than to execute him after the manner of the whites by the humiliating gallows.[24]

During all the Revolutionary years the ominous threat of Brant and his band hung over our valley. Brant's Indian name was Thayendanegea, but he was no ordinary Indian. He had been educated at Moor's Indian Charity School in Lebanon, Connecticut, under Dr. Wheelock, who afterwards became president of Dartmouth College.[25] He had been sent there through the influence of Sir William Johnson, who was married (Indian fashion) to a beautiful Mohawk girl, Molly Brant, a sister of Joseph.[26] One of Brant's schoolmates was John Harper Jr. of Cherry Valley, and Brant was said to have given warning to his friend before the massacre that took place there. Just before the Revolution, upon hearing that Brant was siding with the British, Dr. Wheelock wrote him a letter using every argument he believed would influence an Indian to favor the colonists. Brant replied that he "very well remembered the happy hours that he had spent under the doctor's roof, and he especially remembered the family prayers, and above all how his schoolmaster used to pray 'that they might be able to live as good subjects, to fear God, and honor the king'."[27]

Twice Brant visited England, where he was lionized and received at court. He has been described as a tall, handsome Indian of light complexion, and although he had a fierce expression he was well mannered and in English clothes looked and acted a gentleman. He associated with men of letters such as James Boswell, the Earl of Warwick and Lord Percy—later Duke of Northumberland—and made friends with other nobles.[28] As a warrior he painted himself and wore feathers and enjoyed dressing in finely beaded moccasins, fringed buckskins and beautiful blue blankets edged with vermilion. With these he had epaulets of silver and a cutlass with a silver handle.[29]

Another story about Brant concerns a baby who was captured. He restored the child to its mother with a note saying, "I do not make war on women and children. I am sorry to say that I have those engaged with me in the service who are more savage than the savages themselves."[30] My final story about Brant is told by the Reverend Rockwell in his book on the Catskills. The Indians captured a Captain McKinstry of Hudson near Montreal during the Revolution. It is said they intended to torture him, whereupon he made Masonic signs to Brant, the leader of the band, who spared his life. Brant had become a Mason during one of his trips to England. After the war Brant visited the McKinstrys at Hudson and they always remained warm friends.[31] Rockwell also relates that Brant later went to see personal friends in New York and Philadelphia and even paid his respects to General Washington.

In 1781 Charles DeWitt, who owned the mills at Greenkill that had supplied Washington's troops at Valley Forge with flour and who was on the Committee of Safety and Observation, wrote to Governor Clinton disclaiming responsibility for those who had gone over to the enemy. He said they did not belong to the town of Hurley, where his jurisdiction ended. Fourteen months later Colonel Johannis Snyder, in a letter to Governor Clinton, wrote that a party of rascals—well known to be the deserters from Woodstock who had carried off Short and Miller, and also the Snyders, to Fort Niagara—had arrived back in Little Shandaken and been entertained by Frederick Rowe, Peter Winnen, Nicholaus Britt and others. Having been informed of their whereabouts, Colonel Snyder ordered part of his regiment under Colonel Pawling to pursue them and run them off.[32]

Later, after the Indian forays had subsided, five of the deserters returned to Little Shandaken expecting to find their parents and friends. But since the latter had moved, the party went on to Ackwachgonk (still another version of the place later known as Zena). Finding Lieutenant Van Deusen's guards there, they proceeded to Arie Van Etten's. As he was gone, they were forced by hunger to apply for victuals to one Hommel who lived in Van Etten's house. Hommel was alone and obliged therefore to give them the food they demanded. They acknowledged to him that they had taken part in the raid at Wawarsing but had deserted the enemy for want of provisions and would, if they could count on being forgiven, surrender. But they were afraid their countrymen would take their lives and were not certain how to proceed. Colonel Snyder ends his letter by saying, "No Doubt but they are here yet, or in Dutchefs [sic] County, concealed by their friends."[33]

It cannot be denied that some of the Rowes were on the side of the British during the Revolution, but they were brave men and, according to their tombstones, three Rowe brothers served in the Civil War. Wilson Rowe died of disease contracted in service, William J. Rowe perished as a prisoner of war at Andersonville and John H. Rowe was killed in battle on the Weldon Railroad. Their graves are in Mount Evergreen Cemetery.[34]

Elias Hasbrouck, Woodstock's first supervisor, held the town's inaugural board meeting in 1790 at his home (the house to the right) on Mink Hollow Road. Contemporary photo courtesy of Paul and Karen Goodman.

At last the Indian raids were over as far as Ulster County was concerned, and peace was restored. It must never be forgotten that a large piece of frontier was protected by the forts at Lackawack (Leghweck) and Great Shandaken, with their outposts at Shokan and Little Shandaken. The inhabitants of Woodstock owed their safety largely to the efforts of Captain Jeremiah Snyder, commanding the Militia forces stationed at Little Shandaken.

In his *History of Ulster County*, Alphonso Clearwater lists the following as Revolutionary officers from Woodstock: Captain Isaac Davis, First Lieutenant Philip Miller and Second Lieutenant John Van Etting. He includes as enlisted men Petrus Short, Henry Short, Peter J. Winne, Benjamin Winne, Christian Lanjaar, Abraham Vosburgh and Cornelius Lamendyck.[35]

The Winne and Lanjarr families lived near "The Corner," now known as Mount Tremper—which of course was then part of Woodstock. My files contain the names of Christian Lanjaar's brothers, John and William, as also being veterans of the Revolution. We question whether Abraham Vosburgh was from here, as the Vosburgh family we know did not arrive in Bristol (now Shady) until a later date.

Although they did not enlist from Woodstock, there were three Revolutionary soldiers who lived the rest of their lives in the town. One was Barent Eighmey, who built himself a log house in the Willow valley and was the ancestor of a prominent family—the last of whom was Ralph Eighmey, for years schoolmaster in Woodstock village. The latter was probably the first person seriously interested in the history of this neighborhood and was very helpful, telling me stories of early times and introducing me to the older inhabitants of Willow. He collected books on Ulster County history, some of which were given to the Woodstock Library.

The second Revolutionary soldier was John Yerry, who came to America while serving with the British army in 1776 but soon left the Red Jackets to join the American forces, with whom he fought for five years. He then journeyed up the Hudson to Rhinebeck, where he farmed for several years before crossing the river and settling in Woodstock on leased land along the Bearsville road. Thence he tried living in Mink Hollow, but eventually established himself at a place on the western flank of Ohayo Mountain, which became known as Yerry Hill. His sons, Henry and Jerry, volunteered for the War of 1812 and several of his grandsons took part in the Civil War.[36] The last Revolutionary soldier to be mentioned was the distinguished Captain Elias Hasbrouck, our first town supervisor, whose story is told in a later chapter.

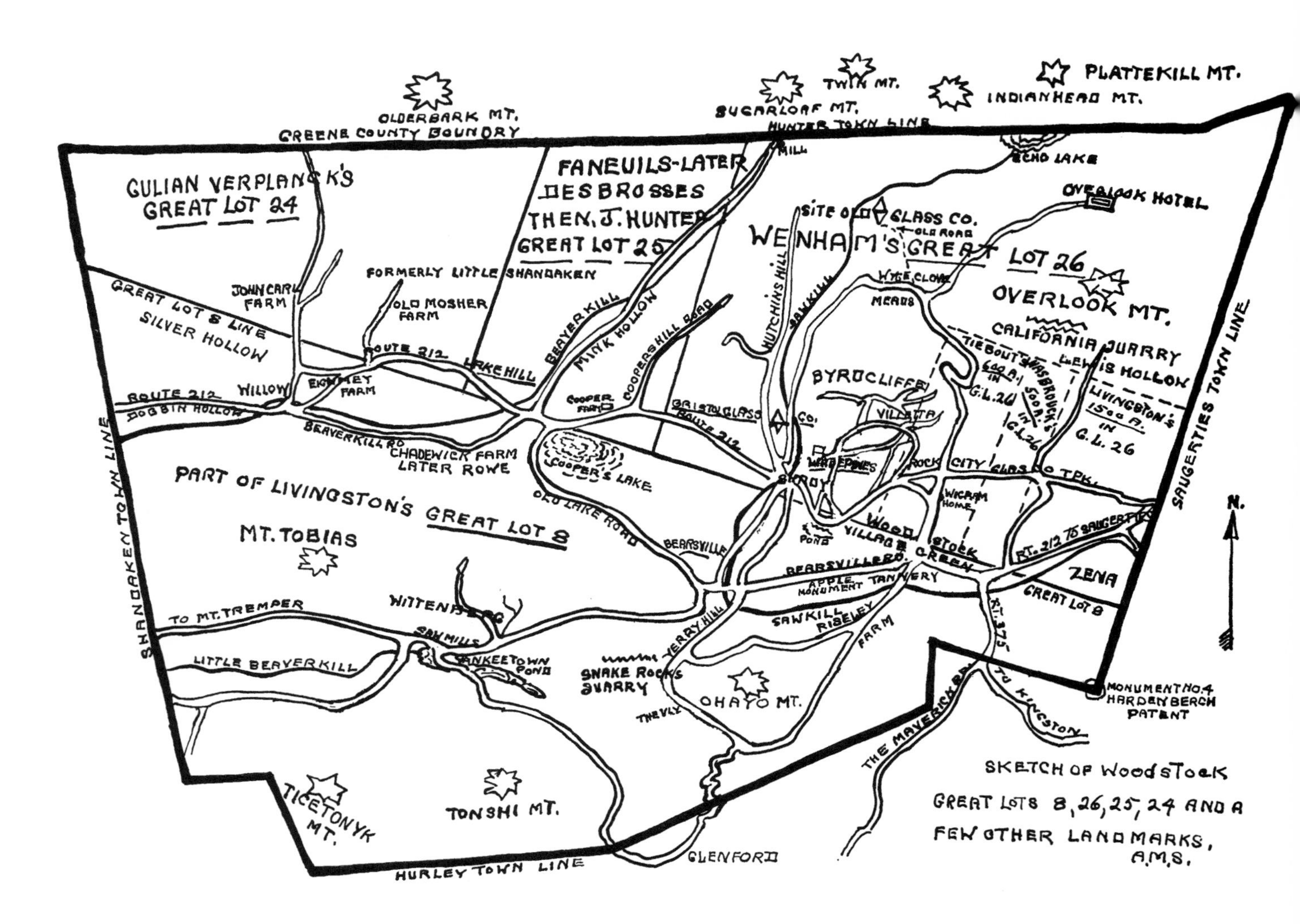

Map of early Woodstock Township drawn by AMS. Note the "Site Old Glass Co." at upper right, location of the Woodstock Glass Manufacturing Society/Company (1809–18) and the Ulster Glass Manufacturing Company (1818–24). To the south, along the Sawkill, is the site of the Bristol Glass, Cotton and Clay Company (1813–24) and, later, the New York Crown and Cylinder Glass Manufacturing Company (1825–30s) and the Ulster County Glass Manufacturing Company (1853–55).
AMS Collection.

Chapter 3

GLASS MAKING IN THE NINETEENTH CENTURY

IMPETUS FOR WOODSTOCK'S GROWTH

When starting my research on the glass factories I had no idea how large and important they had been. Several contradictory articles have been written, including one by me. It has taken eight months and cost me repeated attacks of bursitis (due to lifting heavy deed and mortgage books in the Ulster County Clerk's office) to unravel the truth from these records, old newspapers, company books and other documents.

Five glass companies operated in Woodstock Township during the first half of the nineteenth century. To correlate the deeds with the sites, I found it necessary to begin my studies with the Hardenbergh Patent and one of its divisions known as Great Lot 26. It extends from the village square north to the Greene County line and from the present Saugerties boundary to Lake Hill. In 1803 two New York businessmen, John G. Clark and F. A. DeZeng, purchased eight thousand acres of this lot, becoming owners of present-day Byrdcliffe, Shady and most of Overlook.[1, 2] When they sold the land three years later they doubled their investment. Baron Frederick Augustus DeZeng was a Hessian officer who accompanied the British army to America and stayed to become a citizen. Judging from his letters he had quite a dashing personality. He lived in Shandaken for a time and was on our town board.

DeZeng and his family were subsequently identified with glass manufacture in upper New York State. When he and Clark sold their land to Stephen Stilwell they reserved the mineral rights, thereby assuring themselves and their heirs all benefits if the many legends of silver mines in our mountains should be proved true. Usually the story runs that the Indians led their victims blindfolded to a place where, when the eye covers were removed, they would behold gold or silver, but later would not be able to locate the spot. There was some digging for coal, which was found only in tiny seams in bushel quantities. Speaking of our Devonian age mountains before the Historical Society of Woodstock, Judge Gilbert Hasbrouck said that, as our rocks were of a formation occurring beneath the coal strata, if we wanted to find coal we had better reverse the usual procedure and dig up rather than down! Nevertheless many of the old deeds held clauses reserving coal and minerals, and, for all I know, if uranium were to be discovered on Overlook the Clark or DeZeng heirs might lay claim to it.

In 1806 Stephen Stilwell received a deed for this entire tract, including "mills, forges, buildings and other improvements," showing that it was not completely barren land.[3] On a map made several years later there is a site marked "the old glass factory" just below the summit of Overlook Mountain, which has caused some speculation largely due to the use of the word "old."[4] I went with Bruno and Louise Zimm to try to locate this site but we did not find any trace of it. As the year the map was made coincided with the opening of the Woodstock Glass Manufacturing Company, I concluded there had been a mistake in placing the site about a mile and a half east rather than north of the Wide Clove (later known as Mead's). And as nothing else has confirmed the existence of any such glass works, I have not included it in my list of the five glass companies about which we know.

Stephen Stilwell and his family were identified with Woodstock for many years. He was born in 1760 on Long Island and was a soldier of the Revolution. He engaged in several business ventures and owned a sloop in which he carried flour to distant markets. At one time he conducted his business along the Hudson near Glasco. It was probably from there that he visited Woodstock, where he eventually settled. He lived in the house at Shady now owned by the Staggs, underneath which one can still see his slave quarters. He built and operated a gristmill nearby, and soon took an active part in town affairs—he was Assessor for two years and also Overseer of Highways. He was said to have possessed good qualities of mind and heart and made friends wherever he went.[5]

Woodstock Glass Manufacturing Society/Company

In 1809 Stephen Stilwell and his wife, Nancy, sold forty-two hundred acres in Great Lot 26 to the Woodstock Glass Manufacturing Society.[6] This tract ran the full width of the north boundary of Lot 26—actually it ran into Greene County—and can be easily located on Wigram's map of 1810. The factory was built not far from the Sawkill, about two miles below Echo Lake, and approximately a mile and a half back of Mead's. The factory contained two furnaces, two flattening ovens, several drying ovens, a sawmill on the stream and a blacksmith shop. The stables for the horses and oxen lay up against the hill, and there were also about twenty-four dwelling houses for the workers. Martin MacDaniel, whose grandparents lived there, says there were also a store and a school. The road from the factory went uphill to the Wide Clove and down through Rock City. This was a direct route to the Hudson River, but it must have been a hard climb for the wagons returning laden with the sand necessary for the manufacture of glass. Several early deeds refer to this as the old Glass Company Road. In any case, another route was used, although we do not know when, that connected with Glasco Turnpike at the foot of Van De Bogart Hill in what is now called Shady. It ran back of the Stilwell house and, without crossing any streams, continued its northerly course above the Sawkill back into the valley where the factory was located. Little of this road remains.

A quarter of a century ago the Historical Society of Woodstock made an expedition to the site of this factory, led by their president, Professor Martin Schütze. At that time the ruins of the works were clearly discernible. Many fragments of glass were found, of a clear aquamarine color with a few bits of yellowish hue. Others were darker green, but none of them was as brilliant a green-blue as the glass picked up later at the Bristol works. There were whole hills of broken glass and of pieces of glazed crocks. In a thicket below these ruins the Historical Society uncovered several graves. One was marked with a tombstone showing it to be the burial place of a family member of a well-known glass blower named Greiner. I have a photograph of several members of the Society gathered around this stone and resting on their tools: Professor Schütze, Kenneth Downer, Woodford Royce, Orville Peets, Jean Strain and a few others.

On a 1954 visit to the site the current president of the Historical Society of Woodstock, Alf Evers, his son Chris and I had trouble locating the place, partly because logging operations have disfigured the whole aspect of that side of Overlook. Also, Herb Keefe, the present owner, told us he had tried to cover the ruins because he did not want to be bothered by sightseers. Eventually, however, we did find all that remains of the old factory.

The making of glass requires special skills and many of the glass blowers came from New Jersey, Massachusetts or Pennsylvania. However, the industry also provided jobs for scores of local teamsters and woodsmen. A village of woodcutters was established to supply fuel for the furnaces and to cut the hardwood trees from which certain necessary ingredients were obtained. This community was located several miles away on the slopes of Indian Head Mountain and was known as The Plains. In his "Memoir on the Catskill Mountains," published in the *American Journal of Science* in 1823, James Pierce described a settlement we believe to have been The Plains. This was at a time when the once prosperous community was in decline, due to lawsuits and other difficulties. Pierce proceeded up the Plattekill Clove via a narrow dug-way and found the mountain valley at the head of the clove tolerably fertile but not

Historical Society of Woodstock field trip to old glass factory on The Plains, 1933. Standing behind a gravestone of one of the Greiner family's children are (l to r): Professor Martin Schütze, Kenneth Downer, Orville Peets, Jean Strain and Woodford Royce (sitting). Photo: AMS Collection.

extensively cultivated. He described large tracts covered with hard maple and beech trees that if cleared would have afforded fine grazing for sheep. He found the inhabitants living in log huts without floors or furniture. Bread was in scarce supply and few people had gardens. Their principal food, in addition to an occasional meal of fish or wild meat, consisted of potatoes and pumpkins. "Unfortunately," Pierce wrote, "most of the residents on this part of the mountain are not proprietors of the soil. They preferred stripping the land of its best timber rather than resort to the regular toils of agriculture." This was due to the onerous system of long leases—favoring the landlords—still in place at that time. Within twenty-five years these conditions would lead to the down-rent war, setting Woodstock Township ablaze.

Pierce walked on to Shue's Lake (now called Echo Lake), which he described as surrounded "by an amphitheatre of wild, rocky, and steep mountains," and he wrote of a nearby spring as of a "chalybeate character." This means it was impregnated with salts of iron. A reference of his to the great depth of the lake was not borne out by soundings made about 1910 by Neil Stevens of the Bureau of Plant Industry, U.S. Department of Agriculture, in Washington. When Stevens sent me the article by Pierce, he wrote that he had spent two days on a raft measuring the depth of the lake and found it to be shallow.[7] According to Alphonso Clearwater in his *History of Ulster County*, the name Shue's Lake is a corruption of Schoon Meer, meaning clear water.[8] However, on Wigram's map of 1810 it is marked Athens Lake. Whatever its name, the lake behind Overlook seems full of mystery, as it lies usually without ripple or sound and then overflows into the valley to form the Sawkill. It is not surprising that it has spawned many legends, among them stories of buried treasure. An escaped prisoner during the Civil War named Krauss is said to have hidden himself on its shore.[9] And the last of the Indians are believed to have camped there before they disappeared forever.

One winter day I went with Louise and Bruno Zimm to find The Plains. A few days previously Martin MacDaniel had pointed to the place halfway up the mountain distinguished by a difference in vegetation—where the trees had never covered the scars of a settlement that had been abandoned for a hundred years. We stood in front of the MacDaniel farm looking north toward the recumbent contours of Indian Head Mountain, which in the clear atmosphere appeared to be very close—without showing the difficulties we would encounter as soon as we descended the intervening valley. Upon entering the forest we found it impossible to see the identifying landmarks. The Zimms and I forded the upper Sawkill and jumped at our peril from boulder to boulder over the rushing Pecor and Dymond creeks. We scrambled in and out of several ravines, pushing our way through thickets of laurel and trying to decide if the many rivulets of melting snow we had to cross accounted for the three streams we had been told to pass before turning up the mountain. We found no sign of a trail, and soon, through the gray beech trunks, we could see the winter sun was beginning to glow into a sunset and had to abandon our search and hurry out of the woods before darkness should overtake us.

Our next attempt to find The Plains was made on an April day with daffodils blooming in our dooryards and arbutus lurking among the leaves on the valley bottom. But soon we climbed beyond the line of budding foliage and were back in winter on the slopes of Indian Head. We even had to traverse patches of snow. This time Bruno Zimm was the leader, and having studied old maps he proved a far better guide than I had been. We jumped the streams with no hesitation as we climbed through the deep woods. We found the partly washed-out bed of a road, and it led directly to the site. We ate our sandwiches by a spring that probably accounted for the choice of this spot as a hamlet. We found two cellar holes, a few wild apple trees, the inevitable stonewalls enclosing a couple of acres—and nothing else. Of course we had not expected to find a baby's shoe or a tin can, but we had hoped to reconstruct in our minds a picture of the village street from old bricks or even the door stones, but nothing like these were left. Here for years some forty families had gone about their lives with practically nothing left now to show for it. Their men had chopped down the great forest of hemlocks, but in doing so had removed their livelihood. Now the whole of Indian Head Mountain had reverted to wilderness. We could only speculate over the brooding quiet that emanates from an abandoned site where many people had worked out their destinies. It was as if the old witch had shrugged them off her shoulders to show who was mistress of the Catskills.

Martin Booth was the last to leave The Plains, supporting himself by cutting shingles with his frow from hemlock logs. His avocation was sermonizing and every Sunday he walked to Wittenberg to preach in the Methodist Church; in the afternoon he tramped to Little Shandaken where he repeated his discourse; and in the evening he came back to Bristol where he preached for the third time before walking home to The Plains. He did this for years without any compensation until the parishioners joined together to buy him a horse, which made the twenty-five-mile trip comparatively easy.

Martin Booth's sister Betsy was likewise a vigorous walker who thought nothing of tramping to Saugerties or Kingston and returning with a bag of meal on her back. If it was cold she carried a hot brick for warmth. She married James MacDaniel and lived near the old glass company, and there are many stories about her. She was a pioneer feminist, the first woman on record to have worn trousers in Woodstock. She was seen picking wild strawberries in her husband's breeches—certainly most daring! She was known for her skill at doctoring, and for many years "Aunt Betsy's" concoctions brought comfort to her neighbors. She gathered herbs and made infusions such as sweet fern for fever, spearmint for stomach ache, catnip for jumpy nerves and gentian (called "blue blows stuff") for dysentery. But most prized of all was her syrup of sassafras for coughs. Three of her sons were soldiers in the Civil War and they would write home asking for it. In response, Aunt Betsy would stay up all night to watch her crocks of syrup on the back of the stove, then send it to the soldiers by the case.

The MacDaniels first had a sawmill up on The Plains, which was moved down to the Sawkill to three different sites in turn. In about 1867 one son, Nathan, married a sixteen-year-old girl named Louise Taylor. Nathan's son, Barney MacDaniel, tells of his father's great capacity for work and what he expected from his sons. On occasion he would make Barney and his brothers rise at midnight in winter to start off through the snow into the forest for logs. It was probably on one of these trips that Nathan encountered the devil. He tried to run him off by swearing, but when that had no effect he went down on his knees and prayed. As he told the story: "It was like a fog come up and in it the devil disappeared."

A daughter, Mrs. Cashdollar, also remembered Nathan's industry. She told of seeing him in the evenings working in a leather apron and cutting hemlock shingles with his frow. Filling one corner of their cabin was a big round fireplace into which the children threw the shavings to supply the light by which he labored. Their mother gathered the shingles into bundles and thus they worked late into the night. In the Catskills it was not easy to support a large family. Three generations of MacDaniels cut wood for fuel to sell to the glass factories; they barked the hemlocks to supply tannin for the tanneries. Also, they sawed wood for buildings, made shingles and grew crops. They were a valiant family whose descendants make a rich contribution to the town.

The Woodstock Glass Manufacturing Society or Company (it began in 1809 as Society and was reincorporated in 1812 as Company) ran into financial difficulties within a few years. It would take a Philadelphia lawyer to untangle its affairs from the fragmentary information I was able to find more than a century later.

I have not been able to identify a whole glass piece as having been made at this factory. The shards picked up at the site indicate that they manufactured window glass and possibly some small bottles. No records or account books have surfaced. Of the glass blowers, the names Pecor, Bogardus, Dymond, Short and Vosburgh have been mentioned, as well as Greiner, in connection with this early firm. It is likely some of the blowers went from there to work at the Bristol Company and became identified with that concern.

Ulster Glass Manufacturing Company

In the books of the later Bristol Glass, Cotton and Clay Company there is reference to its doing business in 1818 with the Ulster Glass Manufacturing Company.[10] Therefore we know that the original firm (the Woodstock Glass Manufacturing Company) had been reorganized and was running under a new name. Two years later the *New York Evening Post* ran an advertisement for the sale of the property and works.[11] It is generally thought that by 1824 the old glass companies back of Overlook had run their course.

Bristol Glass, Cotton and Clay Company

On August 13, 1813, in consideration of $6,247, Stephen and Nancy Stilwell signed an indenture that conveyed eight hundred and thirty-three acres of land to the Bristol Glass, Cotton and Clay Company. This tract was in the southwest corner of Great Lot 26 and extended up Hutchins Hill to the land of the Woodstock Glass Manufacturing Company, but did not include any of that holding. It was widest along its northern boundary and spread across the Sawkill for a short stretch, but along the remainder of its course kept to the west bank of that stream on down until it reached Great Lot 8 near the turnpike. From here it ran westerly along this boundary to the junction with Great Lots 25 and 26. At this intersection, as mentioned in many deeds, was an old chestnut tree on flat land below Shandaken Lake (now known as Cooper's Lake). As there was a sawmill on the stream that went with the lake property, this western boundary of Great Lot 26 and the Bristol Company probably ran north along the base of Cooper's Hill. The tract included the entire hamlet we now know as Shady.[12]

The Bristol Glass, Cotton and Clay Company set up their glass works in what is now the Reynolds's barn, and the foundations for their furnaces may still be seen in the bay of the barn. Originally there were more buildings to the factory; one old-timer told me he remembered the drying sheds that occupied all the space in the triangle between the two roads. Looking down from the church hill, one sees that the buildings are connected unevenly and in a slight curve that follows the line of the Sawkill. The different angles and heights make an interesting design

Bristol Glass pitcher. Photo: AMS Collection.

that has intrigued several generations of artists. On the church hill the company built a row of houses for their employees. These dwellings could not have been of sturdy construction, because they did not last long. According to the company books of 1819, J. Lester and his son were paid $425 for building a new house for Dr. Ebenezer Hall. It should be remembered that money was worth far more in those days—even a half cent was considered important and was tagged onto the accounts.

The Bristol Company's store building still stands about a hundred yards from the bridge connecting the Shady road (now Reynolds Lane) with Route 212, but unless a radical repair job is done it will soon fall to pieces. It is being used today by Mrs. Brockenshaw as a pottery, and it still contains a beautiful old iron stove dating back to the time of the glass factories. A generation ago when Charles Reynolds owned the farm, the building was used as a polling station for the upper district of the town. It is a weathered wooden building grizzled from hard usage, having served as a store for three glass companies.

Spafford's *Gazetteer* of 1813 mentions two glass companies in Woodstock Township; therefore we may assume that the Bristol Glass, Cotton and Clay Company began operations very soon after the land was purchased.[13] Hereafter when speaking of the Bristol Company I am referring to this concern—though the name has been loosely used to cover both of the other companies that subsequently did business on the site. The names of the other two glass works were the New York Crown and Cylinder Glass Manufacturing Company, which took over the premises by 1825, and the Ulster County Glass Manufacturing Company, which in 1853 started operations in the same plant but lasted only two years.

The Historical Society of Woodstock has two books of the Bristol Company, one of them donated by the late Mrs. Clarence Shultis of Wittenberg. Both books are for a middle period because they include references to a previous ledger, A, and at the end the accounts are marked to be carried over to a ledger C. One is a book of store accounts, the other a record of the company's business, including glass sales, accounts with other firms, and amounts charged and due to their employees. Of the five glass companies, the Bristol appears to have been the most successful. They did business for eleven years and they carried on their books the names of over three hundred men. The most interesting entries in these ledgers have to do with the blowers, cutters, flatteners, tenders and batch mixers. Unfortunately the first ten and a half pages are missing and other pages are torn or tattered. The earliest notation is for labor in December 1817, and the accounts run to May 1821. I went over the glass records with particular attention, thinking I could get a total for several years' business. They begin with a balance carried over from the old ledger—which, added to the figures up to 1821, brings the total to $11,690.56½. But this may not be the net amount, because the last page under "Glass Dr." (debitor) is torn out and no balance is to be found. Also, a large part of the glass credits were taken in goods for the store instead of cash. For example, there were credits for shoes in exchange for two boxes of seven-by-nine-inch glass. On another occasion glass was traded to Peter Freer of Athens for three barrels of damaged black and white salt—for industrial use, we trust, rather than human consumption. The glass company traded for such diverse items as dried fish, muslin, pork, nux vomica, snuff, tobacco, nails and liquor, to be sold at the store. By April 1821, the amount paid out for labor amounted to the equivalent of $51,791.77½. Of this, over $10,000 was carried over from the previous ledger, which covered less than three years.

A few of the other expenses were noted as follows, all related to glass making:

Lime	$ 518.70
Wood	$15,660.76
Raw Ashes	$ 924.15
Clay	$ 794.90
Furnace Stones	$ 341.43
Iron	$ 47.09½
Broken Glass	$ 144.62½
Sand	$ 767.76
Packing Straw	$ 83.97½

Other costs included teaming, $689.86; scantling, $9.03; and diamonds (several references, but no total given). Besides raw ashes there were pearlash and potash, the latter sometimes brought from the kiln at West Camp. The total paid for freight charges to Captain Lewis Hall of the *Two Sisters* was $759.35. Several woodsmen brought "coal" (charcoal, we assume) for credit at the store. On March 31, 1818, the company paid R. W. Dubois for building the sand house at Glasco. That year they paid a large bill to James Lashar (the name is presently spelled Lasher) for "riding" loads to Bristol Landing, as well as to Glasco. This is the first reference I found to a place called Bristol Landing.[14]

In 1821 the company built an addition to the store and the next year they erected a new "sparling house."[15] There is another mention of a sparling house where men were paid to work—at what, it seems impossible to learn. There are other terms that are puzzling. For example, in several instances men were paid for "picking pot shells."[16] After consulting our local authority, Frances Rogers, author of *5000 Years of Glass*, I was persuaded that the term refers to the job of preparing crockery for firing—especially as one entry is to Moses Lyons for "*breaking clay* [emphasis mine] and pot shells."[17] If the term used had been shards it would be self-explanatory. Thirty-odd years later the Ulster County Glass Manufacturing Company was likewise paying considerable sums for "picking shells."

Glass is made from a mixture of sand, potash and lime, to which waste glass is added to help in melting the mixture. The quality of the glass depends largely upon the properties in the sand, which accounts for sand being brought from as far away as Perth Amboy, New Jersey. One author has written that the Bristol Glass Company owned their own sloops on the Hudson. Of this we find no record, but if it is true, we can surmise they frequently filled the holds with cargoes of sand or broken glass. It is known that these

Page from Bristol Glass ledger regarding transactions with James Lashar. The entry for March 19, 1819, at upper right, mentions Bristol Landing. Courtesy of Historical Society of Woodstock. Photo by Dion Ogust.

goods were shipped to Glasco by Captain Hall of the *Two Sisters*.

It requires skill to mix a batch of glass, and with the addition of small amounts of chemicals it is cleared or changed in color. I have fragments of glass that are aquamarine, green-blue and amber. I found these after the flood of 1935, which tore out the road near the glass house; they may have dated from any one of the three companies. At the same time I discovered the iron tip of a blower's pipe.

It seems somewhat impertinent to be looking into a day perhaps a hundred and forty years past to learn the tastes and weaknesses of these people of Bristol. For example, stories have come down to us of Stephen Stilwell's graciousness while president of the Bristol Company. But it brings him more alive for us to know that on a certain day in 1817 he had to buy a blister plaster and that he drank wine rather than rum. Similarly, it is interesting to note that a gentleman named Augustus Greele purchased forty-three yards of French shirting. Liquor was the most popular commodity at the store and there was hardly a man from the three hundred families mentioned in the accounts who did not stop in often for a gill of rum. Not everyone took four rums at once like Joseph Wigram, son of the Surveyor, one of Woodstock's most distinguished citizens. Maybe Joseph was treating his companions; that we shall never know. Nor shall we understand why Conrad Lester, one of the best-paid glass cutters, bought "muslin for the Hasbrouck girl."[18] He might have been a dashing fellow, as he bought six silk handkerchiefs at one time—and because he was not charged a school tax he may have been a bachelor. One item to his credit was $139.40 for cutting 37,175 feet of glass. Also, he received twenty-five cents for cutting a clock face. (This must have been a small clock because the regular price paid for a clock face was fifty cents.) Other cutters were Aaron Barber and the Arnold brothers, Samuel and Hosea.

John G. Evans was a master blower who received credits amounting to $2,589.69 for about three years' work. No wonder he could indulge in seven yards of bombazette, many yards of ribbons and a pudding dish. He was credited $5.50 "by blowing bottles," which was the most paid over the period covered in the account book for that activity.[19] Charles Herrick owned a bottle stamped with an eagle from the Bristol Glass Company that unfortunately was thrown out.[20]

Stories are still told locally of the glass blowers' success with the girls. We can almost picture Evans when we see that he bought, in one day, buttons, silk and 13½ yards of glazed cotton for $7.72. A notice in the *Ulster Sentinel* gives an idea of how the ordinary young men of the day dressed. A reward of ten dollars was offered by an Ulster County constable for the apprehension of an escaped prisoner named George Plass of Woodstock, who was being held on a petty larceny charge. When he escaped he was wearing "a white wool hat, a bottle green surtout coat" and "light colored linsey woolsey pantaloons."[21] Another item in the local newspaper was an advertisement placed by a disgruntled husband: "Whereas my wife, Polly, has left my bed and board without any just cause or provocation . . ."[22] (So he says!) The man went on to state that, as his wife was fond of riding, he forbade anyone to pick her up in a sleigh, carriage or wheelbarrow. Poor Polly, not allowed a whirl even in a wheelbarrow!

Isaac and Joseph Peet were both blowers but Joseph received special pay for one month as "master blower."[23] They were each charged for half a hat! We wonder which one wore it or if they alternated. Another master blower was Lewis Casstoller, the ancestor of a family now living in Woodstock. The best known of his descendants is Albert Cashdollar, who was our town supervisor, chairman of Ulster County Supervisors and county treasurer and is now commissioner of roads in Woodstock. Lewis Casstoller paid a large school tax, so he presumably had several children of school age, and there is mention of his buying combs for his wife and daughter. He made large purchases at the store beginning in 1816 (when the existing ledger began) and was still on the payroll in 1821.

Another ancestor of a prominent Woodstock family who came here as a glass blower was Richard Vosburgh, who traveled from Amenia, New York, in 1810, when he was twenty-six years old, along with his wife, Polly Rowe. His great great granddaughter, Elsie Vosburgh Rowe, wrote an account of the family in which she says he first went to work for the old glass factory back of the mountain and took a house there in what seemed to his wife and children to be the wilderness.[24] By 1817 he was working for the Bristol glass company. He made good pay blowing and batch making.

Other blowers for the Bristol company were David Robinson, who did not arrive until 1821, Jacob Lott, Green Reynolds, and Allen McCormack, who was also a cutter. Warren Bailey made up the batches of glass in addition to being a blower, and he had the distinction of being fined "$2.00 for neglect of Duty."[25] In addition there were Robert McCoy and Abraham Van Voorhis—the latter also a "scrivner of bay," for which he was paid an extra $2.50.[26] Arnold Robinson was yet another who received extra pay, and he made it by producing "large glass."[27] Finally there was John Sager, who made good pay at blowing yet was willing to earn seventy-five cents for digging a drain; he was also credited $2.25 for blowing bottles. John Clark, the pot maker, was also paid well.[28]

All these men stopped in at the company store to get their gill of rum and their snuff and to do their shopping. It is evident that if their womenfolk asked them to buy a half dozen needles or a twist of thread they took advantage of the errand to get themselves a little nip. How pleasant it must have been, after spending the day near their furnaces, to stop in at the big store and sip a cool drink. There is no mention of beer. The usual drink was rum, which cost 6d (although they spoke in pence, they probably meant our American cents). On at least one occasion our friend the glass cutter Conrad Lester paid for three tumblers of rum! Sometimes the more prosperous blowers such as Richard Vosburgh would buy brandy or wine. Purchases of boxes of snuff or plugs of tobacco were common. They bought flannel and cotton goods for the women and, in terms of food, made large purchases of pork, potatoes, molasses, meal,

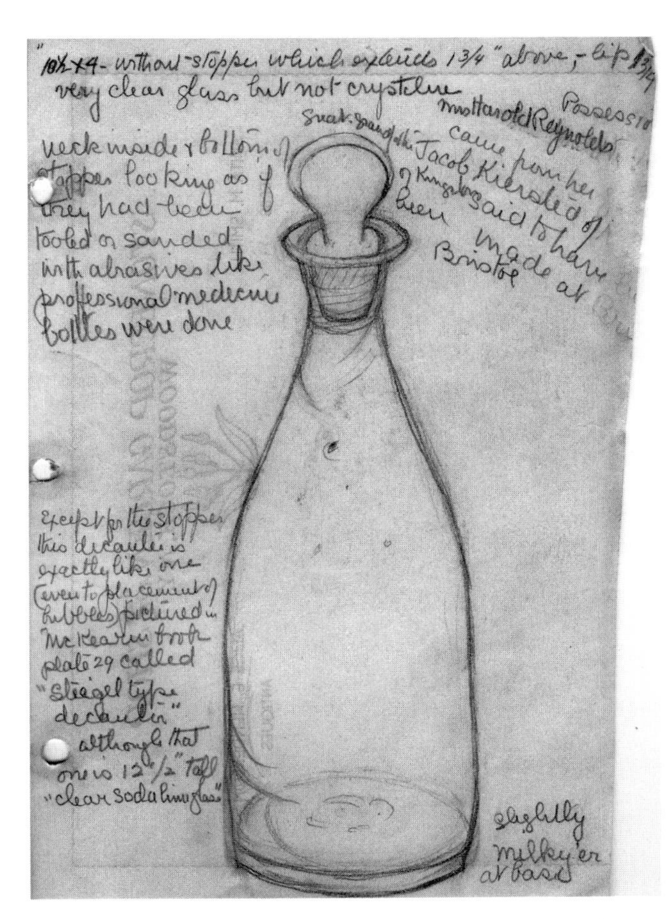

This decanter belonged to Mrs. Harold Reynolds, inherited from her great grandfather, Jacob Kiersted of Kingston. It was said to have come from the Bristol works. AMS noted that the decanter measured 10½ in. without stopper (lip ¾ in., stopper 1¾ in.), that it was of very clear glass but not crystal, and that inside the neck it looked abraded in the manner of a medicine bottle of the era. Drawing by Anita M. Smith. AMS Collection.

salt fish and spices. These, together with what they raised themselves, must have been the staple diet. There were times when the store stocked raisins, blueberries or chocolates, and these found ready buyers. In the fall of 1818 chestnuts were on sale, reminding us of the handsomest of our trees, which abounded throughout the Catskills until a century later when disease destroyed them all.

Dr. Ebenezer Hall was a free spender, buying such things as wine glasses, ribbons and silk. He had a salary of approximately six hundred dollars a year from the Bristol Company as a supervisor, in addition to his income from a medical practice. For instance, he was called in to visit a sick child, for which he was paid twenty-five cents. Little cash was exchanged, although it can be noted that Lewis Casstoller was advanced as much as a hundred dollars at a time. Fortunately most items went on the company books, which we may study. House rents were five dollars a month; a box of seven-by-nine-inch glass cost five dollars. Benjamin Davis did constant business as a blacksmith mending plows, sleds, and chains and providing hundreds of axes. Samuel Culver, the owner of the tannery and supervisor of the Woodstock Town Board, dealt in leather and hair and made harnesses.[29] Moses Lyons was the shoemaker but earned more breaking clay and pot shells. James Lester and one of his sons were paid often for carpentry work, and Stephen Stilwell Jr. was on the books frequently for "grinding clay stuff."[30] Numerous men were paid for tending fires and for tempering pots. For example, Francis Neelis ran up a credit of almost a thousand dollars on the latter job, and Andrew Weatherwax earned several hundred dollars "making . . . glass."[31] Quantities of scantling were needed for boxing and the Edson mill in Mink Hollow provided most of it, totaling almost fifteen hundred dollars by 1819.

The Lewis Edsons, father and son, composed hymns that were famous in their day, but they do not seem to have enriched themselves thereby. In 1844, when the younger Edson died, the town had to provide his coffin. Interest in the Edson hymns has now been revived and a few years ago Sidney Cowell, the musician, was instrumental in having some of them sung at the Shady church. The only story I have in my notes relating to the Edson family came from an old Mink Hollow resident who maintained that Lewis Edson Sr. had Indian blood in him, which accounted for his being a natural horseman, and that he rode the swiftest mare in this locality. Returning one night over the Mink Hollow road he was attacked by a wolf, which sent the mare headlong down the mountain, carrying her rider over rocks and thickets until they passed out of the deep forest. The horse's flanks were torn by the wolf; the bridle was broken and the horse's new shoes were worn away. As the story was related to me, "If that hoss hadn't been a whirlwind instead of hoss flesh, they'd a bin et up by the wolf."

In the accounts are many names still familiar in the town, such as John P. Harder, working in the cutting room, and Michael Smith, who did teaming. John Longyear, Philip Bonesteel, Peter Short, Daniel Hasbrouck, Henry Shultis and Levi Wolfen (the *f* was later changed to *v*) are but a few mentioned. Ebenezer Hall and William Greele received steady incomes for "attendance," which probably meant superintending the works.[32] The largest number were employed in providing fuel. They cut the trees in the forest, and they hauled wood to the factory and split and dried it in enormous quantities. But ever more trees were required and more acreage needed to feed the insatiable fires.

On April 24, 1817, Stephen and Nancy Stilwell deeded a thirty-acre piece of land in the valley west of Stilwell's millpond to "Daniel Elliott . . . and Augustus Greele."[33] On an 1825 map by Wigram the home of Elliott is shown at that locale. We see the names of these two men emerging to greater prominence as the years pass. According to Mrs. Zimm, Daniel Elliott was one of three men chosen to represent Ulster County in a State Road Convention in 1826.[34] He had already established himself in Bristol, but up to then the name of Augustus Greele was infrequently mentioned—although William and Robert Greele, whose relationship to Augustus we do not know, were on the Bristol Company's payroll.

Glass dome said to be from Bristol Glass era.
AMS Collection. Photo by Dion Ogust.

New York Crown and Cylinder Glass Manufacturing Company

The New York Crown and Cylinder Glass Manufacturing Company evidently assumed control of the factory by 1825. Little is known regarding this glass company. It is quite possible that they used the same books and the same personnel as the Bristol Company and that the two companies were alike in everything but name, but they probably did not have as many employees.

In 1825 Daniel and Abigail Elliott and Augustus and Caroline Greele of New York City sold an indenture to the New York Crown and Cylinder Glass Manufacturing Company to make payment of ten thousand dollars for three pieces of land.[35] One of these was known as the Shandaken (Cooper's) Lake property. It consisted of 157½ acres in Great Lot 25 of the Hardenbergh Patent, being part of a tract that James Desbrosses had leased to Thomas Treadway Smith in 1794. Each time the property changed hands it had to be written into the deed that it was subject to an annual quitrent of one shilling per acre, which was not cancelled until the property came into the possession of William M. Cooper. With it went an 833-acre tract upon which the factory stood, and also a thirty-acre lot by the gristmill. In addition to these lands, the New York Crown and Cylinder Glass Manufacturing Company in 1826 acquired 306 acres from the descendants of Jeremiah Reynolds, for which they paid fifty dollars to each of the thirteen heirs. This tract is in Great Lot 25 adjoining the Shandaken Lake property described above, and was under the same type of perpetual lease from James Desbrosses requiring an annual quitrent of one shilling per acre. The new glass company probably also controlled the Sawkill tract of 170 acres, the title of which was in the names of Noble, Hooke, Elliott, Greele, Hall and the two Lesters.

The *Gazetteer of the State of New York* in 1836 mentions the village of Bristol as the location of the New York Crown and Cylinder Glass Manufacturing Company. It says further that the company employed fifty people and made fifteen hundred boxes of window glass per month.[36] There is no mention of any other glass company operating in Woodstock at that time. The fifty employees probably did not include the company's outside workers.

An authority on American glass says the few glass pitchers attributed to our glass companies belong to this period. One of these is described as being of green glass with a yellowish tinge, another as aquamarine in color.[37] It is hard to find a whole piece of glass left in Woodstock. I have a glass dome that is said to be of Bristol glass.

By 1830 the New York Crown and Cylinder Glass Manufacturing Company began selling its holdings.

Perhaps they had stripped the forest so the land was no longer useful, or, more likely, they were in financial difficulties. That year they sold the Shandaken property to John P. Winne of the Court of Chancery, Cyrus Perkins signing the deed for the company.[38] They also sold fifty acres of the old Reynolds tract to Peter Burger.[39]

Even as hard times fell, the company tried to help its workers. The Woodstock Town Records of 1833 show that one John Holland acquired a mortgage as follows:

> Know all men by these presents that I John Holland of Woodstock Ulster County for and in Consideration of the Sum of Thirty 75/100 dollars to me in hand paid by the New York Crown [and] Cylinder Glass Manufacturing Company the receipt whereof I do hereby acknowledge have Sold and Conveyed & by these presents do Sell and Convey unto the Said Glass Company their administrators or assigns a Certain lot or parcel of potatoes now in the ground being in the field Southwest of the house now occupied by the Said John Holland and on the Land belonging to the Said Glass Company and one White Sow two years Old last Spring and one yellowish red Calf being the Same now and lately in my possession [and] promise to Warrant and defend the Same property against the lawful Claims of all other persons...
>
> In Witness Whereof I have hereunto Set my hand and Seal this tenth day of August 1833.
>
> [signed]
>
> X [John Holland]
> mark
>
> Witness present I. J. Grovier and . . . recorded by . . . John Wigram Town Clerk[40]

Two years later Holland's wife and children went on relief.

As there is no record of this short-term mortgage being satisfied, we can only hope the company secured the potatoes before they rotted in the ground and herded the white sow and the yellowish calf into the store before winter set in. In the Town Road Survey of 1837 there is mention of this glass company store being the same building I described earlier.

I have been unable to find another word concerning the glass factory until 1842. At that time Hiram St. John Short and Peter Short, owing the company $570, obtained a mortgage on fifty acres in Great Lot 25 that was subject to an annual quitrent of one shilling per acre. Five years later this mortgage was assigned to Daniel Elliott. Champion Pelton and Leander Pelton signed for the New York Crown and Cylinder Glass Manufacturing Company. In 1845 Daniel Elliott bought the remainder of the old Reynolds tract in Great Lot 25, the thirty-acre mill lot and 710½ acres of the factory tract—the latter being the upper or northern piece of it. The southern section of 122 acres, which included the factory premises, was bought by Peter Reynolds. A year later Reynolds bought on contract all the holdings formerly purchased by Daniel Elliott for three thousand dollars. It was to be paid in six installments and this mortgage was satisfied in 1852. Thus Peter Reynolds became the owner of practically the entire Bristol valley, including the glass works.[41]

Ulster County Glass Manufacturing Company

All of these data on the glass industry may not interest the casual reader, but for those seeking to unravel the history of Woodstock they are worthwhile studying, because glass was the most important product of our town throughout the nineteenth century. It increased the population, bringing in many families of those directly employed in the factory. It also created work for hundreds of the existing inhabitants, who supplied materials such as wood, food and transportation that were necessary to keep the industry alive. It was a large factor in the early development of Woodstock.

The last glass works to operate in Woodstock Township was the Ulster County Glass Manufacturing Company, which opened in 1853 and lasted two years. We have considerable information on this company because Craig Vosburgh turned over to the Historical Society of Woodstock several of its books, including a ledger and a petty accounts record. In addition, there are personal reminiscences, such as that of Mr. John Miller, who, when he was almost one hundred years old, talked to me about the glass company. He remembered visiting the factory as a lad of twelve, when it was operating in the present Reynolds barn. Mrs. Loretta Short, widow of David Short Jr. of Wittenberg, recalled visiting the factory at night and watching a man whirling the molten glass, then throwing it off and fashioning a bird on the end of a stick. She also told me she saw the men making glass mugs with handles and cylinders for

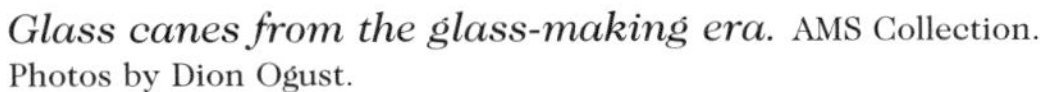

Glass canes from the glass-making era. AMS Collection. Photos by Dion Ogust.

domes to put over wax figures. This was an eyewitness account regarding some of the fancy pieces the blowers made after hours. If still living today, Mrs. Short would be a hundred and thirteen years old. If only I had asked her more questions about the glass works! She did add that the blowers "made big money and threw it around."[42]

Moses Sagendorf, another old-timer who departed this life years ago, likewise told me of the boys and girls of the neighborhood going to the glass factory at night. It was a comfortably warm place for them to gather for a social evening, and the blowers were always willing to make them trinkets. These were shaped from the "metal," as the glass mixture that was left in the pots was called. No doubt the blowers were glad to show off before the girls and present them with glass canes, birds and vases.

Sagendorf's father was clearing his land at that time and built a charcoal pit close to his home on the west side of Shandaken Lake. There the fires would be left to smolder, though well tended, for two or three weeks to make the charcoal. He sold this "coal" to the factory in Bristol where it may have been used to intensify the color of the glass. A good load on his bark rigging would bring six or seven dollars. Moses's father was Peter Sagendorf, the hotheaded down-renter.[43]

The site of the Ulster County Glass Manufacturing Company was owned by Peter Reynolds, a supervisor of the town of Woodstock, who had acquired all the property of the previous glass works. He became secretary of the new company and its largest stockholder, owning thirty-eight shares. Other local shareholders were William M. Cooper, a Democrat who several times served as supervisor in this Republican town[44]; the treasurer, Squire Joseph Miller (father of John, mentioned earlier); James Vosburgh; William Johnson; Isaac Mosher; Christian Baehr; Levi Newkerk; H. St. John Short; William Kerr; Thomas Roney; S. O. Peet; and William

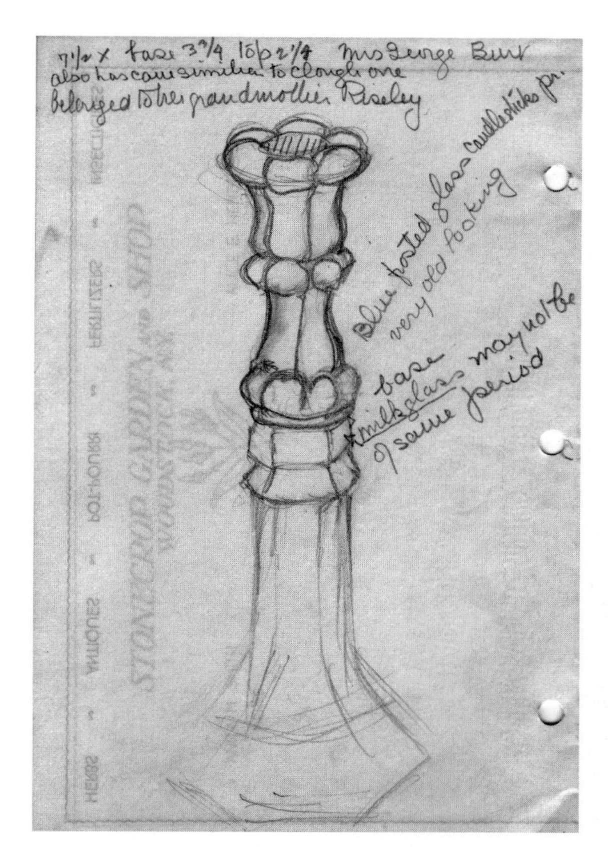

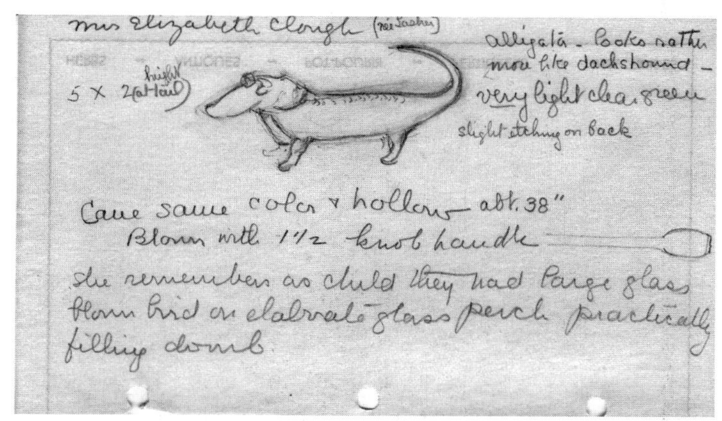

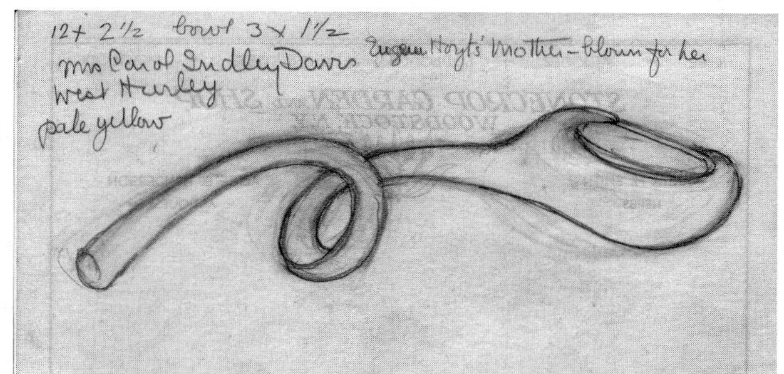

Left: *Drawing of a candlestick owned by Mrs. George Burt. To AMS, the base appeared newer than the top. It was 3¾ in. across at the bottom. The lower post (blue frosted) was 7½ in. high and the uppermost part (milk glass) 2¼ in. high.*

Top: *Sketch of an alligator owned by Mrs. Elizabeth Clough. It was light green in color and had a slight etching on its back.*

Bottom: *Glass bowl with pale-yellow handle, owned by Mrs. Carol Gridley Davis. The handle measured 12 x 2½ in. and the bowl 3 x 1½ in.* Sketches by Anita M. Smith. AMS Collection.

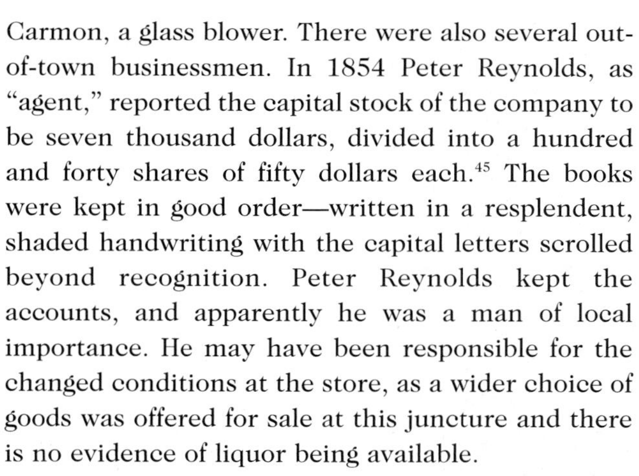

Carmon, a glass blower. There were also several out-of-town businessmen. In 1854 Peter Reynolds, as "agent," reported the capital stock of the company to be seven thousand dollars, divided into a hundred and forty shares of fifty dollars each.[45] The books were kept in good order—written in a resplendent, shaded handwriting with the capital letters scrolled beyond recognition. Peter Reynolds kept the accounts, and apparently he was a man of local importance. He may have been responsible for the changed conditions at the store, as a wider choice of goods was offered for sale at this juncture and there is no evidence of liquor being available.

We believe the old glass company operating behind Overlook Mountain closed around 1824, and a number of people have stated that it was moved down to Bristol. Yet another company had already been established in Bristol before that date. As we have seen, the New York Crown and Cylinder Glass Manufacturing Company had taken over the works in 1825, and it could have inherited something from the old Ulster factory. In any case I have not been able to find any reference to the owners of the concern. The similarity between the names of the Ulster Glass Manufacturing Company and the Ulster County Glass Manufacturing Company suggests a tie-in, yet the latter works did not start until thirty years after the demise of the first. The pay was equal to that of the earlier companies but costs were lower; for instance, house rent had dropped from five dollars a month to two and a half, although perhaps the houses had deteriorated during the intervening years. The workers were paid by the number of boxes of glass they could produce, and bills were sent for so many boxes of window glass—with never any variation unless it were for thick glass. There are also puzzling references to orders received for other glass companies.

We know that the Greiner family was connected with the factory back of the mountain, and that four

Ulster County Glass Manufacturing Company ledgers. Courtesy of Historical Society of Woodstock. Photos by Dion Ogust.

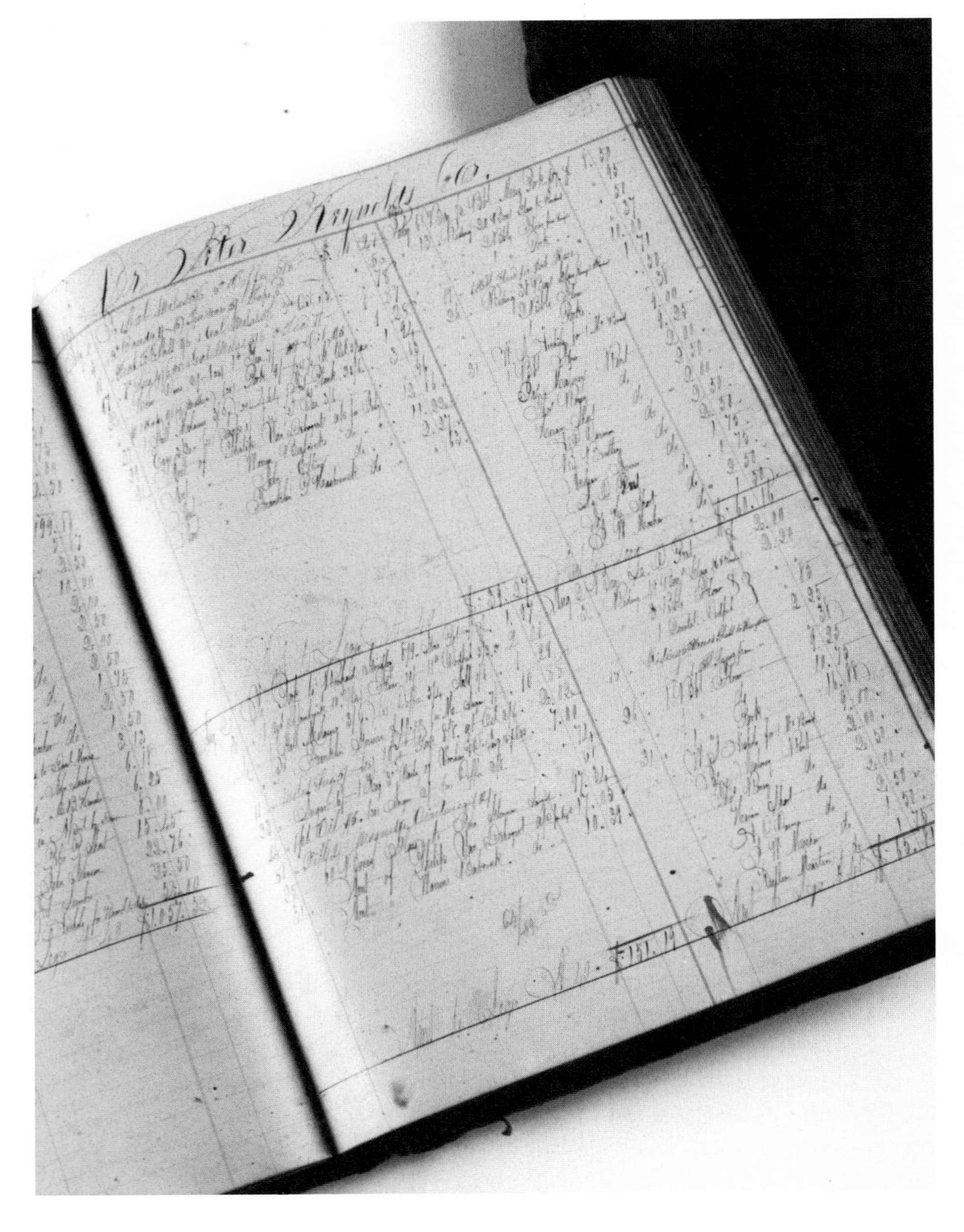

Greiners—Adam, Andrew, John and Franklin—were blowers for the Ulster County Glass Manufacturing Company. The company had fourteen regular and two spare blowers. Besides the Greiners there were Charles and George Roney, blowers; Hamilton Roney, a cutter; and Thomas Roney, who earned more by cutting glass than the others did by blowing. There were two brothers, William and Joseph Gabler, said to have been expert glass blowers from South Jersey.[46] William Carmon was one of the stockholders, Silvester Carmon worked on the pots, Nathan Carmon was a cutter and John Carmon was a flattener. There was Orville Knowlton, a blower, and also Edward O'Hara, who remained but a year. Joseph Short was a master blower who earned $135.49 in a three-and-a-half-month period. Still another blower was Larry Peet. The Peet family had been established in Woodstock Township for years—Isaac and Joseph having been blowers for the Bristol Glass, Cotton and Clay Company.[47] Mrs. Zimm's files show that Isaac Peet leased one hundred acres in the Hunter Patent in 1827 and that a few years later Joseph Peet was made a justice of the peace. There are some Peet family graves in the old Hasbrouck farm burial ground off the Mink Hollow road and others in the Woodstock cemetery, but there is no record of Larry Peet. The two spare blowers were Killian Martin and Nicholas Hackett; the latter was allowed eleven dollars a month by the company for board at Killian Martin's.

Hiram St. John Short was a cutter, and Peter Short, Esq., worked at batch making and tempering pots—sometimes assisted by his son, Henry. It was Hiram and Peter Short who had lost their property in the old Arnold Reynolds tract on a mortgage to the New York Crown and Cylinder Glass Manufacturing Company several years before. In January 1855 the company paid a fifty-five-cent military tax for David Short. He traded a load of wood to them for muslin de laine and trimmings, which leads me to think he was quite a dandy!

Elias Short provided large amounts of wood for the glass works, as did Elizabeth MacDaniel (i.e., Betsy Booth, whose cough syrup was famous). Another who earned a large credit for wood was Abel Hasbrouck. Silas Husted made shingles from wood cut in Hutchins Hollow and bought more snuff than anyone else; it cost 9d a purchase. Richard Gridley, who must have had a sweet tooth, unless the large quantity of candy he bought was for others, supplied the factory with wood that at one time amounted to seventy-nine cords. Joseph H. Miller sold wood in large loads to the company and hired others to work for him. He was a justice of the peace and was usually referred to as Squire Miller. Ezra Calkins was hired to shingle the factory and also the store, which had been built forty years previously. Cornelius Peterson was the general carpenter and glazier. He was paid two dollars for a trundle bed and he built a bookcase for the school. (From records with the Woodstock Town Clerk we know the schoolbooks in use about that time were *Cobb's Speller and Readers*, *Brown's Grammer* [sic] and *Davies' Arithmetic*.[48]) Peterson also made pipe handles for the blowers. John Johnson was the blacksmith. He must have been a hearty fellow, buying two gallons of molasses per month—or possibly he had a raft of children to use it up so quickly. William Johnson, who paid a military tax, was a batch maker and had one of the largest bills at the store, buying such luxuries as lemons and cordial.

Among those who made big money teaming and riding was James Vosburgh, who had a large account at the store and made purchases of goods that included alpaca, palmetto, cashmere and shirting. He bought shoes for his wife and his sons, linen, flannel and a horse blanket. He is credited with selling glass to the merchants of Delhi. Levi Newkerk was on salary, earning forty to sixty dollars a month teaming. Among others doing teaming were Peter Harder and Franklin Hasbrouck. Most of the glass workers were down on the books for a contribution to the church. The minister, the Reverend D. P. Wright, bought sundries at the store but his due bill was returned; evidently he expected his parishioners to help support him.

Richard Shultis was employed regularly in shearing, tending or just picking pot shells. Philip Simmons worked on clay, at batch making and also at picking pot shells. Cornelius Elting earned $2.06 for picking five and one twentieth bushels of pot shells.[49]

Philip Van DeBogert was a hard-working man, chopping wood and teaming for the company. Frequently he paid his sons' accounts at the store, as they did not earn many credits themselves—yet they charged such luxury items as cigars, candy, cashmere and tweeds as well as trimmings for their pants or a silk handkerchief. These young men eventually settled down to useful family lives, but there is a story

Drawing by Lucile Blanch. AMS Collection.

connected with one member of the family that is too good to resist. I cannot vouch for its verity, but this is the way it was related to me many years ago. The young man in question, John, was prone to go to trade in Kingston and return tipsy, much to the amusement of the young bucks hanging about the tavern on the Woodstock Green. On one occasion he proudly exhibited a new pair of shoes he had purchased for his wife—only to be met with a taunt that the shoes were made of hen skin. Thereupon the excitable Van DeBogert threw the footgear into the fire, although the onlookers could plainly see that the stout leather showed traces of critter's hair as was to be expected in shoe leather of that period. One night when he failed to return, the boys were sent out to search for him and found the man up to his neck in the Tannery pond singing for more than he was worth in Low-Dutch, of which he ordinarily knew nothing. On that occasion we hope the cold dip brought him to his senses before he returned home, because John Van DeBogert was known to misuse his family, sometimes even taking a gad to his wife. He was jealous of her, and it is said that one evening when she returned home he would not accept her explanation of having been out to nurse a sick neighbor. He cut a fresh elm gad which he used upon her with such cruelty that the poor woman was taken ill the next day, giving birth to a stillborn child. Before she died she is said to have requested that the elm stick be buried with her, to take root in her heart. From this gad a sapling thrust forth from the grave and grew to be a mighty elm tree that many of us have seen. A few years ago the family had the tree chopped down, which leads us to the conclusion that the story has some truth to it.[50]

The glass company did considerable business with Christian Baehr, who gave his name (with changed spelling) to the hamlet of Bearsville, two miles west of Woodstock and formerly called Bears Ville. There exists a letter to the glass company from E. J. Burhans of Roxbury, dated March 25, 1845, in which he tells of sending "Butts and Shoulders" amounting to $89.05; he was prepared to take glass in return. However, his team "was deviated" and Burhans was obliged to leave the meat at Rondout with Mr. Schoonmaker, "who said he would forward it to you by your own Teams." He added, "I can't get teamsters to go to your place . . . as the road [through Bearsville] is impassable."[51] Around 1847 plans were made to improve the roads between the Hudson River and the Catskill Mountains.

The road improvements were made largely with money subscribed from the tanneries and the villages that would benefit. The towns of Olive and Woodstock raised five thousand dollars for this purpose. The story of the tanneries is too long to take up here, but during the periods when the glass factories were not operating, and for those backwoods families who were not directly employed, the tannery in Woodstock village provided much-needed work. The bark of the hemlocks and oaks was used for its tannin content by the numerous tanneries in the Catskills, while the trees themselves were left to rot in the woods. Millions of feet of lumber were thus wasted until a company was formed to improve the road from Kingston to Pine Hill, and also a branch road through Woodstock, with four-inch planks of wood.[52]

It took several years for the roads to be completed, and it is evident from the letter written by the meat dealer in Roxbury that the section through Little Shandaken and Bristol was not ready by the winter of 1845. It was completed soon thereafter and toll points were established, one of them being located in Bearsville at the tavern run by Harder. Some people were so angry at being taxed for using the road they made a dug-way up the hill and drove to Bristol via Van De Bogart Hill. Another tollgate was established at the top of Cooper's Hill. A toll of eight cents was collected for a one-horse rig and sixteen cents for a team. Mrs. Hannah Cooper Vosburgh, now ninety-four, remembers as a child stubbing her toes on the planks.[53] The road remained in good condition for about fifteen years, when parts of it were replaced by stone to accommodate the heavy loads of bluestone from the quarries.

But let us return to the affairs of the Ulster County Glass Manufacturing Company. Peter Reynolds, its secretary, had the largest account at the store. As the proprietor of nearly the entire valley he had eleven houses to rent and also boarded a few glass workers. He drew up to several hundred cords of wood at a time from Hutchins Hollow, and rode glass to Saugerties, Kingston, Rondout and Rhinebeck.[54] When the company failed he was left with the plant and the store equipment. Most of the property was sold, but it was later bought back by the Reynolds family. A descendant, Fred Reynolds, now owns the main factory building, which was converted into a commodious barn.

William Avery was a shearer, and, like most of the customers, he bought snuff. He made miscellaneous purchases such as tea, buttons, candles, pork, British Oil, mittens, salve and a small pair of shoes.[55] Trask's Magnetic Ointment was a popular item and the store stocked it in large quantities, buying it wholesale from Munde in Poughkeepsie.[56] Other popular medicines were Pain-Killer, Family Pills and Condition Powder.

The company did business with several firms in Albany, the largest account being that of Carmen Peet from whom they bought Ameatiron stoves, furniture, fish hooks, linen and so forth. The largest orders were for broken glass—three tons at a time—and pipe clay, which we assume were used in glass making. In return they sent window glass to Carmen Peet. For instance, by April 1853 eleven hundred dollars' worth was sent from Bristol Landing via the steamer *Mazeppa*. According to its letterhead, this steamer left Poughkeepsie three times a week for Albany, stopping to pick up freight at all intermediate landings. I saw a receipt from D. Livingston, Agent at Bristol Landing, for fifty-five boxes of glass. Other shipments were made from Kingston to New York City via the steamer *R. L. Stevens* under Captain Anderson, and from the city of Hudson via the *Elmendorf*, the *Santa Claus* or the *Columbia*. The days of the Hudson River sloops were past.

Pipe clay was purchased in large quantities in New York. The first year the company bought "from Olriches" almost two thousand dollars' worth of soda ash, which was sent by railroad to Tivoli and Rhinebeck. They also acquired items such as lampblack and chalk, which may have been used in the composition of glass. I have no record of where they obtained their sand in the beginning, but there exists a letter from A. R. Fox of Berkshire, Massachusetts, dated January 12, 1854, in which he says he is sending two cars of sand, twenty tons each, to Rhinebeck Depot—this was in addition to the two cars that had been sent the day before. He adds, "Our order is not to let any freight away until paid in cash or note."[57] This is the first indication that the Ulster County Glass Manufacturing Company was tardy in paying its bills. Soon there would be more evidence of its imminent demise. Another of its customers, Hawley & Co. of Troy, wrote, "It is a hard time to sell."[58] By June 1854 the company was being dunned by Fowler and Company, who said its notes for five hundred and a thousand dollars, endorsed by Peter Reynolds, were overdue at the Bank of the Commonwealth in New York City. The era of glass making in Woodstock was drawing to a close. The Ulster County Glass Manufacturing Company was issuing more and more notes, and creditors were increasingly pressing for payment. The last entry in the cashbook is dated September 1855: "To cash in P. Reynolds' hands—$8.59."[59]

These glass companies were tremendously important in the development of our town. Stories of the glamorous blowers persisted for years. They were said to be "real tony dressers" with their embroidered waistcoats, which dazzled the women. They earned far more than the farm boys and were free spenders. Indeed, there were gay doings in Bristol in those days when the population exceeded Woodstock village and the glass factories were the heart of the township.

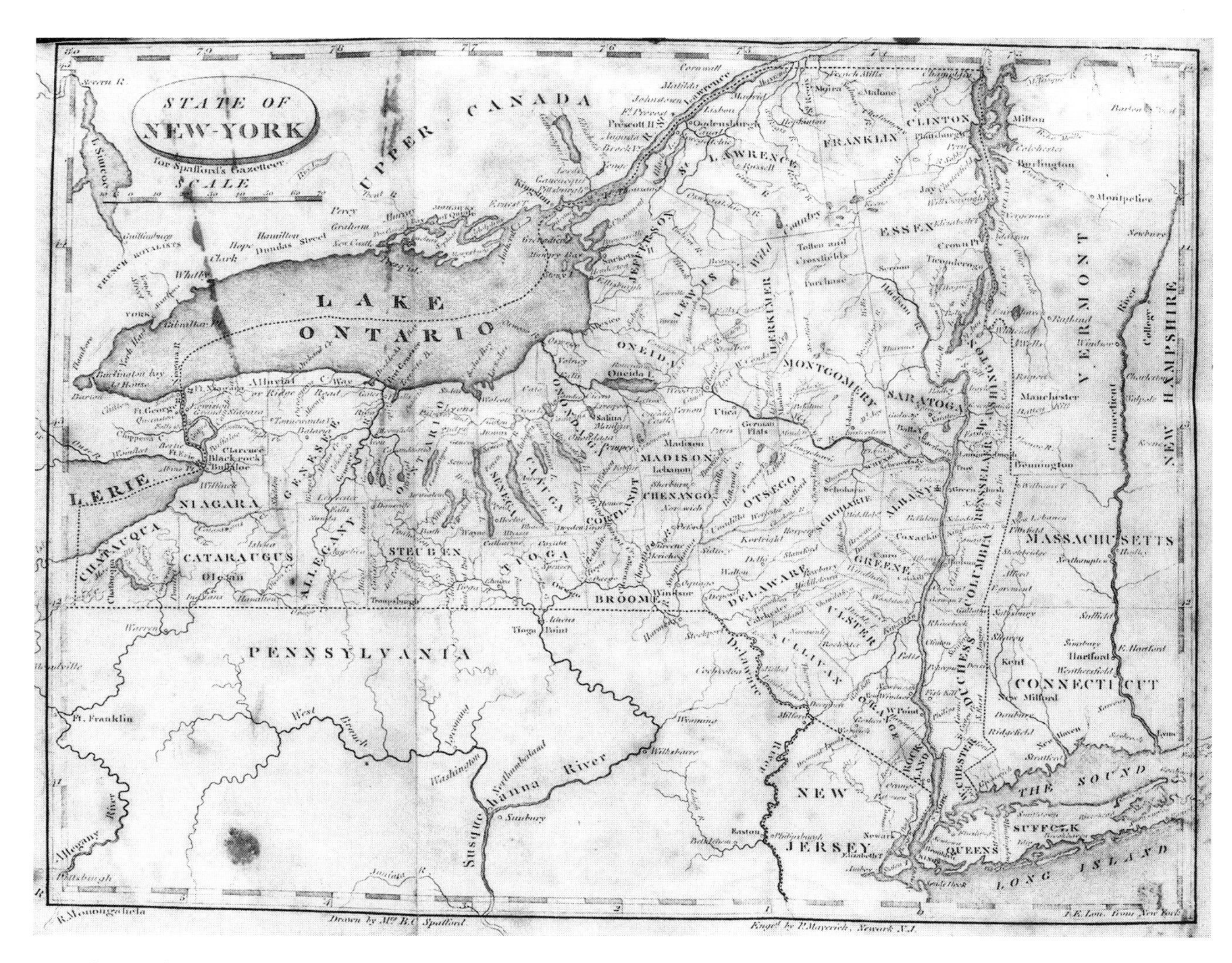

Map of State of New York from Spafford's Gazetteer (1813).
Courtesy of Lawrence H. Slaughter Collection, The Lionel Pincus and Princess Firyal Map Division, The New York Public Library, Astor, Lenox and Tilden Foundations.

Chapter 4

THE DOWN-RENT WAR

CATSKILL FARMERS REBEL AGAINST FEUDALISM

To understand the exciting events of the farmers' rebellion, part of which took place in Woodstock Township, one needs a few background facts. The large patents were granted in New York State before the Revolution to encourage settlement in the wilderness. The holders of these grants were responsible for law and order, for building roads, sawmills and gristmills, and for providing conditions under which settlers could live and make the land productive. The patentees were obliged to pay an annual quitrent to the Crown, and in turn they demanded a quitrent from those under their jurisdiction. The Van Rensselaers, Livingstons, Verplancks, Hunters and others concerned in the rebellion sold some of their lands outright but more often arranged perpetual, two-life or three-life leases. After the Revolution most of the Tory grants were confiscated, but as the patentees named above were on the American side of the conflict they were allowed to keep their lands. When the independence of America was assured it was quite necessary to confirm land title and contracts or there would be chaos. Title to all the land in Ulster County was traceable to colonial grants, and in the first constitution of New York State, drawn up in Kingston, the right of every citizen to the property of which he was the lawful owner was confirmed.

Almost all of Woodstock was included in the patent granted to Johannis Hardenbergh and his associates by Queen Anne in 1708. Edward Hyde, Viscount Cornbury, Governor of the provinces of New York and New Jersey, arranged for the Hardenbergh grant in the name of his cousin, Queen Anne. He is assumed to be one of the dummy signators who subsequently sold his interest to Robert Livingston Jr. (Robert of Clermont) and Gulian Verplanck.[1] A few years later the acquisitive Livingston, whose family already owned a huge tract of land on the east side of the Hudson River known as Livingston Manor, secured about a third of the patent.[2] This was Great Lot 8, which extended from the Kingston Corporation Line (now Saugerties) westward to the east branch of the Delaware River. The northern line of this lot ran diagonally across the Woodstock Village Green and along the Old Forge Road through parts of Bristol (Shady) and Little Shandaken (the Lake Hill–Willow Valley) and for miles beyond. North of the Village Green sat Great Lot 26, which belonged to Thomas Wenham, and this included what would later become Rock City, all of Byrdcliffe and most of Bristol north to the Greene County line.

The proprietors had no difficulty selling their best ground and the subdivisions near the villages. But in the hilly and less desirable sections it was necessary to induce settlers to come—even though they lacked cash. These people were usually allotted a hundred acres of unimproved land and had to clear a designated acreage each year. They were expected to plant two acres of orchards, to build a good house and a suitable barn, to erect fences and so on. They had to pay all taxes and levies and had to provide oxen and drivers for at least two days' work on the roads per year. At the end of seven years they were to receive a deed for their property. During that time the farmer would have improved his holdings, and after building his home and barns and bringing the fields into cultivation he was obligated to sign whatever the landlord required or lose everything for which he had worked. It was an unpleasant surprise for him to discover that instead of a clear title his deed was in fact a lease. The deeds were of several kinds. There were perpetual leases in which the title depended upon an annual payment to the proprietor of one shilling per acre—some were for ninety-nine years—and there were one-, two- and three-life leases. The last were most common in the upper sections of Woodstock, and upon these the tenant could include the names of three living members of his family. When the last-named person died, the property would revert to the proprietor or his heirs. It was further stipulated that the tenant had to pay the landlord an annual quitrent of from fifteen to twenty bushels of wheat and four fat hens for every hundred acres, as well as so many days' work. The tenants had to give the landlord first right of purchase, at a reasonable rate, of all grain, fruit and stock raised on the farm; had to have all their grain ground at his mill, allowing him one tenth of it; and were obliged to return all manure to the land. The restrictions varied with each lease. All so-called deeds carried a provision that the farm could not be sold without the consent of the proprietor, and upon such sale the titleholder was to receive at least one quarter of the sale price.[3]

In the 1830s and 1840s most of the last-named persons on the leases were dead or about to die and the farmers, whose families might have been on the land for three generations, suddenly found that their properties were due to revert to the landlords. It has been estimated that by this time the rent paid by the farmers had given the owners a return of more than three hundred percent on their investments. Meanwhile the proprietors had been relieved of the quitrent paid to the Crown. Law and order had become the charge of the local government, as had the responsibility for upkeep of the roads. The original unimproved lands had been developed by the tenants' labor into farms with homes, barns and bearing orchards upon which they paid the taxes. These people could hardly be expected to relinquish all they had built without a fight.

Many attempts were made to resolve the situation by legislative means, but it proved impossible to change the laws favoring the proprietors. Some of this legislation had been drawn up by Alexander Hamilton, who was kin to the Van Rensselaers. It was evident the legislators were under the domination of the large landholders, as every measure introduced to ameliorate the plight of the farmers was either tabled or turned down. Governor Seward was persuaded to recommend that the legislature appoint a committee to investigate the tenures, but nothing was heard from this committee in four years. The governor believed in the inviolability of the proprietary laws, and when the rebellion started he was determined to crush it as soon as possible.

In Albany County the feudal system of patroon and vassals in its most objectionable form had robbed the farmers of their dignity. This un-American practice was continued long after the Revolution by the Van Rensselaers, who held an annual court where the head of the family sat in state to receive the tithes. This ceremony galled the workers of the soil even more than the payment of the quitrent. Stephen Van Rensselaer, nicknamed the Good Patroon, allowed many of the poorer farmers to skip payment of the tribute. But after his death his heirs demanded all payments that were in arrears, thereby placing an intolerable burden on some of the tenants.[4]

The trouble began in Albany County in 1839. The memory of the Boston Tea Party was still fresh in the minds of all Americans. The men disguised as Indians dumping tea from England into Boston Harbor served as a model for the farmers in New York State who believed an equal injustice was depriving them of their lands. They disguised themselves with sheepskin caps pulled down over their faces. Holes were cut in these caps for eyes, ears and mouth, and feathers, plumes of horsehair or snakeskins were attached.[5] The rebel farmers called themselves such terrifying names as Big Thunder, Black Hawk or Blue Beard.[6] But despite their efforts, Governor Seward took prompt measures and the initial disturbance was soon quelled.

For the next few years the tenant farmers seethed with unrest. Attempts were made to redress the injustices of the feudal tenures by legal means, but these measures always failed. Again in Albany County an outbreak took place, this time in the Helderbergs at Berne. There a deputy sheriff was tarred and feathered, bringing on a civil suit for ten thousand dollars in damages. In Columbia County a

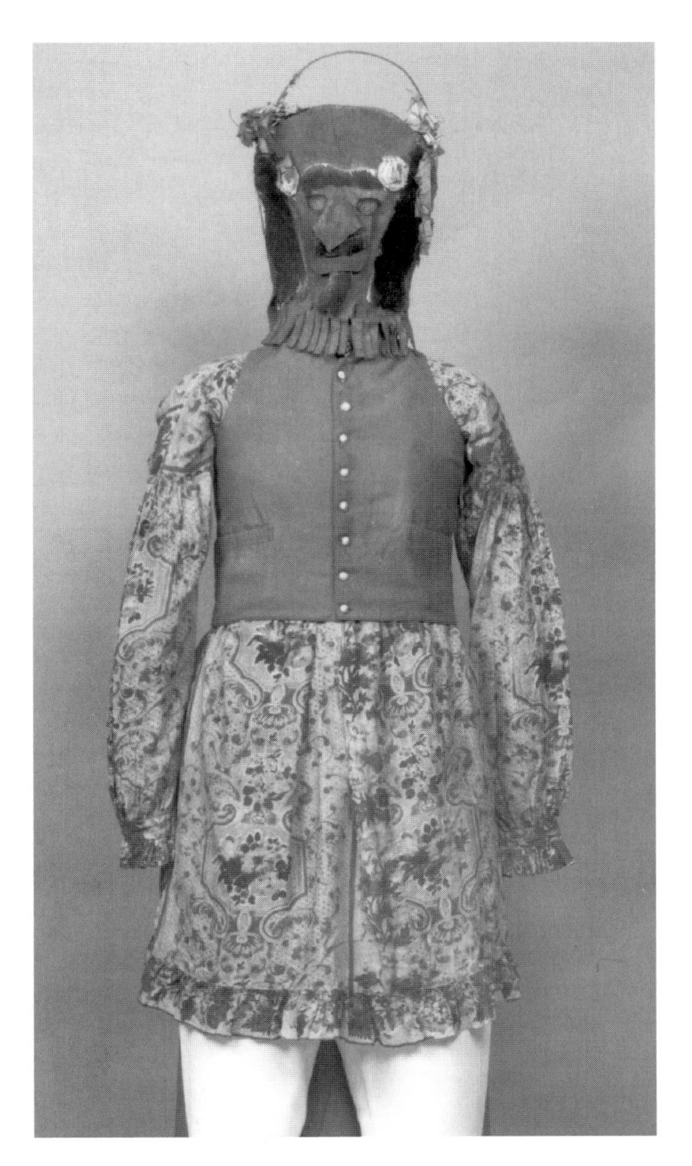

LEFT: *Anti-rent costume: mask, vest and dress, circa 1845.*

ABOVE: *Close-up of mask.* Courtesy of New York State Office of Parks, Recreation and Historic Preservation; Senate House State Historic Site.

sheriff tried to evict from a farm two men who had fallen behind in the payment of chickens and wheat to the Van Rensselaers. Forewarned, the farmers gathered in force, wearing disguises of sheepskin masks and calico robes. Under the leadership of a man called Big Thunder, they raised a fearful din, beating tin pans and shouting—but they also carried loaded guns. The sheriff was forced to relinquish the eviction papers, which the crowd destroyed in a bonfire before they disbanded.

The next meeting of the "Indians" was held in Livingston Manor. It consisted of about a hundred "braves" observed by a large crowd of onlookers.[7] The demonstration got out of control and a young man was accidentally shot, which soon brought a posse from Albany. The posse was led by the district attorney, who arrested Big Thunder. When the Indians tried to rescue their leader a fight ensued, but the officials managed to place the man in the Hudson jail where they discovered their prisoner was Dr. Smith Boughton, a much-respected local practitioner. The insurgent farmers declared they would burn the town of Hudson unless their leader was set free on bail. When rebuffed, they did not burn the town but did cut off much of the food supply. The farmers threatened to come thousands strong to rescue Big Thunder, and the local townspeople became thoroughly frightened. They did not know that Dr. Boughton, in the cause of peace, had refused to be rescued.

Expecting an attack, the police were apprehensive, demanding that guards be sent from Albany. Troops were alerted for trouble at all the towns along the river and Captain Krack's cavalry was shipped by steamer from New York City to Hudson. The cost of maintaining these troops burdened the town. However, the gentry enjoyed themselves entertaining the soldiers with receptions and balls, while the ordinary people grumbled and were glad to see them leave. Meanwhile the local ministers preached the evils of the anti-rent cause: as all power came from the Almighty, they thundered, resistance to authority was rebellion against God. In fact much of the ministry's income was derived from the leases, many of which contained clauses requiring the tenant farmers to contribute to the churches.[8]

At Berne in Schoharie County the first Equal Rights Convention in New York State was held late in 1844. In their manifesto the delegates to the convention proclaimed that all power emanated "from the people, not the few, but all!"[9] The one hundred and fifty delegates elected Hugh Scott as their president. (Scott had been secretary of the first anti-rent meeting five years earlier.) At the convention, in a move to be conciliatory, organizers voted that the down-renters should cease wearing disguises. As if to nullify this effort to please the authorities, the recently inaugurated Governor Silas Wright issued a proclamation outlawing disguises. This move so infuriated the farmers that they brought forth their abandoned calicoes and sheepskins. They were not deterred when the governor maintained that anyone armed in a disguise was guilty of a felony, which was punishable by state imprisonment or even death.[10]

Soon another festering sore erupted, this time in Delaware County, and it was a development of deep concern to the Ulster County farmers. The Delaware "Indians" had been well organized into an association of over a thousand men, all of whom swore to obey their leaders, to keep secret all things connected with their affairs and to stand by each other as long as life should last. Their declared objective was to resist payment of the quitrent and the consequent eviction of owners from the disputed farms. A levy of two cents per acre was made upon each member.[11] They agreed to blow cow horns to warn other farmers of danger and to assist any one of their fellows who might be in trouble.

Among the down-renters were the Burroughs family and William Brisbane, who was one of the movement's cleverest proponents. For several years a fiery Irishman, Tom Devyr, had been working for the cause, and it was he who brought a high level of organization to the so-called Indians. Devyr started a newspaper called *The Anti-Renter*. Other sheets published to explain the farmers' plight were *The Guardian of the Soil*, printed at the Schoharie courthouse, and the *Helderberg Advocate*. I have heard that a paper called *Voice of the People* was published in or about Delhi, although no trace of it seems to be left in the county seat. Verses used by the Indians appeared in these sheets. The following ballad is said to have been sung whenever the Indians gathered.

THE END OF BIG BILL SNYDER

The moon was shining silver bright
When the sheriff came at dead of night;
High on a hill stood an Indian true,
And on his horn a blast he blew—

Out of the way of Big Bill Snyder,—
Out of the way of Big Bill Snyder,—
Out of the way of Big Bill Snyder,—
Tar his coat and feather his hide, Sir!

Bill thought he heard the sound of a gun;
And he cried in his fright: "My race is run!
Far better for me had I never been born,
Than to come to the sound of that tin horn!"

Chorus

Bill ran and ran till he reached the wood,
And there in horror still he stood;
For he saw a savage, tall and grim,
And heard a tin horn not a rod from him—

Chorus

Next day the body of Bill was found:
His writs all scattered on the ground;
And by his side a jug of rum,
Which showed how Bill to his end had come.

Chorus[12]

When the disturbances started in Delaware the neighboring county of Ulster was already in ferment regarding the titles to many holdings, particularly in the upper part of the town in Livingston's Great Lot 8. Most of the farmers dreaded the possibility of bloodshed, yet they believed deeply in the justice of their cause. Of course there were a few characters who enjoyed flouting the law and it was they who were responsible for the excesses that occurred later. In the meantime the farmers continued to gather. In *Tin Horns and Calico*, Henry Christman tells of a meeting in June 1844 near Pine Hill, Ulster County, of five thousand dissatisfied tenants eager to form an anti-rent society.[13]

The rebellion in Woodstock Township, as related to me by the sons of those who participated, began with events that occurred the following winter. Ashley Cooper of Lake Hill told me many stories and showed me the cow horn used to call the "Indians." His father, William Cooper, son of Jacob Cooper, who ran the inn and tollgate at the top of the hill, was in a strategic position to give warning of the approach of the Livingston agents or of the sheriff's arrival from Kingston. Elmira Cooper made gowns for the Indians of red and green calico with strings at the waist and little hoods with holes for the eyes. But to complicate matters William's cousin, who also lived

OPPOSITE: *Tin horn used by Moses Shultis in the anti-rent rebellion. Down-renters blew horns to warn of the approach of Livingston land agents or officers of the law.* Courtesy of Historical Society of Woodstock. Photo by Dion Ogust.

Silas Wright Jr. (1795–1847), governor of New York from 1844 to 1846 and implacable foe of the down-rent cause. Courtesy of U.S. Senate Historical Office.

Masthead of Tom Devyr's newspaper supporting the farmers' rebellion. Courtesy of New York State Library, Manuscripts and Special Collections.

The Anti-Renter.

THOMAS AINGE DEVYR,] "FOR THE LAND IS MINE, SAITH THE LORD; FOR YE ARE STRANGERS AND SOJOURNERS WITH ME."—MOSES. [EDITOR & PUBLISHER.

VOL. I. ALBANY, SATURDAY, APRIL 4, 1846. NO. 34.

COMMUNICATIONS.

For the Anti-Renter.

Roxbury, Delawate county, '45.

It was once remarked by Shakespeare that in order to be considered something, we must commit some notorious act of injustice—and we have reasons for the belief that the superintendent of schools for our town intends to test its veracity—and has already succeeded, we believe, in committing some notorious acts—but what he should be considered for so doing, remains for the public to determine. Permit me to remark that this is an office that should be graced by some of the most intelligent, equitable, and virtuous men of our community, instead of being disgraced by purse-proud aristocrats, whose only aim is to gain the respect of their fellow tyrants by committing some notorious acts of injustice on the friends of equity, and not considering that they are mutilating the tree of knowledge that is fast spreading its nutritious branches over this widespread republic. We confess that we do not approve of the looseness that has been practised in the examination of pedagogues as to their character and ability, &c.—but we have seen, during the present year, several young men of talent turned away with a half-way license, who had, previous to this, received good legal certificates, and for years shone as a bright star in their profession. We are not as versed in law—we do not suppose as those who style themselves law and order m n, for, as we understand things, superintendents are authorized to give license to such applicants as are sufficiently qualified with respect to moral character, learning and ability, and not, as perhaps our honorable superintendent supposes, with respect to law and order, &c. If the superintendents of common schools take the absurdity upon themselves of being partial in the examination of applicants, and of holding back the public moneys of certain districts, we think it time that they should be considered something, if that be their desire; and we think the most appropriate time in future for consid-

their enforcement, not on the moral convictions of the people, but upon the physical force of a standing army. The aristocracy are promot to enforce all their oppressions at the bayonet's point, and yet in the instance I have cited they did not even attempt to bring a single redcoat to the scene of action. They knew how vain it would be to array mercenaries against men, as well armed as the mercenaries themselves, who defended the rights of their wives, their daughters, and their helpless little ones, against the bad men who would reduce them to destitution and distress.

I am aware, my lord, that instead of meeting the controversy upon the broad field of argument, you are resorting to the old barbarous means of putting it down by brute force.—It was perfectly natural for you to do this, you would not be one of the true race if you did not do it—but am I for that reason to suppress facts—to blot out history—to cover past events with a pall—to go back to the letterless times of barbarism—merely that the present times may be suited to the barbarism which you would reintroduce among us.

I cannot do it, my lord, I have spoken and written the truth in more lord ridden countries than this, and in the teeth of men more powerful, if not more vindictive, than your lordship.

But my lord, a word in your ear. The Government, either of New-York state or of the Federated Republic, has neither the will nor the means, to do for you what the British Government did not attempt to do for the forenamed landlord. So long as the people confine themselves to isolated and desultory movements against your rapacity and injustice, and so long as the other citizens of the state look on with apathy, so long are you all right. A sheriff and a *posse* does the work for you—two or three victims are singled out and sacrificed, and there is an end of it. You have nothing to do only sit upon your easy chair and issue your orders; those orders are obeyed—property is siezed upon and sold for your benefit; men are ironed, like thieves, for your safety and pleasure. This is very well so long as it lasts

right to our descendants, whose wants and rights will be equal to our. There is no alternative.

But this State was settled upon very different principles, and the question in the Convention will be, or should be, after deciding the natural right to the soil, how to secure the right under existing circumstances. In choosing the delegates, those who have more land than is their right in possession will be unwilling to part with it; those who have less may not only want their land, but compensation for the time they have been deprived of it. The monopolists will point to their parchments, (if they happen to have any,) and the landless will point to their hard hands, their hungry stomachs, their oppressions and insults, and their children. The people however, as on all former occasions, will neglect to stand up manfully for their entire rights; consequently they will not be fully represented in the Convention, and their representatives will therefore be compelled to *compromise*. What, then, shall be the nature of the COMPROMISE.

In my view, the compromise should in no event permit the wrong of land monopoly to go one step further. No new monopoly should be allowed under any circumstances. With respect to existing monopolies, the monopolists should be required to sell out within a given time to landless persons; or they should be allowed to hold till their death; but after the adoption of the Constitution *no individual should be allowed to acquire more land than may be considered sufficient for the support of a large family.* If the Convention should thus proceed to secure the fundamental right of an Inalienable Homestead, in the best manner possible under the circumstances, their after labors will be comparatively light. If they do not secure this right, their efforts will be apt only to make confusion more confounded, and the landless should immediately strike for a *new* Convention.

It is not too late to pledge the delegates to the LIMITATION PRINCIPLE, the INALIENABLE HOMESTEAD, and the LIBERATION OF THE ANTI-RENTERS. LANDLESSMEN, *and men*

trol or accountability, would have vied with you for grace or beauty in the parlor or in the hall, and have shone like jewels of the first water in the diadem of human society. Now suppose you take an inventory of all your enjoyments, of all the articles of your dress, furniture, food, fuel, &c., and see how many of them you could buy with the money paid to the seamstress for taking twenty thousand stitches on a shirt. Begin if you please, with your boa, muff, bonnet or shawl, and find how long it would take to pay for one of these at the rate at which thousands of your sisters are compelled to labor. Especially when you are out shopping, with papa's purse in your hand, remember this calculation. Have you purchased a boa at $18, and returned delighted with your glossy treasure? Take your pencil and solve this problem: If a seamstress takes 3000 stitches in a seam of one yard in length for two cents, what would be the length of a seam she would have to sew to buy a boa at $18? Problems of this kind would cultivate a lovelier sentimentality in the hearts of susceptible young ladies, than all the tearful novels in the world.

A correspondent of The Tribune indulges in the following:

The "Harmonious Democracy" had a nice time in this city last night. Rows and fights graced their assemblages and we have double delegates from almost all the wards. Assemblyman WATSON got knocked and kicked in his ward, and in the ninth, Attorney General VAN BUREN, and the ex-State Printer were distressingly conspicuous. The full particulars may be found in the Argus and Atlas.

There is nothing up in either House except private claims. There is little of public interest about any of those except one for the relief of Marcus Brown, of which I will take the liberty to make a few remarks. Marcus is the son of Cœnradt Brown, and it is for the Revolutionary services of the latter. He was a resident of Schoharie County in 1781, when Col. WILLETT was sent out there to bring the Tories up to the bull-ring. They were as thick as blackberries, and to cut the matter short, Col. W. ordered all the friends of America to rally at a particular

great expense and trouble in defending himself in said suit. Also, that he has committed oppression and wrong on seven other citizens by a similar vexatious prosecution, obliging them to defend themselves before a distant tribunal, on a charge of a pretended criminal act, at a cost which said individuals are wholly unable to meet. Also, that he has committed oppression and wrong on a religious society which had purchased a lot on which to erect a church, by taking measures manifestly and *avowedly* to drive said society to the necessity of abandoning their design of erecting a church on said lot.

"12th. That he has been oppressive and tyrannical in discharging armorers from employment, refusing to assign any reason for the act, and then using his official influence with private manufacturers to prevent said discharged armorers from obtaining employment elsewhere.

"13th. That he has interfered with the public press and with the rights of workmen, by threats of discharge to armorers if they persisted in taking one of the newspapers published in the armory."

Boys, let us keep a tight reign upon this villanous spirit. Couldn't you try, and put men into legislative halls who would look sharply—sharply after blades of this description—men who would hunt out, and drag into daylight, all the scoundrelism of this nature that is going on in the Republic. Our Reformers are not half Reformers—our democrats are not half democrats—our whigs are not half whigs. When they get into snug quarters they grow sleepy.

HIGHWAY ROBBERY AND MURDER.

A man aged about 50 years, from East Davenport, Delaware county, by the name of Sournberger (Suttenburg, the name is commonly pronounced), was murdered on the night of the 24th inst., about one mile west of the Vly, in the town of Middleburgh, Schoharie county.

on the farm, was a constable. Other neighbors remembered odd bits regarding the farmers' rebellion, but my chief source of information was Merritt Staples, to whom I am most indebted for part of the following account. (He was the carpenter who built my studio at Lake Hill, and ours was a most rewarding association. He was the kind of person who, when the contract was completed to everyone's satisfaction, threw in an extra closet and widened the cellar door to accommodate a rolling cask, which he called a "kag.") His uncle as a boy carried provisions to the Indians when they were in hiding and, being too young to be a full-fledged "brave," was nicknamed "Papoose." His other uncle, Elisha, shot the hat off the sheriff's head during one of the "battles"—the hat was the main casualty of that skirmish.

The Woodstock down-renters chose as their leader Asa Bishop, who became known as Black Hawk. The members pledged themselves to secrecy, to loyally support one another and to obey their leader. At their meetings, speakers exhorted them to refuse payment of the quitrent and to resist the sheriff's men if the latter attempted evictions—but they were not to molest anyone else. It was agreed that all the Indians would assemble upon the blowing of the cow horns.

The first action took place on the road above Little Shandaken (Lake Hill) after the blasts of horns had been relayed down the valley from The Corner (now Mount Tremper). Soon a horseman brought news of a sheriff's attempt to serve eviction papers upon Benjamin Winne, but the latter was not found at home. (Farmers were seldom at home for a sheriff.) Winne's wife detained the sheriff in the house while she managed to sneak out the back door to blow the signal. From farm to farm, the alarm was relayed through the mountains until the news was spread for many miles and brought the Indians on the run.

The sheriff, hearing all the cow horns blowing, became suspicious and started back to Kingston through the Little Shandaken valley. In the dusk along his route hooded figures jumped from the hedgerows, trying to frighten and detain him. Now fully aware of the menace, the sheriff urged his horse into a gallop but was suddenly confronted by a roadblock. The Woodstock Indians had placed a farm wagon across the road and stood around it in forbidding array. The process server whipped his steed, trying to break through, but a strong arm grabbed the bridle to slow the frightened horse. The rider raised his whip again but before he could bring it down a dozen Indians unseated him and he landed ignominiously in the muddy ditch. While a couple of men held him, his coat was torn open and the legal papers removed. Afterward the sheriff was allowed to proceed with a warning that if he tried to serve eviction again in Woodstock the Indians would resort to tar and feathers. The victorious gang turned their wagon around and rode to Shandaken Lake, where they burned the papers in a bonfire.[14] No doubt they danced around the blaze, as was their wont, singing one of their popular songs, such as:

> The horns will toot from door to door,
> While old tin pans they clatter;
> There's Indians scalping all around—
> For Lord's sake, what's the matter?[15]

That night's work freed a savage violence among the farmers, which was well expressed in another of their ballads:

> We are up to our necks by now,
> We might as well finish the row,
> O whow, O whow![16]

The story about the sheriff was told and retold from house to house throughout Ulster County. Though many supported the cause of the farmers, there were some who sympathized with the sheriff and deplored the actions of the lawless down-renters. Around Shandaken Lake the air was charged with excitement, for apart from the few men who had participated, nobody knew with certainty who the so-called Indians were. If the local authorities did not take immediate action it may have been because, up to that time, they had considerable sympathy for the difficulties of the tenant farmers. A charge of robbery was written on the books but there were no persons named. It would require another violation of the law to oblige the authorities in Kingston to take repressive measures.

On a disputed farm across Shandaken Lake a farmer had been cutting trees in violation of the old contract with the proprietors, who held that the timber belonged to them. One day in early March a yoke of oxen was visible plodding up through the woods to the place where the farmer had piled his recently cut logs ready to draw them across the frozen lake to Cooper's sawmill. A group of men headed by John Lasher, who was working for Henry P. Shultis, the

Re-enactors of the down-rent rebellion photographed in 1937 during the sesquicentennial celebrations. Photo by Konrad Cramer. AMS Collection.

agent for the Livingstons, was soon spotted beginning to load the logs onto their sled. Immediately, three blasts of the cow horn sounded from Cooper's Hill to summon the down-renters.

The Indians, hurriedly donning their disguises, assembled by the lake. They were a wild-looking group in their tattered calicoes and sheepskin hoods bedecked with turkey feathers, coon tails or strips of bearskin as would befit Catskill mountain men. A select number sneaked through the woods to surprise the workers and found them rolling the logs off a ledge onto the sled drawn up below. With their usual whoops and bloodcurdling yells the Indians fell upon Lasher and his men. Lasher, armed with a handspike, was prepared to defend himself. He warned them to keep off, shouting that Henry Shultis had ordered him to remove the lumber. The attackers' response was to rush in and try to disarm him. His helpers, Bonesteel and Plass, lost their nerve and flew into the woods, and the oxen took fright and bolted. Lasher continued to fight until he was pushed off the ledge. As he fell he grabbed at two of the Indians, who lost their disguises. Lasher survived the fall and ran, with the Indians in close pursuit.

They captured him on the shore of the lake and in Peter Sagendorf's nearby barn found a cask of tar that had been recently warmed. (It was prepared quite by accident, they later testified!) Here, Lasher, with his hands tied behind his back, had to submit to having his hair painted with tar and sprinkled with chicken feathers (which were also handy); his leather boots were removed and filled with tar and he was forced to step back into them. Then the unfortunate Lasher was allowed to depart amid the jeers of the men.[17] It is said that Lasher was subsequently rewarded by the landowners with the gift of a farm on the lake. In later years whenever William Cooper caught sight of Lasher across the lake, out of deviltry he would blow his cow horn, to Lasher's chagrin.

When this day's work was finished the Indians came to realize the gravity of their position. They knew full well the authorities would come to arrest those men who had lost their disguises, as well as Big Bill Diamond, who had been identified by Lasher due to his store-bought boots. Diamond was a glass blower and could afford the luxury of machine-made shoes. For months he hid in a cave above the lane leading off Cooper's Hill, and when the horns were

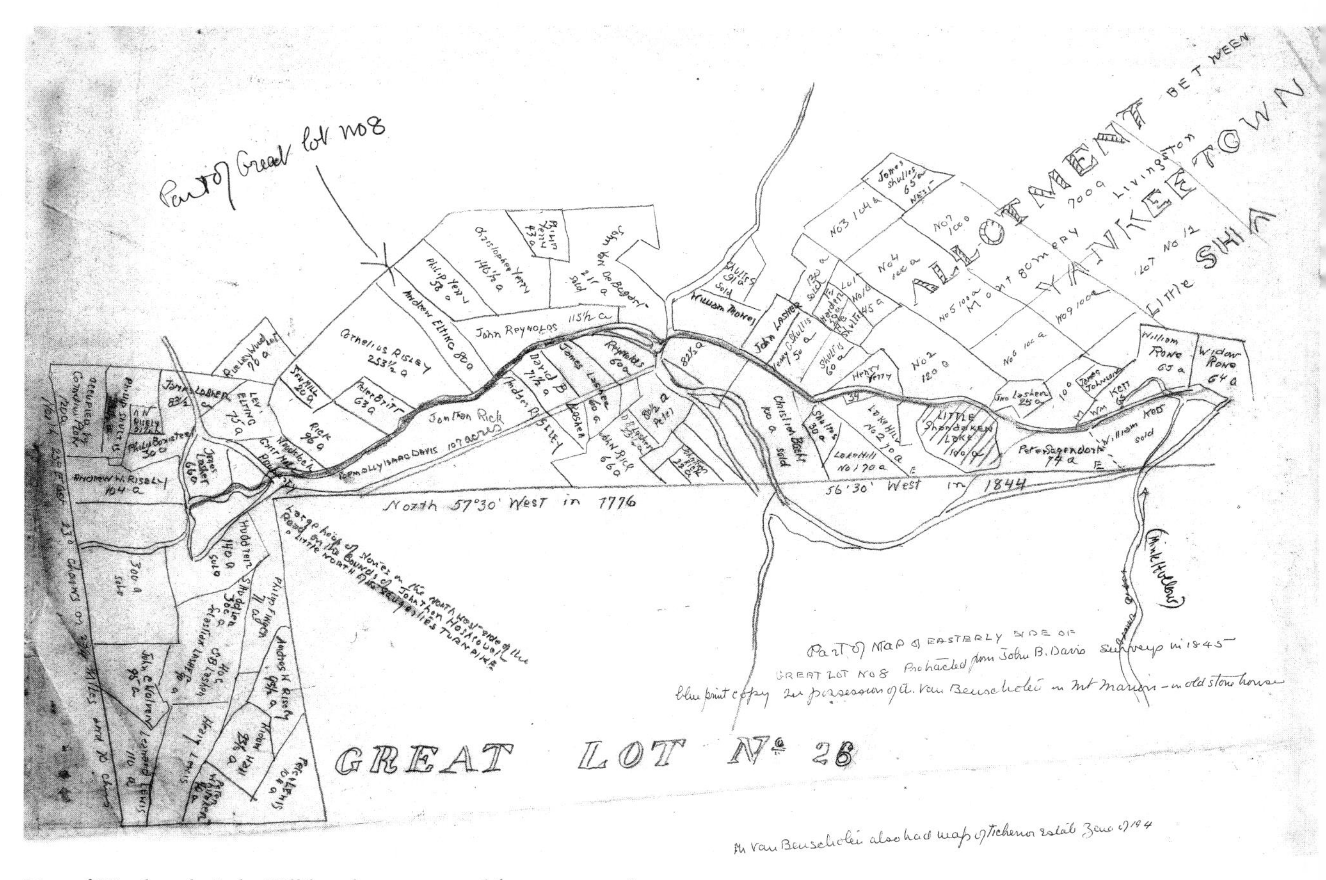

Map of Woodstock, Lake Hill hamlet, protracted from surveys by John B. Davis, 1845. Note Peter Sagendorf's property at far right, center, bordering Little Shandaken Lake. Copy in AMS Collection.

blown he usually received visits from the other Indians who had reason to think the authorities were looking for them. The young Staples lad, "Papoose," carried food to the cave dwellers. Friends of Peter Sagendorf, on whose farm the tarring and feathering had taken place, tried to persuade him to join the others. But he refused to budge from his own land, although he spent several days at a time hidden in the marsh that originally bounded the western shore of the lake. At such times he was invisible from the house and road, secreted in one of his charcoal pits. If his friends approached they would call out, "Hey, Pete, hey, Pete." When my friend Merritt Staples related this to me, he laughed and laughed, making me feel very dull because I failed to see the joke![18]

Joab Eighmey of Willow, trying to deliver his lumber to the mill, would take along a young boy to guide the oxen in the event a constable was spotted and he would be obliged to run into the woods. On the other hand, there is a story of the widow Carl who, while preparing breakfast, heard voices by her door shouting, "Down rent." To this she gave a spirited reply, "Up rent." The unwelcome visitors entered the kitchen and spilled her crock of batter in fanciful patterns all over the floor.

A few uneventful days passed and then the neighborhood once again heard the blast of the cow horn. News was relayed to the Indians that the sheriff's black cart, known as the "tally-ho wagon," had passed on up the valley, presumably to pick up some of their fellow down-renters. On its return the Indians were waiting for the wagon, blocking the road under the brow of Cooper's Hill. This is where, from a distance, Elisha Staples, armed with his squirrel gun, shot the hat neatly off the sheriff's head. Then the gang rushed the "tally-ho," and in the fight that ensued the mountaineers trounced the posse and freed a couple of prisoners they found inside the wagon. The battered enemy was now permitted to reboard the cart and was sent ignominiously down the road as fast as their horses would go. The battle of Cooper's Hill had been won by the Indians![19]

The Delaware County Indians helped to organize the down-renters of Woodstock and fan the flame of courage within them. They included intellectuals who gave our farmers ideas—such as that individually they might be weak but banded together they could have a voice in the state legislature. They maintained that the quitrent was a relic of feudalism, that eviction was unwarranted and that leases cunningly contrived to benefit only the patroons would some day be proved illegal. They challenged the right of a few proprietors to those vast territories that once belonged to the province, and the right of the governor to give them away. They claimed that Tory privilege had to end and that human rights came before property rights. Their speakers would finish by promising that, when necessary, the Delaware County neighbors would come to the aid of the Ulster tribe. That time had arrived, because the Woodstock Indians were now in serious trouble.

It was a clear winter's evening early in 1845 when the clump of many hoofs upon packed snow aroused the farmers of Little Shandaken. Down the length of the valley twisted a line of horsemen in a monstrous snake dance. The lights of flaming torches leaped crimson into the gem-blue sky with sparks flying upward to lose themselves against the brilliance of the stars. Only the mountains that contained the valley showed, in their regal profiles, remoteness from the tumult, for they had been lifted from the bed of a Devonian sea and for millions of years had stood immutable. In the farmhouses the candles were hurriedly extinguished, as if the occupants feared attracting attention, though from their front stoops they watched the spectacle. They shivered as they heard the unrestrained yells, the clanging of dishpans and the wailing of the cow horns that profaned the night. The torches revealed the fantastic disguises of would-be Indians, their nightmarish hoods with rams' horns, fur tails or turkey feathers trailing behind. Their cloaks, fashioned in every color of calico, were belted with straps in which were thrust guns, leaving their hands free to make the metals clang or to hold the horns to their lips.

The noise caused the horses to leap and buck in a frantic effort to break away, but the men curbed them to march along the circuitous route. Their pounding hoofs resounded through the cloves and up the rocky ledges. The smell of horses, leather and sweat mingled with the odor of smoke to stimulate the senses of the men. They were crazed with the electricity that emanates from a gang surging forward with a common purpose. The formation seemed endless as it passed through the valley, knocking down fences and tramping through fields, coiling like a whiplash or slithering like a giant rattlesnake. Several hundred of the horsemen had come from Delaware County and, with a contingent from Ulster, formed a brave army determined to frighten the landlords and to prove the strength of the down-renters in New York State.

The parade ended at the store of Christian Baehr in what is now known as Bearsville. Not far from there a few of the young bucks tarred and feathered the stone marker on the boundary of the farm of Henry P. Shultis, knowing him to be the agent for the Livingstons. In a nearby building the wives of the down-renters had prepared a late supper for the paraders. The men removed their masks and no doubt ate with gusto after their exhilarating ride. It was said that suddenly Black Hawk, their leader, gave them a sharp order to turn to the fire and don their

This section of road was part of the route used by the anti-renters in 1845. "The formation seemed endless . . . slithering like a giant rattle snake . . . the parade ended at Christian Baehr's place in present day Bearsville." Anita Smith's painting hints at this procession and is titled Shady Hill *or* Snake Road. *Oil on canvas, 24 x 20 in.* Courtesy of Anita M. Smith Estate. Photo by Rick Echelmeyer.

masks as there was a spy looking in the window. Although they obeyed quickly they were not fast enough, and a number of the Indians were recognized by the spy and reported to the authorities. When the excitement of the snake-around had subsided, the Woodstock men were very worried indeed.[20]

Meanwhile several articles on the disturbances appeared in the Kingston newspapers, chronicling Deputy Sheriff Schoonmaker's efforts to bring in the down-renters. His efforts were supported by Major General Smith—the local commander—who appealed to Adjutant General Farrington in Albany for muskets, bayonets and cartridges to be used in putting down the rebellion in Woodstock Township. It was understood that a large-scale expedition would be undertaken. Warrants were issued for those Indians who had been recognized, and on March 11, 1845, Sheriff Schoonmaker marched with a hundred men to the Henry P. Shultis farm in Bearsville where they made their headquarters.[21]

The *Ulster Republican* railed against the down-renters:

> We regret to state that the spirit of insubordination and resistance to the laws, that has manifested itself in Schoharie, Rensselaer and Columbia counties, has also been evinced in Ulster, in the towns of Woodstock and Shandaken, where the lease system prevails to a great extent. Whatever may be the complaints of the tenants, whether well or ill founded, the course they have adopted to redress their grievances must array against them every good citizen. They *must* and *will* be put down. The laws cannot be trampled upon, and its officers resisted in the legal exercise of their official duties, with impunity. If these misguided men will not listen to the appeals of reason, but wilfully and deliberately place themselves without the pale of the law, they must abide the consequences.[22]

The editorial goes on to describe Lasher's ordeal.

On March 12, 1845, the *Democratic Journal* of Kingston summarized the troubles spreading through Ulster County, then commented:

> We have had our tawdry "Indians" and vagabond orators on "feudalism" and a great inconvenience has accrued to the owners without producing a cent's benefit to the insurgents. It was hoped that the demonstration of the power of the State in other quarters, would show the folly of a resistance to the law. But our civil officers having been prevented from the execution of lawful process, the last resort to an adequate force, has been considered necessary.[23]

The article also describes the arrest of two of those responsible for the assault on Lasher. Once again, it says, Sheriff Schoonmaker, accompanied by Constable Vredenbergh, had been thwarted by a gang of armed men while attempting to make arrests. It was under these circumstances that the sheriff "very properly ordered out a posse to sustain the Executive power of the county." Further along the article states:

> A formidable force was promptly drafted from this town, Saugerties, Rosendale and other points, and notwithstanding the storm, a body of 60 men proceeded to Woodstock yesterday morning, where they were to meet a like number from Saugerties, fully armed and equipped.
>
> A larger force is still at the disposal of the Sheriff, and will march for the disturbed quarter, if needed to maintain the supremacy of the laws.

I found no Ulster County newspaper articles sympathetic to the down-renters. However, all the stories recounted to me, passed from fathers to their children, now dead, were of a different nature. For these men the rebellion had been a wonderful bid for freedom from injustice, giving them back their self-respect. Theirs was no revolt behind street barricades by a city rabble. Their methods were rustic, involving awesome masks to frighten in a sudden ambush or an occasional charge from a shotgun aimed at the treetops, and only once did they resort to tarring and feathering. They resisted the law only when it became the exclusive instrument of the landowners. Although the men were soon subdued, their cause was never a lost one. How human were the accounts related to me compared to the newspaper editorials!

Among the armed forces brought into Woodstock to quell the rebellion were the Hurley Greens, a swagger organization of young men proud to be seen parading in lightweight frock coats with brass buttons, yellow epaulets and black fringes at the bottom, beneath which they wore duck trousers. This was hardly a warm uniform, nor were their hats practical—with ostrich plumes running along the top. The men provided their own guns, which were of all makes and sizes. Thus equipped they had no enthusiasm for being called out on a stormy day in March to go to the war front in Woodstock. As a matter of record the sheriff had to go in person to order them to depart for the seat of trouble.

That night, encamped on Cooper's Hill, their military ardor is said to have oozed away as, shivering, they faced the onslaught of snow, sleet and high winds, in anticipation of a horrible battle in the morning. There were bloodcurdling yells of wildcats in the mountains, which were probably augmented by the so-called Indians nearby who enjoyed tormenting these heroes. A story is told of one of the Greens on sentry duty. The password for the night was "moon." While walking his dangerous beat the sentry spied a human figure crawling through the brush. Scared out of his wits, he swore at the person, shouting, "If you don't say 'moon' I'll shoot you." Thereafter the renegades had the upper hand. The Hurley Greens remained but a few days in the troubled area, yet it was enough to cure them of any desire for military glory. These gallant cavaliers were completely disillusioned when they found that their pay was to be only seventy-five cents a day instead of the dollar a day the other guard units received.[24] The company never forgot its terrible experience on the field of glory, and from that time interest in the organization waned. Within a few years it was disbanded.[25]

The *Democratic Journal* for March 19, 1845, tells of the arrest of William Cooper, the Lake Hill innkeeper, as well as the posse that went in search of Asa Bishop, known as Black Hawk, the leader of the Ulster Indians. Bishop managed to elude his pursuers by taking flight as far as Whispell's tavern at Mount Tremper. Before he escaped he and several others made a stand high on a hillside where several shots were exchanged. When the Indians retreated, the troops found their footprints in the snow and some of their disguises abandoned behind a stone wall. A few nights later a detail under Deputy Catlin arrested Elisha Staples. Staples was found sitting up in his bed with a pair of loaded pistols by his side, but he made no resistance. The same posse arrested Joab Eighmey, who, in contrast, gave them a good chase before being captured in a black ash swamp in Silver Hollow. The whole campaign resulted in the capture of ten down-renters, who were confined in the Kingston jail to await action by the grand jury. Elias Van Gaasbeek, Samuel Culver and Henry P. Shultis were among the members of the grand jury for March.[26]

During the disturbance, a law-and-order meeting was held in Little Shandaken by citizens of Woodstock—among them many who were known to be friendly toward the anti-renters. The following resolutions were taken:

> Whereas we consider the laws of our country to be just and equitable, and that all violations of them would be productive of deep injury to ourselves and the community in general, and should be frowned upon by all good citizens:
>
> Resolved, That as such, we entirely disapprove of all the acts of violence committed by certain individuals disguised as Indians, against the authority of the laws; and that we will individually use our influence to suppress such acts of riot to the utmost of our power.
>
> Resolved, That a committee of seven be appointed by us to visit the neighboring towns of Shandaken and Olive, to effect the like object in those places, so that our county may be freed without external aid from any further difficulty in regard to the supremacy of the law.
>
> Signed by: Barent Eighmey, as President,
> Hiram Lamont, as Vice President,
> and William H. De Forest and Wm. Theo.
> Van Doren as Secretaries of the meeting.[27]

The names of eighty respectable citizens of the vicinity were appended, among them Benjamin L. Smith, Thomas Elzra, John Bishop, Henry P. Eighmey, Herman Reynolds, Alexander Row, Benson Eighmey, VanLuveren Van Gasbeeck, Peter D. VanDeBogart, Elijah Freeman, Samuel Culver, Elias Van Gasbeeck, John Hasbrouck Jr., Peter VanDeBogart, Peter Hoyt, William R. Row, John Reynolds and S. L. Heath.

On Saturday, March 15, 1845, inhabitants of Shandaken and Olive had convened at the house of Jesse Lockwood. Christian Winne was elected chairman of the meeting and Henry W. Longyear secretary. This resolution, signed by the most prominent citizens of Woodstock, had an immediate effect upon the down-renters, many of whom came forth voluntarily to surrender to the authorities. Their organization was dissolved and there were no more disturbances of the peace in the western end of the town. The farmers were glad to return to their work.

The neglect of farms all through the middle counties was having a bad effect on agriculture. The farms suffered not only because of the workers' absence but also because of the tenants' uncertainty about the ownership of their lands. There was no incentive to keep buildings in repair or to nourish the ground; fields were becoming overgrown, buildings needed painting and the forests were denuded without thought for new growth. Unless this was stopped there would be little of value left for either the farmer or the proprietor to claim. Many of the younger generation were already migrating to the west.

On March 17th the grand jury met to question the down-renters detained in the Kingston jail. Judge Charles Ruggles of the circuit court addressed them as follows:

> Gentlemen:—It is the duty of the court and of the Grand Jury, to abstain from taking any part with the land owners, or with the occupants, in the excitement which has grown out of the recent occurrences in this county. . . . Our business is only to administer the law as we find it established. This is not to be done in an angry or vindictive spirit. The land owners and [the] occupants are equally entitled to favor and protection so long as they have been guilty of no offence; but when the law has been violated, the public peace broken, and crime committed, it is your duty to cause the offenders to be presented for trial and punishment, to which party soever they may belong. The evil must be corrected by the impartial and dispassionate action of the Grand Jury in the first instance.
>
> It is a notorious fact that extensive associations have been formed in other counties, having for their object the forcible resistance of legal process and the obstruction of the due course of law. In more than one instance, human life has been taken by persons acting under, or influenced by, these associations.
>
> . . . Bands of men have been assembled at various times and places, and evidently by concert, for the purpose of committing misdemeanors or higher crimes; and in order to elude detection and escape punishment, they have concealed themselves in disguises . . . with deadly weapons.—The Sheriff and his officers have been threatened with violence and insult, in case they should proceed to the discharge of their official duties; those who were aiding him in the arrest of offenders, are said to have been fired upon; and individuals, one or more, have been attacked, and wantonly beaten and insulted, when in the peaceable pursuit of their lawful business . . .
>
> Combinations and agreements between two or more persons to commit any criminal offence, are termed conspiracies, and are punishable by fine and imprisonment. So combinations or agreements for the perversion or obstruction of justice or the due administration of the laws, are declared by the Statute to be conspiracies, indictable and punishable in the same manner. All resistance, without arms or disguises, to the service by public officers of legal process, is an offence of the same class and character. Assaulting and beating the Sheriff, or any of his officers, or any person acting in their aid, is a felony or state prison offence, if it be done with deadly weapons.
>
> The facility with which felons and other offenders may escape detection, and elude the punishment due to their offences, by disguising their persons, has induced the Legislature recently to pass a statute on the subject, which is now before me, and which will be laid before the Grand Jury.
>
> By this statute every individual, so disguised, may be apprehended, not only by any public officer, but by any citizen of the county, and taken before a magistrate to be committed to the common jail as a disorderly person . . .
>
> Every assemblage of three or more persons, *armed and disguised*, is an unlawful assembly, and is of itself a riot. Every riot committed under such circumstances is a felony; and every individual of the assembly so armed and disguised, is, by the statute now before me, a felon, punishable by imprisonment in the state prison.
>
> It is apparent that these disguises are assumed only for unlawful and criminal purposes. Every individual of such assembly is implicated in any crime which may be committed by any other individual of the same company or assembly. If an assault, or a homicide, or a murder, be committed by any one of the number, all the rest are equally guilty. Being assembled for a common purpose, every one is answerable for the act of his fellows.
>
> On the part of the occupants of the land, we hear it alleged, in justification or excuse of the resistance to the payment of rent or purchase money, that large landed estates are an evil, because they impede the general prosperity of the country. If this is be so, the remedy lies only in the operation of our laws of descent, by which these large estates are broken up and divided among the descendents of the owners. This remedy is gradual and slow. A change in this respect cannot take place during the present generation of occupants. The distribution of these lands into smaller parcels cannot be made against the will of the owners, without overturning the principles on which the very foundations of government rest.
>
> An opinion appears to have prevailed extensively among the occupants, that the title of the land owners is defective because it is derived from the crown of Great Britain through the colonial government before the American Revolution. This opinion, however, could have been entertained only by those who have neglected to enquire, or were unwilling to be informed.
>
> One of the great objects of government is, to establish on sure and permanent foundations the titles to land and the obligation of contracts. At the time of the American Revolution, nearly all the titles to real estate were derived from the King of Great Britain and his Colonial Governors. The whole country had a deep interest in establishing and confirming these grants. Nearly every farm in the state was held under them. The spot on which we now stand is embraced

within a Colonial Patent, and I do not know of a foot of land in the County of Ulster, the title to which is not to be traced to a Colonial grant, unless it may be some small parcels of land under navigable waters. Under these circumstances, the first constitution of the State of New York, bearing date "Kingston, 20th April, 1777," for the purpose of securing to every citizen the lands of which he was the rightful owner, contains a confirmation of all grants of land made by the Crown of England, previous to the 14th October, 1775. After annulling the grants made after that day, the 36th section of that instrument ordains, "that nothing in this constitution contained, shall be construed to affect any grants of land within this State, made by the authority of the said King or his predecessors, or to annul any charters to bodies politic by him or them, or any of them, made prior to that day." This provision may be found in the first volume of the Revised Statutes, 2nd. Edition, p. 32, section 36.

The Constitution of this State, adopted in 1822, contains a provision to the same effect and in the same language. It may be found in the same volume of Revised Statutes, page 46, section 14. Thus, at an early day, were the Colonial patents and grants of land confirmed to the proprietors, by the fundamental law of the state.

But it is understood that the leaseholders expect the Legislature to annul these leases, and to give them the right of soil, without the consent of the landlords . . .

A law to abolish the leases, or to change them into fee simple estates, or to alter them against the will of either party, would be absolutely void. It would afford the occupants no relief. The power of the United States government would prevent such a law from taking effect . . .

The consequences of the forcible resistance to the execution of the laws, which has been made in this and other counties, is not limited to one class of men. The value of the property of the land holder is, beyond doubt, greatly impaired and diminished. But that is comparatively a small evil. It does not reduce the land owner to poverty. It does not take the bread from his mouth—But it will be otherwise with many of the occupants. The sure and inevitable result of this opposition to the due course of law, will be *their* utter and absolute ruin. This is a far more deplorable calamity, not only to them, but to their families, and to the country. The constitution and laws of this State are based on the consent of the whole people. They cannot be overturned. Nor can they be resisted with impunity. Some of those who attempt it, may for a time elude the law and escape punishment, but most of the actors in the outrages lately perpetrated, will become fugitives from their homes, or be brought to that punishment which will render them infamous.

The course of your duty, Gentlemen, is plain. It is indispensably necessary that these disturbances should be speedily checked and terminated. They are inflicting a heavy expense on the county. They will soon lead here, as they have led elsewhere, to bloodshed and murder. They are bringing poverty, misery and disgrace on those who are engaged in them. The prompt and efficient action of all concerned in the administration of the law, is sufficient to correct the evil—to restore order—to establish the supremacy of the law, and to demonstrate to the world that, in this country, the people are able to govern themselves.[28]

The Kingston press claimed that Judge Ruggles had "produced an almost electrical effect upon all around." Shortly thereafter the grand jury came into the court and presented nineteen indictments, of which seventeen were against persons connected with the anti-rent difficulties. The members of the grand jury then retired and on Monday completed their business by presenting to the court nine more indictments. Certain of the persons in jail who were indicted were arraigned and pleaded "not guilty." Several of the prisoners "were remanded to prison" and others "found bail for their appearance" at the next court in October.

Though the jury included Henry P. Shultis, agent for the Livingstons, several other jurors were Catskill mountain men hardly eager to convict their fellow citizens. No matter how much they might have deplored the actions of the down-renters, they were not persuaded that their Ulster County neighbors were conspirators against the State of New York. William Cooper was released immediately since there was no proof of his participation in the anti-rent outrages. The other Woodstock men were set free after payment of small fines.[29]

The public interest now turned from Ulster to Delaware County, where a Sheriff's sale was to take place on August 7, 1845, on Dingle Hill at the end of a remote lane a few miles from Delhi. The stock to be sold belonged to a farmer named Moses Earle who had refused to pay quitrent to the agent of Charlotte Verplanck. The sale was being held under a clause in the lease concerning distress for rent (frequently not understood by the farmers when they signed because the leases were couched in obscure legal verbiage). To prevent the sale, the "Indians" ran the cattle into the hills and stood around the farm in large numbers to intimidate anyone who might be rash enough to bid on what remained of Earle's stock. They interfered to such an extent that Under-sheriff Steel was unable to proceed and, to restore order, shot off his pistol a couple of times. The Indians reciprocated and Steel fell, mortally wounded.

The authorities arrested dozens of onlookers, which caused rioting around Delhi, where those arrested were subsequently imprisoned.[30] Governor Wright, in turn, declared martial law in all of Delaware County. He ordered the civil authorities to be energetic in maintaining the law and demanded the death sentence for the accused, some of whom could not be connected with the slaying.[31] The trial before Judge Parker became notorious for its prejudice. The grand jury indicted the men for conspiracy, riot and highway robbery as well as for murder. The judge stated that all those gathered at Earle's farm had committed a felony and were guilty of homicide whether or not they had fired a shot. He based his conclusions upon Governor Wright's proclamation the previous year. Two of the prisoners, Van Steenberg and O'Conner, were sentenced to die and the others to long terms in Clinton State Prison.[32]

This trial caused an uproar all over the state and created sympathy for the down-rent cause—which until that point had not been well understood. Now newspapers such as the *New York Tribune* under Horace Greeley came forth staunchly on the side of the farmers.[33] Efforts were made to pass bills protecting the leaseholders, but the proprietors still had enough influence in Albany to prevent these so-called radical measures from becoming law. The flood had been loosed, however, and throughout the state new candidates were appearing for the legislature, wooing voters by advocating land reforms. Many men, such as Samuel Tilden, the fiery writer Thomas Devyr and Colonel John Young, a shrewd Whig assemblyman from upstate, were fighting for the embattled farmers.

Most of the Ulster down-renters were by now quietly tilling the lands under dispute. Big Bill Diamond stayed in hiding for six months in the cave, leaving it only to replenish his food supplies. A few others had fled the county, among them Black Hawk. It was September before news came of him, in the form of a paragraph in the Kingston *Ulster Republican*:

> On Monday of this week, under-Sheriff Schoonmaker, assisted by Constables Plough and Vredenbergh, succeeded in arresting Asa Bishop, *alias* Black Hawk, who figured conspicuously as head chief in the Indian disturbances . . . last spring. A bill of Indictment was found against him at the March Circuit [Court], but he . . . managed by absenting himself from the county to avoid the officers until the present time.[34]

Meanwhile the tide was slowly turning and the proprietors were beginning to sense that their absolute power over their vast holdings was seeping away. The change was evident in a notice published in the *Albany Atlas*:

> Mr. Wm. P. Van Rensselaer, of Rensselaer county, announces that he will dispose of his rents and reservations in Stephentown, to owners and occupants, on the following terms . . . rent of lands . . . to be sold for a principal sum . . . at an interest of five per cent . . . Five years credit will be given for the purchase money, on a mortgage of 5 per cent.[35]

This was a clever way of salvaging an income from properties over which Van Rensselaer might lose title. It was not long before other big landowners followed his example. A notice appeared in the *Ulster Republican* on September 3, 1845, reprinted from the *Albany Argus*:

> The following statement, signed by the respective non-resident proprietors of landed estates in the several middle counties, in which the anti-rent feeling has manifested itself, has been addressed to us for publication . . .
>
> "The undersigned, proprietors of tracts of Land in the counties of Greene, Ulster, Sullivan, Otsego, Schoharie, Rensselaer, Columbia, Dutchess and Delaware, having learned that an impression continues to exist among the occupants and others, that they are unwilling to change the tenures of their leased lands, and to make sales *in fee*, take this mode of announcing their readiness to dispose of all their lands in those counties on fair and equitable terms. Some of the subscribers, indeed, have been for several years selling off their leased and other lands, as fast as favorable opportunity presented themselves, and they have taken some pains to make their tenants acquainted with their intentions.
>
> "If the leasing out of tracts of land has sometimes happened by reason of the preference of the owner for this system, it has likewise in many instances been done in compliance with the wishes of the settlers themselves, and to promote their interest: and it is not easy to see how any wrong to them can arise from their exercising the liberty of making such contracts as shall best promote their own convenience. And notwithstanding the complaints made by them against the so called 'feudal tenures,' very little alacrity has been manifested to take advantage of the offers thus made to them, and numbers of the tenants seem to prefer to hold their lands under the so termed, 'obnoxious system.'

Samuel Tilden (1814–86), a reform-minded attorney who came to the aid of the down-rent cause in Albany. Courtesy of The New York Public Library Archives, The New York Public Library, Astor, Lenox and Tilden Foundations.

"The subscribers take this opportunity to renew their offers to sell their rents, and make grants in fee on fair terms—for which they refer either to themselves, or to their respective agents, who have been made fully acquainted with their views and intentions, and who possess their entire confidence.

"Application on the subject will of course be made to them."

Jno. Hunter,	Campbell S. White,
Henry Overing,	G. Le Roy Banyer,
J. D. Overing,	Louise Livingston,
G. C. Verplanck,	Maturim Livingston,
S. Verplanck,	H. B. Armstrong,
Wm. W. Verplanck,	H. G. Armstrong,
S. D. L. Verplanck,	T. K. Armstrong,
Frederick De Peyster,	Robert H. Ludlow.
John A. Livingston,	

New York, August 12th, 1845.[36]

Gradually the way was cleared for the farmers on disputed land in Woodstock to pay the quarter value on it and to acquire undisputed title from the Livingstons. However, it would be years before the anti-rent dispute was completely resolved. Governor Wright did what he could to stem the tide of liberalism. He respected private rights above human rights and upheld the enactments that forbade the state to interfere in contracts. Perhaps he honestly believed it was impossible to give relief to the tenant farmers under the present constitution, but he must have become aware that the people of New York State were prepared to fight for a voice in their government. At last Wright was persuaded to commute the death sentences of the Delaware County insurrectionists to life imprisonment.

At every meeting of the legislature—to which some down-renters had been elected—amendments to the constitution favoring the farmers were offered. The spokesmen for the leaseholders shouted, "Why should they pay other people's levies? Why did the so-called owners not pay any taxes? Why should the lessors be helped by the authorities to collect rent while the tenant has no way to contest that right?" The farmers claimed to have actual possession of the land while the proprietors' ownership was by proxy. They questioned the legality of the state's having given away these public lands and asked that the so-called landlords be obliged to establish their titles.[37]

At Samuel Tilden's instigation the tenants brought suit in the Supreme Court to test the legitimacy of the quarter sales. They lost their case, however—and when they appealed, the matter came before Judge Ruggles, long a foe of their cause. Ruggles determined that the leases drawn up before the Revolution were valid but that those drawn up after 1787 were illegal.[38] However, in May 1846 the legislature outlawed seizure and forced-sale of tenant property as distress for rent. A constitutional convention was called that same year, which William Boyce and William De Forest attended as delegates from Woodstock Township. This convention eventually abolished feudal tenures and perpetual leases.

Late in 1846, while seeking re-election, Governor Wright belatedly admitted that feudal tenures might properly be investigated, but it was too late then to placate the masses. The Whig assemblyman John Young—described at the time as an independent and fearless politician—ran for governor with the backing of the down-renters. He was elected by a large majority and on New Year's Day 1847 replaced Silas Wright. A petition with eleven thousand signatures was tendered to Young demanding that the Delaware County men in Clinton State Prison be freed,[39] and he immediately issued a pardon for all the down-renters.

Ralph Radcliffe Whitehead, Hervey White and Fritz Van der Loo. Whitehead and White, together with Bolton Brown, founded the art colony at Byrdcliffe in 1902. Van der Loo joined White to launch the Maverick art colony in 1905. Courtesy of Historical Society of Woodstock.

Chapter 5

THE BYRDCLIFFE ART COLONY

A UTOPIAN DREAM

Ralph Radcliffe Whitehead was born in 1854 in Yorkshire, England, the son of Francis Frederick and Isabella Dalglish Whitehead. He attended Harrow and in 1880 received his master of arts degree at Balliol College, Oxford, where he studied under John Ruskin.[1] While a student he was a friend and admirer of Algernon Swinburne, but most of all he was influenced by Ruskin and by William Morris; this was evident throughout his life. Morris was soon to give up his socialistic ideas that had caused such a stir among the undergraduates at Oxford and would devote the remainder of his life to art and literature. Although the idealistic community of craftsmen in Whitehead's later plans may have been a social experiment, it was primarily to consist of a selective group of people of fine principle dedicated to creating beautiful objects with their hands. These people were to live under conditions that would be healthy for minds and bodies, without any political overtones. However, twenty-five years would pass before these plans matured.

Hervey White, who helped to found the art colony in Woodstock, wrote in a paper on Whitehead that when the latter left college he formulated a plan to enter his father's business and turn its factories over to the production of beautiful cloth, in place of the ugly felt that had created the family's fortune. Whitehead's father would not agree to this, wishing his son to be a gentleman, not a businessman. The result was a break between the two, ending with the younger man going off to Paris to apprentice himself to a carpenter in order to earn his living with his hands. In that phase of his development the young Whitehead considered this to be the only honorable way of supporting himself. Years later Hervey White accompanied him on a visit to this carpenter, now living in the suburbs of Paris in a house probably provided by Whitehead—although the latter was far too modest ever to admit to such generosity. Whitehead was greeted by the carpenter's family like a beloved son who had done them great honor by visiting. They inquired most solicitously about his family and were shown photographs of Mrs. Whitehead and the two sons—and in turn they informed him of all that had befallen them since their last meeting. Hervey quotes Whitehead as saying wistfully on the return trip, "It was the happiest year of my life, when I worked with that man."[2]

Whitehead must have soon come into his inheritance because we next hear of him in the 1880s living on a beautiful estate in Styria. It is said that there he designed and planted the first of his lovely gardens. He was married at that time but the union did not last long. By 1890 he had gone to Italy and would remain there for several years—probably the most rewarding of his career. He spoke Italian fluently and compiled a volume on Dante in which the poet's ancient phraseology was annotated into modern Italian to enable the average reader to better understand the masterpiece. He wrote numerous essays, a number of which were gathered into a volume called *Grass of the Desert*, issued by the Chiswick Press in England. It was apparent Whitehead's aesthetic development was becoming as important as his interest in political reform. He was still concerned with the individual's place in society but we detect a bit of irony in his words at this time: "A society is not healthy which is composed of a few rich idlers, a few rich workers, many of whom do useless work, and a great many poor, whose sole aim is . . . to get into a richer class."

He was constantly planning the ideal community. Referring to one unsuccessful attempt, Whitehead says, "The surrender of the 'convent' . . . has once more shattered on the rock of social conventions." But then he adds:

> Let us not be disheartened. It was to have been a preparation and a practice for a more comprehensive scheme; let each of us now make it our object . . . to bring to the aid of our scheme what we can, by inquiry and work and contemplation . . .
>
> Let us, as soon as may be, begin to live, each one of us separately, as if we were in the "convent," and according to its rules; following only what we know to be good and healthy, regardless of the opinions of "society," working each of us at whatever art or craft we think we may be able to gain the mastership in.

Elsewhere he writes of a community where there shall be room for all kinds of work:

> You have your painting, that is work enough for you; another may have his music; but to others, such as myself, who have no particular artistic or literary faculty, simpler crafts are still open. We shall want clothes. Why should not the women spin the yarn, and the men weave the cloth? Such work, done on hand machines, and not for too many hours in the day, has nothing degrading in it, and would be a delightful occupation to those whose nerves are overstrung by the irrational life they have hitherto been leading.[3]

This was written in 1891 and is basically the plan that would bring Byrdcliffe into existence a decade later.

Hervey White refers to Whitehead's years in Italy as though they had left only ugly memories. He further defines this ugliness as a palace on the Via Turnabuoni, with liveried servants and the extravagances and inanities of society life, and implies that during this period all ideals had been discarded. Whitehead's own account of these years refutes this interpretation. Perhaps White's personal viewpoint colored his recollections of their conversations. Hervey White was the only genuine socialist I have ever known. He shared all he had with others and his credo was "live and let live," but his lack of sympathy for all formal ways of life became a block in his thinking. White would not admit that there might be grace and freedom in a more luxurious mode of living than he engaged in himself.

Whitehead's writings in Italy attest to his scholarly approach to Dante, whom he always revered. Boccaccio and Petrarch and the artists Cimabue, Giotto and Michelangelo are but a few of the literary and artistic masters whose works he admired and analyzed. He compared them with Plato, Homer, Sophocles and Virgil, and his active mind linked them to the present, suggesting they had the power to influence the conduct of modern man. What Whitehead absorbed during those years in Italy remained with him always. Significantly, at that time he quoted from a Shakespeare sonnet, ". . . the [prophetic] soul of the wide world dreaming on things to come . . ."[4]

Even the casual wanderer through Byrdcliffe in its early days was reminded of Italy. There were the hills and the villas suggestive of the Apennines, and the lovely gardens full of old-fashioned flowers such as lilies, larkspur and Persian roses. The Della Robbia shrine amidst the soft murmur and odor of pines was reminiscent of Italy although it was also in complete harmony with our mountains. He made a collection of the flowers native to the Catskills, and found a greater variety here than in any other part of the country.[5]

Whitehead came to the United States at the end of the 1890s. In 1892 he had married Miss Jane Byrd McCall of Philadelphia and they had two sons. Together they built a large home in Santa Barbara, California, with a fine garden overlooking the Pacific Ocean. Those who have seen the garden describe it as extraordinarily beautiful, planned skillfully to enhance rather than displace the natural features of a rocky coast. When ostentatious houses were erected nearby, the Whiteheads sold their home and moved to Carmel and later to Montecito. The Montecito house has been described as built on a hill with terraced gardens filled with roses and olive trees set against the Pacific Ocean.[6] While at Montecito he gave a talk that was published as a monograph, which Whitehead dedicated as follows: "To my wife to whose knowledge of Art I am indebted for whatever is most useful in this lecture."

A quotation from the monograph may throw a little light on Whitehead's beliefs: "Those who love to live among the Saints and Angels of Perugino and Botticelli will hardly be very coarse in their daily life; those to whom Michael Angelo is a constant presence, will, when they walk in dark and slippery places, feel more really the support of the eternal arms."[7] If these ideas do not sound especially exciting now, remember that they were expressed many years ago when antimacassars were popular and the Turkish cozy corner at the Waldorf was the last word in fashion.[8] Whitehead was soon to launch his experiment at Byrdcliffe, with its communal living, its cooperative workshops, and its insistence on simple designs and functional lines for furniture and textiles that would be both pleasing and practical. There would also be pottery, sculpture and painting, and forges for metalwork.

Bolton Brown, an artist, tells of searching for a place to found an Arts and Crafts colony at the behest of Whitehead. He describes walking through the Catskills, coming to Mead's from behind the mountain and suddenly finding the valley of Woodstock spread out beneath him. From there he walked down to where the meadows began near the Snyder farm (now Camelot) and turned westward, going through what would become Byrdcliffe. He liked the aspect enough to wire Whitehead that he had found the right place. They agreed to meet in Washington to consider the proposal. Brown recalls that when they met they discussed the fourth dimension over a steak dinner, but enough was said regarding Woodstock for Whitehead to agree that he and Hervey White should accompany Brown back to the village to look over the prospect. They traveled by train to Kingston and there hired a team to drive to the Mead's boardinghouse. They traversed the same territory covered previously by Brown and sat on the ground chewing the sweet ends of grass while they considered the terrain. Whitehead was not won over immediately because he had a lingering desire to settle further south. Finally he agreed with the others and even picked out the site for his own house among the white pines. He would later name his home after these beautiful trees. He authorized Brown to buy seven farms on the side of the mountain that were to make up the place called Byrdcliffe, composed from part of his wife's name and part of his own.[9]

It took months, but eventually Brown acquired the land. There was the Chauncy Snyder farm below Mead's, which is now owned by Dr. and Mrs. Frank Boudreau of the Milbank Foundation, and the Rivenberg (or Rifenberg) property next to Levi Harder's. West of this he bought the Fred Keller farm, and he purchased

Bolton Brown, third co-founder of the Byrdcliffe art colony.
Courtesy of Historical Society of Woodstock.

from Mark Riseley the group of buildings later to become the Lark's Nest. Besides these he bought property owned by Catherine Lapo and by Elizabeth Ricks and a further piece described in the County Clerk's Office as having belonged to "Fred Keller and Others."

When the purchases were complete Whitehead came back from California and, to quote Bolton Brown,

> Hervey reappeared from somewhere, bringing along as a chum one Fritz Van der Loo, ex-cavalry captain under De Wet in the Boer War. He showed me a scar on his breast and another on his back where an English lancer stuck a spear through him. He was a jovial party, fond of cooking and used to get up wonderful dinners . . . Carl Lindin, painter, dropped from somewhere—I think it was Chicago. Lindin originated as a boy on his father's farm in Sweden. Aside from painting, his specialty seemed to be making a hit with the ladies. In those days the house in which he now lives, on a rock ledge above the road, was a disused church. Hervey and Lindin camped in it for a while.[10]

Later Carl Lindin bought the house for four hundred dollars and made it into a home.

Brown boarded at Mrs. Ella Riseley's, in Rock City, and hired one of Cal Short's barns on the lower corner. He boxed off a section of it and then put in a window and a stovepipe for a wood stove. That fall he

The Byrdcliffe Library in 1907. Over five thousand volumes on arts and crafts were housed here. Note the wall hanging by William Morris. Courtesy of the Winterthur Library: Joseph Downs Collection of Manuscripts and Printed Ephemera.

commenced drawing up plans for the first house. Construction began immediately. Larry Plass was head carpenter for the group of buildings centering on the library, Charley Waters for Carniola and Fordyce Herrick for White Pines. The two latter buildings were ready for the Whiteheads and the Browns to move into with their children by the autumn of 1902. The Riseley farm was converted to the Lark's Nest. Also, the library, the dance hall and the inn for the students—which later was called The Villetta—were completed that summer. The colony was ready for the great experiment.[11]

According to Mrs. Brown, the following summer Lindin and White took over all the cottages around the Lark's Nest with the idea of developing a club for highly interesting people. These included Professor Martin Schütze of the University of Chicago and his wife, Eve, a painter and photographer, who occupied the lower part of the meadows while Lindin had the studio above them; George Eggers, later to become an art museum director; and Ned Thatcher, who taught metalwork. Before long John Dewey, Clarence Darrow and other intellectuals joined the group. Dewey did not settle in Byrdcliffe but was responsible for bringing some important people to Woodstock, including the Shotwells and the Weyls. Walter Weyl came to Woodstock and liked it well enough to rent the Lark's Nest from Whitehead and to bring his wife, the former Bertha Poole, from Chicago. (It was a long way around for her, descended as she was from the Vanderpoels, who had settled along the Hudson River in the seventeenth century.) Two years later when the Weyls were ready to build their own home they were not content to buy any of the Byrdcliffe land with its numerous restrictions, but decided upon a tract across the valley on Ohayo Mountain. Here they built a large, comfortable house where Weyl did most of his best writing. Weyl's life and work are recounted in a later chapter.[12]

I have a photograph taken against the mantel of the Lark's Nest that shows excellent likenesses of Isabel Moore, Lucy Brown, Carl Lindin, a Swede named

A pitcher from the Byrdcliffe pottery as well as several books from the Byrdcliffe Library, including works by William Morris and Dante Gabriel Rossetti. Pitcher in AMS Collection. Books courtesy of Jacqueline Thibaut Eubanks. Photos by Dion Ogust.

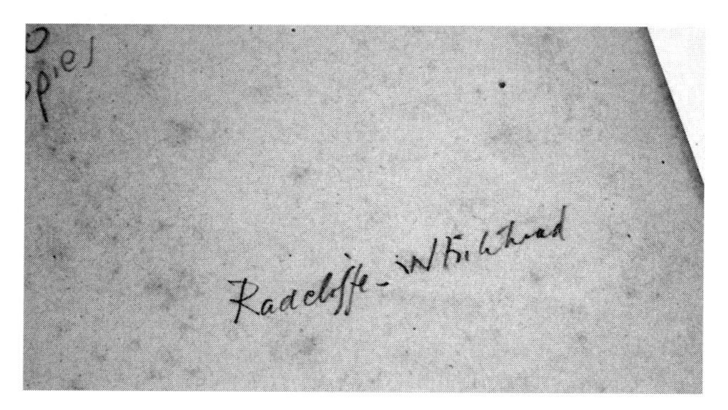

Erlenson, who was the cabinetmaker, and Ethel Canby, who later married Orville Peets. Lindin, with his dark complexion and square-cut features, was an attractive man. One can imagine the pleasure of his companions as he read aloud from the book shown in his hands, his deep, accented voice resonant with appreciation for the beauty or humor of the writing. The stunning Vivian Bevans made a stir when she arrived and subsequently became the wife of Hervey White. Fritz Van der Loo went back to South Africa, and from there, or from Dutch Guiana (according to Brown), escorted his bride-to-be to Byrdcliffe. Brown also describes the Lark's Nest as becoming so full, and people getting on each other's nerves to such an extent, that the place was nicknamed the Wasp's Nest.[13]

Other early teachers of art at Byrdcliffe, besides Brown, were Herman Dudley Murphy and Dawson Watson. Erlenson headed the woodworking shop, Ellen Gates Starr came from Hull House to do book-binding, Edith Penman and Elizabeth Hardenbergh started the pottery, and Murphy and Edwin Slater made picture frames. The students came from different art schools on scholarships offered by the Whiteheads. Thus arrived George Macrum, John Carlson from Buffalo, and Edna Walker and Zulma Steele from the Pratt Institute. The latter two were set to work designing furniture under Whitehead's direction. He admired the large flowers on our native tulip tree and decorations of these blossoms were carved on the furniture built by Erlenson, the master carpenter. It proved expensive to send these heavy chests and cabinets to exhibitions. Although a large order was received from McCreary's, it was impossible to make a profit on the furniture and after a couple of years the woodworking shops were closed. However, Erlenson had made a career for himself and when he left he took up an important position elsewhere. Several of these pieces of furniture may be seen at White Pines. Whitehead engaged Walker and Steele to stay on, and he built a studio for them where they continued making designs, block prints and stencils. Bolton Brown describes Zulma Steele as an "outstanding lady, both visually and in a quality we may call style." Later she made a name for herself with her painting and her luster glazes. She is now Mrs. Neilson Parker.[14]

Within a short time Bertha Thompson built her hillside studio to the west of White Pines where she made jewelry and silver tea services. She is the only artisan who has remained all through the years in Byrdcliffe.

Several Byrdcliffe artisans pose in front of fireplace at the Lark's Nest, circa 1904. From left, Isabel Moore, Lucy Brown, Carl Eric Lindin, the cabinet-maker Erlenson and Ethel Canby. Photo: AMS Collection.

An early comer to The Villetta was Mathilde de Cordoba, an etcher. She arrived with a commission to do a painting of the naturalist John Burroughs, who spent several days there sitting for his portrait. Burroughs was a friend of Whitehead and visited him on several occasions. One of Whitehead's favorite excursions was to drive his yellow car to Roxbury for a talk with a man who knew and loved the Catskills more than any other. Burroughs wrote in a letter that while we can't all be nature students we can all be nature lovers,[15] which was certainly true of Ralph Radcliffe Whitehead. Zulma Steele invited John Burroughs for breakfast, asking him to choose the hour and the kind of eggs she should serve. He was very emphatic about the time, assuring her he would be prompt, and chose

Ellen Gates Starr (1859–1940), at left, with bookbinding pupil Peter Verburg and unknown woman having tea at Hull House Book Bindery, circa 1902. Courtesy of Jane Addams Memorial Collection, University of Illinois at Chicago.

ABOVE: Desk with Three Panel Iris Design, *circa 1904. Green-stained cherry with three painted panels, 50⅝ x 38¾ x 16 in. Designed by Zulma Steele (1881–1979).* Courtesy of Woodstock Byrdcliffe Guild. Photo by Mathew Ferrari, Johnson Museum of Art, Cornell University.

soft-boiled eggs. At the appointed hour Miss Steele had the eggs ready but there was no sign of Mr. Burroughs. In fact she prepared four sets of soft-boiled eggs before he finally appeared. Perhaps the unnatural tempo of Byrdcliffe had thrown him off his farmer's schedule.[16]

Bolton Brown, who was born in 1864, was himself a painter but is better known for his lithography. One of his finest accomplishments was making the lithographs for George Bellows's drawings of prizefights. Brown was an instructor in drawing at Cornell University, a principal of the Government Art School at Toronto, Ontario, a professor of art at Leland Stanford University and a lecturer at the Art Institute of Chicago. He published several books on lithography and was also an experienced mountain climber. And he became a potter, building his own wheel and kiln; he originated glazes and kept the pedigrees and records of seven hundred and fifty pieces with ninety different glazes.[17] I didn't know him until late in his life. During his final illness his former wife, Lucy,

BELOW: Iris Desk Panel Drawing, *circa 1904. Graphite, 18½ x 28½ in. Drawn by Zulma Steele.* Courtesy of Woodstock Byrdcliffe Guild. Photo by Mathew Ferrari, Johnson Museum of Art, Cornell University.

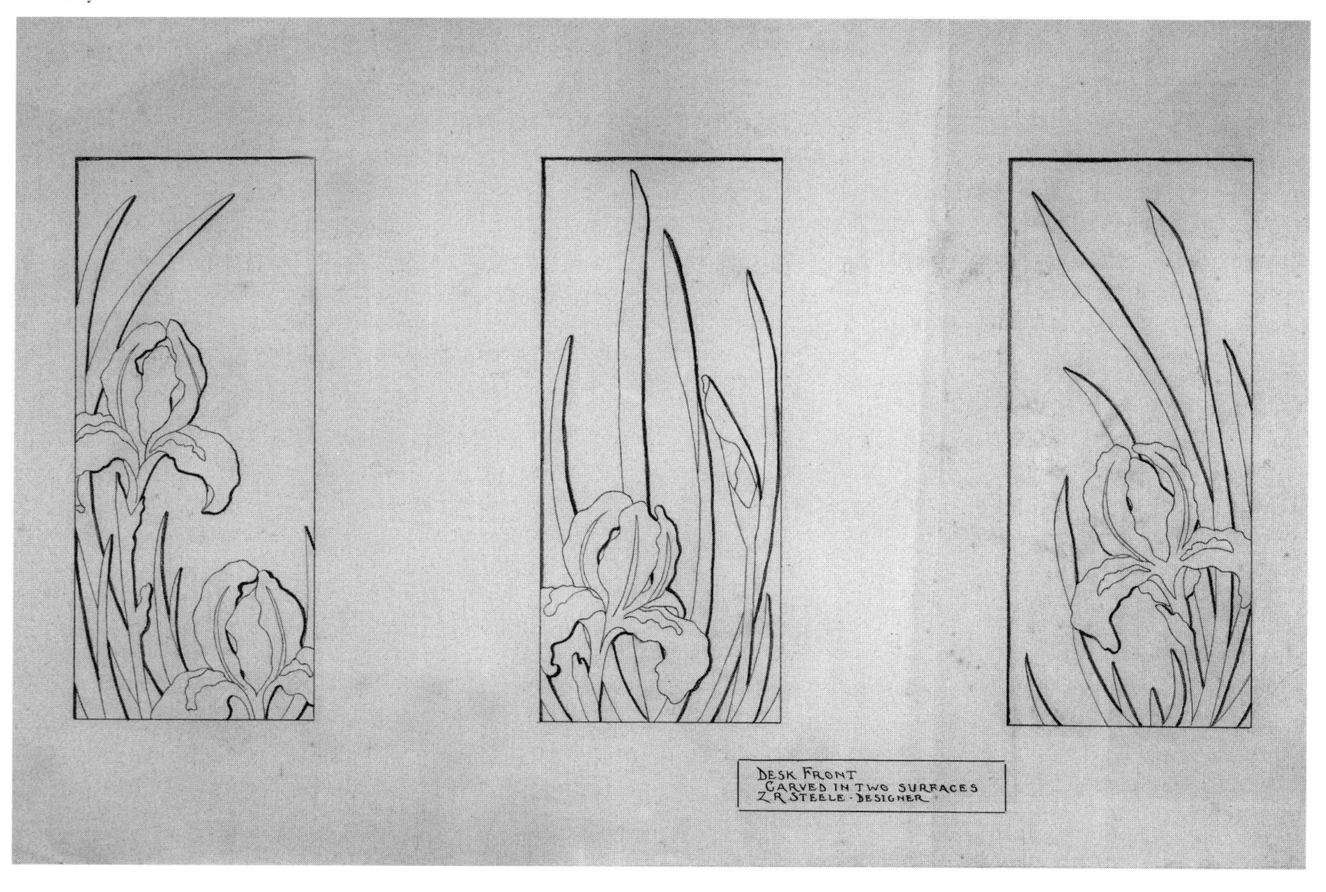

went to nurse him at his home in Zena. I remembered hearing he was near death and therefore was amazed to see him arriving at the Woodstock Artists Cemetery in a truck, from which he directed two workmen in placing a boulder he had brought for a gravestone. A day or two later he was buried as he had requested, his body being carried to the grave on a litter covered with pine boughs. No interment could have been more dignified.

No one who knew Lucy Brown could ever forget her beautiful face; it revealed a keen mind as well as compassion, which are not always mates. She had traveled far and experienced much and could reminisce in picture-making sentences with well-chosen words. She gave an amusing description of Edith Wherry, who came to lodge with the Browns for a fortnight and stayed all summer. Miss Wherry was called "The Flamboyant Bat,"

> for when the dew fell and the stars began to twinkle over the hill-tops she would wrap herself in a somber cape and flitter out, up and down the hill roads, joining the parties of nightriders, or walkers, doing Overlook, or haunting moonlit meadows and streams on the lookout for a pixie or so . . . Edith left Byrdcliffe in the fall with the poetess, Florence Wilkinson, for France; they avowing their intention to open a salon in Paris . . .

Three years later, when the Browns were living on the Overlook road, she reappeared from France to ask if she might borrow the oak tree in their hinterland, which she considered the loveliest spot in the world, for a meeting with a Canadian to whom she was engaged. She stopped only long enough to don a white gown and a virginal wreath and then floated into the woods. Within an hour her fair young man arrived from Canada and was apparently "embarrassed by the stagesetting. However, he washed his face and smoothed his hair (omitting the wreath [which had been provided for him]) and disappeared in the direction of the oak tree." Lucy adds, "That was Edith!" Years later Miss Wherry wrote a successful book on the Boxer Rebellion called *The Red Lantern*. She had been brought up in China, and according to Bolton Brown she would, upon request, recite "The Lord's Prayer" in Chinese.[18]

"The beauty and the joy of life seem too often to be lost through the haste to 'get somewhere' too quickly," writes Whitehead in "A Plea for Manual Work," an article published in 1903. "Nature works

Unglazed vase and pitcher from Byrdcliffe pottery era.
AMS Collection. Photo by Dion Ogust.

slowly . . . and the ties which bind us to her larger soul are torn and weakened by our impotent restlessness and love of novelty . . . —the joy of a man in the work of his hands,—is not a mere passing satisfaction, but is an element in all sane life." It is too early to speak of the work at Byrdcliffe, he continues, but they have proved it is possible to combine manual and intellectual activity with the simple country life. He ends by saying that Byrdcliffe will welcome any craftsman who is in sympathy with these ideas and wishes to act on them.[19]

It might well have been this article that brought to Byrdcliffe a sentimental lady eager to experience the sylvan delights but with no knowledge of country life. She was abashed to be assigned a cabin in the woods and left to her own resources. It was bad enough in the daytime, but at night, when the crickets chirped from the fireplace and the katydids sent forth their clamor, she picked up a carving knife with the threat of making Mr. Whitehead pay for her disillusionment. Forewarned, the occupants of the other studios planned their strategy. They persuaded the most attractive man in the group, Carl Lindin, to call on her in the dashing garb of a beret and cape, using his most ingratiating manner. The lady was disarmed, figuratively as well as physically, and was soon sent away. Needless to say, she ended up in an institution. Woodstock has always attracted eccentrics of one kind or another.

Ned Thatcher was another Pratt Institute graduate who came to Byrdcliffe. At first he was put to work making decorative hinges and locks for the furniture. Whitehead set up a forge for his use, and besides helping with the furniture Thatcher held classes in metalwork. Subsequently, Thatcher taught at Columbia's Teachers College. He was there when the First World War began and immediately turned his efforts to training teachers for occupational therapy. His students were being prepared to work in hospitals with disabled soldiers. Thatcher was most ingenious in this field. For example, he simplified instruction in woodcarving to make it easy for all the doughboys. He was probably the first person to use tin cans in craftwork. His tin toys brought him fame and later he was asked to make models for toy manufacturers. The teachers had such success with the disabled veterans that the Surgeon General wrote Thatcher a laudatory letter commending him for the excellence of the system.[20]

Thatcher continued to come to Byrdcliffe each summer. In 1910 he married, and he and his wife, Isabel, built a home on Van De Bogart Hill. For some three years he held summer classes at Short's Corner near Rock City. Ned Thatcher was a likable fellow with a keen sense of humor. His stories made a large contribution to the gaiety of Woodstock parties. He enjoyed poking fun at the farmers and was clever at imitating their talk. He wrote funny stories for the local newspapers under the name Iddie Flitcher. If one met him on the road or at the post office he always conversed in the idiom of the farmers. Eventually he never spoke in any other way and seemed to take pleasure in sinking his personality into that of a mountaineer. Here is a poem he contributed to the now defunct *Overlook*. With its ungrammatical style I think it has a homely beauty:

WINTER

It's a-snowin pretty out
an' litein' on the pines
'n things

Even the old junk pile
is kivered up
till it looks like the icin
on a cake

It's one [of] them still days
when you kin hear enjine
whistles far off
'n the trains a-roarin
down the track

This snow reminds me of
the crullers
Ma used to make
all thick with powdered
sugar on the top

Pease an' quiet
fer them that kin see
an' hear it
But
These is few.

—Iddie Flitcher[21]

Bottle cap/tin tank model designed by Ned Thatcher. Kits from his designs were used in occupational therapy for disabled soldiers during the First World War. Courtesy of Historical Society of Woodstock. Photo by Dion Ogust.

There were several German-Americans in Byrdcliffe besides Professor Schütze. Peter Whitehead recalls his father telling of meeting Lotte Stoehr for the first time while she was walking in the mountains. She was looking for land to buy. They had a casual conversation which ended in Whitehead inviting her to White Pines for lunch. She liked Byrdcliffe enough to return with her husband and build a home there. This led to the arrival of the Alfred de Liagres, the Jellinghauses and the Beisners, all of whom would be associated with Woodstock for years. There was considerable friction between this group and the English during the First World War but now all have become friends again.

A weaving studio was built for Marie Little, which she called The Cricket. Although she never fully mastered the process she turned out attractive mats, bags and curtains made of cotton strips. Most of Little's dyes she made herself from barks and berries, which gave her materials the tones of the woods and fields. Her studios—for later she too forsook Byrdcliffe for the valley—were always nut brown with accents of black and orange. The sparse furnishings and the floors were always freshly cleaned and oiled. In her youth Little had studied music in Italy where her poplar-like figure and quavering voice were much admired. However, no one had tried to plumb her soul and now she had been waiting fifty years for understanding. There was no one left to remember her music, and as the seasons passed Little withdrew more and more into herself. In this solitary life she vibrated to refinements that common folks ignored. One felt her thoughts were too subtle for expression, her taste too delicate to be exposed.

Occasionally she asked someone to come into her retreat but often cancelled the invitation as if to savor control over another's actions. If guests did enter her house they would be uncomfortably conscious of their dusty footsteps on the floor. They dared not move from the seat allotted to them because they knew they had been placed there to see the graceful branch of an apple tree against the mountain or perhaps for the vista up the path to a sumac. Because Marie Little was poor she scorned what only wealth could bring. In contrast she made a rite of offering beauty that had no price, such as the perfume of a wild flower. Her guests might be required to go on their hands and knees to sniff the odor of her evening stock. If she had a trifle to eat she might serve it on a leaf or in a wooden bowl, yet with ceremony, as though it were ambrosia from a chalice.

Most of the houses, thirty or forty of them, are still standing in Byrdcliffe. Only a few of them have been destroyed, such as Marie Little's weaving studio, which burned to the ground. The roads loop along the hillside as they used to do, separating and unexpectedly rejoining each other and occasionally coming to a dead end on a cottage lawn, to the confusion of the outsider. In the old days these studios were occupied by painters, woodcarvers, metalworkers, potters, weavers and musicians, who walked back and forth visiting one another. One of the early residents recalls with pleasure the evenings when a group would gather at White Pines to read aloud. Whitehead did not usually read himself but is remembered for his comments. This person recalls, "He had so much to give us although part of what he had to say was over our heads."[22] Whitehead once said he would be satisfied if he could make a good pair of shoes but added that his greatest ability might have been in architecture.[23] Bolton Brown quotes him as saying, "Artists are the only people in the world worth living with, and the most difficult." Another person recalls a particular evening when Herman Dudley Murphy interrupted a reading to announce the death of James Whistler, which cast a gloom upon the group. There were also frequent musical evenings with madrigals being played on the red clavichord at White Pines. Whitehead collected a number of folk songs, translating many of the verses from the originals himself; the title was *Folk Songs of Eastern Europe*.

Mrs. Whitehead was poetic and sensitive, belonging to a romantic era that was not appreciated in the twentieth century. The rough art students growing up in the midst of an industrial revolution, fighting for the right to express ugly facts and even to play politics with their art, did not have the patience to spend valuable hours with their patroness, listening to the cooing of her doves or strolling among the lilacs. However, the lady was known to protect herself from visitors who came at awkward hours by showing her head at a window and calling out, "Mrs. Whitehead is not at home."[24]

She expected all work to stop at four o'clock and the students to assemble on the terrace, ready to take part in her Morris dances. She had someone brought in to teach the dances, having no idea that the students might prefer to go on working all the daylight hours rather than bob about on the terrace. Mrs. Whitehead had a vision of the picturesque life remote from reality. One can imagine the reaction of sweaty teamsters goading their oxen to the plow on a hot day when Mrs. Whitehead and Miss Little—resembling figures in a Burne-Jones painting in their flowing gowns and veils—would swoop down on them carrying bowls of mead for their refreshment, especially as the mead was non-fermented honey!

In a 1909 article about Byrdcliffe, writer Poultney Bigelow said of the growing colony: "Here is a city of the forest where every tree is a soul in sympathy with the workers under its branches. [At last one hears what the trees thought about the goings-on!] . . . The idly curious are not invited, and, thank God, automobiles are barred as well; also, all merely mechanical forms of progress." Continuing in his ornate style, Bigelow describes the Saturday night dances:

No dress-suit is permitted on the floor; young men and maidens disport themselves in such studio or working-dress as suits their complexion or purse, and such dancing as at Byrdcliffe is not to be found anywhere else this side of the Hungarian Danube.

The last Saturday of the season brings with it a magnificent fancy dress ball, and such marvels of costuming fished up from chests where have been stored the clothing incident to studios where models must be draped for every taste.

It's all a beautiful dream to me, that final dance of last autumn, the exquisite taste, the simplicity, the absence of money-display, and then the refreshments were not at a long bar, but each bungalow spread a carpet under the trees, hung Chinese lanterns in the branches, and there they entertained the guests who reclined like the gods of Homer and forgot the hours in the joy of festive relaxation.

Byrdcliffe proper is the summer and winter home of the Whitehead family, a home in the best old sense of that word, the house of massive timber, the interior made by artists in woodwork, the whole a thing which appears to have grown out of its happy invironment [sic]. The view from the front takes in an immense range of mountain and valley, blocked to the south by the range of Lake Mohonk [The Shawangunks]. In the foreground is the great barn, for Ralph Whitehead is a mighty farmer in addition to his other many accomplishments. All the buildings are in harmony as to color and design with the main house, none painted, merely stained to preserve the wood in its natural beauty of color.[25]

Bigelow came from a Malden family that around the 1880s headed the largest bluestone company in the country, doing business of over a half a million dollars a year. His father, John Bigelow, had been the American ambassador to France and Poultney attended school with Kaiser Wilhelm II.[26] No doubt this accounted for his prejudice in favor of Germany and for the visit paid him by the Crown Prince and one of his younger brothers after the kaiser had been deposed. Bigelow brought the princes to a reception in Woodstock where many of their former enemies were given an opportunity to shake their hands. Woodstock, the bohemian community, has had its share of visiting royalty. It is well known that the former King Peter of Yugoslavia visited Mead's, but few are aware that Archduke Rudolph, son of the late Emperor Ferdinand of Austria, spent part of his honeymoon in Hickory Hollow.

Bigelow was educated as a lawyer but preferred a more adventurous life and sailed around the world. He was shipwrecked off the coast of Japan and journeyed in China, Java, Australia and Africa. He published a number of books and belonged to learned societies and clubs all over the hemisphere. He was a global adventurer and did not give a whoop for the conventions. Naturally he fitted into Woodstock perfectly. Bigelow had a puckish humor that delighted in the unexpected sally and the contrary opinion. I was invited with many others to his home while the bitterness of war was still prevalent, to find that the occasion was planned as an unveiling of a statue of the kaiser with accompanying eulogies. Another time, walking in the garden after a dinner party, one of my friends remarked, "Mr. Bigelow, what an interesting group of people you gathered here." "They don't eat any more than others," her host instantly replied.

The Bigelow home at Malden was an unpretentious and comfortable frame house with a wide porch and narrow terrace on a bluff overlooking the Hudson River. Standing there you felt as though you were on the top deck of a large ferry that might head across the river to Tivoli at any moment. For many years Poultney Bigelow invited all the old county families and half of Woodstock to help him celebrate his birthdays. We all responded enthusiastically to his invitations because he was a good host and was likely to produce an amusing or provocative surprise. For example, just as the clouds were gathering ominously for the outbreak of the Second World War we found his grounds bedecked with Japanese flags!

The Albert Websters came to Byrdcliffe in 1904, buying twenty acres and building a home that the family would occupy for many years. Mr. Webster was an engineer and architect with much experience in public and private works in Germany and the United States. Among his positions was that of consulting civil and sanitary engineer in New York City. He was a member of many international societies including the Council of National Defense during the First World War and the U.S. Building Code Committee. He also served on the executive committee of the Yale Engineering Association.[27]

What Woodstock liked best about Webster were his lovable personality and his sense of fun and whimsy. He entertained his children, Ben and Aileen, with stories of animals whose fanciful portraits and activities he drew with chalk on a blackboard and then erased. A neighbor photographed one of these drawings and persuaded Mrs. Webster to preserve others in photographs. These became the foundation for the little book *Caleb*, which has delighted many young children over the years.[28]

My favorite Albert Webster story concerns a Christmas tree that he made and set up for the birds, only to have the birds ignore it. His children were disappointed, so he decided to entertain them by pretending to be a bird himself. He attached a feather duster to his rear end and, leaning over to look more like a bird, hopped about the lawn taking pecks at the birdseed on the tree. This brought whoops of joy from the youngsters. It happened that at this moment an important visitor arrived to see Mr. Webster and was nonplussed by the scene he beheld, but his host, with perfect aplomb, finished the pantomime and then greeted his guest without embarrassment.

Among the teachers, Birge Harrison was certainly the closest to his students, yet there are few left in Woodstock who knew him. Harrison was a thin man with old-fashioned spectacles and in no way conspicuous except for the watermelon-pink necktie he usually wore with his tweeds. When talking with him one saw his kindly smile and the fun in his eyes and soon became aware of a man of tolerance and wide experience. Of late he has been associated with a moribund form of painting, yet he always told his pupils that if their art remained in a rut it would die. Further, he claimed that the true artist must be an innovator, and he encouraged his students to be themselves, never to copy him. He had studied with John Singer Sargent in the atelier of Carolus-Duran in Paris and made a name for himself as a landscape and seascape painter before coming to Byrdcliffe at the request of Mr. Whitehead. Two years after arriving here he organized the Art Students League Summer School in Woodstock, which became nationally prominent under his direction.

Harrison and his wife, Jennie, built a home off the Glasco Turnpike near Bearsville and here they held open house every Sunday. To many students their hospitality meant the difference between intolerable homesickness and the happiness of being included in family life. Little Mrs. Harrison, known affectionately as Jennie Wren, had a mischievous streak, but most of all she had a warm heart and listened to all the troubles of the uprooted young students. The Harrisons took into their home John Follinsbee, who was restricted to a wheelchair, and his constant companion, Harry (Tony) Leith-Ross, both of whom became well-known painters. After a few years the Harrisons sold their house to Richard Le Gallienne and in the years thereafter one might come across the poet preoccupied with his own thoughts as he walked the trails in the deep woods.

The Harrisons moved to the eastern end of the village along the turn of the Sawkill, where they did over one of the oldest houses in town using family antiques and creating an old-fashioned garden. Although they lived well, Harrison was for years content to drive his model T Ford. One of his eccentricities was an inability to spend money on tires and for a while he drove the old car with discarded rubber tires wired over his wheels, which made the driving a bit uneven. He received various honors but none pleased him more than being made a member of an Indian tribe while living in Arizona. Although in Europe he was less famous than his brother Alexander, in the United States his paintings did become popular. I saw less of the Harrisons in Woodstock than in Charleston, South Carolina, where Mr. Harrison taught at the art school in the 1920s. They lived at the Villa Margherita where Miss Lisa Dawson fed her guests the finest southern food, as delicious as it was rich. When I stayed in Charleston the Harrisons, with their usual kindness, invited me to join them for dinners at the Villa. By this time Mrs. Harrison had grown rather plump and the doctor had prescribed a diet for her. She readily ate all the items in the diet and then, asking for the regular menu, to our astonishment would proceed to eat all of the dinner she had missed. Nevertheless she continued to live in good health for many years.

Birge Harrison's birthday was celebrated each October with a surprise party that his wife made such a fuss over, it might have been more of a surprise to him if it had *not* taken place. All of his former students and friends would gather in costume outside his house to serenade him, and of course Mrs. Harrison would invite them in for refreshments. Rhoda Chase, the children's book illustrator, recalls one of the first of these parties when the guests were driven by moonlight in a hay cart to the Harrisons' Bearsville house. Poultney Bigelow came attired in Turkish costume, wearing a red fez, and delighted in making shocking remarks to the girls with whom he danced.

Harrison contracted lead poisoning from careless handling of his paints and was not well for years before his death in 1929. "No biography of Birge Harrison would be complete," wrote Harry Leith-Ross, "without mention of his unfailing generosity in

Woodstock Meadows in Winter, *1909, by Birge Harrison (1854–1929). Oil on canvas, 46 x 40¼ in.* Courtesy of Toledo Museum of Art.

giving a helping hand to numberless struggling young painters."[29] No teacher has had the same fatherly concern for the lives of the students or has been so well loved. Yet now I am asked, "Who was Birge Harrison?"

In 1928 the Whiteheads' elder son, Ralph Jr., was lost in the sinking of the *Vestris*. Mr. Whitehead never recovered from the shock of this loss and died himself in 1929. The Della Robbia shrine that holds his ashes was later moved from its ideal setting at White Pines to the Woodstock Artists Cemetery.

Why did the Byrdcliffe plan deteriorate after so little time as an Arts and Crafts community? One former resident of the colony attributed its decline to the First World War and the radical changes that followed. After 1918 there was a revolution in culture as well as in labor, and the old patterns failed to appeal to the young. Most of the survivors of the Byrdcliffe era, however, say that it began to decline before the war because fundamentally artists are egoists and do not, or cannot, fit into a cooperative scheme. The Whiteheads gave generously but they held the reins tight and there were too many restrictions to suit creative individuals. One by one the artists and craftsmen relinquished the opportunities offered in Byrdcliffe and drifted down to the barns and boardinghouses close to the village. Hervey White had already gone on to found the Maverick. Bolton Brown, Carl Lindin, Walter Weyl and James Shotwell had all bought property elsewhere in Woodstock. John Carlson gave up his studio in Byrdcliffe to live precariously for months on beer and cheese in a Rock City barn until his landscapes began to sell.

Occasionally some form of art is revived in Byrdcliffe. For a couple of summers the old library building was used as a theater. In 1925 Ben Webster launched a theatrical group with the cooperation of Robert Edmund Jones, Robert Lytell and Jacob Ben-Ami. Richard Aldrich, who married Gertrude Lawrence, was director. They called themselves the Phoenix Players and the first season they presented *The Importance of Being Earnest* by Oscar Wilde, *The Mistress of the Inn* by Carlo Goldoni and *Foul Is Fair* by Marya Mannes. Rose Hobart, Edward Cooper, Edward Hale and other actors starred in these productions.[30]

More recently opera has had a season in Byrdcliffe. The Turnau company has converted the library into a modern, though tiny, opera house where talented young singers have been presenting good music.

Probably the most interesting cultural venture took place in the late 1930s with the series of talks known as Byrdcliffe Afternoons initiated by Professor Schütze. Martin Schütze was born in Mecklenburg in 1866 and, after studying law in Rostock and Freiburg, came to this country as a Fellow in German at the University of Pennsylvania. While there he met Walter Weyl, and no doubt it was in Philadelphia also that he met the artist Eve Watson, who would become his wife. For many years Schütze occupied the Chair of German Literature at the University of Chicago and spent his summers in Byrdcliffe. Elsa Kimball describes him as a familiar figure in Woodstock with his "gracious presence, his agile step along the highway, the cavalier tilt of his beret, [and] his manifold interests and activities in our local scene."[31] It was he who envisaged our local historical society as an organization concerned not only with the past but also with history in the making. He became the first president of the Historical Society of Woodstock and was responsible, through his initiative and encouragement, for many of its early programs. He founded the Byrdcliffe Afternoons in 1938.

As Schütze explains in his preface to the published papers, he, Mrs. Whitehead and Peter Whitehead were sitting in his garden talking of the early days in Byrdcliffe and the conversation awakened a desire to breathe new life into the beautiful place where they had spent so many years together. Mrs. Whitehead and her son asked him to come up with a project, and a few weeks later he presented them with the plans for the Afternoons, to which they agreed. Schütze next took the idea to Shotwell and to Alfred de Liagre, a cultured businessman who had built a modern home in Byrdcliffe. They both promised to cooperate, and thus the Afternoons were launched.

The first year fourteen papers were read during a three-week session, seven of them by persons closely associated with Woodstock. These were James Shotwell, Henry Billings, Carl Lindin, J. Donald Adams, Pierre Henrotte, Joseph Pollet and Martin

A Della Robbia shrine, formerly located in Byrdcliffe, now marks the graves of Ralph R. Whitehead and his elder son at the Woodstock Artists Cemetery. Postcard by L. E. Jones. AMS Collection.

THE PHOENIX PLAYERS

... Present ...

"THE LOVERS"

By Carlo Goldoni

(Translated by Haroldine Humphreys and William Miles)

Opening Tuesday, August 3, 1926

at the Phoenix Theatre, Byrdcliffe, Woodstock, N. Y.

Production staged under the direction of ETHEL GRIFFIES
and designed by BEN WEBSTER

CAST OF CHARACTERS
(in order of appearance)

Eugenia, Niece of Fabrizio	Haroldine Humphreys
Flaminia, Her Sister, a Widow	Anne Walter
Tognino, a Servant to Fulgensio	William Miles
Fabrizio, an Old Citizen of Milan	Murray Kinnell
Roberto, Count of Otricoli	Philip Leigh
Succianespole, Servant to Fabrizio	Theodore St. John
Lisetta, Servant to Fabrizio	Rose Hobart
Ridolfo, Friend to Fulgensio	Harold Moulton
Fulgensio, Lover of Eugenia	Edward Cooper
Clorinda, Sister-in-Law of Fulgensio	Henrietta Goodwin

ACT I. Room in Fabrizio's house; morning.

ACT II. Same as Act I; morning.

ACT III. Same as Act I; afternoon.

Place: Milan, 1755.

Business Manager	Richard S. Aldrich
Subscription Secretary	Olivia D. Johnson
Stage Manager	William Miles

Program guide for the Phoenix Players production of The Lovers *(second season).* Courtesy of Historical Society of Woodstock.

Schütze. Their themes ran from history and education to the contemporary novel to music and painting and were a real contribution to the cultural experience of Woodstock. To me the papers on art were the weakest. George Biddle's ideology, unlike his painting, was confused, perhaps due to poor transcription of the spoken word. Pollet extolled the detachment of the artist who contemplates a tree or sky undisturbed by wars and alarums (this in 1938). He went on to say, "The clue to the traditional recipe for a good artist . . . [is] the study of nature to educate the senses; the study of great Art of the past to form a mind trained to translate nature in the finest terms of the medium employed."[32] Billings spoke not of how we paint but *what* we paint. Lindin quoted various philosophers (not artists), mostly Hans Wahlin, and ended by saying, "In spite of herd-tactics and a return to so-called paganism . . . the road to culture and art still runs through Plato and Christ" on to the present.[33] Perhaps these ideas played better when voiced by the painters in person than they read in print; the papers are disappointing.

The next year's session was devoted to Latin-American culture, and besides Shotwell, who gave the introduction, the only Woodstocker to speak was Nathaniel Weyl (son of Walter Weyl), whose subject was Mexico. Columbia University Press published these last lectures for the Committee on International Intellectual Cooperation, of which Shotwell was chairman. This session was held in 1939 when the Second World War was breaking and it marks the last attempt to revive liberal thinking in Byrdcliffe.

The war in Europe brought a number of distinguished refugees to Woodstock. I remember meeting Thomas Mann and his daughter—visiting the scholarly Dr. Erich Kahler, who for several summers lived in Carniola above White Pines. To become a friend of Dr. Kahler one had to be a friend of his remarkable mother, Frau Antoinette Kahler, who, like a queen, dominated any gathering. When she was over eighty she took up painting and thought nothing of translating Homer before breakfast as an eye opener. Another of Kahler's friends who came to join him was Austria's foremost poet, Richard Beer-Hofmann, who rented Chanticleer next door. Beer-Hofmann's best-known poem was titled "Schlaflied für Miriam." Miriam, his daughter, accompanied him to America and lived with him at Chanticleer. He was a big man with a massive head and large features who was very gentle and charming in conversation. He was the most sensitive guest who ever visited my herb garden, seeming to delight in learning the virtues of the plants. This whole group later moved to Princeton where they were closely associated with Albert Einstein. They wrote for the magazine *Commentary*, a most erudite publication.[34]

James T. Shotwell, who was born in Canada in 1874, was another Woodstock resident who came on the recommendation of John Dewey. But unlike Dewey, he and Mrs. Shotwell, the former Margaret Harvey, bought a farm to the east of Byrdcliffe on the Overlook Mountain road, where they maintained a hospitable home for many years. Shotwell has been identified with the cultural life of the town from the early Byrdcliffe days, but I knew him as the neighbor who drew us from our houses and studios to view the world through the telescope of his great mind, for this man was never too busy to speak to his neighbors about world events. I recall many a gathering—it might have been Memorial Day on the Village Green, or at the Town Hall, or on his own terrace overlooking the valley—where he would speak of the Versailles Treaty, President Wilson or the League of Nations, never as past history but to show new horizons open to mankind for a lasting peace. In a rich voice he would eloquently sum up the large issues and make us understand our responsibilities to them as citizens of a new world. At an age when other people would rest on their laurels, Shotwell continues to respond to those who ask for his ripe advice. He belongs to the wide world, but he is also a revered citizen of Woodstock.

Just before dark one recent spring evening I drove through Byrdcliffe—entering below White Pines, the Whitehead home. Peter Whitehead had been trying to regain the views by removing the underbrush, but it is an endless task keeping the meadows cleared and the woods open without cultivation or cattle to munch away at the weeds. Anyway, there were spots where Ohayo Mountain and the valley could be glimpsed, and perhaps it is well the ugly real-estate developments near Bearsville are partially hidden.

As I drove slowly along, I could see many of the graceful branches of dogwood in flower glowing moth-white between the trees, and I made a mental note to return when the white wisteria, planted with unerring taste by Mr. Whitehead, would come into bloom. The roads were deserted and nobody was to be seen as I stopped below The Villetta. Nearby was the old library, stripped of all the books collected by Mr. Whitehead. Many of those volumes were moved to the loom room at White Pines. Here one may see whole sections devoted to books in Greek, German and Italian as well as English. These were all languages that he spoke, and he was familiar with the philosophy, science and art of Greece, Germany and Italy. Above the mantel is an inscription in Greek which, roughly translated, means "It is grace that always gives birth to grace."[35]

On my last visit to the loom room, Fritz Kroll's advanced students were playing for his criticism. I sat at one end in the shadows, for the only illumination was from a cluster of shaded lamps near the musicians. The light shone but a few yards along the backs of the books and a short distance along the poles that held the slanted roof. It was good to relax and listen to music, but when Kroll lifted his own violin to show his pupils how the music should be interpreted I became alert and sensitive to the playing of a real artist.

Now it was quiet as I waited on that May evening by The Villetta and a sweet odor permeated the moist air, which I identified as the pinxter flower before I caught sight of the pale blur of pinkish blossoms. Then from far away came that most perfect sound, the song of an evening thrush.

The dream for Byrdcliffe may have evaporated, but it started and nourished the creative art that drifted into the valley and over the mountains where good pictures have been painted, fine music played and important thoughts written. All these are the outgrowth of a plan conceived by Ralph Radcliffe Whitehead.

Hervey White (1866–1944), co-founder, in 1905, of the Maverick art colony. Photo by Konrad Cramer. AMS Collection.

Chapter 6

ON THE MAVERICK

THE FIRST WOODSTOCK FESTIVAL

Hervey White

Many of us remember the gentle-eyed Hervey White with his gray, ruffed-up hair, pointed beard and short smocks belted with scarves of contrasting colors. His clothes were home-dyed, faded purple, blue or magenta—and he wore them with an ease to match his lazy motions. The history of the Maverick is really the biography of Hervey White.

The story begins a couple of years after Ralph Whitehead, Bolton Brown and White started the colony of Byrdcliffe. The concept of a community such as Byrdcliffe was defined in Whitehead's essays, written during the years when he lived in Florence. Hervey White was in Florence several years later but under very different circumstances, because he was tramping through Italy on a budget of twenty-five to fifty cents a day and sometimes his only food was a handful of chestnuts. While just north of Florence he wrote in his journal,

> As I live and learn, I am getting the idea of the true dignity of labor so thoroughly ingrain[ed] that I think I shall never feel it in me to write a speech or tract about it, but, instead, I shall during the rest of my settled life employ a good third of each day at some productive manual labor, seeing therein the only possible method of keeping a vigorous body, a healthy mind, and a conscience free toward my neighbor and myself.[1]

It is interesting to ponder this statement in light of Whitehead's philosophy as described in the preceding chapter on Byrdcliffe. It was inevitable that, having met, the paths of these two men would merge, but it was also inevitable that their natures would not allow them to travel the same route for any length of time.

When Bolton Brown found the valley of Woodstock and Whitehead and White came to live here, it did not take long for the differences in the characters of the three men to cause friction. Whitehead spent a fortune building and developing the Byrdcliffe colony. He was generous to lavish in providing aid to students and teachers in the arts and crafts. Of Hervey it has been said that he would turn his pockets inside out to help a neighbor, but those pockets were usually empty! It was natural that, after all the years of careful planning and building, Whitehead should wish to steer the course of Byrdcliffe along his preconceived path.

Originally everyone came to Byrdcliffe to do creative work, and like all artists they were individualistic and inclined to rebel against restrictions. This does not mean they were licentious, because creative work requires self-discipline beyond the understanding of most laymen; but they were nonconformist, setting up their own rules. Bolton Brown tells of one student who was so full of self-importance he would paint only behind a screen for fear of someone stealing his technique. It is unnecessary to add that his approach would not have been of value to anyone else, and was probably useful in the end only for digging ditches. Many of the scandalous stories about the artists can be attributed to the camp followers who flock around any bohemian settlement.

In Byrdcliffe, Whitehead tried to provide conditions conducive to creative work, and he believed this required order and direction. But it is tricky to set down rules of conduct for artists. And Mrs. Whitehead had plans for the group that may have been picturesque but were even less acceptable. The incidents over which the three founders quarreled are not important, but there was a rift and Hervey White and Bolton Brown moved out—each to settle in a different section of Woodstock. Years later White was heard to say that a rich man and a poor man could never really be friends.

Hervey White was born in a sod hut on an Iowa farm in 1866. His ancestors had all come to America before 1635 and he is said to have been directly descended from Peregrine White, born on the *Mayflower*. When Hervey was twelve years old he moved with his family to Kansas. His mother was dead and his sister married, and the young man was left to cook for his father, his older brother and the farm hands. For this work he was paid six dollars a month, which he saved for his education. For a couple of years he taught school. Then, with one hundred and fifty dollars of savings in his pocket, he was able to enter Kansas State University. There were several financial setbacks to his college career, but by working during the holidays and doing odd jobs around the campus—such as cleaning stables and lighting the street lamps—and even mortgaging the horse his father had given him, he managed to complete three years.

At the end of his sophomore year he had so distinguished himself in the study of geology that he was recommended by the president of the university for membership in a geological expedition—during which Hervey gathered more material for future stories than he did geological specimens. Returning to Kansas, he finished his junior year, devoting himself to the study of speculative philosophy. This course was better suited to his nature but he soon exhausted the field of study available at Kansas State University. Thereupon he went east and entered Harvard College, from which he graduated in 1894.[2]

Soon after leaving Harvard, White departed for Italy—with a steerage ticket for which he had paid eighteen dollars. He had just thirty dollars in his pocket, along with a notebook from which most of this material is taken.

The young man from Kansas with curly hair and wide-open eyes plunged into the foul hole assigned to the steerage passengers on the *Victoria*. He wrote:

> I confess I was somewhat staggered at my first introduction to the steerage . . . a low, black hole, lined on either side with two tiers of narrow tray-like boxes into which the men were hastily clambering . . . however much I might have felt like turning back, the thing was impossible then . . . I hurried deeper into the hole, and saw that the lower berths were already claimed; a few upper ones remained, and, in desperation, I flung my knap-sack into the one at the end of the passage . . . at least, I would not have one of those howling beasts on more than one side of me . . .
>
> My first impression when settled was that we should all smother in the night together. My second, was that if the boat should sink, I, being at the end of the passage, would be the last on deck, and probably left to drown like a rat in a hole.[3]

He forced himself to eat some stale biscuits and tinned beef and waited grimly for the carbon dioxide to asphyxiate him. The men around him were Italian emigrants returning home. "The argument that such men prefer to live as they do is not strong enough to excuse us who allow it," he wrote, adding that the habits of the sailors were as dirty as those of the steerage passengers. When the ship got under way the air became fresher and he slept well the first night. However, it was not long before heavy seas were encountered, the hatches were closed and he became seasick. The stench in the steerage quarters was more than he could endure. Thereafter he slept on the deck unless it rained.

Finally the *Victoria* deposited them in Naples and after a long hunt he succeeded in renting a room with a balcony for three dollars. Hervey joined one of the petty officers from the *Victoria* to do some sightseeing, and soon was exultantly describing the countryside. They went to Pompeii, climbed Vesuvius and looked down into its smoking depths, and from there took in the view of Capri and Ischia across the Bay of Naples. All of this he describes with appreciation.

He went on many excursions, buying a *soldi*'s worth of bread or the equivalent of two cents' worth of hot chestnuts for lunch. In a wine shop a woman overcharged him but also complimented his looks. The comment remained in his memory and left him satisfied with a bad bargain. Fifty years later people seeing Hervey White with his ruffled gray hair, his open collars and his colorful dyed blouses would ask whether he was not conscious of his picturesque appearance. Some of the entries in this diary suggest the answer. The day after the woman paid him the compliment, he spent some time improving his appearance:

> My hair is growing now and the collar of a sweater makes ever a good setting for the head . . . Today I

> met a whole convent of young ladies out with the sisters for a walk. The girls were very pretty in their black dresses and white straw hats banded with black velvet . . . I wondered how I looked . . . It occurred to me that my hands were red, but I folded them carelessly behind me, so that was all right. I believe I once had some foolish idea about neglecting my personal appearance and looking like a regular tramp. I see the folly of all that nonsense now.[4]

Soon he set out for Rome, tramping with a knapsack over his shoulder and stopping at inns where he paid six cents for a bed in shared rooms. There were fleas and dirt and vulgar companions, but he was beginning to like Italian peasants, in particular the farmers who took him in and frequently gave him far more than was warranted by the few *soldi* he could pay for board. At Caserta he was impressed by the palace and gardens built by Charles of Naples:

> For the first time I begin to see what Europe is or has been, to realize that there may be another point of view than that of democracy. I do not mean I am attracted by this magnificence, but I must admit I am tremendously impressed.

He described the view from the cascaded garden to the fruitful plain seen in all its opulence, but as he looked he became surfeited with "its sweating secureness" and longed to

> get away to sterile soil. There is a fulsomeness here [that is] almost greasy . . . but the blue mountains loom on my horizon . . . [5]
>
> As soon as I left the level land and came into the mountains, the poetry of Italy began for me again . . . Now and again I would see a gray castle with its surrounding village crowning an isolated hill-top. I have yet to see a more beautiful thing than a city like this rising from a hill . . . The castles [have] become a part of the landscape.

After walking twenty miles he found lodging at ten cents for the night. Here, with his bread, figs and sausage spread out on a table, with his aching feet and legs under the bed covers and a candle strapped to a chair-back in camp fashion, he managed to feel deliciously at home. "It takes camp life," he wrote,

> to teach one to make a candlestick out of a string, and a library out of a book . . . All this is so different from my loneliness of yesterday . . . I think it was on account of that flat land. Now I know there is a gray, castle-crowned hill just back of me.

A few more days of walking and he wrote,

> The world here is full of pastorals . . . Knitting and spinning women watch the goats, sheep, cattle, geese, and swine . . . Men work with wooden plows, driving the wide-horned oxen . . . Young girls on the road wear the full white sleeves and purple skirts in the old fashion . . . Gardens, gardens everywhere . . . Stern fortresses, grown soft with centuries of sunshine and weather-kissing . . . arched bridges . . . tunneled hill-sides . . . peace, contentment, industry . . . a place to dream but not a place to work in, a poem of the past . . . There may be places in the world more beautiful than this valley at the foot of Monte Casino: I do not know: perhaps I, myself, have seen them: but I do not care to think of them now.[6]

The account of his Italian journey on foot is, to me, the best writing Hervey White ever did.

When he reached Frosinone he noticed that "everything begins to look toward Rome."[7] That day he spent one cent for breakfast, four for dinner and three for supper; his bed was five cents and a candle one cent—a total of fourteen cents. Five men shared his room and they joked and talked throughout the night; the fleas were also active, and sleep impossible. At the next stop he took a room for himself alone that had the added luxury of a lamp. At last Rome came into view, though it was still a long day's walk into the city. He had walked from Naples to Rome in twelve days, at a cost of four dollars and twenty-five cents. It was not easy to find affordable lodging in Rome, but he succeeded in locating a room for five dollars a month.

Up to this time White had been acting like a man of the people, of necessity subsisting on the most meager rations and by choice associating with peasants and the lower classes. In Rome, armed with a Baedeker, he became the tourist, visiting all the ruins and monuments. He went to the Coliseum, making a mental note to return to it by moonlight just as the most sentimental tripper would have done. He visited the museums and St. Peter's and the Pantheon and for a while reacted as any other visitor might. After several days he broke away to tramp through Campagna among the herds of grazing sheep and the shaggy-legged boys watching them. As a Kansan he wondered why this good soil was not being used to grow food. He munched a sprig of pennyroyal and plucked some "daisies" to put in his cap and felt better.

The next day he returned to the museums and fell in with an English party who were having everything explained to them by a Latin professor. "I followed through two rooms and by that time was so filled with mythology and art that I longed to stop and see if there was any of my original self left."[8]

There came a period when he felt impelled to search for a companion but did not find one among the crowds. He remembered the face of a friend in a museum where he had gone. It was the self-portrait of Velázquez. He took a chair to sit by the painting and found that "The man and I can be very happy in each others [sic] company."

He mentioned among his other friends Van Dyck and Guido Reni of the

> delicate, almost querulous face . . . All the time there has been another man with us, though we have given him less attention because he is an old man and must be more or less out of sympathy with us younger dreamers . . . His face is somewhat drawn, he has lived his life, but gradually it dawns upon me that it is not all lived yet and if he has not dreams, he has vigorous intentions, which are much better. He is not satisfied with what he has done any more than the rest of us. My interest in him is growing so that I leave my seat and step over to see if I can find his name, or at least his artist. I find "Michel Angelo, painted by himself."
>
> Strange, I had always thought of him as a heavy muscled man like his own creations. This man is almost wiry. If I could only see his hand[s] as well as his face! . . . There must be something remarkable about those unseen hands.
>
> So we sit in our friendly company, and we talk to each other of the secrets of life and we take good hope and courage.[9]

After three months in Rome he started out again, this time in the direction of Florence—not taking the direct route but allowing himself to follow any lane or view that attracted him. On this trip he wrote lyrical prose about the mountains and lakes and the people with whom he talked, but this prose does not show new sides of his character. Near Florence he came upon many wildflowers:

> The first were clumps of daffodils hiding away under a hedge holding up their yellow lily [-like] flowers safe in the fence of thorns. They were very welcome for all that and it seemed right that they should be the first Florence should offer me. Then there were daisies, too, and one large star-like variety, bright yellow all of them and varnished like the buttercups. I plucked one of these and carried it along with me. Still it is usually a mistake to pluck a flower. After one has enjoyed it what can [one] do with it? To keep it in the hand is only to see it wither. It is cruelty to throw it down to die in the dust. I know a way to solve the difficulty if there is a stream near by. Today I found one only a little out of my way. I walked out on [a] bridge and dropped the daisy over. Then it danced away over the dimpling water, a yellow sun to shine for the fishes and frogs.

This paragraph shows the delicacy of his thoughts in that period of his youth. He noted further about Florence:

> That shining city of the Arno has remained in my memory a place of beauty always in spite of its commonplaces, a place in which I grew toward the beautiful more than in any other city I have known. Why then did I not write of it, you wonder. I can only answer that perhaps the very act of growing was sufficient expression of my feeling and I had nothing left to put down on paper except the ordinary contrasts of sordid life.[10]

Upon his arrival home from Europe, White went to live in Chicago, where he worked for a technological library and spent his evenings at Hull House. He is said to have organized a group that designed and made furniture. This came to the attention of Charlotte Perkins Stetson, who recommended him to Whitehead. He also directed theatricals. "Jane Addams seeing Hervey was a man of unusual talent gave him a high place in her counsel," said Henry Morton Robinson, who lived on the Maverick for years and was a friend of White's. On leaving Hull House he would return to his room and write by an oil lamp until dawn. In quick succession Small, Maynard & Company published his first novels, *Differences* (1899) and *Quicksand* (1900), which were instant successes. Theodore Dreiser said, "Our own American *Quicksand*, by Hervey White, I consider among the six great novels of the world." The friends White made at Hull House included Clarence Darrow, Sidney Webb, Ramsey MacDonald and the Crown Prince of Belgium, then a reporter on a Minneapolis newspaper.[11]

It was through Hull House that White met Ralph Radcliffe Whitehead. I remember Hervey, during a talk before the Historical Society of Woodstock, telling of his first impression of the Englishman, who approached him with a hesitant, almost apologetic gait. The forthright westerner concluded that what the other man needed was a good meal. He invited Whitehead to a thirty-five-cent basement cafeteria and was disappointed to have his guest eat so little of this extravagant outlay. In return Whitehead invited him to dinner at one of Chicago's most expensive hotels. Thinking the poor fellow would never be able to pay for the meal, Hervey stopped at a bank and withdrew thirty dollars, thus being prepared for any emergency.

That evening he was shown into a private dining room where the waiters made a feeble attempt to show respect for Hervey despite his hatlessness and bohemian attire. When his host commenced to order wines and fancy Italian dishes, White could feel the thirty dollars dwindling in his pocket. Little did he know that Whitehead was considered one of the richest commoners in England. He had come to Chicago to investigate certain spiritual mediums for the Society of Psychical Research.

Later Hervey went to California and met with Whitehead at his Montecito home. This gave him an opportunity to become more intimate with the Englishman. Whitehead was already planning a crafts colony in the Oregon forest, where he wished to start a furniture industry utilizing the native woods. He would have a large house built for himself and smaller ones for the workers. He had even engaged a string trio, the members of which were to precede them to this almost inaccessible place and be prepared to produce music as soon as their patron arrived. White was to accompany the Whitehead family, who took the thousand-mile journey slowly with many side excursions. A log house in the forest was ready for them when they arrived. But the musicians had become entangled in romantic adventures and had quarreled among themselves, and there was no music. The entire Oregon project failed before it was under way.[12]

Soon after their return from Oregon, Whitehead and White met with Bolton Brown at his Palo Alto home. They discussed plans for an Arts and Crafts colony to be located in the proximity of a large city. Brown recommended the Catskill Mountains, and after much discussion he was sent east by Whitehead to search for a suitable location. The founding of the Byrdcliffe colony is covered in the previous chapter.[13]

When Hervey White chose the site for *his* colony, he picked a farm on low land. "One gets so tired of climbing a hill to go to supper," he said. "Better [to] live in a valley and climb the hill for a view."[14] He decided to name it the Maverick after a wild or untamed creature.[15] He and Fritz Van der Loo purchased Peter Ostrander's one-hundred-and-two-acre farm just over the Hurley boundary from Woodstock, each paying half. They paid a thousand dollars cash, with a mortgage of five hundred.[16] Van der Loo soon returned to his native land after agreeing with Hervey that if either of them should receive an offer to buy any of the land it would be referred to the other partner, who would refuse to sell.

At about this time, in 1904, Hervey married Vivian Bevans, a girl who had come to Byrdcliffe and has been described as very beautiful. He built a cottage for them called Bear Camp and in due time they had two sons, Dan and Caleb. The primitive life and uncertain future proved difficult for his wife and two babies, although Hervey, trying to be a wage earner, taught school for a while in West Hurley. There was talk of his going to a city to get a regular job to support his family, but when the final decision had to be made he chose to remain on the Maverick and his wife left with the children. Shortly before Hervey's death, Dan, then grown, came to see him. This is believed to have been the only subsequent contact between the boys and their father.[17]

In 1908 White set up a hand press on which he printed his books, plays and magazines—setting the type, stitching, cutting and binding by hand. *The Wild Hawk*, a periodical begun in 1911, lasted about five years, every number featuring White's stories or

Cover of The Wild Hawk, *Vol. 1, No. 1: Hervey White's first Maverick periodical.* Courtesy of Woodstock Library.

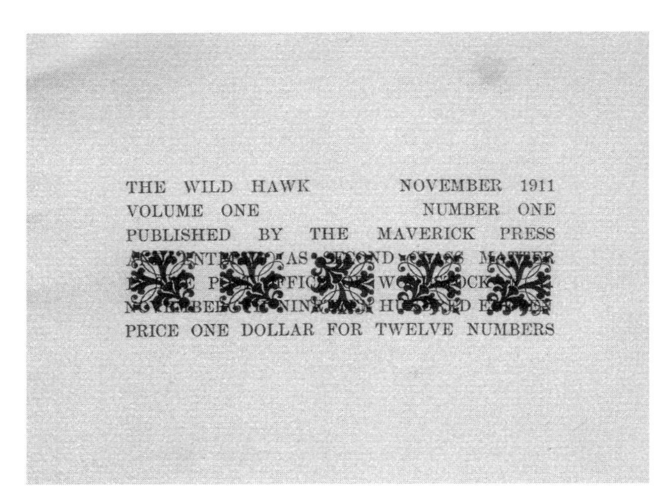

THE WILD HAWK NOVEMBER 1911
VOLUME ONE NUMBER ONE
PUBLISHED BY THE MAVERICK PRESS
PRICE ONE DOLLAR FOR TWELVE NUMBERS

Serial notes from the inaugural issue of The Wild Hawk *in November 1911.* Courtesy of Woodstock Library.

poems or entries from his Italian journal. There were also contributions from the educator Edward Yeomans, poetry by Allan Updegraff, and translations by Edwin Bjorkman and Carl Eric Lindin of stories from European folklore. (The translations, although charming, do not add to our collection of Woodstockiana.) The successor to *The Wild Hawk* was *The Plowshare*, begun in 1916 and "conducted" by Hervey White, Allan Updegraff, Carl Lindin and later Gustave Hellstrom. This was a more versatile magazine, containing editorials, reviews and woodcuts by local artists, as well as poems, stories and even advertisements. These magazines were widely distributed and acclaimed among those interested in independent literary ventures.

In the first issue of *The Plowshare*, Hervey White wrote of Woodstock:

> Our special stock in trade, we think, is our humanness. We even include the institutions and conventions as essential to humanness. We are not revolutionaries; we are but harmlessly tinged with radicalism; we are not the wild anarchists that onlookers might judge us from the freedom exhibited in our clothes. We are just ordinary "nice people" in the main . . . a little nicer than others, it is true, but not so nice as to be devoid of interest and inspiration.
>
> Woodstock is a group of idealists . . . We are not all idealists however. That is the charming thing about Woodstock, that it isn't all of anything, nor yet quite all of everything . . . On the whole we do not vastly differ from the denizens of the city. We are selected from the city that is all. Self selected and of course, well selected.[18]

An early issue featured a play by Hervey White called *The Woodcutter*, which had no dramatic possibilities but did show an understanding of the core of nature. The woodcutter says:

> I've often thought what it must be like when a tree feels the ax in its body . . . Why shouldn't trees have their feelings? . . . tree-feelings, of course . . . I almost wish, sometimes, I was a tree. (*he stands, and lays his cheek meditatively against the bark.*) It's as if I could feel the sap flowing . . . coming up from the million roots down in the ground. There's a power about it that humans don't have; and a peace! . . . like the peace that "passeth understanding."[19]

Over the years *The Plowshare* published many interesting articles. Among the contributors was Bolton Brown, who stirred up a hornet's nest with his remarks on democratic and majority rule, bringing heated replies from Gustave Hellstrom, Norman Boggs and others. Brown maintained that democracy did not favor art, science or education and that the only freedom in a real democracy was the freedom to be like every other democrat. He recommended training the powers of the child and "so to set its face, that it should 'try all things,' that it should, therefore, doubt all things; that it should get outside of mass-hypnotism and see new truth and perhaps God in something else than its own class-image." That "would be for democracy to cut its own throat . . . [and] cease to be a democracy," he added.[20]

The early numbers of *The Plowshare* featured woodcuts by Fernand Léger, Henry Mattson, Konrad Cramer, William E. Schumacher (who would allow that there were only two artists in the entire history of art whose work excelled his), Pamela Brown, Carl Lindin, Ethel Canby Peets and John Bates. They included designs by Hunt Diederich, probably the finest craftsman and designer who ever lived in Woodstock, and numerous others.

The Plowshare most likely ran until January 1920, as that is the last issue of which a copy survives. But it was revived later by Henry Morton Robinson and Ernest Brace, along with Hervey White, this time subtitled "A Literary Periodical of One-Man Exhibits" and each issue devoted to a single author.

In the *Woodstock Bulletin* of September 1, 1928, William Harlan Hale wrote, "Every summer we find thrust upon us a new weekly or bi-weekly paper which we read until autumn and forget completely by next spring, when another paper appears to take its place. And the procession of local publications still passes; it has been a long one." A few years after White began publishing on the Maverick, *The Hue and Cry* was conceived by several young bloods—principally Alex Brook and Josh Billings. Hale went on to say:

> Besides the Maverick sheets [Hale meant Hervey's own publications] and *The Hue and Cry* there have been others, Poet Seaver edited a magazine in 1924, and in that year the *Woodstock Almanac* made its first and only appearance. This April was born *The Woodstock Bulletin*, this August the *Saturday Morning*. What a journalistic bustle! Three papers this summer in a little town like this! Of course the field is overcrowded . . . But they are essentially different from each other, these rivals . . . *Saturday Morning*, Mr. Newgold's house-organ, shows an especial flair for importing great names; another, *The Woodstock Bulletin*, limits itself to strict news, which ranges from notes on the Maverick Festival to the reflection that Mr. G. W. Elwyn has bought a new car; and as for *The Hue and Cry*, it is printed on paper of two colors which change weekly, as does the pen-name of one of its columnists.[21]

Music

The first musician to settle on the Maverick was the cellist Paul Kefer, who had been engaged by the Whiteheads to play in Byrdcliffe and moved across the valley with Hervey White. Kefer brought Horace Britt, an even more distinguished cellist, to the Maverick, and it was Britt who persuaded Pierre Henrotte, the much loved violinist, to join them. Among the early musicians to arrive at Britt's invitation was George Plochmann.[22] He in turn brought Charles Cooper, another pianist, and Edward Kreiner. Thus the musicians gathered on the Maverick. At first they played together informally, but in 1914 Henrotte, accompanied by George Howard Scott, gave a violin recital at the Firemen's Hall in Woodstock village; another recital there featured Britt and Marion Eames, a soprano. In August of that year a string quartet played in the village: Pierre Henrotte, violin; Henri Michaux, viola; and Roger Britt (a brother of Horace) and Paul Kefer, cello. The First World War had begun and the proceeds of this concert were given to the Red Cross. Henrotte remembers that they played Beethoven's Quintet no. 2, opus 59, and numbers by Raff and Glazunov. These concerts were so enthusiastically received that plans were made for a permanent ensemble and a concert hall on the Maverick.

The Maverick Concert Hall opened in 1916 with a performance by the trio of Engelbert Roentgen, Charles Cooper and Edward Kreiner, and the audience loved not only the music but the informality of the musicians playing in their shirtsleeves, the feel of being in the forest, and even the odor of the new pine benches.[23] The hall had been built from trees cut on the grounds—long poles making the frame with rough boards forming the roof and sides. One

Hervey White in front of Maverick Concert Hall. Postcard by L. E. Jones. AMS Collection.

end of this rustic building was open and the other had an addition for a small musicians' waiting room. Inside was a platform and the audience paid twenty-five cents for the privilege of sitting on planks. Here they sat enthralled by the excellence of the chamber music, while the sunshine entered between the whitewashed boards, colored greenish yellow as it filtered through the trees, and an occasional birdsong vied with the instruments. A summer rain might patter on the roof and claps of thunder force the players to pause briefly. In the old days everyone was welcome to bring their pets and babies, but eventually these created such a disturbance they had to be banned. A dilapidated bus brought part of the audience, a few people came in their own cars, but most of the art students gladly walked the few miles from the village to the concert hall, where they sat enraptured listening to Bach, Beethoven, Tchaikovsky and other great composers, an experience to fire their creative spirit.

Engelbert Roentgen, who came from a well-known musical family in Holland, would play his Gagliano cello here for many years and head the first Woodstock string quartet. He was desolate when his cello was smashed into hundreds of pieces by his own car, which had been parked on a slope.[24] An expert undertook to repair it and, although this was an expensive endeavor, mended it so skillfully that the tone was better than ever. The resident musicians also included Henri Michaux, who arrived from the station, three miles away, trundling his luggage in a wheelbarrow. There came Leon Barzin Sr., who was first viola with the Metropolitan Opera Orchestra, Gabriel Peyre from the same orchestra and Georges Barrère of the golden flute. They all played for the love of producing fine music, because the few dollars divided among them after a concert would scarcely pay for new strings for their instruments, which sometimes suffered from the damp air. In 1918 the cost of admission was raised to fifty cents.

For years Pierre Henrotte played in many of the concerts and directed others. During the second season while he was on tour, Edward Deru took over the direction. Deru had been violinist for the Belgian king and more recently had been heard in recitals with Eugene Ysaÿe. It is from Pierre's little notebook that I have taken most of my information about the early Maverick concerts. In the autumn of 1958 I sat with him in his small house, which—with its stone walls and tiled roof—looks as though it might have been built for a character in one of Hans Christian Andersen's fairy tales. I asked many questions, which he answered with his quick, smiling eagerness. His

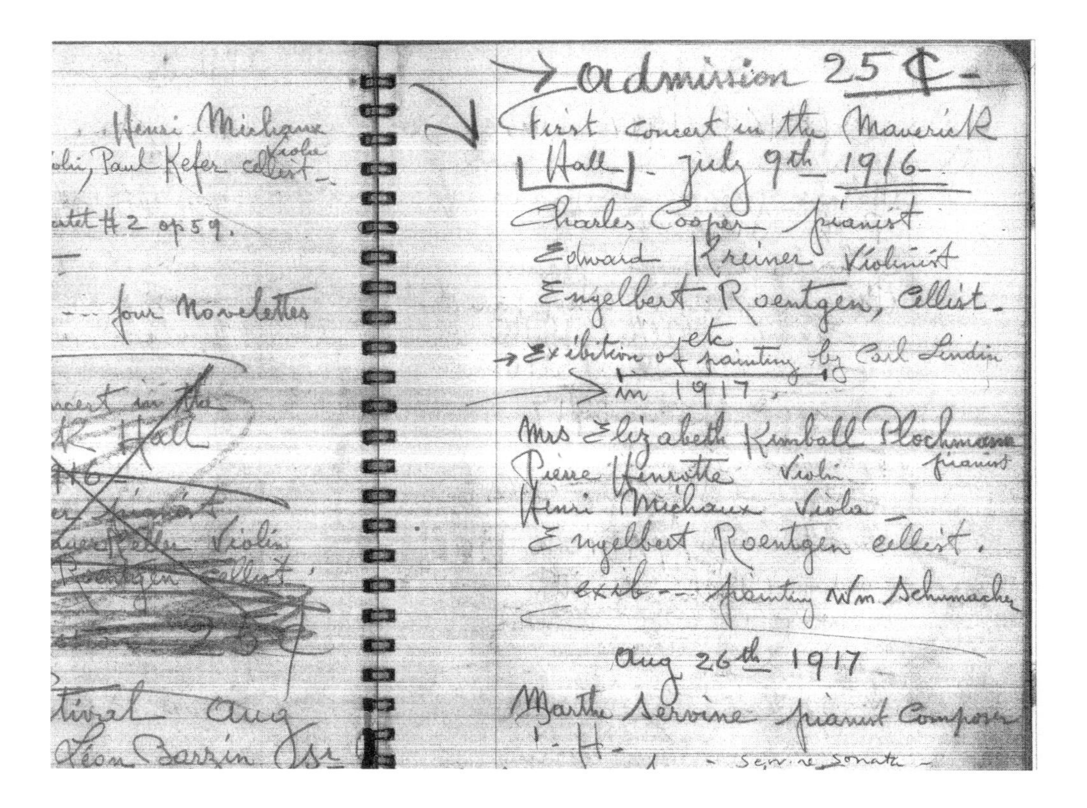
Henri Michaux
Paul Kefer cellist
four Novelettes
Leon Barzin

→ admission 25 ¢ -
First concert in the Maverick
Hall - July 9th 1916
Charles Cooper pianist
Edward Kreiner Violinist
Engelbert Roentgen, Cellist
etc
→ Exibition of painting by Carl Lindin
in 1917
Mrs Elizabeth Kimball Plochmann pianist
Pierre Henrotte Violin
Henri Michaux Viola
Engelbert Roentgen cellist.
exib -- painting Wm Schumacher
Aug 26th 1917
Marthe Servine pianist Composer
Servine Sonata

Detail from a page in Pierre Henrotte's notebook. Courtesy of Woodstock Library.

wife, Elvira, having been disabled with a broken leg, hobbled in to greet me before I left. That was why Pierre would frequently excuse himself to dart out to the kitchen to baste a roast, which was emitting savory odors from the oven.

For forty years the Maverick concerts have continued, and Henrotte remembers most of the musicians and artists. He spoke of baritone Mario Laurenti, through whom Elsa Schiaparelli was introduced to the Maverick. At the time Schiaparelli was not known in the world of fashion and was glad to make a little money knitting sweaters. He recalled Caplinger of "Tompkins Corner" fame on radio and how he ended up running a successful restaurant in Lafitte's Tavern in New Orleans. It was Caplinger who brought the Negro John to the Maverick. John settled down here for the rest of his life. He grew a few vegetables in front of his shack and somehow managed to eat over the years until he received his old-age pension. He refused all offers of work, saying, "Mr. White don't work, why should I?" John did not consider the writing and printing of books to be work.

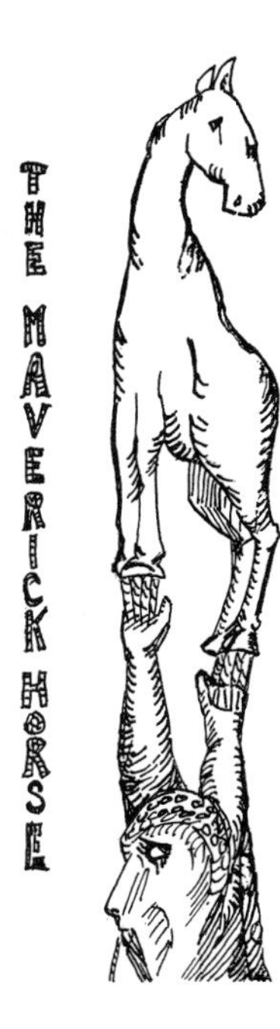

Block print of John Flannagan's sculpture The Maverick Horse. *Until 1960 the sculpture stood at the entrance of the road to the Concert Hall. Now it resides stage right in the hall itself.* Print by Anita M. Smith. AMS Collection.

Hervey persuaded Elvira Henrotte to open the Maverick's only restaurant, called the Intelligencia, which she undertook with the help of several of the artists, including Arnold and Lucile Blanch. Hervey was successful in getting people to work but rarely credited their efforts on his behalf. Later the Intelligencia was run by a character named Hippolyte Havel, who was supposedly an anarchist and in any case was sufficiently bizarre to attract a clientele. It was a pleasant place to dine out of doors after a Sunday concert, and one could always count on the soup being good.

At the entrance to the Maverick stood John Flannagan's remarkable sculpture of a horse. Though Flannagan showed talent in his work, his career may have come to an end before he achieved his peak, for he was said to be an alcoholic. Nevertheless, one day in 1924 he carved *The Maverick Horse* out of a living tree, with an ax as his only tool. For many years it stood on the Maverick, a vigorous sculpture and a symbol of the untamed.[25]

During the next few years the Maverick concert musicians were joined by Sandor Harmati, conductor of the Omaha Orchestra, Gaston and Edouard Déthier of the Juilliard School, and Samuel Lifshey, now of the Philadelphia Orchestra. There was also the Letz Quartet, which at one time included Alfred Megerline, Michel Piastro and our own Inez Richards, whose piano playing gave pleasure for years. There were recitals by Georgette Leblanc and by the Chamber Music Society of San Francisco—which Henrotte marked with three X's, indicating they were unusually good. Paul LeMay, of the Minneapolis Symphony and the Kilbourn Quartet, came to play. The latter included Gerald Kunz, who is still a resident, and Gustave Tinlot. There was a recital by Paul Robeson in 1925, and later Henri Deering played the piano at a concert. One Sunday Clara and David Mannes were heard. William Kroll—according to Henrotte one of the "foremost Chamber music player[s]"—has frequently played his violin for us. Kroll has spent the past twenty-five summers in Woodstock, traveling back and forth between the Catskills and the Berkshires when his services are required at Tanglewood. A few of us remember Leon Barzin Jr. as a boy when he would turn the pages for the piano players. His eyes and ears seemed to absorb all the beauty, so intently were they concentrated on the music. Indeed he learned it well and it was not long before he gave a recital with Gaetane Britt, also the child of a musician. Young Barzin is now leader of the National Orchestral Association and has become famous. It was music that first attracted the community to the Maverick, and now, after more than forty years, the Sunday concerts are as popular as ever.[26]

Pierre Henrotte was born in Liège, Belgium, and his wife, Elvira, was prima ballerina with the Metropolitan Opera Company when he became

The Letz Quartet played on the Maverick with various members over a number of years. Pictured here are (l to r): Hans Letz, Horace Britt, Edward Kreiner and Edwin Bachmann. Circa 1921–22. Courtesy of Woodstock Library.

concertmaster. As a young man Henrotte showed such extraordinary ability with his violin that he was accepted below the age limit as a pupil in the Royal Conservatory. To pay his tuition he took a position as second violinist in a local theater. At sixteen he received his first prize as a violinist. This led to an offer to play in the Sables d'Olonne summer theater. When he appeared for the job the manager almost wept because he looked so small. After he had played, the manager not only was satisfied, but offered him a winter engagement at the Grand Théâtre in Nantes, France. Later he became concertmaster of the symphony orchestras at Nice and Aix-les-Bains and frequently appeared as a soloist with other celebrated artists.

In 1904 Henrotte came to America to play with the Bagby group and toured with Madame Lillian Nordica, Alice Neilsen, Maggie Teyte and other prima donnas. After many years as concertmaster for the Metropolitan Opera Orchestra he resigned to give more of his time to the Williams School of Music at West Saugerties. For a number of years before his retirement he directed the Minneapolis Symphony but always returned in the summer to his home on the Maverick. Henrotte will be especially remembered for his Woodstock Ensemble.[27]

Georges Barrère was regarded as the most celebrated flutist in America, and Woodstock audiences were quick to appreciate his virtuosity. To quote from a recent issue of the *Freeman*: "A flute simply cannot be played as Mr. Barrère plays it; there are no such exquisite gradations in a flute as he gets out of it."[28] He was born in Bordeaux, France, and as a child embarked on a musical career by playing a tin whistle that had been given to him as a toy. This was the beginning, though it

Georges Barrère and Inez Carroll Richards.
Courtesy of Woodstock Library.

was years before he would achieve the pinnacle of his profession and become the "Monarch of flute players."[29] At twenty he took first prize at the National Conservatory. In turn he played at the Folies-Bergère and the Concerts de l'Opéra and founded a wind instrument ensemble before coming to America to play under Walter Damrosch. This led to one triumph after another. In 1929 he conducted the concerts for the Maverick Festival, played in many of the Maverick concerts and built his home here; he was thereafter identified with Woodstock.[30] Barrère's sense of fun is apparent in an account published in a local newspaper:

> Are you an Artist or not? As long as you have elected Woodstock as your rusticating abode, you must do something artistic in Life: dress raggedly and look odd. If not what would be the use for Tourists to come "to see the Artists?"
>
> Opposite the Art Gallery, some of these Pilgrims in a Pierce-Arrow asked me . . . the way to the Colony, pointing inquiringly toward the Bearsville Boulevard. As if I was a stranger or a gloomy joker I asked them: What Colony? The P.A..'s owners looking [disgustedly] at my open shirt and unshined shoes retorted: "The Artist Colony, of course!!!". . .
>
> I told these Aristocrats . . . "You are right in the midst of it." Showing them Paul Rohland emerging from Happy's store with a[n] armful of groceries while Pierre Henrotte was having a fight with Jesse Wolven over the high cost of Frankfurters . . . The Pierce Arrowers stepped on the gas and disappeared towards the Nook, convinced that I was most ungracious to deny them the information so politely required . . .
>
> Never mind! When in the mid-Winter some charming Girl comes to you after a Concert in St. Louis or Seattle and insists on shaking hand[s] with you because she is from Woodstock *too* you feel proud to have obtained your second papers from that Colony of Artists.[31]

Aerial shot of the Maverick Festival.
Courtesy of Woodstock Library.

One of his stories concerned a concert tour to Mexico made by several of the Maverick musicians. In Mexico City they dined together at a French restaurant, where the maître d'hôtel was delighted upon hearing them converse in French and learning who they were. The musicians, who were accompanied by their wives, asked if there were snails to be had at the restaurant. The proprietor was "désolé"—there were none available that evening, but he promised he would have them the following night. The next evening the only person to order them was Madame Britt, and she did not enjoy the dish because the snails seemed soft and had an unfamiliar taste. When asked, the maître d'hôtel explained, "Well, you must know snails are difficult to find in Mexico, but here we have a fat caterpillar that we consider a good substitute." I wonder if Madame Britt wrinkled her nose at that announcement, because it was said she refused to smile for fear of causing wrinkles—which to me is as amusing as the snail story.

Many other musicians played from time to time at the Sunday concerts. I have mentioned the Letz Quartet, which by staying through one winter of practice before going on tour gave us an opportunity to hear fine music. When the audience could no longer keep warm in greatcoats and blankets sitting in the breezy Maverick hall, the concerts were moved to the Art Gallery (Woodstock Artists Association). The musicians included Hans Letz, Horace Britt, Edwin Bachmann and Edward Kreiner.

In Henrotte's little notebook is a list of the artists who exhibited during the first concerts. They were Carl Eric Lindin, William Schumacher, Catherine Watkins, Alfred Hutty, Marion Bullard, Anita Smith, Grace Johnson (sculpture), Henry Mattson and Eugene Speicher.

Festivals

By the time twenty or so cottages had been built on the Maverick, the need for water became acute. Of course there was no plumbing, but even water dipped by the pailful from the dug wells was scarce. Hervey White came to the reluctant conclusion that it was necessary to have an artesian well drilled. No water was found until the drill had bitten over five

The Maverick Festival. Standing third from right is the painter Henry Lee McFee. Courtesy of Woodstock Library.

hundred feet into the Catskill rock and Hervey found himself fifteen hundred dollars in debt, at a time when a dollar was worth a dollar. Several of the musicians living nearby suggested that a fête be held to help pay for the well, and in the summer of 1916 the first Maverick Festival took place.[32]

On the date chosen, when all preparations were completed, it poured rain as if the witch were laughing at the fuss that had been made to obtain and pay for a water supply. Hervey was in despair, seeing all the expense of the preparations being added to the cost of the well. It continued to rain for several days and to cheer Hervey the musicians conspired to give him a tin-pan serenade. They organized a band with buckets and dishpans and created such terrifying sounds that they did exorcise the old squaw spirit that lives above the mountains and the following day was clear. The sun, followed by the moon, shone on the freshly washed Catskills with invigorating purity; the air was more luminous than any city dweller will ever see.

Few of us will forget the beauty of that first festival, although we may not remember the details. There was a dramatic performance of some kind and suppers were eaten on the meadow now used for parking. Many bonfires were lighted, around which gathered gypsy-looking groups of people cooking stews or toasting hot dogs and boiling coffee in blackened pots—there was little liquor in evidence at that first festival. Everyone attempted to wear some costume, as the entrance fee was doubled if one did not appear in fancy dress. It might be only a peasant smock and a bright handkerchief tied around the head, or a wreath of grape leaves such as the one Hervey wore to resemble Pan—a role that suited him well. Later the crowd, in their vivid array, took their seats in the stone quarry. They scrambled to points of vantage among the shelving rocks and tailings left by the stone workers, while above them a white goat frolicked along the rim, adding a decorative note to the sylvan scenery. A small orchestra played—Gabriel Peyre and a few other good musicians directed by Leon Barzin Sr.—and never did Tchaikovsky seem finer to our ears than when his music resounded off that rocky amphitheater. As we listened, it gradually became dark. A

Maverick Festival revelers. Standing are the artists Eugene Speicher and Charles Rosen. Courtesy of Woodstock Library.

full moon appeared above the treetops, providing a gentle light into which the Russian dancer Lada stepped to present her recital. How good she was we could not judge because we were enchanted by the setting, the music and the grace of her movements, all of which enhanced her art beyond evaluation. It was one of those rare occasions when everything seems perfect.[33]

The festivals soon outgrew the quarry as accounts of the revelry spread, until unfortunately they became famous far beyond the borders of the village. The first festival paid for the well and subsequent ones would provide the means of paying Hervey's debts for the preceding year, although after about a week he would be left as poor as when he started.[34] Each year a new theme would suggest the subject for the show and the costumes the public should wear. One of the early festivals was a gypsy carnival, and one of the most attractive groups to arrive consisted of Ethel and Orville Peets with blankets and utensils heaped onto a little cart pulled by that balky western pinto, Teddy. The Peets set up a genuine-looking gypsy camp around their bonfire, and while Ethel cooked their food in a black iron pot on a tripod, Orville—in a Portuguese nomad's outfit—collected wood and chopped it with gusto to keep the fire blazing.

At one of the early festivals the Chase brothers brought a pair of world champion wrestlers to perform. When it came time for the act they did not appear and Frank and Ned Chase went to search for them. The wrestlers were found under a tree completely absorbed in poetry being read to them by Hervey White. As a matter of fact, they were of a higher cultural level than most of the artists who deplored this advent of sports to the Maverick.

One year Bob Chanler, who was more famous for his escapades than his art, put on the show *Nebuchadnezzer*.[35] On another occasion Walter Steinhilber presented *The Pirate Ship*. Other performances included Farrell Pelly's *Circus* and a fantasy from *1001 Arabian Nights*, *Scheherazade*. Yet another year a local group presented a scene from *The Canterbury Tales*. On this occasion there was a

The Maverick Festival welcomed celebrants of all ages. Courtesy of Woodstock Library.

pageant that started on the Woodstock Village Green with knights on horseback and ladies in wimples riding sidesaddle upon very surprised and resplendently caparisoned farm horses, driving them to a friskiness they had not shown in years. After various unexpected sideshows they finally arrived at the Maverick. In 1929 there was a Gay Nineties performance in which Barrère did a caricature of John Philip Sousa. Another time Barrère was a black-faced comedian in a minstrel show. In a few of the earlier performances a trio comprising Frances Rogers, Alice Beard and Phoebe Ropes delighted audiences with clever skits they wrote and played themselves. Sometimes after the festival Hervey invited the workers to a pig roast, which recaptured some of the spirit of the original entertainments.

In 1929 R. L. Duffus wrote an interesting and fairly accurate story about Woodstock in *The New York Times Magazine*, although he began by calling Whitehead "Whiteside," which unfortunately was copied in later articles. He described the Saturday Market Fair, which was then at its best, and told of the Riseley swimming hole, the exhibitions and the theater. Duffus claimed the Maverick Festival was a means for audiences, three or four thousand strong, to shed their inhibitions. He said it began at four in the afternoon and continued until four the next morning. To quote from his account:

> But when people are allowed to take off some inhibitions they are likely to take off a good many. Last year, it was felt, too many were doffed. The two lone State policemen who tried to keep order did not entirely succeed. The fault was not Mr. White's, perhaps not even Woodstock's. The most boisterous of the revelers, it was thought, came from adjoining towns, and perhaps from New York. Nevertheless, the aftermath was that many sober-minded people in the vicinity began to wonder if the Maverick had not got out of hand, and if it ought not to be abandoned.[36]

By this time most of the old crowd had ceased to participate beyond possibly paying the entrance fee and showing up for an hour in deference to their friend Hervey. Seeing the nude figure is nothing exceptional to artists, and they do not find anything lewd in a model posing naked in a stream, but to exploit the body can disgust them. For example, at one festival an outsider, abiding by the stricture to wear some clothing, covered his body with tights but then painted his entire anatomy on the outside. The carousing through the night became increasingly repulsive, stretching the limits of even Hervey's tolerance. Finally, in 1931, the festival was discontinued.[37]

Theater

The Maverick theater as an enterprise started in 1924. The preceding fall the Irish-born actor Dudley Digges, who was well known in New York, motored through Woodstock and met Hervey White. Digges was enchanted by the man and the place. Hervey outlined for him a plan for a rustic theater in which plays of distinction could be produced. Digges, intrigued, agreed to come the following summer as director. The theater was built on a natural slope without flooring, where the patrons took their seats on rough boards amidst a cloud of clay dust. It also lacked so-called facilities. In July the theater opened with *The Dragon* by Lady Gregory, with Helen Hayes, Dudley Digges, Norma Mitchell, E. J. Ballantine and Edward G. Robinson in the cast. Helen Hayes was stopping in Byrdcliffe and came over to the Maverick for the performances. The audience enjoyed the play even though the production was marred by poor lighting and staging.[38]

I received the following letter from Helen Hayes:

June 19, 1957

My dear Miss Smith:

Am without a secretary due to prolonged illness of a member of her family. I am trying to take care of mail on my own. Deadly task!

Woodstock! The Maverick theater! Hervey White. All of us indigent actors so grateful to be there for four weeks room and board. Eddie Robinson, also broke, looking longingly at the paintings of Bellows, Carroll, Speicher, etc. First performance of the lovely Lady Gregory play a huge success—tried a second performance, "popular demand"—got rained out! I remember one dilemma I had during our only performance. Had to lie still in apparent death through nearly all of last act. Mosquitoes settled in large groups for banqueting. They got so they didn't even fly away after a bite—just walked across to a fresh spot! But I kept still!

Don't remember Whitehead—only his younger brother who beaued me around.

All in all, it was a unique spot in the world, wasn't it? Throbbing with creation, flashing with genius—and so placid and countrified withal. Sorry for this incoherent note. I dictate better.

Sincerely,
Helen Hayes[39]

Lady Gregory's The Dragon *was staged on the Maverick in 1924. A young Helen Hayes is pictured second from right.*
Photo by Stowall Studios. Courtesy of Woodstock Library.

This first success led to other performances. The next play was Lord Dunsany's *The Lost Silk Hat*, with Edward G. Robinson and Brandon Peters. This was followed by Eugene O'Neill's tragedy *Where the Cross Is Made*, featuring Rose Hobart, E. J. Ballantine and Dudley Digges. A comedy by Franz Molnar called *Sacred and Profane Art* with David Bell Bridge in the leading role was next, and at the same time Mollie Pearson of *Bunty Pulls the Strings* fame began rehearsals of William Cotton's *Andrew Takes a Wife*. The final performance, presented over the Labor Day holiday, was *Antony and Cleopatra* starring a Finnish actress, Madame Tampieri. Presented with this was a comedy called *Fixin's*. That first year of theater at the Maverick resulted in no crashing success or financial rewards, but it did prove there was a place for good drama in Woodstock.[40]

It is curious how slight has been the artists' cultural influence on those who were born in the village. Important books have been written here, exhibitions shown here by painters who would make history in American art, and some of the finest musicians and actors performed here for all to hear and see. Yet only a half dozen or so of the villagers ever attended the concerts, the art shows or the theater productions, until cheap Broadway hits were presented. The Broadway shows drew a large Ulster County audience and also had the reverse effect of diminishing the attendance of creative-minded people.

For several years there were no resident groups offering plays regularly on the Maverick. But there were special performances—for instance, a French divertissement presented by Edith King and Dorothy Coit, who lived at the Lark's Nest in Byrdcliffe. They spent an entire season training children of all ages—down to Teddy Goddard, who was three—painting scenery and making costumes with infinite patience for detail. The result was a jewel-like performance into which the children fitted like small gems.[41] Later in New York these two women became famous with their productions at the Heckscher Children's Theatre.

In 1925 a beautiful dance recital was presented by Ruth St. Denis, Ted Shawn and Charles Weidman.[42] There was a dancer already on the Maverick: Alexis Kosloff, who was born in Russia and at seventeen had been the youngest pupil to graduate from the Moscow Ballet School. A member of the Imperial Russian Ballet, Kosloff was for seventeen years ballet master of the Metropolitan Opera in New

Alexis Kosloff is pictured on a program guide for a dance recital at the Maverick theater in 1939. Courtesy of Historical Society of Woodstock.

York. He was also well known as a teacher. He and his wife, who was a painter and musician, bought the Barnes farm next to Hervey White's property. Among Kosloff's pupils were Marilyn Miller, John Barrymore, Marion Davies, Maude Adams and Alice Brady.[43]

Hervey White has been described as philosophical about anything that might happen. For example, once when he was listening to a concert, one of the cottages caught fire. Someone slipped onto the bench beside him and excitedly whispered the news. "Oh, let it burn," he replied. "What's the use of doing anything about it?" Afterwards when the topic of insuring the cottages was raised, he said: "It's too expensive. Anyway, if only one cottage burns every five years I would end up better off than if I had paid for the insurance."[44] Certainly the houses were not individually very valuable and almost nothing was done to keep them clean or in repair. Hervey's philosophy was turning to inertia.

The whole place was run down by 1929 when a fresh group took over the theater and a dozen cottages. This ensemble was headed by Allen DeLano, Gladys Hurlbut and Teddy Ballantine—the last named having been a Woodstock resident for several years. They were professionals and wanted their agreements in writing, as well as regular leases. Hervey said he could not provide these without Fritz Van der Loo's consent—which, if obtainable at all, would have taken most of the season to secure. They were starting a school and trying to build a reputation. The Intelligencia restaurant, now run by a Russian, was to be their eating place, but a week before the theater opened the Russian changed his mind and Gladys Hurlbut was obliged to run it with the help of an old Negro cook. She ran back and forth to Kingston for the food supplies and also planned the meals. The food was so good the clientele ate overabundantly and opened charge accounts that Gladys knew would never be paid. The customers were furious when she insisted upon cash payments from everyone. She was willing to allow Hervey free meals but could not permit him to bring along groups of friends to run their accounts into the red. The philosopher was so angry, according to bystanders, that he shook all over. From that time he frequently took a vindictive attitude toward the theater company, an attitude that was extended to anyone who tried to make a financial success of the theater. Hervey maintained he was interested only in experimental work and did not want to see known plays produced. He could never understand that the capital outlay necessary for a summer theater required proportionate box-office returns. Hervey himself wrote plays that everyone knew were not producible.

Advertisement in the Woodstock Playhouse program guide for 1940. AMS Collection.

Allen DeLano tried to get the theater in shape. It was merely a shell of a building in which bats and flying squirrels were domiciled—and would occasionally steal a scene. The stage was tiny and there was practically no space in the wings. They would therefore have to add on storage space and a workroom. There was a homemade electric light plant that was unreliable. The utilities company said they would put electric current into the theater if DeLano would sell twenty contracts to the cottagers, which he did. He was dismayed to learn that Hervey objected, saying he did not want tenants improving his houses. He wanted them left in their primitive state and added that DeLano had no business giving the artists delusions of grandeur. But his protest was too late to prevent the improvements from being made.

The cottages were in terrible condition. Hervey was persuaded to use some of the rent money for new mattresses but would do nothing else. Gladys Hurlbut and a school friend, who had come to run the box office, had to shovel out the dirt and scrub and clean twelve houses. Hervey flitted unhappily from cottage to cottage, convinced that the charm of the Maverick was being destroyed by fresh curtains and flowers in every toothbrush glass, which had been added to welcome the apprentices. The pupils arrived, friendly and stagestruck, and brought all their troubles to Gladys, who said she felt like the mother of the entire mountain. One of the teachers was a spinster with madness in her eyes who was frightened by one of the young students the night she arrived. His name was Harvey Fite, and he was working out his tuition by sleeping at night in the theater as watchman and by keeping everybody's wood box filled. It was raining this particular evening and he wore bathing trunks and nothing else as he carried an armful of wood to the teacher's cottage. In answer to his knock, she opened the door and, seeing his white torso, shrieked and ran through the woods to Gladys, crying that a naked man had come to her door and what would her family say to that? She was past forty and Allen DeLano remarked in his dry way that her family might say be sure to let him in.[45]

Opening night was approaching. They were staging *Wedding Bells*, starring Gladys Hurlbut as Rosalie—for which she had to rehearse besides doing a hundred other jobs. They had a new switchboard, new curtains and freshly painted scenery. But they were most concerned over the holes in the rutted lane that led to the theater, particularly as a new playhouse had been opened in a barn close to the village. Allen decided to take fifty of their precious dollars and persuade the town scraper to level the road. They were in the midst of this on the day of the opening when Hervey came by and made another scene, yelling that Allen was ruining the Maverick and adding that they were merely commercial artists, not real ones, and were to confine their efforts to producing plays.

In a subsequent episode, the town machinery and Hervey White blocked the road as Gladys was heading home for a lysol bath after the "garbage crisis." No provision had been made for disposal of the garbage, and behind the restaurant was an accumulation topped by fish waste. This occurred in a heat wave and the whole Maverick was saturated with a terrible stench. Nobody could be found to handle the situation, so Gladys and Harvey Fite drove a truck to the scene and ladled out the filthy mess by the pailful, took it to a distant ledge, and dumped it. That night when she appeared on stage, looking gorgeous in an evening gown, there was a shout from the back of the house: "My God, it's the garbage woman!"[46]

The second week they produced *Rain*. Allen DeLano worked all week with the ingenious Ned Thatcher to build the rain effect upon which the mood of the play depended. At the dress rehearsal their rain poured down beautifully and was caught in a trough to be carried back and used again. However, on opening night God provided a real storm and it rained so hard and so long that when the curtain went up nobody could hear a line of the play, and when Allen turned on his rain it merely looked as if the theater roof were leaking. These stories were told by Gladys Hurlbut, but I remember that wonderful performance of *Rain* and how enthusiastically it was received. One reviewer said Hurlbut displayed masterful control over every act and gesture, with a perfect interpretation of its deep religious and sexual meaning.[47]

Word had passed among the Woodstockers who counted that the Maverick Players were really good that year, and audiences flocked to applaud the serious acting and to enjoy the old-fashioned melodramas. William Harlan Hale spoke of Gladys Hurlbut's superb ease playing in *Wedding Bells*, which was a particular triumph after her experience of the afternoon. Another reviewer, Grant Allen, likened the Maverick Players to the "famous Abbey Theatre group at Dublin in its early days."[48]

THE MAVERICK PLAYERS

Present

Thursday, June 30	Friday July 1	Saturday July 2	Sunday July 3	Monday July 4

Miss Cecilia Loftus

in the premiere of

"While Doctors Disagree"

A Three Act Comedy of Early America by

LAURENCE EYRE

Author of "Mis' Nelly o' New Orleans", "The Things That Count", "The Merry Wives of Gotham", "Martinique", etc.

Cast in Order of Appearance

Aunt Plez	*Miss Emma DeWeale*
Miss Maria Finch	*Miss Catherine Proctor*
Miss Phoebe Beebe	*Miss Thais Magrane*
Miss Crosby	*Miss Katherine Grey*
The Reverend Mr. Entwhistle	*Mr. France Bendtsen*
Arabella Crosby	*Miss Dortha Duckworth*
Byng Anderson	*Mr. William Post, Jr.*
Dr. Horatio Anderson, an Allopath	*Mr. George MacQuarrie*
Dr. Hector Jonny, a Homeopath	*Mr. E. Laurance*
Deborah Copeland,	*Miss. Cecilia Loftus*
Mrs Govett,	*Miss Irene Shirley*

The period is 1840. The time is the month of May.

The place is the little town of New Castle, Del.

Act I

About noon-day. Mrs. Crosby's parlor at Harmony Street and the Strand.

Act II

Evening. Waiting at Doctor Anderson's house on Delaware Street.

Act III

Scene 1 Same as Act 1.

Scene 2 Deborah's Bedroom

Scene. 3 Same as Scene 1

Play directed by Mr. Laurence Eyre. Production prepared under the supervision of Mr. Arthur Bond assisted by Mrs. Alice Young.

Playbill for a Maverick Players production.
Courtesy of Historical Society of Woodstock.

The last play of the season was a new work by James McCabe Jr., *The Higher Court*, in which Gladys Hurlbut and Ian Wolf starred.[49] They had been successful throughout the summer and had every reason to believe that in the second season they would actually turn a profit. Then Hervey White announced he would not allow them to have the theater another year—and they had no signed contract.

The following season Hervey let the theater to a fresh group, which lasted only a short time. Another year it was the same story, with the theater closing in midseason. I do not have the date, but among my myriad scraps of information is a notation that Cissie Loftus and Laurence Eyre appeared at the Maverick in *While Doctors Disagree*.

Hervey had reached a place where, in his own words, he could "sit and enjoy the solitude and loneliness," and perhaps that was where he was heading all along.[50] The Maverick impulse was beginning to unwind. Even those extraordinary rainbow-hued sheets, *The Hue and Cry*, printed at the Maverick Press, featured an editorial captioned "Criticism of Criticism," which should have been the last word on art.[51]

Hervey made the mistake, from his point of view, of renting the theater a few years later to Robert Elwyn, who made a success of his enterprise. The more popular Elwyn's productions were, the more agitated Hervey became. He tried to persuade Elwyn to go in for artistic failures rather than successes, saying that he did not want a large business to be run on the Maverick and that Bob attracted too big a crowd, yet all the while demanding higher rent. No improvements or repairs had been made to the theater and when Elwyn begged to have plain privies constructed for the audiences, the answer was, "Oh, just tell them to go into the woods." Elwyn had two good seasons as director of the theater, but in the third year Hervey became insistent that Bob present one of *his* plays, and Hervey's dramatic work was very poor. The piece in question seemed to be the most difficult play in the world to produce because all the characters were on roller skates! Elwyn declined to present it and this infuriated White. The next winter, after Elwyn had signed contracts with his cast and bought the rights for his new plays, he received a letter from Hervey saying he would have to leave the Maverick. Thereupon Elwyn built his own theater close to the village. It had the support of the whole community and ran profitably for several years. It was closed only by the gas rationing at the beginning of the Second World War.[52]

There was one more flicker of drama on the Maverick when a group of young players took over with spotty success. However, when they moved to New York City they made a name for themselves with their Circle in the Square Theatre.

Hervey, whose appearance was arresting, was very attractive to most people. To me his flat voice was not appealing and I could never decide whether it was because he was tone deaf or if this was just a Kansas accent. Most of his disputes were in protest against those who tried to make money. In regard to the theater, he was certainly to blame for charging rents that necessitated substantial returns. He was no more prepared to absorb losses than the directors of the companies. He also had quarrels with successful writers and artists. Perhaps he was right in believing that money should not be the standard measure for creative achievement. Faced with the flow of opposite thinking, he became bitter and gradually withdrew from all participation in the arts.

Hervey White Again

In 1931 the Greenwich Village celebrity Romany Marie was running a restaurant on the Rock City road that was formerly known as Ken's Sandwich Shop. At the same time she was advertising soirées at the former Bob Chanler house on the Saugerties road. This house had been owned by one of the few Negro families of Woodstock Township and is said to have been haunted by a youth who was murdered there. Later it was one of the houses occupied by Hunt Diederich, whose bull and toreador weathervane still adorns the roof. Bob Chanler lived in it for several years and while there gave some of his famous parties. From Chanler it came into the possession of Clemence Randolph—who later gained renown, with John Colton, for writing the play *Rain* based on the Somerset Maugham story.

I do not know how Romany Marie came to be there, although she had been in and out of the Maverick for several years. Evidently she was hostess to groups who gathered there in the evening. A visitor to Woodstock tells of sitting outside the kitchen door at a wooden table talking to Hervey White. Hervey was sixty-four at the time, with a head looking as if it were cast in bronze. He gave an impression of serenity and happiness, surrounded by admiring friends. A few days later the visitor attended a Maverick concert where he described Hervey as appearing like an officiating priest at a religious ceremony—although he added, "I know, of course, that he is really a pagan."[53]

People have said that Hervey was influenced by and emulated Walt Whitman, including the bard's interest in nursing. Old Dr. Downer sometimes called him in on a case. Mrs. Walter Weyl remembers with gratitude an occasion when she was unable to secure help in taking care of an ill man who was working for her. Late at night there was a knock on the door, and she opened it to find Hervey White, who had come to nurse the sick man. He reappeared every evening to spend the night until the patient recovered.

Rhoda Chase tells a similar story, set during the Spanish influenza epidemic at the end of the First World War. Harry Brink had not been drafted because he was the sole support of two women in his family. This worried him and he was heard to say, "They'll be pointin' their fingers at me because I haven't done my share in the war!" Brink's dependants did not profit for very long by his exemption, because he succumbed to the dreaded epidemic. It was a virulent type of influenza, sometimes afflicting whole families, turning their skin black and deluding their minds. Brink became violently delirious and the women could not hold him in bed. Members of his church and other organizations were asked to help, but no one responded to this appeal because people were frightened out of their wits by reports of the disease. Wearing as a hat a bag woven by Marie Little, and walking four miles through the freezing winter night, Hervey arrived to help his fellow villager; and he continued to go every night until Brink died.

Another of Rhoda Chase's stories reveals how Hervey lived. She remembers having a visit from a conventional cousin in a black satin dress, a string of pearls and high heels. Her husky cousins, Ned and Frank Chase, thought it would be fun to show the visitor the Maverick—thinking she would be so shocked she would never return to Woodstock. At that time Hervey had his printing press set up in his living quarters in a cottage that was scarcely more than a shack. On one side of the fireplace was his cot, on the other the press and counters of type. It was during the era when he was busiest, printing books as well as *The Plowshare*, and he composed his sentences directly in the type, running the pages immediately on the press. He didn't believe in reworking his writing, and in any case there wasn't enough type to set up a whole chapter at a time. The Chases, with their cousin, paid a visit to Hervey, passing what was obviously his washing bench, with a basin and a pail of water, under a tree. The patron saint of the Maverick greeted them cordially and invited them to stay for lunch. The meal consisted principally of tortillas cooked in a flat pan over the open fire. Hervey handed each person a blob of ground corn mixed with water, which they were to pat into very flat, round cakes; the thinner they were made, the crisper the cakes would be. But it required some skill to get them right, and Rhoda still laughs when she recalls the cousin trying to pat the tortillas, which flapped and tore in her bejeweled fingers. Tortillas were Hervey's standard food, along with the beans he kept in a pot in the ashes of the fireplace, and anybody was welcome to share them. The Chases' cousin was not frightened. Rather, like many conventional persons, she enjoyed dipping into bohemian life for an hour or so. She relished the encounter and expressed a wish to return.

The few painters living on the Maverick were good ones. Lucile and Arnold Blanch did over a house where Lucile still paints every summer. Arnold's story is told in another chapter. Harry Gottlieb had a studio there, as did Eugene Ludins before he moved to Zena. There were also Austin Mecklem and Wendell Jones. The writers were more transient, except for Henry Morton Robinson, who built a home near *The Maverick Horse* and there produced, besides many poems, the books *A Skeleton Key to Finnegan's Wake* (written with Joseph Campbell) and *The Cardinal*, a bestselling novel.

John Flannagan and Carl Walters were introduced to the Maverick by Arnold Blanch, who had known them as fellow students in Minneapolis. Walters arrived around 1922. He had originally made lithographs and also watercolors of circus animals with some success before he turned to pottery. He set up his kiln in Greenwich Village where, like Bernard Palissy, he had to burn his furniture before succeeding in his attempts to duplicate the Egyptian alkaline glazes. Hervey White built a studio for Walters, where he produced bowls and decorative animals that brought him fame. His pieces were not only beautiful but full of humor, the animals in particular. Probably his best-known work is *Hippopotamus*. His work was acquired by the Metropolitan Museum of Art and by permanent collections in Philadelphia and Minneapolis. He tried glass and made a pair of doors for the Whitney Museum in New York City—duplicates of which were bought by Eleanor Rixson for her house in Woodstock. Later, Walters moved to Ohayo Mountain where he set up his kiln, and he was living there at the time of his death.[54]

Hervey White became discouraged with the Maverick, which he feared was dying, and around 1933 decided to start another colony for creative workers in a milder climate. He bought a three-hundred-acre rice plantation on Point Peter at St. Marys, Georgia. For a while a musician and perhaps a writer or two joined him, but he was never able to attract an interesting group there such as the one he had built up at the Maverick. In the spring he would return to his old haunts, but, except for the Sunday concerts, they had all changed.[55]

A few years later Hervey handed over the Maverick Press to James Cooney. The first issue of *The Phoenix*, a quarterly magazine, appeared in the spring of 1938 with J. P. Cooney as editor. It is hard to evaluate this periodical, which sometimes published fine stories and poetry. Cooney and his associates were influenced by D. H. Lawrence, and the first story in the premier issue of *The Phoenix* contained Lawrence's "Pan in America," published with the permission of Freda Lawrence. They seemed to be fighting against machines, chemical fertilizers, the Fascists, the Communists and the Christians—and through the evidence of my own nose I can add that they were also opposed to baths; nonetheless they made a fetish of the human body.

Strange tales came from the Maverick during this era. For example, one man quite openly had two wives of equal status. Another man believed he could acquire a mate by bellowing like a bull in the night, and it was said he was successful! One of the last jobs to come off the Maverick Press was a booklet of mine called *As True as the Barnacle Tree*. It was through this work that I came to know some of the unwashed and unshorn young poets of that community. They liked to visit my herb garden and listen to herbal lore. One of these encounters proved embarrassing when, on a hot summer's day, a young man arrived in very short shorts and asked if he could do a bit of writing on the terrace overlooking the garden. It was swelteringly hot and when it came time to have lunch we took him a sandwich and a bottle of cold beer. Thereupon we forgot about him. Toward the middle of the afternoon very conventional friends of my mother arrived and, while showing them the house, I went to the north window, saying, "Here we have a view of Overlook." Then we all gasped, for behind the stone table upon which sat an empty glass and bottle there appeared a naked and very hairy man who was declaiming at the sun. I said rather lamely, "Oh, that's just a poet from the Maverick." The visitors went away convinced that all the wild rumors about Woodstock were true.

The sequel to the story is that a few days later the young man returned to show me what he had been writing on the terrace. It was called a sermon and had been read at a meeting held Sunday evening on the Maverick. It was quite moral although it showed the prevalent Lawrencian influence. What interested me was that this young man and his friends thought they were being ultra-modern and radical in holding pep-up meetings on Sundays with sermons presented. It showed the complete turn of the cycle from old-fashioned morality to innovative thinking, through abandonment of all standards that led to a surfeit of debauchery, and on back to precepts of common decency.

These young men were not made lily-white by their sermons, and the following winter when their provisions dwindled a couple of them broke into several of the closed houses on the Maverick, stealing and selling everything of value. They were arrested, but in one case a member of the family made restitution, and soon they were gathered up by the army where no doubt they were washed and shaved and taught to respect other people's property.

Image from the cover of Anita Smith's As True as the Barnacle Tree, *one of the last publications printed at Hervey White's Maverick Press.*
AMS Collection.

Adolph Heckeroth, a fine plumber and electrician, tells of warning Hervey about a certain individual. Hervey had given the man a cottage and allowed him to charge up to fifty dollars for food on his account at the grocery store. As soon as the man acquired a dollar he proceeded to get drunk. Hervey said to Heckeroth: "How do you know this man is no good? If I think a man has something of value in him and give him a house and food, I do so because I believe he may make good. If I do this a hundred times and only the ninety-ninth man works out well, I consider it has been worthwhile."

Hervey was growing old and tired. He made himself a primitive shelter in a locust thicket close to *The Maverick Horse*, and here he existed free of the care of a home. Whatever riches he valued were kept in his mind. On October 19, 1944, Raoul Hague found him on his couch where he had died peacefully during the night. Friends provided for his funeral, which was simple yet more beautiful than any other seen in Woodstock. It was autumn and the music hall was decorated with boughs of flaming maple and evergreens. The musicians came from far and near and played all his favorite chamber music. Professor Schütze read a few of Hervey's poems to a packed hall, because his friends had come from New York, Chicago and all over to pay tribute to the man who had brought so much art to Woodstock.

Rock City painters, circa 1912, across from Rosie Magee's. Ned Chase is third from left. Henry Lee McFee and Marion Bullard are second and third from right. Photo: AMS Collection.

Chapter 7

ROSIE MAGEE OF ROCK CITY

MOTHER TO A GENERATION OF ARTISTS

Rock City is part of Great Lot 26 in the Hardenbergh Patent. Unlike many other sections of Woodstock it never belonged to Robert Livingston. Although Livingston was among a number of men who purchased Great Lot 26 from Thomas Wenham, his share was along the eastern boundary. Rock City was in Cornelius Tiebout's tract of six hundred acres, which occupied both sides of the road from the center of the village and ran up the mountain to the Wide Clove (now known as Mead's). Tiebout sold to John Reed of Rhinebeck, who in 1788 conveyed his holdings to William Eltinge, a turner from Kingston. It was then that the settlement of this tract really began.[1]

One of the first surveys shows the road up the mountain as running from the village to the John Wigram home, at which point it turned west and north past the present Speicher house and then north up to Camelot. The survey for the more direct route past the Rock City crossroads was made a few years later, and it mentions the Matthew Dymond house on the way to the Wide Clove. In 1825 Matthew Dymond Jr. and his wife, Margaret, deeded their entire property to their son-in-law, John Sickler, in consideration of his taking care of them for the rest of their lives. He was to provide good and sufficient meat, drink, lodging, washing and clothing as befitting them, to treat them kindly and affectionately, and to pay all necessary funeral expenses at their death. Sickler later sold the property to Robert and Rebecca Carroll.

In 1843 the land was purchased from the Carrolls by George W. Snyder, an uncle of Mrs. Levi Harder, who at a later date lived diagonally across the road. Snyder had a license to run the tavern on the Village Green, but Mrs. Harder remembered hearing that her Uncle Bill Snyder ran a roadhouse from his home at the Rock City crossroads before he moved to the village. She recalled being told that the teamsters from the glass company at Bristol, as well as from the backcountry, stopped there for an early morning meal and again in the evening after returning from Glasco. This could have been because the last glass factory was in existence until 1855. These teams brought white New Jersey sand and chemicals that were shipped by sloop, and later by steamboat, up the Hudson River to Glasco. After depositing their loads in Bristol they carried the finished window glass to the river to be shipped to Albany, Poughkeepsie or New York. We can imagine the scene as the drivers "ye'd" and "haw'ed" at their oxen, which would still have been steaming from the hard pull up the hill or tired from their long haul from the river. It must have been agreeable for them to rest under the cool shade of the maples while their masters disappeared into the welcoming house. When Snyder moved to the village he sold this house to Petrus Stoll.[2]

Petrus was a great one for cussing, and the many stones that snagged his plow while he was tilling his cornfield produced some choice words. One day he swore so hard he called upon the devil himself, and the old demon promised to clear the field of stones if Petrus would deliver up his soul in a year's time. The angry farmer agreed and for a season had no trouble plowing. But the following spring when the devil returned to claim his due, Petrus, in a sassy mood, just threw the sole of his shoe at Satan. The devil was in no mind to be cheated, so the story goes—and he not only returned all the stones to the field, but added twice as many more.[3] As the present owner of this field, I can testify to the large number of stones that are there to this day. According to the stories, Petrus was not a squeamish man. He would gather potato bugs in his hands and when he had a fistful he would squeeze them to death. He had so little inclination to cook that in the autumn he would make a huge pile of pancakes to set down cellar in a crock covered with vinegar, and every morning throughout the winter he would grab a few, rinse them off and eat them for breakfast. It is not surprising to learn that he asked the Magees, Sanford and Rosie, to come stay with him and promised them the farm if they would look after him. He did not live many years after making this arrangement (during his last illness the absentminded Dr. Hall gave him a box of fishhooks instead of the pills he had prescribed).

When the artists spilled down to Rock City from Byrdcliffe there were two farmhouses at the crossroads with their numerous barns and outbuildings, and there were smoke houses, wagon sheds and a little tenant house whose large window had once displayed (of all things!) bonnets for sale.[4] Later the house was occupied by Mrs. Duboise, who wove rugs. Lucy Brown described her as "a tall rawboned figure, with [an] intelligent and powerful visage—it wasn't just a 'face'—of prodigious memory and trenchant tongue."[5] Mrs. Duboise's husband carried the mail and baggage from West Hurley with the help of Teddy, the long-suffering pinto. There was a little mill by the waterfall along the Wide Clove Kill where not many years before a turner named Luke Lewis made chairs with roses carved upon their backs.[6] Within a quarter of a mile there were about a dozen other dwellings. Harriet Lewis's house, toward the village, was later occupied by Captain Jenkinson and his family. Below that lived Ella Riseley, who took in roomers. I stayed there for a while and she was very kind to me. The day after my arrival I noticed a strange odor emanating from the kitchen and upon investigation found Mrs. Riseley busy at her regular fall chore of "rendin' down skunk fat" for the family's chest colds. One of the early boarders at the Riseleys' was Shaemus O'Sheel with his wife and baby, Patrick. One of O'Sheel's poems is called "It Happened Near Woodstock":

There's a patch of moss on a hillside,
With a sheltering tree above.
'Twas only these and a casual cloud
Saw how I loved my Love.

Or maybe that quaint cicada
Somewhere high on the tree,
Grew shrill with passion just then because
He saw how my Love loved me.[7]

Mrs. Riseley's husband was a descendant of Cornelius Riseley, who owned considerable property at Rock City, the upper part of which he sold to the Harder family. The old Riseley homestead is still standing across the road. For a number of years I lived in the stable belonging to the old house and I remember hearing that it had been the original slave quarters. The Ulster County census of 1800 lists one of the first Riselars (more commonly known as Riseley) in the town, named Andrew, as owning two slaves; shortly thereafter he registered in the town records the birth of a female Negro child named Pine.[8]

Cal Short had his farm at the corner where the upper and lower Rock City roads divided. This was where John Wigram, who married Marije Schermerhorn, built his house in 1806. Wigram was a surveyor and acted as agent for some of the large landowners, including the Livingstons. He was well educated and one of the important men of this area, according to Louise Zimm, who also said it was believed to have been his Negro, John, who planted the huge balm of Gilead tree that still leans over the road. The beams from the Wigram house were used in the forge across the way, which was torn down this year. The watering trough was removed several years ago and all that remains of the farm are the red barns.[9]

A quarter of a mile above the crossroads was the Hogans' little house subsequently bought by Ethel Canby; and beyond, on the rise, was the Reynolds's boardinghouse near which Andrew Dasburg, Allen Cochran and Eleanor Rixson built studios, although the last named kept adding to hers until it became a castle. However, these houses did not make a city and the principal rocks were the outcrop of bluestone, or "cobbler." The farmers had for generations stacked these into thick walls to encircle their pastures.

The first so-called barnacles were Zulma Steele and Edna Walker—who, in the early days of Byrdcliffe, came to live in the Reynolds's barn while their house was being built. Mrs. Magee had a spyglass to keep an eye on the doings in the neighborhood and could see up as far as the Reynolds's, where Zulma seemed to have a man as her companion. She walked up to have a closer look and found the man was Edna Walker working in pants. When

Rosie Magee of Rock City. Photo by Konrad Cramer. AMS Collection.

Mrs. Magee surveyed their quarters she exclaimed in amazement, "Why they're livin' like real folks even if it is a barn!" A few years later there were dozens of artists living in stables and barns.[10]

There were several quarries in the neighborhood, one of which was back of Ella Riseley's orchard; another was to the west, worked by Levi Mann. There was also, on the side of Overlook Mountain, the huge California Quarry, which produced thousands of tons of bluestone suitable for paving and curbing. Certain roads leading to the Hudson River that had been paved with hemlock now had to have stone tracks to carry the heavy loads of bluestone to the docks, where they were "dressed" and shipped to the cities. New York City was paved with Ulster County stone before the advent of cement. It is possible the name Rock City came from an accumulation of stone slabs stocked near the crossroads awaiting transport to the river. Every dwelling about Rock City had large flagstones leading from its door to the road.[11]

On the northeast side of the Rock City crossroads was the home of Rosie Magee, who mothered a whole generation of art students and writers. She was far from beautiful in the common sense of the word, with her scarred lip and homely face, and there was always the odor of sour milk about her, yet all the artists in Woodstock wished they could express the grace they felt within her. But how could they paint the sympathy that soothed the hurt of their failures or depict her tolerance of their bohemian goings-on? Who could show the healing current that flowed from her knobby fingers as she stroked the pullet with the broken leg? There were many who understood and loved her.

Mrs. Levi (Marietta) Harder, who lived on the southwest corner, kept her flagstones scrubbed and polished, and she did not approve of the untidy appearance of the Magee yard on the northeast side. Over there, drifts of leaves collected against the picket fence and duck and chicken droppings spattered the walks; these certainly added sustenance to the roses that grew luxuriantly about the place. The tidy Harder veranda held a few upright chairs that did not invite relaxation. Although sadly in need of paint, the Magee porch with its dilapidated seats was thoroughly enjoyed—especially by Sanford Magee. He did not often rouse himself between cussing his cows to pasture in the morning and driving them home at night, except at plowing time when he proudly worked his fine team of horses. As soon as the midday meal was over he would comfortably settle himself on a rocker and stroke his long white beard, of which he was very proud. Looking across the road, Marietta would sniff at him, saying, "There's Rosie's parlor ornament a-settin' on the porch!" But Rosie appreciated her husband's gentle ways and was quite content to let him "set" while she milked the cows and fed the horses, the pigs and the fowls. She also planted and weeded the vegetable garden, washed and mended the clothes, made the rugs, filled the cellar with preserves and pickles, and cooked, baked and cleaned for boarders, with only occasional help from a halfwit who lived down the road. She knew how hard it was for Sanford to bestir himself. Trying to start him off to Saugerties one day, she was heard to exclaim, "He's harder to get going than a British sloop."[12]

Sand was one of those men who ponder, and he was troubled when the First World War began, fearing the Germans might reach Rock City and disturb him. Captain Jenkinson, a neighbor, tried to reassure him by saying the outcome of the war would probably be decided on the ocean. Replied Sand, "That's what I'm a-feared of, that we'll have to fight where there ain't no footin'." When Magee died it was hardly noted on the corner, but Rosie kept his horses in the barn, feeding them for years, because Sand had been so proud of them.

Not many of the farmers were sentimental toward animals that they had to work or kill for food. Yet Mrs. Magee made pets of every creature on her farm. Even when cash was scarce she bought box after box of shredded wheat for the chickens when she realized what a treat it was for them. Occasionally there was conflict. Once, for instance, she put her hand in the barrel where a hen laid its eggs and felt the nose of a skunk. It made no objections to Rosie's pats, but when she placed a cover on the barrel it let loose a blast—before being shot. On another occasion she surprised a fox trotting off with one of her hens thrown over its shoulder. She whisked her apron at the fox, whereupon it dropped the hen, followed her into the kitchen and placed its head on her lap. It created a moral issue that was ended by a neighbor who came and dispatched the fox, but forever after Rosie spoke regretfully of allowing the killing of an animal that had trusted her.

It seems that Rosie Magee was never still except in the hundreds of sketches made of the Rock City corner. For in the days of Impressionist art in Woodstock the first enchanting sight of the crossroads always led the students to try painting a canvas. When one approached from Woodstock village, the composition seemed perfect. Through the branches of the old apple trees was the white house surrounded by a picket fence with splashes of red from a flowering shrub or the apples to match the color of the chimney. There was the hard-to-catch faded blue of Rosie's sunbonnet or the several layers of skirts, or the apron that usually held a few handfuls of grain to cast to the fowls that followed her about. Close to the house were weathered barns and sheds that shone warm gray against the blue of Overlook Mountain. The place was depicted in every season, in spring when the first cool greens crept over the valley under silver skies, and full summer when the sun parched the grass and the mountain seemed to smoke in a heat wave. The students tried again in the autumn when the hard maples flamed red and yellow against a cobalt blue sky that was usually painted as if scraps of denim had been stitched among the branches of the trees. These were sentimental times when painters tried to catch elusive beauty.[13] Birge Harrison encouraged his students to paint with a fluid technique that lent itself to landscapes swooning in moonlight. Every other person passing on the crossroads carried a sketch box over his shoulder.

John Carlson, who lived for years in the barn directly across from the Magee house, in reminiscing about the early days describes what he called the "high-brow group" who foregathered at the Rock City crossroads. "There, of an evening, you might see Andrew Dasburg, Charles B. Cook, Eugene Speicher . . . Henry L. McFee . . . Frank S. Chase, George H. Macrum, Edward Thatcher, Margaret Goddard, Marion Bullard [or] Evelyn Jacus . . . all seated on the famous stone wall or around the community pump, busily talking shop, singing, and playing the harmonica."[14] The group thus described had emerged from the barns and sheds that clustered about the corner. Levi Harder, who owned most of the barns, didn't think much of painting. He told Carlson he had "never noticed that the sky was blue until you fellows came."[15] However, he had been quick to realize it paid more to keep artists than hay or pigs in his buildings. Four or five dollars per month provided a studio for at least two students, who would cut out windows in the upper half of the walls for their painting light. The villagers used to say the only way to tell a studio from a chicken coop was if there was a window on the north side, which of course no respectable chicken would have tolerated.

For winter heat Harder would provide a chimney, but to reduce the cost he built only half the chimney—the upper half, which was hung on a bracket a few feet below the roof.[16] Here the painters set up long pipes for the iron stoves purchased from the mail-order catalogs they had studied in the privies. Wood was cheap and if the wind didn't blow too hard they could keep defrosted by hanging over the stoves. John Carlson swore that when the belly of his stove was red hot he could pick icicles off its bottom. For those who complained of too many drafts Levi would send his wife over to plug the largest holes with his old red flannels. The north lights were made by overlapping window glass set like shingles so as not to cast lines across the pictures. It was a refinement that did not improve the quality of the work as much as it permitted more snow to sift into the barns. On mornings after an old-fashioned snowstorm there was always snow to be shoveled inside as well as outside. Frank Chase argued that it was best to sweep it into a pile just inside the door where it could provide some insulation, but that required one to leap over or go through it to get in or out.

When I moved to a barn at Rock City most of the people Carlson mentioned were in the neighborhood, but there had been some changes. John

Frank Chase pumping water at Rock City. Photo: AMS Collection.

Carlson had built himself a house up the road where he took Margaret Goddard as a bride. Frank Chase had married Evelyn Jacus and they were living in the tenant house recently vacated by twenty-four cats and an eccentric writer named Howe. Evelyn proved to be such a particular housekeeper that Frank, who had become used to barn ways, now had to rinse his hands after he had washed them clean. For years they lived there happily, and husky Frank was always the person called when there was trouble and a real man was needed. This house is now owned by Henry Mattson. Frank's aunt and her daughter Rhoda, who illustrated children's books, built a house in the Harders' orchard.

The stable known as the Hanson studio where I lived was typical. The only warm spot was on the half of the hayloft not cut away for the north light, and here among the cobwebs and the wasps was a place for a cot. Rather than disturb the wasps I left the cobwebs hanging. For several years we had a truce and I was very much surprised when eventually one of their descendants bit me on the tip of my nose while I slept. The walls were of rough boards; the uprights had been nibbled by the horses' teeth, which gave them an interesting texture. The furniture was limited to a few chairs, a table and a cot nicknamed "Gibraltar." The kitchen consisted of a dishpan and a few cooking utensils on a deal table. When the nearby stream was not frozen I made use of a natural dishwasher by placing the greasy pans filled with sand to be cleaned by the action of the running brook. There was a kerosene cook stove that went wrong occasionally, covering everything with oily soot. The refrigeration was a crock with a boulder on top sunk in the nearby stream, and the plumbing was of a chemical type in an adjoining shed. I had the bright idea of having a hole cut through the wall to reach it in winter, but for some mysterious structural reason the hole could be only two feet high. This made it necessary for one to use a most undignified crawling technique in making the passage. The so-called plumbing situation could be rugged.

A few years later when I was living in the Mill house at Rock City I was abashed to be confronted one morning by a privy whose door was frozen shut. I ran over to the Chases', whose accommodation faced the turnpike, only to find its door was frozen open, which was as bad as the other circumstance. Now, almost flying, I tore across the road to Mrs. Magee, who provided me with suitable facilities as well as sympathy.

The heart of all the studios lay in their stoves. Mine was an iron stove that could take two-foot logs, and in very cold weather it was necessary to set an alarm for the middle of the night to feed it. But none of these inconveniences could quell our enthusiasm for this bohemian life. After hard days of painting we would pull on our felts and boots, such as the farmers wore, and struggle through the snowdrifts to see what was taking place in the other barns. The subject of "what is art?" was always good for a discussion until midnight when, warmed by our eloquence, we would face the bleak way home to a cold studio.

For weeks at a time the snow lay pure and unbroken. Only those who have experienced the cruelty of winter can fully appreciate the spring. Then one notices that the tracks along the road have become dirty, the circles of earth showing around the tree trunks have widened, and suddenly the hard maples are festooned with syrup kettles. The barn doors would be thrown open and voices would shout joyfully back and forth on the Rock City corner. Marion Bullard could be seen at the door of her stable on the main road, her black hair confined by a red scarf, her almond eyes sparkling even when they were half closed with laughter—which was frequently, as she was full of good humor. She was Rock City's gay widow, appreciating admiration but seeming never to succumb to her many suitors. Marion was not only handsome but a good painter, exhibiting her landscapes widely. Later several of her children's books were published with considerable success; she also became a journalist and had a popular radio program. For her, Levi Harder had a house moved from one of the villages about to be inundated by the Ashokan Reservoir. It was placed under a pear tree in a field above the corner and is pictured in several of her books.

Dinner at Mrs. Magee's was always lively, with plenty of repartee besides the hearty appetites that made one speculate whether the twenty-five cents, or even the thirty-five cents we subsequently paid, half covered the outlay. There was always chicken or stewed meat with heaps of potatoes and gravy, onions, turnips, pickles and jellies, followed by pies and puddings. Because Mrs. Magee couldn't discipline her pets we often had to brush a setting hen off our plates or chairs, and we always sliced the butter thin so as not to miss a feather.

On one occasion a Boston friend of Marion's made a short appearance. At first Mrs. Magee refused to allow him to come to her house, saying he was "too much of a gentleman" for her table, but she was persuaded by Marion, who "had a way with her." At the Bostonian's first dinner a delicious blueberry pie was served. To his dismay his teeth chomped down upon something hard and resistant among the berries. He proved to be a real gentleman as he quietly removed a shoe button from his mouth and slipped it into his pocket, to the delight of Frank Chase, who sat beside him.

When Mrs. Magee had brought in the last heaping platter of food, she would linger a while to join in the fun or to add a bit of her wise philosophy. Among the farm people she was one of the few who appreciated the humor of the artists, and she was always ready to defend them. She rejoiced over their successes and lamented over their failures, ever tolerant of their behavior even when the other village folks were scandalized. When they were unable to pay for their meals she allowed them credit or accepted their paintings, which hung on her walls, although it is doubtful that she liked them. The boarders were a mixed lot; for instance, there was a bespectacled German who had built himself a box-like house of about ten feet square into which we were not invited. He rarely spoke but hung around the Magees' where occasionally he might be seen chopping kindling or fetching a pail of water from the pump. It was only after his solitary death that we learned he had been an engraver who was always suspect because he had worked at the mint. Then there was the chorus girl who had been stranded unaccountably in Woodstock. As she had no money she of course drifted to Mrs. Magee's, where she remained for months. Suddenly she went away as mysteriously as she had come. But the chorus girl never forgot Rosie's hospitality, and wherever she went she remembered to lift a teaspoon from the dining room to send back to her benefactor. We were always fascinated by these souvenirs from third-rate hotels all over the Midwest, which stood in a glass receptacle in the center of the table.

Sometimes Anne Moore, the poet, would come from her nearby cottage. She was a great friend of Mrs. Magee's. Although she hesitated to paint a word portrait of the old woman, fortunately she wrote this (taken from "The Hen Came Clucking In"):

> The hen came clucking in one day
> and found the chair.
>
> "I declare to goodness," said Rosie Magee,
> "if she ain't got Sweetie's place.

I suppose I ought to drive her out.
But it seems to fit her somehow.
And Sweetie ain't wanting it just now."

The hen stopped clucking long enough
to lay an egg.

"Well, it's nice anyway," said Rosie Magee,
"to have her bring it here to me."[17]

With her strong Carolina accent Anne Moore would amuse us with her stories of the Catskill mountaineers. She had a wonderful sense of humor but was never unkind. She had a doctorate and several other degrees of higher learning, but it only made her laugh when, during the period she was working for women's suffrage, trying to persuade a digger of ditches to support the Nineteenth Amendment, the man looked up from his pickax to say, "What's the use of that? Women ain't edicated enough to vote." Another poetess in the neighborhood was Grace Fallows Norton, who wrote delightfully of faraway things. She married George Macrum, one of the best-known painters of our group, and upon the mountain they built a home that later burned during a communal Thanksgiving.

The summer after they returned from Europe the Eugene Speichers came to board with the Magees, with Gene sharing John Carlson's barn for painting. They remember that Mrs. Magee allowed her kittens to sleep in the warm bread pans. They also recall that the halfwit who worked for Mrs. Magee went home for a few days and was brought back by her irate mother. "Now you set down, Rosie," said the mother, "for I want to tell you something. My girl was all right when she come here, but she ain't all right now. How about it, Dorie, haven't you got somethin' to say?" The girl answered sullenly, "I was all right when I come here, and I'm all right now, I *think*!"

There was the evening when the boarders heard a dish crash in Mrs. Magee's kitchen, whereupon the door was hastily closed. Just then Konrad Cramer came with a pail to fetch his milk and when he emerged from the kitchen those waiting for their supper asked him for news. "It's the peas," he said, "and she is sweeping them up from all over the floor." Thus forewarned, the diners passed up the peas when the dish went the rounds of the table.[18]

The congeniality among the painters suffered when Konrad and Florence Cramer appeared from Munich, talking of abstract art. Florence had been a member of the old Art Students League group who had boarded at the Cooper house. She went to Europe and met a handsome German officer who was interested in art. When they were married they came to Woodstock and built a studio off the Glasco Turnpike not far from Rock City. In 1910 Andrew Dasburg returned from Europe under the influence of the French Moderns and the rift widened. In 1913 several members of the Rock City group, including Dasburg and Henry McFee, went to New York City to see the famous show at the Armory, returning to talk of the *Nude Descending a Staircase* and to discuss Picasso, Braque, Cézanne and Matisse. Woodstock was never the same after that![19]

Andrew Dasburg, chief protagonist for so-called modern art, was by nature a revolutionist, hacking away at conservative painting and showing the way to fresh viewpoints, which had a wide influence upon the other young artists. He had great charm and a boyish look—wide-set eyes, mussed blond hair and a mobile mouth—but this appearance was contradicted by the intense focus of his conversation. Dasburg had been born in Paris in 1887 of Rhineland parentage and was brought to America when he was five years old. He studied at the Art Students League in New York, where he won a scholarship to come to Woodstock and work under Birge Harrison. Much as he liked Harrison personally, Dasburg was not happy painting in the subdued tones recommended by the older man. Eventually he tried expressing the brightness of the sunshine around him. A fellow student, Jim Wardwell, seeing one of these canvases, suggested they form a "sunflower club" in revolt against the moonlight formula. From then on Dasburg found the Woodstock landscape an open door. His rebellion was promoted by Robert Henri, under whom he worked for a period in New York. For the first time he was stimulated, because Henri, as Dasburg said, "not only [had] ideas, but...would live with you through the process of drawing, talking and criticism."

From that time forward Dasburg worked independently and his paintings showed his desire to experiment. One of these had the intriguing title *Absence of Mabel Dodge* and created a sensation. He built a studio below Reynolds's boardinghouse, where he lived with his first wife, the sculptress Grace Johnson. However, Johnson became so engrossed in her sculptures of wild animals that she left him to follow a circus around the country. In time Dasburg went to New Mexico and found there a landscape he

Still Life, *by Henry Lee McFee (1886–1953). Oil on canvas, 20 x 16 in.* AMS Collection. Photo by John Lenz.

preferred, eventually making it his home. In answer to a letter of mine he wrote recently from Taos:

> Mother Magee, as we came to think of her, is still very much alive in my memory. She was even-tempered, hard-working with a twinkle in her eye and always greeted "her boys" with a smile and a joking remark. "Come, Dasburg," she would say, "set down and eat your vittels." Such breakfasts! All the eggs and bacon you could eat and sourbatter buckwheat cakes with maple syrup.

For a while he lived in her house and she would exclaim,

> "My soul's sake alive, you're like a swingin' door, in and out of the house all day!" When I think of her during those early days it is always with strong affection. John Carlson, George Macrum, McFee and I ate our meals regularly at Mrs. Magee's.[20]

Henry Lee McFee, the less flamboyant of the two friends, may have gone deeper below the surface aspect of his subjects. He talked of psychology in art and was an admirer of Clive Bell. His sensitive fingers seemed to envelop the apples and vases in his paintings as he would try to describe their two-sidedness and linear relationship. He had a keen and sensitive mind and it was ironic that he should have been at the apex of a scandal that shook Rock City. The outline of the story is that before McFee came to Woodstock he had been engaged to a middle-class girl, who followed him here. He arranged to have her put up at the home of his friend Isabel Moore—who, as chaperone, became sympathetic toward the girl and subsequently helped her. Meanwhile McFee had become interested in a married woman, whom he later wed. One Christmas Eve the painters were celebrating with a few drinks in one of the studios and were talking of adventures that had befallen them. In response to a question, McFee said, "Oh, nothing exciting ever happens to me." At this instant there was a knock on the door, which opened to reveal a sheriff's deputy serving him with papers. That bombshell was a breach-of-promise suit, which was eventually won by the ex-fiancée. It was years before the McFees were clear of the debt this created, and while Mac painted like a demon his wife, Aileen, baked delicious bread that a few lucky neighbors were permitted to buy. Their house in Hickory Hollow was a rendezvous for the artists; the woods around their home would resound with the laughter of the Speichers, Wilna Hervey and Nan Mason, the Lindins, the Fienes and many others, prompted by Aileen's wit.

When Marion Bullard's brother, James Rorty, returned from the war he lived in one of the Rock City barns. It was his first attempt at housekeeping and he enjoyed the experience, which was a salutary release from long hours spent writing radical poetry. When he became confident about cooking he invited me for supper. Jim was trying out his sister's recipe for muffins—but in the excitement of entertaining for the first time forgot to add the baking powder to the batter. He was too flustered, dashing back and forth from the oil stove in the kitchen to the dining room table, to get around to tasting the muffins himself. But he smiled with pride at their fragrance and handsome brown crusts as he placed them before me, and I did not have the heart to reveal that they were inedible. Instead, as soon as he left the room, I dropped one into the front of my dress. Returning, he offered me another and each time when he sped into the kitchen I would drop another muffin into my bosom. This became a trifle awkward—particularly in those days of flat figures. Jim was too busy to notice and he himself ate only one unadorned chop. Then he dumped the dishes into a pan and prepared to read his latest poems.

In spite of his large size, Jim's thick black hair and wide cheekbones made him look a little oriental as he shouted and shook his fists, voicing impassioned lines that called upon the universe to witness his testament of revolt. It was a vividly engrossing evening and it was late before I started back to the Mill where I was living. Jim held his Rayo lamp aloft to light the bridge I had to cross, but as he waved it above his head the light only served to blind me when I turned away. He called, "Are you alright now?" "Yes, goodnight," I replied, trying to sound normal as I felt myself stepping off the bridge and striking the icy water far below. The noise of the running water prevented his hearing the splash, and as I climbed ignominiously up the far bank I had the satisfaction of knowing that I had not

James Rorty, poet (and brother of Marion Bullard), circa 1913. Photo: AMS Collection.

Teddy, the recalcitrant pinto, being sugared by Maud Robinson.
Photo: AMS Collection.

spoiled the exultant mood of the evening. Nor had the muffins caused me to sink as they might well have done! Nobody would have known about this misadventure had I been able to resist telling the funny story on myself.

In 1920 I moved to the upper end of town, although a few years later I returned to Rock City. It was while living in Shady that I came to know "Grandma Shultis," another of the good souls of Woodstock. She had been born Ophelia Davis and had a brother with the heroic name of Hercules. Herc Davis was a farmer grown crotchety from trying to wrest a living from a few mountain acres. We became acquainted when he cussed me out for picking wild strawberries along the roadside where he planned to cut the grass, which was probably better than any in his fields. Although I tried to show my regrets he continued to make such a fuss that his wife came to the door to tell me not to "mind his goings-on." Sure enough, I found his language was no indication of his true nature and we soon became good friends. Herc was a tall, knuckly man with a bald head. He was toothless except for one long incisor that for years clung miraculously to his gum and made his smile irresistible. When he learned I had previously lived in Rock City, which was three miles away, he asked if I knew Rosie Magee. He said that he and Rosie had "sparked" when they were young but that he had not seen her for forty years. As this was said regretfully it seemed the situation might be remedied.

That was how the little tea party at the "Shanty" (where I was then perched) came about, when Herc and Rosie met again and for the last time. It required considerable planning. Herc's wife would have nothing to do with it, believing it was all nonsense or worse, but his sister, Grandma Shultis, accepted my invitation. At Rock City Carla Atkinson had difficulty persuading Mrs. Magee to trust herself to Carla's model T Ford. It was to be Rosie's first ride in an automobile and in her mind a most hazardous undertaking; however, she finally consented. Dressed in flowered muslin buttoned decorously to her throat, she sat with a gentle smile on her face, trading questions back and forth with her old friend Ophelia. But when Herc strode in, the tempo quickened, and if they didn't "spark," Rosie and her old beau were at least as coy as teenagers!

That was the year Mrs. Magee had an eightieth birthday and her "boys and girls" gave her a surprise party in Carla Atkinson's barn across the road. They came from far and wide, each with reason to bless the old woman and eager to honor her. There were a few good singers in the group, like John Carlson and Charlie Speicher, but the whole crowd burst lustily into "Sweet Rosie O'Grady" as the little old woman was led into the studio. She was placed in an armchair, where she sat weeping with joy as each person in turn squeezed her worked-out hands, expressing their affection and gratitude. When refreshments had been served the singing began again and there was not a song with the name Rose in it that they neglected to sing. As I recall she did not say a word all evening, but just sat there with the tears flowing down her cheeks.

One winter afternoon I went to see Mrs. Magee, who was beginning to fail from the long illness that would end with her death. She questioned me about my neighbors in the upper end of the town. She especially wished to know how the poorer families were coming through the winter. "Now tell me about Teddy?" she inquired, and I related the pony's latest escapade. There was always a fresh story about that western pinto who began his Woodstock career hauling the post from the railroad and subsequently belonged to the Shotwell family and several others. He was a contrary little beast whom one either hated or loved, and of course Rosie and I belonged to the latter group. If he did not like you he would not hesitate to bite and kick or buck you off his back, and there were many stout men who were afraid to enter his stall. He was one of the few male creatures of the time that did not at least temporarily succumb to Marion Bullard's charms. He disliked her so much that it took a half hour to hitch him to a tree near her house, and he always broke a rope or his bridle and escaped. Fortunately we had mutual respect for each other. I described the comfortable box stall in the Shultis barn where Teddy was wintering and continued, "I often take him an apple or a chocolate peppermint, for it's true what Grandma says, 'He's the greatest hand for peppermints even though he don't like watermelon.' And she says the lambs have been breaking out of their pen to get in with Teddy, trying to suckle him; but 'he's so good he don't mind them at all'." "Well, I do declare to goodness!" said Mrs. Magee, so intent upon my story she dropped the pile of rags she was stitching for rugs.

Clara Chichester was a pianist who came in the 1920s to live at Rock City. On one of Mrs. Magee's last birthdays Clara asked her what she wanted. "Oh, don't get me nothin'," the old woman said. "But I am going to get you a gift and it might as well be something you want," the musician insisted. In a shy way Rosie admitted, "Well, you know, I've always wished I had a pair of pink satin slippers, and I'd like to be buried in them." Therefore it was Clara who in Rosie's final days gave her what she most wanted.

On her last visit to Mrs. Magee, Rhoda Chase heard her say wistfully, "What I been thinkin' about is whether when I die I'll be allowed to see the people I care most about. But then when I come to figure it out perhaps it won't matter for I guess up there we'll be lovin' everybody. So's it won't make much difference whether we're near them we loved down here or not."[21]

Not long before she died Rosie asked to see Miss Wardwell. When Alice Wardwell entered the room where the old woman lay she was appalled to find the two nearest of kin waiting expectantly on either side of Rosie's bed keeping a watchful eye on each other and on anybody else they thought might interfere with their inheritance. Mrs. Magee requested that Alice go upstairs and find a cigar box in which she had hidden her money. When the box was opened in front of them, all it was found to contain was several hundred dollars. "Take it to Victor Lasher," she said, "and tell him to use it for a nice funeral." Rosie Magee knew well who she could depend upon, and in that year of 1927 she had a fine funeral and was buried in the pink satin slippers.[22]

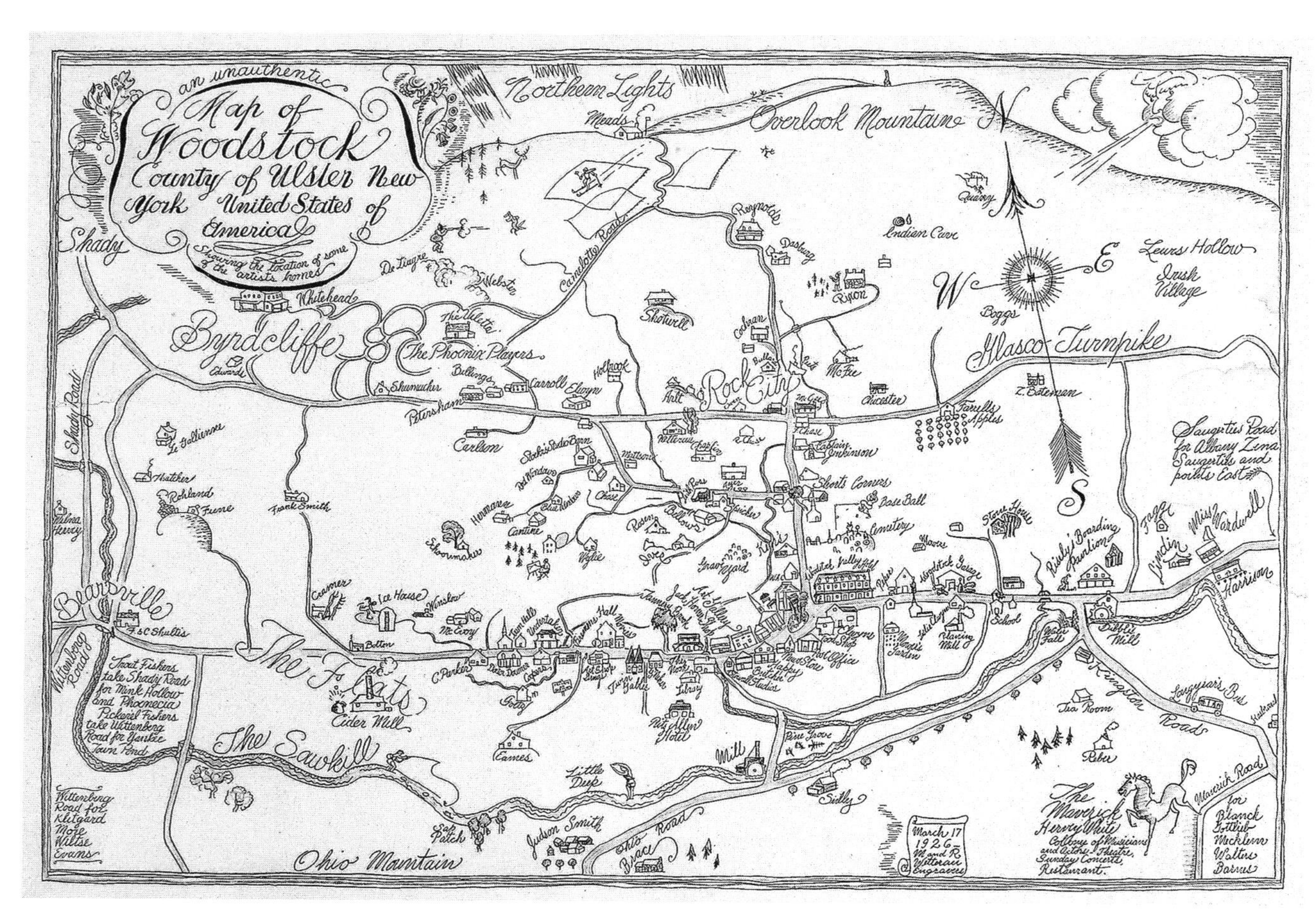

Map of Woodstock, *1926, by Rudolph and Margaret Wetterau. Engraving with hand coloring.* Courtesy of Woodstock Artists Association Permanent Collection.

Chapter 8

THE CREATIVE ENERGY OF ROCK CITY

HOME OF GEORGE BELLOWS AND OTHER LEADING ARTISTS

News items from the *Hue and Cry* in 1923:

> The Rosens and Bellows called
> on the Speichers Monday.
>
> The Rosens and the Speichers called
> on the Bellows Tuesday.
>
> The Speichers and the Bellows called
> on the Rosens Wednesday.[1]

Eugene Speicher was born in Buffalo, New York, in 1883. While a teenager he worked as a tally boy at a local lumber mill and had a newspaper delivery route. He studied art at the Albright School, from which he received a scholarship to the Art Students League in New York City. While there he worked under Frank DuMond and William Merritt Chase, but his strongest artistic impulse came when he studied under Robert Henri, with George Bellows and Rockwell Kent as fellow students. At the League he won another scholarship, which entitled him to come in 1908 to the Art Students League Summer School in Woodstock, under the direction of Birge Harrison. Evidently the award did not provide a good living, because Speicher's studio that season was in the sap patch at the foot of Ohayo Mountain. There, he maintained, he had the best north light for painting in his entire career, but there *were* some disadvantages. For example, one night he found a skunk had sprayed him with its puissant defense mechanism, which cost him his bedding. For a small sum he was allowed to park his gear on the porch of a nearby farmhouse, where he was permitted to sleep as well if it rained but otherwise he spent his nights under the stars.

In 1910 Eugene Speicher and Elsie Wilson were married and they went to Europe, where he had an opportunity to study the old masters at the art galleries. His work never became Europeanized, although his painting was enriched by his admiration for Renoir's technique. When they returned from Europe the Speichers came to Woodstock and spent one season at the Magees'. Although they maintained a studio in New York City they came to Woodstock every summer. Cal Short, in a wildly speculative venture, converted three of his buildings on the lower Rock City road into studios and the Speichers settled into one of these. Speicher received many prizes and awards from all over the United States but always remained modest in regard to his painting. Two of his best-known pictures are *Portrait of Katharine Cornell* and *Red Moore, Hunter*, and his *Dahlias* and *Head of a French Girl* have been particularly praised. He received the Beck Gold Medal for Portraiture, the Temple Gold Medal at the Philadelphia Academy, the Potter Palmer Gold Medal at the Art Institute of Chicago, first Hallgarten Prize at the National Academy in New York, first prize at the Corcoran in Washington and innumerable other honors.[2]

Once success made it possible, Eugene Speicher took over the red barn next to his house to use as a studio. He had the interior whitewashed so that his bright paintings seemed to sing in contrast to the walls. This was a radical departure from the older studios, which were still under the somber influence of cool light and deep shadows. Later Speicher built a studio for himself with special lighting and every convenience. The little frame building where they had lived for a number of years was completely renovated into an attractive stone and wood cottage with a well-kept garden. His art had matured to the point where he was considered the best portrait painter in the country. His still lifes of flowers and his landscapes had a richness of color and painting technique that were outstanding.

Speicher was a fine-looking man and he and his handsome wife attracted admiration wherever they went. There was a special aura around them because they were so deeply in love. Theirs was probably the happiest marriage in the artists' colony. We often speculated as to whether Gene would have gotten as far as he did without Elsie. She had a good business sense, and she protected him from interruption—doing it in such a tactful way the intruder did not realize he was being brushed off. She had a talent for creating a charming home and above all she was a superb cook. She had a maid to clean and wash but she always did the cooking, and the dishes she prepared in her white kitchen with its red polka dots were marvelous. She had attended cordon bleu lectures and could cook a French dinner with sauces and wines that would never be forgotten. She didn't mind spending two days or more in perfecting a special dish. By the time the guests arrived at the kitchen door—which, probably due to off-road parking, seemed to be the usual approach to Woodstock houses—the hostess would be ready with a decorative apron over her gown and the kitchen looking so bare and immaculate that the guests wondered if they had come on the wrong night.

Drinks would be served in a room that was not only comfortable but filled with choice mid-Victorian antiques. Yet it was not in the least museum-like, with its flowering plants, ruffled curtains and bright chintzes. There were so many beautiful pieces that it would be impossible to see them all even if one were not entertained by the animation of the well-chosen guests. Every once in a while Elsie would run in from the kitchen to add one of her amusing stories to the conversation, and as she came in the most delicious odors would follow her. Soon the guests would be seated at a candlelit table at the far end of the room to enjoy a feast for a connoisseur; it might start with a *soupe à la Bonne Femme* or fish with a white wine sauce. It was often said that Gene might be a great painter but Elsie cooked masterpieces. She had the habit of seating herself at a separate small table where she could dash back and forth without disturbing the guests, and there she ate sparingly, if at all. Speicher would assume the responsibility of entertaining, his dark hair glossy above his fine profile and his eyes alert to everyone's needs. His rich voice was ready to boom into laughter, for talk at the Speichers' parties was always gay. And Elsie would proffer a choice of French, Italian or American coffee while Gene would hand around brandy and cigarettes. Then the best conversation would begin.

Robert Henri, whose teachings had a profound influence on several of our painters, spent one summer in Woodstock. Henri was an innovator to whom his generation owed a great debt. With John Sloan, he freed our artists forever from European dependence, allowing them to paint the American scene with a fresh technique.

Rockwell Kent was also at Rock City for a short time, and yet another friend of the Rock City group was the painter Leon Kroll, though he lived farther away. George Bellows, after renting the Shotwell house for two seasons, decided to build a home in Woodstock.[3] He, Speicher and Charlie Rosen were close friends and lived within shouting distance of each other at Rock City. I received permission from the Metropolitan Museum to quote from their catalog for the George Bellows Memorial Exhibition, and I also secured the consent of Mrs. Bellows to use excerpts from the fine book *George Bellows, His Lithographs*, published by Knopf. But then I came to the conclusion that, as these books would always be available to the public, it might be more interesting to present the reader with recollections by the neighbors of this great artist.

My introduction to Bellows's work was a landscape exhibited at the Pennsylvania Academy, probably before 1910. It created a sensation with its bold pattern and harsh colors, or that is the impression it made among the slickly painted canvases that surrounded it. A few years later while studying at the Art Students League I saw and admired a number of Bellows's canvases, and therefore was eager to join a half dozen or more art students who were trying to persuade him to give them criticism. He consented to come in once a week, providing we would locate near his New York studio. It was not easy to find a room with a north light for rent in the neighborhood of Nineteenth Street, but eventually a box-like place was found a couple of flights of stairs above a greengrocer on Third Avenue. Unfortunately the room

PORTFOLIO II

ANITA M. SMITH'S PAINTINGS OF WOODSTOCK, 1920–28

Red Barns in Shady, *n.d., Shady, New York.*

Hay Gatherers, *n.d.*

Shady Hill *or* Snake Road, *n.d., Shady, New York.*

Shady Valley, *n.d., Shady, New York.*

Summer Sky, *n.d.*

Bearsville, *n.d., Bearsville, New York.*

Woodstock Winter, *n.d.*

Shady Barns, *1922, Shady, New York.*

Zero Weather, *1923.*

The Woodpile, *1923*.

Winter Sketch, *n.d.*

would not accommodate all the aspirants, and as I was the last to apply I was dropped. To assuage my disappointment they allowed me to pose for them, which I did and was rewarded by hearing a criticism.

Bellows was a tall man with a slender, athletic figure, an oval head and the clearest eyes I had ever seen. He talked of painting as an expression of one's life. Discovered among his papers after his death is the following, which is approximately what he told us during the criticism:

> The student of art is continually at work both on art and on life. He gathers from the first what other fine minds have found, from the second he searches for new experience[s] . . . The great school is where the great man teaches and where he finds students with heart enough and head enough to meet the ordeal. This truth implies the necessity on the part of every student, however young, of becoming . . . his own editor and judge of who and what is for him worth while . . . Of what importance is art to society? All civilization and culture are the results of the creative imagination or artist quality in man. The artist is the man who makes life more interesting or beautiful, more understandable or mysterious, or probably, in the best sense, more wonderful. His trade is to deal in illimitable experience. It is therefore only of importance that the artist discover whether he be an artist, and it is for society to discover what return it can make to its artists.[4]

He told us about many facets of his own career. To supplement his income he had been a semi-professional baseball player for a time and had also developed several tools for artists. One of his inventions was an implement for squeezing the last bit of paint out of a tube. (Later Eugene Speicher told me he proved to his friend that he could do a better job using the old method of rolling the handle of the palette knife along the tube.) Another of Bellows's innovations was a hinged cover for oil cups, which is still commonly used with sketching outfits. In this period he was using the Maratta color system, which he persuaded the students to follow. He explained that in music, for instance, one did not have to look around the house for the right note and to achieve it perhaps be obliged to use a dishpan (some present-day musicians might argue this point!), because the tones for music are definitely related and spaced on one keyboard, which simplifies the musician's playing. To ensure that the Maratta colors were of equal strength, and to use them correctly, one had to mix them with an equal quantity of white, black or any of the other full colors in order to make halftones. These in turn could be subdivided into quartertones and so on, but there always had to be a definite proportion and the mixtures were not to be scrambled. Faced with a subject, one had to decide on the dominant colors, the secondary colors and so forth, and set up a palette with balanced degrees of color strength. All of this meant that the students had to analyze and choose their color scheme before they could get started. This was probably good for them, but at least an hour was needed to set up the palette and a large proportion of the paint was apt to be left over.

On this occasion Bellows became impatient, searching for words to critique one student's painting, and he started to work it out on the canvas. He had discovered that the proportions of the head were wrong and he suggested that one eye was misplaced. He made several adjustments and repainted the eye. Preparing to daub the highlight on the eye—the keynote of the portrait—he could not find the right color on the Maratta set-up palette. "Oh, hell!" he exclaimed, and, squeezing some fresh color from a tube, mixed it to suit himself. He flicked it on the eye, whereupon the whole portrait came to life. Bellows was too big for any petty rules and he soon abandoned the Maratta system. He was also interested in the Jay Hambidge theory of dynamic symmetry but never allowed it to cramp him into the confines of an arbitrary set of rules. Nor did he close his mind to innovations, and he was ready to try any scheme he considered reasonable.[5]

Frank Crowninshield, in his introduction to the catalog for the Metropolitan Museum of Art's George Bellows Memorial Exhibition, speaks of the muted palette of Bellows's early period. As an example of later canvases, which were more colorful, he refers to the "singing quality" of *The Picnic*.[6] This was painted at Cooper's Lake in 1924, the year before Bellows's death. Cooper's Lake has undoubtedly reflected more historical scenes than anywhere else in Woodstock. It was the site of many of the down-rent episodes, and the first Town Meeting was held nearby at the home of Captain Elias Hasbrouck, who became our first supervisor. Bellows's painting shows his family and the Speichers enjoying themselves by the water. Of course it is not realistic, but it shows the character of the hills beyond the lake and the massive hulks of Sugarloaf, Indian Head, Twin and Olderbark mountains against the rain clouds. It is typical of the beauty that surrounds the lake where we have all picnicked in our day. On other canvases Bellows painted the Cooper barn as well as the Shultis barns under the hill in Shady. *The Picnic* shows one of the men fishing, but I doubt it was meant to be Bellows, who disliked that sport. Robert Henri was an enthusiastic fisherman and on one occasion Speicher persuaded Bellows to take Henri and himself on a fishing expedition to Yankeetown Pond. Bellows did not want to miss an afternoon's painting because he never worked before lunch, but as he possessed the only automobile among the group he reluctantly consented. The whole afternoon was spent in a small boat under a blazing sun without a nibble from the fish. It was Bellows's chore to return to Woodstock to collect their wives, who were bringing a picnic supper—and at least one wife will never forget his bad temper over that fishing expedition![7]

Every summer the threesome of Bellows, Speicher and Rosen would go off on sketching trips with their picnic lunches, returning to make more sketches on succeeding days. Several times I saw them park the Bellows's touring car at a likely place for painting and unpack their gear. Bellows had the best gear because he had made a narrow wheelbarrow, which he hitched to the running board. He would trundle this wheelbarrow, which held all the necessary equipment, up and down the fields until he settled on a spot to work. He needed only a moment to open his sketch box, set up the canvas against two posts conveniently arranged on the barrow, and was ready to paint.[8]

These sketches and the notes he wrote were but reminders, and when he painted his pictures he retained only what would serve the emotional and pictorial design of the canvas. Although the results might look spontaneous, Mrs. Bellows told me there were occasions when he struggled with endless patience to achieve the finished work.

Mrs. Bellows was very gracious when I bothered her with many questions regarding her famous husband. The Bellows's white cottage is next to the Speichers', and it was due to the friendship between the two painters that Bellows came to Woodstock. Eugene Speicher told me of the hard work Bellows put into building his house with the help of another painter, John Carroll. The proportions had been carefully worked out and Bellows wished to keep it simple. He was miffed when he showed it to Mr. Whitehead and the Englishman said he thought it would be very nice when finished. In his direct way Bellows retorted, "You mean it's damn beautiful just as it is now!"[9] The house has not been radically changed, but the studio, in a separate building, has been made into a complete cottage. Originally it was just a workroom where the artist conceived and executed many of his best pictures. At one end was a large model stand, which held the oft-painted horsehair sofa. The remainder of the studio contained only the paraphernalia necessary for a painter.

Mrs. Bellows told of the Bellows Exhibition at the National Gallery in Washington in 1957. It was the first time a one-man show had been given there to honor an artist, and it was visited by members of the Senate and the Supreme Court. All the paintings had been loaned by museums and private collections and it was a wonderful experience for her to view them together. She felt it was of such importance that she took the Bellows grandchildren to the capital to see it.

After Washington the greater part of the collection was sent to Columbus, Ohio, Bellows's hometown, and it seems that for the first time that city realized the importance of their native son. Various people came to Mrs. Bellows with anecdotes of the painter as a boy. It had been natural for him to draw everything he saw. His father was a builder and architect and would give him the long strips of paper cut from the plans he had made. The child would accommodate his pictures to fit the narrow pieces by drawing trains or parades of animals. One of the neighbors told of George coming to their house to play circus with the children, though his contribution was mostly pictorial. He would draw for them anything they requested, from a poster full of wild animals to a boat race or a horseman. He would oblige for just so long and then announce that he was hungry and "I must be fed." As this particular family owned a grocery business, he was sure they would produce fancy foods such as figs, of which he was very fond. When he had eaten he would continue drawing what they wished.[10]

Much as Bellows liked to draw and paint, he also enjoyed physical exercise such as tennis, and he was an excellent ball player. A number of us recall him at the athletic field wearing knickers, an open shirt and a baseball cap. He formed an artists' team whose playing caused great hilarity even if it did not distinguish itself in baseball history. Bellows played shortstop, with Charlie Rosen as umpire. There were two well-remembered occasions when they played the bewhiskered House of David team. The second time this team came to play, the artists were prepared for

Mr. and Mrs. Philip Wase, *1924, by George Bellows (1882–1925). Oil on canvas, 51¼ x 63 in.* Courtesy of Smithsonian American Art Museum, gift of Paul Mellon.

them, wearing false mustaches and beards. Charlie Rosen and Hughes Mearns were particularly effective, appearing with red dust mops tied to their chins.

A conspicuous piece of furniture in the Bellows's living room is the horsehair sofa, which was brought from the studio. It has associations with such famous paintings as *My Family*, *Emma*, *Elsie and Gene*—and above all, in my mind, with *Mr. and Mrs. Philip Wase*. In the Metropolitan catalog for the Bellows memorial show, Frank Crowninshield says of this picture:

> Does it not put before us all that is left, in America, of Puritan austerity and rigour? How completely we are made to feel the discipline and self-denial, not only in the two people before us, but in thousands like unto them. How simply the patience and dignity of Mrs. Wase is suggested![11]

Well, having known the Wases, who lived near Rock City, I do not associate them with Puritan austerity—though Mrs. Wase worked hard and was a confirmed worrier. She tried diligently to keep in check her husband's weaknesses, sometimes locking him inside when she left the house. Sam Wiley, a painter, recalls being invited to view their new bathroom, which had been built to keep pace with the Wases' friends. When Sam dropped by to see the new addition, he heard someone swearing about "my woman" and then calling, "Let me out, let me out, unlock the door!" Finding the key on the outside of the bathroom door, Wiley used it to release the irate husband.

When their bathroom was completed the Wases could find no use for the tub. One day when Phil turned on the faucet, just to show off, he ruined two sacks of flour stored there. Mrs. Wase always referred to her husband as "Phil Waste," and told excitedly of the "grape paragolia" (pergola) built by her neighbors, the Arlts. She was the chief breadwinner of the family with her cleaning and laundering. When Charlie Speicher, the singer, brought her his wash one time he apologized for including a very dirty pair of white pants. "You don't need to mind," she said, "I'll just fill them full of lust."[12] She cleaned house for the Wileys and, having done some modeling, was interested in seeing Sam's latest canvas of a snow scene. Finally her pronouncement came, "Must be easier to paint the trees in the winter when you can see what you're a-doin'."

To appreciate the following story one should keep in mind the Bellows painting of the Wases—especially her pinched face and pithy body. Mrs. Wase said to Elsie Speicher, "Why, you know, we earned a dollar an hour just a-settin' there on the sofa in front of Mr. Bellows. And if we'd been a-willin' to set without our clothes on we'd a-made twice as much; but me, I won't let down my drawers for any artists!"[13]

There were painters to whom Bellows was obligated for opening his path—such as Robert Henri, Winslow Homer and John Sloan—but they never achieved his mastery. He was not limited by New York or by any part of the country. The whole American scene was his field. He never went to Europe, and although he could and did study the European masters at the museums, they never moved him a chit from his American point of view. Consequently he was the first great painter born, bred and nurtured exclusively in and by the United States. He made a profound impression upon the art thinking of his time, and he received nearly every honor and prize available during his short life.[14]

One of the last studios on the lower Rock City road belonged to Frank and Augusta London. He was a good painter and a popular man. He was born at Pittsboro, North Carolina, in 1876, attended the University of North Carolina at Chapel Hill, and studied art at the Pratt Institute and under William Merritt Chase. For a number of years he designed stained-glass windows and objects of ecclesiastical art. When in 1923 he decided to devote all of his time to painting easel pictures, he parted from the restraints of his previous work but kept his command of materials, constantly enriching his color and paint texture. London showed a keen sense of humor in his pictures, often choosing to depict objects that were once prized but then discarded by a later generation, yet choosing them primarily for their pictorial rather than their sentimental value. Occasionally he painted people, but these pictures were not as significantly human documents as were his still lifes. He surrounded himself with baroque memorabilia and had only to juggle his possessions around to make a still life. He might choose a stuffed chair, a piece of brocade, some mounted birds or a water pitcher draped with leaves, but he was never inhibited by realism. These objects would merely form the basis to which his imagination could add or subtract hundreds of forms or ideas until he had made a picture full of his sensuous delight in paint.

Frank London was a good storyteller, and in his drawling Carolina accent with the descriptive motions of his hands he would, without any rancor, entertain his friends by showing up the humorous side in all of them. Sometimes a group consisting of the Londons, Bradley Tomlin, Alice Henderson and myself would drive far into the mountains to attend country auctions. One such auction was held at a place called Hancock, where the contents of a railroad hotel that had been closed for forty years were being sold. It was an eerie spectacle as everything from attic to cellar was dragged out onto the pavement. Closets full of old-fashioned clothes and unclaimed trunks were smashed open, occasionally disclosing intimate garments, to the delight of the auctioneer. There were also love letters, because the last owner of the hotel had closed it after being abandoned by her salesman lover; and now, after all these years, without any delicacy, the letters were read aloud to the curious public and offered to the highest bidder. Both Frank and Bradley bought useless articles, or so it seemed—the latter completely losing his head over a huge moth-eaten Brussels carpet. Thereafter on every breezy day Rock City could hear Bradley Tomlin beating his carpet—which spent most of the summer swinging on the clothesline in his yard. Frank bought some old-fashioned window shades and a few other run-down objects that eventually showed up in his paintings. We had good times at the auctions and at supper parties at the Londons' or at our house. One afternoon when Frank London stopped in to see us we spoke of the delicious mustard sauce Augusta had served a few nights previously. "Oh, there's nothing to it," he said. "Give me mustard, celery seed, vinegar and a cabbage and I'll show you how it's made." When the ingredients had been assembled he began to cook while we hung over the stove watching. He quickly became bored with stirring the sauce round and round the pan so he began telling one of his amusing stories, and every time he made a point be would throw more mustard into his brew. When the tale was finished he considered the sauce was done and exclaimed, "You see how easy it is to make that sauce!" He left us with a product that could serve only to burn our tongues.

Augusta London and I are the only ones left of that group. Frank died in 1945 and there was a retrospective show of his work at the Woodstock Artists Association that was sent on tour. Bradley Tomlin wrote a beautiful and penetrating appreciation of his friend's work that was printed in the catalog. This collection of London's pictures received favorable comment all over the country.[15]

Konrad Cramer, one of the most versatile of the Rock City artists, has been exhibiting over the years in many different styles and media. He has tried everything from montage to abstract painting and has mastered them all. His imaginative grasp of each new phase of art has kept him young in spirit. He has also worked in metal with a sure sense of design, and he is a fine photographer; for several years he had a successful school of photography.

Konrad's wife, Florence Ballin Cramer, is also a good painter, but it was after they left Rock City that her talents truly developed. She now has a one-woman show in New York.

The Albert Heckman studios are on the mountain road above Rock City. Here Heckman has produced many prints and lithographs, besides watercolor paintings. For many years he headed the art department at Teachers College, Columbia, and for a time directed their summer school of art in Woodstock. He is now teaching at Hunter College. Florence Hardeman, his wife, is a violin virtuoso who began her career at sixteen playing solos with John Philip Sousa's band. For eight years she toured with Madame Schumann-Heink. When Sarah Bernhardt made her last tour of the United States, Florence Hardeman was with her and played the violin between acts. She has had several concerts in Woodstock.

Bradley Tomlin was born in Syracuse, New York, and studied art at the university there. He was a delicate-looking man upon whose thin face the veins showed when he was animated. In a refined, clear enunciation he would relate some small incident with real appreciation of the humor in it and the play of the characters involved. For many summers he lived around Rock City, painting canvases that showed a feeling for line and color. Periodically he would leave town in an attempt to avoid interruptions to his work. He would go to Long Island or elsewhere, but always returned to Woodstock—in that respect, defeated. Among the artists there has been a never-ending search for the ideal conditions in which to paint, especially among those who had known pre-war Europe. Here, on a small income, their physical requirements could be cared for, their anonymity preserved and their creative urge encouraged. Woodstock was originally a place where it was inexpensive to live and where one's working time was respected, but later it became filled with people who had no inner resources and who were obliged to gather together or perish of boredom. In Tomlin's case he was always sure he was making the right move and would therefore sell his studio in Woodstock—and be obliged to find another place when he returned. He was fastidious regarding his surroundings and spent valuable time renovating these new homes.

When I first knew him he was a neighbor, having rented the house under the pear tree vacated by Marion Bullard—and there he brought his mother. The house was heated by several stoves, one of them an old iron cook-stove with a cranky personality that Marion had bought from Aileen McFee. Mrs. McFee felt responsible for the stove's behavior and periodically came to poke its interior to make sure its drafts were clear. Mrs. Tomlin, a conventional little lady, was surprised one day to have an eccentric-looking woman arrive at the door saying she had come to clean the kitchen stove. Aileen worked her usual magic on the stove but was not interested in cleaning the ice chest, which Mrs. Tomlin had suggested. When Bradley returned his mother told him about the peculiar charwoman who had been there. He made inquiries and was embarrassed to discover the "charwoman" was in reality the wife of one of the best painters in Woodstock, while at this time nobody in the art world had heard of Bradley Tomlin.[16]

For several years Tomlin had a studio on the lower Rock City road not far from the Londons. Then he did over the mill house by the waterfall near the crossroads. Later yet he bought Judson Smith's big Victorian house at the foot of Ohayo Mountain, using up all his energy to get it into the

Number 20. 1949, *by Bradley Walker Tomlin (1899–1953), 7' 2" x 6' 8¼ in.* Digital image © The Museum of Modern Art / Licensed by SCALA / Art Resource, N.Y.

condition he wished. I rarely saw him during these years and have no idea when he took up abstract painting. His work always retained the old sensitivity to line and color, although it became distinctly modern (meaning among the advanced concepts of the art of the Forties). His pictures began to be noticed, but it was not until the year before his death in 1953 that Tomlin became really famous among the promoters of the last cry in art and was given a one-man exhibition at the Whitney Museum.

On the lower Rock City road the red barn that had formerly been Speicher's studio was bought by the Harry Leith-Rosses. "Tony" Leith-Ross was a tall, handsome Englishman who painted well in a very conservative manner. This probably accounted for his leaving here to settle in New Hope, Pennsylvania, where there were a greater number of artists painting in the traditional way, and where his close associate, John Follinsbee, had preceded him. Along the Speichers' western boundary runs a lane that leads through the Bellows property to the Rosen house (and beyond, to the studio of Harvey Emerich).

When Charles Rosen was sixteen he opened a photographic studio in his hometown of West Newton in the coal-mining region of western Pennsylvania. He soon found that the only time the miners were interested in having their pictures taken was when a member of their family had died. A few years of photographing corpses on the "cooling board" were enough for the young man. He went to Ohio where he worked with a friend who ran a gallery, and this was his introduction to art.

A year later Rosen entered the National Academy of Design in New York and stayed in that city, studying at the Chase School of Art. To pay his way he ushered at the Criterion Theatre. The salary was small but he augmented it under the direction of the head usher, who had a racket whereby he bought cheap opera glasses from a pawnshop and had the ushers rent them to the patrons of the theater at a good fee. The money so earned was split between them, and it provided sufficient income to keep Rosen going.

When Rosen had completed his studies he moved to New Hope, Pennsylvania, where at first he supported his family by working in commercial art. Then his easel pictures began to sell, and he twice received the Hallgarten Prize. He had married Mildred Holden and they had two daughters, Katharine and Polly. He was then working in the traditional style, and it was not until he came to Woodstock in 1916 to teach at the Art Students League Summer School that his thinking on art began to change—though he denied that it had been a conscious effort. He found Woodstock stimulating as it seethed with new ideas. Within a couple of years he gave up his studio along the canal in New Hope and moved to the Rock City neighborhood where he built his home. In 1922, with Andrew Dasburg and Henry McFee, he started the Woodstock School of Painting, which was later taken over by Judson Smith. A few years after the death of his first wife Charles Rosen married Jean Inglis.[17]

The Depression of 1929 hit the artists hard, because buying works of art was considered a luxury that even the wealthy abandoned for a time. When the Roosevelt administration began art projects under the Treasury Relief Program, many artists were provided an opportunity to paint murals in public buildings, enriching the walls of countless post offices throughout the land. Charles Rosen was given the job of painting the murals for the post office at Beacon, New York. It was a large undertaking as it consisted of eight panels, the two largest being eight by twenty feet. He chose to depict the Hudson River landscape from New York City to Catskill, showing twenty-five historical places, including the Kingston tugboat yards. He was assisted by Clarence Bolton and the project required two years to complete. Before the murals were finished the Rosens had a visit from Mrs. Roosevelt and Mrs. Henry Morgenthau Jr., the wife of the Secretary of the Treasury. In her column, "My Day," Mrs. Roosevelt wrote:

> At 9:45 this morning Mrs. Morgenthau and I left in my car to go to Woodstock, N.Y., an artists' colony behind Kingston. We wanted to see the sketches for the murals which Charles Rosen is doing for the Post Office at Beacon, N.Y.
>
> Anyone who knows Woodstock will agree, I think, that it is a charming place. It shows what good taste and imagination can do to create a delightful atmosphere.
>
> In the first place there are a number of attractive spots where you may stop and eat out of doors if you wish. I can say nothing about the food, but I know that if I could eat on a little terrace back of a stone house which we saw I would be satisfied with very simple fare.
>
> I have always loved the Catskill Mountains, and here they loom up very near at hand. In every direc-

John Follinsbee and family in New Hope, Pennsylvania, circa 1913. Follinsbee (1892–1972) studied under Carlson and Harrison from 1912 to 1914 at the Art Students League. He then moved to Pennsylvania and became a leading member of the New Hope American Impressionist movement. Photo: AMS Collection.

Georgina Klitgaard's WPA mural showing the village of Poughkeepsie circa 1839, at the Poughkeepsie Post Office, 55 Mansion Street. Photo by Weston Blelock.

tion there seemed to be attractive spots to paint. We saw one or two easels up and painters so engrossed that they did not even look at passing cars.

We found our artist's house quite easily and spent a delightful time in his studio. The map, which is to go the length of the lobby, is not only lovely in color but interesting in design. The other paints harmonize in color and give additional views which are historically interesting as well as scenically.[18]

In a local newspaper Fritzie Smith tells about Mrs. Roosevelt's having asked a gardener the way to the Rosens' studio. Later when the gardener was told he had spoken with the First Lady, he was so excited he put down his tools and took the rest of the day off!

Rosen was next commissioned to do the murals for the post office at Palm Beach, Florida, where he moved his family for the winter. They depicted the life of the Seminole Indians as well as local scenes. Later, Rosen and Georgina Klitgaard won the competition for the designs of murals to be placed in the Poughkeepsie post office; Klitgaard's subject was an older view of the town, while Rosen's was of a present-day Poughkeepsie regatta. Poughkeepsie, of course, was close to the Roosevelts' home at Hyde Park, and it was revealed the president had a voice in the selection of the murals.[19]

In 1940 Rosen went to San Antonio, Texas, to serve as director of the Witte Memorial Museum, a position that had recently been vacated by another Woodstock artist, Henry McFee. Rosen taught there for four winters, returning to his home each summer. I doubt if he made a single enemy during the forty-eight years he lived in Woodstock. He was a man with strong convictions but with a gentle and smiling manner that would disarm any fanatic.

Charles Rosen won many awards: the Inness Gold Medal, the first Altman Prize and the Jennie Sesnan Prize for the best landscape at the Pennsylvania Academy, to mention a few. But the greatest tribute paid him may have been by his fel-

Charles Rosen's WPA mural of a Poughkeepsie regatta, 1939, at the Poughkeepsie Post Office on Mansion Street. Photo by Weston Blelock.

low citizens—for his sympathy and encouragement to all the young artists of Woodstock, and for his spirit of tolerance toward everyone, even those with whom he disagreed. He died in 1950 and is buried among his peers in the Artists Cemetery.

Earlier I made mention of a house on the southeast corner of the Rock City crossroads where over a hundred years ago Davis the blacksmith lived. Subsequently it was occupied by the Duboises, followed by the woman with all the cats and then by the Frank Chases, and is now owned by Henry Mattson. A short while ago I stopped in to see the Mattsons and enjoyed being shown two of his latest pictures. One was of the sea, a favorite subject that he paints in his Woodstock studio. (I forgot to ask him if he can best paint mountains while he is by the sea.)

This picture of tumultuous waves dashing against somber rocks is different in concept from Mattson's earlier work. He remarked that he could best express himself by painting the waves of the ocean but that his present style is unlike the more lyrical quality of his younger days. The second picture was of the Wide Clove Kill, which tumbles over a falls near his house. It was a twilight scene under a moon hanging in a dark sky, which sparkles on the water and throws silver-green lights on the trunks of nearby birch trees. There is nothing sentimental in this moonlit scene, as it is painted with virility—and unlike most of his canvases is heavy with pigment.

Mattson was born in Gothenburg, Sweden, in 1887, and came to the United States when he was nineteen. For many years he worked as a machinist. While he was in New York he saw great paintings by Rembrandt and El Greco. These inspired him to try painting for himself, and he began working on Sundays. In 1916 he came to Woodstock to study at the Art Students League Summer School but soon realized that he would not find there what he wished to learn and he would have to be his own teacher. He recalls at that time setting up a still life of red onions and eggs, which he was unable to paint no matter how much he studied it. He therefore decided to forget about his picture. Yet whenever he closed his eyes, whether day or night, he saw nothing but red onions and eggs. His models were no longer in front of him, and, "relieved from the subject matter," as he expressed it, he found he could paint those onions and eggs to his satisfaction. Now Mattson never poses anything while he is actually painting it. He works fast, sometimes completing two canvases in two weeks, followed by a rest period. Each day when he takes up his brushes he finds he has lost the mood in which he last painted and therefore begins afresh on the same canvas but with a new impetus.

It was fun to be once again climbing the steep stairs from the Mattsons' living room to the studio, although each step being of individual height and width posed a problem. Everything about the studio stimulated my enjoyment—the smell of paint, the intellectual north light, the workman-like order, and above all the sight of the iron stove in the center of the room with its twisting pipe. Below are two bedrooms, which originally formed the entire space of the house. Two steps lead from these down to the living room, which Daphne Mattson keeps fresh and comfortable. In the windows there are pots of flowers, which even in the winter she can coax into blooming constantly. Daphne has delicately colored red hair with milk-white skin and a smile in her eyes. Henry is tall and thin with a visage marked by troubled thinking, though sometimes the lines break into a humorous twist. But why attempt to describe him when so often he has painted his own portrait? The Mattsons' living room was made from a lean-to that originally was Benjamin Davis's blacksmith shop. Davis bought the property in 1812 from Matthew Dymond Sr. His name appears in the books of the Bristol glass company, for whom he worked at making axes.

Self-Portrait, *1951, by Henry Mattson (1887–1971). Oil on canvas, 16 x 12 in.* Courtesy of Hirshhorn Museum and Sculpture Garden, Smithsonian Institution.

Henry Mattson had his first one-man show at the Montross Gallery in 1921, and ten years later he won the Norman Wait Harris Silver Medal at the Art Institute of Chicago. A few years after that he received the one-thousand-dollar prize as well as the Bronze Medal at the Corcoran Gallery in Washington, D.C. In 1943 he won the two-thousand-dollar W. A. Clark Prize and the Corcoran Gold Medal for his painting *Rocks*. He also won the Clark Gold Medal at the Pennsylvania Academy of Fine Arts. He received a Guggenheim Fellowship in 1935 and was made a member of the National Academy in 1951. His pictures may be seen at the Metropolitan Museum of Art, the Whitney Museum, the Phillips Memorial Gallery and the Corcoran Gallery in Washington, and in permanent collections in Detroit, Brooklyn, St. Louis, Cleveland, Kansas City and elsewhere.

Included in my notes is an account of an afternoon visit the Mattsons paid us several years ago. It was a real call because they were dressed for a special occasion. Henry wore a becoming forest-green jacket with high collar and lapels, evidently of foreign make, probably Swedish. Daphne wore a little skullcap upon her pale red hair, and she carried a basket that I had taken to them the fall before filled with late pears and that she now returned with a batch of homemade cookies. When we had settled down and were sipping highballs, the discussion centered upon a recently published book on flying saucers. It led Mattson to speak with envy of the fields open to young scientists of today to whom the whole universe seems to be a laboratory. "Artists also wish to do original work," he said, "but there are few directions left open to a sincere painter. It must be a growth from within a man's deep convictions, not like the work of one of our neighbors who can turn out a brand new conception on a three-by-nine-foot canvas in fifteen minutes!" We all laughed.

Later Daphne inquired about the birds that had come to our feeders that winter. Our lists were comparable, including jays, chickadees, snowbirds, sparrows, purple finches, grackles, nuthatches, woodpeckers and evening grosbeaks. Also, we had caught occasional glimpses of a pileated woodpecker but it had not come close.

"One winter we had a pet fly," Henry told us.

> We would not have wanted a dozen flies but to have a single one buzzing around was friendly. We noted he slept every night yust about a foot from the stovepipe clinging upside down to de ceiling; den in de morning he comes down and flies about, so we talk to him and he becomes friendly. He would sit on our hands or our heads and he was no more afraid of us. If we were busy he would make fun buzzing our ears, swooping back and forth to attract our attention. De only ting was soon we were going to Florida for a visit and although we considered taking him with us in Luther's taxi we decided it would be too hard for him; yet we didn't know what to do with our pet when we should close the house. Den we tought of a plan which was to take him over to de farmhouse across the road where there were lots of odder flies for him to make friends with, but we weren't sure how Hazel Harder would welcome an extra fly in her kitchen. So we play this strategy to get our pet over there where we knew he would enjoy the winter with all those many friends. He would let us pick him up and I could place him in a covered jelly glass. Daphne would then cross the road to the Harders and as she entered the door she would say to Hazel, "Isn't this your glass?" as she opened the lid, releasing the fly. We planned all dis and had the glass ready just before we were to leave. Den Paul Fiene came in to say good-bye and he sat down to have a little chat. By and by I saw our fly go over and place himself on Paul's forehead and I want to tell him dat is our pet but he is talking so hard I don't like to interrupt him. But he knew dat fly was dere and before I could stop him he took his big sculptor's hand and he clapped it down on his forehead and squashed our friend, and shook it off on de floor. We both stood dere aghast and he says, "What's the matter, what have I done?" "Oh Paul," I shouted, "you have killed our pet fly!" Paul was astonished but when he saw how upset Daphne and I were he says, "Gosh, I'm sorry." And dat is de story of our pet fly.[20]

Maud and Miska Petersham live on the Glasco Turnpike about half a mile from the crossroads. Their stone house is gay with warm-colored stones mixed with the blue, bright pottery in the many niches, and hollyhocks higher than the eaves. For years they have written and illustrated children's books of the finest quality. Miska was born and went to art school in Hungary and in his work he has retained the character of that country's folk art. Maud was his pupil and when they were married they began a long collaboration on books such as *Miki* and *The Ark of Father Noah and Mother Noah*. In preparation for *The Christ Child* they spent three months in Palestine to acquire an authentic background. It is still one of their best-selling books. Almost as popular is *The Circus Baby*. They received the Caldecott Medal for the best illustrations of the year for *The Rooster Crows*. Of their American series, *Story of the Presidents of the United States of America* was taken by the State Department to be reprinted in twelve languages for distribution abroad.[21] When I asked the Petershams how many books they had written they said about forty-five, besides contributing the illustrations to at least fifteen more. They have worked as hard as any artists in Woodstock. This year for the first time I heard them say they were taking a rest.

It is fortunate for the painters that they require a north light for their studios, because this is the direction that faces Overlook. For fifty years the artists have looked at the mountain and loved it, yet few of their pictures express the true power of this massif. They live under its protection unaware that it may be the mountain's subconscious influence that urges them beyond the usual human endeavors to express real creativity. But the mountain can be savage and unpredictable: a Rock City artist, George Ault, fell victim to an Overlook Mountain stream. He worked quietly for years in a tiny box of a building on the Glasco Turnpike. Then he was suddenly swept away in one of the Sawkill's flash floods that periodically remind us we are here only as the tenants of nature.

Woodstock Library circa 1955. This photo was used in the library's promotion booklet. AMS Collection.

Woodstock Library in 2005. Photo by Weston Blelock.

Chapter 9

THE VILLAGE GROWS

FROM A LIBRARY TO THE ART STUDENTS LEAGUE

A large part of Woodstock village was in Chancellor Livingston's Great Lot 8. In 1789 Isaac Davis purchased from him the lower mill property, which was located where the present Kingston and Saugerties roads meet at the bridge. Seventeen years later Davis in turn sold the mill to Philip Sickler. After the Revolution, Davis was in possession of property from the Village Green to where the Methodist Church now stands. In 1806 he deeded the site of the Dutch Reformed Church to the Elders and Deacons of that congregation, which was already established on the Green. The history of the Dutch Church has been written by the Reverend Harvey I. Todd,[1] who was its popular minister for thirty-five years. Besides his regular duties Reverend Todd was always the first to volunteer when there was trouble. He was the man on the roof at a fire; he was at one end of the stretcher when flood rescues were made; and he brought into his parlor the village alcoholics when those poor souls were in need of help. Some of Reverend Todd's war work is told in a later chapter of this book.

According to a map drawn by John Kiersted in 1827, Samuel Culver was then in possession of the Woodstock mill located on the stream that crosses the village. South of the bridge was a dam, and it is probable that Culver established the first tannery there, because he dealt in hides. However, it was Orsen Vandervoort who developed the large tannery remembered by the oldest residents. Of this only a few foundation stones now remain. He had the capacity to turn out sixteen thousand sides of leather a year, using eighteen hundred cords of bark to do it. The hides were processed in twelve vats, in which they progressed each month into a different solution until by the end of a year the leather was well cured. The hides came from as far away as South America and the reason for transporting them into the northern mountains was that here there were plenty of hemlock trees available. Stripping the bark from the trees gave employment to many men, who delivered it to the tanneries in their "bark riggings" for a few dollars a load. At the tanneries the acid was extracted, to be used in curing the hides. As the tannery was situated in the middle of the village, the strong smell must have been disagreeable to its neighbors. The local tanning business failed after the development of chemical acids for curing hides. Before long other industries, such as bluestone quarrying, provided employment to the Catskill mountaineers—although this in turn gave way to the era of cement.[2]

The Woodstock Library

Dr. Larry Gilbert Hall and his wife, Catharine Longyear, were the owners of what is now the library building. The land was part of the tract sold by Chancellor Livingston to Isaac Davis and in turn sold to Philip Sickler. The latter divided it into smaller pieces, and from then on the lots were subdivided and changed hands repeatedly, because this was the tract of Woodstock village with the churches, gristmill and tannery. Philip Sickler sold the library site to

John G. Ring. (According to Orville Elwyn, the library building was constructed by Larry Bogardus, who married Jane Elwyn.) Later, Stephen Force came into possession of it and sold the upper section to Larry Gilbert Hall. By the time Dr. Hall was practicing medicine the lot had dwindled to six acres, with its back boundary along the Old Forge Road. Finally the house and garden were all that remained. After Catharine Longyear Hall's death in 1885, the house came into possession of the Lasher family, who sold it to Mrs. Walter Weyl in 1927, and she gave it to the Woodstock Library Association for a permanent home in memory of her husband. That the library was thought worthy of perpetuating the name of this intellectual has been a matter of pride to the trustees.

Cornerstone of the new Woodstock Library addition in 1948. The stone was from Woodstock, England, and was given as a token of thanks for the help received from the New York Woodstock during the Second World War. Photo by Weston Blelock.

Dr. Hall was born in 1788 and must have had a good education. He kept an account book that began in 1830 and is still in existence—having come to Mrs. Alma Simpkins through her uncle, William Harder, the husband of one of Dr. Hall's daughters, Sally. The Simpkins now live in the Harder house on the village street to the west of the library.

There are a few items in the account book that pertain to the library building. Dr. Hall paid Henry Davis three dollars for three days' work to place the "pilasters" on the front of his office. Evidently these are the star decorations we have all admired. On another occasion he lists paying Joseph Peet a dollar fifty for delivering and planting five locust trees. He had other interests besides doling out pills and tending confinements (the charge was three dollars for that service). He had an extensive medical library and at least once bought a book on astronomy, in which the position of the globe was annotated by Dr. Ebenezer Hall, who was more interested in the glass factory of Bristol than in doctoring. Larry Gilbert Hall also received payment for teaching in the schools. The account lists most of the early inhabitants of the village as his patients and many of them paid their bills in food or wood.

Among the interesting purchases made by Dr. Larry Gilbert Hall was that of sixty shad at five and a half cents a fish. Some of these may have been used for fertilizer, which was then a common practice. He paid John Bonesteel thirty-one cents for one dozen pigeons, which were presumably of the "passenger" variety that used to fly in sky-darkening numbers through our Catskills but have now totally disappeared. In the back of the book are noted some of the recipes he used. He cured Henry Myers's leg of a dark purple sore by washing it three times a day with limewater. The limewater was made by burning oyster shells and pouring water over them. After washing the sore he placed sheet lead over it. He added a notation that the limewater was also a fine mouthwash. Dr. Hall was only forty-seven when he died in 1836, but his widow lived on for another forty-nine years.[3]

In 1913 Ralph Radcliffe Whitehead called together a group of residents that included Walter Weyl, Mrs. Dubois, Edward Simmons, Carl Eric Lindin and Dr. Downer to form a Woodstock Club. Its purpose was to start a community health program and to provide a reading room and library. To help finance their activities, moving pictures were to be shown in the Fireman's Hall. The homemade electrical apparatus frequently broke down, but this did not quell the audience's enthusiasm. A home for the club was found in the former Bovee barn along Tannery Brook in a room rented to them by George Neher. Here, a pool table was set up to entertain the young people. A suitcase full of books brought by Ralph Whitehead and Walter Weyl was distributed among the members, and this became the nucleus of the library. None of the other activities of the club survived, but the handful of books was augmented by many donations and Francis Clough was engaged as librarian for one or two afternoons a week. He took the job because it allowed him time for reading and it was easy work. Compare this with the present circulation requiring three librarians working at high speed handling four to five hundred volumes on an average afternoon.[4]

After 1926 the library moved to its present location in the white frame house originally occupied by Dr. Hall. It is a good example of Woodstock's early farm architecture. At first the library did not require the entire space and the two west rooms (formerly Dr. Hall's office) were rented as an apartment. Yet within a few years it not only had absorbed the apartment but was in urgent need of a large addition. Due to the hard work of a small group of the trustees, funds were collected to build a new twenty-by-fifty-foot room designed by Albert Graeser. It was completed in 1948 with a cornerstone from Blenheim Castle presented by Woodstock, England. This created an entente that led, after the war, to our joining all the other American Woodstocks in contributing to the replacement of the bells in the English town.[5]

The new wing provided space for the cabinets of musical scores and the comprehensive collection of art books, besides the expanding reference library. The large reading table and matching chairs were made by one of the leading craftsmen of the village, Iris Wolven, who cut the lumber from the side of Overlook Mountain. It was then possible to allot one of the original rooms for the children, a cheerful place with small furniture and books both old and new. It also had space for exhibitions of the illustrations for children's books by Woodstock artists, and for the much loved merry-go-round horse. This wooden horse was made by William Spanhake of Wittenberg and painted by the Petershams.[6] At the opening of the new wing Dr. James T. Shotwell gave a talk on the history and purposes of the library, and he made several memorable statements. He noted that our only hope lies in escape from ignorance and that the greatest of all the arts is life itself.[7]

Bruno Louis Zimm (1876–1943) with busts of St. Francis of Assisi and Robert E. Lee. Photo by Konrad Cramer. AMS Collection.

For several years the library circulation was limited to village residents, but early in the 1930s two volunteers began taking books to the hamlets of Zena, Shady, Lake Hill, Willow and Wittenberg. With help from the teachers, the books were distributed out of the schoolhouses. At first there was opposition among the old-time farmers, who considered it demoralizing for the young to acquire what they considered the bad habit of reading. However, the practice of reading spread, bringing new horizons to young and old, and before long the teachers were bringing carloads of their pupils to the library to select their own books.[8] Thus the circulation expanded and with every passing year the Woodstock Library establishes itself more firmly as one of the invaluable institutions of our community. The aid it gives to schoolchildren, to artists and musicians, to research workers and homemakers is known to all the friends of the library, but it has taken the interest and cooperation of the whole town to bring it to its present state of efficiency.

The main support of the library has been the money raised at the annual fair, which accounts for over four fifths of its income. The authorities in Albany hesitated to endorse this source of support and it was only in 1933 that they granted our library a charter as a full member of the State Library Association. However, they have always said for its size our library is one of the best in the state.[9]

The sculptor Bruno Zimm served as president of the library for several terms and was largely responsible for its joining the State Library Association. He worked without consideration for his time and effort.

Zimm was born in Hoboken, New Jersey, in 1876. His talent for sculpture became evident when he was very young, and at age fifteen he was introduced to

WOODSTOCK
LIBRARY FAIR

Woodstock Library Fair during the 1950s.
Postcard by Bob Wyer. AMS Collection.

Karl Bitter. The latter employed him in his studio and a year later sent him to Chicago to supervise a sculpture commission at the World's Fair. Zimm continued his studies at the Metropolitan Museum and the Art Students League and later studied with Augustus Saint-Gaudens. He was awarded the Silver Medal at the Paris exhibition of 1900 and one of his friezes is a permanent part of the Fine Arts building in San Francisco. Other works include memorial sculptures in New York City, Houston, Wichita, Baylor College and St. Pancras Church in Brooklyn, as well as the fourteen Stations of the Cross in St. Clement's Church in Philadelphia. He was engaged on a commission for the Naval Chapel at Annapolis when illness compelled him to stop working.

Zimm was a founder and trustee of the Woodstock (Byrdcliffe) Guild of Craftsmen and the Woodstock Memorial Association. In addition to his art work he made a catalog and complete collection of fossils from local rocks. This collection was subsequently purchased by the Smithsonian Institution. His widow is the genealogist and author Louise Hasbrouck Zimm, and they had one son, Bruno H. Zimm, a scientist.[10]

After his death on November 24, 1943, Marion Bullard wrote in the *Ulster County News*:

> This place named Woodstock is more than a place of hills and brooks, fields and woods. It is the accumulation of the indestructible things of the spirit that men and women leave behind them when they pass away. Bruno Zimm is dead. He rests on the hillside where so many of his friends also rest in peace.
>
> Creative men like Bruno Zimm do not stop with the carving in stone and wood. He can be said to have hewn out of life something as shaped and beautiful in the hearts of his friends as ever he visioned or aspired to make out of wood and stone.
>
> Perhaps the best and greatest epitaph for anyone is the simple one—a good friend.
>
> Looking back down the years, I can remember no time when Bruno failed to respond to the need of anyone who appealed to him for help. He gave without

sparing himself. I believe it probably did not occur to him that he had a choice. There was a need to be met. That was enough. During the later years, he sometimes said to me, "I must not take on anything more. After all, I have my own work to do." Then, at once, he took on something more for his neighbors or his community.

Now that his strong skilled hands are quiet and we can make no more demands on them or on his sympathy, his tolerant kindness and his generosity, we can measure what he has been to us. Bruno Zimm carved his own monument. Day after day, year after year in the materials of friendship and of life lived at its fullest and best.[11]

The Library Fair has now become fairly stabilized. Originally it was run by the artists, who formed the majority of the book borrowers. At one of the first fairs Andrew Dasburg and Henry Lee McFee designed banners for which a few of us dyed yards and yards of unbleached muslin a rich purple, maroon, blue and burnt-orange, which, sewn in uneven patterns, were strung between the trees in joyous brilliance! Indeed they were so decorative they were borrowed by all the organizations in town, including the Maverick Festival, and soon became faded and tattered. For the fair the best musicians played popular songs, the artists gave pictures to be auctioned for a fraction of their value, and George Bellows and other painters made quick sketches of sitters for a dollar. There were pet shows, when the usual collection of dogs, cats, snakes and frogs might be joined by exotic animals such as the Cannons' honey bears or one of their llamas. The latter, on one occasion, came wearing panniers, one of which contained a hundred-pound prize pig to be auctioned. There was a tail-wagging contest and guessing games, shooting galleries and hot-dog stands. Each year there has been an entertainment for the children, such as puppets, a merry-go-round or a seal. It was at the Library Fair that the trained seal Sharky had one of his earliest successes, which led him to Broadway and Hollywood fame. There have always been fortune-tellers and booths for food, flowers and so on. One of the great orchestra leaders might be found peddling balloons or, unknown to the crowds, famous authors might be selling second-hand books or pure junk for a nickel. Incredible as it may seem, the present fairs take in well over two thousand dollars an hour.[12]

Victor and Eleanor Cannon with their honey bears.
Photo: AMS Collection.

People come from up and down the Hudson Valley to attend, knowing they will find bargains for themselves while their children delight in magic shows, pony rides or maybe a carousel. An artists' Gypsy band plays with gaiety while the crowd rushes to buy such bargains as an evening gown for fifty cents or a stove at the flea market for a quarter. Banners wave, tambourines jingle, young people shout with laughter, and all the while the coins pour into the cash boxes so that the library may function for another year.

The Woodstock Guild of Craftsmen

One of the nicer houses on the Village Green is the one occupied by the Woodstock Guild of Craftsmen, now known as the Woodstock (Byrdcliffe) Guild. Like the library site, the land was originally part of the Isaac Davis tract of a hundred and seven acres. It passed through several hands before it came into the possession of William De Forest, whose ownership was marred by the controversy resulting from his building his privy to lap four inches over the Coons's land to the northeast. An 1858 map shows the property in the possession of Samuel Gage, who also owned several houses on the road to Ohayo Mountain. By 1875 F. W. Beers's *County Atlas of Ulster* indicates that Orsen Vandervoort, who operated the tannery and had been town supervisor in 1871, lived on the property. Still later the house belonged to Abram Rose, who had a store next door (the site of the present gallery) but moved to

ABOVE: *Woodstock village in the 1930s.* Courtesy of Historical Society of Woodstock.

BELOW: *Ethel Adams sketch of Woodstock village during the 1940s.* Courtesy of Historical Society of Woodstock.

Kingston, where he became a successful merchant. The store burned early in the twentieth century and the house was sold separately, coming into the possession of Hunt Diederich. He sold it to the Eugene Schleichers, who turned it into the fascinating Jack Horner Shop filled with interesting antiques and Old World folk art.

In 1945 Mrs. Blanche Rosett bought the property as a home for the Woodstock Guild of Craftsmen, and several years later, when the Craftsmen had become established as a village institution, she gave them the house. The organization was begun in 1939 by a few weavers, potters, wood carvers and jewelry workers as a small cooperative enterprise.[13]

The northeast corner of the Green, where the Rock City road begins, was the site of various taverns and hotels until the Woodstock Valley Hotel burned in 1930. It was a picturesque double-decker building dripping with Virginia creeper and had been bought by a group of civic-minded citizens for an inn. Unfortunately it did not last long. This site had been occupied by a tavern since about 1789 when the town board gave a license to a William Snyder. In 1825 Stephen Deforest deeded the tavern to Andrew Newkirk and thereafter it was known as the Newkirk and Deforest Hotel.[14]

The tavern achieved real importance in the middle of the nineteenth century when George William Snyder became the proprietor. He sold it to William Brinkerhoff and it was torn down and rebuilt to become Brinkerhoff House—but Snyder seems to have continued as host and probably part owner. During this period former president Ulysses Grant stopped there, not for the night but for the time it took to change the coach horses for the trip up Overlook. Larry Elwyn remembered seeing Grant and described him as short with a reddish beard. Another former president Elwyn saw at Brinkerhoff House was Chester Arthur, who he said was a tall, noble-looking man with mutton-chop whiskers. (Larry Elwyn, as the village barber, noted their hair!) Several village girls asked to be presented to President Arthur, and Snyder complied with their request. Still another distinguished visitor was General George Sharpe, Commander of the 120th Regiment of New York State, which was made up of men from Ulster—including five from Woodstock—and Greene counties who fought in the Civil War. General Sharpe spent many weekends on Overlook.

General George Sharpe (1828–1900), who led Kingston's 120th Regiment during the Civil War, was a frequent visitor to Overlook Mountain House. Detail from frontispiece of The One Hundred and Twentieth Regiment, by C. Van Santvoord. Courtesy of Research Library, New York State Historical Association, Cooperstown, New York.

Elwyn told of the four-horse stages driven by Leydendecker, who galloped them around the corner and brought them to a smart stop in front of the hotel. The main tavern was on the northwest corner, and it contained a bar, a large box stove and a wooden bench along the south wall. There was a ballroom on the east side of the building.[15]

Mrs. Will Russell of Shultis Corners remembers that when she was a young girl, in about 1874, the stagecoaches brought visitors from the old Catskill Mountain Hotel above Palenville for excursions to Overlook. The stages would stop at Wolven's shop at The Corner for refreshments and would be served "turnpike pancakes," which she helped cook; they were made of Indian corn meal with hop tea for leavening. Everyone agreed that the true destination of these trips was Overlook Mountain House, which at that time was run by John E. Lasher. When the Overlook hotel finally burned, its register was taken to Mead's, but the distinguished guests stopped at Mead's and the other taverns only for rest and refreshment.[16]

Until a few years ago there was a tavern in the village, dating back a hundred and fifty years, which had always been in the Elwyn family. It was midway along Tinker Street in a building that has now been converted into apartments and a beauty parlor. The first Elwyns, three brothers, came from Wales in the late eighteenth century. There is an unconfirmed story that they were owners of the ship in which they crossed the Atlantic Ocean and that they sold the vessel to finance themselves in the New World. One of them, John M., was called Captain Elwyn, which supports the ship story. He evidently had some money and was an able wagon maker and blacksmith. He first went to Saugerties but soon moved to Woodstock. At first he may have leased land, because he was issued a license by the town board to run a tavern in 1812—whereas the deeds for most of his property, which he bought from Alexander Hunt and Samuel Culver, were not recorded until later. The home where he died is now owned by Joseph Fitzsimmons, our present town supervisor. Elwyn was a religious man, being one of the trustees of the Methodist Church when they purchased ground from Culver. He did not wish to operate a tavern himself but had no scruples against his wife running a hotel and bar across the road. Eventually the Elwyn holdings ran from halfway along the village street (excepting a few lots) to the DeVall farm, and to the south extending to the Sawkill, including the tract now owned by the Comeaus. John M. Elwyn had four sons: Alexander, Peter, William and Larry. The last was the father of George Washington "Wash" Elwyn, who was on the town board for years. Peter became a farmer on the property later owned by the Hasbroucks on the Kingston road. William left town and Alexander became the well-known tavern keeper. It was said he was over-fond of eating and became too fat for his health. The meals at the tavern were delicious and salesmen were known to travel many extra miles after dark just to enjoy the food and comfort of Elwyn House. The tavern finally petered out under the management of Alexander's bachelor son, Sam. It was Alexander's great grandson, Allen Dean Elwyn, who revived the family tradition of providing good food by giving Woodstock Deanie's restaurant.[17]

Ethel Adams sketch of Deanie's, a popular gathering place in Woodstock. Courtesy of Historical Society of Woodstock.

The Art Students League studio in 1917. It is now the Christian Science Church. Postcard by L. E. Jones. Courtesy of Historical Society of Woodstock.

The Art Students League

In 1906 Birge Harrison was asked to start a school of landscape painting in Old Lyme, Connecticut, but, as he had built his home in Woodstock and preferred the mountains for a school, he persuaded the Art Students League to locate here. His classes were an immediate success and students gathered from all over the country to study under the gentle guidance of Harrison, who, although an ultra-conservative painter, was ever tolerant of fresh ideas in art. Out of his classes came some of the most dynamic artists Woodstock has ever produced.

In June the stagecoach driven by Eddie, from whose mouth dripped a perpetual ooze of tobacco juice, would pick up the students at West Hurley station and as the horses headed north the first view of Overlook Mountain threw its never-to-be-relinquished hold upon the hearts of the young people. The accounts of the early League activities in the village tell of hard work during the daylight hours and fun in the evenings when the irrepressible high spirits of the students would leap forth. For many of them it was an exhilarating experience to be free of home conventions and to associate with creative people. Boardinghouses were filled and there was money circulating—although the villagers complained of the bohemian goings-on, not realizing that prosperity would soon follow.

The leading boardinghouse was the Coopers,' where an exceptionally large room with meals could be had for eight dollars a week. Walter "Pop" Goltz sat at the head of the table. He was not expected to live more than a few months as he was afflicted with an incurable disease, but the climate of Woodstock kept him alive for over forty years. The students would gather on the porch after supper every night. Sometimes they sang, led by Cecil Chichester, who had a talent for piano playing and mimicry and was considered a leading student at the League school. There was A. B. Titus, who produced a students' magazine called *The Pochade*, which appeared in 1912. That was shortly after Hervey White began *The Wild Hawk*, the first Woodstock periodical. As far as we know, the inaugural issue of *The Pochade* was also the last. Chichester and Eddie Ward did an imitation of a trainer and dancing bear act that had recently passed through the village; the performance was so amusing it lingered for years in the memories of those present. There were hayrides and dances and picnic suppers on the flat rocks along the Sawkill, and always singing and hilarity.[18]

Marion Bullard described her arrival in Woodstock by bus. From the Village Green she saw three students emerge from the barber shop and, to her astonishment, observed that one had his head shaved to resemble a checkerboard, another's hair was cut to leave polka dots upon his scalp, and the third had part of the hair on the back of his head removed, leaving the outline of a face with eyes, nose and mouth. That was her introduction to *la vie bohémienne* in Woodstock.[19]

After six years John Carlson succeeded Birge Harrison as instructor for the Art Students League Summer School, with the assistance of Frank Chase and sometimes Pop Goltz when the classes were filled to overflowing. One hundred and fifty pupils enrolled at a time for instruction in landscape painting, and the class had to be divided into two. Each section would be assigned to either a blue or a red group, which, according to flags stuck in a map, would indicate at which pasture the students were to take their field criticism. Out the students would go, laden with sketch boxes, easels, canvas, umbrellas and stools. One old lady trundled her gear in a baby carriage. Another student, having torn her umbrella in a dozen places, patched the rents with various colored pieces of paint cloth, which created a landscape in itself. John Carlson and his assistants would appear in the field and conscientiously make their way through the multitude of would-be artists. I knew a couple who were on a walking trip through the Catskills. At dawn, after a disturbed night on Overlook caused by a skunk digging bones out of their campfire, they moved down the mountain and settled in a quiet pasture. It seemed a lonely spot far above the village. They were awakened by voices, and to their amazement found themselves in a crowd of people who were dotted every few feet throughout the field busily splashing paint on canvas and even taking advantage of them as free models. This reminds me of a story Tony Leith-Ross told about painting a farmer plowing. Tony was a tall, well-built man and he sketched the scene sitting on a campstool hunched over a small box. Gradually the farmer's furrows came near the artist; the plowman stopped, ejected a stream of tobacco juice and said with scorn, "Gosh, you look strong enough to do a day's work!"

On Saturdays the best of the canvases would be hung at the League studio and Carlson, and occasionally Harrison, would rip the work to pieces for the benefit of all the students. Carlson would open the criticism with a talk on one of the problems of landscape painting, such as perspective or the drawing of clouds or trees. He was often accused of giving formulas for painting because he explained the laws of growth, atmospheric conditions or weight and balance in nature. But, after hearing him lecture, none of his students would ever again be satisfied to paint the ground without solidity, mountains that had no weight or trees that were not rooted in the earth. Carlson not only loved nature but respected and made a study of it, and he instilled this attitude in others.

At first the League's studio was in the tannery barn. Later the League rented a house among the pine trees south of the village and eventually built its own classroom, which is now the house occupied by the Christian Science Church. After Carlson resigned from teaching at the League, Charles Rosen and later Hayley Lever headed up the Summer

Walter "Pop" Goltz and John F. Carlson (at center) study a canvas at an Art Students League criticism. Photo: AMS Collection.

John F. Carlson (1875–1945), the landscape painter and charismatic Art Students League instructor, at his home on Glasco Turnpike. Postcard by L. E. Jones. AMS Collection.

School. Then it remained closed for twenty-four years until it was revived largely through the efforts of Arnold Blanch. It now occupies the former National Youth Administration buildings on the Saugerties road.[20]

John Carlson was born in Sweden in 1874. He immigrated with his parents to this country as a young boy, was educated in Buffalo, New York, and came to Byrdcliffe on a scholarship. He was one of those hardworking students who preferred to leave behind the easy life of Byrdcliffe with its accompanying obligations. Carlson moved into a Rock City barn where he subsisted on a near-starvation diet of cheese and beer but where he could devote all of the daylight hours to painting, and also to music, as he had a fine voice. During the years when he taught at the League he attracted more students than had ever attended the Summer School. His paintings are represented in museums all over the United States. His awards include the Altman Prize at the National Academy in New York City (of which he was elected a member), the Silver Medal at the San Francisco Exhibition in 1915 and the Carnegie Prize in 1918. He married a student, Margaret Goddard, and they had three sons. John Carlson died in 1945.[21]

During the early days of the Art Students League the character of Woodstock was that of an art colony. Easels were set up not only in the fields and woods, but also in the center of the roads, where considerate drivers would swerve around them. Frequently, too, canvases were set up along the brooks where nude models shivered in the mountain water and callow villagers peeped at them from the bushes. There were some wild parties in the studios, which were greatly exaggerated in the telling and gave the colony a bad reputation.

The playing and drinking did not appeal to all the students; some had come to Woodstock at considerable sacrifice to escape from social life. These dedicated youths would work on large canvases each morning and think nothing of walking several miles with their heavy gear to places such as Shady, Zena or Lake Hill to sketch every afternoon. When their early boardinghouse supper was over, they might whip up a quick picture of a sunset or a moonrise. To them Woodstock meant freedom for work rather than for play. Ever more important art was produced, and Woodstock's fame for creating masterpieces obliterated the gossip. The more serious artists built their studios off the main road where they could work without interruption.

Original concepts burst forth in every field, although some enterprises, such as the cooperative shop and the civic center, failed. Among the more picturesque were the camping trips organized by Edith and Dyrus Cook. The donkey, Jackie, driven by

Dyrus, would carry the equipment over the easier routes to a designated site near a spring. There, fires would be lighted and food cooked for the clients, who would have climbed over the mountains guided by Edith. She was an outdoors type filled with the lore of the birds and the flowers, which she enthusiastically imparted to the city dwellers who would arrange to join her on these trips for a weekend or longer at a nominal fee. Early in the 1930s the Cooks went on an eight-month hike that was written up in a book, *Donkeying Through Seven States*.[22] Later, Dyrus launched a project that was successful for years. He established a group of hillbilly dancers called the Cheats and Swings, which started the rage for square dancing. They performed in costume and were invited to dance for audiences in New York City and Hyde Park, where they gave a special performance before the president of the United States.[23]

By 1919 Woodstock's reputation as an art colony was well established and the dream of the painters to have their own exhibition hall was soon to be realized. Stock had been sold for an Artists Realty Company to build a gallery on the Village Green. The gallery was to be rented to the "Art Association," and the plan was to leave the exhibitors free to run their own shows. Only a few persons were naive enough to believe their investment would pay dividends other than the satisfaction of promoting art, and even here opinion would be divided as to whether the returns were worthwhile. These differing views no doubt accounted for the arguments and even fights that have always kept "art thinking" alive in the town. The chief organizers of the Art Association were Andrew Dasburg, John Carlson, Henry Lee McFee, Frank Chase and Carl Eric Lindin.

The preamble of the constitution of the Art Association stated that both conservative and radical artists were to be represented on the board of directors, and a real effort was made to have the exhibitions reflect both schools. But over the years the constant influx of younger and more liberal artists has gradually replaced the conservative group. At one of the early shows I was on the jury, which consisted of an equal number of representatives from the two sides. Unfortunately Birge Harrison was ill and unable to attend, which left the conservatives one juror short. Andrew Dasburg solved the problem by offering to vote for Mr. Harrison if we would all agree to his doing so. As each exhibit was presented to the jury, Andrew would vote for the painting or sculpture if he believed it to be progressive, and then, as Birge Harrison, against the same offering; if he considered the work belonged to the old school he would reverse the votes.[24]

Harry "Tony" Leith-Ross was the first secretary and treasurer for both the Artists Realty Company and the Art Association, and later I was asked to take his place. In retrospect it seems incredible that I should have attempted to take the job, as I was unable to spell or add. The Art Gallery books of that period must be unique, if even legible. However, Tony Leith-Ross was not too businesslike himself, and when he left he handed me an enormous coat box into which he had jammed all the correspondence and bills concerning the building of the gallery. Soon fresh invoices arrived, which required checking with past records, but it was impossible to find the right documents in the mix-up within the box. In desperation I called for aid from the other trustees and several, including Dasburg and McFee, came to help. After a couple of hours of futile effort one of them took the box and fed the contents into the good old iron stove. We were quite pleased with ourselves for solving the problem—that is, until the spring when Carl Lindin returned from California and had to hire a lawyer to untangle the legal snarl that had ensued. None of us had considered the fact that the Artists Realty Company was incorporated and the State would require an accounting. Lindin served many terms as president of the Artists Realty Company and the Art Association and frequently helped them to recover from disorganization and quarrels. His recollections of the early days at the Art Association provide a valuable picture of the painters and their work:

> This paper is concerned not so much with the present exhibition as with a review of the life of the Gallery and the people connected with it during the last ten years.
>
> The youthful enthusiasm of fourteen years ago, when Dasburg first introduced Cézanne to his friends and pupils, has given way to a more individual and conscious attempt to reach beauty and truth, perhaps more congenial to the American background.
>
> Dasburg was always the experimenter, the innovator, the fighter; I believe he loved contention for its own sake—but in the main he was right, for he had dreams and visions of a new beauty and the strength and intelligence to create it.

Sketch, by John Striebel, of twelve Woodstock art personalities, 1924. Charcoal, 12 x 9 in. Courtesy of James Cox Gallery, Woodstock, New York. Photo by Dion Ogust.

Standing on his own legs and seeing things in his own way, Eugene Speicher grew sturdily and from year to year revealed his great powers in exuberant flower pieces, robust landscapes and delightful portraits of young women.

Henry Lee McFee learned during these years how to distill the most exquisite and significant beauty into his still-lifes, his landscapes and figures. His art has been tagged "intellectual," but it is more than that: it is also deeply emotional and reserved; the word "classical," in its best sense, seems to me appropriate in speaking of his art.

George Bellows gave us his whole boyish enthusiasm and strength, hitting the mark in art as often as he hit the ball in baseball or tennis. His interest in the American theme, in the portrayal of individual character or of the blatant, commonplace crowd surrounding the prize-ring, always grew stronger and stronger, and blazed forth in great pictures, in innumerable drawings and lithographs. No one since Winslow Homer has been so peculiarly and sanely American.

Then there is Charles Rosen, with his knowing and disarming smile, who quietly worked his way out from an academic career and is now painting strongly constructed landscapes, of a modern but unmistakably American origin.

Then John Carroll, more than clever, though somewhat sensational, with his fine portraits of young girls, his spectacular nudes and his rhythmical line. He has easy and heathen ways which make him attractive to all kinds of people.

Then Judson Smith, romantic and seeker after new and impossible things, but finding his own way and expression more and more. Neil Ives, gentle and quiet, painting flowers, still-lifes and landscapes with that serenity which sets him apart from his fellows. Paul Rohland, vigorously expressing his enjoyment of fruit and flowers, of sunny landscapes and peaceful pursuits, but with a mischievous glint in his eye, which suggests that there are many things in his make-up—"wir schlafen alle auf Vulkanen." Ernest Fiene, young and strong, seeing the poetic and dramatic in the Woodstock landscape, and often reaching mastery in his lithographs. And Herm[o]n More, who paints landscapes of a deep-toned quality that make one think of good cello music. And, "last but not least" Henry Mattson, the Swede. A real strain of Nordic melancholy, enlivened by humor and a gay color sense, sings through his flower pieces and landscapes and makes one think of his native folk-songs and fairy tales.

From the Maverick colony come Mr. and Mrs. Arnold Blanch, bravely attacking the American scene, but equally interested in the life of the circus . . . sideshow. Harry Gottlieb belongs in this group and paints characteristic landscapes around his own place, or down at the Rondout, as well as still-lifes and portraits, with a fresh and unbiased eye.

Then there is Bateman with his austere still-life arrangements and his abstract landscapes, almost religious in their severe simplicity. Konrad Cramer, versatile and experimenting with technical methods; his last flower pieces have a decided charm and the quality of a well-considered decorative problem. Up in Bearsville live the two Klitgaards, producing very original and delightful landscapes and amusing pictures from Biblical sources.

Alexander Brook, with his Mephistophelian countenance, his mocking and refreshing laughter, has also lived in Woodstock and helped to make it known by his essays on some of the painters, and also by his own pictures. Peggy Bacon, his wife, has seen and depicted the comic side of Woodstock life; and as in most good caricature, it almost makes one weep to see how sad a really funny thing can be!

Among the other artists Alfeo Faggi, the sculptor, stands out as one who has seen and understood the eternal beauty of the great Greek and Italian traditions. His sculpture has a stern and spiritual quality that is rare in our day.

At the time the Gallery started, a rather fine cooperation existed between the academic and radical groups. Gradually the differences between them widened, until the younger and more radical group took possession of the Gallery. Finally the academicians withdrew almost entirely from the exhibitions, and out of many misunderstandings and much small talk there developed the scornful and bitter feeling which seems to follow all new moves in any community. Perhaps opposition is necessary in life and art, but fair play and respect for your opponent make the fight more interesting and dignified. A good picture is a good picture, even if it is painted by an academician, and there are many good ones in Woodstock—Birge Harrison, John Carlson, Leith-Ross, "Papa" Goltz, Frank Chase and others . . . Birge Harrison is not with us any more! His charm and sweetness remained with him to the last, and undoubtedly it was this charm and sweetness which constituted the strongest connecting link between the academic group and the youthful conquerors of the Gallery. Harrison refused to take sides and he sent his pictures to the annual exhibitions as if there were no "rival groups." Art to him was "beauty, refinement, and gentleness," a world full of the silvertoned colors of night, where all could meet on equal terms, to enjoy and dream in a temple built by the gods, where there was plenty of room for all expressions and creeds.[25]

Mrs. Roosevelt at her home in Hyde Park, New York, accepting salt and pepper shakers made by NYA woodworkers in 1940.
Courtesy of Woodstock Library.

The Great Depression

The 1929 break in the stock market did not make itself felt as noticeably in Woodstock as it did in richer communities. Here, there was not much money to be lost as very few artists owned stocks or played the market. In their hand-to-mouth existence it was a mercy to have prices drop on food and clothing. However, soon it became apparent that pictures and sculptures were not selling. When the Artists Project under the Public Works Administration was set up, some members of the community fared better than ever before, and the large number of those who registered as artists for federal aid was surprising. No doubt the project did serve a legitimate need; various public buildings were enriched by murals, and many old Woodstock records were copied and thus saved.

That the town fared as well as it did may be due to its reputation as a place where people could live cheaply. Hence, those in higher income brackets moved to the rural community, real-estate values here were maintained, and the shops were well patronized throughout the Depression. Judson Smith, as a technical director and supervisor of Works Progress Administration art projects for artists in New York State, initiated an art caravan, together with Eugene Ludins, to set up exhibitions of the WPA artists in communities where there had not previously been an opportunity to see the work of New York State painters and sculptors. Later Ludins replaced Smith, taking the art caravan on visits to most of the towns throughout the state.[26]

Meanwhile, under Roosevelt, a National Youth Administration was formed to combat the effects of unemployment among young people. The Civilian Conservation Corps set up camps in various localities for forestry, road building and outdoor jobs. In Woodstock an arts and crafts center was opened, drawing unemployed boys and girls from all over New York State. It is doubtful if these young people absorbed an appreciable amount of culture from the artists, because the latter were busily engaged in their own work and kept to themselves. The NYA center in Woodstock was fortunate in having as its director William Phelps and later a Mr. Mathison, both of whom set high standards. On the teaching staff were exceptional persons from Woodstock such as Towar Boggs, Educational Director, and Tom and Elizabeth Penning. Tom Penning, the sculptor, taught his pupils stonecutting and setting, which was of more value to the students than trying to become indifferent sculptors. He had them build the walls for their workrooms, and a fine job they made of it. The teacher in woodworking and carpentry had the boys complete the building, and in so doing taught them the principles of constructing a house. These buildings along the Saugerties road are now occupied by the Art Students League Summer School.

When, in 1939, the buildings were to be dedicated by Mrs. Franklin D. Roosevelt—whose pet project the National Youth Administration had been—it was agreed there would be a minimum amount of ceremony. The only attendees would be the young people involved, the staff, and a small committee that had been appointed to serve as liaison between the village and the students. Mrs. Roosevelt, in her charmingly informal manner, drove alone in her car from Hyde Park to Woodstock. Unfortunately the news leaked out and the mayor of Kingston was on hand to welcome the wife of the president of the United States. Not one to have his prerogative usurped, the mayor of Saugerties arrived in great haste, claiming that the site was under the jurisdiction of *his* township. The two mayors, with their staffs, jockeyed for the most conspicuous position nearest to the First Lady. Most of the young students, who were her real interest, were pushed to the rear. The mayor of Kingston managed to turn the situation to his own advantage and began a long speech, while Mrs. Roosevelt tactfully inclined her head to listen. It was not a political speech; it was a contrived piece of advertising with microphones and cameras. After many pompous phrases of welcome, the mayor approached his real objective, saying he had read in the newspapers of the recent visit of King George and Queen Elizabeth to Hyde Park. He spoke of the president and Mrs. Roosevelt's having entertained their royal visitors with a picnic at which hot dogs had been served. His voice rising to a crescendo, the mayor shouted, "And I hope, Mrs. Roosevelt, you served them Kingston's own FORST'S FORMOST SAUSAGE!" A tiny flicker of amusement crossed Mrs. Roosevelt's face, but she retained her impeccable manners and thanked the mayor for his speech of welcome. The remainder of the time she devoted to inspecting the buildings and talking to the NYA youths.[27]

With the approach of the Second World War more and more of the NYA young people entered the armed services. A few who were not taken volunteered to help in civilian defense work or the Aircraft Warning Service, and soon the NYA closed its Woodstock center. A few of the boys married local girls and returned to live in Woodstock after the war.

The Ku Klux Klan

The Ku Klux Klan was revived in 1915 but did not make itself felt in the north until after the First World War. It seemed very remote from the life of the Woodstock colony, until suddenly in July 1924 we became aware of organizers who had come to the village and enrolled members from the less intellectual elements of the population. These misguided souls imagined they were being patriotic. The KKK was a menace because it was secretive and difficult to combat. In a short time the outside organizers collected six hundred dollars from the village, for which they never accounted. The atmosphere became ominous with whispered threats directed not only against the foreign-born in our population, among whom there were many distinguished artists and musicians, but also against any resident who might oppose the Klan. One day posters appeared announcing a meeting to be held in Sherm Elwyn's sand pit, where there would be the burning of a fiery cross. This gave us an opportunity to fight back. We circulated petitions protesting such a defilement of our town; but, though we secured some signatures, there were few villagers or merchants willing to sign, as they feared reprisals. One of the storekeepers said to a friend of mine, "Aren't you, as a woman alone with young children, afraid to fight the Klan?" Of course we used this as an example of the evil in the KKK, willing to threaten unprotected women and children.

Within a few hours a committee had been formed among whose members were Mrs. Walter Weyl,

Andrew Dasburg, Mrs. Leaycraft, myself and, I believe, Dr. Shotwell and a few others. The Firemen's Hall was engaged for the evening when the burning of the cross was scheduled and, through the intercession of Justine Wise at "Red Roof," her father, Rabbi Wise, was persuaded to be the speaker at the meeting. The firehouse was crowded and Rabbi Wise was most eloquent. His splendid voice resounded with denunciation of the Klan as defamers of Jews, Catholics and all foreign-born of whom America was proud. Unfortunately some of his talk misfired because there were scarcely any Catholics there and, as Alfred Cohn said, his was the only Jewish family residing in Woodstock. But the famous preacher's voice was cello-beautiful, thundering against intolerance, and he ended with a recital of the Psalms of David. After his talk everybody went to Sherm Elwyn's sand pit where the Klan was gathered.

It was a black night and we had a dark field to stumble through between the road and the sand pit. We could hear the terrifying mumblings of a brewing mob. Nobody appeared to have flashlights and the gathering was mysterious and threatening. It took some time before our eyes could discern the white-hooded figures of the Klansmen faintly silhouetted against the sky and our ears could decipher the illiterate pronouncements of the speakers. They denounced all those freedoms of race, creed and equality with which we are endowed by our Constitution. At one side, converts were taking oaths and undoubtedly being fleeced of ten dollars for membership. It was like attending an obscene ritual in the Dark Ages. On several occasions the speaker was nonplussed by the questions put to him but he brushed these aside with meaningless threats. Certainly there was dramatic suspense as we waited for the climax of the show, and everybody was silent as a large cross was lifted into place. We were tense with excitement when suddenly a crude voice asked, "Ain't yer got the can? Where's the kerosene?" It broke the spell and there was a burst of laughter. The next moment the flames ignited the cloths wired to a huge cross and the blaze illumined the crowd—but the mystery and the apprehension had vanished and we looked into the faces of as many friends as Klansmen.

The KKK tried to salvage their prestige with persuasive speeches, but they were a poor lot of uneducated men who could not answer the charged questions well aimed to place them in a ridiculous position. I remember the childish voice of our dear Jennie (Mrs. Birge) Harrison naively asking, "Do they permit Unitarians to join?" The speaker was confused, not knowing what a Unitarian might be, and his reply showed he was sure it was something subversive. Again the artists shouted with joy. Never has heckling paid off better. The Klansmen's discomfiture was complete and they made a hasty retreat. (The river rats returned from whence they had come.) We were rid of them. Although after the Second World War a couple of crosses were burned, presumably to frighten Communists, it was obviously done by halfwits and accomplished little more than to disgust the few who heard about it.[28]

There was an amusing sequel to the Klan meeting in the sand pit. It was said that an artist of uncertain age living in Zena had taken into her heart and home a young man whom we shall call Buck. As a prank, a couple of the painters went in the night and scrawled a *KKK* on their door, as well as on the doors of several other unmarried couples. Buck and his friend (long since dead) were immediately married and should have lived happily ever after. However, not far away, another young man brought home from Europe a beautiful, sophisticated bride who, it was whispered, had been the model for a character in Hemingway's *The Sun Also Rises*. It was evident she was not the type to settle down in the woods for the winter, and before long the welkin rang with the report she had eloped with Buck. The news was detailed enough to allege that when she crept from the conjugal couch in the middle of the night she left a note saying, "I know you both need me, but Buck needs me most."

This reminds me of two other couples who came to an amicable agreement to switch partners—an exchange that has long since been regularized. At the time they debated who was to do the moving but this was decided by the wives, who were determined to keep their own kitchens, and the husbands were required to change residences.

These stories make it sound as if the artists were very free and easy. This certainly was often true, but many of the excesses were committed by those whom we called "camp followers." And every scandal concerning the artists could be matched with one concerning a native-born citizen. It was merely that the latter were better at hiding their peccadilloes.

The Rescue
as Told by an Old-Timer

Many years ago when the winters were hard and the summit of Overlook was a half day's journey by carriage from the village, there lived alone on the mountain a caretaker named Clint. All the men liked him, for he was a good fellow ready to crack a bottle at the village pub whenever he came off the mountain. An enormous structure of white boards, Overlook Mountain House clutched the windswept rock to keep from being hurled into the treetops a thousand feet below. In season the sun-drenched ledge, suspended in the clear air, was a promenade for the boarders who gazed in fascination over the Hudson Valley. When they were surfeited with infinity, they turned to follow the trails through the woods of stunted pines, or perhaps to hunt for the tiniest harebells that grew in the crevasses of the glacier-scored rocks. By November the guests had left and the dark clouds swirled around the peaks of the mountains sending squalls of snow skipping off the bald rocks to gather lower in the woods or to block the leaf-strewn trails. Then the hotel was left in chilled loneliness to the care of Clint. About once a month when the weather was not too ugly, he would walk to the village of Woodstock at the foot of the mountain to buy fresh supplies.

It was after the New Year, and the mail was being sorted as fast as the storekeeper could manage and still keep track of the village correspondence. The usual winter-idle farmers were seated in armchairs behind the potbellied stove in the combined store and post office when someone asked, "How long is it since anyone here seen Clint?"

"Don't just know when last he come down to git his supplies," the storekeeper mumbled through his fringed mustache. "But I tell you, he ain't likely now to get offen that mountain till there's a thaw. For if there's two foot o' snow down here there's more'n likely six foot on Overlook." He turned to finish reading a card before thrusting it into a letterbox. A stocky fellow with an enormous midsection nodded. Then his slack mouth gathered muscle-tight as he aimed for the spittoon, hitting it with a loud splat. Pushing his plug of Plowman's Delight into one corner of his red face, he conjectured, "This is the deepest snow I've ever known. I'll bet it don't melt for three months. Do you suppose Clint has enough to eat?"

With the finality of the last sentence of a book, an old man answered, "No tellin'," and, as he clapped his lips together, he tilted back in his chair and hooked his boots over the nickel guard that encircled the stove. By this time the iron filigree on the fancy stovetop was steaming, the potbelly was glowing red and all conversation ceased. The ninety-degree heat was penetrating their flannel shirts and fleece-lined caps, making them too drowsy to talk. The fumes of tobacco were heavy and added another film upon the flyspecked windows and upon the labels of the less popular canned goods that remained on the top shelves.

The next day when the same men were gathered around the stove one of them asked, "Any news of Clint?"

"Nope," the storekeeper replied. "How could any news come offen that mountain, I'd like to know." He chawed on his quid until the back of his jaws jutted out like a squirrel's. Then he commenced to hollow his cheeks in preparation for a shot at the spittoon. Thus relieved, he began once more: "How much food do you figure he keeps in his cellar up there?"

"Oh, he wouldn't starve for a few weeks."

"But he hasn't been down for eight or nine weeks."

A week passed and after the mail was sorted the fellows again settled down to talk over any news that might have developed in the valley. One of them remarked, "Wonder how Clint's making out since this last foot of snow fell? Do you figure we should try and dig him out?" He pushed his cap to the back of his head and took a long, satisfying scratch at his scalp before he continued. "Well, if he don't come to view within the next few days perhaps we better do something. My wife says she's going to bake a double batch of bread this week in case we do try to break open the mountain road and take him some food."

A couple of days later the storekeeper had sorted and figured out all he could glean from the mail before he noticed that the usual group of men were not gathered around the stove but instead were stamping impatiently by the door. When he emerged from behind the tier of letterboxes they shouted, "How about it, man, what you going to donate? We have a sack of potatoes, one of onions and another of apples, and a stock of bread and doughnuts, a crock of butter and a keg of rum. Here comes someone with a whole ham too."

"I'll give you a bag of canned goods," the storekeeper said (and he added, to himself, "They can have those slow-moving cans, and maybe the cost can be tacked onto their bills later on"). He reached for the flyspecked cans on the top shelf and dumped them into a box. There was a loud, "Gee, and a haw!" from the Village Green. A span of black and white oxen had been brought to a halt beneath the maple trees. The flat wooden sled to which they were hitched was full of bags and baskets and a cask that was firmly tied on the back. From every direction came stout fellows stomping through the snow with shovels over their shoulders. When all had arrived there were more than thirty men to participate in this splendid show of village concern for the safety of a neighbor. Off they started with a crack of the whip that caused the oxen to free the sled from the clinging snow with a squeal. They marched proudly past the hotel where the two lone guests came out on the upper porch to cheer them. The children ran along beside these heroes, shouting encouragement, and they rounded the corner to the lively notes of "Yankee Doodle" whistled by the village veteran who watched with envy showing in his pale eyes. On they marched toward the mountain, which they could now see as blue and white with plum-colored shadows above Short's barns. What a brave band of mountaineers they were, their spades flashing in the sunlight, their mufflers and caps, brown, blue or red, showing bright upon the snowy landscape. Their faces were lusty and they felt so fine that they soon left behind the plodding oxen that wore red top-knots, like the woodpeckers tapping in the trees along their way. These birds at work and the chatter of chickadees were all they could hear from the mountain except for an occasional crack from a frost-bound tree in the forest.

Soon after they passed the Rock City corners, they came upon a snowdrift that was the first challenge to their strength, and eagerly the most ambitious men started to demolish it. The first workers cleared a narrow track and those who followed widened it enough for the oxen to pass through a snow corridor that was as high as the tip of their horns. The men who had worked at this drift now followed the sled, for their exuberant strength had met the test and they were content to allow others to go ahead. Without difficulty the caravan progressed for a few hundred yards up the mountain until they found a place where the wind had banked the snow six feet deep. The trees on one side and the mountain on the other made a detour impossible; therefore they set to work digging through it, throwing the snow far out of the way where it fell like spangles upon the unbroken crust, making a faint tinkle of ice music. Soon, with a higher sun, the snow became heavier and clung to their shovels. And it was not long before the most stouthearted men were glad to rest. Thus during the next hour there were several relays before the huge drift was cleared away. One of the diggers called, "We need some refreshment."

"Sure, we all do," several of the others shouted. "We can't be expected to keep a-going if we don't have refreshment. How about a doughnut and a swig of rum!"

They broke open the keg of liquor and gave themselves a round of cheer as they leaned against the banks of snow they had piled into two high walls. When they had finished they resumed their trek with fresh vigor. Soon the route became steep and they were exposed to a sharp wind that blasted the cold through them, but the wind had blown some of the snow into the woods, and the way was passable except on the turns when they were obliged to do a little spading. The oxen dragged the sled with their peculiar wallowing gait exaggerated by the uncertain footing.

When they reached the fields below Mead's they encountered deep snow, and there was another long drift to be cleared. The workers now demanded food and drink at regular intervals, and by noon when they pulled into Mead's the oxen's load was considerably reduced. The boardinghouse was not open at this season but from the backyard many loud voices could be heard. To their surprise the farmers discovered there twenty men from Bristol, a village on the other side of the mountain. These good fellows had not been willing to let Woodstock assume all the glory so they had also climbed halfway to Overlook to join in the rescue of Clint. The hospitable Mead family were hard put to warm these heroes in their cottage kitchen, and when the thirty men arrived from Woodstock they decided to build a large bonfire in the shelter of the barn and to make coffee in the boardinghouse pot, which could serve dozens at a time. In this way everyone was thawed inside and out. But the men from Bristol smelled the rum, and the Woodstockers belatedly suggested that all hands celebrate this union of fifty men dedicated to a noble cause—which, of course, made everybody happy!

The day was well advanced when the rescuers continued their campaign to scale the white walls of Overlook. They started up the unbroken route that followed the hip line of the mountain. This road made a dip downward before it finally led up the steep grade to the summit. The fortified strength of this valiant army cleared the snow at double time along the first mile, but when they reached the rise their ambition sagged. They maintained that, being farmers, not ditch diggers, they needed sustenance to keep up this pace. Again the sad-faced oxen were rested while slices of bread and jam were distributed, and this gave them a thirst that could only be slaked by drinking the last of the rum. They did not worry over this, or the fact that it had grown dark, because they were within a quarter of a mile of their objective.

The sun had dropped like a ripe pippin beyond the western mountains and, with the dusk, the frost strengthened and nicked at their noses and fingers and their voices rang crisp upon the air. At last they staggered around the final turn of the road to the summit, and were met by an icy gale that blew in from the north. There, they came upon a tall figure with a lantern, shouting, "Who comes there, what the hell goes on?" It was Clint himself, alive and hearty, who had come out to discover what was causing the hubbub on the mountain road.

"We have come to rescue you," they cried, pushing forward to crowd around the object of their deliverance and to clap him on the shoulder. "We have dug our way up the mountain to bring you food and help."

Clint looked surprised but responded with heartiness, saying, "Come right in, boys!"

The food was unloaded from the sled and the weary oxen were bedded in the woodshed. Carrying the food into the kitchen, the men exclaimed, "Here is the provender we brought you, Clint." But all that was left were the canned goods, the flour, some partly frozen potatoes and the ham. This was barely enough to feed the fifty hungry heroes who crowded into the kitchen. The chairs and benches were full and many sat on the floor and leaned against the walls.

In due time the smell of frying ham was mingled with tobacco smoke and the odor of sweaty bodies. Clint said that, seeing it was like a celebration, he guessed he would bring up pitchers of hard cider to make the evening real sociable. It was not long after supper when the men began to nod, and one by one they fell asleep on the hotel blankets. If they did not smother in the polluted atmosphere it was only because there was always somebody who needed to step out the door, and this would permit a blast of pure mountain air to rush through the entrance to refresh the sleepers' lungs.

The next morning Clint was up at dawn and had built up the fire in the stove and made batch after batch of biscuits with the donated flour. He emptied his crocks of water-glassed eggs and dumped all of his coffee into kettles of boiling water. The rescuers were well breakfasted in preparation for their long descent, and the heroes started away in the morning sunshine that made their return to their village seem like a holiday excursion, with the thanks of their host ringing in their ears.

Clint re-entered the kitchen, saying to himself, "They sure picked me clean. As soon as they get a good start, I'll take my knapsack and start down the mountain to get me some provisions or I'll sure starve to death!"

Fred Dana Marsh (1872–1961) documented the advances of industrial development through his art in the early 1900s. He and his second wife, Mabel Van Alstyne Marsh, created artistic showplace homes in Boothbay Harbor, Maine, Woodstock, New York, and Ormond Beach, Florida. He was the father of Reginald Marsh, the celebrated urban realist painter.
Courtesy of Robert Slater.

Chapter 10

OHAYO MOUNTAIN

A PLACE THAT PAINTERS AND SCULPTORS CALL HOME

Only twelve hundred feet high, Ohayo Mountain forms the long southern boundary of the Woodstock valley. Just across the Sawkill it rises mostly on Livingston tract number 8, but over the hill its southern face runs into the Hurley Patent at Glenford, which is now part of Olive Township. According to the John B. Davis survey of 1845, Cornelius Riseley was the largest landowner on Ohayo, holding 253½ acres, which ran from the Sawkill well up the mountain. Parcels of this property remained in the Riseley family for the next hundred years. To the west, Andrew Elting had eighty acres, which was the farm later owned by the well-known etcher Alfred Hutty. Beyond that was the John Reynolds tract and above it the Yerry holdings. Other early settlers who lived on top of the hill were the Degraffs, the Nehers, the Bonesteels and the Herricks.

Griffin Herrick tells a story about the naming of the mountain now known as Ohayo. There was an old man named Alec Bonesteel who lived on top of the hill, and when he had to climb up from Woodstock he would complain every step of the way. There were "thank-you-ma'ams" across the road, which afforded a run-off for water as well as a convenient flat area to hold the wheels of the carts when the horses needed a rest. When old Bonesteel reached each of these hollows he would utter a great sigh of relief. "O hi o!" he would say, and when other wayfarers heard this they named the hill—in a slight variation—Ohayo. Another theory is that the name derives from a gambling game played in the old days. Yet another explanation, and the one generally accepted, is that Ohayo is an Indian name.

When the artists arrived, Griffin's father, Fordyce Herrick, was one of the best carpenters in Woodstock, and he built many of the studios. He was elderly when he talked with me about old times. He told tales of Ohayo Mountain where, as a boy, he lived in the farmhouse recently owned by the Walter Weyls. He recalled the old man Alec Bonesteel who lived higher up (in the house now occupied by the Frank Meyers). They would play checkers almost nightly and one game might last a week. Bonesteel was a great one for telling stories. One was of a witch who came from over in the Vly and hung around his orchard stealing apples while assuming the disguise of a deer. So many apples were stolen he finally had to take notice by trying to shoot the deer, but no shot took effect until he added a silver piece to his charge. That grazed the deer's back, frightening it away forever. Bonesteel knew who was behind it all because the old woman of the holler was "took right away with an awful pain in her spine, which just goes to show what a bad one she was." Herrick said he was scared by Bonesteel's stories and would run home—so eager to get there he would jump over the picket fence instead of going around by the gate.

The Vly, a valley whence the witch came, contained a little settlement beyond the Neher house (which is now owned by Nina Bull) and from it ran a wood road to Yankeetown Pond. Several families lived along there, the most respected being the Clappers. They were charcoal burners and also made splint

Wilson and Alec Bonesteel at Snake Rock Quarry, Ohayo Mountain. Photo: AMS Collection.

hickory baskets. One of their sons, Jacob Clapper, was killed in the Civil War.[1] Some of the other families were not overly bright and eked out a dubious living telling fortunes, working in the forests in the winter and picking wild berries in the summer. One family made willow baskets. As they were continually in need of cash, these families had the reputation of being light-fingered. Consequently they did not have a good name, and mothers used to threaten naughty children by saying they would give them to the Vly-Yonders, as they were called. In the early years of the twentieth century there was one family left in the Vly that is remembered as tending charcoal pits, but most of the community was scattered. However, their "innocent" behavior continued to foster stories. Herrick said one of these men tore up his marriage certificate and thereby considered himself "unmarried." Another descendant of the Vly-Yonders had such an itchy elbow he just had to play the fiddle for the square dancers.

Wilson Bonesteel, later caretaker for Cooper's Lake, was a descendant of Woodstock's first tavern keeper. Wilson and his uncle Alec were the last of the family to work their quarry at Snake Rock on Ohayo Mountain. He gave me a photograph of one of the last operations at the quarry, showing him dressing a flagstone with Alec beside him. Alec was reputed to be able to give the weight of any piece of bluestone down to the last pound. The quarrymen had special skills and distinctive names for their tools. For example, a "jumper" was a steel drill held by one man while another hit it with a sledgehammer. The jumper was given a turn between each blow to form a circular hole in the stone, and the wielder of the sledge had to hit the head in the center or there might be a bad accident. One time Lute Cashdollar was holding the jumper for cross-eyed Mose Plimley. "Whoa," Lute cried, "are ye goin' t' strike wher ye look?" "Yep," answered Mose. "Then ye can hold your own damned jumper," his nervous co-worker declared.[2]

Bonesteel's other uncles were David, nicknamed Blue Pete, and Brownie. They were in the woods boiling sap one March afternoon when, at dusk, they heard a panther up on Snake Rock. The maple syrup was practically finished and they decided to fill their pails and hurry home. Their dog was no help because every time the panther howled it cowered in terror. The panther crept so close they could see its eyes glowing, but it dared not leap at them because it feared the steaming pails of sap. The danger of an attack by one of these animals was very real to them. Wilson Bonesteel's grandmother remembered an incident in the early settlement of Woodstock when a man stopped by the mill with his flintlock gun, saying he was going hunting. He started up the mountain and they heard one shot fired but evidently he did not have time to reload before they heard terrible shrieks. The miller picked up his rifle and ran to the hunter's aid—and he arrived just in time to save the man's life. With his clothes torn off, the man was almost spent—trying to defend himself against a big cat with the barrel of his gun, the stock having been splintered into fragments.

For the last years of his life Jim Twaddell and Mrs. Park, who kept house for him, lived on the farm that had belonged to Egbert Riseley on the low meadows (the place now owned by the George Laws). During Woodstock's early days as an artists' community, Twaddell was a picturesque figure, riding horseback on his western saddle, his deeply notched profile resembling that of an Aztec under a wide-brimmed hat. He was entirely at ease on a horse and continued to ride until he was over ninety. Most of the stories about Twaddell concern horses. He is said to have trained racehorses, and it is a fact that he operated a horse-and-buggy mail route between West Hurley and Willow. His favorite mare, Daisy, once was stuck in the mud so firmly that the fire company had to be called to extricate her from this ignominious position. Twaddell had been born in 1843 to Nathaniel and Abagail Twaddle (as it was then spelled), and it is said they came from Massachusetts to Woodstock, where they ran a boardinghouse. Nathaniel Twaddle was the contractor who built the Stony Clove road, which connects Phoenicia with Hunter and Tannersville. Their son Jim married the daughter of Charles Krack, who was also an unusual character in Woodstock annals. The Kracks lived at the top of the hill where the Glasco Turnpike descends to Shady. The daughter worked at the Harder Hotel, which was located beyond the bridge in Bearsville. It was said she had but one pair of shoes, which she carried to work, saving them to wear on duty. This must have been exceptional or it would not be remembered a hundred years later, perhaps because Krack was considered a man of substance. In an 1871 county directory Charles Krack is listed as a member of the Assembly and the proprietor of a bathing establishment at the foot of Grand Street in New York City. He also owned the property on the Village Green where the Rock City road begins. Evidently this came into Twaddell's possession upon the death of his wife, because in the early days it was run as a hotel by Twaddell with the help of Mrs. Park. In the barn, faded to a rich pink (to the delight of the painters), Twaddell kept his horses. This building is now named the "S. S. Seahorse."[3]

Mrs. Park was the widow of a Dutch minister and was a kindly person although not very efficient. Over the years she had several jobs, which she undertook with compassion. At one time she was postmistress, always accommodating about credit for a stamp or cashing a check, although the postal authorities took a dim view of such practices. Later she ran the telegraph office. Some of our friends were worried about their family, who were in a flooded area, and they telegraphed to inquire if all were safe. Mrs. Park was very sympathetic. When our friends did not receive any answer they finally went to the telegraph office

Jim Twaddell in Maverick Festival attire.
Photo: AMS Collection.

Judson Smith, *1923, by Andrew Dasburg (1887–1979). Oil on canvas, 29⅞ x 24 in.* Courtesy of Dallas Museum of Art, gift of Mrs. A. Ronnebeck.

to inquire. "Oh, yes, I heard they were all right," said Mrs. Park, "but I have been busy and I knew that no news is always good news, so I did not hurry about notifying you." On another occasion she received a telegram addressed to Mrs. Bullard saying one of her admirers would arrive shortly. Knowing that Mrs. Bullard was away, Mrs. Park telegraphed the man not to come! All of this was understandable, just as one can sympathize with the taxi driver who profited from the long wait for customers by painting pictures from the taxi window—and sometimes became so inspired by his work that he refused to carry any dull passengers. There was also the handyman who left his lawn cutting when it was only half finished. When his irate employer asked for an explanation, he replied, "Well, I have to take some time to write if I'm to win the ten-thousand-dollar *Atlantic Monthly* prize, now, don't I?" In Woodstock it is sometimes hard to distinguish between the artists gone native and the natives who have gone arty.

Ohayo Mountain went through a gay period during the early 1930s when a group of village businessmen promoted the Winter Sports Association. The young people enthusiastically supported the project by helping to build a ski slope at Bearsville under the direction of the Norwegian painter Arnold Wiltz, who was also an expert skier. The bobsled run was located to the west of the main Ohayo road, starting at the top of the hill and running to the lower road where a refreshment booth was stationed. It was an exciting run and not without danger. Special winter sports trains ran from New York to West Hurley, and over the weekends the village would be overrun with sportsmen in colorful caps and sweaters. Even the most demure rooming houses would be decorated with skis rakishly protruding from snow banks. The bobsled run was a bright spectacle at night, the route dotted with torches that could be seen all through the valley. Unfortunately there followed a succession of winters with little or no snow, and the whole project failed.

Fifty-odd years ago Abram Wilbur ran a mill at the foot of Ohayo Mountain on a stream that is scarcely a thread of water now. To the west of his mill was the Cornelius Riseley farm, where descendants of the family lived until George Riseley sold the remaining property to Judson Smith.

Judson Smith was a businessman turned painter. He studied under John La Farge and John Twachtman and also at the Art Students League. He executed several murals before coming to Woodstock in 1921, but from that time he painted landscapes and figures. He was awarded prizes at various exhibitions, including a gold medal at the Detroit Institute of Art, First Honorable Mention at the Carnegie Institute International Exhibition and the Logan Prize at the Art Institute of Chicago.

In 1931 he co-founded and became the director of the Woodstock School of Painting, whose classes were held in his barn studio. The roster of instructors included—in addition to Smith—Henry Lee McFee, Yasuo Kuniyoshi, Charles Rosen, Henry Mattson and Konrad Cramer. It was opened at a time when the Art Students League was not functioning in Woodstock, and it was quite successful for several years before the war.[4]

Soon after Judson Smith bought the Riseley property on Ohayo Mountain, he sold the original farmhouse near the creek to Dr. Eleanor Van Alstyne and her sister. George Riseley remembered living there as a small boy when it was heated by just two fireplaces. When Dr. Van Alstyne took possession she

The Marsh home on Ohayo Mountain Road with several of Mabel Marsh's celebrated Americana pieces in the foreground.
Courtesy of Friends of Historic Kingston.

LEFT: *Figurehead of the* Mary Powell, *the fastest and most famous side-wheeler boat on the Hudson River during the late 1800s. This was one of the first purchases by the Marshes for their Americana collection.* Courtesy of Friends of Historic Kingston.

ABOVE: *This sea horse was part of the Marshes' carousel collection.* Courtesy of Friends of Historic Kingston.

OPPOSITE: *Carousel horses from the Marshes' oceanfront home in Ormond Beach, Florida.* Courtesy of Friends of Historic Kingston.

made many alterations to the low clapboard house and added a studio to stable and repair her collection of merry-go-round horses and primitive wooden figures and carvings. Gradually the appearance of the farmhouse has changed, although the living room still contains the big fireplace decorated with mementos from a century ago. After Dr. Van Alstyne's death, her sister, Mrs. Mabel Van Alstyne Marsh, lived there for many summers with her distinguished husband, Fred Dana Marsh. Together they added to Dr. Van Alstyne's collection of primitive folk art until it became one of the country's finest collections of Americana.

Fred Marsh received his art training at the Art Institute of Chicago. While there he made some murals and decorations for the World's Fair; this led to his interest in mural painting. Until his father took him to Europe in the 1890s young Marsh had done little besides cartoons to earn a living, and his father—who was a businessman—was skeptical regarding his future. Marsh remembers the excitement of seeing the Arc de Triomphe in the Place de l'Étoile on their first night in Paris, and he recalls thinking that the city was too beautiful to leave. He persuaded his father to give him enough money to stay on for further study, and through economies

such as sharing his room in the Latin Quarter with another American he managed to remain in Paris for several years. For a while he studied in the atelier of Jean-Paul Laurens but soon worked by himself on a painting for the Salon. The first picture he submitted, which had murder as its theme, was hung in the Salon to the astonishment of his friends. He tells an amusing story about taking his painting to submit to the jury: he passed André Derain returning after the jury had rejected *his* painting. In 1900 Marsh won the International Bronze Medal for a portrait of his wife, an American art student he had met in Paris.

When he returned to the United States with his wife and two sons (one of whom became the well-known painter Reginald Marsh), Fred Marsh noticed the acceleration of industrial development in this country. Instead of being repelled he saw the pictorial possibilities for an artist in New York. He was inspired to begin a phase of painting such industrial subjects as sky-piercing towers and far-thrust bridges. His work led him to dizzying scaffolds where he made sketches, often under hazardous conditions. He told me of an experience he had while drawing the riveters who were engaged in fastening the last span of the Williamsburg Bridge. The temperature was below zero and the men, crazed by the cold and danger, could work only ten minutes at a time. The foreman warned Marsh to keep out of the way of the men but he crept out upon the girders to get closer to his subject. During a rest period the riveters had to rush by him and one of them, seeing him making notes, threw a wrench at him. Marsh succeeded in dodging it, but he realized the risk as he watched the tool fall into the East River far below. The pictures he made of those works brought him renown as a painter of industrial subjects, and when the First World War began the Navy used his services for patriotic displays.

After the war his work underwent a change and he made a number of historical murals for private homes and clubs; unfortunately many of these works have not been preserved. Soon after the death of his first wife his interest turned to architecture and sculpture. Like many artists of the period he grew increasingly unorthodox and experimented with modern materials and methods of handling them. He is still exploring new fields in art.

Fred Marsh loves the ocean and he built two houses close to salt water. The less important of these was constructed on an oil-soaked half acre just off the town of Boothbay, Maine. This tiny island had been in use as a marine gas station and seemed an unfavorable site for a house. But this only proved a challenge to the Marshes and Dr. Van Alstyne, for they all collaborated on the project. Dr. Van Alstyne made her quarters on an old dock that was anchored to the rocks. A long walk was constructed above the water, upon which she placed two of her merry-go-round horses prancing toward the bay, resplendent in fresh paint and glittering harness. Behind them were window boxes full of wooden marigolds that would never wilt from the salt spray. On the roof of her building was a metal turret made from a large garbage can, which was one of their many ingenious conversions. The distinction between a creative and an ordinary mentality may be seen in the former's propensity not to accept objects or ideas at their face value but to consider them apart from their conventional associations. Marsh has the ability to make use of whatever is available, and to invent any missing ingredient.

In the Boothbay house the lounge was made from a scow that had been stranded above the high-water level and was now brightly painted. The Marshes built their own apartment to resemble a blue and silver lighthouse; indeed, for a number of years their lamp served as a harbor beacon. The problem of furnishing the circular areas of the rooms in this tower stimulated the Marshes to design furniture with rounded backs to fit against the walls. Most of the windows faced the water but a few overlooked the center of the island. Here, many boatloads of earth had been dumped to provide a fresh green lawn and immaculate beds of petunias. There was a tiny dock to which was moored a handsome little cruiser designed by the owner, and there was a flock of little dinghies to provide mobility for each member of the household. The whole island had a brilliant fairy-tale luster, which war conditions eventually dimmed.

The house Fred Marsh built in Florida is his masterpiece. It is made of white concrete, on the sands of Ormond Beach facing the Atlantic Ocean. The style is modern, the form clean-cut, but there is a touch of whimsy in the decorations—from the merry-go-round horses that prance toward a tropical sea, to the sculptured fish, shells and sand monsters in the courtyard and within the house. Very imaginative, they are made of innovative materials with which he experimented until he found the ones most durable.

The largest work realized by this versatile artist is a piece of sculpture that was placed in Tomoka State Park, a few miles from his home. It is forty-five feet high and includes nine copper-colored Indian figures upon a base of coquina rock. It was inspired by a legend that is a variation of the fountain of youth theme. After seven years the work was completed, and the official dedication ceremonies were held in 1957 with Dr. Hanna of the Florida Board of Parks accepting the gift for the State. The tropical surroundings were developed as a park and a pool was added to reflect the sculptured group. The Florida Symphony Orchestra played and a plaque was unveiled—honoring not only the sculptor but also his wife, Mabel Van Alstyne Marsh, in recognition of her large contribution to the project.

Fred Dana Marsh is now eighty-five years old, but he has the exuberance of a young man, always bubbling with plans—which is probably the true secret of the fountain of youth. He is fortunate in having a wife who assumes responsibility for the mechanics of living. It permits him to devote all his energy to creative work. He strides along a busy thoroughfare

Dr. Eleanor Van Alstyne's cottage on Artist Island, Boothbay Harbor, Maine. Photo: AMS Collection.

with his gray hair flying above pink cheeks, a ready smile on his lips as he surveys the world with an ever fresh outlook. His artist's hands are often in the pockets of a stylish tweed suit. Maybe they are feeling for a pencil or his eyeglasses, but never coins, because he goes about without a cent on him—showing a disregard for money that occurs only when wealth has never been an objective.[5]

Halfway up Ohayo Mountain Road is a studio built by one of Woodstock's most celebrated painters, Yasuo Kuniyoshi. He was born in Okayama, Japan, in 1889 and came to the United States when he was about seventeen years old.[6] He did odd jobs for a living, working in gardens in the Imperial Valley of California while attending school to learn English. As a bellhop a few years later in Los Angeles he attended the School of Art and Design, and this led him to think seriously of becoming an artist. In 1910 he moved to New York where he lived precariously while studying painting. It was a long while before Kuniyoshi's pictures sold and he had one-man exhibitions, but there were always a few fellow painters to encourage him. He became a photographer, specializing in reproductions of paintings and sculpture, which provided him with an income and allowed him to pursue his art career. When his paintings began to sell he went to Europe and also built a studio in Woodstock.

Kuniyoshi returned to the Orient on visits but his art has been identified with America. "I grew up here. The most important part of my life has been here," he said. "My friends are here. My work is here." Both his marriages were to Americans. His first wife, Katherine Schmidt, was a painter, his second, Sara Mazo, a journalist. His white clapboard house and studio are more conventional than his modern painting might suggest. There is a wide view from the garden (which I helped him with) across the valley to Overlook Mountain. My conversations with Kuniyoshi were usually on the subject of flowers. Once he came to photograph the rock plants on my back terrace and it was amusing to watch the awkward positions he twisted himself into in order to get close-ups of the rosettes of sempervivum or the alpine minutiae that grew between the flagstones or through the crevasses in the steps. He held his camera a few inches from the plants, sometimes directly above or almost beneath the leaves. I never saw the results of these "candid" shots.[7]

Mask, *1948, by Yasuo Kuniyoshi (1889–1953). Lithograph.* Courtesy of Woodstock Artists Association Permanent Collection. Art © Estate of Yasuo Kuniyoshi / Licensed by VAGA, New York, N.Y.

During the Second World War, "Yas," as his friends called him, offered to serve as an observer on the Aircraft Warning Service, but as a non-citizen he was rejected. He was quite frank about condemning Japanese aggression and later was cleared by the State Department to perform valuable service through propaganda broadcasts to Japan.

After the war he replied to my letter of inquiry:

> Actually what I have done is very little. At any rate here is the material as well as I can recall it, for the record:
>
> For Coordinator of Information—short wave radio scripts on "Japan vs. Japan" which were rebroadcast from San Francisco to the South Pacific and the Orient.
>
> For the Office of War Information: war posters—"Nature of the Enemy." Also illustrations for a booklet on Japan.
>
> Short wave radio broadcast: A reply to [a] Sheridan School, Grand Rapids, Michigan school boy's letter explaining my attitude and feelings about democracy as against oppression and militarism in World War II.

> "Twenty Years Retrospective" exhibition of my work held in aid of United China War Relief. Also donated a painting to raise additional funds.
>
> Participated [in] and donated my works [to] all the major United Nations War Relief and War Bond drives.[8]

It is not my province to evaluate the work of Yasuo Kuniyoshi. Among his best-known paintings, besides the figures, are many still lifes and pictures of animals, of which he had a special understanding. One of his works is a portrait (no less) of an iron stove. It is the type used to heat all the Woodstock studios and it arouses such nostalgia that it is impossible for me to judge it as pure art. Kuniyoshi's painting was not realistic but he depicted the particular significance of each subject. His pictures won innumerable prizes in important exhibitions and his work is represented in many museums. But Kuniyoshi was more interested in selling his paintings to individuals, who often had to purchase by installments, than in getting the highest price from important collectors. Above all he was a painter's painter.

During the 1930s Woodstockers were occasionally invited to the Brain Research Laboratory on Ohayo Mountain to hear a talk by Dr. Joshua Rosett of the Physicians and Surgeons College, Columbia University, and the Neurological Institute. One presentation was titled "Physiological Mechanisms of Thought." It is not easy for a layman to comment upon Dr. Rosett's theories, but I do know he divided the functions of the brain into three categories, each influenced by the "degree of disorientation of an individual's brain." When *thinking*, a person tends to detach himself from his immediate surroundings but his processes of deduction remain consecutive and logical. Under the classification of *imagery* he placed the poets, painters and writers, whom he called the "daydreamers" because their thinking is not practical. This concept led to many conversations between Dr. Rosett and me. He had a brilliant mind and now it amuses me to look back upon my efforts to argue with him against his theory. These spirited discussions sometimes took place in his stone house, the greater part of which he built himself, where he would serve supper before a large open fire. He had other interests besides the study of brains and could talk knowledgeably and enthusiastically about gardening, the forests, wildflowers or mushrooms. Collecting fungi was an especial hobby and Dr. Rosett's unique method of casting them in metal and giving them realistic touches of paint made his collection permanent.

Dr. Rosett's third category of the functions of the brain was *hallucination*, and this he described as a state of almost complete unconsciousness or thorough disorientation from one's physical surroundings. He was particularly interested in studies of abnormal thinking processes.[9]

According to one of the doctors associated with him in the neurology department at Columbia, Dr. Rosett later turned his research to the investigation of the "conduction systems of the cerebral hemisphere" and "developed a revolutionary technique" whereby he "burst apart the compact tissues of the brain" and separated the fibers. This permitted detailed dissection. Subsequently he invented a method for continued study by preserving slices of brain tissue in Bakelite. (At the Ohayo Mountain laboratory he used wax models to illustrate his talks; these probably antedated the Bakelite invention.)

A collection of tributes to the memory of Dr. Rosett, published after his sudden death in 1940, includes these remarks by Dr. Adolph Meyer:

> [I]t was characteristic of him that he had to bring his idea to realization and to a concrete and effective form . . . [T]here was that same interweaving of a sense of structure with function, and a sense of philosophy that still kept him on the ground of concreteness . . . He was a man who to a rare degree combined imagination and action.[10]

At the top of Ohayo Mountain Road, in the old house formerly occupied by the quarryman Alec Bonesteel, the Alfeo Faggis lived during the 1920s with their son Giannino (who later anglicized his name to John). It was here that Faggi made some of his finest pieces of sculpture, working in the one-hundred-and-fifty-year-old barn that stood across the road from the dwelling. Subsequently he built his own home and studio in the woods along Plochmann Lane. He was born near Florence, Italy, in 1885 and his initial appreciation of plastic work came at the age of six when at a puppet show he noticed a small figurine of a man playing a flute. He became so enamored of this trinket that he could not resist the impulse to take it. Handling that figurine awakened his passion for creative art, but his conscience destroyed his pleasure and in obedience to his mother's command he returned it to its owner. His father was a fresco painter and gave the boy lessons in drawing; after a few years this was followed by study at the Accademia di Belle Arte di Firenze. He rented a little hole vacated by a shoemaker, and this became his studio. For the next five years he attended life classes and visited museums—meanwhile winning the three highest medals at the Accademia.

While studying an early Michelangelo sculpture at the Casa Buonarroti, Faggi was told by an aged guard that the master said "the artist should represent things not as they are but as they ought to be."[11] These words pronounced by an elderly caretaker were a revelation to Faggi of the true field of art—the realm of the imagination. Toward the end of his studies in Florence he began to understand the inner significance of primitive Christian art and it was from this comprehension that his genius sprang.

There is a story about a beggar woman who came to the house of Faggi's parents and read Alfeo's fortune. She predicted that he would make a name for himself in sculpture but that this would not happen until he went to America. The prediction came true. He traveled to Chicago, which at first appeared to him as a barren land, but this desert-like atmosphere spurred him on to the fruition of all he had derived from the great masters of Florence. He made a resolution that, freed from traditions, he would work as if he were the first artist under the stars. This determination gave him strength, and within a period of some three years he created his large *Pièta*, now in the Church of St. Thomas the Apostle in Chicago, the St. Francis of Assisi in Wheeling, Illinois, and several lesser works. Soon after the outbreak of the First World War, under the stimulus of deep emotion, Faggi began the *Stations of the Cross*, commissioned by Mrs. Frank Lillie, an early patroness of his sculpture. Work on the *Stations* was interrupted by his service as an officer in the Italian army. He recalls toward the end of the campaign seeing the tragedy in the figure of his general—who stood alone facing the enemy as all his soldiers were fleeing south, because this was the disaster at Trentino. The *Stations* were not completed until after he had settled in Woodstock in 1921. They are probably his most significant achievement, although they caused controversy before being placed in the Church of St. Thomas the Apostle. There is a Giotto-like simplicity to Faggi's work that is particularly noticeable in the *Stations of the Cross*.[12]

Alfeo Faggi has a theory that climate and background are responsible for the encouragement or deterioration of the artistic impulse. He cites Florence, Paris and Woodstock as places where creative imagination is stimulated—but, he adds, the prime qualification for intellectual development is the structural shape of the person's head. He believes that cultural background must fit the temperament; hence the large numbers of mystics in Tibet, intellectuals in Boston and cranks in California! This last comment shows that Faggi has rare insight and a sense of humor.

Faggi is one of the most dedicated artists in Woodstock and nothing is allowed to interfere with his work. He has stripped living requirements to the minimum, particularly since the death of his wife, the musician Beatrice Butler. Now he leads a Spartan life with work and just the inspiration of Dante. Yet at an occasional dinner party he can be an entertaining guest after a couple of drinks and his sudden hearty laugh always carries companions along with his merriment. One evening during a dinner party at Stonecrop he was reminded by Kami, our Siamese, of an experience he had with a cat. It was the day he was taking his wife to a sanitarium and they were walking along the lane when a strange cat appeared, rubbing its back against Faggi's legs and trying to wrap itself around his ankles. "Beatrice told me, 'It is because you are going to be lonely that he has come to be your companion; please keep the cat'." He replied, "If you ask me, I will," and he took the cat home. He observed that the animal had one eye open and one closed, and likewise one ear erect and the other down. Looking at him, Faggi realized the cat was more intelligent than he. However, he said to him, "I not like fleas and though I don't see any fleas maybe you have them, so I feed you but you must sleep outside on the porch. 'Yes,' the cat replied. He stay around for several days and I make drawings of that cat, and then the cat he say, 'You not artist but a business man. I go away now.' Soon he disappear and I never see him again, but I sell all those drawings and he was right—I do business from that cat!"

To my regret I have not kept more notes of Alfeo's remarks. For example, he said, "The spirit whispers, never shouts," "Self-criticism and the creative process must go hand in hand," and "The true artist wrests anew each day against death of the spirit."

During the intermediate years Faggi made several portraits, including one of the Indian poet Rabindranath Tagore. While Tagore was posing he sang melodic poems. At the time a curious incident occurred: Faggi had been given a room at a hotel close to Tagore's apartment, and one day he inadvertently left the key inside and neither the desk clerk nor anyone else who would be able to unlock the door could be found. When Faggi related the misadventure to him, Tagore said, "Do not worry; you will find when you return that the door will be unlocked." And to Faggi's amazement this proved to be true. His sculpture of Tagore shows the great spiritual quality of the Hindu. Another of his portraits was of the Japanese poet Noguchi, whose work is not well known in America. He met Noguchi in Chicago at the home of Mrs. William Vaughn Moody and describes Noguchi's face as resembling ivory smoothed by a thousand years of handling. His modeling of the sensitive face of the poet has overtones of intellectual subtlety that are impossible to describe. Noguchi wrote Faggi that the bust was very well received when hung in the Imperial Museum in Tokyo.

The afternoon I read Noguchi's letter I was sitting in Faggi's orderly little house at a big square table polished to a dark luster; it was a pleasure to feel it under my palms as we talked. He brought photographs of all his important pieces of sculpture to spread around me, and although I had seen most of the originals it was rewarding to study the photographs. Seeing the reproduction of the Whitman figure, which is now in the Buffalo Museum, I asked, "How did you decide to do this statue without clothes?" "Because Walt Whitman was always naked to the world," the sculptor replied. "I had thought about it for a long while until I saw the finished statue outside among the trees and then I could carry it out. Most of my work has come to me like that; after long thinking it suddenly appears to me out in the woods in its final form." The winter afternoon was passing and Faggi turned on the lamps and made coffee as we continued the conversation. He spoke of the Martin Ryersons of Chicago, who had invited him for dinner when he first arrived in America. Fortunately they spoke Italian and Mrs. Ryerson asked him, "How do you like our native oysters?" as these were being served. He replied, "Signora, I find them horrible, like dead mice." Nevertheless the Ryersons remained his good friends, with human understanding and solutions to his problems. "I have been blessed by the people I have known," continued Faggi. "They connect and have helped me in my work."

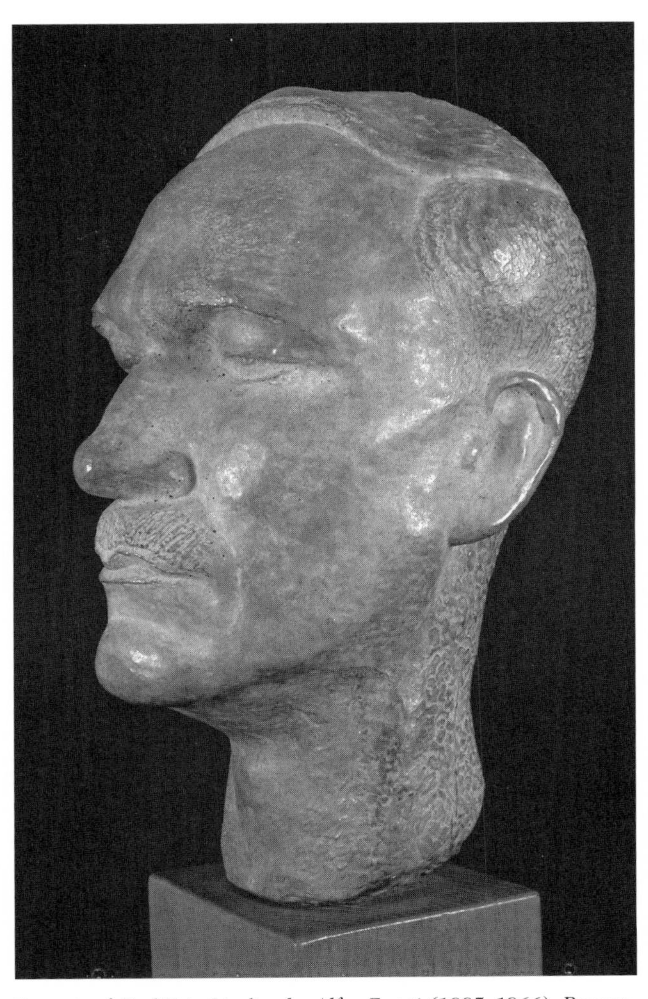

Portrait of Carl Eric Lindin, *by Alfeo Faggi (1885–1966). Bronze cast, n.d.* Courtesy of Woodstock Artists Association Permanent Collection.

There was the sound of bounding footsteps along the path and onto the porch. It was John, his son, come from New York where he is a professor at Columbia University. John is a distinguished-looking man with Italian charm and Yankee forthrightness.

Alfeo Faggi has now returned to modeling the more classical religious themes, which stimulate his creative impulse more than secular subjects. It is a rare spiritual experience to have him show his work in the studio. The odor of wax and metal, plaster and wet cloth dominate the senses. With the solemnity of a priest before a shrine, the sculptor uncovers the pieces one at a time, or pulls from a cabinet one of his drawings. The cool studio light falls upon the bronze or stone, or perhaps an unfinished work in green Plasticine, casting shadows to enhance the design. No form exists for itself but is an integral part of the whole, as one line in a poem is dependent upon another.

Lincoln MacDaniel frowing shingles.
Photo by Konrad Cramer. AMS Collection.

Chapter 11

TALES OF THE UPPER HAMLETS

THE SUGARLOAF MOUNTAIN WITCH AND OTHER CHARACTERS

Shady and Lake Hill

During the 1800s Shady was more densely populated than it is now. The Bristol glass company attracted hundreds of people, some of whom made the window glass that was its chief product, while others supplied the fuel for the factory or "teamed" the sand and the glass back and forth to the Hudson River. Many of the workers' houses have disappeared. For example, there was a row of little homes along Church Hill, one of which belonged to "Aunt" Sophronia Burger, the widow of a glass blower. When the last company failed she was left with a baby and took up sewing, going to live at the houses where she worked. She became a good tailor of men's clothes but also had the reputation of being a great taster when meals were being prepared. Her employers were kind to her and always sent her home with enough food to last the weekend. Hers was the last dwelling to stand on the hill; all that now remains are the few roses that still bloom along the road in June.

Behind the church is a large hall built through the zealous work of the King's Daughters Society. A small group of them sewed and cooked the building into existence. Fortunate were they who ate those old-fashioned church suppers and bought the patchwork quilts that paid for the hall. There was a store in the hamlet, and for years Clark North, who was almost blind, walked there from West Hurley with the mail in a bag slung over his shoulder. During the bluestone era there was a stone dock near the store run by Peter Havey. Later, John Johnson had a smithy and a post office near the store, and the few letters that arrived were kept in a drawer with the horseshoe nails. Bristol also had a gristmill, two sawmills and a turning shop.

A man from Connecticut by the name of Ferguson set up grindstones at the foot of Hutchins Hill beside an outcrop of shale, which he ground to extract red pigment for paint. This product was used locally and I have a sample from a barn at Bearsville, proving its durability. But like so many other projects it did not last and all that remains to attest to Ferguson's ingenuity is the hole in the shale bank; this can be seen at the head of Shady Valley just beyond the old Vosburgh home.

The valley winds and narrows between mountains so high that only the midday sun shines into it. No wonder that, when the name had to be changed (because there was another Bristol in New York State), Shady was the one chosen, but the secondary meaning of the word should have been considered in order to avoid the inevitable quips.

In 1860 James Vosburgh, son of Richard, the glass blower, bought the powder keg shop that had been run by Timothy Colburne and converted it into a turning mill, which is still operated by the Vosburgh family. Originally it was powered by a waterwheel. This was later replaced by a motor but the same precision handwork is required to form the spindles for banisters, posts for beds, and legs for the tables and chairs that the company sells to the furniture store in Kingston with which it has done busi-

Invitation to a picnic at the John Kingburys.
AMS Collection.

ness for three generations. We are told that an expert turner had to learn his profession in youth. The ability runs in certain families in Woodstock, among whom the Vosburghs and Wilburs are the best known. The shop is a fascinating place to visit and watch the spindles whirl. The workers hold their chisels against the spindles with varying pressure to conform to a pattern, while the wood shavings and sawdust stream out, giving off the rich scent of hardwood. The dust covers everything, smoothing the floors and tables and even powdering the heads of the men, creating a haze that catches the light from the many windows. The engine roars, the conveyor belts clap and the chisels hum until the work stops, and then the only sounds are the Sawkill spuming through the race outside and the gentle voices of the turners. They are kindly people, always willing to turn a baseball bat for the neighborhood boys.[1]

The Vosburghs lived in the three last houses in the valley where it narrows and the Hutchins Hill road commences to climb until it comes to an indeterminate end on the top of the mountain. Hikers may be lured further along an old wood road that in the past connected with Mink Hollow. Up this road lived the Roses, old Doc Hasbrouck—who ran a sawmill and fathered innumerable children (so they say)[2]—John Hutchins, and later the Burns family. The Burns farm is about a mile off the main road up a lane that leads to a plateau with open fields and a fine outlook. In recent years this place has belonged to the Kingsburys.

Dr. John Kingsbury was a former commissioner of public charities in New York City and a member of Governor Sulzer's committee that revised the health laws. He was also a member of Governor Roosevelt's New York State Public Health Committee and general director of the New York Association for Improving the Condition of the Poor. During the First World War he was an assistant director of the Red Cross in France and Italy, and later was on the executive committee of the Serbian Child Welfare Association, besides working for numerous other relief organizations. For fourteen years Kingsbury was director and secretary of the Milbank Fund, and it was during this period that he traveled in the Soviet Union—studying the Communist plan for combating disease and managing the aftercare of patients. He admired the Russians and was frankly critical of his own country, which alienated many of his friends. There were other sides of his character that were endearing. One of these was his love of nature. He had made a study of the mushrooms of the Catskills, and in his rambles through the pastures and woods he gathered many species of edible fungus, some of which had previously been considered poisonous. The only party I regretted not having been invited to was a dinner given by the Kingsburys where mushrooms were served with every course and where, for a short period, the lights were turned out and the guests continued the meal under the eerie illumination of fungi.[3]

Kingsbury was president of the Amateur Astronomers Association and the star parties he gave during the season's busiest meteor showers were memorable, especially in the earlier days. The guests would arrive at nightfall with blankets, prepared to lie on their backs out on the terrace all night, watching the stars and counting the meteors that fell. As they watched it seemed as if the bounds of the universe would retreat until they were gazing into space beyond time and comprehension. Each group would watch a section of the sky, counting the meteors, and the total was reported to headquarters in New York City. Dr. Kingsbury would give an informal talk on the night sky, informative but always accompanied by stories of the mythology and poetry of the stars. At one of the star parties the head of the Hayden Planetarium made a presentation. I remember during one special Perseid shower the constellation Perseus was outlined by candles anchored in the swimming pool, adding beauty to the night scene. Kingsbury collaborated with Sir Arthur Newsholme on *Red Medicine* and was the author of several other books. He was a member of the Council of the World Peace Congress and chairman of the American Council on Soviet Relations.

Star gazers setting up camp; John Kingsbury is at left (in knickerbockers). Photo: AMS Collection.

Front of an 1893 brochure for Overlook Mountain House.
AMS Collection.

According to Wigram's map, John Hutchins, for whom the hill was named, had a three-hundred-acre lot that apparently included the present Kingsbury property. In the old days there was a connecting lane from the Hutchins "outroad" east to the old Glass Manufacturing Association's plant. Here, under the mountain, was the village described in chapter 3. Among several families who lived there, the MacDaniels were prominent. Martin MacDaniel is now the only member of his generation left. He remembers the old roads. For example, as a boy he walked a route up to The Plains, the village deserted for over a hundred years, and from there to Echo Lake and beyond to Plattekill Clove. He is familiar with all the woods and streams as well, and also remembers the people of the old times. For years now, Marty and his wife have operated the Cold Spring boardinghouse behind Mead's on the Shady Road, a route that did not exist when he was born. In the summer the boardinghouse is always full of people who return year after year to enjoy hiking, riding and swimming in the mountains. The food is good and it is a cool place to stay, exposed as it is to the winds that blow off Twin and Indian Head mountains.

On a winter's afternoon when the boarders were gone and the farm work was finished, I drove up the steep road to visit the MacDaniels in their comfortable, overfilled kitchen. Marty MacDaniel patiently answered my questions. Occasionally he said something most significant, as when he remarked, "You know, there are tides in the mountains as well as in the sea." It sounded like a line from a poem! He had been speaking of an incident in his boyhood. He had tagged along when the older men had gone coon hunting in the moonlight on Indian Head. There had been a prolonged dry spell, and therefore they were surprised to find a spring bubbling up and overflowing near the Dymond Hollow bear trap. His father told him to go to the house and fetch all the pails and kettles he could carry. They filled all of these, and it was well they did because the next morning they found the spring dry. To this Mrs. MacDaniel added: "Yes, and I've seen it happen to the spring back of this house. All at once on a moonlight night it will rise and overflow for no reason we can see unless it's the pull of the moon."

Martin talked of the two Overlook hotels for which his father had hauled the lumber. After the first one was destroyed by fire, his father provided the wood to rebuild it. He showed me a prospectus for one of the openings, dated June 1874 and listing J. E. Lasher as manager. Among the attractions were "cumulative

On the back of the brochure, Overlook Mountain House can be seen on the ridgeline. AMS Collection.

exercises or health-lift rooms for ladies and gentlemen in the hotel under the charge of an experienced instructor." H. T. Wagner of New York City furnished the music. Alf Evers wrote an interesting account of the recreation and social life of the Overlook hotel for *The New York State Conservationist* magazine. I have another prospectus for the Overlook from 1893 when the hotel reopened under the management of Neal & Company. From what MacDaniel says, I gather that the company was largely in the hands of Ira H. Hasbrouck of Kingston. MacDaniel's sister, later Mrs. Wilbur Cashdollar, recalled that every afternoon when she was a girl they took large cans of milk by buggy to the hotel. On one occasion a bear followed the rig and frightened her "'most to death because the road was too steep for the horse to run on." However, she kept the animal away with flicks of the whip and delivered her milk.[4] As we were talking in the kitchen, MacDaniel's son came in from a hike to Echo Lake. He was very animated because he had seen an enormous wildcat. "It was the largest one I have ever seen!" he said. There is a photograph of one of these bobtailed lynx shot by a member of the Wilbur family. It measured over five feet.

This led to talk of wild-animal adventures recalled by the MacDaniels. Years before, Martin's brother Lincoln had been out on the mountain fighting a fire when, exhausted, he threw himself down to sleep at the edge of the forest. He awoke to find a panther nuzzling him. Keeping still, he realized the panther was covering him with leaves. As soon as the animal left, MacDaniel arose, and after placing a log in the leaves he climbed a tree. Soon the panther returned with cubs, but they were cheated out of their feast. The man remained in the tree until daylight before daring to return home. Martin's father, Nathan, married Louise Taylor from another back-of-the-mountain family. She was a strong girl like her mother-in-law, "Aunt Betsy." Louise was able to saw through a four-foot log without difficulty. While walking to his hay field one morning, Nathan encountered a panther. When the animal advanced toward him he held up his scythe, facing the big cat, and retreated down the mountain backward to eventual safety. All of Louise and Nathan's sons were taught before they were ten years old to handle a yoke of oxen and to draw logs from the woods. Their farm could never support the family through cultivation of the soil alone. Consequently they resorted to the forests—cutting wood for fuel and hauling out logs to the sawmills for planking and making shingles. They stripped hemlock bark for the tanneries and during the Civil War cut alder for the manufacture of gunpowder. After the failure of the Woodstock Glass Manufacturing Company, the MacDaniels moved to farms along the newly opened road between Mead's and Shady; along there were strung out five of their homes.

At the corner where the Fern Hollow Road begins, the one-armed Oscar Howland built his home. It was not an old house at the time I lived in Shady. He came from the Mink Hollow family that were famous hunters, his father having shot fifty bears during his lifetime. For several terms Oscar Howland was tax collector for the town. With one arm he could hoe or shoot a gun with the best of men. He had a large family and eked out a livelihood selling skins and rendering down skunk fat, which produced a cup of fat per animal, worth fifty cents. He also gathered medicinal herbs such as ginseng (Panax), which grew in the mountains under beech and butternut trees. In China it was used for many purposes including as an aid to fertility. It happens that our chipmunks are very fond of the plant's red berries, and it is obvious that the disappearance of the ginseng and the increase in the number of chipmunks are tied together. Howland tried cultivating golden seal and ginseng in his garden. They require lath covering for shade and an exceedingly acid soil. As the seed of the latter takes eighteen months to germinate and two more years to grow to harvest size, it isn't a very profitable crop—especially considering that the roots have to be dried for market and bring only six dollars a pound.[5]

In the old days there was a distillery at Phoenicia where the oil of wintergreen (Gaultheria) was extracted. Gathering the wild berries provided an income for women and children. Mrs. Van Wagner of Willow, who was in her nineties during the early 1930s, told of many home remedies made from the plants of the fields and woods. Arbutus was known as gravel weed because it was used for kidney troubles. "We never thought of it as a flower," she said. Mayapples served as a substitute for calomel, and pennyroyal and sassafras were used to treat croup. She would apply crushed plantain leaves to her children's bruises and make onion syrup for their colds. She said, "There's not a weed that grows which isn't good for something." It was from her I learned the method of making vinegar from maple syrup. Water is added to make it spoil, and when kept in a warm place it will ferment and turn to vinegar.[6]

After leaving the hamlet of Shady, the main route follows the course of the brook that flows from Cooper's Lake. Before the rise of the road, the home of Sidney and Henry Cowell is on the left. They are musicians who settled in Woodstock Township without knowing it was an art center. They had come at Percy Grainger's suggestion to the Williams Band School at West Saugerties. Liking the mountains, they had searched for a house and found this one at Shady. They both belong to those dedicated few to whom the world outside their art is merely a background.

Sidney Cowell was a California concert pianist who studied in Paris with Cortot and later with Bauer. As a student of Ernest Bloch and Henry Cowell, she became interested in folk music. During the Great Depression she worked in the Resettlement Administration to encourage folk music among the new householders. This led her to make a study of the music of various communities among national groups that settled in the United States. The Library of Congress has many of her recordings of the music brought to this country by the Finns, who provided their traditional chants, of the songs of the Portuguese in California and of the Yugoslavs, the Armenians and others. She has probably provided the congressional library with folk recordings from more places than anyone else. She has traveled all around the world with her tape recorder, leading her to adventures in Ireland, the Orient, Greece and Iran.

Sidney Cowell was also interested in Early American hymns. In the Library of Congress she accidentally came across the names of the Edsons, both father and son, of Mink Hollow, who composed hymns over a century ago. This led to a meeting with their descendants, with whom she went on a trip to Mink Hollow to find the grave of Lewis Edson Sr. The descendants could remember only that it was beside a stone wall. Here they assembled, probing and scratching through a century's accumulation of leaves, hoping to locate the slab that marked the grave. With rumps uppermost they were far too intent to notice the irate owner of the farm who had posted himself above them. He was amazed to find this usually quiet corner of his pasture astir with city folks. When he demanded to know what on earth they were up to, the honest answer only added to his disbelief. "A likely story!" he scornfully exclaimed.

However, he did not volunteer any opinion as to what he supposed they might actually be doing. No doubt he thought it was a subversive occupation, and certainly it was sub-something. Unfortunately the search had to be abruptly halted. Subsequently another Woodstocker, Harold Manierre, came forward with a photostatic copy of a rare Edson hymnbook to present to the library. Sidney Cowell trained a choir to sing these hymns at the Shady church.[7]

In the early days of our friendship we invited the Cowells for dinner. After the meal, seated comfortably in an easy chair, Henry Cowell said, "If you will get your recorders we can have music." We did not have recorders, and didn't even know what they were. He later chided me, saying that I could not be very familiar with Shakespeare. That evening he made do by playing shepherd's music on a reed flute. The Cowells enjoyed our flowers, particularly the herb garden. Shortly after one of his visits Henry wrote two compositions for us to whistle while we gardened. These were included in a collection of his work published a few years ago, but they are missing the distinctive instruction that they are to be whistled while gardening.

The first time I heard Henry Cowell play was years ago at the New School for Social Research. It was an exciting experience seeing him pluck the strings, pound the keys with his fists and even go behind the piano to get a particular effect from its innards. His radical departure from conventional composition and playing created a storm of criticism. Yet now his symphonies are played by the great orchestras and his original work is considered a prelude to contemporary American compositions. In his earlier work there was talk of "tone cluster" experiments, and the shrieks of his "Banshee" were the subject of long discussions.

Henry Cowell was born in Menlo Park, California, and raised in San Francisco. He attributes his interest in Oriental music to his early association with Asian playmates. Another influence was a neighbor's fascination with Gregorian chants, an enthusiasm he shared. At eight he abandoned a career as a child prodigy of the violin. At sixteen he began formal training in composition under Charles Seeger. Later he traveled in the Orient and made several trips to Europe—one under a Guggenheim Fellowship to study non-European music in Berlin—and these experiences left their impression upon his music. His world tour was sponsored by the Department of State, the U.S. Information Agency and the Rockefeller Foundation. He has written an enormous collection of all kinds of music, among them some thirteen symphonies. Many of his compositions may be heard on recordings. Aside from the symphonies, his best-known works include the *Persian Set*, recorded by Stokowski and his orchestra, and *Ongaku*, a two-movement piece of Japanese character. Cowell taught at Columbia and at the New School, and for four years was president of the American Composers Alliance. One of his recent achievements was writing the life of the composer Charles Ives, in collaboration with his wife. He was associated with Ives for years and was his chief publisher.[8]

Henry Cowell and Alexander Semmler at Maverick Concert Hall for a performance of their chamber works, circa 1965.
Photo by Jack Weisberg. Courtesy of Historical Society of Woodstock.

Beyond the Cowells' the road comes out of the woods and lies coiled in an *S*, ready to rise up Cooper's Hill. But just before the ascent begins there is a road on the right leading past new cottages and through the fields to one of the older houses. This house lies in a depression of the hills where the rivulets gather the rain and keep the grass green. It was a hundred years old when the artist John Taylor bought it in 1927, and although Taylor has made improvements he has retained its quaint aspect. It still looks like an old farmhouse, with low ceilings above the parlor, dining room and lean-to kitchen. When it belonged to the Lapo family, it is said, thirteen little Lapos were born in the attic.

Musicians, *by Andrée Ruellan. Ink sketch, 8 x 9 in.* AMS Collection.

Now it reflects the taste of its cultured owners. The living room is painted a special tone of pink above the white wainscoting. Upon the walls are small paintings, French in character, that somehow fit in with the simple furniture and rag rugs. This has been the setting for many perfect French dinners cooked by Lucette Ruellan.

John Taylor was born in 1897. He worked under S. MacDonald-Wright in California and Boardman Robinson at the Art Students League, and went to Paris to finish his art studies. While in France he met and married another artist, Andrée Ruellan, and brought her and her mother, Lucette, to his home in Shady. Meanwhile they tore down an old barn and in its place built two large studios for themselves. Here the husband and wife each achieved success in their work and considerable recognition in the world of art. John Taylor received a Guggenheim Fellowship, served as instructor at the Art Students League Summer School, and taught at Pennsylvania State College and at Tulane University in New Orleans. He received the gold medal from the American Watercolor Society in 1949 and a grant from the American Academy of Arts and Letters. He was elected a member of the National Academy in 1958, and his work is represented in many museums throughout the United States. It is interesting to follow his development through various phases of naturalistic painting to his present expression in abstract designs. He will not stop there, because he is constantly experimenting and growing.

Andrée Ruellan was born in New York of French parents. While she was still a child her work was selected to be shown at St. Mark's in the Bowery, where noted artists such as Robert Henri and George Bellows were exhibiting. Naturally this encouraged her ambition. She studied sculpture with Leo Lentelli and drawing with Maurice Sterne. She was fortunate to receive an art scholarship in Rome, and at the end of a year continued on to Paris where she studied with Charles Dufresne and Henri de Waroquier.

She had her first solo exhibition in Paris. After five years in France she returned to the United States with her husband. Since then her studio in Shady has been headquarters, although she has spent many months painting in New York, New Orleans and Paris. She has had nine solo exhibitions and her work is represented in a number of the large museums and art collections. She has received an arts grant from the American Academy of Arts and Letters and in 1950 a Guggenheim Fellowship for creative painting in Europe.

Andrée Ruellan's work shows the subtle humor and delicate insight into character that is both French and feminine. She has said that she believes the artist must go to nature for renewal of his impulse but it is imagination that enables him to dominate his material and to create what is truly personal.

The Sugarloaf Mountain Witch

Three quarters of the way up the Lake Hill road there is a lane leading north and up toward the skyline of Sugarloaf Mountain. The lane peters out when it arrives at the old Van de Bogart house, but there were wood roads in use a hundred years ago leading into Mink Hollow and the Burns farm, which is off the Hutchins Hill road. Once upon a time not far from the Burns house there lived a witch who coveted one of her neighbor's piglets. The neighbor refused to give it up, which so enraged the wicked woman that she bewitched his entire litter until they would do nothing but dance on their noses. The farmer, realizing what had befallen his pigs, was obliged to cut off their curly tails and throw them into the fire. This cured the piglets of their compulsion to dance, but it injured the witch. She was found scratching in the farmer's fireplace trying to save the charred remains of the tails and was badly burned. Thereafter she limped around with one misshapen foot upon which she wore three socks. Otherwise she was a comely person who married and had a family, but she would never give up her bad practices and even boasted about her powers instead of being ashamed of them. One man, who if he were living now would be over a hundred years old, remembered seeing her and described her to me. "She was a short woman with black hair and bright eyes and a complexion white as snow." On more than one occasion she was tested with a three-cent piece, and it was found that if a broom were laid across the threshold of a door it would bar her entrance. She had special magic words she used such as "Pocks E'Rollins," and whoever heard her utter these words was sure to fall upon evil experiences unless he or she resorted to the services of a witch doctor.

One of the most famous witch doctors was Doc Brink of Lake Katrine. I may use his name because his grandson, Theodore Brink, readily confirmed the man's practice—even describing the simple herb remedies he used to cure his patients. The old doc used cathartics and carminatives as well as mumbo jumbo to exorcise the evil. He was careful never to demand a fee out of respect for the law, though he did not refuse gifts of eggs or meat. He held to the belief that to be efficacious the salves had to be made from water running *with* the stream, not against it. Theodore showed me a hand-blown bottle in which his grandfather kept the wash for sore eyes and told me it had to be made of snow water from the last fall of the season.[9]

This witch had a granddaughter, the lovely Dianthe with whom Enoch Purdey kept company, notwithstanding the witch's disapproval. The Purdeys lived on the lane in the house later owned by Hercules Davis. One afternoon Enoch set out to visit his girl, feeling reasonably sure Dianthe would accept his proposal of marriage. However, there were obstacles to their romance that were beyond his ken. The first problem was to find a few minutes to speak to the girl in private, because the grandmother contrived to have members of the family with them throughout the afternoon. When it was time to do the evening chores, the witch, accompanied by the other children, was obliged to go to the barn to do the milking and other tasks, and this gave Enoch his opportunity. Immediately he began his impassioned plea, but the words were left hanging on his lips by the loud and untimely crowing of a cock just outside the door. It jolted Enoch out of his romantic mood, and each time he brought the conversation around to the subject of marriage the cock would begin to crow. The suitor was completely baffled, and as night was approaching he reluctantly bade farewell to the beautiful Dianthe. When he opened the door he found a white cock on the threshold, staring at him with its beady eyes. In a fury he gave the bird a mighty kick, which sent it flying off. The crow was unhurt but the youth was left with a bruised toe. The sore spread up his leg and eventually caused his death. Doc Brink was called in to see the wound but could not cure it—yet he refused to accuse the witch lest he incur her wrath. Thus ended the romance of Dianthe and Enoch.

Enoch's father was Gilbert Purdey, whose near neighbor was John Rowe. The two men had married Eighmey sisters but they were continually in disagreement. According to my informant, old Justice Sickler, who was born in 1857 and knew of these people, Rowe did not have "much principle and Purdey was hot-tempered." (The town records of 1845 show that one James Bogardus received a judgment for damages against John Rowe but do not state what the damages were.) The quarrel between Purdey and Rowe was aggravated by the six sets of bars that had to be let up and down on the lane to keep their cattle confined to their pastures.

Mrs. Purdey was expecting a child and one winter's day Gilbert went off with the oxen to fetch the "granny woman" who lived at Shandaken. He was in such a hurry that he neglected to replace the bars and when he returned he discovered that Rowe had put them back and nailed them in place. Purdey took his ax and shattered them into kindling. There is no record of the baby's arrival, but the quarrel that developed has never been forgotten. Both families were members of the Methodist Church in Little Shandaken (now Willow), and a church trial was held there with Barnett Eighmey as moderator. During the trial the reliability of each man's word was questioned.

To prove that his opponent did not tell the truth, Rowe brought up an old argument about a dog. One of the Riseleys, who lived in the gristmill house at Bristol, claimed that his dog had been shot. Rowe said Purdey was guilty, which Gilbert denied. Rowe

William Cooper summer sleighing. Photo: AMS Collection.

tried to prove the deed had been done by Purdey: pointing to the remains of the dog, he indicated it must have been shot with Purdey's gun. Purdey claimed he had bought the gun from Rowe after the dog had been killed. The fight about the dog became so heated that the original cause of the trial was forgotten. The inquest continued for a long time. Eventually Purdey was persuaded to say he was sorry for his anger, but Rowe refused to admit as much and the preacher suspended him from church for six months. Subsequently Rowe left the church, with many members of the congregation following. He brought to Little Shandaken a Wesleyan preacher named Lowerie, who established another church that was built a mile east of the Methodist one. This is the little white church on the corner of Mosher's Lane that stands out so starkly from the hill with its tower cocked skyward. For years it was called the Dog Church.[10]

In 1847, according to a paper in the possession of Philip Van de Bogart, an agreement was signed by Gilbert Purdey, John Rowe and Martin Booth to open and maintain the road that ran between the Cooper and Booth properties and those of Purdy and Rowe. It was fully sixteen years later that this agreement was attested to before A. Elwyn, Town Clerk. The matter had been kept boiling for many years![11]

Most of the hamlet of Shady is in Great Lot 26 of the Hardenbergh Patent, but Great Lot 25 begins at the foot of the road to Lake Hill. This was the property of Benjamin Faneuil, a merchant from New York City. Later it was owned in succession by James Desbrosses and John Hunter. Desbrosses sold lots on perpetual leases to various local people, including Jeremiah Reynolds and Thomas Treadway Smith. Each deed stipulated that the purchaser pay annually a quitrent of one shilling per acre in Spanish milled dollars valued at eight shillings per U.S. dollar. In 1794 Smith acquired his tract, which included 157½ acres known as the Lake Farm. For a while the glass companies held title to this property, but in 1842 the farmhouse was being run unprofitably as a tavern by John Winne. At this time William M. Cooper, traveling as a salesman, stopped there overnight and, liking the place, decided to purchase it on lease. Eight years later, after the anti-rent rebellion, he was able to buy the property outright from Elias and Ann Hunter. Later still he extended the farm across the pond, then known as Shandaken Lake, and acquired the water rights.[12]

The Jacob Cooper family first came to Woodstock in the 1820s and settled in Yankeetown, now Wittenberg. Jacob had been a colonel in the War of 1812. The town records show that he was an overseer of highways and in 1833 was elected a justice of the peace. His son, William M. Cooper, married Catherine Eltinge, left Wittenberg, and later returned to settle his large family in Lake Hill. According to his grandson, Ashley Cooper, besides farming he ran a sawmill, the tavern, the post office and a store. When the plank road was built, the Cooper family also operated the tollgate.[13] In recent times the City of Kingston bought the lake for its water supply and removed the barn that was across the road from the house. I wept when the barn was destroyed because, like poetry, the barn was beautiful in line and color and as rhythmical as the surrounding mountains. I was able to salvage only a few of the rafters, which are now incorporated into my stone house. The barnyard was almost surrounded by buildings weathered silver gray, their sagging roofs of different heights, their forms pushed crooked by the winter gales until they seemed to be bowing toward each other in a crazy dance. The hand-hewn timbers, carefully pegged, might lean but they would never break from the storms. They could have stood for another century, protecting the yard, which in the sun at noon was like a steaming bowl. Here the cattle wallowed knee-deep in manure, the chickens scratched around for grain and the smell was rich with the essence of the farm. Inside, the barns were impressive, with huge rafters aloft in the dim light—and the beams below were fourteen inches thick. Above the stables someone had tacked illustrations of buxom ladies in tights—the kind of pictures given with chewing tobacco. Here in the bay of the barn was the sweetish odor of hay and grain. The soaring rafters and the great height created a feeling of awe, as in a cathedral.

The house has double-decker porches from which doors lead into halls with comfortably large rooms on either side. On the ground floor are the parlor and the room that formerly held the bar. Behind this is a spacious kitchen painted Dutch blue. Mrs. Hannah Cooper Vosburgh has written of her life on the farm as a girl. She tells of the quilting bees and of the big dinners during the butchering when the neighboring men gathered to help with the work outside while within the women made sausage and headcheese. She writes of the husking contests when a boy lucky enough to find a red ear could choose a girl to kiss. In the fall the barn would be cleared for the harvest dances and she recalls the fiddling of Kit Lindsley. After the square dances sweet cider and pumpkin pie would be served.[14]

It was forty-five years ago that I made my first sketch on that farm. My work was engrossing and I paid no heed to the hour or the thought of a five-mile walk back with my gear. The farmer had done his evening chores and had long since carried the milk across the road when he returned with a glass of milk for me. It was Ashley Cooper, concerned because I had not eaten. He invited me into the kitchen where I met his wife, Jessie Van de Bogart Cooper, and thus began a friendship that lasted as long as they lived. I bought a lot and built a studio on their farm. Ashley Cooper proved to be the kindest of men and whenever there was a storm he would tramp up the hill to make sure all was well. Mrs. Cooper taught me how to live in the country without any of the modern conveniences. Every movement of her trim body was efficient; that

Old Man of Cooper's Hill, *by Anita M. Smith.*
Block print: AMS Collection.

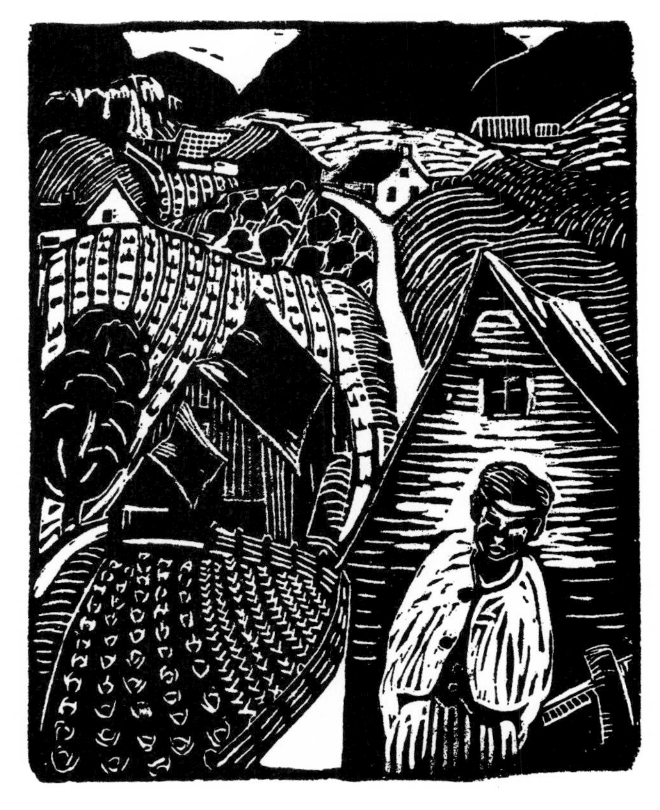

The Return of the Wilbur Family. *Primitive watercolor by Helen Ophelia Howland showing the Mink Hollow homecoming of Mr. and Mrs. Rufus Reno Wilbur after a sojourn in New York City.* Photo: AMS Collection.

is why she could always spare a few minutes for reading to keep her mind alert. The cellar was her refrigerator, an outhouse served for plumbing, and the water was hand pumped from a well and brought in by the pailful. On the stoop her blonde head might be seen above the blue chum, paddling the golden butter in a wooden bowl or preparing the vegetables. Occasionally she would look beyond the wash bench in the maple shade and through the gray-limbed apple trees to the last dip before the ground fell away to disclose the valley. She was never indifferent to nature; between her and her environment there was peace, and in that lay her strength and her charm.

Many years ago there lived a farmer along the Little Shandaken road who believed he had worked harder than anyone else in the region. By the end of the summer the hay and grain that was packed into his barn was valued at six hundred dollars and he was very proud of this accomplishment. One Sunday in the fall it became this farmer's turn to entertain Dominie Waters for dinner. The dominie told the farmer he had "no call" to be over-proud of his crops because the Lord had provided the sunshine, sufficient rainfall and the fine haying weather that had made the bumper crop possible. Then he called upon the farmer to give thanks to the Lord for his success. The farmer replied that it had been his work, not God's, that had filled his barn to overflowing and that he was beholden to no one.

It was a beautiful day without a cloud in the sky but in mid-afternoon suddenly a thunderhead reared over Mount Tobias. It stayed compact and ominous as it moved to the center of the valley and hung above the proud man's farm. As the neighbors watched, a ball of fire descended from the thunderhead and dropped plumb down upon the barn, reducing it to ashes. Ben Lane, his wife and many others testified to seeing this happen.[15]

The Mink Hollow road runs from Lake Hill along the Beaverkill almost to the Greene County line. A hundred years ago this area was well populated but now most of the houses have been torn down to protect the City of Kingston's water supply. There are no longer families living there by the names of Howland, Edson, Gridley, Mosher or Sickler, and there is but one family of Wilburs left.

There used to be a sawmill near the upper bridge in Woodstock but it burned down in a thunder and lightning storm around 1916. It was called Sully's Mill although it had been built by Ulysses Boice. It was sold to that interesting character Dan Sully, who with his wife spent his last years at what is known as the Mill Stream Farm. Sully was a comedian of considerable reputation when he married Louise Arzula Dulaney (herself an actress) from a family who lived in Mink Hollow. In that remote valley they would return to rest between engagements and to invest their savings in real estate.

Mrs. Sully's mother had taken for a second husband Charles Fox, who was a circus clown before he acted in vaudeville, and his wife became a bareback rider in the circus. Other members of the family were a nephew, Wilbur Crane, who was an actor in the movies and later a director, and his sister, Edith Crane, who married an actor named Frederick Tyrone Power. But all these people are long since gone from Mink Hollow. Years ago a neighbor told me that when Mrs. Fox retired there was such a gay aura regarding her career (at any rate in the thoughts of the village bucks) that at night she was obliged to take pot shots at the loiterers outside her windows. A niece of the Sullys' is Mrs. George Wilbur, who was taken by them when she was two years old to be the baby in one of their acts and remained with the troupers, touring the whole country in one-night stands until she was sixteen. At that point she reversed the usual process, becoming disillusioned by the stage and marrying a wood turner. As there was no suitable place for rehearsals in Mink Hollow, Sully, who had a fine pair of sorrel horses, would drive his troupe down to the Methodist Hall in Woodstock where there was space for them to work. Mrs. Wilbur remembers the Sullys when they had sold their holdings in Mink Hollow and were at the Mill Stream Farm. Here in the barn they rehearsed the country comedies, which were often written, at least in part, by Dan Sully. Mrs. Will Elwyn, in her "Gay Nineties" recollections, describes the Kingston Opera House when it had a fine auditorium and was filled with well-dressed audiences; she recalls seeing Dan Sully there, acting in a play he had written about Woodstock village life.[16]

The road over the clove to the higher Catskills was in use at the time of the Revolution. Several Tories were known to have fled through there to avoid capture by the Committee of Safety and Observation, which was rounding up British sympathizers, and they became the first settlers in Hunter Township. In 1921 I drove the last carriage to go through the clove when the road was scarcely more than a freshet run. It was too rough for me to keep seated in the buggy, and, at great peril from the vehicle careening behind us, I guided the horse from the ground by the reins as he plunged down the mountain. Soon after that the bridge over the Beaverkill was washed away and the road became a trail.

This path through Mink Hollow was a favorite hike for one of the Catskill Mountains' best-known poets, Bliss Carman. He was born in Canada but for many years spent his summers in a slab-bark cabin in the woods above Kaaterskill Clove. He wrote many poems showing his love for the mountains, among them "The Mountain Gateway." He was a tall man

At Michaelmas, *a lyric written in 1895 by Bliss Carman (1861–1929).* AMS Collection.

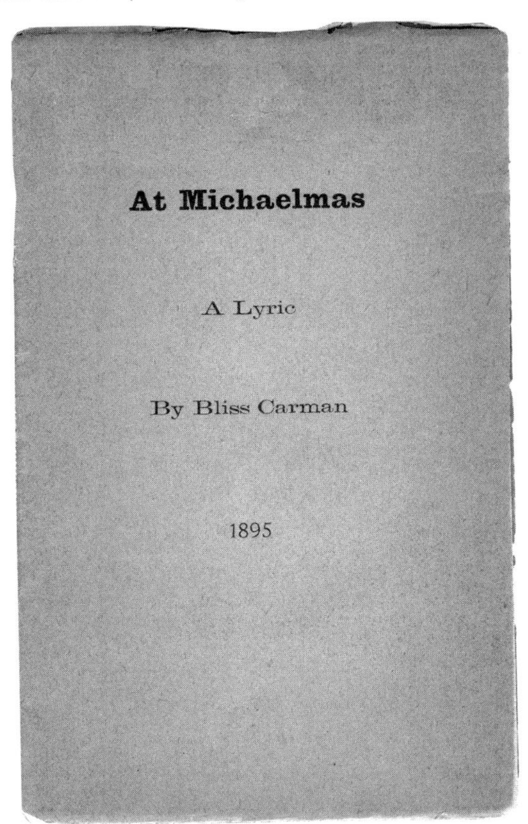
At Michaelmas

A Lyric

By Bliss Carman

1895

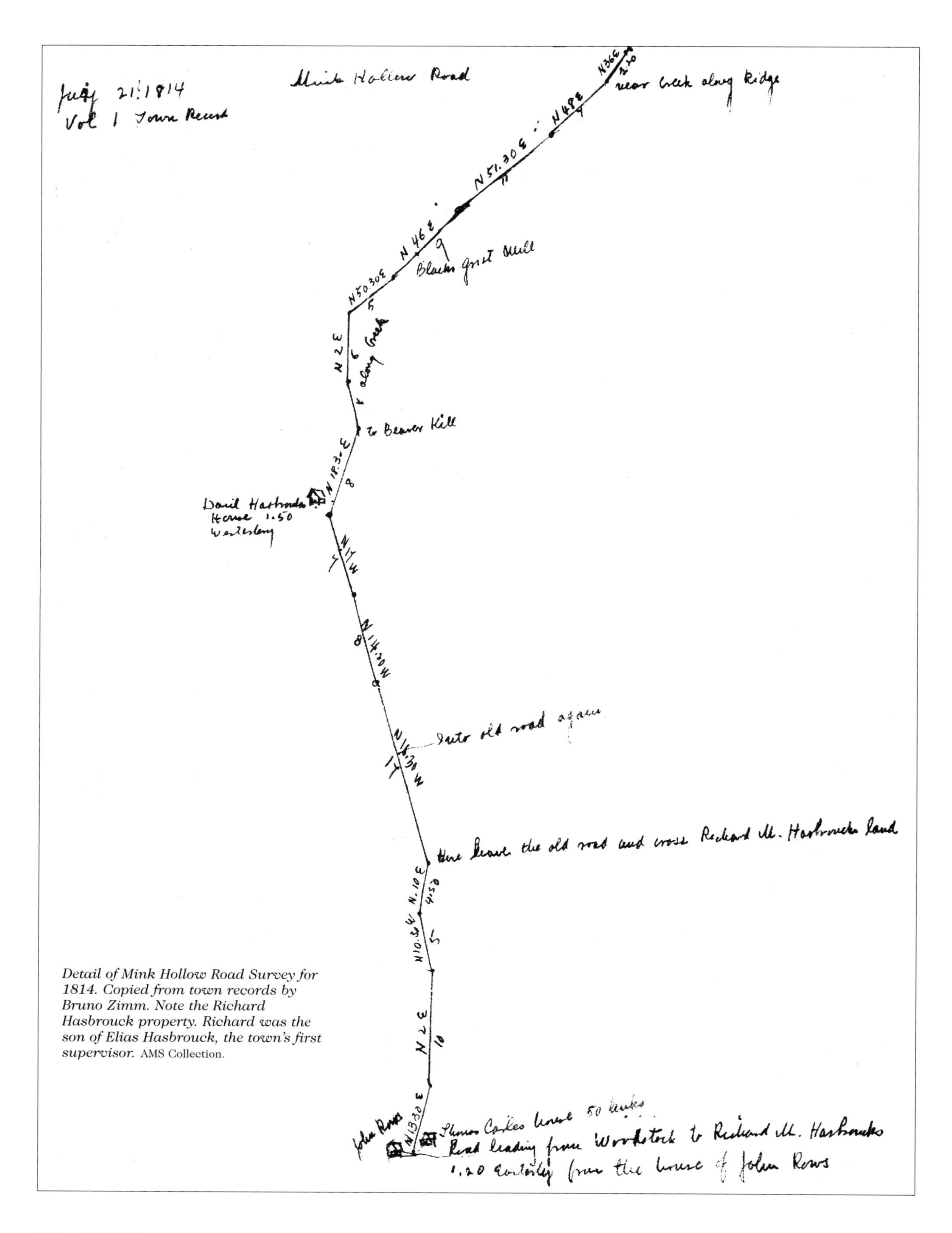

Detail of Mink Hollow Road Survey for 1814. Copied from town records by Bruno Zimm. Note the Richard Hasbrouck property. Richard was the son of Elias Hasbrouck, the town's first supervisor. AMS Collection.

with long hair combed flat to his head, heavy-lensed eyeglasses and a gentle smile inviting friendly conversation. Sometimes when he tramped through Mink Hollow he would be going to visit his friend, the English writer Richard Le Gallienne, who lived in a cottage on the Daily place. The latter was as tall as Carman but his fine head was capped with graying curls and he was not easy to approach. Le Gallienne, probably for greater privacy, moved from Byrdcliffe to Mink Hollow. He would occasionally be seen stepping silently along the mountain paths as only a hunter or a lover of the forest would. He seemed ever ready to absorb the beauty of the wild places, and he shared with Carman an understanding of the Catskills. He wrote an essay on Woodstock printed in the first catalog of the Art Association. It was written with charm but unfortunately provided only a fragment of the story of our town.

Bliss Carman was known as the "unofficial Poet Laureate of Canada." While in Woodstock he became a good friend of the writer Richard Le Gallienne. Photo: AMS Collection.

About half a mile from Route 212 on the Mink Hollow road there stands one of the oldest houses in Woodstock Township, built soon after the Revolution by Elias Hasbrouck. In that period this locality was the most populated section of Woodstock and it was here that the first town meeting was held in 1787. Elias Hasbrouck was elected supervisor; John Row, town clerk; Petrus Short, Samuel Mowers and William Snyder, assessors; Petrus Row and Samuel Mowers were made constables; Zachery Short, collector; Andries Riselar and Bement Lewis, overseers of the poor; Petrus Short, William Snyder and Hendrick B. Krom, commissioners of highways; and Aurey Newkerk, John Karl, Hendrick B. Krom and John Longyard, overseers of highways.[17]

The grandson of one of the Huguenot founders of New Paltz, Elias Hasbrouck was born in 1741. He became a merchant in Kingston, with his place of business as well as his home near the corner of Main and Wall streets. When the Revolution began, Hasbrouck was one of the first patriots in Kingston to sign the Articles of Association. In 1775 he received a commission as a captain of the line in the Third Regiment. He recruited his own company and led it to Albany, where they became part of the American army under General Richard Montgomery and marched under him to Montreal. From there Captain Hasbrouck was ordered back to Ulster County and was appointed Captain of the Scouts and Rangers, guarding the frontier, which included Ulster County. He was one of the few soldiers who tried to defend Kingston when it was burned by the British General Vaughan. He sometimes served as quartermaster, supplying food to the French as well as the American armies along the Hudson River.

Although his house had been burned by the British soldiers, Hasbrouck tried to re-establish his business in Kingston after the war. However, by 1787 he had moved to Little Shandaken, where he built himself a home and farmed the land. The exterior of the house has been changed to stucco but the old outlines remain and much of the interior is believed to appear as it did a hundred and seventy years ago. Captain Hasbrouck died when he was fifty, and he and his wife, Elizabeth, are buried in a little cemetery on the east side of the entrance to Mink Hollow. A lane has been run across his grave but the stone was reset a few yards away. Here, quite neglected, is the grave of our first town supervisor and a most distinguished early citizen.[18]

France Forever

BASTILLE DAY CELEBRATION

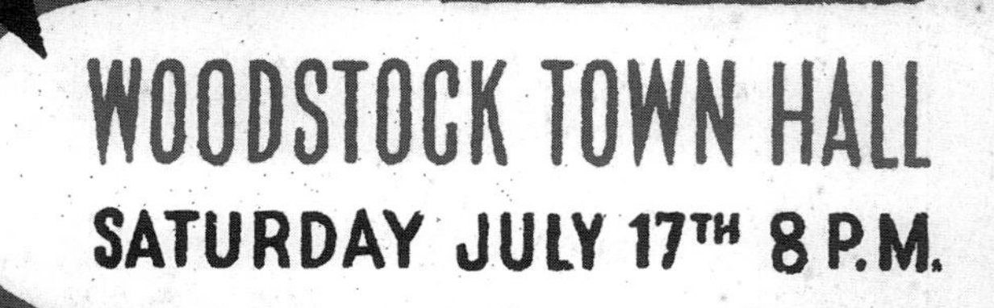

TICKETS 55¢ ON SALE AT WOODSTOCK 5 AND 10

Poster for the Woodstock chapter of France Forever. This Bastille Day celebration took place on July 17, 1943. AMS Collection.

Chapter 12

THE SECOND WORLD WAR

THE COMMUNITY UNITES TO LEND A HELPING HAND

In September 1941 there was a spectacular display of northern lights that hovered in the sky above Woodstock and up and down the Hudson River Valley. The pulsating streaks of fire were a magnificent sight, but awe-inspiring like an omen; those watching spoke in strange tones or just looked at each other as if made mute by the eerie light. There was a tendency to seek one's friends or neighbors to watch and wait together. There were rocket-like projections and waving flags of gold and silver and bands of light in rainbow hues. One person discerned a giant *V* of fire, another an eagle. The patterns continually changed as the flames leaped and fell and gathered into fiery tongues that licked the sky. The tension increased as if electric currents were being discharged upon the earth beyond man's ability to absorb. These fireworks continued far into the night—disrupting radio reception and, according to the telephone company, slightly affecting their service. Nobody could recall a greater display of northern lights in this locality.[1] Perhaps it was a foreshadowing of the war years for Woodstock.

Dr. James T. Shotwell, former professor of history at Columbia University and Woodstock's most distinguished citizen, had the idea of recording the war activities in this village. He came to me with a plan for collecting the war records—and that plan developed eventually into this book.

This chapter tells the story of our village, a tiny fragment of America in the Catskill Mountains, and how it met the emergency of the Second World War. Now that it is over and the reckoning added up, I think we can be proud of Woodstock.

One of the first drives took place several months before Pearl Harbor, when Thomas Carey and Carl Eric Lindin went into action to secure funds for the United Services Organization. In all the years he lived in Woodstock, Lindin never spared himself, and soon after this drive he joined the Ration Board. There he overworked himself to such a degree that it contributed to his death in November 1942. Another drive for the USO took place the next year, and one of the events was a talk on Mallarmé given by Werner Vordtriede at Alice Wardwell's studio. The total raised was $1,018, which exceeded Woodstock's quota.[2]

In 1941 many Woodstock men volunteered for service. There is no list available of these boys but there were many who did not wait to be drafted. Among them were the seventeen-year-old Pierpoint twins, Bill and Charles, who joined the Navy; Caleb Milne, who became an ambulance driver in the American Field Service and was sent to the British Eighth Army in North Africa; his brother, Aubrey Milne, who became a Paratrooper; Clifford Wells, who went into the Navy; Walter Sarff, who, as an artist, was assigned to Camouflage; and John Faggi and Bob Carlson, who were assigned to a Cavalry unit that was stationed at Fort Devens before being sent overseas to take part in the Normandy invasion. The first of our young men to go into combat was Buddy Striebel, who went to Canada to join the Royal Canadian Air Force; after intensive training he was sent to England and then to Malta, where as a pilot he took part in many missions, distinguishing himself and receiving numerous medals before being transferred to the U.S. Air Force in 1943.[3]

On December 7, 1941, the Civilian Defense was activated in Woodstock. Albert Cashdollar had been made head of the Ulster County organization and Martin Comeau was appointed director in Woodstock. Offices were opened in the Comeau Building, and here a twenty-four-hour telephone watch was maintained—in readiness to alert the town in the event of an emergency. This came under the supervision of the minister, Reverend Todd. It was a tiresome job but the room was warm and reading and writing were permissible. The American Legion and the National Youth Administration boys volunteered, in addition to many other citizens. An emergency police organization was set up, headed at first by Theron Lasher and later by Allen DeLano. A station wagon was outfitted as an ambulance and many other disaster precautions were planned. Fire Chief Murphy came from Kingston to instruct the volunteer firefighters, who were led by Reggie Lapo; food experts arrived to lecture on the preservation of foods; and an inhalator was secured. When an alert was sounded most of these departments turned out with their armbands hastily pinned on and began to patrol the roads, to stop traffic and exert their authority to have all lights extinguished. There were frequent test blackouts when the siren would give its ominous wail. It was amusing to find our local artists, who made up the bulk of these brigades, directing traffic or tapping authoritatively upon doors to warn householders to turn off their lights. Some of them felt very important, some did the job wishing they could do more and some felt just plain silly in their armbands.[4]

Isabel Doughty headed the Red Cross unit, which was prepared to deal with all forms of health crises. It had two hundred and thirty active workers, including two doctors and eight trained nurses, as well as trucks registered for immediate duty. In the early days Dr. Cohn held classes in first aid at the firehouse. These lessons were difficult and by the time everyone had passed the advanced course they had reason to be proud of their certificates. Occasionally there would be an alert with a simulated disaster to be faced and some poor dumb souls would have to pretend to be burned or have sustained a fracture and allow the "experts" to manhandle them. However, it was dramatic as the siren with its banshee howl started things going, sometimes with the fire engine clanging its way to the designated spot, followed by the ambulances that carried the "victims" to headquarters where doctors and nurses waited. The citizenry were never quite sure whether or not it was the real thing.[5] Alice Wardwell was appointed chief of Social Services for Evacuees, a job that did not materialize.[6]

Charles and William Pierpoint. Charles was lost on the USS Meredith *during the Battle of the Coral Sea.* Photo by Stowall Studios. AMS Collection.

Alice Henderson headed the Housing Division of Civilian Defense. It began with a survey for the evacuation of children from New York City. Ben Webster made a large-scale map of Woodstock, and within a couple of weeks a corps of volunteers had visited every house in the township (covering approximately thirty-six square miles) and had ascertained how many children could be accommodated on each premise. A minimum amount of money was to be allowed for the children's food, but this would not begin to cover all the expenses involved in caring for them. It would entail real sacrifice on the part of the householders. In this survey the artists did not show up as being very generous. It was the homes where there might be several children already that would sign up for the most evacuees. In each of the seven school districts there was a committee appointed to receive and distribute the evacuees to their new homes. Miss Henderson never forgot that Wittenberg was the first district to telephone headquarters announcing it was prepared to accommodate more than a hundred children. Under the leadership of Mrs. Viehmann, Mrs. Van De Bogart, Mrs. Everett

Cashdollar, Mrs. Griggs (a trained nurse), Mrs. Hegner (who collected clothes) and others, a detailed plan was set up, ready to be activated at an hour's notice. A short time later a rehearsal was held in which the schoolchildren from Zena were taken to Wittenberg.

The children from the Zena School were to pretend they were evacuees from New York City. Each child had his or her name and address pinned on—except for two little ones who were to make believe they had lost their tags and could not remember their names. The young people played the game all the way to Wittenberg, pretending to be city children who had never seen the country before: "Is that a cow?" "I never saw a cow before." "I know how to milk a cow; you pump the tail up and down!" This was followed by shrieks of laughter.

Wittenberg lies in the valley, where there is an old mill, one store and a bumpy road coming finally to the church and school. As they drew near the church, men wearing Red Cross bands were standing in the road to help them park. They got out feeling solemn and shy. There was a reception committee, and the chairperson was at a table at the foot of the altar. She sat with her lists and her index file and an imaginary telephone. She had four assistants. Over at one side was a trained nurse in a white coat with a first-aid kit. It was she who had taught the Wittenberg women how to handle the youngsters: If they are nervous, you massage their necks just a little as you help them take off their coats. You hold their hands when you welcome them, to determine if they are hot or cold. You tell them you want to look down their throats to see how empty they are. She impressed the women with the need to be very quiet but to assure the children that they were most welcome. She said that little children show shock in various ways, some by being noisy and silly, some by crying or shivering, and some by just smiling at you and not speaking at all, and these were the ones a grown-up must stay with and watch most carefully.

The children (there would be eighty for Wittenberg in the event of a real evacuation) were put into pews and taken a few at a time to the desk where their names were checked. The women played along just as seriously as the children did:

"Was the trip a long one?"

"Have you a brother or sister? We want to keep the families together."

"We're so glad you've come. We hoped you'd come up here if New York had any trouble."

The chairperson pretended to telephone: *Ding ding!* "This is Wittenberg calling Miss Henderson. I wish to report that the children have arrived. We have one who is not on our list and two who have lost their tags. We will hold these children until we have further information."

Then they went upstairs—one of those old-time church social rooms with a kitchen leading off it, a long white room over the old carriage shed. On the floor along the walls were beds; the men of the village had made them out of lumber, just wooden frames with wire springs and bedding. The children ate, and there was no pretending about this! There were cookies and cocoa at long tables covered in white. While they were eating, a local character named William Spanhake played his accordion. He was very tall and skinny and redheaded. A former barber who had been on the *Titanic*, Spanhake also volunteered to cut the children's hair. First he played "The White Cliffs of Dover" and the children sang along. While they were singing the women walked around the tables with their cards and tried to decide which would be the best home for each child (getting a little acquainted with the children without their being aware of anything).

Then a man arrived to call for his guests. He had just been notified that they were ready. He was to take three. They stood over in a corner and shook hands. He said, "We sure are glad you came. We got a cow and you can help milk her if you want to. Let's go home and see her." So they went out. Then a lovely big country woman stood up. (This had not been planned.) She said, "I'll take the last four children—don't make any difference what they are, boys, girls or both; I want the ones that's been left 'til last."

The ladies asked the bus drivers to come and have coffee and doughnuts while the children sang songs. They sat down at the long table and wanted Miss Henderson to tell them how she thought it had gone. One of them said, "Our hearts are in it. We want it to be just right!" Another said, "Of course it won't be as easy as this when they really come, but we ought to know what to do, no matter what."[7]

Alice Henderson said she was proud of them and particularly liked the way they had learned to be so quiet and happy about everything. She said that of course they were wondering if the children were really coming, but that was not their job at all; their job was to be ready. She wished the mothers in New York could see this—they would be so comforted if the time came when they had to send their children away.

The above is taken from an account I wrote to friends in New York, who then told *Life* magazine about it. In consequence the whole rehearsal for evacuees was done over again before *Life*'s photographers. The story was never published, however, because the government did not wish to frighten the population of New York City.

The Woodstock Observation Post

The Woodstock Observation Post for the Aircraft Warning Service became active when the United States declared war in December 1941. Bruno Zimm was in charge of one of the three posts set up in Woodstock Township. The other two, run by the Legion, were never properly organized and were subsequently closed by the Army. Mr. Zimm found himself alone—responsible for reporting all airplanes flying over the valley. It was midwinter and the people whom he had enlisted to help were unable to get up the mountain to assist him. For over two months he carried on, spending most of the daylight hours on a hilltop where he kept watch while he chopped wood. When an airplane appeared he would rush downhill and within a minute telephone the information to headquarters. At night he slept fitfully with one ear always cocked toward an open window. Mr. Zimm kept his vigil with great patience and courage, until the strain seriously impaired his health. Then, realizing that the setup was not efficient, he applied to the Army to move the post nearer the village.[8]

The Woodstock Observation Post, used for plane spotting in 1942–43, was manned twenty-four hours a day. This drawing by Charles Rosen was turned into a postcard. AMS Collection.

On February 26th the Woodstock Observation Post was relocated to Stonecrop, Rock City, and Anita Smith was appointed Chief Observer under the U.S. Army Air Force First Fighter Command. In the beginning the telephone was placed in a reconditioned tool house and the observers, sitting in a nearby field, would hurry, at the first sound of an airplane motor, to flash their report to the Filter Board in New York City. Teams of instructors were sent by the Army to help recruit personnel and to make the post function better. At first the observers stayed for four hours on duty, but as more help was enlisted this was reduced to two-hour shifts with two persons on duty together. In addition to the Chief Observer, the staff consisted of Allen Cochran, Assistant Chief Observer, and Eugene Ludins, Recognition Officer.

The story of the building of the Observation Post will long be remembered. Everyone on duty contributed pennies, nickels and dimes. Anita D'Costa waved a model plane before the audience at the Playhouse to collect funds. Benefit concerts were given by Clara Chichester, Inez Richards, Engelbert Roentgen, Horace Britt and others. Nelson Shultis, Bruno Zimm, Victor Cannon, Clark Neher, Joe Friedberg and Arthur Wolven brought lumber. The local building-supply companies donated matériel. Nearly every electrician and carpenter in the township, led by Arthur Wolven, gave supplies and a day's work to construct the little building, which was on stilts and had a staircase. Charles Rosen, the well-known landscape painter, and Alexander Peacock, the house painter, helped to paint the exterior. How

U.S. ARMY AIR FORCE
FIRST FIGHTER COMMAND
Aircraft Warning Service
Certificate of Authority

This is to Certify that Observation Post ADAM 51 *of the* NEW YORK *Region, to which this certificate is issued, has been established by authority of the Commanding General of the First Fighter Command, U. S. Army Air Force, and vested with the power and duty to act as a part of the Aircraft Warning Service, in accordance with present and future orders of the First Fighter Command.*

Witness my hand and the seal of the First Fighter Command this 18TH *day of* NOVEMBER *in the year One thousand, nine hundred and forty-* TWO.

REGIONAL COMMANDER

BRIGADIER GENERAL, U. S. ARMY
COMMANDING

Certificate of Authority for Adam 51 (the official name of the Woodstock Observation Post), issued in 1942.
AMS Collection.

BELOW: *Recruitment poster for Woodstock Observation Post.*
AMS Collection.

proud the "spotters" were when their gay little post, painted white with blue trim and a red door, was commissioned by Lieutenant Drum on July 21, 1942. By this time there were over one hundred observers and the post was manned continuously by two spotters.[9] Every week, publicity director Gladys Hurlbut wrote articles under the heading "Looking Up." Usually these were items about the spotters or pleas for new recruits to help on the post. Sometimes she wrote rebuttals of criticism. One of these ended, "How can we forget that some members of the Woodstock colony gave a party to celebrate the fall of Warsaw?"

On June 14th she wrote:

> This was to be . . . gossipy and gay . . . We were going to end with the news that a foundation has been laid for our post. Under the cornerstone is a four-leaf clover. [But] this . . . morning we read about Lidice. When we got to the Post our youngest spotter was on duty. His name is Don Randolph and he is twelve years old. He started as an assistant observer but he was so good he was promoted. He knows more about the planes than most grown ups . . . That morning he stood out in the field, "looking up." He ran to the telephone when he saw [the] planes. His face was very

serious. When his time was up he got on his bicycle and went home. His mother was waiting for him. She had his dinner ready. He was safe.

Lidice was a town in Bohemia as all the sad world knows. There is nothing there now. The homes have been burnt. There are no men. They have all been shot. There are no women. They have been taken to "camps." The children have been placed in "suitable institutions." There is no Lidice today because not one soul would tell if he knew anything about the hero who shot the Nazi hangman, Heydrich.

As Don went home to dinner our village was quiet. Women worked in their gardens. Men went about their business. The mail came in. The little Carey boy ran his fire engine up and down in front of his father's store. It looked like any summer day. But it was not. Something was happening to all of us. A rage was swelling in us as we thought about the children of Lidice crying for their mothers. Woodstock is about the same size as Lidice.[10]

It took real stamina to operate the post throughout the following winter. One night the temperature dropped to thirty-two degrees below zero[11] with a gale blowing, yet the listening window was never closed. The little stove puffed valiantly and showers of blessings fell on those kind friends who, unable to serve themselves, gave fuel. From Kingston came Frederick Snyder to give a dramatic lecture that brought in over a hundred dollars.[12] The town truck brought donations from the Roentgens and the Weyls, and LaMonte Simpkins brought a truckload of logs. The Anderson brothers and Herminie Kleinert sent checks for wood to fill that ravenous stove, and the skies were searched through every kind of weather, all day and all night. Many observers had never before heard the bark of a fox or seen one at midnight race across a frozen patch of moonlit meadow. They listened to the hoot owls and heard the eerie call of a pileated woodpecker, and when summer came they listed all the birds and held a contest to count the repetitions of the whippoorwill. The coldest weather merely strengthened their determination not to fail. Rarely did they skip a night shift, which would necessitate calling out the Chief Observer. Pushing their cars to reluctant starts, sliding over ice and digging through snowdrifts, they came! A couple of times their cars had to be abandoned and they walked miles on foot. Once the FitzPatricks' station wagon slid beyond control and left its owners to seek shelter overnight along the road. One icy day Rhoda Chase was able to arrive for duty only because she had commandeered a mop to help her walk on the ice.[13]

The first attack upon the post was made by mosquitoes, which arrived in the trillions before a smudge pot was set up. Another attack was made by gremlins. Wilfred Bronson took issue with them at once and captured their likeness. He placed in captivity the pictures of the gremlin that blew down the chimney to choke the observers, the gremlin that steered the ax off the kindling block, and the gremlin that glued the firewood with ice and snow. Nancy Chase then captured the gremlin that flew over the mountain making sounds like airplane engines to confuse the spotters. Hung in the Observation Post, these reproductions helped subdue the gremlins. One dawn a strange figure was observed in the herb garden below. Fortunately the sheriff was not notified, for it turned out to be a wonderful female scarecrow made by Lucile Blanch to be auctioned at the Library Fair.[14]

Many of the high-school pupils volunteered for daytime duty. Dick Lapo was the Junior Chief Observer and he brought in many recruits. The youngest spotter was five months old: Pixie, daughter of Marianne Appel and Austin Mecklem. She came on the midnight shift, wrapped as a papoose. She slept peacefully, propped by the stove while her parents were on watch.

One day the Chief Observer found a comic strip tacked on the wall. It was a "Dixie Dugan" strip by J. P. McEvoy and J. H. Striebel. It depicted a fat and bossy CO named Smith, and the observation post was unmistakably our own. It showed a spotter arriving with a child, whom the CO refuses to allow on the post. Just then an airplane flies overhead, which the CO hastens to report but is unable to identify. The child screams, "That's a Boeing B-17 Flying Fortress," which saves the record. The child, Imogene, is then made an honorary spotter by the discomfited CO. The story gave us a hearty laugh. Fritzie Striebel was responsible for the cartoon.

For several months Ruth Downer held the record for the most planes spotted, but Elsie Speicher surpassed her until the Wetteraus took the final lead.[15] Besides the airplane records to be sent weekly to the Army, there was a register on the post. However, as the observers were most articulate it was impossible to keep this book unmarred. Eventually one side of the sheet was kept for comments and there began a

Scarecrow observed outside the Observation Post. This was fashioned by Lucile Blanch and was later auctioned at the Woodstock Library Fair. Photo: AMS Collection.

series of humorous entries. Two old friends who had not met since returning from Paris years before found each other through these pages, and as their correspondence continued the other observers breathlessly followed their weekly notes. Bits of bad poetry soon appeared and caricatures were pinned up on the bulletin board, which started an avalanche of repartee.

VERSE FLIGHT OF ELSIE SPEICHER

Wish to hear "Spot" history?
No longer a mystery.

Full of experiment
(Just full of merriment.)

But with our concentrate,
Three planes we contactate!

High in the sky
We see them fly.

And send our clarity,
Without hilarity,

But hearts that palpitate
To ARMY FLASH 68![16]

Half the people serving on the post had some ax to grind. Religious tracts were left around, and anti-smoking propaganda was discovered in the matchboxes. Many complaints and constant ranting by the CO on the subject of alertness and order were scratched across the pages of the register. One morning she found among the airplane reports to be sent to the Army: "2 a.m., 1 skunk—high—smelled—N.—close!"[17]

The second winter there were stove troubles. It was difficult for the old-timers to realize that the present generation did not know how to keep a wood stove going. Many urged that we get a coal stove, and we were offered one that had been discarded at the Lutheran Parsonage. The problem was that it had to be carted up to the post. One late afternoon when the thermometer was rapidly falling, the CO saw one of the spotters at the corner with his truck. On duty at the post were two husky men and this combination held irresistible implications for the CO. Soon the truck and driver, who had taken a couple of drinks too many, were commandeered. A second reluctant man was lured into the vehicle, and, with the CO fluffed up in a sheepskin coat serving as ballast in the rear, they made a careening passage to the Lutheran Parsonage. Here it occurred to them that there was something unorthodox in their arrival before the minister this Sunday afternoon—even if they were concerned only with the contents of his former chicken coop. However, the minister, himself a midnight spotter, sympathized with their cause. The stove—of the parlor-ornament species—was carried out dripping legs, lids and iron filigree, making dirty marks on the clean snow. Later it was assembled on the post, and after the usual stovepipe cussing it was lighted—whereupon it burned so fiercely it became a hazard to the surrounding walls. Meanwhile the old wood stove was inched out upon the deck with its pipe still attached and the fire from

FLASH MESSAGE FORM

Call your telephone central and say: "ARMY FLASH 68 "
(Give your phone number)
Central will connect you with an Army Information Center.
When you hear: "ARMY, GO AHEAD PLEASE", you say: "FLASH"
and continue message you have checked on form below, in the order indicated:

1	2	3	4	5	6	7	8
NUMBER OF AIRPLANES	TYPE OF AIRPLANES	ALTITUDE OF AIRPLANES	WERE AIRPLANES SEEN OR HEARD?	YOUR OBSERVATION POST CODE NAME	DIRECTION OF AIRPLANES FROM O. P.	DISTANCE OF AIRPLANES FROM O. P.	AIRPLANES HEADED TOWARD
1 (Number) FEW MANY	SINGLE-MOTOR ✓BIMOTOR MULTI-MOTOR	VERY LOW LOW ✓ HIGH VERY HIGH	✓ SEEN HEARD	Adams 51	NW N NE W E SW S SE	4 (Miles)	NW N NE W E SW S SE
					If airplanes were directly over O. P. cover columns 6 and 7 by reporting: "OVERHEAD"		Omit if it will cause delay in report.

5:45

RPB—7-2-41—3,000,000

Plane recognition report for Woodstock Observation Post. This was used to record aircraft sightings for transmission to U.S. Army Air Force Command. AMS Collection.

the dismembered elbow belching wildly into the night. (The CO still maintained that it was a good stove, and from that time on there was coal trouble instead of wood.)[18]

In March 1943, Eugene Ludins was chosen to go to New York at the Army's expense for intensive study of airplane recognition. Having successfully gone through this course, he was made Recognition Officer of the Woodstock Observation Post and came back to instruct the observers. He was a gifted teacher and two nights a week classes were held at the Town Hall. Within two months ninety-six observers were given certificates as qualified Recognition graduates. A second class was held for forty more and when in July the Army ordered them to report the names of the airplanes they were spotting, the observers did an excellent job. There were several who were outstanding in identification and a team was formed to challenge other posts. The Woodstock team consisted of Alma Simpkins, Doris Barclay, Anita Mower, Jack Taylor, Hannah Ludins, Wendell Jones, Konrad Cramer, Elizabeth Carter and Reverend Todd. The only qualification they lacked was an ability to win contests. Other good times were enjoyed when the spotters met for "fish fries" at the Maverick Restaurant. Doris Barclay would play the piano and the Allen Waterouses sang popular songs, while Wilna Hervey and Nan Mason sang and played the guitar.[19]

On October 4, 1943, at eleven in the evening, a call came to the Chief Observer from Captain Patterson confirming General Arnold's radio orders regarding the curtailment of the work of the Ground Observer Corps. Paul Fiene and Eugene Speicher, who were on duty at the Woodstock post, signed off with mingled emotions of relief and regret. The fire was allowed to die out and the little house on posts with the windows open to the sky was left silent and alone for the first time. The CO gathered up the records and made one final midnight tour around the deck before closing the door. Night and day for nearly two years the spotters had kept faith—part of an army of six hundred thousand volunteers guarding the coast of America from sneak attacks.[20]

When the Observation Post was dismantled and the lumber sold, there was $213 left in the treasury. At a special meeting of the observers it was voted to give this money for the pleasure of the young people. Subsequently part of this sum was given to the Woodstock baseball club for uniforms and the remainder spent on games, which were given to the American Legion Post.[21]

In closing this story of the observers it is nice to record the names of those who received medals for serving over two hundred and fifty hours of faithful duty on the post: Louise Bolton, James Carter, Mabel Chase, Allen Cochran, Konrad Cramer, Isabel Doughty, Margaret FitzPatrick, Philip FitzPatrick, Lura Haupt, Julia Leaycraft, Eugene Ludins and Malette Davis Russ. The Chief Observer, Anita M. Smith, served more than twelve hundred hours.

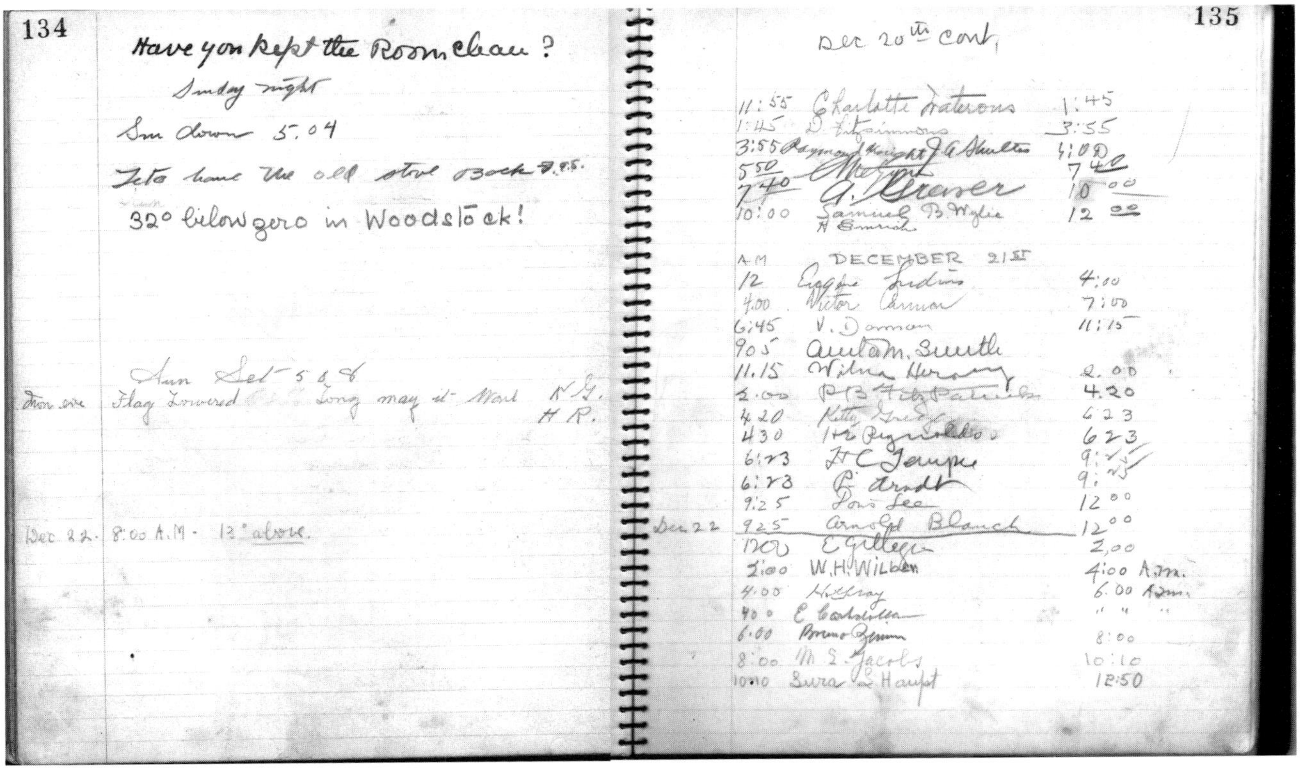

134

Have you kept the Room clean?

Sunday night

Sun down 5:04

[illegible] have the old stove Back [illegible]

32° below zero in Woodstock!

Sun Set 5 [illegible]

Mon eve Flag Lowered [illegible] Long may it Wave N.G. H.R.

Dec. 22. 8:00 A.M. 13° above.

135

Dec 20th cont.

11:55	Charlotte [illegible]	1:45
1:45	D. Fitzsimmons	3:55
3:55	Raymond [illegible] J. A. Shulte	4:00
5:50	[illegible]	7:40
7:40	A. [illegible]	10:00
10:00	Samuel B. Wylie, H. Emrich	12:00

A.M.	DECEMBER 21ST	
12	[illegible]	4:00
4:00	Victor [illegible]	7:00
6:45	V. Damon	11:15
9:05	Anita M. Smith	
11.15	Wilma Hervey	2.00
2.00	P. B. FitzPatrick	4.20
4 20	Kitty [illegible]	6 23
4 30	H.E. Reynolds	6 23
6:23	H. C. [illegible]	9:25
6:23	P. Arndt	9:25
9:25	[illegible] Lee	12:00
Dec 22 9:25	Arnold Blanch	12:00
12:00	E. [illegible]	2,00
2:00	W. H. Wilber	4:00 A.M.
4.00	H. Gray	6.00 A.M.
4:00	E. [illegible]	" " "
6.00	Bruno [illegible]	8:00
8:00	M. E. Jacobs	10:10
10:10	Surd E. Haupt	12:50

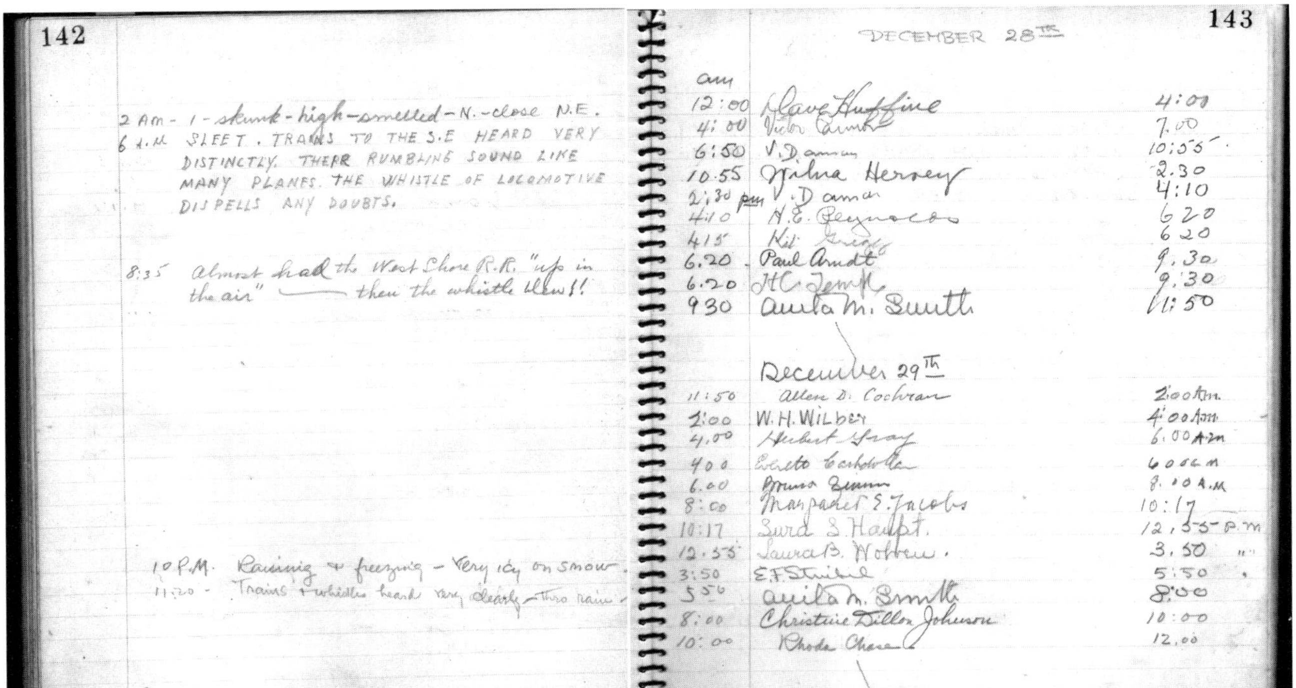

142

2 AM - 1 - skunk - high - smelled - N. - close N.E.

6 A.M. SLEET. TRAINS TO THE S.E HEARD VERY DISTINCTLY. THEIR RUMBLING SOUND LIKE MANY PLANES. THE WHISTLE OF LOCOMOTIVE DISPELLS ANY DOUBTS.

8:35 Almost had the West Shore R.R. "up in the air" —— then the whistle blew!!

10 P.M. Raining & freezing - Very icy on snow.

11:20 - Trains & whistles heard very clearly - thru rain [illegible]

143

DECEMBER 28TH

am		
12:00	[illegible] Huffine	4:00
4:00	Victor [illegible]	7.00
6:50	V. Damon	10:55
10.55	Wilma Hervey	2.30
2:30 pm	V. Damon	4:10
4:10	H. E. Reynolds	6 20
4:15	Kit [illegible]	6 20
6.20	Paul Arndt	9.30
6.20	H. C. [illegible]	9.30
9 30	Anita M. Smith	11:50

December 29th

11:50	Allen D. Cochran	2:00 A.M.
2:00	W. H. Wilber	4:00 A.M.
4.00	Herbert Gray	6.00 A.M.
4 00	Everett [illegible]	6 00 A.M.
6.00	Bruno [illegible]	8.00 A.M.
8:00	Margaret E. Jacobs	10:17
10:17	Surd E. Haupt	12,55 P.M.
12.55	Laura B. Wolters	3.50 "
3:50	E. F. [illegible]	5:50 "
5:50	Anita M. Smith	8:00
8:00	Christine Dillon Johnson	10:00
10:00	Rhoda Chase	12.00

TOP: *Notes section in Woodstock Observation Post log for December 20 to 22, 1942. See reference on left to temperature.* AMS Collection.

BOTTOM: *Log entries for December 28 to 29, 1942—including skunk encounter.* AMS Collection.

On the first Memorial Day after Pearl Harbor, Lieutenant Bob Browning spoke on the Woodstock Village Green. He is a veteran of the First World War and is now known as the dean of the Hudson River radio commentators. He said, "There is no room for brotherhood and Fascism in the same world." Later he added, "This war we are engaged in is a total knockdown, winner take all, loser lose all fight and there isn't one act by any of us that doesn't have a direct bearing on the outcome of the struggle." He warned, "Don't forget that the winners write the history . . . If Hitler wins who is going to write the history . . . of the things we love? Who will define the meaning of the words: life, liberty, freedom?" The words of Browning were impressive, for they were spoken from a wheelchair. "It is a lot easier to die for a cause," he said, "than to live for one."[22]

Corporal Alexander Peacock in Royal Scots Regiment regalia photographed for his 20th Memorial Day parade in 1952. Peacock's father fought in the Crimean War and his grandfather was at the Battle of Waterloo. *Daily Freeman* photo: AMS Collection.

Taking part in that Memorial Day parade were the boys of the Drum Corps with their spirited music. Two of their members, Roger Cashdollar and Ronald Mower, sounded taps at the cemetery. Afterwards, the Legion entertained the Drum Corps and a beautifully decorated cake donated by the baker Lenhard Scholl was cut and served.

For twenty years Woodstockers have enjoyed the sight of Alexander Peacock walking in the parade in his Royal Scots Regiment kilt. Born in Dunfermline, Scotland, he was a veteran of the Boer War and served with the British army in Egypt and India. He wore two medals presented to him by Queen Victoria, besides service medals, ribbons and the Royal Scots Badge. He continued to take part in the parades until he was over ninety years old, and invariably attracted all eyes: Mr. Peacock was a fine figure even in old age, and the kilts were conspicuous. He had a keen wit, which, with his strong Scottish speech, made him popular to have around as a house painter. His grandson, Jackie Peacock, was lost in a bomber over France.

The Red Cross

Mildred Todd, wife of the Dutch Reformed minister, headed the Woodstock chapter of the Red Cross before we went into the war. She had always responded wholeheartedly to the needs of the village and county, and to the appeals of suffering people everywhere. After the war began in Europe one of her projects was a Red Cross table set up every week at the market fair. Under the direction of Mabel Robeson and Mrs. McDougall, flowers—contributed by the townspeople—were sold for the benefit of the Red Cross. One of the best flower growers in the town was a Japanese man, Mr. Kimura, who brought enormous bouquets week after week, contributing in large part to the success of the table. Marion Bullard collected prints by local artists that were sold for the Red Cross at another table. By fall Mrs. Todd was able to announce that they had raised enough money, from these tables and other donations, to provide three completely equipped cots for air raid shelters in England. Meanwhile other workers knitted socks and scarves for the British soldiers.[23]

Woodstock, England, appealed to its namesake in New York State for aid. Binoculars and many other items, including emergency kits by the dozen, were assembled by our sympathetic townsfolk to be shipped to the embattled British Isles. Mrs. Todd also directed the Bundles for Britain drive.[24] She gave me a canister to be placed in my herb shop, but it did not fill up very fast. Most of its contents were the bits of change I myself dropped in. Determined to remedy this situation, I devised a plan whereby every day numbers of clients were shown through my herb garden for a free lecture and then given bouquets of fragrant or interesting herbs. I would interrupt this routine in front of sweet cicely, saying, “The virtue in this plant is that when carried it makes one irresistible to the opposite sex. It is too precious to give away, but if you contribute to Bundles for Britain you may have a sprig.” Within a very short period the canister provided sixty dollars for the cause. If the client was an elderly man he usually gave a dollar. And nobody looked at me to ask if I had tried it! Mrs. Todd and Mrs. Shotwell were also active in raising money for the British when Colleen Moore’s fairy castle, which was exhibited around the country, came to the village.[25]

After Pearl Harbor the whole town responded to the call of the Red Cross. A workroom was set up at the Twin Gables under the supervision of Helen Buttrick, and later another workroom was opened in Willow under Mrs. Wilfred Bronson’s direction. Hospital jackets, pajamas, dresses, crib quilts and baby flannels were among the items produced. It is impossible after all these years to trace all the work done. Even the county records have been destroyed. Within two weeks a waltz ball was held for the Red Cross at the Town Hall, with Julia Leaycraft as chair. Vladimir Padwa directed the string ensemble for the waltzes, and Percy Hill of the Cheats and Swings provided music for square dances. Several hundred dollars was raised at this one party.[26]

In February a Valentine’s ball was held for the same purpose. It brought out the largest crowd ever to assemble at the Town Hall. Marion Bullard was chair and Norbert Heermann and Ben Webster were masters of ceremonies. Before me now is one of the programs made by Maud and Miska Petersham—a delightful valentine with Cupid amidst the traditional frills and flowers and lovebirds. These programs were sold, and there was an auction of the posters, which had been made by local artists. On the program were listed many waltzes and polkas; one of the polkas was composed by Vladimir Padwa, who lived for years in Woodstock. In reminiscing about this gay ball that was attended by people from all over the county, I am reminded of an amusing incident. It was a cold night and everyone came in heavy coats that were checked (at a good price!) in the cloakroom. There was a punch sold by the glass but it contained no hard liquor, and a few of the guests repaired to the local pubs for serious refreshments. One of these gay blades returned to the checkroom as the attendants were giving out the wraps. He was in just the right mood to be free of any inhibitions and proceeded to start his own drive for the cause by forcing the reluctant guests to pay a premium for the release of their coats. He would hold up a garment saying, “Surely it is worth a dollar to redeem this beautiful fur” or “this handsome greatcoat,” and he would refuse to release it until the furious customer paid up. The committee was unable to stop this outrageous form of blackmail, and they would not have been surprised if future Woodstock entertainments were shunned. People are tolerant, however, especially if it is for a good cause, and the trick did bring in many extra dollars for the Red Cross.[27]

Looking back on those war years, I believe the musicians were as generous as any one group in giving of their talents. Many of their efforts have gone unrecorded. One benefit concert was held at the home of the Cohns. Another was held at the Town Hall by the Britt String Sextet, composed of Horace Britt, Carlo Piscitello, Gerald Kunz, Conrad Held, Remo Bolognini and Edwin Ideler. On another occasion Mildred Dilling gave a recital for the Red Cross at her home. For each named, there were probably a dozen more who contributed.[28]

The teenage set staged two amateur theatricals. *Little Women*, with Nellie Robinson, John Heller and James Carter in the leading roles, netted $295 for the Red Cross. This performance was so successful they tried again the next year, presenting *Junior Miss*, which made $200, half of which went to the Health Center and half to the Red Cross.[29]

One of the entertainments about which we have little information was the variety show held in April

THE BRITT STRING SEXTET

Violins	Cellos	Violas
REMO BOLOGNINI	HORACE BRITT	CONRAD HELD
EDWIN IDELER	CARLO PISCITELLO	GERALD KUNZ

Benefit of AMERICAN RED CROSS
TOWN HALL - Woodstock, N. Y.
June 10th, 1942 at 8:30 p.m.

PROGRAM

Sextet in G major, opus 36................J. Brahms
Allegro non troppo
Scherzo
Poco Allegro

Sextet in B flat major, opus 92............V. d'Indy
Entree en sonate
Divertissement
Theme, Variations et Finale

Sextet in A major, opus 48 ....A. Dvorak
Allegro Moderato
Dumka
Furiant
Finale

By special courtesy of
BERNARD R. LA BERGE, INC. NEW YORK

1944, of which Mrs. Hugh Elwyn was chair. If the proceeds for this and other parties were known it would undoubtedly increase the total amount raised for the Red Cross during the war years, but Mrs. Todd's accounts are not available and the county chapter has not saved its records. The incomplete figures we now have come to a total of $7,148.

If the articles made and collected were piled together they would make a sizeable mountain. In 1942 there were eight cartons of books collected and sent off under Isabel Doughty's direction. I remember a party given just after the war for the collection of used clothing to be distributed by the United Nations, including several boxes of good shoes donated by the village cobbler, Ross Pagliaro. It amounted to six trucks of garments![30] I have forgotten what the attraction was at the Town Hall on the next occasion, but I

LEFT: *Flyer for American Red Cross benefit at the Town Hall in 1942.* Courtesy of Historical Society of Woodstock.

BELOW LEFT: *Program guide for* Little Women, *which raised $295 for the Red Cross.* Courtesy of Historical Society of Woodstock.

BELOW RIGHT: *Program guide for* Junior Miss. *This local production also raised funds for the Red Cross.* Courtesy of Historical Society of Woodstock.

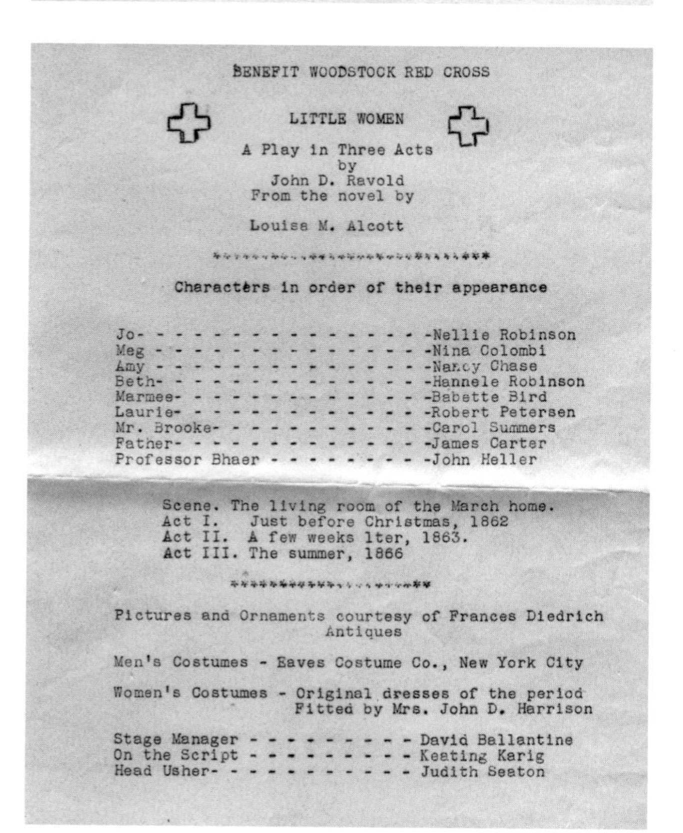

BENEFIT WOODSTOCK RED CROSS

LITTLE WOMEN
A Play in Three Acts
by
John D. Ravold
From the novel by
Louisa M. Alcott

Characters in order of their appearance

Jo- - - - - - - - - - - - - - - -Nellie Robinson
Meg - - - - - - - - - - - - - - -Nina Colombi
Amy - - - - - - - - - - - - - - -Nancy Chase
Beth- - - - - - - - - - - - - - -Hannele Robinson
Marmee- - - - - - - - - - - - - -Babette Bird
Laurie- - - - - - - - - - - - - -Robert Petersen
Mr. Brooke- - - - - - - - - - - -Carol Summers
Father- - - - - - - - - - - - - -James Carter
Professor Bhaer - - - - - - - - -John Heller

Scene. The living room of the March home.
Act I. Just before Christmas, 1862
Act II. A few weeks lter, 1863.
Act III. The summer, 1866

Pictures and Ornaments courtesy of Frances Diedrich Antiques

Men's Costumes - Eaves Costume Co., New York City

Women's Costumes - Original dresses of the period Fitted by Mrs. John D. Harrison

Stage Manager - - - - - - - - - David Ballantine
On the Script - - - - - - - - - Keating Karig
Head Usher- - - - - - - - - - - Judith Seaton

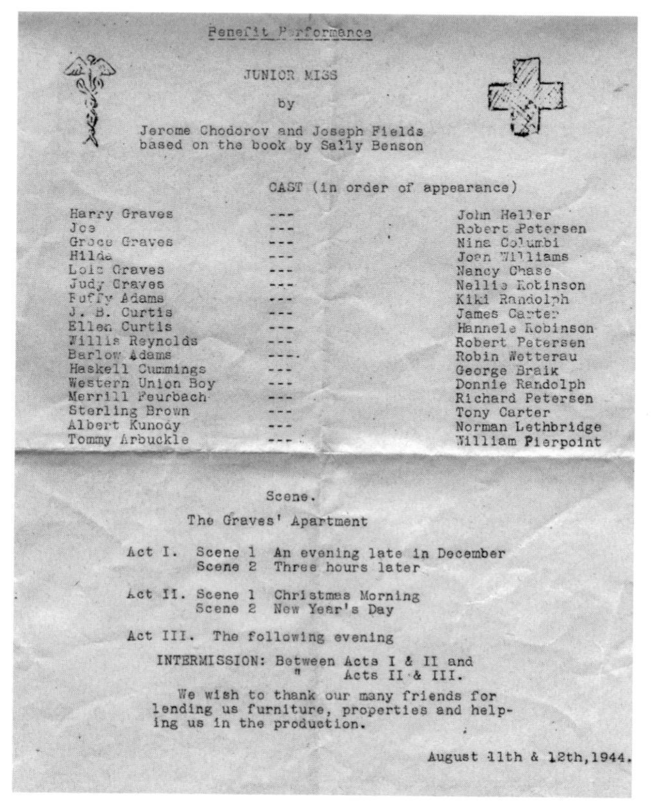

Benefit Performance

JUNIOR MISS
by
Jerome Chodorov and Joseph Fields
based on the book by Sally Benson

CAST (in order of appearance)

Harry Graves --- John Heller
Joe --- Robert Petersen
Grace Graves --- Nina Columbi
Hilda --- Joan Williams
Lois Graves --- Nancy Chase
Judy Graves --- Nellie Robinson
Fuffy Adams --- Kiki Randolph
J. B. Curtis --- James Carter
Ellen Curtis --- Hannele Robinson
Willis Reynolds --- Robert Petersen
Barlow Adams --- Robin Wetterau
Haskell Cummings --- George Braik
Western Union Boy --- Donnie Randolph
Merrill Feurbach --- Richard Petersen
Sterling Brown --- Tony Carter
Albert Kunody --- Norman Lethbridge
Tommy Arbuckle --- William Pierpoint

Scene.
The Graves' Apartment

Act I. Scene 1 An evening late in December
Scene 2 Three hours later

Act II. Scene 1 Christmas Morning
Scene 2 New Year's Day

Act III. The following evening

INTERMISSION: Between Acts I & II and
" Acts II & III.

We wish to thank our many friends for lending us furniture, properties and helping us in the production.

August 11th & 12th,1944.

do remember Reverend Todd and myself at the door accepting old clothes as the price of admission. A group of county orphans who had been farmed out to private homes were herded down off the mountain to see the show, and through some misunderstanding the coats and hats they were wearing were donated to the cause. All went well until the performance was over and they came to ask for their wraps. By that time the cloakroom was filled ten feet deep and up to the ceiling, and we were obliged to lend them coats and hats to wear home through the very cold night air. Provided with descriptions of the missing garments, Reverend Todd and I spent hours the next morning trying to locate them. The clothes gave out a nauseous odor that made us feel faint and we were in peril of being smothered by an avalanche of garments as we sweated in that small enclosure. A few of the hats and coats were retrieved but others had to be replaced with the best clothes available. The youngsters were angry with us even if they were given better garments than those they had lost.

There were several U.S. Bond drives; during one of these a concert was presented at the Town Hall where Dr. Shotwell spoke at the intermission and $9,262 worth of bonds were sold. I believe another of these drives was headed by Mrs. Walter McTeigue. In any case, on the last day she organized a "pretty girl raid" on every restaurant, at the Art Gallery (Woodstock Artists Association), where there was some entertainment, at the country club and at the movie house. It took place on a beautiful summer evening, they secured an incredible number of pledges, and our quota was surpassed. Julia Leaycraft was chair of the fourth and fifth bond drives. On the last drive Woodstock achieved the fifth-largest sale of bonds in Ulster County. This was partly due to the efforts of Lillian Downer and Mrs. Joe Friedberg, representing the Legion, operating a booth in front of the post office. It is reliably recorded that during the war years Woodstock purchased more than $175,000 worth of bonds.[31]

Salvage Efforts

One of the major village activities was collecting scrap, and it continued for years. Even before Pearl Harbor we were asked to donate aluminum to be placed in an open cage on the Village Green. In this way eight hundred and ten pounds of aluminum was collected. Many housewives gave their favorite pots and pans and in some cases were chagrined to find later that they were missing from the heap. Then some bright person conceived the plan of puncturing all utensils before they were added to the collection, thereby rendering them useless for cooking. This happened at a time before we were *all* pulling together for victory.[32] About four months before Pearl Harbor, Marion Bullard wrote in the *Ulster County News*:

> Surely no village of its size has so many nationalities, races, varieties of political conviction, so many shades of religious belief, and so many languages spoken in front of the Post Office on a summer morning at mail time. Matching every group is an opposition group and a reporter with fingers crossed holds a notebook and pencil gingerly. We have Isolationists in our midst, apparently well financed under the banner of America First, and its representatives are working furiously to undermine all that [the] Aid to Britain, Free France and Fight for Freedom groups are building up.[33]

Later she wrote:

> During the past week or so, disruptive publicity has been spread in Woodstock by paid agents of America First [which backfired] and the result has been a much more rapid increase in Free French sympathizers with considerable outspoken condemnation of the methods of the isolation[ist] element for their efforts to disunite the nation at this time.[34]

Considering all these diverse elements, it is to Woodstock's credit that when the need arose we all united in our quest for victory.

We were soon asked to save paper and metal, rags and rubber. The Boy Scouts did a fine job collecting old paper, which sometimes amounted to a thousand pounds to be rounded up in our station wagons. To publicize the scrap drives Helen Buttrick wrote and produced a radio skit, *Presents for Uncle Sam*, in which Reverend and Mrs. Todd took leading parts. *The Woodstock Press* carried a story about Marion Bullard's Scottie, the Bold Keppoch, who was chair of the Dogs' Rubber Drive.[35] He urged all his canine friends to donate their rubber toys by placing them in a container in the portico of the Dutch church. There is no record of how successful the dog was, but we do know of people who collected a great deal. At Lake Hill alone Jules Simpson assembled over a ton

Marion Bullard with Jackie Playboy Smith (middle) and Bold Keppoch. The latter was chairman of the canine rubber drive. Photo: AMS Collection.

of rubber during one drive. These collections were usually brought to a reception center where Joe Friedberg was very active with helpers baling paper or rags and weighing rubber or metal to be taken to nearby towns, where it was sold. The town trucks under Joseph Hutty did a big job in carting.

Early in the salvage collections it was decided to use the money from these sales to buy Christmas presents for our service men and women. The committee formed to buy and send these gifts to the soldiers was chaired by Myron Hall and included Bertha Thompson, Lura Haupt, Ray Allen, George Braendly, Frank Hall, Henry Houst, J. Augustus Shultis, William Van Wagner, Craig Vosburgh and Lloyd Woods. Helen Buttrick worked on publicity, Donald McLennan was secretary, Reverend Todd was treasurer, Joe Friedberg was a salesman and LaMonte Simpkins worked on trucking arrangements. It was no easy job this group took on. The metal scrap came not only from cellars and kitchens but also from abandoned quarries, choked streams, fill-ins and barnyard muck. For instance, somebody would report a piece of farm machinery rusting on the mountain, or a wrecked car pushed into a deep ditch. The salvaging of such an object might entail a powerful hoist or an acetylene torch to dismember its parts, and then the backbreaking work of loading and unloading would begin. In the first drive the amount collected came to nearly eighty pounds per every man, woman and child in the town, and this was sold for $689. In 1943 a further collection was made, which sold for $324.53. Thus over a thousand dollars worth of metal was recovered for the government. This money from salvage was used to send each young man and woman in service from the Woodstock area at least eleven articles, which included subscriptions to weekly magazines, cigarettes, socks, fountain pens, shirts, candy and Christmas cards. These presents were sent for Christmas 1942 and 1943, and we presume for the following Christmas, although there is no record of what was done after Myron Hall resigned.[36]

By February 1942 a victory garden program was being planned, with the actor Harrison Dowd as chair. Various persons donated land to be planted, close enough for the gardeners to walk to the plots without consuming precious gasoline rations. Dowd had certain hours at the Civilian Defense headquarters when he could be consulted, and several times during the growing season he visited each of the registered gardens. Awards were offered for the best garden and that year Ethel Adams won first prize, Lucy Brown (who was over seventy) took second place for a thrifty little garden at her Zena home and Sonia Bronson in Willow won third prize. The following summer the garden plots for the village were concentrated near the country club. It was here that eight-year-old David Minor, who spaded and planted his own land, grew the best garden. Alfred Hutty, the etcher up on Ohayo, raised a potato weighing one and a half pounds that held the title of largest potato until the painter Ned Chase produced one that weighed one pound eleven ounces. Another artist, Allen Cochran, raised a tomato that weighed a pound and a half, and as far as we know these sizes were not challenged throughout the war years.[37]

Other projects to produce extra food included raising squab, ducks, pigs and guinea hens. The last named will always be associated with Rock City, where their hilarious shrieks advertised them to the whole neighborhood. Allen DeLano decided to raise snails, supposedly the most nourishing of foods, and he sent to France for a stock of these mollusks. His garden was full of grape leaves, said to be their staple diet, and the Department of Agriculture and Markets provided a leaflet on the *Love Life of Snails*, which might not have been allowed through the mails if it had not originated in a Washington bureau. Unfortunately at this time shipping from Europe became disorganized and it was many weeks before the snails arrived. When the box was opened all but two of the hundred snails were very, very dead. The two survivors from France were placed among the grape leaves and no further history of them is available. We can only hope an entente was reached with the American snails.

China Relief

Many people in Woodstock were concerned by the plight of the Chinese people, but Mrs. Walter Weyl, who had been to China and had followed its efforts to be free of Japanese rule, was the person most responsive to their need. She was the leading spirit in the effort to raise money for medical aid and, with her co-chair, Mrs. Rosett, provided an entertainment that was long remembered. A gala performance was put on at the Woodstock Playhouse on August 17, 1942. The Chinese ambassador to Washington, Dr. Hu Shih, accepted an invitation from Dr. and Mrs. Shotwell to visit them and be the principal speaker. Mrs. Weyl and her assistant, Miss Bollman, made several trips to New York City to collect material from Chinatown and the Chinese Relief Committee, to be sold at a bazaar that preceded the entertainment. Before the sale a Chinese dinner at the Dutch church hall was provided by Charlie Wu, a restaurateur.

Every detail of the entertainment had been beautifully planned. The painter Yasuo Kuniyoshi designed the program cover, based on a quotation

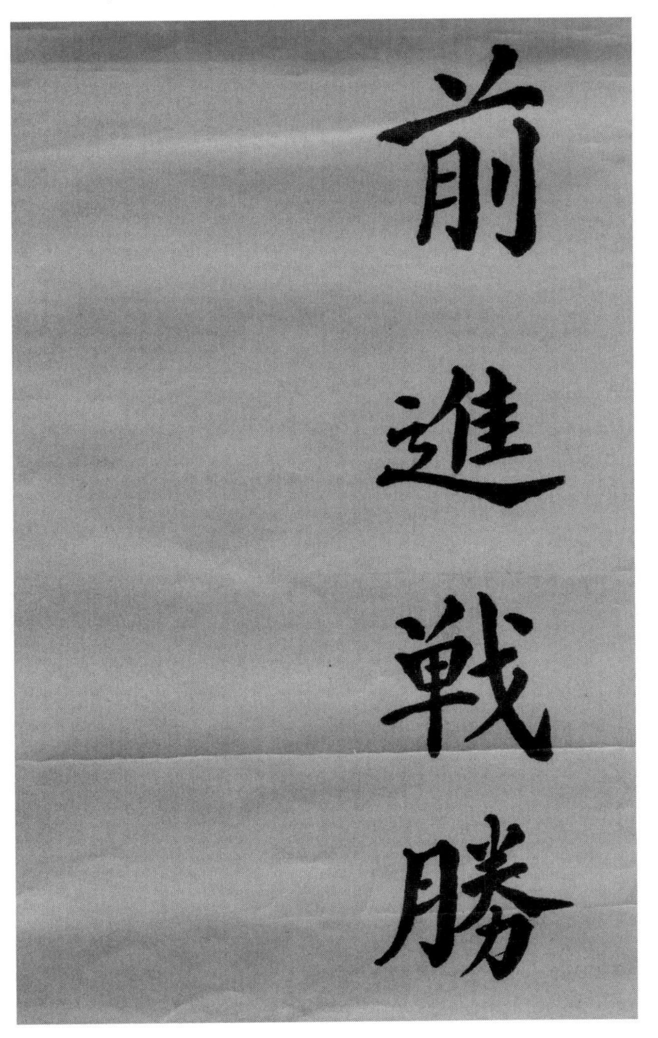

Cover of China Relief program guide, designed by Yasuo Kuniyoishi. The Chinese characters roughly translate to "Forward for Victory." Courtesy of Woodstock Library.

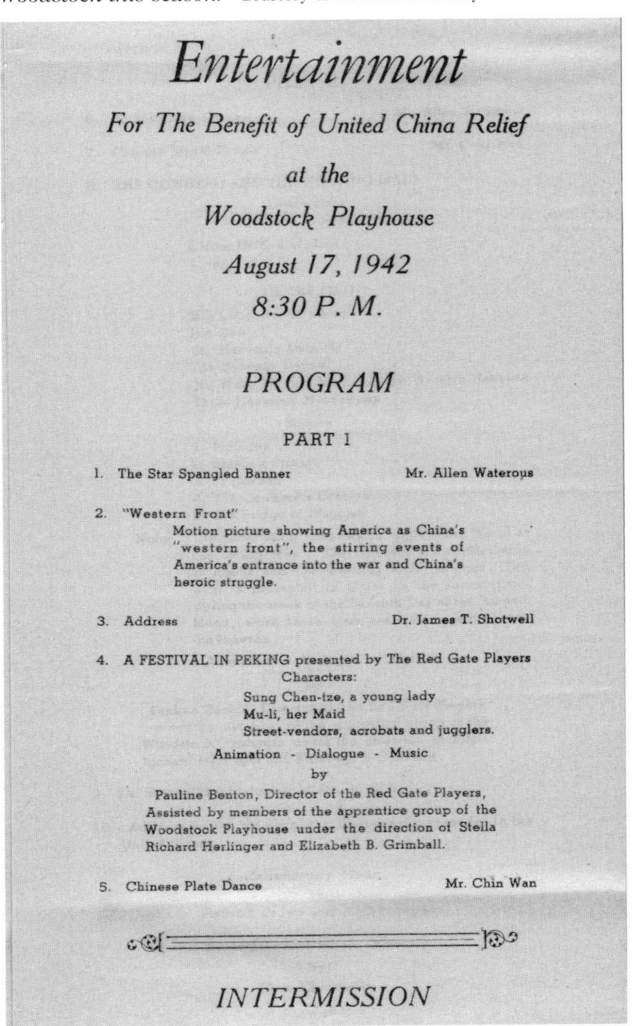

Entertainment

For The Benefit of United China Relief

at the

Woodstock Playhouse

August 17, 1942

8:30 P. M.

PROGRAM

PART I

1. The Star Spangled Banner — Mr. Allen Waterous
2. "Western Front"
   Motion picture showing America as China's "western front", the stirring events of America's entrance into the war and China's heroic struggle.
3. Address — Dr. James T. Shotwell
4. A FESTIVAL IN PEKING presented by The Red Gate Players
   Characters:
   Sung Chen-tze, a young lady
   Mu-li, her Maid
   Street-vendors, acrobats and jugglers.
   Animation - Dialogue - Music
   by
   Pauline Benton, Director of the Red Gate Players, Assisted by members of the apprentice group of the Woodstock Playhouse under the direction of Stella Richard Herlinger and Elizabeth B. Grimball.
5. Chinese Plate Dance — Mr. Chin Wan

INTERMISSION

First page of the China Relief program guide. This event was noted in the Kingston Daily Freeman *as "the most colorful in Woodstock this season."* Courtesy of Woodstock Library.

from Confucius, with decorative Chinese characters brushed in black ink on an orange-colored scroll. Even the acknowledgments at the back were couched in suitable language: "The Unworthy Committee in charge of the entertainment wishes to express its heartfelt thanks to the following most noble and generous contributors of gifts." This was followed by a list of Friends of China. Allen Waterous sang the "Star Spangled Banner," accompanied by Clara Chichester on the piano. The first feature was a motion picture and the next was a play presented by the Red Gate Players. There was also a Chinese "plate dance" by Chin Wan. After the intermission Dr. Shotwell spoke, and then introduced Dr. Hu Shih, who had been called the father of the Intellectual Revolution in China. Hu Shih spoke about present-day China in his usual scholarly fashion. The music was provided by Vladimir Padwa and Adrian Siegel.

The net amount raised was $1,200. As reported in the *Kingston Daily Freeman*, the Chinese benefit performance was "the most colorful in Woodstock this season." With the proceeds from the United Nations fête that took place the following year, the Committee for Medical Aid for China raised a total of $1,703.

The afternoon following the entertainment at the Playhouse, the Shotwells hosted a garden party in honor of the ambassador. It was a gathering of friends on their wide terrace overlooking the Woodstock valley that we all recall with pleasure. On close acquaintance Dr. Hu Shih proved to be a very genial personality and there was good conversation, fine music and a delicious buffet supper served on the porch.[38]

France Forever

In April 1941, Philip Buttrick—who had served with the French army in the First World War, for which he received the Croix de Guerre—told a few friends about an organization called France Forever. This was started after the collapse of France to promote resistance and to keep alive the spirit of "Liberté, Égalité et Fraternité." Soon afterwards a meeting was held at Stonecrop in Rock City where almost a hundred people gathered for a talk by Jean Steck, a representative of France Forever. Steck began by relating his own experiences as an officer in the French army, explaining that his regiment had been sent to face the mechanized German army with rifles dating back to 1872. "The French were brave," he said, "but what could they do?" He had been taken prisoner and placed with thousands of other Frenchmen in a cave where they were ignored and would have starved if it had not been used by Champagne growers: they sustained life for weeks by drinking bottles of Champagne. Steck brought with him a film about the Free French forces in England that Reverend Todd ran through the church's moving-picture machine. General de Gaulle was shown making a speech that ended with the stirring words, "Soldiers of France, wherever you may be, *arise*!"

It was decided to launch a chapter of France Forever in Woodstock, which had the distinction of being the first begun by Americans rather than by exiled French nationals. Philip Buttrick was elected the first chair, Alice Henderson vice-chair and Anita Smith secretary-treasurer.[39] By the end of 1941 $173 had been collected in membership dues and sent to headquarters in New York City.[40] Before the end of the war almost three hundred people in Ulster County belonged to the Woodstock chapter. After Buttrick went to Washington on a special assignment for the government, Elsie Goddard became chair.

To raise money for France Forever the committee decided to hold a fête on July 14th. For this the Woodstock Playhouse was loaned by Robert Elwyn. Andrée Ruellan and Stanley Crane designed a souvenir program, Elizabeth Cowan-Griffith served as stage manager, and Harry Kaufman of the Shubert theaters sent several acts from New York. Evelyn Case, singer on the Ford Foundation program, opened the evening with the "Star Spangled Banner" and also sang the "Marseillaise" and some *chansons populaires*. A string quartet composed of Vitetta, Lenard, Britt and Cohn played Debussy. Paul Haakon danced, giving a very fine performance. There were ballet recitals by Rosina and Milo Snyder of the Paris Opera and a scene from Shaw's *Saint Joan* with Richard Kendrick, Kay Strozzi, Don McHenry and Ivan Triessault. In addition there was a Degas Tableau with Marion Lloyd and Joen Arliss. The comedy of the evening was supplied by the vaudeville team of Master and Rollins, who made the audience roar with delight, as the female member of the duo appeared to be made of rubber! It was a gala performance said to have been the best show ever presented in Woodstock.[41]

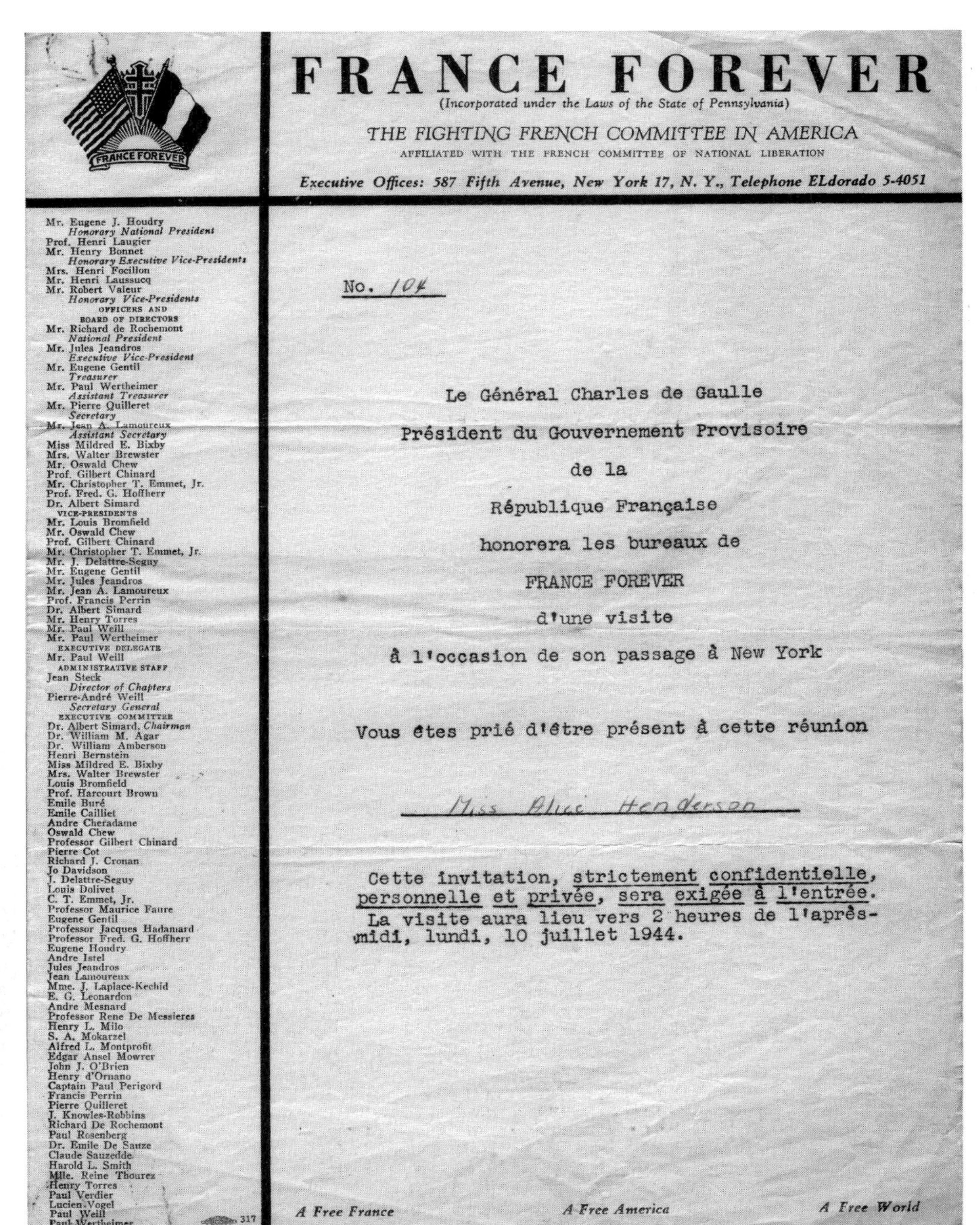

FRANCE FOREVER

(*Incorporated under the Laws of the State of Pennsylvania*)

THE FIGHTING FRENCH COMMITTEE IN AMERICA

AFFILIATED WITH THE FRENCH COMMITTEE OF NATIONAL LIBERATION

Executive Offices: 587 Fifth Avenue, New York 17, N. Y., Telephone ELdorado 5-4051

Mr. Eugene J. Houdry
Honorary National President
Prof. Henri Laugier
Mr. Henry Bonnet
Honorary Executive Vice-Presidents
Mrs. Henri Focillon
Mr. Henri Laussucq
Mr. Robert Valeur
Honorary Vice-Presidents
OFFICERS AND
BOARD OF DIRECTORS
Mr. Richard de Rochemont
National President
Mr. Jules Jeandros
Executive Vice-President
Mr. Eugene Gentil
Treasurer
Mr. Paul Wertheimer
Assistant Treasurer
Mr. Pierre Quilleret
Secretary
Mr. Jean A. Lamoureux
Assistant Secretary
Miss Mildred E. Bixby
Mrs. Walter Brewster
Mr. Oswald Chew
Prof. Gilbert Chinard
Mr. Christopher T. Emmet, Jr.
Prof. Fred. G. Hoffherr
Dr. Albert Simard
VICE-PRESIDENTS
Mr. Louis Bromfield
Mr. Oswald Chew
Prof. Gilbert Chinard
Mr. Christopher T. Emmet, Jr.
Mr. J. Delattre-Seguy
Mr. Eugene Gentil
Mr. Jules Jeandros
Mr. Jean A. Lamoureux
Prof. Francis Perrin
Dr. Albert Simard
Mr. Henry Torres
Mr. Paul Weill
Mr. Paul Wertheimer
EXECUTIVE DELEGATE
Mr. Paul Weill
ADMINISTRATIVE STAFF
Jean Steck
Director of Chapters
Pierre-André Weill
Secretary General
EXECUTIVE COMMITTEE
Dr. Albert Simard, *Chairman*
Dr. William M. Agar
Dr. William Amberson
Henri Bernstein
Miss Mildred E. Bixby
Mrs. Walter Brewster
Louis Bromfield
Prof. Harcourt Brown
Emile Buré
Emile Cailliet
Andre Cheradame
Oswald Chew
Professor Gilbert Chinard
Pierre Cot
Richard J. Cronan
Jo Davidson
J. Delattre-Seguy
Louis Dolivet
C. T. Emmet, Jr.
Professor Maurice Faure
Eugene Gentil
Professor Jacques Hadamard
Professor Fred. G. Hoffherr
Eugene Houdry
Andre Istel
Jules Jeandros
Jean Lamoureux
Mme. J. Laplace-Kechid
E. G. Leonardon
Andre Mesnard
Professor Rene De Messieres
Henry L. Milo
S. A. Mokarzel
Alfred L. Montprofit
Edgar Ansel Mowrer
John J. O'Brien
Henry d'Ornano
Captain Paul Perigord
Francis Perrin
Pierre Quilleret
J. Knowles-Robbins
Richard De Rochemont
Paul Rosenberg
Dr. Emile De Sauze
Claude Sauzedde
Harold L. Smith
Mlle. Reine Thourez
Henry Torres
Paul Verdier
Lucien Vogel
Paul Weill
Paul Wertheimer

317

No. 104

Le Général Charles de Gaulle

Président du Gouvernement Provisoire

de la

République Française

honorera les bureaux de

FRANCE FOREVER

d'une visite

à l'occasion de son passage à New York

Vous êtes prié d'être présent à cette réunion

Miss Alice Henderson

Cette invitation, strictement confidentielle, personnelle et privée, sera exigée à l'entrée.
La visite aura lieu vers 2 heures de l'après-midi, lundi, 10 juillet 1944.

A Free France *A Free America* *A Free World*

France Forever invitation extended to Woodstock representative Alice Henderson. She was to meet the leader of the Free French Movement, Charles de Gaulle, in New York City on July 10, 1944, at the Waldorf-Astoria Hotel.
AMS Collection.

Between the acts a resolution was submitted and passed by the five hundred people in the audience authorizing the secretary to send telegrams to President Roosevelt and Secretary of State Hull favoring recognition of the Free French forces of General de Gaulle by the government of the United States. It was signed by John W. Taylor, Charles De La Vergne and Albert Grasier for the Woodstock chapter.[42] This performance netted $527. Thus encouraged, the committee held fêtes on the two succeeding Bastille Days. In addition, concerts, moving pictures and lectures were presented. The first concert was given by Inez Richards, William Kroll and Horace Britt, who donated their talent in a long-remembered program of French music that included Fauré's Sonata in A Major.

The day Paris was liberated. From left, Rev. Todd, young Luguet, Father Nangle and Rev. Denman. The young boy was the son of General Luguet of the Free French Movement.
Photo by Adrian Siegel. AMS Collection.

On June 26, 1942, Lieutenant Richard de Roussy de Salles spoke at the Town Hall after a movie screening. A surprise guest at this time was Captain of Gunnery François Picard-Destalon. Alice Henderson had known this naval officer since he was a child but had no knowledge of his whereabouts since the surrender of France. When the newspapers mentioned the arrival of the battleship *Richelieu* in New York for repair of damage sustained at Casablanca, on a hunch she wired the captain inquiring if Picard-Destalon was on board. He was, having guided the enormous battleship to dry dock—with its stacks and funnels dismantled, in order to pass under the bridges on the way up the East River. As the only officer who could speak fluent English, he was the ship's spokesman in the United States. He knew the U.S. authorities were prepared to re-outfit the vessel but was amazed to find that the donated supplies included clothes—down to warm underwear for the sailors. Coming from Casablanca, they had been in dire need of woolen clothing for the New York winter season.[43]

A second concert was held in 1945, featuring Florence Heckman, Inez Richards and Engelbert Roentgen. On this occasion there was an address by Louis Dolivet, International Secretary General of the Free World Association, who spoke about France and the San Francisco Conference on the United Nations charter.[44]

The total amount raised for the Free French, including the proceeds from the French booth at the International Bazaar, was $4,089.79.[45] In addition to the money, as soon as France was cleared of the enemy, about twenty-five persons made "package" adoptions of French children. In this way they not only sent the children much-needed food and clothing, but also began an entente that has lasted for years. It is impossible to calculate the number of clothing collections that were sent to France.

There is another story connected with the friendship many Woodstockers feel for France that is worth telling. On August 25, 1944, news came over the radio that Paris was liberated after four long years of German occupation. In the village the church bells rang, and reverberated through the hills and into the hearts of the people, because most of them loved Paris for her art, her science or, at the least, for her gaiety. The news spread rapidly and soon about a hundred people gathered on the Village Green to listen to the ministers and the priest give prayers of thanks. A group of children had been summoned from the French Camp in Byrdcliffe, and one little boy was chosen to raise the Tricolore along with the American flag. He was a tiny boy made over-serious by the war, a son of General Luguet, head of the Free French Air Force, and his heart burned with patriotism. Ever since he had been in exile he had remembered every morning to raise the French flag above his bed and every night he took it down and carefully folded it. At a signal from Reverend Todd, the minister of the Dutch Reformed Church, he pulled the rope that lifted the flags. When the Tricolore and the Stars and Stripes hung free on the staff he stood proudly at attention, though a trifle bewildered by the sudden ending of a familiar dread that had become a pattern in his short life. Joyously the crowd around him sang the "Marseillaise."

Russian Aid

Although later the Russians fought bravely for their fatherland, it will never be forgotten that they signed an infamous pact with Germany on August 23, 1939. With this pact the Soviets were given an all-clear signal to annex small nations such as Lithuania, Latvia and Finland, and to be acquiescent to Hitler's armed aggression throughout the remainder of Europe. When this alliance was made public, many of the idealists who had sincerely believed in the ultimate good of the Soviet concept resigned from the American Communist Party. Those who remained in the party showed their obedience to the Moscow edict by passive resistance, if not outright attempts to discredit the cause of Britain and France. However, when Germany threw in her armies to invade Russia, suddenly the Soviet-American puppets made an about face and declared themselves for the Allies—which before long would include the United States.

The Russian people soon underwent a terrible ordeal and the whole free world sympathized with them. They were now on our side in the war; our government's policy was to help their army with vast stores of munitions, and we were encouraged to send aid to their suffering population. At that time a branch of Russian War Relief, Inc., was formed in Woodstock with Mrs. Vladimir Padwa, the wife of the pianist, as chair.[46] A sewing group was formed that did quantities of work of various kinds. Mrs. Ned Chase and Mrs. Henry Morton Robinson collected seven hundred and thirty pounds of used clothing; Neva Shultis had charge of assembling fifty-two relief kits; and Mrs. Sluizer and Mrs. Kingsbury, head of the knitting project, produced twenty-five sweaters, twenty-two scarves, two helmets and twenty pairs of socks. All of these were for a single shipment.[47]

One of the early benefits for Russian War Relief was a basket picnic held on the Shotwells' terrace. There was a tremendous crowd present. Girls in costume sold caviar, vodka and cigarettes amongst a typical Woodstock crowd that was at its most colorful. Horace Britt, Vladimir Padwa and William Kroll played a musical program of Tchaikovsky. There were a few works of art sold, including a Persian blue bowl by Carl Walters, a mirror in a carved frame by Ludins, a drawing by Archipenko, a lithograph by Lucile Blanch and a signed copy of Edmund Gilligan's new book, *The Strangers in the Vly*. This party netted $279.[48]

Subsequently the movie *Tanya* was presented in Kingston for Russian War Relief, a meeting was held at the Town Hall in Woodstock at which General Victor Yakhontoff spoke and another talk was given by Nadia Krinkin. The last two events netted $239.95. There was a concert given by Padwa and a "Tribute to Russia" supper held where the guests were Lieutenant Arkady Sedoc of the Soviet navy, Lydia Palmina, on duty with a Russian convoy, and Nicolai Zemennoff of the Moravian Republic. The speaker on this occasion was John Summerville, and LaMonte Simpkins was auctioneer. Another benefit was a dance recital by Alexis Kosloff.[49]

Finally, in 1945, there was a fourth Christmas party for Russian War Relief at which the Reverend Howard Melish was speaker.[50] I have no record of the three other Christmas parties or of how much was collected from these or many of the other entertainments. The Russian War Relief totals are the most incomplete of any of the war efforts in the village; the only figure obtainable, including the sum from the United Nations fête, is $931.

The Little Nations

Dr. Shotwell was chair of a meeting held in the summer of 1942 to raise money for the smaller European countries. Before this meeting a smorgasbord was given by the Norwegian Americans in the basement of the Dutch Reformed Church at which two hundred and forty persons were served. Later in the main church there were speakers for seven nations.

Belgium was represented by George Potie, a member of the city council of Brussels. Unfortunately we do not have a record of what the speakers said. Felix von Kahler, who had escaped from Prague early in the war, spoke for Czechoslovakia. Mr. Van Dissel gave a moving account of Dutch resistance under Nazi rule and told stories of the Spanish Republican Army. He also sang Dutch songs. Eistein Drogseth spoke for Norway, Reinald Matheson sang the Norwegian national anthem and children in their national costume sang Norwegian folk songs. Matheson had been on the

New York police force and was known as "The Singing Cop."

Kasmer Hudela, a tailor and head of the Kingston Polish Relief Society, gave a speech in broken English about the plight of his people under the Germans that aroused considerable sympathy. George Radin spoke on Yugoslavia, and as he stepped upon the platform a recording of the song of the Chetniks was played. Mr. Radin pointed out that a short time before, the guerrillas of General Draja Mihailovich in Serbia had been the only United Nations forces fighting in enemy territory.

A collection was taken for these little countries. Due to the smorgasbord the Norwegian group was entitled to a larger amount of the money raised, but Mr. Drogseth said the seven nations were to share the whole amount equally. Shortly thereafter Dr. Shotwell announced that $700 had been collected and distributed. That same season the artists held a ball, "Rendezvous in Rio," to benefit the smaller nations, raising $600.[51]

Nine Nations Fête

During the first week of September 1943 a fête was held on the Village Green to raise funds for the relief of nine nations. By this time most Woodstockers had given their limit for each national drive as it came along. The new plan was to hold a joint fête for two days and make it so unusual that it would have countywide appeal and bring forth those who had not hitherto been reached. The artists Anton Refregier, Marion Greenwood and Wendell Jones arranged for a street of booths to be placed along the west side of the Green with the Dutch church and the dark maple trees making a handsome background. The street was barred to vehicles and the effect was a row of peasant cottages gorgeous in color and design. It took weeks of preparation but the result was spectacular. Each group produced a booth or house with its own national characteristics.

The British booth was run by Mrs. Llewellyn Summers, Mrs. Stagg and Helen Shotwell. Miss Shotwell was responsible for the main decoration, a brilliant thirty-by-forty-inch painting of the royal coat of arms. They sold cakes that could not be transported from their cars to the booth before being pounced on by customers. I know that costume dolls were also sold because Mrs. George Bellows related the story of the hard work she put into dressing Scottish figurines. Helen Shotwell gave her six dolls to be dressed in authentic Highland clothes. Fortunately Mrs. Bellows's sister was visiting her and helped, or she would never have finished them in time for the fête. Miss Shotwell received donations of sugar coupons in order to make a Scottish marmalade that required three days to cook, some of it sold in jars decorated by Toni Drake. Helen relates an amusing though rather tragic incident about one of the batches. She was finishing it up when an air raid blackout sounded, and four gallons of marmalade was burned beyond retrieval. She must have cooked quantities because they made $70 on marmalade alone. The total amount raised for Britain was $402.44.

The Yugoslavian booth was one of the most colorful, with a painting of the double-headed eagle on its roof. On either side was a giant-sized figure of a peasant in bright costume waving a flag. The interior of the little building was decorated with warm-colored Oriental rugs, embroidered blouses and other readily salable articles. Mrs. John Kingsbury and Mrs. George Radin were in charge of this booth. The Radins had come to America in 1941 with a group from the Yugoslavian government, including the young King Peter and General Simoviç, who had been premier shortly before the Germans took over Belgrade. At the invitation of Dr. Kingsbury and Dr. Shotwell, General Simoviç and Mr. Nicolich, a minister of the government, came with the Radins to Woodstock. General Simoviç soon left to take over the direction of their army in exile. The pilot of a commercial plane that carried most of the Yugoslav government to Athens was Savo Milo, an officer in the reserves. Milo later served as a captain in the U.S. Air Force, and in 1945, when his wife and son joined him after their escape from Belgrade, the family settled in Woodstock. The Milos purchased Mead's Mountain House and have been running it successfully for several years. These Yugoslavians were staunch backers of General Draja Mihailovich and his Chetniks, and were very sad when Tito, the Communist, was recognized as head of the government and had Mihailovich killed. Apparently they considered the Russian occupation of Yugoslavia an act of aggression rather than liberation.

French Relief booth with Antoinette Schülte and Bradley Tomlin. Postcard: AMS Collection.

Those who sympathized most with the plight of the Chinese people erected a round pavilion brilliantly decorated with gold paint and glittering jewels. It was not long before they had to hang up an "all sold out" sign owing to the popularity of their tea, drapes and other Chinese goods. Mrs. Walter Weyl and Blanche Rosett were in charge, assisted by Mari Bollman and Mrs. Charlie Wu. Miss Bollman designed and built the pavilion. During the two days of the festival they collected $503, which was more than any other group contributed to the total.

The Norwegian booth was under the charge of a Mrs. Schon of Ohayo Mountain, who had done so much work for Norway during her winters in Brooklyn that she had been decorated by King Haakon. The design of the booth featured a rampant lion surrounded by mountain peaks. It was edged with a typical Scandinavian border motif. The main product sold was canned fish, although they also offered embroidered vests and other items of clothing. Mr. and Mrs. Eistein Drogseth were very active helpers. They were the first of the Norwegian group to settle on Ohayo Mountain. Their booth made $260. Mrs. Drogseth also worked on the smorgasbord served in the basement of the Dutch church the first evening of the fête, but she gave to the chair, Mrs. Buttrick, all the credit for its success in collecting $160.50. After the supper the crowd danced on the Green to the music of William Spanhake of Wittenberg and his square dance band.

In its simplicity the French booth showed up most distinctly among its more ornate neighbors. It was white with a decorative knot of blue, white and red ribbons beneath a golden cock, with the ribbons swirling down one side. Gold letters on the white background spelled out "Liberté, Égalité et Fraternité," and of course there was "Vive la France" in jaunty script across the entrance. It had been designed by the artists Antoinette Schülte and Bradley Tomlin (this was before his abstract period). The booth was enthusiastically manned by Antoinette Schülte, Alice Henderson and Andrée Ruellan along with her mother, Lucette Ruellan. When they were sold out they would rush home for another bottle of French wine or go to the bakery for more ladyfingers, of which several were tied together with tricolor ribbons and dispensed at an outrageous profit.

The village baker, Lenhard Scholl, was a German who spoke with a strong accent, and due to his brusque manner he was not always accepted. However, when the committee for the French went to pay him for the hundreds of ladyfingers they had purchased he quietly handed them a receipted bill and refused to take a cent in reimbursement. Whenever there was a benefit for the Red Cross or other worthy cause, Mr. Scholl always donated a big layer cake, which was frequently auctioned off at a high price. He refused to make any profit from the Christmas cakes that were sent to the soldiers, selling them for the cost of the ingredients. Among these cakes was one I sent in a gift parcel to a friend who was an ambulance driver with the British army in Italy. Heaven only knows how the package found him on Christmas Day huddled under fire in a cellar trying to nurse a desperately wounded enemy soldier just eighteen years old. It was impossible to move the boy and all that could be done was to make him more comfortable. The ambulance driver opened his package and, finding the fruitcake, offered the wounded soldier a piece, placing fragments of it on his tongue. "It tastes like cake I used to have at home. Thank those who sent it," the soldier whispered in German. A contented expression came over his features as he relaxed upon the stretcher. A few minutes later when the ambulance man looked again the soldier had died. Thus a circle was completed. A few months later the baker's only son, Lenhard Scholl Jr., was killed with the American army in France.

The Dutch booth was made by William Cramer and Brock Brockenshaw, who painted upon it an antique clock tower with blue delft tiles. Inside there was a fireplace covered with more tiles. Miss von Sturm, Liesje Cramer and Mrs. Paul Reiff sold the goods, which consisted mostly of small replicas of Dutch tiles and cheese, mustard and cocoa, all products of the Netherlands. They wore Dutch costumes that they had made themselves, and offered other such outfits for sale.

Among the colored photographs of the international fête there is one showing the Greek booth on which appears an inscription in large letters, "The Glory that is Greece." On the counter can be seen a Grecian statue and flowers; the Greek national flag is in the background, in front of which are two pleasant-looking ladies whom nobody now recognizes. Evidently there were no Greeks living permanently in the town at that time, and it was from a newspaper clipping I learned that a musician, Mrs. Raisse Tselentis, had taken charge of this booth. When questioned, Helen Shotwell could not give much information, but she said the booth had looked so empty she had given them a collection of her paintings, which promptly sold. She said further that her friends were mean enough to quip that it took the Greeks to sell them! This I will not confirm because I know that many other pictures by Helen Shotwell have been sold. In any case, the Greeks brought in $116.93.

The Russian booth, designed by Wendell Jones, was probably the handsomest in the show. On it were painted scenes of churches and icons, peasants and their sheep, and singers, all produced with Oriental lavishness of color. On the roof there was a large figure of a soldier and two workers done in a masterful style. Mrs. Padwa was in charge of selling peasant skirts, blouses, and handkerchiefs and many smaller items. They made $412.79.

The last of the nine nations was Czechoslovakia, whose building was dominated by two large decorative figures of a peasant man and woman painted on long panels that flanked the booth. The roof was unusual because it was cut to resemble the skyline of a city, which, presumably, was Prague. Although they did not have many things for sale and brought in only $109, the booth was admired and it added enormously to the attractive aspect of the street of many nations. Mrs. Felix von Kahler was in charge. She, her husband and her daughters left their home for Paris when the Germans entered the city of Prague. A few years later when France capitulated they again had to flee, and joined the refugees crossing into Spain. They were among the last to leave over the International Bridge from Hendaye to Irún before that gateway to Spain and on to Portugal was closed. They described seeing acres and acres of fine cars abandoned on the French side by the refugees. Nobody could take with them more than they could carry as they walked across the bridge spanning the river. I have seen photographs of the von Kahlers' beautiful home in Czechoslovakia, but they had to leave everything behind except for one certificate of stock that they managed to hide from confiscation by the Germans, and it enabled them to live for a few years in freedom here in Woodstock.

The second night, after the booths were all closed, there was a ball at the Town Hall that ended the festivities. Norbert Heermann, an artist, was master of ceremonies. Mrs. Wetterau had collected small pictures from the artists that sold for a total of $275. The *Catskill Mountain Star* published a good account of the whole fête. "One of the highlights of the ball," it said, "was the appearance of the English soprano, Dorita Court, who presented a program of light operatic numbers." The "best costume" prizes were given to Amy Paul (the sister of Eugene Ludins) and Murray Hoffman. Gail Feeley was crowned "Miss Woodstock of 1943" by a committee of judges comprising Doris Lee, Alfred de Liagre Jr., Henry Morton Robinson and Joseph Kesselring. This ball brought in $637.50. The grand total for the whole fête came to $3,402.24.[52]

American Friends Service Committee

From 1943 to 1948 a group of about eight women met every week at the home of Mrs. Anton Otto Fischer to sew and knit for the American Friends Service Committee. They had no idea how much they had accomplished, only remembering that "a lot of material had come in and gone out made up." Some of the workers were more enthusiastic than skillful and on a couple of occasions sewed the little boys' pants hind side before, but this was remedied before the clothes left Woodstock. Fortunately the Friends kept a record and upon inquiry divulged that Mrs. Fischer's group made seven hundred and forty-four garments. All of these required careful labor and included items such as mittens, jackets and five hundred and ninety-eight boys' shirts.[53]

Other people sent what must have been hundreds of pounds of used clothing to the Friends, but it is impossible now to trace the amount. In one effort Alice Henderson with Marion Bullard's help collected and shipped a hundred and thirty-two pounds of candle ends to the Friends Service Committee. At another time they collected dozens and dozens of spectacles, including the lenses, to be shipped overseas.[54]

There were other churches and organizations that contributed to the war effort or sent help to the liberated people of devastated Europe. For example, in one campaign the parishioners of St. Joan of Arc Chapel donated seven hundred pounds of soup, milk and baby foods to be shipped overseas through the Catholic Welfare Conference. And they probably duplicated this gift many times. The Christian Scientists worked hard for years collecting clothes and food that they sent to people in the freed countries of Europe.[55]

In assembling the story of what was accomplished in Woodstock during the war it was possible to study the few records that were saved and to use material remembered by those who were in the midst of the activity, but trying to check dates and amounts through contemporary newspapers was most difficult. The local papers were weeklies and of these there are no complete files. In fact only a few scattered copies of Woodstock's own newspapers are extant. Of the county publishers the only office that has archived files is the *Catskill Mountain Star*, whose coverage of Woodstock was not very full during the war years. The publishers of the *Ulster County News* have not preserved their files; nor were these to be found in the Kingston Library. The *Kingston Daily Freeman*, which is in the library, restricted its Woodstock news items to a few inches per week. This may be accounted for by the fact that Marion Bullard's pages in the *Ulster County News* gave such excellent coverage of our village events. She kept a fairly complete file of her own articles, and these, after passing through several hands, have fortunately ended up in the attic of the Woodstock Library. After a thorough search I discovered them in an old unmarked carton.

In reading Marion Bullard's editorials, called "Sparks," I have been deeply impressed by her wit as well as her indefatigable energy in fighting for the important issues in our village. When she was convinced of what was right she plunged into it with all her strength, without consideration for her own popularity or whom she might alienate. Thus she irritated many persons, but they respected her integrity as a newspaperwoman, and as the years have passed most of the reforms she advocated have been realized. She never allowed her feelings to become encrusted with disillusionment, and she was always ready to work to alleviate hardship. Her wit, which was considerable, made her best editorials sparkle. Yet her greatest success was on the radio, broadcasting the *Woodstock Hour*. This program was filled with news and interviews, and she excelled at getting people to give an interesting account of themselves. Whether they were great scholars, politicians, artists or just old-timers, all were given time for expression. If there were recordings of these interviews they would form a contemporary history of Woodstock, and would show the great talent that Marion Bullard possessed as an interviewer and reporter.

It is impossible to estimate all the individual work, money and gifts that went—often at a real sacrifice—from Woodstock to the war victims. If all the other villages in the United States gave an equal amount, it must have helped a little to alleviate the hurt and suffering of the world.

Manuel Bromberg, Olin Dows and Pablo Picasso in the latter's Paris studio in 1945. Courtesy of Manuel Bromberg.

Chapter 13

THE SOLDIERS' STORIES

WOODSTOCKERS SHARE THEIR WAR EXPERIENCES

During the Second World War over two hundred young men and women from Woodstock were moved into positions all over the world. Some of them belonged to families who were accustomed to travel, but to those who were born in the village and who had never been away the great adventure must have seemed particularly catastrophic. They are older men now and glad to be home at jobs in garages, in restaurants, driving trucks or working for firms that require the technical training they received in the armed forces. Aware of their service records, one asks if they remember the Coral Sea, Guadalcanal, the Philippines or Japan—or perhaps Tunisia, Sicily, Italy, Normandy or the Rhineland—to see if these bring an interested light to their eyes. Their knowledge of the world has expanded far beyond the Catskills. One man especially remembers the mules and the mud at Monte Cassino; another recalls the GIs slogging along through the Normandy hedgerows; a third tells of finding a reproduction of one of Speicher's paintings in an abandoned Japanese command post; and still another remembers the stench of Japanese corpses, which seemed so much more odoriferous to him than our own dead. A pleasanter memory is that of one youth who recalls sipping wine at a café along the Riviera as the German shells screamed overhead. It was just General Kesselring firing from the heights along the Italian frontier toward the American position behind Antibes, and it did not spoil his enjoyment. They called this the Champagne Front because it was easy to get passes to the Riviera and luxury.

Some Woodstockers were able to use their artistic talents to advance the war effort. Among those was Manuel Bromberg, Sergeant and U.S. War Artist for all services in the European theater of operations. Similarly, Anton Otto Fischer, whose story is told later in this chapter, went on special assignments to make pictorial records of U.S. Coast Guard engagements. Other Woodstockers, in fields of endeavor besides the armed forces, also contributed to the winning of the war—such as those employed in defense plants. Unfortunately we do not have them listed, although we know, for instance, that Ruth Downer, Jean Lasher and many others worked faithfully to produce matériel to keep the armed forces supplied. Anne Leaycraft worked on charts for the Navy in the Hydrographic Office in Washington.[1] Then there was Phil Buttrick, who collected detailed maps of France from me for a secret purpose, which undoubtedly had to do with invasion plans.

Some of our people worked in the Office of Strategic Services, and even now, after ten years, will not divulge their experiences. These included Frank Schoonmaker (of wine fame but whom we knew as the publisher of the *The Hue and Cry*), who was brought up in Woodstock; and Walter O'Meara, who told us his story privately but refused to allow it to be published.

Of those in the Merchant Marine there were Kaj Klitgaard, an artist, who wrote of his experiences as a sea captain; and Jack Feeley, a veteran of the First World War. He was Chief Pumper on a tanker that crisscrossed the Atlantic during the war, carrying oil from South America and the Dutch East Indies to Europe, Africa and the United States. They sighted enemy submarines and had several narrow escapes. Henry Barrow worked in three theaters of the war and while captain of the latest type of oil tanker had his ship torpedoed and sunk in the Caribbean Sea. Kenneth Downer was Regional Director for the United Seamen's Service under the Shipping Administration in the Pacific, and was attached to the Army in New Guinea. He had some close calls with typhoons and with a fire on a ship filled with ammunition and high-octane gasoline that was tied to a dock. Downer volunteered to help the crew cut the lines and dump some of the inflammable cargo, which, although there was a minor explosion, prevented loss of lives and saved the ship and the dock.[2]

Some might suggest that this chapter is not Woodstock history. In a narrow sense they are right, for it is really the stories of what befell our people when they were sent away from the village. But who can deny that when these boys and girls left our valley they carried the image of Overlook and the Village Green in their minds and hearts? When they returned they were different because of their foreign experiences. I have tried to record some of their individual adventures because they are now a part of the Woodstock character. I have attempted to reach every person who served in the war to get his or her story. Here are a few of them, usually told or written to me. Several of the soldiers ended their letters with "Thank you for including me in the history of my hometown."

Hans Cohn

Hans Cohn was the doctor in Woodstock when the Second World War broke out. Since he had come as a refugee from Germany in the 1930s, he knew the worst side of the Nazis. By 1941 he was an American citizen and ready to serve his new country. While waiting for his commission, besides his regular practice Dr. Cohn taught classes in first aid, but not many months passed before he was called by the army. Dr. Marie Biebe filled in for Dr. Cohn as village doctor for the remainder of the war years.

When Dr. Cohn returned to Woodstock he was asked to write an account of his war experiences, but he said he was too busy. However, enough people pestered him to tell his adventures that one winter evening friends were invited to his house. He told those gathered that he would relate his story just this one time. After the talk was finished I went home and stayed up all night writing everything I could recall. Later, this manuscript was typed and sent to Dr. Cohn, and within a half hour of receiving it he was at my door prepared to correct my mistakes. This was my indirect method of procuring the following account.

After his basic training, Dr. Hans Cohn, then a lieutenant, was sent to Camp McCall, North Carolina, in February 1942. Reporting to the head of the medics, he was ordered to join a glider battalion of the Eleventh Airborne Division but ended up with the paratroops instead. Dr. Cohn said smilingly that he hadn't volunteered as a paratrooper to be a hero, or for the adventure; after working out with the gliders he concluded it was the safer branch of the two! On his first glider trip, sitting next to the pilot, he was aware that they were not on their course and he wondered what would happen to the jeep tied behind him if they should crash. They came down on an emergency field and if he hadn't pulled up his legs they would certainly have been fractured, because the aircraft burst a hole in its hull and the sandy earth flew up into their faces. If this was what could happen on an ideal take-off, he wondered, how might it be in enemy territory? So he joined the paratroops. The latter were being given very stiff training, and their doctor naturally had to keep up with them. As the average age of these men was twenty-one or twenty-two, he felt like a grandfather.

The Eleventh Airborne left for Pacific duty on May 5, 1944, and saw service in New Guinea, Leyte, Luzon, Okinawa and Japan. The night before the paratroopers made their first combat jump was a difficult one, and the next morning they had no heart to eat their breakfast of powdered eggs. Dr. Cohn said it was impossible for him to eat; even the familiar sounds of the airplane engines warming up made him uneasy. He knew it was different this time as they climbed into their C-47s. The smell of gasoline made them sick. Everyone looked grave, and one boy read his Bible. It was cold but they were sweating, and every soldier's eyes were alert for the little light up front. They were part of a large fleet of transports and a command plane would give them their orders. At last it came, the light flashing green, which meant they were two minutes from the target. They stood up to prepare themselves and when the light flashed red they jumped one right after another, barely seconds apart. They were dressed alike, with no distinction between officers and soldiers, for the Japanese tried to pick out the leaders to shoot first. Dr. Cohn's medical supplies were carried in an ammunition belt and he was weighed down with other equipment, including a couple of hand grenades. Upon landing they abandoned their parachutes and ran to a rendezvous. It is essential that paratroopers assemble quickly, for they have little strength as individuals and their power depends on getting together as a fighting division. Without heavy equipment, these troops are obliged to do more man-to-man fighting in battle than troops of the other services.

It was the end of October 1944, one week after the main invasion, when the Eleventh Airborne Division landed on Leyte. The Japanese had been pushed back into the mountains and the Eleventh was camped some distance back from the port, expecting to be sent over to the north coast where the front then was. Up beyond them a regiment of Negro engineers was working at some construction, and as they believed that area to be cleared they had not posted guards around their camp. In the night the Japanese counterattacked, sneaking down from the mountains in considerable force. These engineers were holding a small perimeter and had sustained a number of casualties. The Eleventh was ordered to march to their relief, but Dr. Cohn was asked by his Colonel to accompany him to their immediate assistance in a cub plane. There was a small airfield close to the engineers that the Colonel hoped had not been captured by the enemy. They flew over the spot and, not seeing any Japanese, landed and ran for the woods. They hurried as fast as they could but floundered in mud up to their hips. Dr. Cohn told of how he got stuck and began to swear so hard that the Colonel had to shut him up for fear it would bring the Japanese snipers down on them. They did reach the engineers, and he began giving blood plasma immediately. The casualties were in a hut on the outskirts of the camp, and while the doctor was working on a wounded Negro there was a burst of shellfire through the hut. He dropped to the floor—except for one arm, which was holding the transfusion bottle. The firing grew worse and they had to evacuate the wounded. Shortly thereafter the Japanese captured the hut.

Meanwhile the main force of the airborne troops arrived, but instead of a full division they had only three hundred and fifty or four hundred troops—which were so inferior to the Japanese strength that if the latter had stepped up their attack they would have had a good chance of winning. Dr. Cohn remarked that this was typical of the enemy, who in this case had a good plan to counterattack and capture the port of embarkation with its enormous supplies, while the main American forces were occupied on the far side of the mountains. But their fighting strategy was not equal to the task. Just at dusk that evening a great formation of Japanese heavy planes flew over, evidently as a cover for a low-flying group of bombers. "Crump." Down came the bombs, the Americans trying to shoot them with their carbines, for they lacked heavy firepower. In the following days the Japanese were gradually pushed back and their attack failed. As soon as the individual Japanese felt pressure they would generally commit hara-kiri. The American losses were serious, especially among the engineers and signal corps. One hut where the attack had started was full of signal corps boys killed in bed, as they had not considered it necessary to set a guard. One man who had tried to escape was shot when he became stuck in the mud.

When this area was cleaned up the paratroopers were sent to their original objective on the front—back of the mountains. It was a wild place and difficult to dislodge the enemy, who continually sniped at them. Few prisoners were taken, although headquarters ordered that some be sent back for questioning. It was a five-hour climb through difficult jungle mountains to the base, subject to sniping, and it was easier not to take prisoners. The Japanese finally cut the U.S. supply line, leaving them without food or medicines. The doctor had to do what he could with only his hands to help the wounded. They had a number of casualties, but for every American lost there were at least two hundred Nipponese killed. The Americans had encircled a group of the enemy and were waiting to attack when their Japanese interpreter intercepted a message from the enemy's commander to his field officer, saying that reinforcements would be brought up during the night. Forewarned, the Americans ambushed this large force and killed them all. Their bodies were piled high, and as there was no opportunity to bury them they soon stank. The stench of dead men pervaded the air all through the camp, and for some unexplained reason the decomposed Japanese smelled worse than the American dead (at least to the Americans). Dr. Cohn, or Captain Cohn, as he then was, said he did not know which was worse, the smell or the hunger they suffered, but he would never forget either one.

For days they starved there, high in the mountains, until they were obliged to retreat. The soldiers went first to clear the path, followed by the doctor and his group, who carried down the casualties on improvised stretcher poles. The trail was almost perpendicular, requiring sixteen or more men to carry one stretcher. As the first units descended they saw on the trail a Japanese soldier standing for surrender with his hands above his head. When the Americans motioned for him to come forward he hesitated, trying to make them come to take him. The officer in command became suspicious and ordered his men to shoot. The troops bypassed this spot, but when Dr. Cohn and the stretchers came to it they were obliged to stay on the trail. As they reached the dead Japanese soldier, they ran into a line of enemy fire. Miraculously nobody in the group was hurt. However, it proved that the dead soldier had been a decoy.

Dr. Cohn was with the American forces that arrived on Luzon in January 1944. These units were even larger than the ones of the Normandy landing. After disembarking, the troops were sent by forced marches toward Manila. The main group rather unwisely moved ahead of their protecting flanks. This spearhead was advocated by their general, who was racing to arrive at the capital first. When they reached a mountainous ravine, the Japanese attacked without warning, shooting down on them with little opposition from the surprised American column. Reinforcements were rushed up, but to everybody's horror they were not armed. They were fresh youngsters hurriedly trained and shipped overseas ahead of their weapons, and here they were defenseless against Japanese fire. Dr. Cohn said the destruction was terrible. The medical corps worked desperately. One of the doctor's comrades was killed by his side, the blood spattering over him. He saw young boys dead all around him. Perhaps, Dr. Cohn said, it had been a necessary choice to equip the army in Europe ahead of the eastern forces, but he could never forget the sacrifice of these youngsters on Luzon.

The final chapter of Dr. Cohn's experience with the army took place at dawn on August 29th when the Eleventh Airborne Division made the first American landing on the Atsugi airstrip in Japan. It was here, eight hours later, after the airfield had been completely secured, that they welcomed the Supreme Allied Commander, General Douglas MacArthur. It was the Eleventh Airborne band that ushered him in as the conqueror of Japan. When they had finished playing, General MacArthur said to the conductor, "I want you to tell the band that that's about the sweetest music I've ever heard."

Dr. Cohn returned home to Woodstock in November 1945.

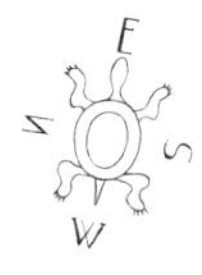

The narrative that follows is told from the point of view of a couple of Woodstock sailors, Warren Riseley and Bob Brinkman, who took part in the battle of Leyte Gulf. Riseley was aboard the USS *Gatling*, a destroyer, and Brinkman was on the carrier *Princeton*. This battle was one of the key naval engagements of the war, and included some of the largest ships of the Japanese fleet. Their vessels had been concentrated into two task forces to fight off Allied landings on the Philippine Islands. Over a dozen of the enemy carriers and many of their lesser ships were sunk or damaged. Although the American fleet was of greater tonnage, some of their battleships were not in top condition because they had been salvaged from the sneak attack on Pearl Harbor. In all, the Americans lost six combat vessels, against twenty-six for the Japanese. It was a tremendous victory for the Allies and it destroyed the might of the Japanese navy.

Warren Riseley

Warren Riseley, on the USS *Gatling*, took part in the rescue of survivors from the *Princeton*, which was damaged during the battle. As Riseley recalls it, about ten o'clock one morning there was an attack by the enemy, but they were driven off without damage to the U.S. Fleet. After this interchange the *Princeton* was landing her planes when Riseley saw an aircraft circling the carrier—and then crash upon her flight deck. It penetrated to a lower deck where planes were being refueled and created a terrible blaze. At first it was hoped the *Princeton* could control the fire, but Riseley's ship as well as three other destroyers and the cruiser *Birmingham* were ordered to stand by. These vessels took turns pulling alongside the stricken carrier, trying to help fight the fire and rescue its crew. After the second approach Riseley's ship came under heavy attack from Japanese planes, and for the next hour he was kept busy at his 20 mm gun station on the starboard side without a view of the burning *Princeton*. He saw a squad from the *Gatling* jump into the sea with lines around their waists to rescue sailors swimming in the water. He asked several of those saved if they had seen Bob Brinkman, whom he believed was aboard the *Princeton*, but none of these men knew Brinkman. It was impossible to inquire further because the enemy aircraft were flying close, attempting to shoot the men in the water, so the ship's guns were kept busy trying to hold them off. After the air was cleared the *Gatling* was about to make another run for the carrier when the *Birmingham* signaled she would go first, and indicated that Riseley's ship was to follow closely behind. By now the *Princeton* was burning badly. As the *Birmingham* went alongside, the ammunition magazine exploded, breaking the carrier in two, and the stern sank at once. The *Birmingham* was damaged and almost everyone aboard was killed from the concussion. Riseley could see her crew spread out topside, mortally wounded.

Now two ships were out of commission. There were still men to be seen on the bow of the *Princeton* and the destroyer pulled alongside to pick them up. They already had about two hundred rescued men aboard who needed attention, most of them with severe burns and other wounds. The *Gatling's* crew applied salve to the burns, replaced their clothes and gave them cigarettes—although there were many who could not manage their smokes. Riseley remembers holding a cigarette to the lips of a sailor whose face, hair and eyes were terribly burned, yet who managed to take a few puffs before the doctor came to give him a shot of morphine. There were wounded sailors lying all over the decks until room could be found for them below.

Meanwhile the other destroyers fired torpedoes to sink the section of the *Princeton* that was still afloat. About dusk the *Gatling* headed back to her base, obliged to go slowly to keep pace with the stricken cruiser *Birmingham*. The next morning as they passed the Japanese air base at Yap they came under attack once more, but passed through unscathed after shooting down one enemy plane. Later that day they arrived at their base on the atoll of Ulithi where they tied up alongside another destroyer that was carrying survivors. Warren Riseley heard his name called and discovered it was Bob Brinkman from Woodstock! He took his friend below deck and gave him clothes and cigarettes, because Brinkman had jumped into the sea without any possessions. Fortunately he was not injured and Riseley was able to notify Mrs. Brinkman that her son had been rescued.

The next day the *Gatling* was ordered back to Luzon to rejoin the fleet, with which they saw more action. Their ship was at sea continuously for sixteen months, participating in nine invasions and two naval engagements. They were credited with downing about eight enemy planes and sinking two ships. After Iwo Jima they returned to the United States for repairs and afterwards resumed duty in Asiatic waters. From Guam they accompanied the *Missouri* to Tokyo, where they put in three months of occupation duty. The *Gatling* received many awards, including nine stars for Asia-Pacific service.[3]

Bob Brinkman

After hearing Warren Riseley's story of the sinking of the *Princeton*, I wrote Bob Brinkman. This is his reply:

> Well, it has been quite a long time ago since I was on the USS *Princeton* (CVL 23). To be exact it was on the 24th day of October in the year of 1944 that the best ship in the Third Fleet met its untimely death.
>
> I shall give you as much of her history as I can, up until the day she was sunk.
>
> First off, I enlisted in the regular navy on July 17, 1942. I went through my "boot" at NRTS, Newport, R.I.

On September 10, 1942, I was assigned to the Aircraft Carrier USS *Sangamon*. We took this ship on a "shakedown" in Chesapeake Bay and on October 10 we set sail for the island of Bermuda. We arrived there seven days later, and anchored off of Hamilton, the capital. We provisioned, took on bombs, small arms ammo, and aviation gasoline. Six days later we sailed for parts unknown.

Then one day, much to our surprise, we met up with the largest convoy of ships I had ever seen in my life. We knew then that something big was coming up. Our Captain passed the word, telling us that we were to help support the first landing in French Morocco. Immediately preparations were made for the coming D day. We had practice landings, gunnery, fire drills, abandon ship drills, etc. We got so that before the first sound of the gong had died we were out of our bunks and halfway up to the flight deck.

Finally the day dawned, November 10, 1942: I was assigned as an aerial gunner to a TBF [torpedo bomber]. We crossed the coastline at 0500 hours on the dot. The French people were in the streets, waving and jumping around when they saw our insignia. We met no opposition in the air. We had it made easy, as the saying goes. This wasn't to last though. All of a sudden, from out of nowhere, there were planes all around us; we were caught unawares. They had come out of the sun, and no one knew what was up for a second or two. We fought them off with no losses to us, and headed for home. This went on for seven days. At one time we were [the ship was] so close to the shore that the coastal batteries opened up on us. At the same time they spotted a periscope in the wake of our ship. Immediately a can [destroyer] came across our fantail [rear] and dropped her depth charges. Scratch one sub.

On the 17 of November 1942, we headed back for Norfolk, Virginia. What we called that city in those days couldn't be mentioned in any book, or this letter as far as that goes.

We ran into a North Atlantic storm of all storms three days later. The waves were mountainous; they smashed our flight deck to splinters; ruptured our catwalks and gun mounts, so that they were unsafe for use, and washed away all our life rafts and small boats. Our aircraft were also damaged, and we lost six of those on the third day. Finally, when we had ridden out the storm, we were off the coast of Labrador. We had Thanksgiving at sea. Spam, cold tea, peas and crackers. Real choice. At last we reached Norfolk, and disembarked for the NAS [Naval Air Station] which was to be our home for two weeks.

Some of our men were being transferred to the USS *Princeton*, which was being built in Philadelphia, Pa.

The rest of us departed Norfolk for the blue Pacific. We went directly to Nouméa, New Caledonia, where we met three other aircraft carriers; the *Saratoga* was the biggest.

We were at Nouméa about ten days when the whole squadron was sent to Henderson Field on Guadalcanal, to support or soften up the invasion of Munda. We lost no planes but "Washing Machine Charlie" kept us awake all night. Went through a few night bombing raids, but no casualties so far; we were far too lucky. Our first casualty was not due to combat. A plane went through the barrier and killed my best friend. It was a pretty gory sight, one that I will never forget as long as I live.

You'd be surprised what a prop [propeller] can do to a man.

After a series of raids on Munda and Bougainville, we returned to the States for dry dock. We got to stay thirty days, and headed for Pearl Harbor again. This is where I was transferred to the USS *Princeton*.

We went through the Marshalls, Gilberts, made raids on Mindanao, Truk, Ponape, Kwajalein, Eniwetok, Roi, Majuro, etc. We met stiff opposition there. My plane was shot up pretty badly at Majuro, and we had to ditch at sea. We were picked up an hour later. Next we went to Saipan, Tinian, Guam and Rota. This was the big "Turkey Shoot." Our squadron alone knocked down 286 planes that day. We also connected [with] the Japanese fleet for the first time. Admiral Mitscher immediately dispatched all available aircraft to attack. We had flown about 100 miles when we spotted the Japanese force. Immediately the TBFs went to the sea level, dive-bombers from out of the sun, and fighters came in from all angles, strafing and bombing. We sank our "fish" into the guts of a cruiser, and saw her head for Davy Jones locker. We were well pleased. The aircraft carriers were so badly damaged that the Japanese planes couldn't land or take off.

We winged our way home; it was getting dark; we couldn't find our carriers; finally, thanks to Admiral Mitscher, the ships put on their lights to direct us home. No prettier sight had we ever seen. All the planes were low on gas; we landed on the first carrier that could take us. We were split up all over the place. We were lucky we got home. Just as we landed we ran out of fuel. Some of the other planes weren't so lucky. We lost seventy five that night in the drink, compared to a loss of ten in the attack. We also lost thirty men that night. Some of the flight crews were found the next day.

One incident did happen that shook us up. We had given a plane a wave off; when it went by the island we could see the meatball on the side. It landed in the sea, exploded; it was loaded with a high explosive, enough to do great damage to our flight deck, not counting the number of lives that would have been lost.

The next day we pulled into Saipan for ammunition, gasoline and provisions. We were there one day. We could see the fighting still going on. They had not invaded Tinian yet. They were softening up the beaches with artillery fire then. The Battle of the Marianas was drawing to a close.

Upon scouting around Guam, we saw a man running on the beach waving an American flag. We found out later he had been teaching the natives, during the Japanese occupation, in guerilla warfare. He had been on the island ever since the Japanese took it over.

We then headed out for a raid on Ulithi atoll, where we met no opposition at all from the air. The atoll was taken in a matter of weeks. When we anchored in Ulithi we had to keep guards all night as the Japanese would tie explosives to their backs, swim out to one of the ships, and blow it up, themselves with it. We spotted one our last night in port, but he didn't get very far.

The next day we headed out and were told we were going to raid Mindanao. The first raid since 1942. I had been grounded by then, so I was in the gasoline detail [refueling planes].

We had raids every morning and every night. The reason these raids are mentioned and not the others is these were last-ditch defenses by the Japanese and they threw everything they could at us. We stayed there for three days, never getting a full night's sleep due to the air attacks.

We then got a surprise. We were to go to Formosa. To tell you the truth we were all shaking; no force had ventured that close to Japan before and nobody knew what to expect. We found out all right. After our first day of raiding everyone was lined up for chow when the G.Q. [General Quarters] went off. No one had a chance to do much. I and two buddies of mine were on the flight deck on watch, when all of a sudden there were Jap planes all around us. We ran to a 20 mm. I was in the mount; we started firing at a twin engine "Betty." We pumped at least two magazines into her and she blew up just about fifty yards from us. We were all singed from the heat, but no serious burns. We got the Navy Commendation Medal for that.

That night, the 23rd of October, 1944, we were told to meet the rest of the Third Fleet at Leyte Gulf in the Philippines.

By 0400 on the 24th we were preparing our first attack on Leyte. We were close enough to see the mountains. We had no raids on the ship; everything was peaceful. We had reported a "bogie" [unidentified aircraft] was in the area. No one paid any attention to it.

I was in the hangar deck on the phone watch when, all of a sudden, I heard a loud explosion and saw smoke about half way down the deck. We had been hit. It was a lucky hit. It disrupted all electrical and water power. Our hangar deck was loaded with torpedo planes fully loaded with "fish," gasoline and auxiliary gas tanks. Fire broke out immediately. I saw ten of my friends vanish down that gaping hole in the deck into a fiery inferno. Their screams were ear splitting; then all was silent. Most on the hangar deck had been killed or were badly wounded. My phone wires had been cut, so I immediately went to start extinguishing the fire with anything I could lay hands on. We were trying to keep the "fish" from exploding. We didn't succeed. I was blown half way up the deck and I went out on the catwalk and up to the flight deck. We started pushing the planes over the side to make more room for the men. We ditched ammunition, everything.

Finally the "fish" started going off in succession; our flight deck looked like somebody had gone down the middle of it with a huge can opener. We were told to abandon ship; I jumped overboard and tried to blow up my life belt; a friend of mine didn't have one and was fighting—he couldn't swim. I pushed it over to him, but he never got it; he had gone under. So there I was, no life jacket, my clothes starting to drag me under, when I looked up. There was the Chaplain; he threw me a mattress. I was never so thankful in all my born days. I picked up two more men and we floated past the burning ship to a group of men that had a life raft. This may seem like a tall tale to you but it actually did happen. There were twelve of us all told.

We talked about nothing else but our rehabilitation leave in the States. What we were going to do (which can't be mentioned, by the way); where we were going, and when were we going to get paid. It was the only way to keep our minds off of things. The Japanese attacked about three more times but didn't hit the ship. Finally after six hours in the water we were picked up by a can.

We circled the *Princeton*, helping when we could, looking for buddies and fighting off air attacks.

We got a warning that twenty five enemy planes were in the area, so we had to leave the *Princeton*. They were driven off, and we proceeded to the aid of the *Princeton* in hopes of saving her. But fire had leaked into the aft bomb storage and gasoline tanks. Just as the cruiser *Birmingham* pulled alongside the aft part of the *Princeton* blew up, also damaging the cruiser. Three hundred forty-two men, including the captain of the *Birmingham*, were killed instantly. The decks were nothing but a mass of blood, etc. These men were the fire fighting crew, that were going to board the *Princeton* to try and put the fire out.

At five o'clock that afternoon all the ships left the *Princeton*'s side and put fire torpedoes into her hull and sank her. There were tears in more than one man's eyes when she went under. She went up in a sheet of flame; when the smoke had cleared away she was gone. She died hard, just like she fought.[4]

Anton Otto Fischer

Due to his reputation as a painter of sea subjects, the artist Anton Otto Fischer was asked in 1942 to join the U.S. Coast Guard by its commandant, Admiral Waesche, and was given the rank of Lieutenant Commander. His first series of pictures on Coast Guard subjects appeared in *Life* magazine and he was then asked by the Coast Guard to go on active duty to record what the convoys were up against in escorting merchant ships through the submarine zone in midwinter. He was assigned to the USS *Campbell*, a Coast Guard cutter on North Atlantic convoy duty, and in January 1943 found himself on a ship where he was old enough to be the father of every man on board, including the captain. On the return trip the *Campbell* ran into a wolf pack of German submarines. The U.S. ship fought them off all day with depth charges but in the evening there was close combat with one that surfaced suddenly right off the *Campbell*'s bow. The fight ended with the submarine sunk, but the *Campbell* itself was hopelessly disabled. The engine room was flooded and the ship was left without light or power. She drifted helplessly for three days about eight hundred miles off the U.S. coast until a valiant naval tug managed to make its way out to the *Campbell* and tow her back to St. John's, Newfoundland. Fischer painted the whole episode in a series of dramatic pictures that were reproduced in *Life* magazine. At war's end he retired with the honorary rank of Commander.

Anton Fischer was born in Munich, Germany, in 1882. At the age of five he was orphaned and at sixteen ran away to sea, where he spent the next eight years on various types of ships traveling all over the world. In 1906, with savings of $750, he went to Paris and studied at the Académie Julian under Jean-Paul Laurens for two years, after which time his money ran out. At that point he returned to the United States and began his career as an illustrator. He married the daughter of Admiral Sigsbee.[5]

The Campbell Meets Her Enemy *shows the USS* Campbell *bringing to bear her firepower on a U-boat. The submarine is caught in the beam of the twenty-four-inch searchlight and is being punished by 20-mm tracer shells. A three-inch shell has slammed into its side, sending a geyser of water into the air. This painting by Anton Otto Fischer (1882–1962) was featured in a* Life *magazine spread in 1943. Oil on canvas, 24¼ x 36¼ in.* Courtesy of the National Museum of the U.S. Army, Army Art Collection.

Taking Off the Survivors of a U-Boat, *1943, is another Anton Fischer painting of the encounter. Oil on canvas, 24 x 31½ in.* Courtesy of the National Museum of the U.S. Army, Army Art Collection.

James Kinns

As soon as James Kinns was inducted into the army his adventures began. This young man, who had lived quietly with his wife and babies here in Woodstock, was suddenly crisscrossing the United States from one training camp to another. In 1945 he was sent overseas as a member of the Signal Corps and found himself in India where at first the poverty-stricken masses depressed him. It was hard for him to understand the Hindu faith, a tenet of which was the veneration of all white cows. Nobody dared oppose them and the cows had their own old-age home where they were pastured in comfort. Even in one of Calcutta's finest hotels, when a white cow entered it was treated with respect as the staff gently persuaded it to leave. The monsoon came on while Kinns was in India and he watched with amazement as two feet of rain fell within a few minutes; the thirsty soil sucked it up and then within a day became powdery again. A slim Moslem boy, who might have been stunted from hunger, attached himself to Kinns and was determined to follow him to America. He did not get that far but he accompanied Kinns on the Burma adventure. The boy saw photographs of a paradise that we call Wittenberg, Ulster County, New York. In these were pictured Kinns's wife and their home—and, what astonished the boy most of all, the various automobiles belonging to Kinns and his in-laws. He tried to tell the Indian that he was just a workman, but with this the boy became even more convinced that everyone in America was a millionaire. When Kinns was sent to Burma the Indian boy sneaked aboard the transport and went along to serve him faithfully.

In Burma, Kinns found himself among many wonders and in places with strange names that in time became familiar. Among these were Rangoon and Mandalay and the Irrawaddy River—sites that he had never expected to visit. He was put to work driving a supply truck over the Burma Road and he recalls the magnificent mountains, the flamboyant sunsets and the gorges dropping a mile or two below the road. Sometimes they drove to altitudes of eleven or twelve thousand feet where it was cold when their convoy stopped to eat. They were not allowed to build fires so Kinns devised a rack close to the manifold of the engine where he stowed the cans of daily food. When he was ready to eat he had only to open a can to have hot chow. The other drivers were surprised to see him eating warm food and soon he was asked to fit up dozens of similar racks for other trucks. There would be as many as three hundred and seventy vehicles in a convoy. They were not allowed to travel in groups of fewer than six because bandits were likely to attack smaller units. Radio trucks were distributed along the convoy to keep them advised of danger spots. There were also pockets of Japanese guerrillas to be encountered at such places as Myitkyina, Bhamo or Paoshan—exotic-sounding names to be remembered by the young man.

They were carrying military supplies and personnel for General Terry's army in China. At Kunming, warehouses were filled with supplies guarded by native police who were watched by a population half-starved and ready to steal whenever there was an opportunity. If the thieves were caught they were hastily judged guilty or not guilty: if it was the former verdict they were shot; otherwise they were freed. Jimmie Kinns drove his truck over the Ledo, the Stilwell and the Burma Road—and an extension in China known as the West Road, which ran from Kunming to Kweiyang and on to Chungking. In some places the road was so narrow it did not provide enough track space for the multiple tires on their huge vehicles, and the outside treads might have to hang over a precipice. He had photographs of one such place, which showed a lake far beneath the road. They would frequently encounter remnants of the Chinese First Army in groups of fifty or a hundred, trudging their way to homes thousands of miles away near Shanghai. They had been boys when inducted in 1933 and had been pushed back further and further into the southern provinces. Those who survived the fighting, starvation and cholera now looked like old men as they crept northward.

Among the photographs Kinns took are ones of a monastery in the mountains of Burma with the Temple of One Thousand Gods. It is a beautiful building with roofs that curve upward at their base, seen behind a lotus pool, with high mountains forming the background. He told of the many-hued lilies in the pool and of the two twenty-foot-high statues of gods that are pictured in terrifying aspect on the portico. Perhaps they were placed there to keep evil spirits from entering the temple. There was a monk who spoke English and told them that a wooden carp they admired had been carved a thousand years ago. Centuries of meditation seemed to hang above the temple even as the ten-ton trucks rushed noisily by on the new road. But to Kinns a year in the Orient seemed a long time, and he was glad when he was ordered home.

There were three wars progressing in China. The Nationalists were fighting the Communists, the Japanese were still at war with the Chinese and the Americans were fighting the Japanese. One of the last photographs Kinns took was of some of the fifteen thousand trucks they left behind, and he would never know who benefited from them. He was sent back via the Suez Canal and the Mediterranean, but fortunately they stopped first in India where he parted with the young Moslem lad. It was winter and they had boarded the aircraft carrier *Essex* to cross the North Atlantic when they encountered a terrible storm; it severely damaged the ship, bashing in its prow and leaving a hole wide enough to allow several trucks to drive through, but they finally made their port in the United States.[6]

Robert Carlson

Robert Carlson was brought up in Woodstock, one of three sons of the well-known landscape painter John Carlson. When the United States entered the war he was a member of New York's famous Squadron A, which became a cavalry tank unit and was absorbed by the regular army. After officers' training Carlson was assigned to the 635th Tank Destroyer Battalion and as First Lieutenant was sent to England preparatory to the Overlord invasion. It is thirteen years since Bob Carlson rode his armored car onto Omaha Beach with his guitar tied on top. Now he is not sure exactly when it was, although he thinks it was with the second or third wave of troops. His battalion had previously been given a map of the landing area to study, and while waiting to board the transport he had busied himself making a relief map of that part of the Normandy coastline. It was dark when their ship approached France and the officer in command was uncertain regarding the location of Omaha Beach. He used Carlson's contour map showing the exact outline of the bluff.

They did not have a bad time climbing the escarpment, because the enemy batteries had already been silenced. After assembling their battalion they

Robert Eric Carlson at Aachen, Germany, in February 1945. By his side is his guitar in its wooden case. Courtesy of Historical Society of Woodstock.

camped in a hedgerow about a half mile back from the beach. It was while they were waiting for the next move that Carlson saw some French "characters," as he called them, come from a nearby farm, driving a donkey on which were two panniers holding jugs of Champagne cider. Ignoring the danger, they toured the entire field, giving long drinks to each man in every unit hidden in the *bocage*. Other French people brought gifts of eggs and milk to show their gratitude to the Americans. It surprised Carlson to see the farmers going about their daily chores in the midst of the battleground—which extended for miles. There were rumors of German agents left behind who telephoned their positions to the enemy, but this he could not verify. During their next advance with the First Division, the 635th was constantly under fire and every night they would sleep in a trench covered with a camouflage of shrubs.

One morning they awoke at dawn to the sound of enemy planes circling their position and to their dismay found that the Normandy cows had eaten their camouflage. In a letter to his parents Bob describes their advance across France as following roughly the route he and his older brother had taken a few years previously on a bicycle trip, but time and the war had changed the aspect of the places he remembered. He and another officer went ahead of their Tank Destroyer Company to choose sites for guns in preparation for possible counterattacks. He felt like a pawn on a chessboard but realized he was very lucky to be alive. As an example of his good fortune he described the night before they were to start on a "drive forward." He decided to change the position of their armored car and his foxhole—to be nearer to the command post so he would be the first to know when the orders came to start. German planes roared overhead, dropping bombs, and the spot where he had been before the move received a direct hit. His guitar also survived, and whenever there was an opportunity Bob played and sang as he had done all his life.

When asked if he had any dealings with the Underground, Carlson remembers that once, in the middle of the night, a little Renault full of men woke them to ask for help in capturing a group of Storm Troopers who were holed up on a farm in no man's land. The Germans were reported to be sleeping in the house and every morning hiding in the nearby forest. His commanding officer gave orders for Carlson to lead a platoon in two armored cars to help the civilians, and off they started, with the Renault leading. As they were passing through the American lines they were fired upon until they established their identity and were allowed to proceed—but now the little French car went second. They drove onward to a house, where they picked up a man who was familiar with the farm where the Germans had been hiding. He told them there was a dog on the premises and they would have to be very careful not to arouse it. When they reached the place the men were deployed in a circle around the house. One of the armored cars took up a strategic position hidden near the gate, and they all waited for the dawn. At daylight a girl emerged through the gate and they grabbed her before she could shout a warning. Though they kept her prisoner for a couple of hours, no Germans appeared. The girl told them that the soldiers had left two days before. Finally they decided she was telling the truth, but before they entered they sent a volley of shells into the roof of the house. This set the house afire, which Carlson said he regretted because it was an attractive group of buildings (he did not think it was destroyed). They proceeded to search the premises thoroughly and, although they did not find any Germans, they discovered an escaped American aviator hiding in the hayloft who was very pleased to be rescued. The band of soldiers returned to their base without capturing any Storm Troopers but with a grateful GI.

Carlson's battalion went a short distance into Germany and it was there he experienced the most comfortable living of the campaign. For several peaceful evenings the men were invited into a farm cottage owned by an old woman who had a daughter—and a cow named Luna. There it was warm and they could play games or write at a table. The woman gave them milk to drink, and for these soldiers it was a wonderful interlude between battles. They were sufficiently relaxed to enjoy the rooster they called Herman—it did a perfect goose step and they'd "count cadence" for it to march. Carlson felt sorry when the time came for him to turn the old woman out to stay with her neighbors so that other soldiers could occupy her cottage. It was not long before the direction of the war changed, but he never forgot the woman's kindness.

A little while later they had occupied a hill to relieve some battle-weary boys. There they received orders to fight their way to yet another hill; this was accomplished with the aid of tanks and only a couple of casualties. But the Germans poured into the small valley between the two hills and their battalion was directed to pull out. Then they were ordered to withdraw to a position deep in the Hurtgen Forest and from there they retreated back to Belgium. His platoon was put into the reserves as they had been taking a beating. This was the time of the Ardennes breakthrough when Carlson's friend, John Faggi, was wounded in the Hurtgen Forest, and another Woodstock boy, Charles Carnright, lost his life with Patton's army in the withdrawal behind Metz. The German army completely surrounded a town named Bastogne on an important crossroad where yet another Woodstocker, Aubrey Milne, was fighting with the 101st Paratroop Division.

After a rest period Carlson's battalion was assigned to join fresh troops of the Seventy-first Infantry to accompany them into the next engagement. In his letters home he was not permitted to detail the battles but he did describe the endless rain and cold of the European winter. Their clothes were never dry and they had to ignore the discomforts, but he survived—as did his guitar. In Germany he was able to have a wooden box made to cover the instrument, which he calls "the juke." In describing the men of his group he tells of the Indian driver who was by nature lazy but who, when needed, was always on the spot; of their machine gunner who had a talent for picking up rumors and passing them on; of their radio man who was a farmer; and of another gunner who was a Filipino and a deadeye shot. But in the whole platoon there were only two men who were even remotely interested in his music, whether it was classical or jazz; therefore he curtailed his playing. In the old days of the Cavalry, whenever he strummed his guitar the men gathered around him, hungry to join in the singing or simply to listen. But these soldiers were deaf to music even when it might well have eased their boredom, for the war was almost over except for the waiting. As for Bob, he couldn't have lived without his music.[7]

Jean Barrère

Jean Barrère was from the Maverick in Woodstock, where he spent all his summers in his parents' home. His father, Georges Barrère, was the famous flute player.

> First I went to Africa—Casablanca, Oran, Algiers, Bizerte, Tunis . . . From there I was sent to Italy where I remained for a while doing what I considered . . . not quite as important a work as I wanted to be doing. The main thing in this job which was at all attractive to me was the fact that it permitted me the opportunity of travelling a great deal. I went to Corsica, Sardinia, Sicily, and all over part of southern Italy.
>
> After a couple of months in this capacity I "worked a deal" and got myself transferred to another organization. It was rather a unique one at that—it was a signal detachment which had served with the French Corps Expéditionnaire Français through the African and Southern Italian Campaign. We went to France—entering at St. Raphaël and became members of the First Airborne Task Force. We remained there with them for three months on what was called the "Champagne Campaign" front which stretched from Menton to Grenoble. Our job was to hold the Germans in Italy so that when General Clark and his Fifth Army came up from the south they would be bottlenecked there. We did a lot of liaison work with the FFI [Forces Françaises Intérieures, or French Forces of the Interior] and the Maquis in the Maritime Alps around Barcelonnette and Briançon, etc. My activities consisted mainly of maintaining wire communications for the Task Force and also for the French. Our "matériel formidable" was just a little too complicated for the average maquisard to cope with.

I utilized the P.T.T. [Postes Téléphone et Télégraphes] facilities a great deal—in fact did quite a lot of work renovating their systems for our use. I only had thirteen men with which to do this work but fortunately they had mostly all been associated with the Bell Telephone Company, and with the cooperation of the French linemen we did what I consider a very efficient job. The Task Force was relieved by the Forty-fourth Brigade at the end of three months and fortunately for us we remained with them. Our work was the same and went on until March of 1945.

It was the most amusing front one could really be on—for instance, one could sit on the terrace of the hotel at Monte Carlo sipping dry martinis and watch the shells from the artillery that was behind us in and around Nice sailing over our heads. The PT boats in the bay could be seen firing shells into the hills around Ventimiglia and Menton where the Germans sat and looked down our throats.

I might also add as a sidelight that we had with us, when the Brigade took over, the 442nd Infantry Regiment—that wonderful bunch of American Japanese. Really, it's a shame when one reads some of the things they are subjected to on the [West] Coast in this country—they were just about the best soldiers I have encountered anywhere.

Then in March they took our little detachment and brought us up to Vittel. They kept our outfit around Sixth Army Group headquarters but fortunately my thirteen men and myself were placed on Detached Service. We would go beetling off into the various outfits scattered out for a few weeks at a time, keeping in their wire or putting in switchboards and all that sort of thing—first into Alsace and then into Germany, entering at Saarbrücken, Kaiserlautern, Worms, Darmstadt, Ludwigshafen, Mannheim, Heidelberg, Kaufbeuren, Ulm and down towards Nürnberg and Munich. At this point the war in Europe ended.

A few weeks later we found our little band in a staging area in Rheims awaiting shipping someplace. However, from the cholera shots and the khaki-colored helmets we were being issued it was obvious to even the meanest of intelligences that it was not USA bound. Fish heads not agreeing with me, plus the fact that I had not yet seen "la ville lumière," prompted me to pull another "deal." I got myself transferred to a Signal Photographic Battalion that was stationed in Paris and so in the beginning of June I bade my fellows farewell in Rheims and went on my way to Paris. It so happened that if I had stayed with my outfit I would have gotten home a great deal sooner than I did, as they started out for the Pacific and en route the war ended there and the ship turned around and headed for the United States.

However, I did not regret my decision in the least because it offered me probably the most interesting four and a half months that I spent in Europe throughout the whole war. I sat around in Paris not doing much of anything—taking care of administrative details for the Battalion for a while—and suddenly the executive officer called me in and asked me if I would like to go out on an extended trip of Europe with a motion picture crew that was going to make a film for the War Department. It sounded interesting and I volunteered my services. It was to be for three months but I had the assurance that as soon as this mission was completed I would be able to come home almost immediately.

And so I started out with this crew making this picture. The picture was being made at the request of Governor Lehman to show the destruction that had been caused by the war in Europe and to show what was being done about it (i.e. UNRRA [United Nations Relief and Rehabilitation Administration]). The writer and director of the picture seized this opportunity to show in the film also the German plan of systematically weakening the neighboring nations to such an extent that in another twenty five years they will still be the strongest nation in Europe and will be able to again try their plans for world domination—a fact which unfortunately not enough people are aware of and something which I thoroughly believe to be true.

So we left Paris and off we went. Here follows the itinerary: Normandy, all Belgium, most of Holland, straight to Berlin, then down the Rhine to Nürnberg, Munich, across to Pilsen, then Prague and environs, then down through Linz to Vienna, south across the Yugoslav border to Belgrade. Then by plane to Athens, across by plane to Naples where our vehicles rejoined us, north to Rome, Florence, Leghorn, the Italian Riviera, the French Riviera to Marseille, then up La Côte d'Or to Lyons, Dijon, and then back to Paris. Quite a little tour, what?

And those damned jeeps—if I never see one again I shall be very happy—after bouncing along in one for eleven thousand miles the lower regions of one's anatomy become very, very sensitive. Obviously I cannot go into detail as to the many, many experiences we met up with on this trip—someday perhaps I'll write a book on this myself. They are far too numerous.

However, in general I can say that we went into each country looking for the worst possible conditions that existed in that country in order to photograph it and I have never dreamed that so much misery and want could exist. You have to see it really to appreciate it. As for UNRRA—a great deal is said pro and con and as the world of today is prone to indulge in what I consider that gravest of sins—generalizing—you cannot judge really the good, or the bad, in UNRRA unless you see it for yourself. Myself, I feel this way: if all UNRRA did was to give one can of milk to one starving European child a year I would still consider it worthwhile. This of course is a ridiculous example, however I believe it conveys what I mean.

The people of UNRRA seem to me to consist of three distinct types: those who are there simply to get a free tour of the world; those who have been overseas and who are bored with conditions over there and who have taken jobs with UNRRA because they have nothing else in view; and thirdly, that minority, as in all organizations, that really try to do a good honest job. Oh, there are many people who are sincere welfare workers and do their best. Unfortunately they sometimes are swamped by the uninterested and incompetent surrounding them, but as a whole UNRRA is a very important and worthy enterprise; also the fact that idealistically it is the way the world should be run—think of it, forty-seven nations all contributing to a cause and working together. Of course it can't go without hitches and of course incompetents infiltrate into its ranks—with such a young organization it is inevitable—but be that as it may, the vast good and the relief that UNRRA brings to the millions suffering throughout the world far outweigh its many faults.

Now which of all these countries do I believe to be the most destroyed and the one which will take longest to get back to normal? It is without the slightest shadow of a doubt "La Pauvre France." Why? For numerous reasons. First of all, one fact which many people do not see, is that France had a terrible time during the last war and is still suffering from it, to say nothing of this one. It lost a lot; the men and women who are supposed to be the leaders of France today were most of them the war kids of the last war.

Then, too, the German occupation of France was a masterpiece of organization and it went on for a long time—four years. All those who resisted and were caught were deported to concentration camps. All the leaders of the country—the writers, the doctors, the priests were sent away; the farms were then systematically pillaged; the farm equipment shipped off to Germany or wantonly destroyed; and then, malnutrition. The people, to coin a phrase, were "devitaminized" and when your system is lacking in the necessary amount of corpuscles and calories, etc., a lethargy sets in that takes a long time to get over.

It was considered patriotic to be dishonest during the occupation and that is another thing one does not get over immediately. I don't say the French are dishonest, no, not that, but instead of squarely attacking a thing they have a great tendency to get at what they want by circumventing it—in other words, "se debrouiller." It's as if a great fat slug had settled itself over all of France and the people are going to have to do a lot of pushing to get out from under. This same thing happened in all other countries—yes, but still and all not to the extent that it did in France.

The Frenchman also has several characteristics that are not so prevalent in other countries that permitted the German plan to take hold. He is "très rouspétteur"; he loves to kick—if something goes wrong he will sit and kick about it for an hour before doing anything about it; secondly, the little Frenchman has a genius for complications. Both of these characteristics were like antennas and without realizing it permitted the German wrought disruption to take a very firm hold. I could go on in this vein at great length but I think it's unnecessary as I am sure you see what I mean.

The worst thing in Europe on the whole is the situation which the kids are in. Many times as I would find myself among a group of children and could see their thin faces, their swollen bellies, rickety legs and thin wrists, I asked myself, "Is this the face of the future?" Well, if it is, something had damned well better be done about it and quickly too.

At the conclusion of this trip I was on I went to Southampton from where I sailed for America, coming across on the Aircraft Carrier USS *Enterprise* which made the crossing in five days. A few weeks later I was discharged from the army as a Captain and there ends a rather long interruption in my life.

My only hope is if I have any children that this same thing should not happen to them. Unfortunately we see things going on, in our country and abroad, that don't make for a very bright future. I may have a prejudiced viewpoint but it seems to me the same old cliques are working again to set the world in chaos. I'm afraid the Wheelers and Tafts and Nyes are not satisfied yet.

One rather amusing incident happened to me after I was in Paris and before I started on this long trip making the film I told you about. I received a cable from General Tobin who was the Commanding General of the outfit I was with on the Maritime Alps front, telling me to come down to Berchtesgaden, where the brigade was then, to receive a decoration for services rendered during the Southern France Campaign. I hopped a plane and went down there and found that the French Government had decided that I should receive the Croix de Guerre for my activities with them while we were down there.

A strange thing existed however—I have to go back about seven or eight years. A person born of French parents in this country, whether his parents are citizens or not, has to, when he comes of age, go to the French Consul and state whether he wants to be a Frenchman or an American. No matter where you are born, if it is of French parents, in the eyes of the French Government you are considered as a French citizen unless you go through this administrative formality of saying that you do not choose to be a French citizen. Well, I didn't know about this and when I came of age failed to do so.

Alright—one fine day before we got into the war I received a card from the French Consul telling me to pack my bags and go and join such and such a division in Martinique. Well, I beetled down to the Consulate and said, "Look, boys, there must be some mistake." "Non, non, Monsieur," they replied and then explained this business that I have outlined above. Well I was happily submerged in "Life with Father" and had no intentions of going to Martinique or any place else with the French army. Alright—I was declared a deserter and told that I could never go back to France, etc., etc., etc.

Well, now we switch back to where I get the telegram from General Tobin. I go to Berchtesgaden and in a very beautiful setting on the shores of the Hintersee, with much flourishing and kissings on cheek by the French General, and a very spit and polish military ceremony, I am given the Croix de Guerre. After the ceremony I am at a party at General Tobin's quarters where the French General was holding forth also. I went up to him and said, "Mon General, do you know that you have probably committed the gravest error of your whole military career?" With a look of terror he looks at me and says, "Que voulez vous dire?" To which I replied, "You have just given the Croix de Guerre to a deserter." Since I have come home I haven't been to the Consulate to see what situation I am now in but somehow or other I feel that it will get straightened out . . .[8]

Peter Carlson

It takes the Army a mere four weeks to make a parachutist out of a civilian. He may not be experienced at the end of this month, but he has accomplished the primary purpose of his training. He has jumped from a plane in flight by means of a parachute.

There are four phases of training. The men spend a great deal of time in a mock plane. In the plane they learn jump procedure and the proper means of leaving the plane quickly, but safely. During a real jump, twenty-four men can clear a plane in ten seconds without mishap. A man now becomes fully aware of what he is training to do; hence, if any men are thinking about quitting, they usually wash out at this point.

The last stage is mostly a pleasure because the men are dropped from 250 foot towers in open 'chutes, and float gently to the ground. These towers are precisely the same as the one used at the World's Fair.

On the eve before the first jump, each student packs two parachutes. Since he himself must jump with both of these, he takes great care in packing them. He dampens both 'chutes with the perspiration from his streaming brow ere he is fully satisfied that both have an excellent chance of opening properly.

At 7:30 P.M. everybody is in bed. There are a few who doze fitfully, but the majority lie on their backs chain smoking, listening for a board to creak, and wondering if their 'chutes will work okay. The usual train of thought about this time starts working: "Wonder what's on the menu for dinner tomorrow, and for crying out loud, will I be here to partake of the same?—Joe, your bitterest enemy. Darn nice guy. Too bad we don't hit it off better together. Heck, I didn't really have my heart in it when I placed cigar ashes in his beer the other night. I didn't think it would make him sick—much. Yeah, I'll have to see Joe tomorrow and square things."

That's only one sin. By 11 P.M. all past mal-doings have swarmed to the fore, and our student finds his pillow soaking wet. Suddenly this miserable train of thought is snapped by a piercing scream from the far end of the barracks. Nightmares? And how! This new character whom I shall call the Victim, starts to splutter: "No, you can't make me do it! The air is too loose. Stay away from me I tell ya eeee ahhhh a!" At this point our victim awakens. He knows he is shot for the night, so he joins the chain-smoking group who appear to be on the verge of bursting into flame.

At 6:30 our victim finds himself in the mess hall trying to follow good advice by attempting a hearty breakfast. It takes all the intestinal fortitude he can muster to even so much as stir a cup of black coffee. He lights a Camel. Good for the nerves, if he remembers the slogan correctly. He looks lovingly around him. Today the mess hall looks unusually cozy. He firmly believes he could sit there for all eternity drinking coffee and smoking Camels. His reverie is interrupted as the purring voice of the mess sergeant reaches his ears: "Where y'all think you is, at home?" Our victim is fully aware that he is not at home, but at Ft. Benning, Ga., and that he is on the verge of committing himself to someone or something. At 7:30 A.M. a grim, but determined, formation of men sets out for the airfield. Their heavy, plodding steps stir up strange, hollow echoes among the barracks along the road. Presently, through the chilly morning air comes a spine tingling roar. Planes warming up. Our victim strains his 20/20 orbs, and can barely make out the bulky shapes of the C-47s roaring into take off position.

Upon reaching the hangars, little time is wasted as 'chutes are drawn and fitted. The men rush furiously about checking one another. An instructor blows a whistle, and the men line up according to their plane rosters and move out on the tarmac to load up. Our victim finds himself scrambling through the door of a plane named "Come Back." He decides that he is going to make one gigantic effort to do just that.

Strange that "Come Back" is the lead plane. Or is it? Our victim draws the brilliant conclusion that someone has planned it this way so as to eliminate him first. A personal grudge, perhaps.

"Come Back" idles gently into position, then suddenly starts to vibrate and scream for mercy, as the pilot gives her the full throttle. "Come Back" sails down the cement at 100 miles per hour and the ground falls away. A seemingly nerveless character opposite our victim screams, "We're airborne." Two minutes pass. "Come Back" is clawing for altitude. Our boy is smart enough to know that he must be well upstairs by this time. He must take just one quick look at the ground. He tries to glance briefly but finds himself freezing. Premature rigor mortis sets in and his eyes bulge slightly beyond the bridge of his nose. Terra firma it is, but so far away. The view makes him think of the quilt on his bed at home.

Our victim turns from the window to gaze at his buddies across the aisle. He is proud to be part of them even if they do look a bit sick.

The jumpmaster who has been peering out the door turns and screams to be heard above the roar of the motors, "First stick, stand up and hook up! Check your equipment." The twelve men follow his commands like a group of robots. "Stand in the door!" The men push forward, not too enthusiastically, but forward nonetheless. "Go!" A short shuffling of feet, and one side of the plane is vacant. The plane leaps into a steep left turn and in a matter of seconds is back over the DZ. The jumpmaster shouts again, and our victim hooks up and stands numbly by. He must make good. To make sure, he turns to the grim, helmeted giant behind him. "Give me a big kick if I hesitate." The giant nods. "Go!" The line rushes toward the door, and before our victim has time to think the matter over, he is standing in the door. Above the roar, he hears the Sgt. cursing him up and down. He sticks an experimental foot out the door, and is sucked into space.

The prop blast whistles and whines in his helmet. He sees sky and ground alternately, but has no sensation of falling. Wham! A terrific jerk all but tears his shoulders from his body, and then stars, thousands of them. Next he sees an unsurpassable view of the country for miles around. He finds himself babbling his thanks to God for sparing him, and he has never been happier in all his life.

In approximately nine seconds our victim hits the ground and tumbles in his silk. In spite of its terrifying aspects, jumping is very safe. A 'chute may be counted on 99 times out of 100.

I am not qualified to say anything about combat jumping, but I have gone through the stages leading to one. Our outfit was alerted several times while we were at Amiens, France. On each occasion, the mission was cancelled. This alone is enough to wear a man's nerves to a frazzle. We could have dropped on any point in Germany within an hour, and knowledge of the fact made it utterly impossible to lead a normal life. The general feeling among the fellows was, "Hell, let's get up there and get it over with! We gotta die someday."[9]

Richard Crane

Richard Crane gave me a well-written account of his experiences in the 1943 invasion of Europe. Unfortunately it is too long to reproduce in its entirety. The Normandy landing and a large part of the Seine crossing are included. I regret that the section on the fighting along the Southern Bulge has had to be omitted because it was there Crane received the Silver Star for gallantry.

He begins his story with a description of the army waiting in England. At last the marshalling orders came for D day. These the men received in silent awe and relief, because "there could be no end to the conquest of Europe without a beginning."

A REPLACEMENT ON THE BEACHHEAD

In a few days our orders came, taking us to Plymouth. We had seen bombed cities, but this was in a different category altogether. It was devastation and annihilation, it was utter, it was the end. Here we stayed a few days more. The night of June eleventh we were trucked in blackout to Weymouth, where we boarded a steamer. When day broke, the coast of Normandy was in sight, with long lines of ships moving towards it ahead of us. Two explosions shook the vessel from bow to stern. By public announcement we were informed that they were only depth charges, with nothing to fear. Only depth charges? Do they drop such things for the fun of it? However, nothing further developed as we crept closer to the shore. The USS *Nevada* was dueling with a German gun on shore, which seemed to be on underground tracks, coming up at several distinct places to fire. The hulls of many vessels dotted the bay, ships that would sail no more. Activity was seen more clearly now: engineers at work on shore, amphibious vehicles taking on loads from the ships, plowing through the light surf, and rolling away over the hills. Finally it was our turn to go over the side and down into the landing craft.

As we neared the beach, a hundred thoughts passed in a strangely leisurely manner through my consciousness. I was in the prow and would be first off. Our arms

The Rescue, by Manuel Bromberg, depicts a scene near Carentan during the 1944 invasion of Normandy. Charcoal wash, 7¾ x 9 in.
Courtesy of Manuel Bromberg.
Photo by Dion Ogust.

were loaded. "The wind stood fair for the Coast of France"; was this from Campbell's Ballad of Agincourt?[10]

What lay over the hill rising from the beach? We stopped; the pilot let down the gates forming the prow. "It is only a few feet deep here," was all he said. I stood a moment that seemed an hour, and then stepped into the cold water, nearly to my hips, pistol in hand. Walking quickly to shore, I arrived well ahead of the others. While waiting I looked about me. A few canvases covered objects, very still, almost formless. Partially out of a hole in the bank ahead was one of those nasty little robot-tanks, like a huge fabulous beetle. I shuddered. It had been stopped before it could do any damage. As far as one could see, all about, the land was blasted, torn and burnt, as if cursed and withered by the gods. It was strangely silent. So were the soldiers at work, dirty, grim, and haggard. A knapsack lay to one side, the pitifully few personal effects scattered about. Whose was it? But what difference did that make? It was one of those "cross sections" of war, of the men who fight. "Let's go," quietly came from the lieutenant.

Up over the bank and along a road of heavy iron latticework, still under construction, we went. The lieutenant left us to determine the route, so we fell into conversation with some engineers. They told us that occasionally the enemy strafed and bombed the beach. Nobody would ever know what we owed the initial assailants, the paratroopers and amphibious forces. The Germans had been unspeakably cruel, and we had retaliated in kind. Bands of airborne troops still roamed about, sometimes forcibly taking German prisoners away from the military police and killing them. Such was the psychological effect of the first onslaught. German snipers were still abroad in the vicinity, and we still were within range of roving enemy artillery pieces. The land had been thoroughly mined by "slave labor," but the engineers had found that frequently the mines were un-fused. Investigation among the natives revealed that the harmless fields had been laid by Russians, so that it soon became standard procedure first to determine whether a field had been laid by them, and if so, forthwith to declare it safe. Our lieutenant returned to take us farther along the road; then we halted again near an extensive group of repair shops. A sudden embarrassed hush fell, and as I circumvented an officer with his back to me, I caught a glimpse of his profile. He was interestedly watching the work, now and again asking questions of the men and passing occasional remarks to a naval officer with him. His bearing was modest, and something about his shoulders indicated books and a desk: the thinker, the planner. Yes, it was he, it was Gen. Eisenhower, on the beachhead with us in the hour of determination.

Presently, another officer joined the pair and they departed. The last was Gen. Bradley and the naval officer, Admiral King. They were with us now, they would not be far from us tonight, I thought, as we were ordered to be sure that ammunition was in our chambers and to start inland.

The road led along hedgerows and ditches. Now and then small groups of natives passed us. Where did they live? What did they eat? We invited them to share our rations, which they did diffidently, saying that as yet our supply system could not be well established and we might need the food more than we thought later. Always they told us the same thing, that they had waited four years for us to come. They seemed quietly happy, as if a great weight had been lifted from them, but we were still insecure and, though they never said it, they must have realized what vindictive vengeance they would suffer if we were unseated. We passed on up through Ste. Marie du Mont, where a Nazi priest had machine gunned our troops from a church tower. The town was a shambles, our first sight of the fury that was our air force, the whirlwind of destruction, of fire and concussion, that was sweeping the whole land, from Normandy to Alsace. In the countryside again, we passed a farm, where a little girl stood watching us, envying our trench knives and carbines. There was written in her face and on her body what could never be set on paper. Here was reason enough for at least one soldier to fight. Could there be as many like her as there were soldiers?

At last we found our bivouac: just a field, with ditches under the bordering hedges in which to sleep, and a few wrecked gliders, one of which became the kitchen, another the command post. Here I stayed a month, awaiting assignment. As it was raining daily, these ditches in which we lived were lined with muddy slime. The supply problem, however difficult, was solved, and I was amazed at how much we were apportioned. Every few days men would go out, but always more came in, until many neighboring fields were full of replacements. At night the military police could be heard, exchanging shots with enemy snipers. Once they captured the French wife of a German officer, who had shot eighteen Americans. At night, too, Germans were up, strafing and bombing us, dropping flares which turned the dark into ghastly day, and made you want to shrink into nothingness. Our anti-aircraft guns were active, with their lurid red "flak." By day, transports wheeled like buzzards, parachutes drifting down like dandelion seeds. British Spitfires, like huge dragonflies, and our Thunderbolts, like pigeons, raced overhead with their bomb loads. Big bombers also passed again and again on their way to Cherbourg and inland. At first, light artillery could be heard, moving off as the days passed; then the medium [field guns], and finally the ground was rocked with the firing of heavy pieces; then these grew faint, too, as our lines advanced. The officer of the guard told us one day that our forces had finally cut off the peninsula; it had taken a desperate, hard, final push, but now one more wall had been reared against the Germans' drive to repel us. News was sketchy and oral, but we knew, from the bombers' flights, when the attack on Cherbourg started . . . and when the second assault, which brought success, was launched.

Then all efforts were turned to the south, and soon it was my turn to leave for the Seventy-ninth Division, whose insignia was the Cross of Lorraine. I thought of posters that I had printed in civilian life for the de Gaulle movement. It was Bastille Day, and the people were decorating soldiers' graves in the little cemetery. They brought us butter, eggs, and wine. My French surprised them; they could not believe that I was not at least Canadian. I had heard of physicians falling back on Latin at international medical conventions, but never, never, did I ever expect to hear that language used myself. Yet here it happened: A French boy and an American soldier talking together in the classic tongue!

AN ARTILLERYMAN AT THE SEINE BRIDGEHEAD

Our observation post overlooked the town of Mantes-Gassicourt. Occasionally French people passed back and forth across the river, which the Germans were planning to use as part of a stabilized frontline. The natives pointed out some of their comrades laying wreaths on the grave of a British aviator near the bank; the enemy had drawn back from the verge, and numbered only a holding garrison. An observation plane was gliding over a hill to one side of the town. Suddenly a German anti-aircraft gun fired. We plotted its position and reported it. The plane dived under the flak and returned to our lines. Our artillery began firing: what a hornet's nest was uncovered! The hillside was suddenly alive with Germans retreating into the woods above; this was more than just a gun position. So we shelled it, and the woods above. The French told us where the German artillery was, and we shelled that, too. They told us more: the enemy were sending up two divisions. It would be a week before our armor was due, but the decision was made: we were to cross and hold the bend in the river against all comers without armor, since that would be easier than dislodging a couple of SS divisions.

Finally, it was my turn to go up to the front lines with the forward observer, to conduct fire for the infantry. I had watched, day after day until my eyes were bloodshot and swollen, the slow, painfully slow, progress of these incredible men. And all night, it had been two hours on, two hours off, reporting flares indicating where fire was needed, and our progress as pinpointed by the small-arms fire. Now we were setting out to work with the real heroes and martyrs of war, who live next to death, who for weeks, even months at a time would never be dry or warm, day or night. After a couple of months in combat, the fear of going forward had been more or less dulled: I knew what was coming, but not how much. The Germans were using everything they had to dislodge us, to reestablish an unbroken line along the Seine. We had paid a terrible price, but theirs had been higher. The terrain was torn and pitted with shell holes and bomb craters. Trucks and planes were twisted into fantastic shapes. Everywhere were German horses, French cattle, and men: mangled, bloody, stinking, bloated. Trees were uprooted and shattered, buildings gutted and leveled. Far off was the rumble of our armor, with us at last; and nearer, the roar of the ever faithful Thunderbolts. Our men had held the first ridge of hills and now fought their way to the second. It was up to our tanks to break through into the open country, after we had taken the third and last ridge, and initiate that brilliant sweep to the Belgian border under Patton's command—when, as all too seldom, our infantry was to ride from pocket to pocket, in the longest, swiftest drive against resistance in history. But the last ridge was still before us.

We relieved the other party about noon; they were gaunt and haggard, nervous and irritable. Setting out immediately, we toiled across a muddy valley and up a thickly wooded hill. Resistance was light, shooting occurring only on our flanks. We heard a tank, and gingerly bypassed it, leaving it to the care of more heavily armed troops. What it was doing in the thick woods, we did not know or want to discover. Then it began to rain. There were tuberculosis hospitals in the woods, whose terrified inmates peered at us from under porches and cellars. We had been forewarned that some of the inmates might not be real cases and might give us trouble, so we had introduced ourselves with a little artillery, and our first line bristled with machine guns; so that was that, without any shooting! Finally, towards dark, we broke out of the woods; skirting them, we found a well hidden barn, with only a few leaks! So we spent the night in the hay, relatively warm and dry. The Germans must have suspected something, for they fired at it all night with "Nebelwerfer," more graphically and colloquially known as "Screaming Minnies," an invention of the Devil.

We had been the first of all the allied troops across the Seine, and we had held it against all odds. The so called defunct Luftwaffe had been very much alive. But now, at least for a while, tanks would bear the brunt across the flat lands that stretched ahead of us. Yet the dead and the crippled were none the less dead and none the less crippled for all the success of the Bridgehead.[11]

Ludwig Baumgarten

Sergeant Ludwig Baumgarten is still in the Army (1957) and his story had to wait to be told until he came home on leave and we could talk together. He is a fine-looking man of whom Woodstock is proud.

He talked of the Salween campaign and described the near-starvation diet of the Chinese army on which he and his companions subsisted for weeks at a time. It was so unappetizing to the Americans that some of them frequently refused to take it and consequently suffered from malnutrition. He said he had to thank his mother for disciplining him in childhood to eat whatever was set before him. Due to this training he ate the strange Chinese rations and was the one American in his group who kept well.

Baumgarten was twenty-one when he entered the U.S. Army and after a couple of months' basic training was sent to India, where, after stops at Bombay and Karachi, his unit arrived at Ramgarh. This was the site for the training and combat command of the Chinese army, where he attended radio school. He was then assigned to the 993rd Signal Company and sent to Chabua to be shipped by air over the Hump. As they waited their turn to go, they finally moved into what was called Death Row, close to the take-off, so named because so many accidents had occurred on previous trips over the Himalayas. However, Baumgarten landed safely in Kunming, China. Shortly thereafter he volunteered to serve in the field and was sent into the Salween offensive in western China, where he went with several members of the Signal Corps for liaison with the Chinese Seventy-first Army. Their group consisted of a captain, two radio operators and two cryptographers (cipher experts), of whom Baumgarten was one. There is a Signal Corps photograph of him with another man in a Chinese bamboo hut sending messages back to General Stilwell's headquarters. Their job was to keep Stilwell informed regarding the situation and progress of the Chinese army. In 1944 the Japanese controlled the Burma Road and the task of the Chinese was to clear it for the Allies' use.

This campaign of the Salween offensive was to have been started in October 1943, which would have given them six months before the monsoons set in. But the Chinese allowed months to slip by before they moved, and they were caught by the storms and obliged to fight their way along the Salween River under terrible conditions. The terrain was as rugged as any encountered in the war in the Pacific. They had to fight at altitudes of up to twelve thousand feet in the Kaolikung mountain range and through gorges where there was not room even for a footpath along the river—so they were obliged to cut across the mountains. Baumgarten described the rough going, particularly at the start of the campaign when their food consisted of a little rice twice a day and nothing else except for a twenty-five-pound can of coffee they had brought with them. Later they obtained some Chinese sugar in cakes that were shaped like cookies but were full of straw. Their communications equipment and a few supplies were carried by scraggly Chinese horses. These were so precious that a Chinese company commander could order a soldier shot but it took a Group Army order to shoot a mule or a horse. At one place they obtained food for the horses that they recognized as buckwheat; they had a Chinese man grind some of it by hand to make into pancakes for themselves. The little horses could scarcely hold their footing on the slippery trails and occasionally one of them would fall into the mile-deep ravines. However, they were strong and on the steepest grades the men would sometimes have to hang onto the horses' tails to pull themselves up. The Americans slogged along in mud up to their knees and their clothes were never dry. Raincoats were useless and it was futile to wear leggings because the mud oozed under them, causing blistering sores. They could carry only their carbines and a canteen of boiled water, because they needed their hands to pull themselves up the mountains. The Japanese army, in retreat ahead of them, cleaned out the food from any village through which they passed, and it was a rare event when the Americans found a cow to butcher. The U.S. Army made airdrops that were mostly of ammunition for the fighters and included very few C ration packages. If the men stopped to rest, their muscles would stiffen and it would be torture to get going again. Often the paths were so high in the mountains they would see airplanes flying far below their positions. The Chinese army traversed the very rapid Salween River on rafts that required four men to row an equal number of soldiers across; the horses swam. (This was before the American engineers built a bridge.) They fought their way to the Japanese stronghold of Sungshan, whose guns dominated the thirty-six miles of the looping Burma Road. Their position was impregnable from assault. It was equally hard for the Japanese to send reinforcements except by airdrop, but they would not surrender. It was necessary to use mountain trails to bypass this spot. Eventually a tunnel was bored into the hill beneath their position and the whole cone of the mountain was blown off to demolish the Japanese stronghold.

Cryptographer and generator man Ludwig Baumgarten of Woodstock (right, with radio operator Herbert Yasgur of Highland Park, New Jersey) while attached to the Chinese 71st Army during the Salween Campaign of 1945. "The Jap Zeros used to come over this spot and we would report them to the air corps on the radio," said Baumgarten. Photo by U.S. Army Signal Corps.

Baumgarten had the greatest respect for his superior officer, Colonel John J. Sells. Although he was an older man, Sells shared all the hardships of their group. When he was offered a horse to ride he refused, because he would not accept better conditions than were available for his men. He kept their morale high. An interpreter had been assigned to their unit but as they advanced they came to villages whose dialect he could not understand. Sometimes these people still had their women's feet bound and they had never before seen Caucasians. Most of the food had disappeared from these villages and when they found a farmer who still had potatoes in his fields they treated them like gold nuggets.

A battle was fought at Lungling, which the Chinese won but at a terrible price. They would never learn to advance and then at once dig in to consolidate their positions. Baumgarten could see bodies strewn all over the flank of the mountain as neither side had time to stop and bury their dead.

The whole of the Burma Road was opened by 1945. Soon after the road was freed, our group of American liaisons was sent back to Kunming. By this time they were so unused to good food that some of them became sick on American rations and were hospitalized. Meanwhile the Chinese were beginning to fight among themselves and Kunming was infiltrated by Communists, so the liaison men were flown to India. According to other histories Chiang Kai-shek and Stilwell could not agree on the conduct of the campaign, and rather than antagonize the Chinese the Americans recalled Stilwell to Washington.

Ludwig Baumgarten also served with the Eighth Army in the 226th Signal Company in Korea. He received as many ribbons and medals as any soldier from Woodstock.[12]

Aubrey Milne

Lieutenant Aubrey Milne of the 463rd Parachute Field Artillery Battalion of the Eighty-second Airborne Division under General Ridgway landed in Casablanca on May 10, 1943.

Aubrey Milne. *Portrait by Arnold Blanch.* Photo: AMS Collection.

Early in July his unit was transported by plane to the airfields at Kairouan. It was there that General Ridgway gave his men that famous beefsteak dinner preceding the invasion of Sicily—which carried the suggestion it might be their last meal! At about eight o'clock in the evening of July 9th the paratroopers were loaded into C-47 transport planes. The sky was full of airplanes buzzing like a swarm of bees as they flew around and around to marshal a whole division for the first invasion of Europe by way of Sicily. The fellows had known this was coming and the entire Eighty-second Airborne, who were to become famous for their bravery, spent a nervous, frightening week of anticipation before their first combat jump. As soon as the planes took off the men became actively sick. They were crowded in a small space with the stench of vomit. Fear kept them looking at each other to see how their companions were "taking it." Ahead was a "damn little blue light," which made them look worse than they felt. The trip was prolonged as the planes were ordered to swing over to Malta before heading toward Sicily. None of them knew that General Eisenhower was watching them from the Malta lighthouse, murmuring a prayer for their safety and success.

At last they neared the coast and the minute—the second—came to bail out. Milne's parachute jerked open and he felt a wonderful moment of freedom from noise and stench as he sailed down through the night sky. Far off to his right he could see flashes of fire from the warships that were bombarding the coast. They had been prepared to hit the earth in thirty seconds, based upon the instructions issued to their pilots to drop them at an elevation of six hundred feet. At the right time he pulled himself up on his shrouds to ease the landing, but there was no contact. He pulled himself up and down several times before he gave up and went plop as he collapsed on the ground. Fortunately no bones were broken and he looked around expecting to find familiar landmarks, but nothing in this terrain was recognizable. He learned later that he had been dropped near Marina de Ragusa, thirty miles from the objective. After thrashing around in the dark to no purpose he was forced to wait until dawn. At daybreak he crawled toward a farmhouse. From a wall above, a rifle began to spit at him. He dived to the ground shouting "George," which was their password, and to his relief the man behind the wall called back the counter-word, "Marshall," proving he was one of their own. All through the dawn men could be heard crawling around and at the slightest rustle would whisper "George," and soon would come "Marshall"; "George," "Marshall" echoed from everywhere about them. For those first hours each man seemed to be fighting his own independent war. At last a colonel gathered most of the men together and they received orders to proceed to Gela, where they had originally expected to be dropped. Part of the division had landed there and was fighting for the airports: reinforcements were needed. The paratroopers were ordered to the road and there began a thirty-mile march that took them all day. For the last part the troops slouched along, tired and footsore, totally unlike the picture of a modern army. They finally reached Gela and helped secure the airports.

Meanwhile the main army successfully carried out the invasion of the Sicilian beaches, and the paratroopers joined up to clean out the island. Colonel James M. Gavin had jumped with his men and now led the troops in combat. They proceeded in trucks through Licata, Agrigento and Castelvetrano to Trapani. They did not encounter much opposition. Occasionally concrete pillboxes slowed them up along the roads. These pillboxes were frequently built to look like a house or a shed. There would be a few bursts of fire, but as soon as the American artillery opened up the Italian soldiers would run out to surrender. The Germans were in retreat ahead of them, but when encountered would put up a stiff fight. It was not uncommon for one paratrooper to bring in forty or fifty Italian prisoners. The biggest fight they had with the Italians was at Trapani. There the paratroopers dug into foxholes in an almond orchard. Near them on a mountain they could see a large mass of rock partly hidden in the fog. When the mist lifted they caught sight of the medieval town of Erice perched on the cliffs a thousand feet above them. By this time they were able to supplement their rations with lemons, peaches, plums, tomatoes and melons.

Later they were bivouacked among olive trees on a typical Sicilian farm where the house was being used as headquarters. The soldiers slept on Italian army blankets and used enemy mess kits and other captured equipment. They made a stove from the radio box of a shot-down Messerschmitt 110, which worked very well. The paratroopers could not bring their cooking gear or extra clothes with them, and it was three weeks before the Army could supply them with changes of clothes. During this time the men fought, ate and slept in their jump suits. The western part of the island was being cleared of enemy troops. Their casualties were considered light, although several hundred paratroopers from the Eighty-second had been killed. They had routed the Fifteenth Panzer Division and had successfully battled everything from Messerschmitts to sixty-ton German tanks that were covered with seven-inch armor plate. By the end of July the battle for Sicily was almost over. Milne had traversed about a hundred and forty miles of the island. The civilians had been very friendly, which made their job easier. They cheered and applauded when the American soldiers arrived, and brought them fruit and water.

Milne found the country beautiful as they drove along precipitous roads that wound around hairpin turns with occasional views of the blue Mediterranean in the distance. In the towns the buildings were of masonry with little balconies hanging over narrow and crooked streets. The large cities were almost deserted due to the bombings, and the people were living in caves cut into the limestone cliffs. There they existed in primitive fashion. Hitler's troops had occupied most of the palatial homes, leaving their Italian friends to shift for themselves; then the Germans had gone away, leaving the Italians holding the bag. In Sicily Lieutenant Milne contracted sand-fly fever and jaundice. He was flown back to Africa and hospitalized at Bizerte.

When he was released from the hospital in North Africa he hopped a plane to rejoin his battalion in Sicily. The 463rd was sent on a Liberty ship to Naples. On December 22nd trucks took them to the front at Venafro. The army they joined had pushed up from Salerno to capture Naples, and, fighting as they went, had advanced up the Italian peninsula until they were checked near Cassino. The terrain was rough, the weather in the mountains very cold, and the men and machines became bogged in mud. These highly mechanized troops had to employ mules to drag their equipment through. The casualties were high and the suffering endless. Thoughts of death hovered over the whole army that Christmas season of 1943.

Milne's artillery battalion was attached for the next six months to the First Special Service Force of Commandoes. This unit, called the Black Devils, was made up of handpicked Canadian and American paratroopers and had already served in the Aleutian

Islands before being sent to Italy. They were given the most hazardous jobs, and before the war was over their losses were nearly one hundred percent. To give cover to their activities, the 463rd Field Artillery observers were sent up Mount Summucro overlooking the valley, where stood the battered town of Cassino. This mountain, along with Camino and Trocchio, will always be remembered as the terrible battlefield of jagged peaks and stony ridges won at the cost of many lives. The pack mules could get only halfway up these mountains and then the soldiers were forced to load the supplies on their own shoulders and climb over rocks, which cut their shoes and shredded their clothes. Milne and a few others were sent to the top of Mount Summucro to set up an observation post. *Life* magazine ran a picture of these men in their bulky clothes—top-heavy with packs of food, bedding, guns, ammunition, a radio set, batteries and wire. Only the hardiest would survive this ordeal. The last part of their four-thousand-foot ascent was so steep that it was all the humans could do to mount it, even holding a rope. On top they found a hole that the Germans had previously used and they dug themselves a larger den in the rocks—with a very leaky roof, as they discovered later. They were not permitted to have a fire and were obliged to keep their canteens of water in their beds with them, to prevent their freezing. The day before New Year's a strong wind made walking on the slippery rocks perilous when they had to clamber around the hill to signal. Once Milne slipped on the ice, and to recover he grabbed at an object that projected from the rocks—and found it to be the frozen arm of a dead German. Thereafter he crawled on his hands and knees. That night the snow came with a terrific wind. They covered themselves completely to keep out the snow that blew over them, but their blankets remained wet until they froze, making sleep difficult. In a letter home he wrote:

> We were munching chocolate when around midnight the telephone rang and I shook off the snow to answer it. Listening in the receiver I heard a dance band with people yelling and shouting "Happy New Year"—while around me the wind howled and the snow fell on the God-forsaken mountaintop. It is difficult to describe the feeling it created as the sound was definitely coming from a nightclub in New York. I never did find the explanation but I think somebody had a radio and at midnight piped it into the telephone line. The blizzard lasted for thirty-six hours until the snow was three feet deep. I think I stayed in bed for three days and I have never been so miserable in all my life as I couldn't get warm and had no food or water left. At last relief got through to us and we descended the mountain. I got a slight case of frostbite on the way down.

A hot meal revived them. They were kept at the front, and while Milne wrote that letter the concussion of guns kept blowing out his candlelight.

The check of the Allied armies at Cassino was being criticized on the home front. General Eisenhower answered the critics by pointing out that the Anglo-American drive had already proved itself by securing the Foggia airport, by eliminating the Italian fleet and, above all, by creating another front that put them in a position to outflank the Germans. Further, it pinned down approximately eighteen German divisions.

The Black Devils were credited with taking several mountain peaks on the road to Cassino. They were then moved to the Anzio Beachhead and Milne's battalion accompanied them on an LST (landing ship tank). These commandoes with blackened faces infiltrated the enemy lines at night to get prisoners and information, and undertook the most hazardous tasks. In the diary of a German soldier was found this entry: "The Black Devils are all around us every time we come into line, yet we never hear them come."[13] Again, Milne's battery was used in their support, and was with them when the Allied soldiers broke out of the beachhead toward Rome.

Milne arrived at Anzio about February 1st, a week after the first invasion. It was quiet when they moved through the town and took up their position on the right flank of the Allied forces. Soon the whole front was ablaze with stiff artillery fire from the Germans entrenched on the mountains above them. The earlier optimism about the beachhead proved unjustified. The Germans had all the advantages of terrain on the heights, and the entire area was within range of their artillery. Their air force also made constant raids during those difficult days. The ten-square-mile area held by the Allies was flat, without any natural protection. Even their hospital was within range of artillery fire and received direct hits.

The British and American troops under General Truscott were obliged to dig into the ground for shelter. Here they remained for over three months, and there was no rear area for rest and recovery.

The weather turned cold and rainy and Milne told of being wet to the skin for days at a time. His foxhole caved in and buried all his equipment, blankets et cetera under three feet of mud. In March he wrote that his battery had been credited with destroying six tanks and two airplanes. One of these planes had been hit in a "million-to-one-shot," for the battery had been firing at an objective back on the hills and by accident the airplane flew into the trajectory of one of their shells and was blown to bits. The Germans sent over plenty of planes and he witnessed many air battles until the U.S. Air Corps finally gained control. The beachhead became littered with more wrecked planes than in any other battle area. At last spring came, bringing the soldiers from under their blankets to enjoy the warm Italian sun, although mosquitoes appeared, making them uncomfortable.

Cassino had finally been captured on May 17th and the Fifth Army was moving up the coast. On May 22nd and 23rd the push on Rome started and the whole beachhead poured out. Milne's battalion was sent to cut the famous Appian Way near Cisterna. They reached the edge of the highway to find it put them under direct fire from the Germans. Locating a culvert, the men dived into it. By the time the last man was crowded in, there was no room for Milne. He crouched down in a drainage ditch but it gave little protection against the violent German artillery, and soon a shell burst, landing twelve feet away and spattering him with fragments of steel. Pieces entered his hand and his face and caused a serious wound in his chest. In the excitement he did not feel any pain. Not far away a solider was badly wounded and as soon as the firing eased Milne became engrossed in getting help for him. Milne was in charge of his battery because their captain had previously been killed. Before he could leave he had to get somebody to command his men, and it was the following day before he found time to get to the medic himself. Rome fell to the Allies on June 4th but Lieutenant Milne was not with his troops. He was sent back to a field hospital and then shipped by boat to Naples, where he had an operation to remove the shell fragments—and it was two more weeks before be was allowed to return to his outfit. They were then resting in the hills above beautiful Lake Albano, where there was good swimming for these weary soldiers. Milne was now promoted to Captain. On August 13th they moved to the airports of Grosseto and Fallonica, where odd airborne units were made into the First Airborne Task Force. This was to become part of the Seventh Army under General Patch, which invaded southern France on August 15, 1944. This invasion was preceded by a great aerial bombardment. Captain Milne's group was flown over the tip of Corsica toward France's Riviera. They should have been taken inland to Le Muy but only half the planes reached their destination; the others ran miles off their course and their paratroopers were dropped near St. Tropez along the coast. A number of the men hit the sea and, being heavily loaded, sank immediately to their death. Milne, with about five hundred others, landed safely near St. Tropez. He wrote home:

> The jump was the easiest I have ever made, no airsickness like that fateful night over Sicily. I was the first one to jump and had to push 300 lbs. of equipment ahead of me, which made me leave the plane in rather an undignified position. About a quarter moon was showing so I could see around me some of the other men as they drifted down. Soon a cloud cut off all my view of everything and I was left by myself. It was a very queer feeling as I began to oscillate back and forth very violently in the pea soup cloud that was around me. Finally the clouds gave way and I saw trees, rocks and the vineyards of Southern France under me. I came down in the soft earth between two rows of grape vines and only ruined my gas mask, which I threw away. After trying to contact the rest of the planeload without success I decided to go to high ground and wait for daylight. On my way I ran into a Frenchman hiding in a ditch whom I must have scared badly as my face was camouflaged with grease paint to blend in with my clothes. He gave me the position of the nearest town so I was more or less oriented. When daylight came I headed for the town as I saw some of our infantry doing the same thing so I figured that I would be able to get in contact with some of our own men. The French were very helpful with directions, food and wine. Many of them wore armbands with F.F.I. and the French tricolor marked on them and quite a few had weapons. Just outside the town I met some Infantry so I joined them and went into the center of the town where the French told us there were a lot of Germans holed up in a stone barrack that was situated on a little hill in the town itself. I went forward to see what it looked like and found the barrack was set inside an old stone wall that had slits cut into it so the Germans had a nice field of fire over the 100 yards of open ground between the wall and houses of the town. Through a break in the wall I could see a couple of German sentries walking around but I could do nothing about it as I only had my pistol with me. Finally they saw me and fired a machine gun

in my direction and I made a hasty retreat—and I mean hasty! Going back to the center of the town I found we had a considerable bunch of men both American and French assembled in the town square. This force moved forward and brought the stone barrack under fire but the Germans had the advantage of the masonry which was quite solid so the fighting consisted of desultory shooting at anything that showed around corners and over windowsills. The Germans had managed to get some snipers down in the town so they were taking occasional shots at us from the rear. Whenever that happened any suspected window or door was immediately blasted with every available weapon until the woodwork was in shreds. The French people set up a first aid station in the village square and did everything possible for the wounded. In the afternoon the Germans decided it was hopeless to fight further so they put up the white flag and we went up to the barrack and got quite a few prisoners. After bringing the prisoners of war down into town we received sniper fire and found that a considerable number of Germans had hidden before the rest surrendered, so we had to go back. It took nearly three days before the last sniper had been cleared out so it was not very healthy to wander about. Several times I had one of them shooting at me and although they never got closer than four feet it scared the wits out of me. Late in the afternoon I joined forces with my own outfit, so ended my jump into France.

The Maquis proved very helpful to the paratroopers, serving them well in those first days. The French people greeted them with a genuine enthusiasm that was very different from the questionable sincerity of the welcome they had received in Italy. The troops fanned out quickly after the German coastal batteries were captured. Milne's paratroopers were loaded into "ducks" and driven to join their companions at Le Muy. In a few days his battery was ordered back to the coast and joined the battle near Cannes. They fought the Germans back along the sea to Antibes. The war rolled over Cannes and into Cagnes. These particular troops were then sent by truck to Barcelonnette. Here they stayed three weeks and Milne suffered a severe attack of malaria that hit him "like a ton of bricks." When he had recovered, finding there was a good trout stream nearby, he went fishing right there in range of German artillery. The French inhabitants brought them eggs and potatoes and chickens, and refused to take money in payment—and had to be persuaded to take even a cigarette in exchange. The next move for Milne's men was back to the Riviera behind Nice, where they went into position on a ridge by Roquebrune to shell the Germans on the Italian frontier behind Menton. The Germans were also under bombardment by the Navy offshore. The Americans, from their mountain position, could watch the shells falling amidst the crack mountain troops of German Field Marshal Kesselring. During one nine-minute period, Milne's battery fired over five thousand rounds of ammunition. For weeks this artillery battle continued from the Swiss border to Monte Carlo.

On December 13th Milne's battalion was ordered to proceed by train from Antibes to Rheims to join the 101st Airborne Division. These troops, called the "Screaming Eagles," were having a short rest after an intense engagement in Holland. The respite was abruptly ended on December 18th when they were alerted at dawn and, after hastily snatching their equipment, were sent in large carrier trucks into the Belgian Bulge under the command of Brigadier-General McAuliffe. Two days before, German Field Marshal von Rundstedt had struck at the American lines in the Ardennes Forest and thirty German divisions poured through a breach. Patton's Tenth Armored Division rushed through Bastogne and continued on out to the east, where their tanks engaged the Germans in heavy fighting. The 101st hurried into the town from the west. Bastogne was the hub of seven roads and the fighting spread from spoke to spoke until the Germans had captured every road and the town was surrounded by the enemy. When Colonel Kinnard replied to a corps headquarters inquiry, he said, "Visualize the hole in a doughnut, that's us." The 101st, with elements of General Patton's 9th and 10th Armored divisions, was completely isolated within a fourteen-mile perimeter. Von Rundstedt's main advance was being held up by this little outpost of Americans. The best German divisions were hurled against it but our troops held fast. The weather favored the enemy as the fog clung to the land for days, grounding the Allied Air Force. The German panzer and parachute troops and the Luftwaffe beat harder at Bastogne. Where tanks penetrated our lines they were blown up by head-on small arms and field artillery fire. One of the heaviest losses for the 101st was the capture of their field medical unit. As their casualties mounted they ran out of medical supplies and all they could do was wrap their wounded in blankets against the bitter cold. Finally their hospital was hit. Food became scarce.

On December 22nd two German officers arrived under a white flag and offered an ultimatum: "Surrender or be annihilated in two hours." General McAuliffe wasted neither time nor words sending back his soon-to-be-famous answer: "Nuts." To his officers he added, "They can't have much more than they have already thrown at us. Let it come!"

It came. The Nazis threw everything they had against the Screaming Eagles. When the German tanks broke through the Americans fought back with bazookas and antitank destroyers. During the siege they destroyed a hundred and forty-eight tanks and twenty-five half-tracks. Shells had to be rationed. Captain Milne's battery was down to eighteen rounds of ammunition. Finally the weather cleared and C-47s roared over, dropping supplies. This was the day before Christmas. That night Milne went to a church service in a hayloft. The building was being shaken by concussion bombs and it was impossible to hear most of the service. From there they went out to fight the toughest battle of the Bulge. After hours of bitter fighting the enemy was driven out. The Eagles' line held! The day after Christmas a small detachment of Third Army tanks under the command of Lieutenant-Colonel Abrams fought their way through to Bastogne and the siege was over. In the great German offensive in Belgium one small division had held fast. Thereafter on a road junction in the town a sign read, "This is Bastogne, Bastion of the Battered Bastards of the 101st Airborne Division."

On March 15, 1945, for the first time a full division was cited by the War Department in a Presidential Citation for gallantry in action; it was given to the 101st.

At this time they were heartened by news of the Russian advance. The most popular quip amongst the soldiers was, "Be careful when you shoot to be sure it isn't a Russian you are hitting." Their next move was to Rheims and later by truck through Liège and Aachen—which was in shambles—to the Rhine. At Neuss the battery was set up to shell Düsseldorf, across the river. Milne recalled one curious incident while there. Among his comrades was a man who had Nazi relatives in Düsseldorf whom he disliked. His dislike was strong enough for him to suggest that they find this family's address in a telephone book, and, checking this on their maps, the battery proceeded to concentrate their fire upon this spot. It was at Neuss that the 463rd were given a new weapon to try. They were the first command unit to use the recoilless 75s. These were light enough for a man to lift onto his shoulder and could be fired from that position.

The news of President Roosevelt's death on April 12, 1945, had been a blow to everyone, Milne wrote, even to the British soldiers, with whom Roosevelt had been exceedingly popular.

Milne's next move was past Cologne and on to Bonn, near which the 101st crossed the Rhine on a pontoon bridge. They spent a couple of weeks holding one of the flanks in the squeeze of the Ruhr. This was one of the most brilliant campaigns of the Allies. The Germans in the Ruhr were encircled and then split into two parts and systematically mopped up. This was the last big battle for the American armies in Europe. From then on, the war was one of pursuit. Captain Milne's battalion went by truck through Germany, chasing the enemy down through Bavaria. The German surrender came as he was riding through a snowstorm in the mountains. The end was so gradual the soldiers were hardly aware the war was over. There was no celebration and the day felt like any other. They had not met any organized resistance for two weeks and their work consisted of collecting German soldiers, who were everywhere, waiting to be captured. The slave laborers were wandering around the country in immense droves, constantly jamming traffic. They went into camp at Bad Reichenhall about fifteen miles southwest of Salzburg, near Berchtesgaden. The place was very beautiful, nestled in the Kitzbühler Alps.

The officers set up their own mess with a Belgian chef, waitresses and a seven-piece orchestra. They ate well, with fried trout and mushrooms from Hitler's private supply, and they had wines and cognac to drink. It seemed an easy life, but, as Milne wrote, "Since the surrender I have felt like a man who has been taking dope and suddenly has the supply cut off." He could not get used to seeing Germans in uniform about the roads. The poorer Germans were alright but he had little respect for those of the upper classes. It had been his job to requisition houses for the troops on their way through Germany. He had been disgusted with the people in fine houses who invariably tried to avoid giving up their homes, pointing to those of their neighbors instead.

Early in July, Captain Milne, having a hundred and twelve points, was sent back to the United States. He arrived in Boston at the end of September 1945, after two and a half years overseas and four years in the Army.[14]

Eugene J. Hagemeyer Jr.

Corporal Eugene J. Hagemeyer Jr. was with the Ninth Infantry of the Second Division in the Ardennes, Rhineland and Central European campaigns. He received a Presidential Citation with one Oak Leaf Cluster, three Bronze Service Stars, E.T.O. Ribbon, Combat Infantryman's Badge and Good Conduct Medal. Here is an excerpt from a letter he wrote when the U.S. Army entered Czechoslovakia. It shows the welcome the Americans received. All too soon our army was withdrawn and the Communists were allowed to march in.

> Czechoslovakia is so nice—it was great to be welcomed by signs of greeting stretched across the roadway of each town we entered. Quite different from being shot at or receiving sullen or blank stares as was the rule in Germany. The people here would line the streets and cheer wildly—some with tears streaming down their faces. Flowers, streamers and flags are everywhere. As we would ride by they would throw them into our trucks and on our tanks until by the time we had passed a few towns our convoy looked like floats in a parade rather than fighting machines. If we happened to stop in a town for a moment the people would about mob us, kiss and hug us, fight to get close enough to touch us and give us every kind of food and drink imaginable.
>
> I had tears streaming down my face several times I was so happy for them. Lots of the younger Czech men would join us, grab weapons and ride along with us. As we would leave one village and start for the next several would jump on motorcycles and tear ahead of us to spread the news of our coming. Everything was just like holidays or festivals of Europe as seen in a movie. The bright reds, greens, oranges—all colors imaginable in the dresses and caps of the women are beautiful. Some of those peasant dresses must be worth quite a bit. It's an experience and thrill I'll always remember and wouldn't have missed for anything. I only wish all who helped to make this victory possible and who fought to free Europe could be here to see all this.[15]

Carl Schleicher

Following are excerpts from a letter that Carl Schleicher wrote to his father:

> I am now allowed to tell you that for the past three years . . . I have had the dubious honor of being a small cog-wheel in the giant machinery of scientific research [that] has led finally to the exploding of the atom bomb which electrified the world but three days ago . . . When I first started working we were told the whole story about what we were doing. No mention was made of how the thing was to be used—even the higher-ups where I work were not told that. I had visions of the stuff being used for fuel since in those days the gasoline and coal shortage was acute. For some reason the prospect of high explosives in the form of bombs never occurred to me . . . the announcement of the dropping of the first bomb came as much as a surprise and shock to me as to everyone else . . . So that is the story I have been waiting to tell you and all my other friends for three years.
>
> This is not just a new invention like the telephone, radio, steam engine, etc., but a source of energy so infinite, so powerful and so relentless once it is unleashed . . . it will completely revolutionize our life . . . No man can now say what the full results will be . . . What horrible prospects are in store for all of us if man cannot for once and at once humble himself before God and his neighbor and cease strife . . . It would have been far better that the atom had never given up its secret to man—at least until man was grown-up enough to use the knowledge. The only hope from the discovery of this devastating force is that the use of it on Japan will be so convincing to every man on the face of the earth that the next war CAN ONLY LEAD TO TOTAL DESTRUCTION, that no one will dare to declare war in the future. I think the time has finally come when a statement like this makes some sense.
>
> Was I happy in the work I was doing? Am I proud to be associated in a scientific endeavor which has overcome all obstacles to gain its end? I realize the great experience it has been to be connected with something which has stunned the world . . . True pride can only be felt in work which is the product of the heart as well as the brain . . . a step forward or, to be trite, a boon to humanity. At this stage it is hard to see how the result of this discovery is a boon to anything except destruction and more frustration for the human race. To quote from *The Prophet*, ". . . all work is empty save [when] there is love; and when you work with love you bind yourself to yourself, and to one another, and to God."
>
> Can I have love for work which results in a bomb—one single bomb—which demolishes four square miles of buildings and disintegrates one hundred thousand living souls in less than one second? . . . Can you wonder now why I have been so confused? Why I have been searching for values—for truth? Why I have been questioning my desire to go in[to] science? Whatever I do for a living, I want to do with pride—I want to work with my heart and feel that I am doing something good for myself and others. I do not say this cannot be done with science—but it is more difficult.[16]

Dr. and Mrs. James T. Shotwell with their daughter, Helen, at their home on Shotwell Road. Courtesy of Historical Society of Woodstock.

Chapter 14

SOME LOCAL PERSONALITIES

INTELLECTUAL CURIOSITY THRIVES IN PEACETIME

James T. Shotwell

I have described James T. Shotwell as our neighbor and friend, but he is far more than this, and some of his story must be told no matter how inadequate the telling. I will relate one small incident to show his worldwide reputation. Between the two world wars a friend of mine entering one of the railroad stations in Paris saw a crowd of waiting people. When they were asked whom they were expecting, one of them replied, "Monsieur Shotwell, the great American leader for peace."

His chief contribution to this era has certainly been his work for peace. Right after the First World War Dr. Shotwell declared that the one final lesson history had taught was that, in the complexity of modern industrial life, war had undergone a revolution that made it no longer a controllable agency of national policy; as it was unjustified on the ground of necessity, to resort to it would henceforth be an international crime.[1]

In 1918 he was appointed by President Woodrow Wilson to the American delegation to negotiate peace in Paris. At the Peace Conference he headed the Division of History of the American delegation. He secured the cooperation of the French and British governments in providing background information on the political, economic and social problems under negotiation. Dr. Shotwell also played a major part in shaping the constitution of the International Labor Organization, the one institution created for the League of Nations that lasted through the Second World War. Previous to this there had been no federal labor legislation in the United States to cover an international organization, and Shotwell had to negotiate provisions that would be acceptable to the U.S. government and the public.

After the rejection of the Treaty of Versailles by the American Senate, Dr. Shotwell devoted his efforts to strengthening the policies of pacification in Europe and to reversing the isolationist policies in his own country through a program of cooperation with the League of Nations at Geneva. He labored untiringly as chairman of the Committee on Security and Disarmament, drafting an American plan that was incorporated into an official text of the League of Nations. To continental Europe the passage of this protocol was the high-water mark in the history of the League.[2] However, a new Conservative government in Great Britain rejected this protocol on the ground that it limited Great Britain's freedom to act independently in time of crisis. To address this criticism Sir Austen Chamberlain turned to negotiations that led to the Treaty of Locarno.

Shotwell worked without respite for disarmament. The Kellogg-Briand Pact of 1928 was originally based on the conclusions of the one-hundred-and-fifty-volume *Economic and Social History of the World War* as outlined by Shotwell in his role as general editor.[3] It was a "frank denial of the theory of Clausewitz and Bismarck that war was the legitimate instrument of national policy."[4] In the United States Dr. Shotwell led a nationwide campaign to force the reluctant State Department to negotiate with

Aristide Briand. "U.S. Secretary of State Kellogg, under the influence of Senator William E. Borah, changed the nature of the offer to a renunciation of *all* war, although he continued to insist upon the validity of fighting a war of defense. Dr. Shotwell attacked this confusion in a series of editorial articles in the *New York Herald Tribune*, but upon the signature of the Pact of Paris supported it while continuing to work for clarification along the lines of the original Briand offer of the renunciation of 'war as an instrument of national policy'."[5]

From 1919 to 1924 Shotwell had labored on the monumental *Economic and Social History of the World War* under the auspices of the Carnegie Endowment for International Peace. Previously he had made an outline for this work at the request of Elihu Root, then president of the Foundation. There were no models to follow, as there had never been such a scientific study of war. Fifteen countries collaborated in this work. The group comprised experts who had held wartime government positions or were closely associated with wartime activities, including thirty-five cabinet ministers. It dealt with every phase of the impact of war upon the peacetime life of the nations involved, but omitted purely military events.

Before the conclusion of the Second World War the U.S. Secretary of State, Cordell Hull, called upon Dr. Shotwell's scholarship and experience to help develop, through a committee led by Sumner Wells, a program for the building of an international body envisaged in the Roosevelt-Churchill Declaration for a United Nations organization. Subsequently Secretary Hull appointed Shotwell to serve on five national committees. Shotwell was made Chairman of the Consultants of forty-two national organizations in the United States, in the fields of industry, labor, agriculture, education, religion and women's issues. Throughout the conference, held in San Francisco, the consultants exercised real influence upon the drafting of the charter of the United Nations. They succeeded in having non-governmental organizations recognized in the charter. They also helped to determine the nature of the United Nations Educational, Scientific and Cultural Organization (UNESCO). "The insertion of the human welfare provision in the Charter . . . was largely due to its sponsorship by the consultants who insisted upon a specific provision in the Charter rather than merely including human welfare in the generalized statement of the 'Purposes and Principles' of the United Nations." In this epochal work on the Declaration of Human Rights, Dr. Shotwell took a leading part.[6]

It would require a book in itself to adequately report on all of the work accomplished by James T. Shotwell. Among the many jobs he undertook, here are a few. He was president of the League of Nations Association from 1935 to 1939, director of the Institute of Pacific Relations from 1927 to 1929, and director of the Social Science Research Council from 1931 to 1933. In 1938 and 1939, with the support of the Rockefeller Foundation, he organized a conference on international copyright. He served as chairman of the American Committee on Intellectual Cooperation, the Commission to Study the Organization of Peace (1939–49) and the Carnegie Endowment on Atomic Energy (1946).

For forty-two years Shotwell served on the faculty of Columbia University as professor and lecturer in history. In 1937 he was nominated chair of the Bryce Professorship on the History of International Relations.

In 1948 he was unanimously elected to head the Carnegie Foundation for International Peace. At the present time he is president emeritus of that body.

He has written many books and received innumerable honors. Among his decorations are: Commander, Order of the Crown, Belgium, 1919; Commander, Order of the Saviour, Greece, 1925; Commander, Order of St. Sava, Yugoslavia, 1925; Officier, Légion d'Honneur, France, 1927; Commander, Order of the White Lion, Czechoslovakia, 1927; Commander, Légion d'Honneur, France, 1946.[7]

William K. Gregory

Dr. William K. Gregory, paleontologist, morphologist and anthropologist, has had a summer home in Woodstock for over thirty years. The list of his achievements and honors is so impressive that the thought of interviewing him intimidated me. He proved to be an elderly man with a modest attitude regarding his accomplishments. He was sympathetic when I told him that what I know of anthropology would not fill a thimble. Fortunately he is a reader of subjects outside his particular field and he lent me an interesting book on Alaska written by former

Woodstock neighbors Henry and Susan Barrow. We wandered away from talk about his work to discuss painting, literature and religion, until his nice wife would tactfully bring us back to the subject at hand. She was probably afraid I would stay all night; indeed, after we had partaken of coffee and a rich dessert she had prepared, I was quite ready to stay for hours longer.

Dr. Gregory was born in Greenwich Village, New York City, in 1876 and attended Trinity Church School. For his last year there, as he had to make a choice between art and science, he chose science. Consequently, upon winning a scholarship, he entered Columbia University as a student in the School of Mines. It took him two years to realize this was not the right place for him, and upon winning further scholarships he entered the field of human sciences.

When I asked him what had been the greatest influence in his career he said he owed most to three men: Henry Fairfield Osborn of the American Museum of Natural History, under whom he worked; Bashford Dean, Professor of Zoology at Columbia; and Professor F. J. Woodbridge of the Philosophy Department at Columbia. Then, with gravity, he added, "I have probably learned most through mistakes; I often opened the wrong doors but came through the right gardens." After years of teaching and research, Dr. Gregory is now professor emeritus of vertebrate paleontology at Columbia University and curator emeritus of ichthyology at the American Museum of Natural History. For several winters Dr. Gregory has gone to a coral island in the Bahamas as senior research officer of the Lerner Laboratory of Marine Biology, which is a field station under the auspices of the Museum.

The story of this now permanent laboratory is interesting. When Dr. Gregory was the active curator of ichthyology at the American Museum of Natural History, he was eager to acquire specimens of large fish. He enlisted the help of the National Geographic Society as well as the Amateur Fishermen's Association. Fishermen were catching huge sailfish, marlin and other big fish, but these were not being listed. Nor were there any international records of the varieties and sizes of fish caught around the world. The International Game Fish Association was founded, later naming Ernest Hemingway as its president. In a sense these organizations were the parents of the laboratory, which was financed by Michael Lerner, the New York merchant, and a group of his colleagues. Upon hearing of the harrowing experiences of Eddie Rickenbacker on a raft after his plane had crashed in the ocean, Lerner became interested in developing survival equipment, which included a shark repellent. Mr. and Mrs. Lerner went with Dr. Gregory and three museum employees who were expert in preparing specimens on a trip to Australian and New Zealand waters to collect fish for the Museum. Mrs. Lerner proved to be the best fisherman among them.

Evolution Emerging is the title of a two-volume work written by Dr. Gregory and published by Macmillan in 1951. It is the summation of fifty years of his research based upon developments in this field on the part of past generations of scientists. Now, at eighty-two, he is busy studying and classifying cone shells for a new book. He led me upstairs to see the collection of shells and other examples of marine life that fill two bedrooms of the house. As he described the spiral growth of the cones and the multiple patterns of the shells, it was as if a new world were emerging before my eyes.

Dr. Gregory drew my attention to a lacy fan of coral that hung upon the wall, onto which were attached three sea horses. He pointed to one of these, saying, "Do you want to see a pregnant sea horse? Would you suspect it is a male sea horse? After fertilization it is the male who produces the young. He must be very uncomfortable at the final stage because he practically explodes the issue when the birth occurs." After pondering this information I said to myself, "Humph, it's too bad the evolutionary process didn't stop right there!"[8]

Walter Weyl

Walter Weyl was born in Philadelphia in 1873. He attended the University of Pennsylvania and continued his formal education in Germany, France and England. Upon his return to the United States he threw himself into labor problems. This eventually led to his investigations into the anthracite coal strike, his statistical data becoming the basis upon which the miners rested their plea for better pay and working conditions. Previous to the strike he had been associated with the University Settlement in New York, where he came to know numbers of articulate reformers with whom he discussed world problems.[9] His brother-in-law, Ernest Poole, recalled some of these talks and pays tribute to Weyl's teaching, in which he never acted the part of the pedagogue. "He made you feel he was learning from you—or, rather, that you were learning together."[10] Poole accompanied Weyl on trips to study the Patterson strike and to a Socialist convention in Indianapolis, where the "Wobbly" crew created wild excitement. Weyl stayed up all night writing his notes, Poole recalled,

> . . . his face gray with fatigue and strain. And yet . . . we laughed a good deal . . . for he was a great companion. I know that he did for men and women, old and young, rich and poor, Jew and Gentile, what he did for me. And what he did for me was this: He made me feel that in this bewildering modern world the truth about any question is broad as a great countryside; that to see it whole you must take time to open one window after another; that you must learn to be tolerant, fair, but that one can be fair without losing the fire of his quest; that the fascination of this quest, for the great keys to the better days, is deeper, always deeper, the more patient you can learn to be.[11]

Walter Lippmann writes of Walter Weyl as an editor at *The New Republic*:

> He was not conscious of personal rights that he had to defend, nor touched by jealousy. He was too much interested in a thousand things outside himself . . . But he was a perfect colleague . . . [T]he fundamental idea of *The New Republic* [founded by Mr. and Mrs. Willard Straights and Herbert Croly] was to build on a group. The event which really decided the selection of that group was the Bull Moose adventure of 1912. All of the original editors had been in that affair, Croly and Weyl very deeply in it. No two books had done more to shape the thought of that period in American politics than Croly's *The Promise of American Life* and Weyl's *The New Democracy*.[12]

With a twinkle Lippmann relates this story:

> Up in Woodstock one day I asked him how far he carried this habit of statistical judgment. There had been a burglar around, and Walter had just told me that hearing a noise he had gone downstairs unarmed, carrying a candle to see what was the matter. "You're crazy," I said, "a lot of good your quantitative habits are to you if the best you can do is to offer a burglar a nice bright mark to shoot at."
>
> "Not at all," he insisted, "the chances that a burglar would make such a racket were not one in nine hundred; the chances that a door was banging in the wind were as one in four, there being four doors in that room; and the chances of my breaking my neck if I did not take a candle were at least five to one against me." "And you thought all that out in the middle of the night?" I inquired feebly. "Yes," he said, "I'm not naturally brave and the law of probabilities is a great comfort to me."[13]

Richard Le Gallienne said that Walter Weyl "could make political economy almost as attractive as a love affair."[14] Certainly he had an unusual ability: for a man with a passion for statistics and analysis to be able to understand any opposing point of view made Weyl unique among the intellectuals of his time. However, he was far more than just a brain, as all his friends attest to his having been a delightful comrade who brought out the best in everyone. They also recall his infectious laughter and describe him as a good listener, ready in conversation to give and take.

One member of the Byrdcliffe coterie remembers Weyl's first visit to Woodstock, when he seemed rather out of place walking in a rural community dressed in city clothes with a stiff straw hat. It was so attired that he climbed Overlook Mountain with Clarence Darrow, Zulma Steele and Edna Walker. But it was not long before he adjusted to country life and even planted a vegetable garden.

In a little booklet, *Fallen Leaves*, given to his friends, Carl Eric Lindin said:

> There is still another figure that at times walks with me through the darkening landscape, though he has long ago left us! The kind and witty Walter Weyl, who had the welfare of the community so much at heart: a gay and indomitable spirit! And often when I think of life, of art and the passing fashions, I think of a remark that he frequently made: "Well," he would say, "don't you think this year's chicks are very much like last year's?"[15]

I was one of the many young persons after the First World War searching for answers, and became an avid reader of *The New Republic*. Of course I admired what Mr. Weyl had to offer, but unfortunately knew him only slightly. I remember some of the comments at the time of his death—which were to the effect that both labor and management had lost a real friend because he alone had been able to understand and reconcile their diverging points of view.

For the last thirty years I have been fortunate in being welcomed to Mrs. Weyl's home, where she has kept alive her husband's tradition of intellectual curiosity and a politically open mind. She has given more than her share to every good cause in the nation and the village. She does this thinking of Walter Weyl, whose name is engraved on the building she gave to house our public library. Her home reflects their travels, particularly their tour of the Orient, which provided the Chinese paintings and hangings in the spacious living rooms and halls. But it is in the library one feels closest to Weyl. Here one can find the character of the man through what he read. He had a large collection of reference books; there are many volumes on history, economics, labor, socialism and statistics.

My final quotation is from his friend Francis Hackett, who said of Walter Weyl, "His mind was incorruptible."[16]

Hughes Mearns

Hughes Mearns and his wife live off the Wittenberg road only a few pasture fields and a hollow away from the home of Harold Rugg. The latter came to Woodstock to visit the Mearnses and liked it well enough to build a home here himself. Both Mearns and Rugg have worked in the field of education. As my car mounted the steep road to the house, I thought of the courtesy with which all these well-known people had responded to my questions. With some of them, like the Mearnses, I was barely acquainted, yet they welcomed me with cordiality.

Mearns has been in retirement for several years but is full of enthusiasm over a new edition of his best-known book, *Creative Power*,[17] which is being republished as a huge paperback sponsored by the National Educational Theatre Association. To bring the cost down, Mearns has waived royalties. When this book was first published it was received with enthusiastic praise, not only by those connected with education but also by other writers. Lewis Mumford and Carl Sandburg each spoke of it as one of the great contributions to education, and the poet Robert Frost said it was the best story of a feat of teaching ever written. *Creative Power* is one of a series, which also includes *Creative Youth* and *The Creative Adult*.

Besides the books on education, Mearns has published several novels, the best-known of which is *Vinegar Saint*. He first came to Woodstock more than thirty years ago to write a novel. He was directed to the Maverick, and once there he asked Hervey White for a quiet place in the woods to work. Hervey led him high up behind the quarry, expecting to discourage this stranger. When Mearns said he would take it, Hervey was prepared to let him have the cottage for nothing and was evidently surprised when Mearns gave him fifty dollars for rent. The Mearnses spent several happy summers on the Maverick, not objecting to the lack of facilities. They have real admiration for Hervey White.

Hughes Mearns taught at the Lincoln School of Columbia's Teachers College and at New York University. Perhaps the greatest tribute to his books on education is that they are often carried by teachers on their vacations—because the titles rekindle their dormant creative spirit.[18]

Musicians

Alexander Semmler is a composer, conductor and pianist. He was born and received most of his training in Germany, then came to New York in 1923 to do some "concertizing." A few years later he became the conductor at the Neighborhood Playhouse. In 1927 he joined the Columbia Broadcasting System as pianist and assistant conductor of the symphony orchestra. Since then he has been freelancing, writing music for radio, television and movies. A few years ago Semmler went to Berlin on a special assignment for the State Department, taking over the music administration of radio in the American Sector.

The summer of 1959 Semmler was in Spain making recordings of American music. When he returned he resumed direction of the Maverick Sunday Concerts—which he took over a few years ago when William Kroll resigned.

The Semmlers made several visits to Woodstock before 1943, when they finally bought a home in Zena. They have lived there at least part of the year ever since. Alexander Semmler says that in Woodstock he has worked on some of his best compositions and that he has been "creatively very happy" here.

Adrian Siegel has had a home in Bearsville for a number of years, but his work as cellist with the

Philadelphia Orchestra has drawn him away for many summer tours and special concerts. He is known not only as a cellist but also as a painter and photographer. His photographs of his fellow musicians and the conductors of the Philadelphia Orchestra—including Toscanini—have been reproduced in *Life* magazine and elsewhere.

H. A. Schimmerling was born in Czechoslovakia and served as conductor of the German Opera House in Prague. He is a composer of various works, including folk dances and a Slavonic rhapsody. He now lives high on Ohayo Mountain where he composes and teaches.

Sam Eskin, the folk singer, lives on the Cannon road (now Chimney Road). He has probably been heard around the United States more often than most of our musicians. Another singer of folk songs is Peter Seeger, who is here only occasionally. He is married to the daughter of Takashi Ohta, a Japanese-American who served his adopted country well and who will always be remembered as co-author, with Margaret Sperry, of the enchanting book *The Golden Wind*. Seeger's wife spent her childhood in Woodstock.[19]

Dr. Boudreau succeeded Dr. Shotwell as president of the League of Nations Association. Photo: AMS Collection.

Herbert Spinden

Not far above the Rock City corners is the summer home of the anthropologist Herbert Spinden, who is particularly well known for having solved the mystery of the Mayan calendar. He explored several Aztec and Mayan sites under the auspices of the Peabody Museum. He has lectured and written on archeology and ethnology for years. Spinden is a Fellow of the Royal Geographical Society and has received many honors for his research.

Frank Boudreau

Beyond the Spindens and higher on the mountain is Camelot, the home of Dr. and Mrs. Frank Boudreau. He served in the First World War as an American officer with the British army—first in England and later in France, where he was attached to the Twenty-sixth Field Ambulance. In the period between the wars Dr. Boudreau served for twelve years (1925–37) as an official with the League of Nations. He served the League as epistemologist-statistician of the Health Service. He says his most interesting assignment was making a survey of the ports of China.

Dr. Boudreau was president of the League of Nations Association, receiving this mantle from another Woodstocker, Dr. Shotwell. Boudreau has been active both in the field of health and for the cause of peace. He also served as chairman of the Food and Nutritional Board of the National Research Council and as technical consultant to the United Nations Interim Commission on Food and Agriculture. He was on the executive committee of the American Association for the United Nations and the steering committee of the Commission to Study the Organization of Peace. Boudreau has been for years the executive director of the Milbank Memorial Fund. He has received numerous honors.[20]

Other Well-Known Woodstockers

One of our famous authors is Manuel Komroff, who came to Byrdcliffe years ago. At that time he was editor of the Modern Library and could stay for only a few months in the summer. Later he built his own house on Ohayo. It is high on a bluff with a wonderful view of the whole valley and Overlook Mountain. He told me it is called "The House That Rank Built" because J. Arthur Rank paid for it by producing a movie of one of Komroff's stories. Komroff and his wife have an apartment in New York but spend half the year in Woodstock.

Komroff considers this a fine place for doing creative work. People respect his time and do not intrude while he is writing. He has written many short stories and for a period turned out one a month for *Esquire* magazine. It would usually be a sweltering hot day in July or August when he would be called from the *Esquire* office to write their annual Christmas story.

While in Woodstock, Komroff has written several historical novels. He is the author of *The Magic Bow*, which is about Paganini, *Jade Star* and *Echo of Evil*. *Mozart*, which was written on Ohayo Mountain, received the Mozart award.

Komroff was responsible for bringing two important persons to Woodstock. J. P. McEvoy, of cartoon, special-article and master-of-ceremonies fame, bought an old farm along the Bearsville road, which he converted to an up-to-date home with swimming pool "and everything." His son, Dennis McEvoy, who attended school in Woodstock, was a correspondent on the Eastern Front during the Second World War. Meanwhile the senior McEvoy moved to New York, spending the winters in Cuba until his death a short time ago.[21]

The other person Komroff mentioned was William Pachner, who came after the war. He has been a valued addition to the artists' group. The first paintings he showed here had a special quality of sadness, almost torment, but perhaps now the mood of his work has changed.

Because John Pike did not come to live here until 1944, his record in the Second World War is not

John Pike's Weathervane *once graced the top of the Woodstock Fire House at 76 Tinker Street. Pike, a civic booster as well as a celebrated water colorist, served a number of terms on the Woodstock Town Board.* Courtesy of the *Daily Freeman*.

Harvey Fite in his studio on Fite Road, High Woods, New York.
Courtesy of Opus 40.

included in the stories of Woodstock's soldiers. In painting he is best known for his watercolors. He has had twenty-five one-man shows and has received many prizes, in addition to being made a full member of the National Academy. Pike's interest in civic affairs was aroused when in the middle of the night he witnessed the chopping down of one of the village trees that graced a town street. He surmised it was being done at that hour to avoid criticism; thereupon he decided to participate in village affairs. For his contribution to the improved appearance of Woodstock the Square Club declared him Best Citizen of the Year for 1959. He has been a town councilman since 1954.

Another artist who has received considerable recognition is Alfred Hutty, who died in 1954. He painted canvases but is best known for his etchings—for which he received numerous awards. His etchings are represented in the permanent collections of museums in New York, Chicago, Detroit, Los Angeles, Washington and many other cities. His work may also be seen in Toronto, Paris and London.

Two of our fine sculptors live at High Woods in Saugerties Township but have always been associated with the Woodstock colony. They are Harvey Fite and Tomas Penning. Each of them has built an interesting house and studio next to one of the quarries, using the bluestone for sculpture as well as

Tomas Penning created Our Lady of the Hudson *to honor the sailors who lost their lives on inland waterways between New York City and the Great Lakes. It is located at the Presentation Church in Port Ewen, New York.* Photo by Weston Blelock.

building. Beyond this there is little similarity between them. Fite could be said to belong distinctly to the modern school. Penning is modern in some of his sculpture but his religious subjects tend to be conservative. One of his statues that has become famous is *Our Lady of the Hudson* in Port Ewen, across the Rondout creek from Kingston. It was created to commemorate those men who lost their lives on the inland waterways between New York City and the Great Lakes. The money for the park and statue was raised by longshoremen, tug and barge men, boat builders and others affiliated with the waterways. The statue was unveiled by a descendant of a barge captain on the old Delaware and Hudson Canal. This elderly lady had made the trip between the two rivers on her father's barge.

Everyone remembers *The Invasion from Mars*, the radio play directed by and starring Orson Welles that caused the greatest commotion in the history of radio and created panic in its reputed locale of Grovers Mill, New Jersey. This script was written by Howard Koch, playwright and author or co-author of many other scripts. These included the feature films *The Letter*, with Bette Davis, *Letter from an Unknown Woman*, with Joan Fontaine, *Sergeant York* and the Oscar-winning *Casablanca*. Koch says he likes it here for both writing and living. He also finds it a convenient location when he is called to

Howard Koch (1901–95) wrote the radio script for Orson Welles's The War of the Worlds *and went on to win an Academy Award in 1944 for co-writing the screenplay for* Casablanca. Courtesy of Peter Koch.

London, New York or Hollywood. He says Woodstock is known in all these places, adding that he is surprised a great novel has not been written about it. He remembers Sinclair Lewis telling him that he planned to write a book on the subject.

Other well-known writers who live nearby are Joseph Kesselring, author of the play *Arsenic and Old Lace*, and Edmund Gilligan, who has a great talent for storytelling. Of Gilligan's novels, *The Strangers in the Vly* is probably the most popular. His sportsmen's column in the *New York Herald Tribune* is full of lore on the forests and streams. I remember one in particular, which included a fine description of wild ducks flying over the Hudson River marshes.

Ira Wolfert is a wonderful novelist. In 1959 he received the Page One Award from the Newspaper Guild. He was a writer who came here without knowing it was a colony of artists. When he was free after the war he joined his wife at Mead's, and later they bought a summer home at Lake Hill. Soon "Rondo" Robinson came to see him, and on one of his first walks Wolfert saw Will Durant, who lived on the corner of his road and with whom he was acquainted. Thus he learned there were numerous writers in the community. He prefers to spend his time quietly at work and is now finishing a book on the pace of American progress. Mechanization has necessitated the development of new capacities and patterns of work, and that is its theme. Wolfert tells me he finds Woodstock a wonderful place to work.

Kurt Marek rose to prominence when he produced *Gods, Graves and Scholars* under the pseudonym "C. W. Ceram," a phonetic-reversal version of his name. A friend asked him why he had moved to Woodstock and he is quoted as replying, "Where else could I go into a delicatessen and talk philosophy with the man who waits on me?" Marek at present is overseas collecting more archeological material.

Will Durant, who writes history in an interesting style, spent parts of many seasons in a home he owned at Lake Hill. Others who stayed for a short period include Sinclair Lewis, who acted in *Shadow and Substance* at the Playhouse, and Eugene O'Neill, who is reported to have spent a lost week in Woodstock. The latter's son, Eugene O'Neill Jr., came to a tragic end, after spending a rather tempestuous few years here, in a cottage on the Ohayo Mountain road.[22]

Houston Richards is the director of the successful Little Theater group in Kingston. He joined the Woodstock colony following his marriage to the pianist Inez Carroll. Since then he has received the admiration of almost all of the stage-struck youth in the county—as well he should, because he has been a well-known trouper. He has supported some of the greatest stars on Broadway, including George Cohan, Bob Hope and Ethel Merman. Richards says he spends much of his time now deflating the talented amateurs, figuring that unless they can ignore discouragement they should not take the bus to New York.

Harold Rugg

The Harold Ruggs live in Bearsville, high above the road to Wittenberg. From their terrace may be seen one of the most beautiful views in Woodstock Township. With their backs against Tonshi Mountain they face the series of hills that rise gradually beyond the flank of Overlook to the distant blue of the mountains in Greene County. There is space to watch the play of shadow and sunlight and the

Harold Rugg (1886–1960), author of Culture and Education in America, The Great Technology *and* American Life and the School Curriculum. *His final book,* Imagination, *was published posthumously in 1963.* Photo by Mary Morris. Courtesy of Photographic Records, Rauner Special Collections Library, Webster Hall, Dartmouth College.

thunderclouds bubbling to the northwest. If the air becomes too transparent and the hue of the mountains turns pale blue, a spell of rain will follow. (Or the Ruggs may prefer to inquire about the prospects of a fine day from their neighbor, Tom Shultis, who is considered the best weather prophet in the Catskills.)

Rugg has been in the field of education for many years. He graduated from Dartmouth in 1908 and has successively served on the faculties of the University of Illinois, the University of Chicago and Teachers College, Columbia University, as a Fulbright lecturer in Egypt, and as a part-time educational advisor for the University of Puerto Rico. He has served on various commissions and national research committees on education, and he has made surveys of education in the Philippines, Puerto Rico, the Union of South Africa, Australia and New Zealand.

The Ruggs frequently have informal dinners with well-chosen guests and good food. Their low-eaved house set on the mountainside, with its wide terrace and large living room, is well suited to parties. I recall groups gathered there from among painters, writers, musicians and philosophers, who, under Rugg's guidance, contributed to lively evenings of good conversation. Rugg is adept in the art of keeping talk alive on any subject.

Rugg is envied for his study, which is lined with interesting books and half-filled by a desk that surrounds the writer on three sides. One wall is taken up by a large fireplace. It was close to the hearth we talked one winter afternoon about his current manuscript on the creative process.

Harold Rugg has been versatile in his accomplishments. Since taking his doctorate at Illinois in 1915 he has lectured primarily on civilization and education in America. He is probably best known for his imaginative ideas on modern educational theory. He has received innumerable honors and is certainly one of Woodstock's most distinguished citizens.

When I asked Harold Rugg why he had chosen to live in Woodstock, he wrote to me:

> Billy Mearns, my friend and colleague at Lincoln School, brought me here thirty years ago. From his house I saw a bare mountain plateau, overlooking the most beautiful valley in the world; I bought the land around it, and on it slowly built the nucleus of a house. Then Elizabeth came and she and I together designed our house, appropriate to the life that we would live there . . .
>
> The human landscape drew me too, a community of creative men and women who might, when a day's work was done, cultivate with me the art of conversation and throw light on the creative way of life. On some rare evenings that has happened.
>
> *The Child Centered School*, *The Great Technology* and the fourteen-volume *Man and His Changing Society* for young Americans were written before I settled down in Woodstock. But my best work has been done here in the midst of happy moments of companionship. *That Men May Understand*—my reply to the patrioteers who maligned the schoolbooks—was written that I might understand. Here, during the war years, *Now Is the Moment* and *Foundations for American Education* took shape. And here in the early 'fifties were written *The Teacher of Teachers* and *Social Foundations of Education*. Best of all, since retirement in 1951 freed me from academic bondage, I have lived six years of exciting discovery working on *The Imagination of Man*—a forthcoming book on the nature of the creative act.
>
> Where could one find a scene and a climate more hospitable to the quiet mind of creative discovery than in our house above the valley in a community of artists?
>
> That is why I came to Woodstock.[23]

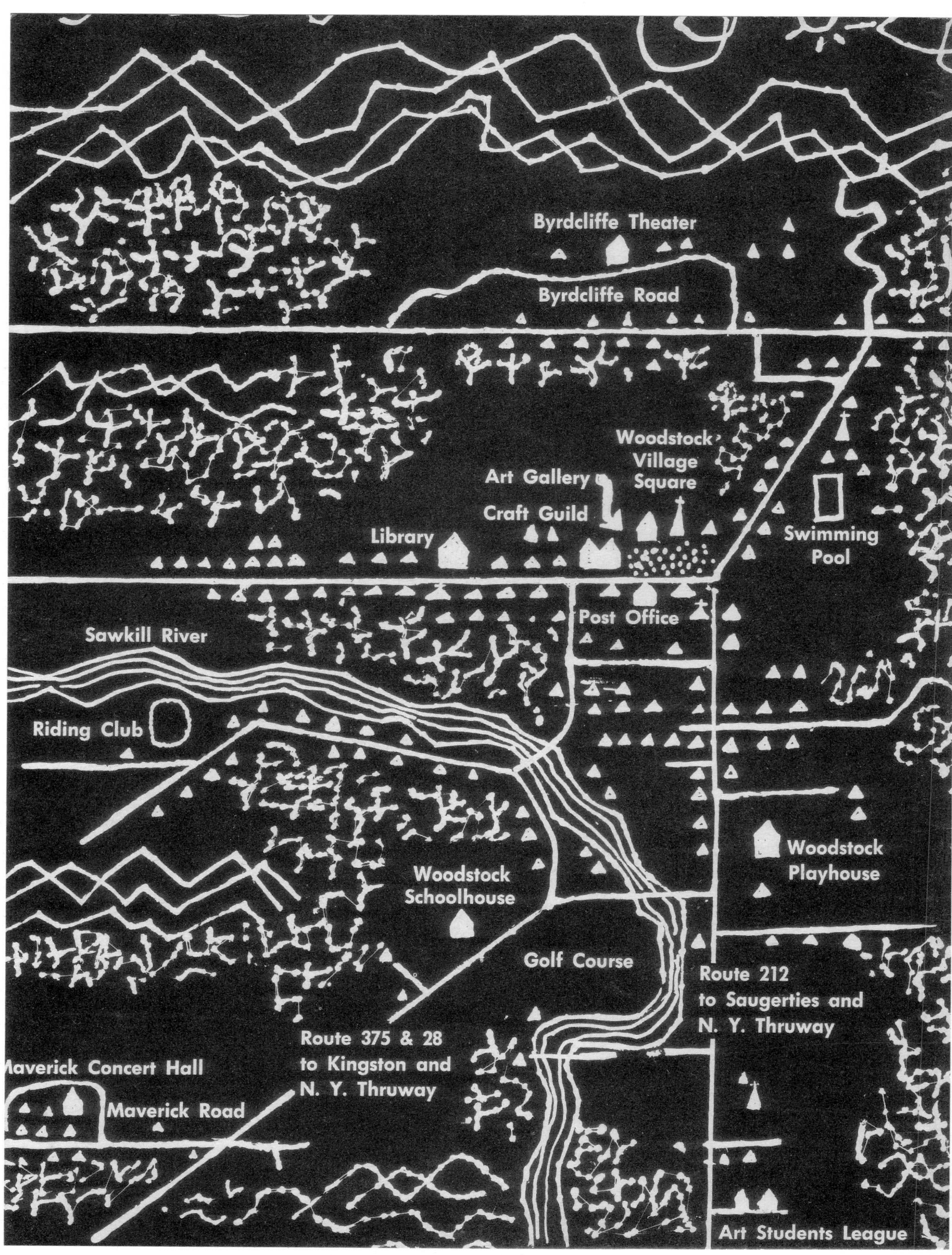

Map of Woodstock by Arnold Blanch. This appeared on the back cover of a Woodstock Festival *program circa 1959.* AMS Collection.

Chapter 15

ARTISTS TALK ABOUT ART

PROJECTING INTO THE FUTURE

Originally this history of Woodstock was to have ended after the account of the Second World War, but questions arose as to where the village is heading in peacetime, as well as to what is its ongoing role as an art colony. If answered, this last could project the story into the future. To secure opinions on this subject I thought it best to allow the artists to speak for themselves. My first inquiry was to Anton Refregier.

The music of Beethoven could be heard as I entered Refregier's barn studio. On the tables and walls were small-scale paintings for a Nebraska mural depicting the history of that state. Each figure and scene was symbolic on several levels but would be understandable to an intelligent person. That is important to him, because he has faith in the ultimate judgment of the people. Temporarily they might accept what is false, just as they could be forced by circumstances to live in crowded developments with ersatz chimneys made of cardboard while all around are miles of unoccupied country. But he believes that, given the opportunity, in the long run people would make a better choice.

Where does Refregier think art in Woodstock is heading? He suspects many of the young painters all over the United States are in a pocket confined by their egoism and intolerance. They are divorced from life, and if they are not to dry up they will have to return to the world. The flow of art advancement was interrupted during the war. Meanwhile the thinking of young people became self-centered, their work an expression of their ego. They rejected the humanist point of view. The period immediately after the war was lonely for real artists, but, fortunately for Woodstock, not long after this a group of painters arrived from the west, bringing with them a fresh understanding of life.

Refregier himself has participated in many world events. For example, he covered the beginnings of the United Nations organization for *Fortune* magazine. One of his important murals was commissioned by the San Francisco Post Office. Most of his murals are historical, requiring long research, and were executed in various media, including ceramics. He spoke of work he had done for public schools, the decorations he had made for the USS *Independence* and the USS *Constitution*, and murals he had created for a synagogue.

As to the future of art, Refregier spoke of the difficulty for the artist of making a living from painting pictures. A composer or writer might derive an income for years from each creation, but a painter sells his work and that ends his profit. The galleries and museums do not offer enough opportunity. He thinks the government should give the artists patronage. During the era of the Works Progress Administration the government's sponsorship helped the arts. The artists were given freedom of expression and were stimulated by the opportunities offered. Above all, Refregier says, he has faith in his fellow artists, and for art to survive they must return to humanism.[1]

When Doris Lee and Arnold Blanch were asked where they thought Woodstock is heading as an art colony they suggested that, as they now belong with the older artists, I listen to what the avant-garde set might say. They offered to invite a representative group of younger artists to meet in their home.

Before the meeting with the younger painters I spent a morning remembering many pleasant associations with Doris Lee and Arnold Blanch. I spread reproductions of several dozen of Doris's pictures over tables and chairs. Many of them, such as the illustrations for the musical *Oklahoma*, were cut from *Life* magazine. Her works also accompanied such articles as "The Harvey Girls," "The Hollywood Gallery," "Modern Living" and "An Artist in Africa." In addition, there was the book *Doris Lee*, from the American Artists Group, and illustrations for *The Great Quillow*, along with reproductions in various other art books and magazines.[2]

It does not require a second glance to recognize any of these as the work of Doris Lee. They are all full of gaiety, color, imagination and humor—not the low-comedy variety but a fanciful type that one can enjoy again and again. The color in these pictures may seem a little strong because they were intended for reproduction, yet the tones always fit the subject. For example, someone who has seen North Africa might take a quick breath of pleasure over the color in the Tunisian *Oasis*. The river winding through the canvas is what Doris herself calls "the blue of bluing"[3]; it complements the drab earth tone, the green foliage, and the notes of dulled copper in the costumes and cooking utensils. These paintings are more typical of North Africa than any number of those pictures of harem ladies and Arab fretwork that abound in European galleries.

It is easy to learn the details of Doris Lee's life, the pictures she has painted and the prizes she has won, from the American Artists Group monograph. But the monograph does not describe her home in Woodstock. She and her husband no longer live in their old house on the seventy-acre farm that she painted in her whimsical *Helicopter* canvas. They have sold all but a few acres and upon the remainder they have built a very modern home. Unlike the old farmers, they chose the best spot for viewing Overlook Mountain. But one must admit those old fellows had more respect for the cranky character of our streams. At the bidding of the old witch, the Sawkill sometimes leaps its banks by the bend and floods across Route 212, seeping under the doors of the newer houses but never under those of the old ones. It always happens when Doris and Arnold are away, and their friends fear that the souvenirs of their travels may be damaged. No doubt they have now learned to stow aloft all their favorite objects, because in looking around the studio recently I noted that every treasure was in its own secure place. There are Early American woodcarvings and ceramics. There are pieces of pottery and fabrics from Europe and Mexico. There are gods and dolls, pictures and decoys, both primitive and modern, each one situated with a feeling for line and color that makes it look right in the setting of a modern house. Doris says she prefers to live here, in a community of professional people surrounded by the rolling Catskill landscape.

This is where we met for the conference with the avant-garde group. On a humid July afternoon we assembled in the studio. A fresh breeze blew in from the mountain and, with the addition of cool drinks and comfortable chairs, conversation became a pleasure.

The only two among the group who were known to me were Bob Angeloch, an abstract painter, and Ed Chavez, who is a fine metalworker as well as a modern artist. The others were Lynfield Ott, Walter Plate, and Jane and Manuel Bromberg. The last named is a portrait painter who first came to Woodstock in 1941 to stay with Arnold Blanch on the Maverick. He was the forerunner of the group of artists who came from Colorado. Bromberg received a Guggenheim Fellowship and is now on the governing board of the Artists Association. Of course, Doris Lee and Arnold Blanch were also present.

In answer to my question regarding the future of Woodstock as an art colony, Lynfield Ott said that, speaking for himself, it was just about over; to see interesting exhibitions and find incentives he had to go to New York. If that were true, I asked, why did he not live in New York? Ott replied that he could not afford to live there. He regretted that a painter had to be practically a hermit in Woodstock, depending upon himself for motivation. Angeloch said he did not feel he had to be "charged up" all the time! Later, Ott added, "There's a different climate now for artists compared to the Thirties, when they were accepted by society and sponsored by the government. Being accepted, they painted more intelligibly. Artists feel that by living like other people they

Helicopter, *1948, by Doris Lee (1905–83). Lithograph, 8⅞ x 12 in.* Courtesy of Keith Sheridan Collection.

become closer to their fellow man." Chavez remarked that he liked living in Woodstock because here he *could* withdraw into his studio to think. There was little exchange between fellow painters, he said. Occasionally there might be a symposium at the galleries, but for exciting stimulation he went to New York. However, he received most of his inspiration for painting from the west, where he had spent his childhood.

There was general conversation regarding the tapering off of good music and musicians in Woodstock. When reminded that there were modern composers around, like Henry Cowell and William Ames, the artists conceded that these men were producing vital work. Blanch recalled the year Frank Mele directed the Festival of Modern American Music, sponsored by the Artists Association—when compositions of contemporary music were produced before an audience that packed the Town Hall.

Plate said that nowadays an artist has to work at another job to get enough money to paint. His wife, he said, was a teacher, and he worked part time. The others agreed that it was necessary to earn money at something other than their art. This work took about half their time. But why did they have to work this much and make so much money? Because they could not live decently without it. Somebody remarked that they could not be expected to make do with less than an untrained workman. Another said they did not want to live in an unusual way. I remarked that in the old days the painters lived in barns without plumbing. Plate answered that there were no barns available. I asked if it were not really that they were soft. Arnold Blanch noted that Sara Kuniyoshi had offered her husband's studio for a student's use. There were no takers because the water had to be carried a few feet and the toilet was outside. Later he amended this statement by adding that the offer had been made a little late in the season.

In connection with the changing pattern of the artists' habits, Blanch remarked that in the early days on the Maverick the creative people would get together and discuss interesting topics. Now when one met artists they would talk about their mowing machines or their babysitters. Referring to my last statement, he said one must take into consideration the fact that many of the young people now had families. Rather dryly I added that formerly the artists had not been able to afford children. This remark was followed by a significant moment of silence. Angeloch said that his job as a janitor at the League made his painting possible but that he could not hold a job and paint at the same time and therefore he was an artist for only eight months of the year. Blanch commented that Bob Angeloch made more sweeping floors than he did as an instructor!

Bromberg made statements from time to time suggesting he agreed with the others that Woodstock had deteriorated as an art colony and that artists today were conditioned to comforts. Ott remarked that he had lived as uncomfortably as any painter, and at times as well as many of them. Bromberg added that not too long ago there were places in Woodstock where one could meet with other artists, drink a glass of beer and play pool. Now there were only the hard-liquor spots. Angeloch said he could not afford to frequent those places even if it were the only way to have conversation with other painters. All agreed about the need to associate with other creative persons. Blanch recalled that Paul Burlin used to go in the afternoon to sit on the terrace of the Irvington.[4] After a while another artist passing along the road would notice him there and go sit at the same table. Along would come a few more painters, and soon a little coterie would have gathered for conversation.

Doris Lee regretted there were no informal gathering places such as the Parisian cafés. Now, one was specially invited to an entertainment and it was necessary to dress up for it. Angeloch asked if it were not because Woodstock has grown too big. Blanch said it was full of people but most of them were on the fringes of art. Plate agreed that the French type of café offered much to the artist. He had been a GI student for three and a half years in France. When questioned, however, he conceded it was no longer cheap to live there. As for the quality of the work to be seen in Paris, he said the most exciting paintings to be seen there now came from America. The trend has been reversed and now French artists were being stimulated by pictures arriving from the United States. He described the little Left Bank galleries receiving bundles of rolled canvases from New York. They all said that there were more good painters here in America than anywhere else.

If they could not find the right living conditions in Europe or New York, I asked, where did they think they might be found? There followed a discussion of other art colonies. Bromberg said his first choice was Paris, his next Woodstock. "After all," he said, "here there is a set of built-in values developed from fifty years of creative thinking in the valley. Artists might fade out for a period but later they might zero back in again. There is an advantage in that artists are not second-class citizens in Woodstock." "Painters do not sell their work as easily as they did formerly," volunteered Ott. "Good painters are not trying to sell as much as they are trying to paint better."

Blanch said there was a creeping mediocrity in the Woodstock Artists Association exhibitions. Bromberg's retort to this was that the gallery group wanted good work. This past spring, he said, there were only nine or ten persons submitting work for membership in the Association, of whom only three were accepted. There were scholarships available, but the kids would not accept them and thereby sacrifice the seven or eight hundred dollars they could make at other jobs.

Plate periodically repeated that he could not find any stimulation among the pictures shown in the Woodstock exhibitions. But because he loved nature, he said, the Catskills gave him an impulse toward creative work. He said he found it a horrible as well as a wonderful feeling to paint; art is a personal conviction that the artist has to work out for himself. Bromberg asked why more of the younger men did not exhibit at the Artists Association shows, implying that if they were to do so the exhibitions might become more vital. Arnold Blanch referred again to the old days when everyone exhibited there. The New York dealers would come to see the shows and invite the painters whose work interested them to exhibit at their galleries in New York. That was how many of the young painters got their start, including Doris and himself. He said one explanation for the present situation might be that now the city was only a couple of hours away and the artists could make their own contacts with the New York dealers. It developed from the conversation that Plate would soon have a one-man show at the Stable Galleries in New York.

I noted that for forty-five years people had been heard to say Woodstock was dying, but after all it is very much alive. Chavez remarked that even if he did not find stimulus for painting here he still liked living in Woodstock. Ott, for all his criticism, admitted that after trying other places he was always delighted to return. He said he liked being able to look at the mountain. Both Bromberg and Blanch said that, notwithstanding the poor quality of the exhibitions, there was actually better painting being produced in the community now than twenty years ago, and that more exciting people were about. Their conclusions were that for an artist Woodstock was just about the best year-round place in which to live. Manuel Bromberg offered the final *bon mot* when he remarked that probably the last hero would be the artist who was on his own and starved.

In a later conversation Ed Chavez remarked to me that though the village has certainly changed and there is no longer a community of artists in the sense of meeting-places and cafés, this year he has been aware of fresh impetus. New galleries have opened and new cultural activities are developing.

Chavez, who was born in Wagonmound, New Mexico, has painted numerous murals in the west. Besides the Fulbright Award, he received a two-thousand-dollar Tiffany Grant, the Childe Hassam purchase award and the Lathrop Prize, among other awards. He is represented by paintings in many museums and in the Library of Congress Print Collection. For the past five years (1954–58) he has been an instructor at the Art Students League.

When Arnold Blanch read what had been jotted down at this meeting he said it was not fair to be critical of the artists just because they wanted comforts. He added that most of the members of this particular group were not students but mature painters. He recalled that most of the original Woodstock artists had been grateful for comforts as soon as they could afford them.

He made another comment, which seems interesting, about the general attitude regarding art. He said that throughout the United States artists have become an important cultural force in their communities. The visiting artist is received enthusiastically and his pictures are considered important.

After talking with these avant-garde painters I came to the conclusion that some of them liked to grumble and I took to calling them the angry young artists. One evening soon after, I happened to speak with a teenage student who was working under Arnold Blanch at the League, and it was refreshing to listen to his enthusiasm. He was called Bobby, and when asked whether his fellow students at the League felt as he did, he said yes and suggested bringing a couple of them to talk with me. Unfortunately there was not time to do this. But it was interesting to know that these very young initiates in art were bursting with zeal and grateful for the opportunity to study in Woodstock. It was reminiscent of the very early days of the League Summer School. This opportunity was not being handed to them freely. In Bobby's case he was working for his bed and dinner, doing chores for his landlady, and when that obligation was met he did odd carpentry jobs in the evening to cover other expenses. He said that for him the most important stimulation was being in the environment of Woodstock with other students who were thinking about art and had the same goal. He quoted Blanch as saying that no teacher could do more than guide and that the only way to grow was by application. He was working so hard at painting and as a handyman that he did not have time to hang around the pubs, although he said he liked to have an occasional glass of beer. Arnold Blanch said Bobby was an unusually hard-working student and was accomplishing as much as any among them. Looking into the intelligent face of this youth, I felt that the future of the Woodstock tradition in art was in good hands.

As the artists continued to speak, in many instances they inadvertently admitted that Woodstock has a spiritual energy. There is an aggregate tone or mindset that emanates from mass creative thinking. To encourage the interchange of ideas, why can there not be sidewalk cafés with tiny metal tables where the artists could gather over a beer, a coffee or a glass of wine? If this could be established, and creative people attracted, Woodstock might come into its rightful place as the center of art in America.

Arnold Blanch

Arnold Blanch was born in Minnesota and first studied painting at the Minneapolis School of Art. His aunt paid his tuition for one term. Thereafter the youth won scholarships to study at the Art Students League in New York, where he worked under John Sloan and Robert Henri. American art owes a great debt to these two masters, who in their day had a liberating influence upon a whole generation of students. Blanch's art development was interrupted by the First World War, during which he was sent to France to make maps for the Intelligence Corps. Whenever possible he visited Paris and the museums. After the war he returned to the League for a short period to study under Kenneth Hayes Miller and Boardman Robinson. This was followed by a summer during which he painted in France, along the Loire.

Blanch arrived in Woodstock in 1923, when he and his first wife, Lucile, built a studio on the Maverick. To supplement their income he set up a loom for weaving, worked in a bohemian restaurant called the Intelligencia, which was being run at the time by some of the musicians, and also did any odd job available. This enabled him to paint part time. Gradually he sold a few pictures, had a one-man show at the Dudensing Gallery in New York City and was launched upon a successful career. He and Lucile were separated, then divorced, and several years later he and Doris Lee were married.

In 1933 Blanch returned to France on a Guggenheim Fellowship. Throughout his life he has periodically returned to Europe, especially to France. He has also traveled in North Africa, Spain, and Mexico and absorbed something of their culture. But while on a trip across this country he became fully aware of the beauty and expanse of the United States, finding here the true orientation for his talent. Since then he has received many medals and prizes from the foremost exhibitions and his work is represented in most of the American art museums and large galleries.

During the 1930s Arnold Blanch was keenly aware of the evil that Fascism was spreading. It may have been this, added to a curtailment of his hitherto superabundant energy, that led him into what has been called his angry period of painting. To me it seemed a necessary adjustment to the tragedy in the world. From that time he developed a greater understanding of humanity and a more buoyant viewpoint. He has looked closely at life and now he expresses a mature appraisal of this era. He has always been popular as an instructor. One of his artist friends remarked that Blanch is a born teacher and is fortunate in that his teaching has not detracted from his creative ability.

As he has received honors too numerous to list, I will describe Blanch only as a neighbor. His hair changed from blond to gray when he was still young. He wears it rather long and allows it to fall naturally over his forehead. His features are square and his body stocky in informal tweeds. If it were not for the brooding intelligence in his face, one would never take him for an artist. He can be seen driving a station wagon to the village and standing before the post office to chat with friends, or bobbing in and out of the Artists Association in the midst of planning an exhibition or symposium. He was one of those responsible for the modern music festival held in the village, and for various art conferences, and he helped with the Art Film Festival initiated by Sydney Berkowitz. However, now he does not have much to do with the Woodstock Artists Association, having yielded his place to the younger painters. In his time he has illustrated several books and made designs for textiles and pottery. There is another side to his character: he loves to fish and hunt and to talk to the old mountaineers who are wise in the lore of bear hunting or know the best pools for trout. On several occasions I have returned home to find a few trout strung from the door latch, and I knew Arnold Blanch had been around.[5]

Sigmund Menkes

My over-the-fence neighbor, Sigmund Menkes, lives in the old home of Rosie Magee and teaches at the Art Students League. When asked what he wished to say regarding present-day Woodstock, his reply was spontaneous. Here he is happy, and here he has found suitable surroundings and painted his best canvases. There have been definite changes in the village since he arrived, and the art students are also different. Now the pupils are not only against tradition but even against learning. They start from zero and in three weeks consider themselves ready to exhibit. In spite of all their talk about individualism, there is in their painting far greater unanimity than in the art exhibited by students in years past. To be important, said Menkes, the painter has to have found himself and be aware of the human senses. The artist cannot lose contact with nature—which he may change for his own purposes but cannot ignore, or he will reach a dead end.

Menkes was born and educated in Poland. As a young man he went to Paris and painted there for twenty years. His work was well known in Europe before 1935, when he came to the United States. Shortly thereafter he arrived in Woodstock, which he considered a fortuitous event. From the first moment in this beautiful countryside he found peace, contentment, and the equilibrium necessary to thrive as a human being and as an artist. He believes only intimate contact with nature can provide this.

As a painter he has exhibited all over America, including a number of one-man shows in New York and elsewhere. His pictures have been acquired by the Metropolitan, the Whitney and other important museums.

When speaking with Sigmund Menkes one finds him modest about the success he has achieved. He ended our conversation by saying, "When a little town like Woodstock becomes big, one must preserve the things that have made it different."[6]

William Ames

William Ames first came to Woodstock to visit Henry Billings in 1922. The next year he returned to spend the summer and has been here for part of the season ever since. He says he finds it a good place to work, among understanding people, and it is here in Woodstock that he has developed his style of composition. He refers to Brahms and Beethoven, whose ideas came from nature. Ames finds the countryside emotionally stimulating. He does not have many so-called conveniences in his Maverick cottage, but he does not consider that comforts are a requisite to creative work.

From 1928 to 1938 William Ames taught at the Eastman School of Music. During these years he specialized in chamber music. Probably the most successful of his earlier works was a quintet for clarinet and strings that was followed by a sextet for oboe, two violins, two violas and a cello. Each of these compositions was stimulated by his surroundings on the Maverick. For the past fifteen years Ames has been attempting to explore the possibilities of different tonal combinations in concise forms.

For twelve years or so Ames and his wife lived during the winter in New York City. Now he is at Cornell University in Ithaca, associated with a modern dance troupe. For this group he has composed a number of pieces. Besides his work with the dancers, he has given recitals and participated in music conferences. One of his latest orchestral compositions, *Prologue*, was performed at the Bennington Composers' Conference in 1957 and at a composers' conference in Dallas, Texas.

He has since composed a concerto for clarinet and orchestra that is now being tried out. When asked how much work he completes during an average year, he said that in the past twelve months, besides a few short pieces, he has produced two piano compositions, the above-mentioned clarinet concerto and two pieces of chamber music.

Mr. and Mrs. Ames were kind enough to drive over to see me at Rock City for a little talk. When I asked his opinion regarding music in Woodstock he said that although there is considerable musical activity now, there were a few exceptional years in the late 1940s when particularly interesting modern music was performed. He believes there is a future for the creation of contemporary musical compositions here. He likes the different points of view expressed in Woodstock and expects to remain here permanently.[7]

Dachine Rainer

The poet Dachine Rainer has faint praise for Woodstock when she says that "in these times [it] is no worse than any other place to live, and despite its gradual but steady deterioration since its inception as an artists' community over half a century ago, it is substantially preferable to the mass psychoses of cities." She and her husband, Holly Cantine Jr., live about a mile from a back road that to most of us seems remote, on the old route to Lake Hill. Cantine built their house of logs he felled himself, and it has real character and charm. From there he and Dachine have produced an "anarchist-pacifist" periodical, *Retort*, and a volume of writings by conscientious objectors to the Second World War. Also, for two summers he published a local paper called *The Wasp*, which has stung many of us!

Cover of Retort, *a literary publication edited by Holly Cantine Jr. and Dachine Rainer that featured poetry and short stories.* AMS Collection.

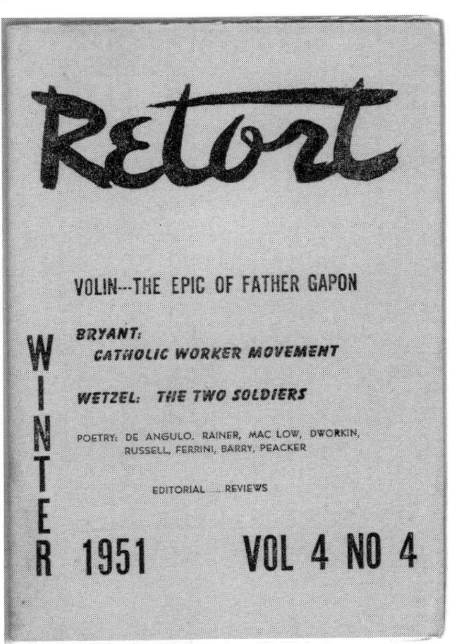

In addition to her poetry, Dachine Rainer writes fiction and criticism. Her poems have been published in several anthologies, including W. H. Auden's *The Criterion Book of Modern American Verse*. She has also published two novellas, both from her longer work, *The Unbeat*. She defines her credo thus:

> Today the only revolutionary position in art consists in upholding the very traditions of the arts—in craftsmanship and integrity. A desire for mastery of one's medium and a deep appreciation of other epochs and other civilizations and their creative answers is of as grave importance as the artist's perception of the disastrous seductions of commerce, fad and the modern academic.[8]

Mountain Valley, *by Ethel Magafan.* Photo: AMS Collection.

Bruce Currie and Ethel Magafan

Bruce Currie, his wife, Ethel Magafan, and their little girl, Jenne, live on one of the mountain roads up which a car has to clamber in second gear. To reach their studios, one parks, then crosses a high bridge above a brook that tumbles through ferns and mossy boulders. Coming from the hot village it is refreshing to be in the cool shadows of Overlook, but one speculates about the snow and ice of winter, because the Curries live here year-round. They tell me that people in Woodstock respect their working hours. Possibly this would not be true if they lived in the hubbub of the town.

These two artists have disciplined themselves to work at regular hours in their studio without interruptions. They try not to interfere with each other and, as Ethel said in a happy voice, "I admire Bruce's painting and he likes mine, so it goes very well between us." Even the redheaded baby is contented and regular in her habits. Ethel kept working right up to the time little Jenne was born, and now as soon as the baby takes a nap she hurries to her studio to paint.

The Magafan twins, Jenne and Ethel, were among those painters who, after the war, came here from the west to inject fresh impetus into our valley. They arrived from Colorado where their father had settled after migrating from Greece. He was unusual in that he encouraged his daughters' interest in art. Both Magafan girls became good painters. After they came to Woodstock, Jenne married Ed Chavez just before he went into the army and Ethel married Bruce Currie after his release from the service. In 1951 all four of them went to Europe, Ethel having received a Fulbright Award for the study of Byzantine and Grecian art, and Ed a Fulbright for painting in Italy.

Sadly, Jenne Magafan died soon after their year in Europe. However, Ethel has continued to develop her painting. Greek culture, as well as the landscape, has had a deep influence upon her. Her inheritance may have given her a greater appreciation of the rugged country, which in some respects reminded her of Colorado. She has always loved mountains, and that is one reason why she has been happy in Woodstock and has often painted abstractions of Overlook. Looking for a picture that would show the spirit of our Catskills, I went to Ethel Magafan; she has allowed me to reproduce one of her paintings in this book.

Her work has been represented in several museums, including the permanent collection of the Metropolitan Museum of Art. She has received eleven awards, among them the first Hallgarten, the fifteen-hundred-dollar Altman Prize and the two-thousand-dollar purchase award of the National Exhibition of Contemporary Art in Pomona, California.

Bruce Currie's work is distinctive; he has developed a highly personal style of painting. He came from Iowa and before he painted he was a musician, playing the clarinet with the University of Chicago Symphony and later at our Maverick concerts.

He has had several one-man shows, the first of which was in Athens in the exhibition hall of the American embassy. He has received various awards, most recently the American Watercolor Society Silver Medal and the purchase award of the Butler

Institute of American Art. He has exhibited in most of the big shows from New York to San Francisco.

Ethel and Bruce Currie have a mature attitude toward their work and the life around them. They appreciate what Woodstock has offered them—the opportunity to paint amidst beautiful surroundings and among congenial fellow artists. They are attractive, well-balanced people.[9]

Reginald Wilson

In talking with Reginald Wilson one senses his intellectual honesty. He has not used his art to attract attention by sensationalism. He has arrived at his kind of painting through a long process of questioning and growth. It has taken him years to acquire his equipment and technical knowledge, but he now feels he can paint naturally. Accepting his sincerity, one studies his pictures with genuine interest, even though they may seem rather startling.

Reggie Wilson was born in 1909 in Butler, Ohio, of a family that had no interest in art. He was a cartoonist before he studied at the Art Students League. He worked for a while with John Steuart Curry, Guy Pene DuBois, Thomas Benton and Harry Wickey, but is convinced that an artist has to evolve his personal convictions and technique and must be his own critic. He belongs to no school and has refused to teach because he cannot accept the responsibility of directing someone else.

His work was interrupted for three and a half years while he served as an airplane mechanic in the Second World War. He came to Woodstock in 1945 and bought a home along the Sawkill, where he lives with his wife and two children. A number of his paintings are inspired by his children and their toys because he is interested in figures as well as objects; all of these he reduces to their fundamental forms. Wilson likes Woodstock and thinks there is much interesting work being created here in both abstract and representational schools.[10]

Howard Mandel

Howard Mandel is an exuberant young man full of enthusiasm for painting and with enough vitality to experiment in other media. On my visit to his studio, which is high off the Wittenberg road, the initial impression was of a varied but orderly collection of easels, working tables, pieces of sculpture, paintings, tiles and heaven knows what else. My eyes lingered upon dozens of apothecary jars full of what looked like colored lozenges. He told me they were mosaic stones but we did not go into his plans for using them. He did tell me about the incomplete papier-mâché sculpture arranged on shelves. These pieces had been used in a Fifth Avenue shop-window display for several successive weeks to illustrate a do-it-yourself method of making sculpture. It had been of sufficient interest for Doubleday to ask him to write a book on the making of papier-mâché figures.

Our conversation revealed that Mandel had started his art career as a sculptor. He had gone to the Pratt Institute, where a teacher told him he could never be an artist. This did not deter him and eventually he left Pratt as top man in his class. After that he worked at commercial art. Mandel believes it is good for a young artist to get into the stream of life, perhaps designing wallpaper or textiles. The best European painters, like Picasso, made pottery, designed ballet sets and so on. Mandel did not work under any particular master but developed his own unique style of painting. There was an incomplete canvas on an easel and I noted that in it he had not painted the heads of the figures in triangles. No, he said, he had gone as far as he wished with that format and for the last year or two had become interested in another point of view. When working out his ideas he had not known that they were in a great Italian tradition until he finally went to Italy and saw the Giottos in Florence and Assisi—and almost went wild with joy.

Asked what he thought about Woodstock as an art colony, he became enthusiastic. Mandel is one of those persons who came for a weekend and had to return. As soon as he was free after his war service he came back to live here and, except for a year in Europe on a Fulbright Award (1951–52), he has worked here ever since. He spoke of the opportunities Woodstock offers, such as the chance to be with other creative people, writers as well as painters. He mentioned the good theater productions, the Turnau Opera in Byrdcliffe and the play-reading group.

When I spoke of the unhappy artists with whom I had talked, he said it was extremely important to hear them give expression to their gripes and confusions. However, he added (and perhaps there was no connection between this and his previous remark) that there is something very wrong if one has to write a three-page essay to explain one's work. This was a reminder of the statement Matisse made when he was asked what advice he had to give students: he said to tell them to cut out their tongues!

Mandel's mother kindly brought in glasses of iced tea. Shortly thereafter a young man in a pink shirt walked in from the kitchen and I realized my visit had been overlong.

Alexander Archipenko

Woman Combing Her Hair, *1915, by Alexander Archipenko (1887–1964). Bronze, 13¾ x 3¼ x 3⅛ in. including base.* © The Museum of Modern Art, Licensed by SCALA / Art Resource, N.Y. © 2005 Estate of Alexander Archipenko / Artists Rights Society [ARS], New York.

The sculpture of Alexander Archipenko is too well known all over the art world to require any description. Nor is it necessary to place him in any category beyond saying he is very modern and has been ahead of the trends for years and years. He gave me a paper of an exhibition covering a half century of his work—the one hundred and tenth one-man show held at Associated American Artists Galleries in 1954. On it were fifteen photographs of his sculptured figures, the earliest having been executed in 1909. It is a most impressive showing.

When I went to see him he did not look old enough to represent all those years of work. He was born in Kiev in the Ukraine in 1887 and it was there he studied painting and sculpture. When he was twenty-one he went to Paris. After exhibiting in several European cities he opened his own school of art, first in France and then in Germany. By 1923 he had moved to New York and soon became an American citizen. He has for many years had schools of sculpture in New York City and Woodstock.

One torrid morning I drove to Wittenberg, turning onto a side road and up into the woods to reach Archipenko's studio. It was in a clearing surrounded by trees and underbrush where no breeze could penetrate. We sat under a sort of open canopy surrounded by hunks of different kinds of stone, some of which were translucent. There were tools, benches, a table, a lathe, a drill, a stand that might have been used to treat metals, and a variety of other impedimenta. I did recognize two exotic birds swinging in a cage hung on a tree. We had hardly launched into our conversation when the birds set up wild chirpings, which brought an attractive young student almost flying out the open door of the studio. She searched frantically through the grass, mumbling something about a snake. The master bade her be calm, assuring her there were no snakes about. We then resumed the interview, only to have the bird scene repeated. This time Archipenko told the girl the parakeets were only fussing because they had heard an automobile approaching. A car did soon arrive, bringing a young man who greeted the sculptor and then set to work chipping stone nearby.

Half my allotted time was gone before I was able to get an answer regarding Archipenko's opinion of our mountains. He had come to Woodstock in 1929 to enjoy nature. He said the place is too relaxing for creative thinking. There is iron through the underlying rocks, which makes the earth magnetic and people sleepy. It takes him about two weeks to fight this relaxed feeling before he can get to work.

When asked where he finds his artistic impulse, he said he is inspired by a universal force. He carries his motivation within himself. Of course, he added, artists put their emotional experiences into their art. One has to have creative consciousness and be aware of creative ability, without which there can be no progress. An artist has to be persistent and work frantically before he is able to touch the universal forces. It is as Christ said: "Knock and it shall be opened." Frequently problems are solved in a dream.

Archipenko will not take more than four pupils at a time. When asked how he chooses those students he made the surprising statement that ability is partly hereditary. He said art is more complicated than science. We were interrupted before he could follow out this theme.

In closing the conversation Archipenko said he was preparing for a tour of Europe in 1960. Already nine countries and fourteen cities had scheduled exhibitions of his sculpture. Evidently he was looking forward to returning to Europe.

Dorothy Varian

Driving down the Wittenberg hill, I stopped in to see Dorothy Varian. She lives in one of the old story-and-a-half farmhouses that used to dot the hillsides in the Woodstock landscape. I remembered her flower paintings, which had displayed her former preoccupation with delicate lines and colors, and I wondered what she was doing now. In her studio she showed me several canvases of an intermediate development. But it was in the house, upon the white walls, that her latest paintings hung. To me they were arrangements of lines and dashes in a non-objective style. They showed she was still concerned with color, but there were depths of patterns and movement that made them more than mere decorations. I was out of my depth talking of contemporary art, but not in the evaluation of her home. She had retained the character of the little rooms and mid-Victorian furnishings, even to a Brussels carpet in the front parlor. Unlike the custom in old farmhouses, she did not have the shades drawn to prevent the sun from fading the upholstery; consequently there was a happy atmosphere without the musty smell. Surprisingly, the modern paintings seemed particularly suited to these surroundings.

Gwen Davies

Marianne Gwendoline Isabel Francisca Mary-Winifred Wallis-Davies—known to us as Gwen—is one of the few artists still to be found in a barn, and here she paints and lives with exuberance. I remember taking her a bouquet of orange calendulas and finding that they exactly matched her hair. Wearing a pink waist and bluish skirt, she glowed against the weathered boards. Her conversation is full of dashes and exclamations. Her shouted "Darling!," hands flung high, is the greeting with which we are all familiar.

Years ago she arrived on the Maverick, where Hervey White placed her in a tiny shed—built as the men's dressing room for the theater. She paid thirty dollars rent for the year, which was enough because there was no plumbing and the rough boards scarcely protected her from the weather. There were other, rather terrifying, elements on the Maverick for which her only protection was a wire wound around a nail each night as a way of locking the door. However, she survived to enjoy the bohemian life and to work at her music. She sang modern songs in a blithe French style for our pleasure.

When she is not teaching, Gwen Davies now paints in her Rock City barn. She is not one of the young artists, but her work is decidedly avant-garde. This is the safest term to use, because if one were to call it abstract, contemporary or non-objective one could be making a serious mistake. She belongs with those showing their art as the Kaaterskill Group. When asked about the philosophy of her work, she became very serious. Here are a few of her remarks.

She says an artist *is*. He cannot be one just by wishing. And even if he is one, this does not mean he will make it, because he may not have the purity and insight to arrive at a state of grace where he expresses, through his medium, a glimmer of a revelation, if he is lucky. It requires nothing short of dedication for the layman to understand art. It requires a super-sensibility to recognize a little more truth and beauty—in other words to discover new values. In the world, in the universe, in art there is mystery and wonder. The artist has to penetrate beyond the surface and beyond imitation. It is his job to make order out of chaos. He becomes aware of overtones, and his emotions react to dynamic tensions, speeds and the wonders unveiled in our atomic age!

Gwen Davies has more enthusiasm for painting than any artist with whom I have talked. And she thinks Woodstock is a wonderful place for creative work.[11]

A Museum Director Speaks

Hermon More has been associated with the activities of Gertrude V. Whitney since 1923, when he joined the Whitney Studio Club. In 1929 he was given a one-man show in the Studio Galleries. He was appointed curator of the museum when it was founded in 1930. He served in that capacity until the death of Juliana Force, that well-loved friend and patron of many Woodstock artists, whom he succeeded as director in 1948.

During his administration the museum moved from its original home on Eighth Street to its new building on West Fifty-fourth Street, where its average annual attendance has increased from seventy thousand to two hundred and sixty thousand. Funds for acquisition have increased in like proportion: now, some thirty thousand dollars is spent annually for the purchase of works, almost entirely by living artists. A constantly growing collection presents problems of storage space, which is largely overcome by loans to other institutions. Three hundred such loans are made each year so that the collection is enjoyed in many places outside New York City.

More has always maintained a home in Woodstock and has now returned to live here permanently. We were together at the Art Students League long ago, and as we talked we spent time reminiscing. At the annual Summer School "Concours" he had received one of the top prizes, whereas I had been awarded an honorable mention. Buoyed up by these awards we felt that we were well on the way to success, and indeed in that less complicated era when the limits of art seemed fixed, steady progress toward the summit seemed not impossible. He recalled the awkward charm of the Woodstock of forty-five years ago:

> In that pre-neon age there were more trees, more time, fewer tourists and not a gift [shop], delicatessen or antique shop in the place. Parking space was adequate for the town's four automobiles. Then the town belonged to the original inhabitants—and, of course, art students—for then, as now, Woodstock was the home of the Art Students League Summer School. Today when students of art do not give nature a second glance, our concern with her every mood must seem to them a quaint preoccupation. But in those innocent days we looked upon nature as a willing model and a beneficent friend, never dreaming that she might be capable of blowing up in our faces.
>
> Even in those halcyon days dark clouds were forming. We had heard echoes of that "explosion in a shingle factory," but in 1914 the Armory Show and the war seemed mostly the concern of Europe and were heard only as faint reverberations in our peaceful valley. Our isolation was soon shattered by the world revolution in art. Dasburg, Cramer and McFee felt the influence of Cézanne and of Cubism. Some form of modern art has been predominant in the young generation until today the romantic realism for which Woodstock was noted has been superseded by various kinds of abstraction.

When asked what art movement is now in the ascendancy, More said,

> Unquestionably abstract expressionism . . . a movement that is difficult to define because it is so personal an expression of the artist's innermost consciousness, an art of extreme sensitivity and intuitive perception, with no objective reality beyond the surface of the canvas itself. Charged with emotion, an art of spontaneity and improvisation, its proponents are in revolt against the movements that dominated American art since the turn of the century, which in the main are forms of realism: the American Scene, Regionalism, Social Realism, as well as the more abstract art of Cubism. On the more positive side, Abstract Expressionism, or "Action Painting" as it is sometimes called, is another manifestation of each new generation's quest to find new symbols by which to express themselves and interpret the times in which they live.

Asked which Woodstock artists of the new movement are most widely appreciated today, he mentioned the late Bradley Tomlin and Philip Guston, whose work is known beyond the borders of the United States. For the first time our artists are innovators whose influence is felt in Europe and indeed throughout the world.

The changes that have occurred in art led our conversation naturally to the changes in living conditions experienced by Woodstock's contemporary students and young professionals. He recalled the way we lived and worked in the early days:

> Rents were cheap for studios in barns and our way of life was simple, even primitive: kerosene stoves and lamps, water from a well, often drawn in buckets. Outhouses, because of their architecture, were drafty on cold mornings. Our pleasures, too, were simple: music from a phonograph served as an invitation to the dance. Until prohibition made applejack our national drink, very little liquor was consumed. Our

Ref's Back Porch, *1947, by Philip Guston (1913–80). When the Philip Gustons first came to the Maverick they rented Anton Refregier's house, and his back porch was the repository for many of the odds and ends referenced in Guston's work. Pen and black ink on paper.* Courtesy of Woodstock Artists Association Permanent Collection.

stimulants were love, hope and the excitement of the occasional sale of a picture. In retrospect it seems a golden age, but we must admit that as soon as economic circumstances permitted we succumbed to the lure of bourgeois comforts. Then, as now, artists had to depend on outside sources of income. Few could devote their whole time to their vocation. Considering the flood of works of art that overflow the Woodstock Artists Association and crowd the walls of museums, galleries and sports arenas in New York, productivity has not been greatly inhibited by part-time jobs.

Some thirty-five years ago Hermon More and his wife built a house on a rocky hillside just off the road to Wittenberg. Now permanent residents of Bearsville, they seldom take advantage of the opportunities afforded by the nightlife and cultural life of Woodstock. What means most to them, they say, is living among the kind of people they like.[12]

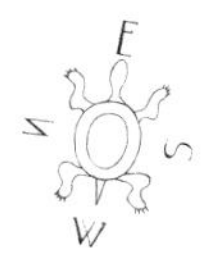

This story of Woodstock has taken three years of research and writing. As it progressed, more and more incidents and personalities were brought to my attention. If all of them were to be included, the book would be enormous. Those people who have not been mentioned are quite as interesting as those who are portrayed. There are plenty of subjects for another history of the town, which should be written, perhaps along with refutations of what I have said! If this arouses others to preserve and write stories that have made Woodstock a special village, then I would consider my book worthwhile.

Sometimes we have worried that the nightspots or commerce might supersede the artistic tradition of Woodstock. However, after talking to many painters, writers and musicians, I realize there are more of them here than ever before; they have merely retreated into the woods to work.

The legendary witch sometimes casts her angry floods upon us, but I think there is another force that prevails now, throughout the hills and valleys. It is the power generated from years of creative effort. Manuel Bromberg mentions it in this chapter and others have indicated they are aware of it. Nothing is ever lost. For over fifty years the dominant thinking has been toward higher ideals in art. Some of us may die without achieving success, but our thoughts live on and serve to lift another generation's ambition toward perfection.

This is a sparkling September day with Overlook clearly outlined against the blue sky. How powerful it looms, with its ledges of bluestone hidden beneath the foliage of summer; yet one is aware of the bones of the mountain rising tier upon tier to the sky. It is a smiling landscape and probably the old witch up there is contented. It seems a propitious moment to write *finis*.

WOODSTOCKERS IN SERVICE

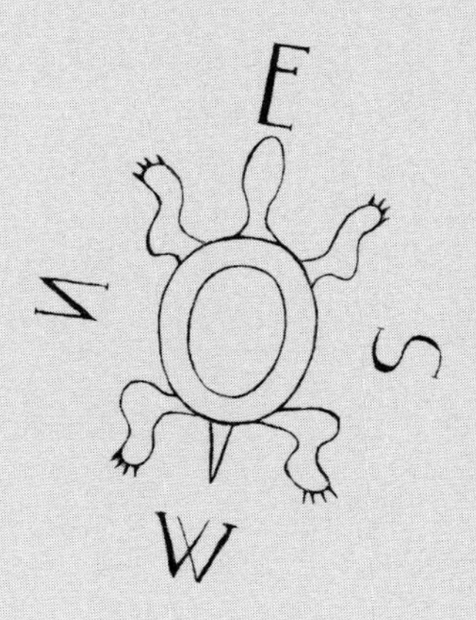

War Memorial, Woodstock Cemetery, Memorial Day 2005.
Photo courtesy of Dion Ogust.

MEMORIA

On the Woodstock Village Green stands a memorial to our war dead, designed by Marianne Mecklem and made possible through the hard work of a committee serving under Wilna Hervey. It is a circular stone container for flowering plants with a flagpole rising from the center. The base of the pole is wrapped with a bronze tablet on which are engraved the names of those who lost their lives for their country in four wars. Also, there is a quotation from a poem by Archibald MacLeish and this line from the Bible: "I will make darkness light before them" (Isaiah 42.16).

CIVIL WAR DEAD

Isaac Barber
Jacob Clapper
Alonzo Sylvester Lewis
Egbert Lewis
John Moe
James Mosher
Gilbert Myers
Hiram Ploss
Jacob Shultis
Philip Van Der Bogart
John Theodore Van Gasbeck
Peter Lewis Welderhouse
Abram Whispel

SPANISH AMERICAN WAR

Sheldon Benjamin Elwyn

WORLD WAR I

Louis Harrison
Henry P. Longendyke

WORLD WAR II

Charles Sherwood Carnright
Eno Compton, Jr.
Charles Anthony Di Andrie
George De Freese
Paul LeMay
Caleb Milne, IV
John Alexander Peacock
Charles Benjamin Pierpoint
Roger Paul Peyre
Robert Oren Russell
Leonhard Scholl, Jr.
William John White[1]

Private First Class Charles Sherwood Carnright was raised and went to school in Zena. Carnright entered the services in May 1943. He was assigned to an armored division and was later sent to join General Patton's Third Army in France. The delay in clearing Antwerp for the entry of supplies slowed the Allied offensive in the autumn of 1944 and the Third Army could not advance into the Saar as Patton wished. Patton was forced to withdraw his troops from around Metz and it was near there that Charles Carnright was killed on October 2, 1944.[2]

Second Lieutenant Eno Compton Jr. was raised in Woodstock and went to school here. He enlisted on December 8, 1941, and after receiving his wings at Moody Field, Georgia, was sent to the 729th Bomb Squadron of the 452nd Bomber Group stationed in England. He was a flight leader engaged in bombing targets on the Continent and had been on one bombing mission over Germany. At the start of a second sortie, on February 9, 1944, his plane exploded when it left the ground at Attleborough, England. He is buried in the U.S. Military Cemetery at Cambridge, England.[3]

Seaman First Class George De Frees of Zena enlisted in the Navy when he was very young. He was but eighteen years old when he lost his life in the sinking of the USS *Ingraham* off Nova Scotia.[4]

Private First Class Charles Anthony Di Andrea lived at West Hurley in a section that is in Woodstock Township, but he had no other association with our village. He was killed in action, but as his family has moved away no details are available.[5]

Lieutenant Colonel Paul LeMay came to play his viola at the Maverick concerts for many summers. He was with the Minneapolis Symphony Orchestra as First Viola and Assistant Conductor. Upon our entry into the Second World War he volunteered for the Air

Force, as he had previously learned to pilot a plane. In due time he was assigned as Wing Intelligence Officer with the Fifty-third Troop Carrier Wing in England. He was on an A-20 (Havoc) aircraft with photographers who were taking pictures of the flight and dropping paratroopers in Holland on September 18, 1944, when his plane disappeared with all on board. A year later Mrs. LeMay received a letter from General H. H. Arnold saying that her husband was presumed dead and that he had been posthumously awarded the Medal of the Legion of Merit. General Montgomery's famous attempt to turn the northern flank of the German army by dropping three divisions of paratroopers into Holland did not succeed, but it will always be remembered as a valiant fight. It might have succeeded if the weather on the 18th had not turned too bad for supplies and reinforcements to land. It was on this day that LeMay's plane disappeared.[6]

Caleb J. Milne IV joined the American Field Service before the United States entered the Second World War and was sent to North Africa. Although he had attended school in Philadelphia, all his summers had been spent in the Catskills. Woodstock became his home when his mother and brothers moved here permanently in the early 1930s. He tried to obtain work in the New York theater, but except for one happy interlude when he was chosen to be an apprentice at the Civic Repertory Theater under Eva Le Gallienne he was unable to make good as an actor. It was at this lowest point in his career, when he was ill and half-starved, that he perpetrated a kidnap hoax to gain publicity and a job. It created a nationwide sensation but brought only notoriety to himself and his family. After a very serious illness he started afresh and this time made a success of his life.

When the war began in Europe he tried to join the U.S. Army but was rejected on account of his eyesight, and the Free French Army turned down his application to serve with them. In December 1942 the American Field Service sent Milne with a group of ambulance drivers to Egypt to serve with the British Eighth Army. He arrived shortly before the battle of El Alamein and accompanied Field Marshal Montgomery's troops on their advance across two thousand miles of North Africa. The ambulances crisscrossed the desert for hundreds of extra miles as they picked up the casualties, both British and German, and drove them back to dressing stations and then to the hospitals in the rear. The story of Milne's experiences is told in his letters published under the title *I Dream of the Day*.[7]

The victorious British army arrived in Tunisia in the spring of 1943 and met the Free French Army, which was engaged in gallant attacks on the main German forces in the mountains above Enfideville. These French soldiers under General Leclerc had completed an epic march from Lake Chad in Central Africa through the desert to Tunisia. They were short of supplies and had almost no medical units. On May 11th a group from the American Field Service responded to a call for volunteers to remove French wounded under fierce fire, and Caleb Milne was among them. He was giving aid to a French Légionnaire when he was hit by a mortar shell that caused his death. The next day the war was over in North Africa.[8]

Caleb J. Milne IV lost his life in Tunisia in 1943. His wartime experiences are captured in a series of letters posthumously published as I Dream of the Day. Photo: AMS Collection.

Sergeant John "Jack" Peacock was brought up in Woodstock and attended the local school. He went to Kingston High, which he left to work at the Woodstock Garage. He was a likeable youngster, popular with everybody. He enlisted in the U.S. Air Force in November 1942, when he was eighteen years old, and was sent to England with the Eighth Air Force, Ninety-fourth Bomber Group, as Ball Turret Gunner. He was on a bombing mission to the Continent on December 5, 1943, when his plane was hit over the target at Bordeaux, France. According to pilots of the other planes, his aircraft exploded in mid-air and all within were killed.[9]

First Lieutenant Roger Peyre was born in Paris, France, in 1912. His father, Gabriel Peyre, a musician, came to New York to play the viola with the Metropolitan Opera Orchestra and remained with that organization for fifty-two years. When the younger Peyre was two years old Madame Peyre emigrated with her son to join her husband in New York. They spent their summers on the Maverick and built a house with a beautiful view over the Ashokan Reservoir, and it was here that Roger Peyre and his younger sister spent their summer holidays for many years. In January 1940 Roger enlisted in the U.S. Infantry, with which he remained for four and a half years. After service at Midway and the Gilbert Islands he was sent to Saipan in the Marianas where he was killed in action on July 26, 1944. Most of the details that follow are taken from a letter sent to his mother by Major Malcolm M. Jameson, who was with him at the time of the tragedy.

Lieutenant Peyre was in command of Company K, his captain having died of wounds sustained in the battle for Saipan. Organized resistance had ceased but about a hundred and fifty civilians, largely women and children, were holed up in a cliff above the sea at a spot so precipitous that one needed a rope to reach it. Peyre directed operations from above the cliff and ordered his men not to fire while he persuaded some of the enemy to give themselves up. A number of them did so and Peyre was still negotiating through a public address system with interpreters when a shot rang out and he was hit and rolled over the cliff. Major Jameson had just joined the lieutenant but the fatal shot came too suddenly for him to catch hold of his friend. The fall from the cliff would certainly have killed him, but the doctor who examined him afterwards said death from the shot had probably been instantaneous. The body was recovered at considerable risk by a Japanese soldier who had just been captured (and volunteered out of shame for the treachery of his comrades). Peyre had the love and respect of the men under him, and at the time of his death he was to have been promoted to the rank of Captain.[10]

Charles Pierpoint and his twin brother, William, enlisted in the U.S. Navy on their eighteenth birthday, January 2, 1941. "Buddy," as Charles was called, was a member of the crew of the USS *Meredith* when she was commissioned in 1942. The destroyer *Meredith* was one of the escorts during the conference held at sea between Winston Churchill and Franklin Delano Roosevelt. The ship had seen duty in the North Atlantic and the Strait of Denmark before being sent to the Pacific. She was part of Admiral Halsey's Task Force and took part in the "Shangri-la" bombing raid on Japan.

The *Meredith* was sent on escort duty to accompany a supply ship with rafts of matériel for the relief of the gallant First Marine Division fighting on Guadalcanal to keep Henderson Airfield operating for the use of American airplanes. All their supplies were low but their aviation gasoline was almost exhausted, and an attempt had to be made to bring in the fuel. The Japanese were making regular bombing runs over the Coral Sea and through the straits of the Solomon Islands to prevent aid arriving from Guadalcanal. Enemy reconnaissance planes discovered the little convoy, and within a few hours Japanese torpedo planes and bombers attacked. The *Meredith* was severely damaged and sank within a few minutes on October 15, 1942. Many of the crew, including Charles Pierpoint, went down with her. The survivors drifted around on rafts for a couple of days before they were rescued by another destroyer.[11]

Private Robert Oren Russell of Shady enlisted in the Army Infantry in May 1942 and had his training at Camp Wheeler, Georgia. He took part in the North African campaign and in the fighting around Medjez el Bab, which was an important road center. This place was the key of our offensive for Tunisia that winter, but the weather prohibited flying and the mud bogged down the ground offensive. General Eisenhower reluctantly ordered the attack stopped until more favorable weather would allow a better chance of success. This order was given on December 24th (Christmas Eve), the day Robert Russell was killed.[12]

Private Lenhard Scholl Jr. attended grammar school in Mount Tremper and then Kingston High. When he was quite young his parents bought the bakery business in Woodstock and for several years their son helped them. He was inducted into the U.S. Army in 1943 and received his training at Camp Campbell, Kentucky. From there he was shipped to England, remaining for several months with the 480th A.I.R. of the Twentieth Division. Sent to France, he was a flamethrower with an armored division—and it is believed he was attached to Patton's Seventh Army when it made its spectacular rush to the Seine to contain von Kluge's retreating forces. On August 21st Lenhard Scholl Jr. fell from shrapnel wounds in his chest. He lies buried in the U.S. Military Cemetery at St. André, not far from Évreux. Two years after his death I visited St. André. I placed a bouquet of asters on the grave of the Woodstock boy and (against Army regulations) took a photograph to bring back to his parents.

Thirteen years later his parents were gone, and to learn a few facts I visited Lenhard Jr.'s sister, who lives on the part of Route 212 known as Dobbin's Hollow. With deep emotion she talked of this younger brother, bringing out his treasured last letters and one photograph. There was not a word about the war in his letters; they were filled only with concern for his family. He begged his sister to make sure his elderly parents were alright at the bakery. His sister gestured down the hill to the houses of her other relatives. "We are all close together here and very fond of each other," she said. I looked at the photograph she had chosen from among a dozen for me to see. It was of the little boy, Lennie, who had turned with surprise to see the camera. Though the picture was slightly blurred, it showed a wonderfully gentle and elfin face beneath wisps of mussed hair. What ironical fate had forced this sensitive youth to be a flamethrower in a mechanized battle and had finally left him forever in the soil of provincial France?[13]

William J. White attended the Zena School and Kingston High. He enlisted in the U.S. Navy in December 1941 when he was eighteen years old. He was reported missing within a year when the USS *Sterett* was engaged by enemy fire in the fifth battle of the Solomons on the night of November 12, 1942. The ship and crew received a Presidential Unit Citation for extraordinary heroism displayed in action against a Japanese task force.

The newspapers carried a description of the battle, though at the time no naval units were identified. The battle had begun two days before with an attack by enemy dive bombers protected by Zeros. They made two attempts but were driven off without the loss of any of the American transports they were after, although both sides suffered airplane casualties. The next day more of our transports approached under convoy and all day there was fighting in the sky. At nightfall a large Japanese naval force, including sixteen warships, sneaked into the straits of Guadalcanal expecting at daylight to shoot out the American forces dug into the beach. But just before dawn our far smaller naval force plunged into combat under the command of Admiral Callaghan, who was on the *San Francisco*. If the Japanese heavy battleships had stood out to sea they could easily have knocked off the American fleet, which consisted of no units heavier than cruisers and destroyers. The Japanese were deployed in a great circle between Guadalcanal and Savo Island in the narrow straits when the U.S. ships sneaked into the circle, zigzagging and twisting as they fired point blank into the enemy lines. Most of the time they were too close for the Japanese heavy guns to be depressed sufficiently to hit their hulls, but several shells tore into the superstructures. The bridge of the *San Francisco* was shot away, and it was there that Admiral Callaghan was killed. Some of the American cruisers were mortally wounded, but the Nipponese lost at least one of their heaviest battleships and many other units. Their surviving ships crawled out of the straits and were repeatedly attacked by the U.S. Air Force. This battle was so costly to the enemy that they attempted only one more naval raid on Guadalcanal. It was in this battle, which saved Guadalcanal, that William White, aged nineteen, lost his life.

The following letter was sent to William's mother, Mrs. Edward F. White:

> The Chief of Naval Personnel takes pride in forwarding the following award made to your son the late William John White, Seaman 2/c U.S.N.R. for meritorious conduct as a member of the Naval Service.
>
> Facsimile and ribbon bar with Star of the Presidential Unit Citation awarded the USS *Sterett* for extraordinary heroism displayed by her crew in action against an enemy Japanese Task Force during the Battle of Guadalcanal on the night of 12 to 13 November 1942.
>
> Chief of Naval Personnel
> Joe H. Floyd, Lt. Commander[14]

SECOND WORLD WAR

Soon after the end of the Second World War every member of the armed forces listed below was sent a questionnaire to fill out. Repeated attempts were made to contact those who did not return their cards. Eventually material was obtained from most of them or from their families, but in a few instances the information was derived from newspapers. The names of others are merely listed. I have made every effort to be accurate but cannot guarantee this information.

Names preceded by an asterisk denote those who died in the service.

Allen, Victor, Cpl., Military Police. Philippines. 1943 to 1946. One battle star.

Allen, Willard, Pvt. U.S. Army Air Force.

Arlt, Arthur W., Capt. U.S. Corps of Engineers. Post engineer work. Ninth Service Command. Seven stations. 1942 to 1946.

Arnold, Elroy, T/Sgt.

Arnold, Milton J., Cpl.

Avery, Lester, Pvt. Med. Dept. Stationed Haddon Hall Hospital at Atlantic City, N.J., October 1942 to February 1943.

Baldinger, Ernest. Navy Seabees. 1942.

Ballbach, William.

Barrère, Jean Clement, Capt. U.S. Signal Corps. Part-time liaison officer with French Army. 1941 to 1945. Croix de guerre.

Barrow, Henry D., Capt. Merchant Marine. Atlantic, Pacific and Mediterranean theaters of war. Oil tankers. Torpedoed in Caribbean Sea. 1942 to 1945.

Baumgarten, Ludwig, Sgt. U.S. Army Signal Corps. China-Burma-India theater, January 1943 to December 1945. Good Conduct with three awards; Europe-Africa-Middle East Ribbon; Asiatic-Pacific, three stars; World War II Victory Medal; National Defense Service Medal; Korean Service Medal with three stars; U.N. Service Medal; Republic of Korea Presidential Unit Citation. Korean War, May 1952 to August 1953. Still in service, 1957.

Baumgarten, Rudolph, Machinist Mate 3/c. Navy. Destroyer Escort, Atlantic Fleet. Also served on LSD. American Theater Ribbon and Victory Ribbon. January 1945 to April 1946 and September 1950 to January 1952.

Bell, Byron, Cpl. U.S. Air Force. Crew chief. Member of crew of B-29, B-25, AT-9, AT-10, ATC-6, BT-17, among other vessels. American theater. November 1942 to December 1945. Good Conduct Medal.

Berryan, Willard, Pfc. Air Corps. American theater. November 1942 to May 1945. Good Conduct Medal. Injured in training; hospitalized and medically discharged.

Blazy, Nicholas, Second Lt. First Army, 3072nd Truck Company Normandy, Northern France, Rhineland, Battle of the Bulge and Central Europe—two and a half years. Five combat stars.

Bodie, Burton, T/Sgt. Technical Transport. Six months in infantry. Two and half years in San Francisco as heavy-duty truck driver, 1942 to 1945. Army life "wonderful experience."

Boggs, Norman Towar. Field Director, Red Cross. In Italy, later stationed at U.S. Disciplinary Barracks, Green Haven, N.Y.

Boudreau, Frank George, M.D. Not in armed forces.

Brinkman, R. William. Seaman 1/c. In African campaign on the USS *Sangamon*. In Pacific and Philippines on the USS *Princeton*, which was sunk. Picked up by a destroyer in which was stationed Warren Riseley from Woodstock. Princeton was sunk by one lucky hit at the Battle of Leyte Gulf. This naval battle broke the Japanese naval strength, 1942. One Silver Star; three Bronze Stars. Still in service, 1957.

Bromberg, Manuel, Sgt., U.S. war artist for all services in ETO. Two and a half years overseas. Covered London bombing, Normandy invasion and six other battle campaigns. Legion of Merit and five battle stars.

Bronson, Richard F., Jr., Pfc.

Buley, Benjamin, Carpenter's Mate 3/c. U.S. Navy ship-repair unit. Asiatic Pacific American Theater Victory Ribbons. April 1944 to December 1945.

Calamar, Donald, Sgt. Some of the film *The True Glory* was photographed by him during the Battle of the Bulge.

Calamar, Gloria.

Cantine, Robert.

Carlson, David, Lt. Comm. U.S. Naval Air Corp. Aeronautical Engineers, 1943 to 1946.

Carlson, Peter, Pfc. Paratroops. Stationed at Amiens, France. No combat jumps before (Armistice) VE day. ETO Ribbon; two stars.

Carlson, Robert E., First Lt. In 1940 Squadron A, National Guards—became 101st Cavalry. Tank Destroyer, 635th Battle of Normandy, Northern France, Rhineland, Ardennes and Central Europe. January 1941 to December 1945. "Underwent the usual run-of-the-mill hole-digging, sniper-hunting, shell-dodging, hash-eating, sleepless routine enjoyed by all frontline troops."

**Carnright, Charles*, Pfc. Armored Division assigned to Patton's Third Army. When Patton's forces were forced to withdraw from Metz for lack of ammunition Carnwright was one of those killed early in October. He is buried in the U.S. Military Cemetery at Épinal, France. Killed in action in France, October 2, 1944. Served from 1943 to 1944.

Carnright, Palmer.

Cashdollar, E. E.

Chaplin, Bigelow.

Chaplin, William W. War correspondent. Covered Ethiopia for NBC and every European front including Russia, Egypt, Iran, Iraq, England and most of Africa. Went into Normandy with the army of invasion "slogging along with the GIs."

Chase, Charles D., T/5. Corps of Engineers, Thirty-eighth Regiment. Sent to Ascension Island February 1942 to construct an airport, tank farm and camps. Completed by August 1942 and left "Rock" for Leopoldville, Belgian Congo, to construct airport; later Dakar. Sent to England in 1944 to construct camps and for pre-invasion training. Attached to First Engineers and went with invasion forces to France for clearing mines, unloading ships, reconstructing roads and so on. Helped in the development of "Vologn Staging Area, Red Horse Assembly Area and the construction of camps 'Twenty Grand' and 'Old Gold'."

Chase, Dennison, Sgt. Fifth Air Force on Pacific duty. Twenty months in Guam, Saipan, Okinawa, Iwo Jima and final station near Tokyo. Three and a half years.

Chase, Edward Tinsley, First Lt. U.S. Navy. Operations Officer in U.S. Navy. First Lt. of carrier aircraft service Unit No. 2, Oahu, Hawaii. March 1942 to January 1946.

Christiana, Earl L., Pvt. U.S. Army Air Corps. April 1943 to August 1943.

Cohn, Hans J., M.D., Capt. Medical Paratrooper. Pacific Theater. Silver Star; three battle stars. February 1943 to December 1945.

**Compton, Eno, Jr.*, Second Lt. Pilot, U.S. Air Force. Flight Leader, 729th Bomb Squadron of 452nd Bomb Group. Enlisted 1941. Killed in action at Attleborough, England, February 9, 1944. Buried in U.S. Military Cemetery, Cambridge, England.

Compton, George B., Cpl. U.S. Air Force. Instrument specialist. 1942.

Cosgrove, James R., Seaman 1/c. U.S. Navy. European and Pacific duty. In Normandy invasion, D day. Three battle stars and five combat ribbons. May 1942 to 1945.

Cosgrove, Joseph.

Crane, Richard, S /Sgt. 311th Field Artillery. Three and a quarter months basic training, twenty months scout, twenty months supply. Normandy invasion D day plus six. Assigned to the Seventy-ninth for scout and survey duty. Star for bravery under fire during assault on Siegfried Line; ETO—four campaigns; Silver Star for gallantry in action. April 1943 to October 1945.

Cunningham, Robert.

D'Albis, Rolande.

Davis, Mildred. WAVES. December 1943.

De Frees, Edward, Sgt. U.S. Army. North Africa, Sicily, Normandy. Drove ammunition truck in Normandy when it blew up, sustaining wounds with quantities of shrapnel. Several campaigns; Purple Heart. 1942.

**De Frees, George*, Seaman 1/c. U.S. Navy. Went down and was lost with the USS *Ingraham*, which sank off Nova Scotia. Eighteen years old.

De Frees, John, Capt. Stationed at Pearl Harbor when Japanese attacked, December 1941.

DeLano, Allen, Capt. Special Services. First and Second World Wars.

Denman, Thomas, Rev., Lt. U.S. Navy Chaplain.

Di Andrea, Anthony J., Pvt.

**Di Andrea, Charles*, Pfc. Killed in action.

Di Andrea, Frank.

Dock, Norman, Sgt. U.S. Army for one year, Forty-fourth Division. Ship Fitter 2/c, U.S. Navy Seabees, three years. While in Navy, served in Guadalcanal and Bougainville. Asiatic-Pacific Ribbon; American Defense Ribbon. 1940 to 1945.

Downer, Kenneth. While Foreign Representative of United Seamen's Service, in South Pacific he voluntarily went aboard merchant vessel on fire and loaded with high-octane gasoline and ammunition to assist crew in cutting lines so ship could be moved away from dock. Later at Le Havre.

Drogseth, Harold N., Pvt. Field Artillery. Italy with Tenth Mountain Division in Po Valley and Upper Apennines campaign. Two battle stars. June 1944 to 1946.

Drogseth, Norman.

Du Bois, William N., Pvt. Army.

Duffy, Charles E., Torpedo Man 2/c. USNR. On the USS *Sea Owl* out of New London submarine base. Sixteen months in Pacific, most of the time near Japan. The *Sea Owl* was given credit for sinking two Japanese destroyers, one patrol craft, one merchant ship and one cargo-type submarine. Rescued six navy fliers. The Japanese submarine they sank was near Wake Island; this was the last attempt the Japanese made to send supplies to 1,500 starving enemy men on that island.

Earley, Robert, Seaman 1/c. U.S. Navy. Spent entire service in Pacific theater. Landings at Okinawa Easter Sunday, April 1, 1945. Two battle stars; Third Fleet Presidential Citation; Pacific Theater, Atlantic Theater and Victory medals. August 1943 to May 1946.

Easton, Alex, Sgt. U.S. Air Force. Radio technician. Duty in Hawaii, 1941 to 1944.

Elting, Arthur Roger.

Elwyn, Allen Dean, Ship's Cook 1/c. U.S. Navy. Asiatic-Pacific Ribbon. Two years. On LCI, Philippines, Formosa; two months at Shanghai. Three stars.

Elwyn, Grant, C.P.O.

Elwyn, Hugh, Sgt.

Elwyn, William, Jr.

Faggi, John Alexander Butler, Capt. Infantry. Joined (Squadron A) 101st New York Cavalry, 1941. Cherbourg, October 1944. Germany, November 1944. Wounded in Germany. Rhine Crossing with "Timber Wolf" Division, First Army. Purple Heart; Combat Infantryman Badge; two Bronze Stars.

Feeley, John. Merchant Marine.

Finch, Clarence, Pfc. Infantry 28th Division. Left U.S. in 1943 for Cardiff, Wales; later stationed in England. Went into France and fought at St. Lô. Shifted to Northern France and wounded. Recovered and moved through Belgium and Luxembourg where his unit held the line until the Third Army made a break through the Siegfried Line. His company was trapped and had to burn the town to escape. Next went to Cologne and was wounded for the second time, in the Hurtgen Forest where his company suffered ninety percent casualties. Sent to hospital in England. He had participated in the battles of Normandy, Northern France, Colmar and Rhineland besides Hurtgen. Good Conduct Medal; three battle stars; Purple Heart Medal with three Clusters; Presidential Unit Citation. April 1943.

Finch, Harvey, Coxswain. U.S. Navy. At the Marshalls, Siapan, Gilberts, Guam, Philippines, Iwo Jima, Okinawa, Uluthi. "We had a lot of fighting until the ship I was on got hit." USS *Sigsbee*—DD502. Service record "very good." October 1942 to 1946.

Fischer, Anton Otto, Lt. Comm. Special Reserve. U.S. Coast Guard. Special assignments to make pictorial records. Went on convoy duty in North Atlantic on the cutter USS *Campbell*, which was disabled in fight with German submarine. October 1942 to October 1945.

Fisher, John.

Ford, Richard, Signalman 2/c. Navy. Anti-submarine Warfare Amphibious Forces—Asia. Vessels and stations served on (copied from discharge papers): NRS-New York, N.Y.; NTSNOB Norfolk, Va.; the USS *Lee Fox* (DE65); ATB-Little Creek, Va.; the USS *LSM76*; PSC-Lido Beach, Long Island, N.Y. Victory Medal, one star; Good Conduct Medal; European Theater Ribbon; Asiatic-Pacific Ribbon. December 1942 to February 1946.

Fortess, Karl E., S/Sgt. Field Artillery. Omaha Beach Landing on D day plus six. With first unit into Germany as Operations NCO. Saw a good part of Europe. "Memory of most experiences, unpleasant." After war received a Guggenheim Fellowship to return to Europe to paint the reconstruction. Five battle stars. March 1942 to December 1945.

France, Clarence.

France, David.

France, Howard, Jr. Two stars; Purple Heart.

France, Irving.

Frankling, Douglas P., T/Sgt. Air Corps. Senior Gunner on B-29s for two years. Completed thirty combat missions. Spent twelve months in India. Five months in Tinian (Mariana Islands). Distinguished Flying Cross; Presidential Unit Citation; seven battle stars; three Oak Leaf Clusters; Air Medal. December 1942 to October 1945.

Frankling, Ruth, Service Pilot. Army Air Force, Air Transport Command. Delivery of fighter aircraft from factories to ports of embarkation. December 1942 to December 1944.

Gardner, Donald, Pfc. Infantry training at Ft. Sam Houston, Texas; San Luis Obispo. Sailed to Europe; took part in Normandy invasion with 86th Black Hawk Division in Germany (342nd Infantry). Sent back to U.S. and on to Manila while fighting was underway and helped capture Japanese. February 1944 to April 1946.

Gardner, Ernest J., Lt. Pilot, U.S. Air Force, C-47s. Evacuated wounded from France to England during Normandy invasion. Later assigned to India-Burma Theater. Flew route from India to China. Eight battle stars; Air Medal; Oak Leaf Clusters. 1943 to 1945.

Garrison, Lawrence.

Goetz, Faith. Cadet Nurse.

Gonzales, Boyer, Jr., Major. Air Corps Instructor. Asst. Operations Officer HQ. Far East Air Force, Manila, P.I., and Yokohama and Tokyo, Japan. April 1942 to June 1946. While he was serving in the East a companion brought him a Japanese book found in an enemy dugout. It was an illustrated art book containing a reproduction of a painting by Eugene Speicher of Woodstock, a close friend of Gonzales.

Grazier, Ruth. S.C.N.

Hagemeyer, Eugene J., Jr., Cpl. Ninth Infantry Regiment, Second Division. Trained in Aircraft Artillery in the U.S. Took part in European, Ardennes, Rhineland and Central European campaigns. Three Bronze Service Stars and Presidential Citation with one Oak Leaf Cluster; Combat Infantryman's Badge; ETO Ribbon; Good Conduct Medal. December 1942 to December 1945.

Hagen, Elsie.

Hale, Bayard Hadley, Capt. Signal Corps. Spent first year as pole climber and truck driver for construction battalion. Then to OCS. After graduation, instructor. Six months as Regimental Adjutant and Intelligence Officer. Transferred to Signal Corps Intelligence. Four months training, mostly in London. Ran an intercept station on English south coast. Then in First Army where he served as both Chief of Radio Intelligence and Commanding Officer of the 113th Signal Radio Intelligence Company from Normandy to Leipzig. Bronze Star for work as First Army's Intelligence Chief. May 1941 to October 1945.

Harcourt, William C., Sgt.

Harder, Clayton N., Mate 3/c. Motor Machinist Mate, U.S. Navy. Repair and maintenance of amphibious landing craft. April 1944 to January 1946.

Harder, Kenneth L., Seaman 1/c. A/S. V-12. Navy Seabees, Fourth Naval Construction. NYS Sampson, N.Y. NTC Davisville, R.I. Camp Parks, Calif., Saipan, Okinawa. ROTE University of Missouri (V12). July 1944 to July 1946.

Heinlein, Abram, Sgt. Wounded. Purple Heart.

Heinlein, Homer, Jr., Cpl. With Patton's army in Europe. Three years.

Heinlein, Joseph, Sgt.

Held, Philip, Capt. Quartermaster Corps. Motor Transportation Units in U.S. and European theater from February 1944 to October 1945. Four campaigns: Normandy, Northern France, Rhineland, Germany. Enlisted. January 1942 to January 1946.

Holumzer, Erwin, S/Sgt. Ninety-eighth Infantry. Was in Hawaiian Islands and Japan. Expert Infantry Badge; Good Conduct Medal; three campaign ribbons: Pacific Ocean Area, American Defense, Japanese Occupation. November 2, 1942, to February 1, 1946.

Holumzer, John, T/5. Army Infantry. Battles: Normandy, Northern France. Wounded in France, sent to hospital in Hereford, England. GO 33 WD 45 as amended; Combat Infantry Badge. April 1943 to December 1945.

Hoover, Hiram.

Hopper, George.

Houst, Milton R., Pfc. In Germany.

Howland, Barnet.

Howland, Emil, Pfc.

Howland, Eugene. Merchant Marine. Oiler and Third, Second and First Engineer on seagoing tugboats. Atlantic Ocean, Gulf of Mexico and Pacific. European Combat War Medal. March 1941 to February 1945.

Howland, John.

Howland, Leon.

Hung, Edward A., Jr., Cpl.

Hung, Edward H., Sgt.

Hung, Henry, Pvt.

Hung, John, Pvt.

Hutchins, James Carson, M/Sgt. U.S. Air Force. Flew as Flight Crew in North Africa with First Bomber Group after invasion in France. Shot down in Northern France. In charge of U.S. Air units in Brentwood, England. Pre-Pearl Harbor Ribbon; Good Conduct Ribbon; North African Campaign Ribbon with three stars; Central European Campaign Ribbon with five battle stars; Presidential Unit Citation; Letter of Commendation from General of Air Forces. October 1941 to November 1945.

Hutty, Doris D., 1st Lt. U.S. Army Nurses Corps.

Hutty, William, S/Sgt. Army Airborne 677th Artillery. In 1942 won Sharp Shooter's Medal; in France October 1944; France and Normandy, one star. 1942 to 1945.

Hyatt, Harold.

Janson, Frederick William, G.M. 2/c. Navy. Served on the USS *Savannah*, USS *San Diego*, USS *Meredith* (was sunk) and USS *Chicago*. The *Savannah* was part of battle force based at Pearl Harbor. Was transferred to Atlantic Fleet convoy duty and neutrality patrol from June 1941 to March 1942. Transferred to San Diego; stayed until December 1943. Commissioned the (new) destroyer *Meredith*—she had to be abandoned on Normandy beachhead. Commissioned the *Chicago* January 1945 and joined Third Fleet in an operation off Japan. Forty-five points by September 1945. February 1939 to September 1945.

Janson, Royal Walter, Boatswain's Mate 1/c. Served aboard the USS *Savannah*, USS *San Diego* and USS *Pasadena*. Put the *Savannah* in commission and served on her for three years until 1941. Commissioned the *San Diego*. Moved west again with "Shoestring Fleet" and engaged enemy several times. Returned to U.S. and commissioned the *Pasadena* and moved through Panama Canal for third time to join Third and Fifth fleets in engagements and visited several of the islands. Steamed into Tokyo Bay to accompany the USS *Missouri* for Japanese surrender. May 1937 to May 1941. Re-enlisted January 1942.

Jerominek, W. J., S/Sgt. Engineers. Special Intelligence Assignment at Fort Belvoir, Virginia, 1941 to 1944.

Kelley, George N. S., S/Sgt. In Germany. Two years, ten months.

Killduff, Campbell, S/Sgt. In France.

Kinns, James W., Sgt. Army. American, Asiatic, Pacific ribbons; China War Memorial; American Victory Medal. Three years.

Kinns, Wilmot, Lt.

Klein, Marcus, S/Sgt. Signal Corps.

Klitgaard, Kaj, Capt. Merchant Marine.

Klitgaard, Peter, Midshipman. Navy. In New Guinea.

Knettel, Howard.

Lane, Alfred C., Pfc.

Lane, Arthur.

Lane, Leslie.

Lane, Louis R.

Lapo, Richard B., Pharmacist Mate 3/c. Hospital Corps. July 1945.

Lapo, Victor N., Pfc. Marines. With First Division in China. November 1943 to April 1946. Re-enlisted June 1946.

Larson, E. Richard, Lt. Engineer Survey Officer for Artillery. In Italy with Eighty-eighth Division. "Now stationed at Trieste." June 1944. Still in service, 1946.

Layman, George Church, T/Sgt. In Netherlands East Indies.

Layman, Muriel. WAVES. 1945.

Leaycraft, Edgar C., Jr., Sgt. In Guam.

**LeMay, Paul*, Lt. Col. Air Force Wing Intelligence Officer, Fifty-third Carrier Wing. Missing from England on A-20 (Havoc) mission to Holland. 1941 to September 18, 1945.

Lenard, Leon V.

Lewis, Louis A., Warrant Officer. Chief Carpenter D, USNR. Began service at Pearl Harbor as carpenter; Pacific later. Pacific-Asiatic Star; Caribbean Ribbon; American Defense and Victory Ribbons. February 1944 to February 1946.

Lilly, Joseph, Major. Air Corps. G-2 with added duty as historian, First Concentration Command; Asst. Enemy Appreciation Sec. A-2, Allied Air Forces, SWPA; Chief, Radio Intelligence Sec. A-2, Advance Echelon, Fifth Air Force, New Guinea, Morotai, Philippines; Chief Duty Officer, 309th Bomb Wing; Lingayen Landing Operation; Chief, Radio Intelligence, Far East Air Forces. Four battle stars. June 1942 to March 1946.

Lindin, Gregory E., Lt. Jg. U.S. Naval Reserve. Duty in and about Central America on logistical work. Saw no action. February 1944 to June 1946.

Lock, John, Pfc. Army. Sent home from European theater after being wounded twice in 1945. Bronze Star with Oak Leaf Clusters; Purple Heart.

Longyear, Stanley B., T/Sgt. Aerial Engineer, Forty-first Troop Carrier Squadron. His plane was first over Luzon dropping paratroopers. Served 111 combat hours; 1,170 pilot hours. Bismarck Archipelago, New Guinea, Luzon, Papua, Southern Philippines. Bronze Star; Air Medal with two Clusters; Service Medal; Asiatic-Pacific Medal; Good Conduct Medal; Philippines Liberation Ribbon (in all, six Bronze Medals). September 1942 to July 1945.

Ludins, Eugene. Red Cross.

Lund, Lloyd, Lt.

MacDaniel, Calvin C., Pfc. Fourth Marine Division, Medical Battalion, Ambulance Driver. Asiatic-Pacific theater. Bronze Star; three battle stars. Served to 1945.

MacDaniel, Robert, Sgt.

Mangold, Jo. Engineers. On Attu. Served fourteen months.

McClellan, John, Cpl. Army Field Artillery. Basic training Camp Gruber; Visual Aids Fort Sill. ASTP (Swedish). France, Germany, Austria with Seventy-first Division Artillery; American Division, Shrivenham, England, 1945. June 1942 to December 1945.

McDonnell, Robert H., Lt.

McEvoy, Dennis. War Correspondent. Pacific theater.

McShane, Donald T.

McTeigue, Jean G., Capt. Army Air Forces. Anti-aircraft 207th CAAA Commissioned 1943. Mess Superintendent 313th Bombardment Wing. Saipan and Tinian. February 1941 to February 1946.

McTeigue, Robert, Sgt. Army Air Forces, 3010th Army Air Forces BV Financial clerk and typist. American Campaign Victory Medal. March 1939 to November 1945.

Metzger, Warren, T/Sgt. Twentieth Air Force as Intelligence NCO. Saipan and Iwo Jima. Asiatic-Pacific Ribbon with one star. April 1942.

Milne, Aubrey R., Capt. Parachute Field Artillery Battalion 82nd and 101st Division European theater, Sicily, Naples, Foggia, Rome, Arno, Southern France, Ardennes, Rhineland, Central Europe. Wounded at Anzio breakthrough. Purple Heart; Bronze Star; EAME; Theater Ribbon with Bronze Arrowhead; American Defense Service Medal (in all, seven battle stars); Belgian Unit Citation; Distinguished Unit Citation. Enlisted July 1942 to December 1945.

**Milne, Caleb J.*, Vol. American Field Service. Rejected by U.S. and Free French Army due to eyesight. Stretcher-bearer and ambulance driver with British Eighth Army in North Africa. Served from El Alemein to Tunisia. Volunteered to go to the assistance of French légionnaires and was killed by mortar shell. Killed May 11, 1943. African Star; Eighth Army Clasp; American Field Service Medal; French Citation by Gen. LeLong. April 1942 to May 11, 1943.

Mitchell, Alexander V.

Moncure, Adam T., First Lt. Fourth Armored Division; had one of the first batteries of self-propelled 105 mm. howitzers, popularly known as "priests," which trained in California desert in preparation for North African campaign. This weapon became the standard field artillery carriage for the armored forces in European campaign. February 1941.

Moncure, William P., Second Lt. Infantry. 156th FA 12th U.S. Infantry Georgia, Oklahoma, Camp Ritchie, Md., and so on. No overseas experience until after war in Manila, Japan and Korea. September 1940.

Morrell, Harold, Pfc. Wounded in Normandy, hospitalized in England.

Morrell, Joseph. Navy. In First and Second World Wars. In South Pacific in October 1944.

Morrell, Ord J., Aviation Machinist Mate 3/c. Navy. French Morocco, Sicily, Truk, Leyte, Asiatic Pacific and North Atlantic. American Theater Medal; European Theater Medal, one star; Asiatic-Pacific Medal, one star; Presidential Citation and Medal, one star; Victory Medal. March 1943 to February 1946.

Mousseau, Roland, CM 1/c. Navy.

Mower, Anita John, Seaman 1/c. U.S. Naval Reserve Women's Reserve. Boot Service Hunter College, 1943. Chicago School Aircraft Instrument, graduated. Stationed Quonset Naval Base, R.I. Worked on Aircraft gyroscope instruments, Rating Petty Officer 1/c. Due to training on aircraft at Woodstock Observation Post was offered position of instructor at Boot School, but chose to go on to Chicago instead. November 1943 to September 1945.

Muller, Ragnwald, Lt. Jg. U.S. Navy. Appointed Midshipman 1940 at Annapolis; Ensign 1943; Lt. Jg. 1944. Designated Naval Aviator at USNAS, Pensacola. Fifteen months aboard the USS *Texas*. Invasion of Normandy, Battle of Cherbourg, invasion of Southern France (Gulf of St. Tropez) and numerous convoy trips to British Isles. Duties, Junior Fire Control Officer Main Battery. September 1940.

Mundy, Terrence P., T/5. Headquarters Co. Third Battalion, 504th Parachute Infantry. Ardennes, Central Europe, Naples, Foggia, Rhineland, Rome, Arno, Sicily GOWD. Forty-five as amended. Wounded MTO, September 25, 1943. Eighty-second Airborne Division. Distinguished Unit; EAME Service Medal; Good Conduct Medal; Purple Heart. June 1942 to September 1945. Re-enlisted in 1945.

Mundy, Wilbur, Cpl. Served in England, France, Belgium and Germany. Three years in service.

Murphy, William. Marines. Guadalcanal invasion.

Nemser, William, Pfc. Medical Corps. Hospital attendant in a veterans' hospital; also an attendant in army hospital at Fort Devans, Mass. September 1942 to February 1946.

Neponski, Chester.

Newgold, Wilburt D. Staff Sgt. Infantry. After special services training, assigned to Headquarters First Army where he was an assistant in Publicity and Psychological Warfare Section. Ardennes, Rhineland, Northern France, Normandy and Central Europe. Bronze Star Medal with Conspicuous Service Citation; European-African Middle Eastern Theater Medal; Good Conduct Medal. "Greatest personal thrill was in entering Paris the day of the liberation." June 1942 to October 1945.

Nichols, John C., Pfc. Quartermaster Corps. Duty at Camp Shanks, Orangeburg, N.Y. Worked after being discharged because of his age at United Aircraft Plant, Bridgeport, Conn. October 1942 to April 1945.

Oakes, D. T.

O'Brien, John E., Sgt. Army Air Force. American Campaign Medal; Victory Medal; Good Conduct Medal. April 1942 to December 1945.

Ohta, Takashi. OSS in China-Burma-India theater and USSBS in Japan. Officer as technical representative of War Dept. March 1945 to February 1946.

O'Meara, Donn.

O'Meara, Walter. Two years in Office of Strategic Services under Col. William Donovan.

Ostrander, Edward.

Ostrander, Paul, Pfc. Army Air Corps. December 1942 to October 1943.

Owen, William.

Park, Harry R., T/5. Twentieth Armored Division. Twentieth Tank Battalion.

Parker, Irving.

Parker, John A., Pfc. Army Infantry Forty-fifth Division, Seventh Army. France and Germany; Dachau Prison; battles of Nuremberg and Munich. August 1944 to May 1946.

**Peacock, John "Jack,"* Sgt. Air Force, Ninety-fourth Bomb Group. Bombing missions in European theater. Lost over Bordeaux, France. Ball turret gunner on B-17. (His father served with AEF, First World War. His grandfather, Alexander Peacock, served with British Army in Boer War.) November 30, 1942, to December 5, 1943.

Penning, Tomas, Cpl.

Peper, Arthur William, Sgt. Air Corps. Airplane mechanic. Asiatic Pacific Theater. On Oahu. August 1942 to February 1946.

Perkins, Edward R., Jr., First Lt. 156th Field Artillery. On March 30, after receiving commission, assigned to the Office of Strategic Services in the China Theater. September 1940 to September 1941 and October 1942 to November 1945.

Peters, John R.

Peters, Robert.

Petersen, Martin, Jr., Lt. Jg. U.S. Naval Reserve. V-12 Hobart College; Midshipman School, Columbia University; diesel engineering, North Carolina State

College. Amphibious training. Engineering Officer aboard LSM 293. In closing campaign on Okinawa. Occupation China. Lighterage duty between Pacific Islands. July 1943 to September 1946.

Petersen, Robert.

Petersham, Miska, F/0 Air Corps. Navigator B-24. Graduate Army AM School, Yuma, Ariz. Fourteen combat missions in South Pacific, 487 hours in air (112 combat). Air Offensive Japan Star; Eastern Mandates Star; West Pacific Awards; Air Medal; Asiatic-Pacific Medal. August 1942 to January 1946.

**Peyre, Roger P.*, First Lt. Infantry. Midway, Gilbert Islands, Mariana Islands. Killed in action at Saipan. January 1940 to July 26, 1944.

Phillips, Francis.

**Pierpoint, Charles B.*, Fireman 1/c. U.S. Navy. The USS *Meredith*—was commissioned March 1942. Bombed and sunk by Japanese planes in the Coral Sea. She was part of Adm. Halsey's task force carrying ammunition and aviation gasoline to the marines at Guadalcanal. She was one of the escort destroyers during the conference of President Roosevelt and Prime Minister Churchill at sea. Pierpoint enlisted at eighteen years of age. January 1941 to October 15, 1942.

Pierpoint, William. Navy. Honorably discharged due to heart condition. Enlisted. January 1941 to February 1941.

Plochmann, George Kimball, M/Sgt. Detached enlisted men's list. Fort Jay; Whitehorse, Y.T.; Edmonton, Alta.; Dawson Creek, B.C. October 1941 to October 1945.

Quick, Helene M. WINGS (Women's International Ground Service). March 1943 to September 1945.

Rade, Henry S., Capt. Ordinance, Second World War, two years' service, 1917 to 1919. Reserves and Second World War (in all, seventeen years, six months). In First World War, machine-gun instructor, Thirtieth Division; designing small arms and ammunition; CO Camp Travis Ordinance Depot. In Second World War, instructor at Aberdeen Proving Grounds; supplies officer, Savannah Ammunition Depot; supplies officer, Raritan Arsenal; General Supplies. July 1942 to August 1944.

Reynolds, Kenneth, T/4. Medical Corps, Ninth Air Force. Truck mechanic for Ninth Air Force Field Hospital. Eight months overseas. American Service Medal; Bronze Star for extraordinary service in Germany; Good Conduct Medal; World War II Victory Medal; African-Middle Eastern Service Medal; two battle stars. January 1943 to January 1946.

Richards, Houston. USO. Entertainment for soldiers overseas.

Riseley, James, Seaman 1/c. Wounded by Japanese sniper on Saipan; sent to hospital at Puget Sound.

Riseley, Warren, Baker 3/c. U.S. Navy. Pacific duty. USS *Gatling*. One Silver Star; four Bronze Stars. May 1942.

Ritterbusch, William. Office of War Information.

Ronk, George, Sgt. U.S. Army Air Force. Airplane crew chief, Eighth Air Force, Ninety-fourth Bomb. Group. April 1942 to September 1945.

Rose, Arlington, Cpl. Signal Corps. Attached Fifteenth Air Force. Chief telephone operator. MTO Ribbon; three battle stars; Expert Rifle Medal; Meritorious Service Wreath; Certificate of Merit; Good Conduct Medal; Victory and American Theater Ribbons. North Africa, Rome, Arno, Foggia, Naples, Anzio. "Did some sightseeing while at rest camp. Saw Capri, Tiberius' Castle, Vesuvius in eruption, Blue Grotto. In Rome saw St. Peter's, Coliseum, catacombs. Saw Mussolini at his death. Was in last air raid the Germans made in North Africa, September 6, 1943." December 1942 to December 1945.

Rose, Donald, Pfc. Glider Field Artillery. Member machine-gun crew in a Glider Troop Unit. Operated gun in close combat. Served in England, Holland, Belgium, France, Germany. Battles: Central Europe, Normandy, Rhineland, Ardennes. Distinguished Unit Badge; European African Middle Eastern Service Medal; Dutch Order of William; Presidential Unit Citation; Good Conduct Medal; Belgian Fourragère. October 1943 to January 1946.

Rose, Durand, T/5. Glider Field Artillery. Machine-gun crew in Glider Troop Unit. Operated gun in close combat. Served in England, Holland, France, Belgium and Germany. Battles: Ardennes, Central Europe, Normandy, Rhineland. Distinguished Unit Badge; European African Middle Eastern Service Medal; World War II Victory Medal; Dutch Order of William; Presidential Unit Citation; Good Conduct Medal; Belgian Fourragère. October 1943 to January 1946.

Rose, Harrison K., Cpl. 269th Field Artillery. Battery A. Served in England, France, Belgium, Holland, Luxembourg and Germany. Battles: Normandy, Ardennes, Central Europe, Northern France, Rhineland. Five battle stars; American Defense Medal; European-African-Middle Eastern Service Medal; Good Conduct Medal and Clasp; Expert Rifle Medal; ETO Medal; World War II Victory Medal. April 1941 to October 1945.

Rose, Malcolm, T/Sgt. Army Air Corps. Four hundred hours of combat flying in C-46 transport plane in China-Burma-India Theater as flight engineer. Air Medal; American Service Medal; Good Conduct Medal; World War II Victory Medal; Asiatic-Pacific Service Medal. January 1942 to November 1945.

Rose, Milton, Cpl.

Rose, Muriel, Lt. Jg. USN Nurse Corps. USNH, Sampson, N.Y.; USNH, San Diego, Calif.; USNH, Oakland, Calif. April 1944 to July 1946.

**Russell, Robert* (of Shady). Infantry. Camp Wheeler, Ga. Within eight months died at or near Medjez el Bab,

Tunisia, on Christmas Eve. Purple Heart awarded posthumously. Killed December 24, 1942.

Sarff, Walter, T/Sgt. (Camouflage Tech. 804). Combat with Engineers, Eighty-seventh Infantry, Third Army. Last outfit with HQ Company, Twenty-fifth Armored Engineer Battalion. Intelligence, Map-making Dept. G-2 and Reconnaissance in Cologne campaign. At end of war attended Grenoble University. February 1941 to October 1945.

**Scholl, Lenhard, Jr.*, Pfc. Killed August 21, 1944.

Schoonmaker, Frank. Civilian, and assumed rank of Col. Office of Strategic Services. Bronze Star; Croix de guerre for work with Secret Intelligence. August 1942 to September 1945.

Schultz, Donald. Seaman 1/c.

Seaton, Richard.

Shultis, Crystal M., ASN

Shultis, Dorothy, Capt. U.S. Nurses Corps.

Shultis, Eugene, T/Sgt.

Shultis, Lois Witte, WACS Public Relations Training, but after brief service received medical discharge.

Shultis, Newton, Pfc. Army Infantry. Campaigns: Europe, African, Middle Eastern, Normandy, Northern France, Ardennes. Wounded in Rhine crossing. Four battle stars; Combat Infantry Badge; Good Conduct Medal; Purple Heart. April 1942 to October 1945.

Shultis, Rudolph, Cpl. Air Force. Guard duty in Florida. Sheet metal school in England and in machine shops repairing B-26s. Moved with Ninth Air Force to Normandy. Prepared first airstrips of metal. April 1942 to September 1945.

Shultis, Sherwood.

Shultis, Stanley.

Shultis, Victor R., Pfc. Army Artillery (Mountain Troops). Campaigns: Central Europe, Rhineland, Southern France, Rome, Arno. Pack driver with the Mountain Artillery, which carried ammunition and supplies to the frontlines over terrain that was considered practically impassable. His battery consisted of 150 men each having three mules in his charge. Travel was always rough going, the men and mules having to scale ledges and edge their way through ravines. They were always traveling at night, often under heavy bombing. Five battle stars; Good Conduct Medal; ETO Ribbon. April 1942 to September 1945.

Shultis, Warren C., T3/c. Aviation radio technician. Navy. July 1944 to 1946.

Sinnock, Donald (of Zena).

Smith, Arthur Francis.

Smith, Donald.

Smith, Frank Leon. Chief scenario writer, Training Film Branch ASF. Quartermaster Corps and Training Corps. Because of motion picture experience requested by War Dept. to report to Camp Holabird, Md., to aid in setting up a training-film division. Army had already purchased one million military vehicles and was training officers and men in motor maintenance. Finished work at Holabird and returned to Woodstock. After Pearl Harbor volunteered at Signal Corps but civilians were not accepted until August 1942. Stationed at Signal Corps Photographic Center, Long Island, N.Y. Detached service at Pentagon, Washington, D.C.; Fort Monmouth, N.J.; Fort Jay, N.Y.; Fort Monroe, Va.; Fort Henry, Va.; and Army War College, Washington, D.C. At completion of training film program, resigned. "I do not consider that I merit a place in your record." June 1941 to September 1944.

Smith, Reese, Pvt.

Smith, Robert N., Fireman 2/c. Navy. November 1944.

Sonnenberg, Ethel. WING.

Spanhake, Charles, Cpl. 316th Reg. Wounded as a runner in Rhineland when Germans made breakthrough near Metz. Purple Heart; Bronze Star.

Spanhake, William, Jr., S/Sgt. Infantry. Sixteenth Reg., Third and First divisions. Trained with Marines in Puerto Rico. Three and a half years overseas. Landings at Oran, North Africa; Tunisia; Sicily; Salerno; Cassino; Anzio; Southern France; Germany; Rhineland; Berchtesgaden. Volunteered. 1939 to 1947.

Stone, Walter D.

Stowater, Rev. Arthur, Chaplain. Navy.

Stowell, John, Pvt. First World War: Company C., Fifty-eighth Ammunition Train. Second World War: Service Battery 116, Field Artillery Bu., 31st Division ("Hoxie"). Enlisted November 1917 to December 1918 and November 1942 to March 1943.

Stratton, Frederick C., Pfc. Corps of Engineers. Eighteen months in Hawaiian Island defense; four months in Japan. Asiatic-Pacific Medal; Good Conduct Medal; World War II Victory Medal; American Services Medal. November 1942 to January 1946.

Striebel, John, Jr., Capt. American Eagle Squadron Flying Officer. First Woodstocker to go into combat, having gone to join the Royal Canadian Air Force as a volunteer. Cited for gallantry; Distinguished Service Cross. Royal Canadian Air Force, 1940. U.S. Air Force, 1943.

Summers, James Carol, T/Sgt. Marine, Third Air Wing. Guam, Iwo Jima and so on.

Summers, Llewellyn, Lt. Comm. USNR. Stationed Naval Communications Center, Washington, D.C. November 1943 to January 1946.

Surdam, Lloyd.

Syversen, Hjordis.

Tamassy, Julius, Pfc. A service unit.

Taylor, Morton, Pvt. Army. Overseas. Hospitalized.

Thaisz, Fred A., Jr., T/3. Medical Corps, Third Army. Stationed for a while in Northern Ireland. Campaigns: Central Europe, Normandy, Northern France, Rhineland, Omaha Beach D day plus forty. Four stars;

Good Conduct Medal. March 1941 to September 1945.

Thaisz, J. Louis.

Todd, Stephen Langwith, Cpl. Signal Corps. Staging Area in New Caledonia. Placed with Eighty-eighth Signal Bn. (Special) in Bougainville. Campaigns in northern Solomons and Luzon. "Exciting experiences at Bamban and on drive in military truck to Legaspi." Hospitalized for wounds and battle fatigue. With occupation forces at Sendai, Japan, then transferred to Sapporo on Hokkaido. Asiatic Service Medal; Good Conduct Medal; Philippines Liberation Medal; World War II Victory Medal; Purple Heart. September 1943 to February 1946.

Tuck, William S., S/Sgt. 14th Air Force, 164th Signal Photo Co., 373rd Bomb. Squad, 308th Bomb. Group (Heavy), Kunming, China. Motion picture camera. Served in China, Philippines, Central Burma and western Pacific campaigns. Accompanied Chinese troops in Kwaljalein and Salween and photographed retreat from Kwaljalein. Used all types of cameras in white and color film. Devised a bomb camera to record ship identification on night sea. Flew waist and tail positions on B-24s. (Most of this taken from Army Qualifications Record.) Five battle stars; Distinguished Flying Cross; Air Medal; two Presidential Citations; Asiatic-Pacific Service Medal. December 1942 to September 1945.

Van der Loo, Cornelius Hervey Diedrick, Capt. Diplomatic and Special Services. Royal Netherlands Army. Special Services Medal. December 1941.

Van Kleek, Ethelbert, Pvt.

Van Wagner, Kenneth, S/Sgt.

Van Wagner, Roy, Sgt. Air Force. August 1943 to February 1945.

Walker, Chauncey Goodrich, Seaman 3/c. Navy aviation storekeeper. December 1943 to February 1946.

Walker, Wilbur.

Wangler, Albert, Capt. Chemical Warfare Service. Commanding Officer of Gas Mask Assembly Plant, Fall River, Mass. Inspector, March to June 1943, Edwood Arsenal. CO Gas Mask Assembly Plant, Denver, Colo., in 1943. Executive officer, First Battalion First Regiment, Camp Sibert, Ala.; later CO Field Commander Co. D. First training officer First Battalion Camp Sibert. On sick leave September 1944, Ft. McClellan Hospital. Also in First World War. March 1942 to December 1944.

Ward, Raymond.

Waterman, James Tuck, Bosun. Merchant Marine. Trips into all areas of operations—Pacific, south Pacific, north and south Atlantic, Middle East and Mediterranean. Torpedoed in south Atlantic. Bombed in eastern Mediterranean. On high-test gasoline tanker partially destroyed at Okinawa by Japanese bombing plane. Sailed her home despite Navy's protest that it couldn't be done! June 1943 to September 1945.

Waterous, Donald C., Sgt. Infantry. Sixty-third Division. With a unit of Seventh Army from Colmar through to Munich. Was assigned also in 1944 to 1945 in EAME theater. November 1942 to November 1944.

Wells, Clifford. Navy. Was in Iceland three months. Suffered injury (wrench—fell from mast on head) and was discharged. His ship went on to Ireland and Scotland and was sunk.

West, William R., Sgt. Army. Second Traffic Control in Italy. July 1944 to 1946.

Weyl, Nathaniel, T/5 Infantry. Writer military subjects. 273 MKM. M 1 rifle. Rome, Arno, Southern France, Rhineland, Central Europe. Served in GI Headquarters Third Infantry Division. Good Conduct Medal; Bronze Star; Distinguished Unit Badge; EAME Ribbon; World War II Victory Medal. September 1943 to December 1945.

Whipple, James, Sgt. U.S. Army Ordinance Dept. Asiatic-Pacific theater, one star, Ryukyu Campaign; Victory Medal; Good Conduct Medal; American Theater Unit Citation. Occupation of Japan.

**White, William*, Coxswain 3/c. Navy. Died when the USS *Sterett* was engaged by the Japanese in the Pacific on the night of November 12/13, 1942. Posthumously awarded Star of Presidential Unit Citation USS *Sterett* for extraordinary heroism displayed by her crew in action against Japanese task force during the battle on Guadalcanal. Enlisted December 3, 1941. Drowned November 13, 1942. Nineteen years old.

Whitehead, Peter.

Whiteley, Daniel S., First Lt. Army Air Corps. Radio Operator and Mechanics course. Trained at Miami Beach. Assigned as communications officer at Boca Raton Airfield. Later stationed in Hawaii. September 1942.

Whiteley, Harry W., First Lt. Air Corps. Two years in anti-aircraft unit. Six months air cadet. Taught radio from July 1943 to April 1945. Controller, Air Sea Rescue work, California. January 1941.

Whiteley, Robert M. Aviation Cadet. Basic training, BTC Greensboro, N.C. CTD Marshall College, W.Va. On-the-line trainee, Victoria, Tex. Pre-flight School, San Antonio. On-the-line cadet Eagle Pass Army Airfield. March 1944 to November 1945.

Wilbur, George La Rell, Jr., T/5. Infantry. Truck driver for ammunition and gas supplies. Served in Iceland, France, Holland, Germany. His assistant on truck was killed. American Defense Service Medal; European-African-Middle Eastern Service Medal; Good Conduct Medal. February 1941 to October 1945.

Wilbur, Harry.

Wilbur, Hubert.

Wilbur, Norman S., Sgt. Far Eastern Air Force. First years with HQ First Battalion 156th Field Artillery,

44th Division In 1942 re-enlisted, was assigned to AAFTTC Radio School. Served at various training schools. Overseas in June 1944. At Nouméa, New Caledonia, assigned to Eighty-second Engineer Aviation Battalion and while en route to join unit worked for several weeks as landscape gardener in Memorial Cemetery at Lunga Beach, Guadalcanal. In October left for Leyte, P.I., landing with initial forces where unit constructed Dulag Aerodrome. Left for Samar, P.I., in February 1945 where unit worked on naval air base. American Defense Medal; American Theater Ribbon; Good Conduct Medal; Asiatic-Pacific Theater Ribbon with four Bronze battle stars; Philippines Liberation with one Bronze Star; Victory Medal; Unit Meritorious Award one Gold Star. (Six stars altogether.) September 1940 to September 1942 and October 1942 to December 1945.

Wilbur, Roland M.

Wilbur, Washington L.

Wiltz, Eric, GM 3/c. Navy. GM the USS *Brush*. Under direct attack six times by Japanese dive-bombers. In constant action for months. Went to aid in raiding of Tokyo. Shot up a Japanese convoy three miles off Tokyo Harbor. Picked up aviators shot down at sea. Crew members swimming out to put lines around pilots to haul them aboard, later delivering them to carriers. Crew of the USS *Brush* awarded four stars, Philippine Liberation Ribbon with star.

Wingert, Fred F., Cpl. Army Medical Corps. Army Service Forces. Training at Camp Pickett, Va.; Fort Jackson, S.C. Desert training Indio, Calif. Overseas: France, Luxembourg, Belgium. Transferred to Engineers Corps. October 1942 to October 1945.

Winslow, Marshall Ladd, T/Sgt. Field Artillery. HQ. Battery, 232nd Field Artillery, 42nd Infantry (Rainbow Division). The Forty-second Division replaced the veteran Forty-fifth Infantry Division in the lines at Wimmenau in Alsace, February 1945, in the Rhineland campaign. They broke through the Siegfried Line as part of Seventh Army. Crossed the Rhine at Worms and followed general direction of the Main River. Took Wertheim-am-Main, Würzburg and Schweinfurt and aided in the fall of Nuremberg. Then turned south across the Bavarian plain to take Dachau, participate in the fall of Munich and strike at the great national redoubt of the Bavarian Alps. The Rainbow Division was just crossing into Austria near Berchtesgaden when VE day came. Four years in service. June 1942 to March 1946.

Wolvan, Sterling, Sgt. Army Air Corps. August 1942 to February 1943.

Wolven, Elsie F., Lt. Nurse. September 1944.

Wolven, Everett, S.

Wolven, John B., Pfc. Army. Co. C, 1288th Engineers Bn. (combat). Left New York Harbor in December 1944; arrived Glasgow, Scotland. Had advanced training in bridge building at Chipping Norton, England. Landed at Le Havre via LST on April 1. From there by truck through France and Belgium and into Germany. Helped build a large floating Bailey bridge across the Rhine above Cologne. Named the bridge after war correspondent Ernie Pyle. The bridge was 1,504 feet long and it helped shorten the war, as troops and supplies were sent over it. After end of war was stationed at Aachen. From there to southern France. Had a week's Riviera pass, all expenses paid by USRRA. Entertained at Marseilles, expecting to be sent to Manila when orders were changed because the Japanese had surrendered. May 1943 to November 1945.

Wolven, Milton, T/5. Army Chemical Warfare. Normandy campaign—beachhead and battle. Northern France, Rhineland. While in Scotland married a Scottish woman. Three battle stars; Presidential Unit Citation; Purple Heart. June 1943 to December 1945.

Wolven, Willard E., Cpl. Army. CMP Luzon campaign. According to newspaper clipping "has been stationed on practically every island in the Pacific." World War II Victory Medal; Asiatic-Pacific Service Medal; Philippines Liberation Medal; American Service Medal. January 1942 to December 1945.

Zelie, George H., Seaman.

NOTES

CHAPTER 1
EARLY SETTLEMENT

1. E. M. Ruttenber, "Footprints of the Red Men: Indian Geographical Names," in *Proceedings of the New York State Historical Association*, vol. 6 (n.p.: New York State Historical Association, 1906), 155; Augustus H. Van Buren, *A History of Ulster County Under the Dominion of the Dutch* (Kingston, N.Y.: n.p., 1923), 5, 14–15.
2. A source for the translation of Onteoras cannot be found.
3. Benjamin M. Brink, "Vaughan's Second Expedition," *Olde Ulster* 4: 8 (Aug. 1908): 234–35.
4. In the first edition of *Woodstock History and Hearsay*, AMS cited a letter from Donald Whiteside to Louise Zimm, dated Nov. 16, 1957, stating that the Doomsday Book (begun by William the Conqueror in 1085 and completed in 1086) recorded all the townships in England south of the rivers Ribble and Tees, and that it referred to Woodstock variously as Wodestock, Wodestok and Wodstok—meaning a royal forest. In a letter to AMS dated Dec. 13, 1957, Victor Tolley, Town Clerk's Office, Woodstock, Oxfordshire, quotes the historian Adolphus Ballard as saying that the name means "a woody place" and quotes a second historian, Miss Shelmerdine, as indicating that it originally meant "a stockaded settlement in a wood." In an e-mail note dated Nov. 5, 2003, the current town clerk, Marian Moxon, cites R. B. Ramsbotham's guide in which he contends that the name comes from two Saxon words: wudu, meaning wood, and stoc, meaning place. Ramsbotham's guide, according to Ms. Moxon, is actually a list of documents on deposit with the Borough of Woodstock, Oxfordshire; the reference to Woodstock itself comes in a monograph by Edward Marshall titled *The Early History of Woodstock Manor and Its Environs in Bladon, Hensington, New Woodstock, Blenheim* (Oxford: n.p., 1873).
5. Neil Stevens, "Geological History of Woodstock," *Publications of the Woodstock Historical Society* no. 8 (Aug. 1932): 12, 15, 17. Stevens was a pathologist with the Bureau of Plant Industry, U.S. Department of Agriculture.
6. Petition of Albert Rosa, Indorsed Land Papers, vol. 3, 40, New York State Library.
7. Petition of Johannis Hardenbergh, Indorsed Land Papers, vol. 40, 125–26, New York State Library.
8. Benjamin M. Brink, "The Hardenbergh, or the 'Great' Patent," *Olde Ulster* 6: 5 (May 1910): 131–32. This refers to the grant application made on Apr. 20, 1708.
9. Bruno Zimm, "A Chain of Woodstock Land Titles," *Publications of the Woodstock Historical Society* no. 5 (Aug. 1931): 15.
10. Robert Livingston Sr. (1654–1728), known as the first lord of Livingston Manor, was also the first of many Robert Livingstons associated with the Hudson River Valley. He had sailed to the New World from his native Scotland, arriving in 1674. During his lifetime he amassed the 160,000 acres that became Livingston Manor—comprising the southern third of modern Columbia County.

    He and his wife Alida were parents to ten children, one of whom was a second Robert Livingston (1688–1775). This son inherited from Robert Sr. a 13,000-acre estate at the southwestern end of Livingston Manor. Known as Robert of Clermont after the gracious home he built overlooking the eastern bank of the Hudson River, he acquired close to half a million acres of the Hardenbergh Patent, including portions of Woodstock.

    Robert of Clermont's only child was named Robert Robert Livingston (1718–75). Robert R. augmented the family's holdings through his marriage to Margaret Beekman—the daughter of Colonel Henry Beekman, another powerful landowner. Appointed to the Admiralty Court in 1759 and to the Supreme Court four years later, Robert R. was known as Judge Livingston.

    The eldest son of Judge and Margaret Beekman Livingston was named Robert R. Livingston Jr. (1746–1813). Robert R. Jr. was made Chancellor of the State of New York, among many other appointments during his lifetime. From his home at Clermont, Chancellor Livingston could gaze across the Hudson River at his vast holdings—encompassing much of Woodstock and the Catskill Mountains region.

    For more on the Livingstons, see George Dangerfield, *Chancellor Robert R. Livingston of New York 1746–1813* (New York: Harcourt, Brace, 1960), 8–9, 13, 25–28 and family tree at page 516.

11. Louise Zimm, *Woodstock During the Revolution* (unpublished manuscript, 1939), 2–3 (AMS papers).
12. For Indian legends see Richard M. Bayles, "Modern Catskill," in J. B. Beers, *History of Greene County, New York With Biographical Sketches of Its Prominent Men* (New York: J. B. Beers, 1884/Saugerties, N.Y.: Hope Farm Press, 1969), 119; Saxe Commins, ed., *Selected Writings of Washington Irving* (New York: Random House, First Modern Library Edition, 1945), 19–20.
13. R. Lionel De Lisser, *Picturesque Ulster* (Kingston, N.Y.: Styles & Bruyn, 1896), 223. For more on Philip Bonesteel, see J. H. French, *Gazetteer of the State of New York* (Syracuse: R. P. Smith, 1860), 668 n. 8; Nathaniel Bartlett Sylvester, *History of Ulster County, New York* (Philadelphia: Everts & Peck, 1880), part 2, 317.
14. Benjamin M. Brink, "Resolutions of the Kingston Trustees," *Olde Ulster* 4: 5 (May 1908): 146.
15. According to Sylvester in *History of Ulster County, New York*, part 2, Shandaken is of Indian origin and probably signifies "rapid waters" (p. 306). However, this interpretation is contradicted by Ruttenber in "Footprints of the Red Man, Indian Geographical Names." Ruttenber writes that Shandaken probably derives from *Schindak*, meaning "hemlock woods," or *Schindak-ing*, for "at the hemlock woods" or "place of hemlocks" (p. 169).
16. Louise Hasbrouck Zimm et al., *Ulster County* (New York: Lewis Historical Publishing Co., 1946), 200, 210.
17. *Heads of Families: At the First Census of the United States in the Year 1790, New York* (Baltimore: Genealogical Publishing, 1971), 186.
18. Ulster County Deed Book, Liber GG, pp. 364–66.
19. Ulster County Deed Book; supporting citation not found.
20. French, *Gazetteer of the State of New York*, 668 n. 8.
21. Byde [sic] Snyder, "Woodstock in Olden Days," *Woodstock Weekly* (Sept. 27, 1924): 4.
22. Ulster County Deed Book, Liber 18, pp. 178–80, covers the land transaction between Margaret Livingston and F. Rowe and also mentions the farm of John Carrol and the leased lands of the Chadewicks and Henry Haniger.
23. Livingston letter: Benjamin M. Brink, "Vaughan's Second Expedition," 234–35.
24. Personal communication from a member of the Rowe family (given name unknown) to AMS.
25. Personal communication from Wilna Hervey to AMS.
26. Wild turkeys: According to *The Wild Turkey in New York*, a pamphlet published by the New York State Department of Environmental Conservation and the New York State chapter of the National Wild Turkey Federation, Susquehanna Longbeards, "Around 1948, wild turkeys from a small remnant population in northern Pennsylvania crossed the border into western New York. These were the first birds in the state after an absence of 100 years." Now, many years later, they have made their way back to the Woodstock area as well. This pamphlet can be found on the Web site of the New York State Department of Environmental Conservation: http://www.dec.state.ny.us.
27. *Ulster Sentinel* 1: 36 (Feb. 14, 1827).
28. AMS, "Hearsay and History," *Publications of the Woodstock Historical Society* no. 4 (July 1931): 17.

CHAPTER 2
FRONTIER DAYS

1. Signers of Articles of Association: Sylvester, *History of Ulster County, New York*, part 1, 70–77.
2. Benjamin M. Brink, "The Committee of Ulster County," *Olde Ulster* 6: 10 (Oct. 1910): 311.
3. AMS, "Stories of Mink Hollow: Hearsay and History, No. II," *Publications of the Woodstock Historical Society* no. 8 (Aug. 1932): 21. According to Louise Zimm, Simms came to America in 1800 and lived hereabouts for ten years. On the other hand, according to the Town Records 1804–71, on Jan. 19, 1827, a James Symes complained that a "red heffer with a white spot on the forehead . . . Came into My Inclosure last summer" (p. 136).
4. Meeting of Committee of Safety and Observation of the Town of Kingston, Apr. 9, 1777; Benjamin M. Brink, "The 'Tories' of the Revolution," *Olde Ulster* 2: 9 (Sept. 1906): 270–72.
5. Kate S. Curry, "The Minutes of the Committee of Safety of the Manor of Livingston, Columbia County, New York, in 1776," *New York Genealogical and Biographical Record* 60: 3 (July 1929): 239.
6. Personal communication from Merritt Staples to AMS.
7. Marius Schoonmaker, *The History of Kingston, New York* (New York: Burr Printing House, 1888), 255.
8. Benjamin M. Brink, "The Loyalist Problem," *Olde Ulster* 3: 6 (June 1907): 169.
9. *Public Papers of George Clinton: First Governor of New York, 1777–1795, 1801–1804*, vol. 4 (Albany: James B. Lyon, State Printer, 1900), 164–65, letter no. 1846.
10. Ibid., letter no. 2277, 807–808.
11. Benjamin M. Brink, "The Fort at Lackawack," *Olde Ulster* 3: 2 (Feb. 1907): 42–43.
12. Benjamin M. Brink, "The Fort at Great Shandaken," *Olde Ulster* 2: 6 (June 1906): 172. Colonel Pawling wrote from Marbletown on May 24, 1779, "The fort at Shendeken is done (I heard yesterday) but by means of the late Heavy Rains, little has been done at Lagewack."
13. Benjamin M. Brink, "Lieutenant Van Hoevenberg in the Revolution," *Olde Ulster* 8: 3 (Mar. 1912): 80–81.
14. H. A. Haring, *Our Catskill Mountains* (New York: G. P. Putnam's Sons, 1931), 58.
15. Letters from George Washington provide background on the run-up to the Sullivan initiative. On Feb. 11, 1779, Washington wrote to General Schuyler about mounting a campaign against the hostile tribes of the Six Nations (*Public Papers of George Clinton*, vol. 4 [1900], 602–604, letter no. 2120). On Mar. 4, 1779, he wrote to Governor Clinton about the composition of the troops (*Public Papers of George Clinton*, vol. 4 [1900], 615–17, letter no. 2129). On May 31, 1779, he issued instructions to General Sullivan (*Public Papers of George Clinton*, vol. 5 [1901], 123–24, letter no. 6425). For more on the Sullivan initiative, see Benjamin M. Brink, "An Ulster County Boy in the Revolution," *Olde Ulster* 1: 9 (Sept. 1905): 276. See also Benjamin M. Brink, "Governor George Clinton," *Olde Ulster* 5: 6 (June 1909): 169. For another perspective, see Rev. Charles Rockwell, *The Catskill Mountains and the Region Around* (New York: Taintor Bros., 1867), 104.
16. For more on Sullivan, Brant and Minisink, see Rockwell, *The Catskill Mountains and the Region Around*, 100. See also Elizabeth Eggleston Seelye assisted by Edward Eggleston, *Brant and Red Jacket* (New York: Dodd, Mead, 1879), 261.

17. Rockwell, *The Catskill Mountains and the Region Around*, 47.
18. Benjamin M. Brink, "A Threat From Joseph Brant," *Olde Ulster* 7: 2 (Feb. 1911): 53.
19. Richard M. Bayles, "The Plaaterkill and Kaaterskill Cloves," in J. B. Beers, *History of Greene County, New York With Biographical Sketches of Its Prominent Men*, 81.
20. For the Drake citation, see Rockwell, *The Catskill Mountains and the Region Around*, 101.
21. "The Captivity of Capt. Jeremiah Snyder, and his son Elias Snyder of Saugerties, Ulster County, (N.Y.) During the Revolutionary War," *Ulster Sentinel* 1: 34 (Jan. 31, 1827); 1: 35 (Feb. 7, 1827); 1: 36 (Feb. 14, 1827); 1: 37 (Feb. 21, 1827); 1: 38 (Feb. 27, 1827); 1: 39 (Mar. 7, 1827).
22. Benjamin M. Brink, *The Early History of Saugerties 1660–1825* (Kingston, N.Y.: R. W. Anderson & Son, 1902), 174.
23. Benjamin M. Brink, "The Captivity of Short and Miller," *Olde Ulster* 2: 11 (Nov. 1906): 339–43. For Short and Miller's encounter with Joe Dewitt, see Rockwell, *The Catskill Mountains and the Region Around*, 99.
24. Eggleston Seelye, *Brant and Red Jacket*, 245, 282–83.
25. Ibid., 164–66.
26. Ibid., 130–32.
27. Ibid., 194.
28. Ibid., 195, 310.
29. Ibid., 286.
30. Ibid., 305.
31. Rockwell, *The Catskill Mountains and the Region Around*, 103–104; Eggleston Seelye, *Brant and Red Jacket*, 200.
32. *Public Papers of George Clinton*, vol. 6 (1902), 562–63, letter no. 3480.
33. Benjamin M. Brink, "The Loyalist Problem," 170–71.
34. Louise Zimm, "Neglected Graveyards of Woodstock," *Publications of the Woodstock Historical Society* no. 2 (Aug. 1930): 12.
35. Alphonso T. Clearwater, *The History of Ulster County, New York* (Kingston, N.Y.: W. J. van Deusen, 1907), 147, lists several Revolutionary officers from the Woodstock area who served. For additional names, see Louise Zimm, "Neglected Graveyards of Woodstock," 9–11.
36. "A Family of Remarkable Longevity: John Yerry," transcribed newspaper clipping in AMS papers, 1, 2.

CHAPTER 3
GLASS MAKING IN THE NINETEENTTH CENURY

1. Ulster County Deed Book, Liber 16, pp. 522–28.
2. Edward F. De Lancey, "Biography of Baron De Zeng," *New York Genealogical and Biographical Record* 2: 2 (Apr. 1871), 49–53.
3. Ulster County Deed Book, Liber 19, p. 353.
4. Town Records 1804–71, p. 18. Survey no. 18 mentions, besides the Bristol Glass house, an "old glass factory near James McDonoughs."
5. Samuel Stilwell Doughty, *The Life of Samuel Stilwell* (New York: Brown & Wilson, 1877), 6–7.
6. Ulster County Deed Book; supporting citation not found.
7. Neil Stevens, "Woodstock and Its Surroundings as They Appeared to a Visitor in 1820," citing James Pierce's paper, "A Memoir on the Catskill Mountains With Notices of Their Topography, Scenery, Mineralogy, Zoology, Economical Resources . . . ," *American Journal of Science* 6: 1 (1823): 89, 92.
8. Clearwater, *The History of Ulster County, New York*, 24.
9. Personal communication from Barney MacDaniel to AMS.
10. Bristol Glass, Cotton & Clay Co. ledger (1817–21), Sept. 7, 1818, p. 120 (Collection, Historical Society of Woodstock).
11. *New York Evening Post* no. 5717 (Oct. 16, 1820): 12.
12. Ulster County Deed Book, Liber 20, pp. 590–93.
13. Horatio Gates Spafford, *A Gazetteer of the State of New York* (Albany: H. C. Southwick, 1813), 331.
14. Bristol Glass, Cotton & Clay Co. ledger (1817–21), Mar. 19, 1819, p. 76.
15. Ibid., June 21, 1820, p. 114.
16. Ibid., Dec. 12, 1818, p. 142.
17. Ibid., June 20, 1818, p. 119.
18. Bristol Glass, Cotton & Clay Co. day book (1817–18), July 15, 1817, p. 2.
19. Bristol Glass, Cotton & Clay Co. ledger (1817–21), May 7, 1819, p. 56.
20. Personal communication from Fordyce Herrick to AMS.
21. *Ulster Sentinel* 1: 16 (Sept. 27, 1826).
22. Ibid., 2: 89 (Feb. 20, 1828).
23. Bristol Glass, Cotton & Clay Co. ledger (1817–21), June 13, 1818, p. 60.
24. Elsie Vosburgh Rowe, *The Story of Our Family Heritage* (Woodstock, N.Y.: privately published, 1956).
25. Bristol Glass, Cotton & Clay Co. ledger (1817–21), Sept. 4, 1819, p. 138.
26. Ibid., June 13, 1818, p. 20.
27. Ibid., Jan. 20, 1820, p. 124.
28. Ibid., Feb. 13, 1818, p. 109.
29. Town Records 1804–71, p. 173.
30. Bristol Glass, Cotton & Clay Co. ledger (1817–21), Jan. 5, 1818, p. 15.
31. Ibid., Jan. 7–27, 1821, p. 212.
32. Ibid., Mar. 7, 1818, p. 28; Aug. 22, 1818, p. 128.
33. Ulster County Deed Book, Liber 22, pp. 618–20.
34. *Ulster Sentinel* 1: 8 (Aug. 2, 1826).
35. Ulster County Deed Book, Liber 27, pp. 355–59.
36. Thomas F. Gordon, *Gazetteer of the State of New York* (Philadelphia: n.p. [privately printed by T. K. & P. G. Collins], 1836), 743.
37. George S. and Helen McKearin, *American Glass* (New York: Crown, 1941), 181.
38. Ulster County Deed Book, Liber 60, pp. 159–61.
39. Ulster County Deed Book, Liber 38, pp. 168–70.
40. Town Records 1804–71, p. 176.
41. Ulster County Deed Book, Liber 63, pp. 416–17; Liber 63, pp. 359; Liber 63, pp. 360–62; Liber 68, pp. 425–27.
42. Personal communication from John Miller to AMS.
43. Personal communication from Moses Sagendorf to AMS.
44. *Commemorative Biographical Record of Ulster County, New York* (Chicago: J. B. Beers, 1896), 776–77.
45. Capital stock, Ledger A, Ulster County Glass Manufacturing Co. (1853–55), loose paper between pages 302 and 303.
46. George S. and Helen McKearin, *American Glass*, 178.
47. Petty Ledger A, Ulster County Glass [Manufacturing] Co. (1853–55): William Carmon, stockholder, p. 386, Oct. 11, 1853. Silvester Carmon, pots, p. 17, Nov. 11, 1854. Nathan Carmon, cutter, p. 45, Feb. 28, 1854. John Carmon, flattener,

p. 48, Feb. 28, 1854. Orville Knowlton, blower, p. 303, May 30, 1855. Joseph Short, $135.49 in a three-and-a-half month period, p. 360, May 31, 1855. Larry Peet, blower, p. 19, Feb. 28, 1854.

48. Town Records 1804–71, p. 246.
49. Petty Ledger A., Ulster County Glass [Manufacturing] Co. (1853–55): Killian Martin, blower, p. 337, Feb. 26, 1855. Nicholas Hackett, $11 a month rent at Martin's, p. 277, Nov. 20, 1854. Hiram St. John Short, cutter, p. 42, Feb. 28, 1854. Peter Short, batch maker, p. 91, Feb. 1, 1854. David Short, wood, p. 257, Jan. 29, 1855, Feb. 24, 1855, and Dec. 26, 1854. Elias Short, wood, p. 150, Nov. 4, 1853. Elizabeth MacDaniel, wood, p. 80, Oct. 12, 1853. Abel Hasbrouck, wood, p. 120, Nov. 19, 1853. Silas Husted, wood and snuff, p. 322, Nov. 1, 1854. Richard Gridley, wood (seventy-nine cords), p. 205, Apr. 5, 1854. Joseph H. Miller, wood, p. 7, June 23, 1854. Ezra Calkins, shingles, p. 311, Apr. 30, 1855. Cornelius Peterson, pipe handles and glazing, p. 170, Nov. 30, 1853; trundle bed, p. 225, Feb. 9, 1855; bookcase, p. 171, June 20, 1854. William Johnson, Godfries cordial, p. 353, Dec. 28, 1854; batch making, p. 40, May 29, 1854; military tax, p. 353, Jan. 22, 1855. James Vosburgh, alpaca, p. 273, Jan. 5, 1855; palmetto, p. 273, Mar. 2, 1855; cashmere and shirting, p. 272, Dec. 15, 1854; boys' boots, p. 272, Nov. 4, 1854; linen, p. 272, Dec. 15, 1854; flannel, p. 62, Oct. 22, 1853; horse blanket, p. 272, Nov. 30, 1854; selling glass to Delhi, page 281, June 12, 1855. Levi Newkerk, teaming, p. 126, Mar. 1, 1854. Peter Harder, teaming, p. 109, Jan. 31, 1854. Franklin Hasbrouck, teaming, p. 103, Jan. 26, 1855. Reverend D. P. Wright, sundries at store, p. 204, Apr. 20, 1854. Richard Shultis, shearing, tending and picking pot shells, p. 71, Jan. 26, 1854. Philip Simmons, batch maker, p. 70, Dec. 8, 1853. Cornelius Elting, pot shells, p. 255, May 31, 1854.
50. Personal communication from Louise Zimm based on Philip Van De Bogart's stories about his family.
51. Supporting letter not found.
52. Benjamin M. Brink, "The Building of Plank Roads," *Olde Ulster* 8: 10 (Oct. 1912): 294.
53. Personal communication from Hannah Cooper Vosburgh to AMS.
54. Peter Reynolds, Petty Ledger A., Ulster County Glass [Manufacturing] Co. (1853–55), cords of wood, p. 238, June 29, 1854; Saugerties, p. 243, Mar. 3, 1855; Kingston and Rondout, p. 239, July 21, 1854; Rhinebeck, p. 243, Mar. 8, 1855.
55. William Avery, ibid., shearer, p. 172, Apr. 30, 1854; snuff, Feb. 25, 1854; tea, Jan. 21, 1854; buttons, Dec. 31, 1853; candles, Apr. 25, 1854; pork, Apr. 3, 1854; British oil, Feb. 14, 1854; mittens, Apr. 25, 1854; soap and salve, Jan. 4, 1854; small pair of shoes, Mar. 21, 1854.
56. Trask's Magnetic Ointment, ibid., p. 391, Aug. 22, 1854.
57. A. R. Fox; supporting letter not found.
58. Hawley & Co.; supporting letter not found.
59. P. Reynolds entry; supporting citation not found.

CHAPTER 4
THE DOWN-RENT WAR

1. Secretary of State, Albany Book of Patents, no. 7, p. 310 (copy, Senate House State Historic Site, Kingston, N.Y.).
2. Henry Christman, *Tin Horns and Calico* (New York: Henry Holt, 1945/Cornwallville, N.Y.: Hope Farm Press, 1975), 77.
3. Dr. David Murray, "The Anti-rent Episode in the State of New York," in *Annual Report of the American Historical Association for the Year 1896*, vol. 1 (Washington: Government Printing Office, 1897), 144–45.
4. Edward P. Cheyney, *The Anti-rent Agitation in the State of New York 1839–1846* no. 2 (Philadelphia: Publications of the University of Pennsylvania, 1887), 25; Christman, *Tin Horns and Calico*, 5–7.
5. Jay Gould, *History of Delaware County and Border Wars of New York* (Roxbury, N.Y.: Keeny & Gould, 1856/New Orleans: Polyanthos, 1977), 261–62.
6. Murray, *Annual Report of the American Historical Association for the Year 1896*, vol. 1, 151.
7. Christman, *Tin Horns and Calico*, 102, 107.
8. Ibid., 111–14, 118.
9. Supporting citation not found.
10. John D. Monroe, *The Anti-rent War in Delaware County, New York: The Revolt Against the Rent System* (n.p. [privately printed], 1940), 52–53.
11. Christman, *Tin Horns and Calico*, 84, 118.
12. Benjamin M. Brink, "One of the 'Down Rent' Ballads," *Olde Ulster* 10: 10 (Oct. 1914): 306–307.
13. Christman, *Tin Horns and Calico*, 79–80.
14. Abram W. Hoffman, "The 'Down Rent' War," *Olde Ulster* 10: 9 (Sept. 1914): 262.
15. Ibid.
16. Supporting citation not found.
17. Hoffman, "The 'Down Rent' War," 264–66.
18. This was a pun on Peter Sagendorf's occupation as a peat harvester (for his charcoal pit) and the fact that he hid himself in the marsh (peat lands).
19. Personal communication from Hercules "Herc" Davis to AMS.
20. Hoffman, "The 'Down Rent' War," 262–63; also, personal communication from Hercules "Herc" Davis to AMS.
21. "Down-Rent Disturbances," *Democratic Journal* 5: 17 (Mar. 12, 1845).
22. "Anti-rent Disturbances," *Ulster Republican* 12: 45 (Mar. 12, 1845).
23. "Down-Rent Disturbances," *Democratic Journal* 5: 17 (Mar. 12, 1845).
24. "The Ulster Posse," *Democratic Journal* 5: 23 (Apr. 23, 1845).
25. Benjamin M. Brink, "The Hurley Greens," *Olde Ulster* 10: 3 (Mar. 1914): 80–82.
26. "Grand and Petit Jurors," *Democratic Journal* 5: 16 (Mar. 5, 1845); "Down Rent in Ulster," *Democratic Journal* 5: 18 (Mar. 19, 1845).
27. "For the Ulster Republican," *Ulster Republican* 12: 47 (Mar. 26, 1845).
28. "Judge Ruggles' Charge to the Grand Jury," *Democratic Journal* 5: 19 (Mar. 26, 1845).
29. "Anti-rent Difficulties," *Democratic Journal* 5: 19 (Mar. 26, 1845).
30. Christman, *Tin Horns and Calico*, 176–82.
31. "Governor Wright's Proclamation," *Ulster Republican* 13: 18 (Sept. 3, 1845).
32. Monroe, *The Anti-rent War in Delaware County, New York*, 44; "The Anti-rent Trials Ended," *Democratic Journal* 5: 48 (Oct. 15, 1845).
33. Monroe, *The Anti-rent War in Delaware County, New York*, 16; Christman, *Tin Horns and Calico*, 233.
34. "Arrests," *Ulster Republican* 13: 20 (Sept. 17, 1845).

35. "Rent Lands in Rensselaer County," *Ulster Republican*, 13: 1 (May 7, 1845).
36. "The Land Proprietors in the Middle Counties," *Ulster Republican* 13: 18 (Sept. 3, 1845).
37. "Land Tenures," *Ulster Republican* 13: 40 (Feb. 4, 1846).
38. Christman, *Tin Horns and Calico*, 293.
39. Ibid., 282.

CHAPTER 5
THE BYRDCLIFFE ART COLONY

1. Sir Ivo Elliott, ed., *The Balliol College Register, 1833–1933*, 2nd ed. (Oxford: Oxford University Press, 1934), 83; Joseph Foster, *Alumni Oxoniensis: 1715–1886*, vol. 4 (Oxford: Parker & Co., 1888), 1542.
2. Hervey White, "Ralph Radcliffe Whitehead," in *Publications of the Woodstock Historical Society* no. 10 (July 1933): 18–19.
3. Ralph R. Whitehead, *Grass of the Desert* (London: Chiswick Press, 1892), 72, 70–71, 62.
4. Ibid., 171, drawn from lines one and two of William Shakespeare's Sonnet No. 107.
5. "From the Editor's Scrapbasket," *The Overlook* 1: 2 (June 20, 1931): 14.
6. Details on Whitehead's home in California: personal communication from Peter Whitehead to AMS.
7. Ralph R. Whitehead, "Pictures for Schools," in *Arrows of Dawn* no. 3 (Montecito, Calif.: n.p., 1901), 12.
8. For a discussion of Turkish cozy corners, see Sarah Abigail Leavitt, *From Catherine Beecher to Martha Stewart: A Cultural History of Domestic Advice* (Chapel Hill: University of North Carolina Press, 2002), 98–100.
9. On choosing the site for the colony: Bolton Brown, "Early Days at Woodstock," *Publications of the Woodstock Historical Society* no. 13 (Aug.–Sept. 1937): 6.
10. Ibid., 9.
11. Ibid., 10–11.
12. Lucy Brown, "The First Summer in Byrdcliffe, 1902–3," *Publications of the Woodstock Historical Society* no. 2 (Aug. 1930): 16–19. Information on Walter Weyl and John Dewey: personal communication from Jean Rosen to AMS.
13. Bolton Brown, "Early Days in Woodstock," 13.
14. Arrival of Macrum and Carlson: personal communication from Jean Rosen to AMS. Quote regarding Zulma Steele: Bolton Brown, "Early Days at Woodstock," 13. Regarding early craft work: Bertha Thompson, "The Craftsmen of Byrdcliffe," *Publications of the Woodstock Historical Society* no. 10 (July 1933): 8–10.
15. Letter from John Burroughs to "Our Boys and Girls," Apr. 9, 1914.
16. Personal communication from Zulma Steele to AMS.
17. Carl Eric Lindin, "Bolton Brown," *Publications of the Woodstock Historical Society* no. 13 (Aug.–Sept. 1937): 17; "Bolton Brown," *The Overlook* 1: 13 (Sept. 5, 1931): 9–10.
18. Edith Wherry story: Lucy Brown, "The First Summer in Byrdcliffe, 1902–3," 18–19.
19. Ralph Radcliffe Whitehead, "A Plea for Manual Work," *Handicraft Magazine* (June 1903): 58, 59, 72, 73.
20. Letters from Bertha Poole Weyl to AMS dated Dec. 8, 1945, and Jan. 2, 1946 (AMS papers).
21. Ned Thatcher biographical details: personal communication from Ned Thatcher to AMS; also, "Ned," *The Overlook* 1: 2 (June 20, 1931): 4–6. Iddie Flitcher poem, "Winter": *The Overlook* 1: 5 (July 11, 1931): 10.
22. Supporting citation not found.
23. Personal communication from Zulma Steele to AMS.
24. Information on Mrs. Whitehead: personal communication from Federico Stallforth to AMS.
25. Poultney Bigelow, "The Byrdcliffe Colony of Arts and Crafts," *American Homes and Gardens* 6 (Oct. 1909): 389, 392.
26. John Bigelow background information: Allen Johnson, ed., *Dictionary of American Biography*, vol. 2 (New York: Charles Scribner's Sons, 1929), 258–59. Bigelows and bluestone: Rockwell, *The Catskill Mountains and the Region Around*, 23.
27. Albert Webster biographical details: Martin Schütze, *Publications of the Woodstock Historical Society* no. 1 (July 1930): 27–28.
28. Martin Schütze, "Albert L. Webster in Woodstock," *Publications of the Woodstock Historical Society* no. 1 (July 1930), 27–29.
29. Harry Leith Ross, "Birge Harrison, 1855–1929," *Publications of the Woodstock Historical Society* no. 4 (July 1931): 33–34.
30. "The Phoenix Players," *The Hue and Cry* 3: 10, 11 (1925): 48.
31. Elsa Kimball, "Martin Schütze," *Publications of the Woodstock Historical Society* no. 16 (Sept. 1951): 4.
32. *Byrdcliffe Afternoons: A Series of Lectures Given at Byrdcliffe, Woodstock, New York, July 1938* (Woodstock, N.Y.: Overlook Press, 1939), 115.
33. Ibid., 127.
34. "Dr. Richard Beer-Hofmann Dies; Vienna Poet a Refugee in U.S.," *New York Herald Tribune* 105: 36110 (Sept. 27, 1945): 20.
35. Loom room mantel: Carla Smith, executive director of the Woodstock Byrdcliffe Guild, says that according to Adam Pinsker, classics scholar at Vassar College, this is a rough translation of line 322 from Sophocles's *Ajax*. The word "grace" may also be translated as "kindness." In the first edition of *Woodstock History and Hearsay*, AMS gave the translation as "Love gives love back to itself."

CHAPTER 6
ON THE MAVERICK

1. Hervey White, "Youth and Italy: The Journal of a Student Afoot," *The Wild Hawk* 3: 8 (June 1914).
2. James P. Cooney, "Hervey White, Noted Hermit of Letters, Is One of Nation's Significant Figures, Theodore Dreiser Says in Written Tribute," *Ulster County Press* (Kingston, N.Y.) (Nov. 12, 1937): 9.
3. Hervey White, "Youth and Italy: The Journal of a Student Afoot: The Steerage," *The Wild Hawk* 1: 7 (May 1912).
4. Hervey White, "Youth and Italy: The Journal of a Student Afoot: A Question of Vanity or Practicability," *The Wild Hawk* 1: 9 (July 1912).
5. Journey to Rome: Hervey White, "Youth and Italy: The Journal of a Student Afoot: Casserta [sic]," *The Wild Hawk* 1: 10 (Aug. 1912).
6. Travels in mountainous regions: Hervey White, "Youth and Italy: The Journal of a Student Afoot: A Roadside Tavern," *The Wild Hawk* 1: 11 (Sept. 1912).
7. From Frosinone to Rome: Hervey White, "Youth and Italy: The Journal of a Student Afoot," *The Wild Hawk* 2: 1 (Nov. 1912).

8. Hervey White, "Youth and Italy: The Journal of a Student Afoot," *The Wild Hawk* 1: 11 (Sept. 1912).
9. Thoughts on painters: Hervey White, "Youth and Italy: The Journal of a Student Afoot," *The Wild Hawk* 2: 2 (Dec. 1912).
10. In Florence: Hervey White, "Youth and Italy: The Journal of a Student Afoot," *The Wild Hawk* 3: 4 (Feb. 1914).
11. Hervey White, "Who's Who in Woodstock," *Woodstock Bulletin* (Sept. 1, 1928): 28. Supporting citation for Henry Morton Robinson's Jane Addams quote not found; may have been a personal communication to AMS. See also Cooney, "Hervey White, Noted Hermit of Letters." For arrival in Chicago and meeting Ralph Radcliffe Whitehead: "Hervey White," *The Overlook* 1: 4 (July 4, 1931): 4–5.
12. White and Whitehead in Chicago, California and Oregon: Hervey White, "Ralph Radcliffe Whitehead," *Publications of the Woodstock Historical Society* no. 10 (July 1933): 14–15, 23–25.
13. Meeting of the three founders: Bolton Brown, "Early Days at Woodstock," 3–4.
14. Joseph Q. Riznik, "Bohemia Goes Native: Woodstock, Once One of Those Different Places, Is Doomed to Be a Summer Resort," Aug. 1929 newspaper scrap, source unknown; found in AMS papers.
15. Choice of name: *Autobiography of Hervey White* (unpublished manuscript, 1937), 114–15 (copy at Woodstock Library). The word "maverick": *Woodstock Bulletin* 1: 9 (Sept. 1, 1928): 20.
16. Details of purchase: *Autobiography of Hervey White*, 170–71.
17. Hervey White's marriage and children: "Who's Who in Woodstock," *Woodstock Bulletin* (Sept. 1, 1928): 28. Dan's visit: *The Hue and Cry* 1: 6 (July 14, 1945): 4.
18. "Editorial and Comment," *The Plowshare* 6: 1 (Dec. 1916).
19. *The Plowshare* 7: 2 (Jan. 1918).
20. Brown's remarks: "On Democracy and Majority Rule," *The Plowshare* 8: 1. Hellstrom's and Boggs's replies: *The Plowshare* 8: 2 (Jan. 1919).
21. William Harlan Hale, "The Woodstock Press," *Woodstock Bulletin* 1: 9 (Sept. 1, 1928): 16. For information on *Saturday Morning*: "Came Another Publication," *Woodstock Bulletin* 1: 8 (Aug. 15, 1928): 8.
22. Martin Schütze, "George and Elizabeth Plochmann in Woodstock," *Publications of the Woodstock Historical Society* no. 3 (Sept. 1930): 23.
23. Description of concert hall: "From the Hawk's Nest," *The Wild Hawk* 4: 12 (Oct. 1915).
24. Roentgen's Gagliano cello: "Comment and Chronicle," *The Overlook* 1: 6 (July 18, 1931): 3.
25. "The Maverick Horse," *Woodstock Bulletin* 1: 9 (Sept. 1, 1928): 1. According to Cornelia Hartmann Rosenblum on the Maverick Concerts Web site (www.maverickconcerts.org) concerning the location of the horse, "Th[is] heroic sculpture standing eighteen feet high marked the entrance of the road to the concert hall (and the now-vanished theatre) for thirty-six years. For a while the sculpture had a little roof over it as protection from the elements but it began to weather alarmingly and artist Emmet Edwards, a painter who knew Flannagan well, moved it into his nearby studio to protect it. It remained there, hidden from view, for twenty years. In 1979 through the generosity and cooperation of Edwards, the horse was moved on large wooden skids from Edwards' studio to the stage of the Maverick Concert Hall. Woodstock sculptor Maury Colow undertook to stabilize the sculpture and mount it on a stone base. It is most appropriate that this mysterious and magical sculpture presides over the last and most enduring expression of Hervey White's original Maverick."
26. For information on Maverick musicians and concerts, see Elsa Kimball, "A Brief Account of Chamber Music in Woodstock," *Publications of the Woodstock Historical Society* no. 3 (Sept. 1930): 9–12, 14–15. For recital at Fireman's Hall, for Maverick concerts from 1914 to 1937 and for citation on William Kroll, see Pierre Henrotte's Maverick Notebook 1914–37 (at the Woodstock Library). In 2005 the Maverick concert series celebrated its ninetieth season of fine music.
27. Henrotte biography: *Art Notes* (ed. by Helen Ayres), July 18, 1931; "Pierre Henrotte," *The Overlook* 1: 10 (Aug. 15, 1931): 6–7. Woodstock Ensemble: Pierre Henrotte, "The Woodstock Emsemble: How and Why It Was Founded," *Woodstock Bulletin* 2: 7 (Sept. 1, 1929): 26.
28. "Barrère's Perfect Flute," *Woodstock Bulletin* 3: 4 (Apr. 15, 1930): 12.
29. Clara Chichester, "Music," *The Overlook* 6: 9 (July 8, 1938): 5.
30. "Georges Barrère," *The Overlook* 1: 3 (June 27, 1931): 5–6.
31. Georges Barrère, "To Be or Not to Be," *Woodstock Bulletin* 1: 9 (Sept. 1, 1928): 6.
32. *Autobiography of Hervey White*, 198.
33. Festival: Eve Schütze, "Comment and Chronicle," *The Overlook* 1: 13 (Sept. 5, 1931): 3 (at Woodstock Library).
34. Henry Morton Robinson, "The Maverick," *Publications of the Woodstock Historical Society* no. 11 (Aug.–Sept., 1933): 7.
35. Eve Schütze, "Comment and Chronicle," *The Overlook* 1: 13 (Sept. 5, 1931): 1.
36. R. L. Duffus, "An Eden of Artists Fights a Serpent: Its Name Is Change and It Disturbs Those Who Would Retain the Old Simplicity of Woodstock," *New York Times Magazine* 78: 26146 (Aug. 25, 1929): 6, 7, 23.
37. Discontinuation of festival in 1931: Henry Morton Robinson, "The Maverick," *Publications of the Woodstock Historical Society* no. 11 (Aug.–Sept. 1933): 7.
38. Dudley Digges, "The New Maverick Theatre," *The Hue and Cry* 1: 2 (July 5, 1924): 6, 17.
39. Letter dated June 19, 1957, from Helen Hayes to AMS (AMS papers). Whitehead had no brother; the person to whom Hayes refers was probably Ralph Whitehead Jr.
40. Dudley Digges, "Plans for the Theatre," *The Hue and Cry* 2: 3 (July 19, 1924): 14. About Madame Tampieri: "Woodstock Sentinel Echo," *The Hue and Cry* 2: 6 (Aug. 30, 1924): 9.
41. Georgia Carter Eldred, "A Children's Play at the Maverick," *The Hue and Cry* 2: 4 (Aug. 2, 1924): 8, 18.
42. "The Denishawn Dancers," *The Hue and Cry* 3: 6 (July 25, 1925): 7.
43. "Kosloff Company: Two Nights in July," *Woodstock Bulletin* 2: 3 (July 1, 1929): 14.
44. White's philosophy on insurance: supporting citation not found.
45. Maverick Theater under direction of DeLano: "On with the Drammer!" *The Hue and Cry* 7: 1 (June 29, 1929): 1, 7.
46. Garbage crisis: personal communication from Gladys Hurlbut to AMS.
47. "Woodstock After 8:45," *The Hue and Cry* 7: 4 (July 20, 1929): 1, 3.
48. Review of *Wedding Bells*: "Maverick Laughter," *The Hue and Cry* 7: 2 (July 6, 1929), 1. Maverick Players: Alice Ann Baker,

"Summer Theatres," *Woodstock Bulletin* 2: 7 (Sept. 1, 1929): 24.

49. James McCabe, "Legal Diversions," *The Hue and Cry* 7: 10 (Aug. 30, 1929): 4.
50. "Woodstockers Have Written," *Woodstock Bulletin* 3: 4 (Apr. 15, 1930): 12.
51. "Criticism of Criticism of Criticism," *The Hue and Cry* 7: 3 (July 13, 1929): 2.
52. Cancellation of Maverick Theater plans: letter to Robert Elwyn from Hervey White, Dec. 14, 1937 (AMS papers).
53. Romany Marie: "Plans and Projects," *The Overlook* 1: 1 (June 13, 1931): 5. Hervey resembling an officiating priest: Leonard Abbott, "An Impression of Woodstock," *The Overlook* 1: 7 (July 25, 1931): 12, 14.
54. "Woodstock Oleos: No. 1 Carl Walters," *The Hue and Cry* 7: 2 (July 6, 1929): 3–4.
55. White's moving to Georgia, returning in spring: personal communication from a Maverick student to AMS.

CHAPTER 7
ROSIE MAGEE OF ROCK CITY

1. William Eltinge sold part of his land to Petrus Newkirk. Matthew Dymond must have acquired a considerable section of Great Lot 26, although there appears to be no recorded deed, because as early as 1802 he had sold a lot to John Newkirk that was subsequently sold to John Wigram. Dymond had a farm outside of Lot 26 but also owned the land on the east side of the Rock City crossroads, and a road survey of 1808 places his barn there.

   Eltinge gave to his son Isaac the property to the west of the crossroads, but Isaac soon exchanged it with Michael Smith for land in Beaverkill (now Wittenberg), which was then much more settled than the lower end of town. The Michael Smith farm later came into the possession of Cornelius Riseley and then the Harder family. Across the road, Matthew Dymond Sr. sold the land on the southeast corner to Benjamin Davis, who erected a blacksmith shop there, attached to his home. Dymond's son occupied a house on the northeast corner, and it was here that the Magees lived during the early days of the artists. For more information see Bruno Zimm, "A Chain of Woodstock Land Titles," *Publications of the Woodstock Historical Society*, no. 5 (Aug. 1931): 22–23.
2. Bill Snyder, Rock City innkeeper: personal communication from Mary Harder to AMS.
3. Personal communication from Henry Gridley to AMS.
4. Personal communication from Mary Harder to AMS.
5. Lucy Brown, "The First Summer in Byrdcliffe, 1902–3," 14–15.
6. AMS, "Old Woodstock Crafts," *Publications of the Woodstock Historical Society* no. 9 (Sept. 1932): 20.
7. Shaemas O'Sheel, "It Happened Near Woodstock," *Woodstock Bulletin* 2: 5 (Aug. 1, 1929): 15.
8. Sylvester, *History of Ulster County, New York*, part 2, 319.
9. Louise Hasbrouck Zimm, "The Wigrams of Woodstock," *Publications of the Woodstock Historical Society* no. 4 (July 1931): 21, 28–29.
10. Personal communication from Rosie Magee to AMS.
11. Ibid.
12. Personal communication from Ethel Peets to AMS.
13. Richard Le Gallienne, *Woodstock: An Essay* (Woodstock, N.Y.: Woodstock Art Association, 1923), 14.
14. John F. Carlson, "The Art Students League in Woodstock," *Publications of the Woodstock Historical Society* no. 9 (Sept. 1932): 14–15.
15. Le Gallienne, *Woodstock: An Essay*, 14.
16. Personal communication from Rosie Magee to AMS.
17. Anne Moore, "The Hen Came Clucking In," in *A Misty Sea* (Portland, Me.: Southworth-Anthoensen Press, 1937), 122.
18. Personal communication from Eugene Speicher to AMS.
19. "Konrad Cramer," *The Overlook* 2: 2 (June 25, 1932): 7. Andrew Dasburg: "Henry McFee," *The Overlook* 1: 9 (Aug. 8, 1931): 6.
20. Letter dated July 10, 1957, from Andrew Dasburg to AMS (AMS papers).
21. Personal communication from Rhoda Chase to AMS.
22. Personal communication from Alice Wardwell to AMS.

CHAPTER 8
THE CREATIVE ENERGY OF ROCK CITY

1. "10 Years Ago in Woodstock From the Hue and Cry July 1923," *The Hue and Cry* 1: 1 (May 26, 1933): 3.
2. Personal communication from Speicher to AMS; also, "Eugene Speicher," *The Overlook* 1: 1 (June 13, 1931): 6–7.
3. Shotwell house: personal communication from Mrs. Bellows to AMS.
4. Quoted in Emma S. Bellows, *The Paintings of George Bellows* (New York: Alfred A. Knopf, 1929), x–xi.
5. Maratta color system: According to AMS, Hardesty C. Maratta (1864–1924) had a house in Woodstock. In responding to a query from a Miss Hardy on the Maratta system (Dec. 19, 1967), AMS wrote: "I recall seeing them [Maratta and his wife] occasionally. The most prominent artist to use the Maratta colors probably was George Bellows." Edward John (Jay) Hambidge (1867–1924) was a reporter-illustrator for the *Kansas City Star* who received his art training from William Merritt Chase; he taught his theories of dynamic symmetry in New York City and wrote several books on it, including *The Elements of Dynamic Symmetry* (New Haven, Conn.: Yale University Press, 1948).
6. Frank Crowninshield, *George Bellows Memorial Exhibition* (New York: Metropolitan Museum of Art, 1925), 19.
7. Personal communication from Mrs. Bellows to AMS.
8. Personal communication from Eugene Speicher to AMS.
9. Personal communication from Mrs. Bellows to AMS.
10. Ibid.
11. Crowninshield, *George Bellows Memorial Exhibition*, 18.
12. This appears to have been a malapropism; Mrs. Wase probably meant Lux soap flakes, popular at that time.
13. Personal communication from Sam Wiley to AMS.
14. Crowninshield, *George Bellows Memorial Exhibition*, 11–17.
15. Bradley Walker Tomlin, *Frank London: A Retrospective Showing of His Painting* (Woodstock, N.Y.: Woodstock Art Association Gallery, Sept. 1948).
16. Personal communication from Bradley Tomlin to AMS.
17. *The Overlook* 1: 6 (July 18, 1931): 4.
18. Eleanor Roosevelt, "My Day," *New York World-Telegram* 69: 38 (Aug. 14, 1936): 13.
19. President Roosevelt's influence: "Po'keepsie P.O. Mural Designs on Exhibition," *The Overlook* 7: 2 (May 19, 1939): 1.
20. Personal communication from Henry Mattson to AMS; also, *The Overlook* 2: 12 (Sept. 3, 1932): 7–8.

21. “The Petershams,” *The Overlook* 1: 8 (Aug. 1, 1931): 6–7.

CHAPTER 9
THE VILLAGE GROWS

1. History of Dutch Reformed Church: Reverend Harvey I. Todd, *Historical Sketch of the Dutch Reformed Church of Woodstock, N.Y.* (unpublished manuscript, July 7, 1934, held with Historical Society of Woodstock).
2. Tannery production figures: Hamilton Child, *Gazetteer and Business Directory of Ulster County, N.Y. for 1871–2* (Syracuse: Hamilton Child, 1871), 148. Tannery of Vandervoort vats: personal communication from Ashley Cooper to AMS.
3. Information on Dr. Hall (1788–1836) drawn from his account book (whereabouts unknown).
4. Formation and founders: Woodstock Club minutes, Woodstock Library, pp. 1–2. Purpose of club: Woodstock Club constitution and bylaws, early history, Woodstock Library. Early book donations: Alf Evers, “Woodstock Library,” Mar. 1958.
5. Laying of cornerstone for new wing: “State, Town and Library Officials Join in Library Cornerstone Laying,” *Ulster County Sunday News* (May 9, 1948): 12–13. Replacement of Woodstock, U.K., bells: Woodstock Library, Special Executive Committee Meeting, Minutes, May 26, 1954, p. 2; copy of letter from A. H. T. Robb Smith, M.D., Chairman, Woodstock [U.K.] Chimes Committee, to Historical Society of Woodstock; Woodstock Library, Membership Meeting, Minutes, June 10, 1954, p. 4 (Committee Reports, 1940–59, Woodstock Library).
6. Information on Iris Wolven: AMS, “Old Woodstock Crafts,” *Publications of the Woodstock Historical Society* no. 9 (Sept. 1932): 23–24. Children’s room and “Peter” the horse: “Horse Auction at Library Fair,” *Kingston Daily Freeman* 83: 237 (July 27, 1954): 11.
7. “‘A Proud Day in History of Woodstock,’ Says Dr. Shotwell,” Marion Bullard, Editor, *Ulster County News and Kingston Leader* (Dec. 2, 1948): 12–13; *Opening of the Woodstock Library, November 26, 1948*, draft of Shotwell’s speech, Committee Reports 1940–49, Woodstock Library.
8. Distribution of books to hamlets: “Bruno Zimm Again Named President of Library Assn.,” *The Overlook* 4: 8 (June 22, 1934): 8.
9. Funding: Alf Evers, “Woodstock Library,” Woodstock, N.Y., 1958. One of the best in state: University of the State of New York Library Efficiency Records, Woodstock Library, 1946, Committee Reports 1940–49, Woodstock Library.
10. Zimm biographical details: “Bruno Zimm Expires; Widely Known Sculptor,” *Ulster County News* (Nov. 24, 1943): 6.
11. Marion Bullard, “Sparks,” *Ulster County News* (Nov. 24, 1943): 4.
12. “Country Fair Plans Develop,” *Woodstock Press* 2: 19 (Aug. 14, 1931): 1; “Country Fair Plans Perfect,” *Woodstock Press* 2: 20 (Aug. 21, 1931): 1; “Hollywood Contract Signed for Sharkey [sic], the Seal,” *Ulster County News* (June 25, 1942): 12.
13. Woodstock Guild of Craftsmen building: “Eugene Schleicher Property Acquired for Craft Guild,” Marion Bullard, Editor of Woodstock Section, *Ulster County News* (Feb. 15, 1945): 4.
14. Hotel fire: Bruce Herrick, “Old Woodstock: Fact & Fable,” *Woodstock Press* 10: 28 (Nov. 20, 1942): 4, 6. Details on transfer of hotel from Stephen Deforest to Andrew Newkirk: Ulster County Deed Book, Liber 26, pp. 385–87, 387–89. Application for license: Woodstock Town Records 1804–71, p. 126.
15. Transaction between Snyder and Brinkerhoff: Ulster County Deed Book, Liber 151, pp. 61–63. Descriptions of Brinkerhoff guests: personal communication from Larry Elwyn to AMS. General Sharpe story: personal communication from Zia Hasbrouck to AMS.
16. Overlook Mountain House/John E. Lasher: Clearwater, *The History of Ulster County, New York*, 407.
17. Elwyn family history: personal communication from Orville and Will Elwyn to AMS. Methodist Church property: Ulster County Deed Book, Liber 28, pp. 702–704; Liber 44, pp. 27–28; Liber 43, pp. 52–53. Elwyn obituary: “Larry Elwyn, 84, Dies,” *Woodstock Press* 9: 50 (Apr. 17, 1942): 1.
18. Early Art Students League stories: personal communication from Alice Owen to AMS.
19. Rose Oxhandler, “Woodstock Years,” *Publications of the Woodstock Historical Society* no. 17 (Dec. 1955): 10–11.
20. John Carlson as instructor: Carlson, “The Art Students League in Woodstock,” 13–14, 17–18.
21. Carlson biographical information: Marion Bullard, Editor of Woodstock Section, “Memorial Exhibition of Paintings by J. F. Carlson, N.A.,” *Ulster County News* (Sept. 6, 1945): 4. Carlson’s birth date is recorded in many sources as 1875. After his death Robert Carlson, his son, determined the true date as May 5, 1874, through a review of some personal papers. Robert Eric Carlson, *John F. Carlson, N.A. 1874–1945* (Boston: Vose Galleries of Boston, May 3, 1978).
22. “To Explore the Forgotten Trails: Cook Tours Announced for Woodstock,” *Woodstock Bulletin* 3: 1 (Mar. 1, 1930): 18; Dyrus Cook, “Contrasts Along Cook’s Tours: Guide or Mule-Skinner Ruminates,” *Woodstock Bulletin* 3: 8 (June 15, 1930): 10, 12.
23. Cheats and Swings: “Cheats and Swings Write Supervisors,” *The Overlook* 6: 30 (Dec. 2, 1938): 3.
24. Artists Realty Company/Art Association: Dino Ferrari, “Tenth Anniversary of the Woodstock Art Association,” *Woodstock Bulletin* 2: 7 (Sept. 1, 1929): 16, 20. Preamble to the Constitution, Woodstock Artists Association, WAA archives. The Artists Realty Company was officially launched in 1920 and rented the Art Gallery to the Woodstock Artists Association until 1971, at which time it gave the building to the Association for $1. “Gallery, Funding Mark Woodstock Artist Meeting,” *Kingston Daily Freeman* (Sept. 1, 1971): 20, Woodstock Artists Association archives.
25. Carl Eric Lindin, “Gallery Reflections,” *The Hue and Cry* 7: 6 (Aug. 3, 1929): 3, 6.
26. Judson Smith and the WPA: “24 Artists Approved for Government Art Project at Kingston and Saugerties,” *The Overlook* 2: 40 (Feb. 8, 1935): 1; “Judson D. Smith Resigns as Supervisor of Art Projects; Eugene Ludins Succeeds Him,” *The Overlook* 4: 48 (Apr. 2, 1937): 1, 3; “Woodstock WPA Art Goes on Tour,” *The Overlook* 6: 20 (Sept. 23, 1938): 1; “Caravan Interests Upstate Centers,” *The Overlook* 6: 28 (Nov. 18, 1938): 1, 5. Eugene Ludins, supervisor of art projects/art caravans: *The Overlook* 13: 52 (May 1, 1936): 5; see also *The Hue and Cry* 1: 6 (July 14, 1945): 3.
27. “Mrs. Roosevelt Officiates at Woodstock N.Y.A Center as Cornerstone Is Placed,” *Kingston Daily Freeman* 68: 213

(June 27, 1939): 1, 2; "Mrs. Roosevelt Visits Woodstock; Lays N.Y.A. Center Cornerstone," *The Overlook* 7: 8 (June 30, 1939): 1, 7. National Youth Association: "Towar Boggs Appointed Educational Director at Lake Hill N.Y.A. Center," *The Overlook* 6: 45 (Mar. 17, 1939): 1.

28. Ku Klux Klan account: "Letters to Editor," *Woodstock Weekly* (Oct. 4, 1924): 4–5; "Fiery Cross Burning Disturbs Woodstockers," *Sunday News* (Mar. 28, 1948): 13; "Citizens Committee Presents Petition to Town Board on Cross Burnings," *Ulster County News* (Sept. 16, 1948): 13.

CHAPTER 10
OHAYO MOUNTAIN

1. Louise Zimm, "Civil War Records of Woodstock Township," Town Clerk's Office, *Publications of the Woodstock Historical Society* no. 17 (Dec. 1955): 20–21.
2. Story about Lute Cashdollar and Mose Plimley: Bruce Herrick, "Old Woodstock: Fact & Fiction," *Woodstock Press* 10: 27 (Nov. 13, 1942): 4, 6.
3. Jim Twaddell obituary: *The Overlook* 7: 8 (June 30, 1939): 1. Charles Krack: Child, *Gazetteer and Business Directory of Ulster County, N.Y. for 1871–2*, 299. Anecdotal information: personal communication from Victor Lasher to AMS.
4. "Judson Smith," *The Overlook* 2: 5 (July 16, 1932): 8; *Judson Smith: Fifty-five Years of Painting* (Woodstock, N.Y.: Woodstock Art Gallery, 1952) (the exhibition ran from Sept. 6 to 27, 1952).
5. Fred Marsh biography: personal communication from Fred Dana Marsh to AMS.
6. Kuniyoshi's birth date: *Yasuo Kuniyoshi 1889–1953: A Retrospective Exhibition*; Hideo Tomiyama, *Yasuo Kuniyoshi and His Native Country, Japan* (Austin: University Art Museum, University of Texas at Austin, 1975), 59–60 (Woodstock Artists Association Archives, Folder no. 11).
7. For more on Kuniyoshi: Morris Gilbert, "Portrait of the Artist: Kuniyoshi, Born in Japan and Widely Traveled, Feels at Home Only in New York," *New York World Telegram* 72: 200 (Feb. 23, 1940), 2nd ed., 19; "Yasuo Kuniyoshi," *The Overlook* 1: 11 (Aug. 22, 1931): 6.
8. Letter dated Sept. 16, 1945, from Yasuo Kuniyoshi to AMS.
9. Rosett's Brain Research Laboratory: "Winter Activity Is Plan of Foundation," *Woodstock Press* 2: 3 (Nov. 20, 1931): 1; "Talk Is Given by Dr. Rosett," *Woodstock Press* 2: 24 (Oct. 2, 1931): 1; "Second Lecture by Dr. Rosett," *Woodstock Press* 2: 25 (Oct. 9, 1931): 2.
10. *Dr. Joshua Rosett: A Living Memory—Tributes to the Memory of Dr. Joshua Rosett Given at a Gathering of His Colleagues and Associates from the College of Physicians & Surgeons, the Neurological Institute of New York, and the American Neurological Association on April Twelfth, 1940*. Archives, Historical Society of Woodstock.
11. *The Art of Alfeo Faggi: To Commemorate an Exhibition of His Drawings* (Carbondale, Ill.: Southern Illinois University, Feb. 1953), Woodstock Artists Association Archives, Folder no. 1; also, personal communication from Alfeo Faggi to AMS.
12. Beggar woman: "Alfeo Faggi," *The Overlook* 1: 5 (July 11, 1931): 5–6. Faggi's years in Chicago: personal communication from Alfeo Faggi to AMS.

CHAPTER 11
TALES OF THE UPPER HAMLETS

1. Early Shady: Elsie Vosburgh Rowe, *The Story of Our Family Heritage*; also, personal communication from Mr. and Mrs. Van Rensellaer Smith to AMS.
2. Doc Hasbrouck: personal communication from Marty MacDaniel to AMS.
3. Dr. John Kingsbury background information: "Dr. John Kingsbury Dead: Ex-head of City Charities," *New York Herald Tribune* Section 1, 116: 40074 (Aug. 4, 1956): 8; "Difference of Opinion Causes J. A. Kingsbury to Resign from Milbank Fund Administration," *The Overlook* 2: 51 (Apr. 26, 1935): 1.
4. Overlook hotel: Clearwater, *The History of Ulster County, New York*, 407. Alf Evers article: Alf Evers, "Overlook Mountain," *New York State Conservationist* (Feb.–Mar. 1958): 2–6.
5. Oscar Howland: personal communication from Oscar Howland to AMS.
6. AMS, *Woodstock Legends and Cures*, 4 (draft in AMS collection).
7. Edson recital: personal communication from Henry and Sidney Cowell to AMS; "Religious Music Program Planned," *Kingston Daily Freeman* 81: 246 (Aug. 6, 1952): 5.
8. Henry Cowell biography: "Local Composers Will Sponsor Event for Artists Association," *Ulster County Townsman* (Aug. 9, 1956): 4; also, personal communication from Henry and Sidney Cowell to AMS.
9. Sugarloaf Mountain witch: AMS, "Stories of Mink Hollow: Hearsay and History, No. II," 22–23.
10. Gilbert Purdey: personal communication from Mrs. Vosburgh and Moses Sagendorf to AMS.
11. 1847 legal agreement: Town Minute Books 1788–1963, p. 263, roll #1. (This transaction was actually recorded in 1863.)
12. Deed between James Desbrosses and Jeremiah Reynolds, referring to Spanish Mill dollars, is in the possession of Mrs. Stanley Vosburgh. (A copy resides in AMS papers.)
13. Cooper family: "William F. Cooper," *Commemorative Biographical Record of Ulster County, New York*, 776–77.
14. Mrs. Hannah Cooper Vosburgh's memoir: Elsie Vosburgh Rowe, *The Story of Our Family Heritage*; Hannah Catherine Vosburgh, "Fifty Years Ago in a Farm House," *Publications of the Woodstock Historical Society* no. 6 (Sept. 1931): 19.
15. Personal communication from Henry Gridley to AMS; also, AMS, "Stories of Mink Hollow: Hearsay and History, No. II," 24.
16. Sully family: personal communication from Victor Lasher to AMS; "Daniel Sully," *Commemorative Biographical Record of Ulster County, New York*, 805–806; Bertha F. Elwyn, "The Gay Nineties in Woodstock," *Publications of the Woodstock Historical Society* no. 12 (Apr. 1935): 26.
17. First town meeting: Road Book (Town Minute Book) vol. 1, 1784–1847, Town of Shandaken, p. 0.
18. Elias Hasbrouck: Louise H. Zimm, "Captain Elias Hasbrouck, 1741–1791," *Publications of the Woodstock Historical Society* no. 16 (Sept. 1951): 25, 27–30, 32–33.

CHAPTER 12
THE SECOND WORLD WAR

1. "A. Borealis and Co. Stages Sky Show," *Woodstock Press* 9: 21 (Sept. 26, 1941): 7.

2. "U.S.O. Collects $138 in Week," *The Overlook* 9: 13 (Aug. 8, 1941): 1; "More Donors Aid USO Total Now at $1018," *Woodstock Press* 10: 16 (Aug. 21, 1942): 1. Wardwell/Mallarmé event: *Woodstock Press* 10: 16 (Aug. 21, 1942): 1.
3. Volunteers mentioned in local press: Pierpoint Twins: Grad, "The Meanderer," *The Overlook* 8: 36 (Jan. 10, 1941): 4 ["Grad" was the nom de plume of the editor, Charles Gradwell]. Aubrey Milne: "Town Talk," *Woodstock Press* 9: 24 (Oct. 17, 1941): 4. Clifford Wells: Grad, "The Meanderer," *The Overlook* 8: 38 (Jan. 24, 1941): 4. Walter Sarff: Grad, "The Meanderer," *The Overlook* 8: 43 (Feb. 28, 1941): 4. John Faggi and Bob Carlson: Grad, *The Overlook* 8: 42 (Feb. 21, 1941): 4. Buddy Streibel: Grad, "The Meanderer," *The Overlook* 8: 51 (Apr. 25, 1941): 5, 4.
4. "Many Appointments to Defense Tasks Announced by Chairman," *Woodstock Press* [formerly *The Overlook*; the name was changed in late 1941] 9: 35 (Dec. 31, 1941): 3, 7; "Comeau Organizes Town Defense," *Ulster County News*, Marion Bullard, Editor of Woodstock Section (Dec. 30, 1941): 7.
5. "Health Group May Organize Home Nursing," *Woodstock Press* 9: 35 (Dec. 31, 1941): 3, 7; "New First Aid Course Formed," *Woodstock Press* 9: 35 (Dec. 31, 1941): 3, 7; "Firemen, Red Cross to Run Aid Course," *Woodstock Press* 9: 23 (Oct. 10, 1941): 1; "First Woodstock Blackout Test Monday: It's Really the McCoy," *Woodstock Press* 9: 41 (Feb. 13, 1942): 1, 8.
6. "Victory Garden Project Mapped," *Woodstock Press* 9: 43 (Feb. 27, 1942): 1.
7. Child evacuee plan: letter to "Sticky" from AMS, Mar. 28, 1942 (copy in AMS papers); "Town Prepared for Evacuees," *Woodstock Press* 9: 47 (Mar. 27, 1942): 1.
8. "Army Places Air Wardens on Duty Here," *Woodstock Press* 9: 32 (Dec. 12, 1941): 1.
9. Gladys Hurlbut, "Looking Up: Woodstock Observation Post," *Ulster County News* (May 1942) (Observation Post scrapbook, AMS papers); "Officers to Inspect Woodstock's Air Warning Service," *Kingston Daily Freeman* 71: 231 (July 20, 1942): 5; "Observation Post at Woodstock Is Accepted by Army," *Kingston Daily Freeman* 71: 234 (July 23, 1942): 5; "Public to See Post, Army Man to Speak," *Woodstock Press* 10: 11 (July 17, 1942): 1; "Army Officers Praise Post, Explain Air Spotting Duties," *Woodstock Press* 10: 12 (July 24, 1942): 5.
10. Gladys Hurlbut, "Looking Up: Woodstock Observation Post: Woodstock Is About the Same Size as Lidice," *Ulster County News* (June 14, 1942) (Observation Post scrapbook, AMS papers).
11. "Mercury Tumbles to 32 Below for December Record and Never Rises to Zero Mark on Sunday," *Kingston Daily Freeman* 72: 54 (Dec. 21, 1942): 1.
12. "Snyder Predicts Momentous Event in Next 20 Days," *Kingston Daily Freeman* 71: 283 (Sept. 19, 1942): 3; "Snyder Sees 'Crisis' Ahead, Lecture Nets Post $125," *Woodstock Press* 10: 21 (Sept. 25, 1942): 1.
13. AMS, "Looking Up: Woodstock Observation Post: Skidding Spotters," *Ulster County Press* (Feb. 1943) (Observation Post scrapbook, AMS papers).
14. Gremlins: AMS, "Looking Up: Woodstock Observation Post," *Ulster County News* (Mar. 1943) (Observation Post scrapbook, AMS papers).
15. "Looking Up: Woodstock Observation Post," *Ulster County News* (Nov. 1942) (Observation Post scrapbook, AMS papers); "Looking Up: Woodstock Observation Post: Mrs. Eugene Speicher Record Spotter," *Ulster County News* (Dec. 1942) (OP scrapbook).
16. "Looking Up: Woodstock Observation Post," *Ulster County News* (June 25, 1942): 12.
17. Woodstock Observation Post 1026A logbook (Aug. 11, 1942, to Feb. 16, 1943) (Dec. 28, 1942): 142 (AMS papers).
18. AMS, "Looking Up: Woodstock Observation Post," *Ulster County News* (Dec. 31, 1942) (Observation Post scrapbook, AMS papers).
19. Eugene Ludins appointed: "Looking Up: Woodstock Observation Post," *Ulster County News* (Mar. 1943) (Observation Post scrapbook, AMS papers). Spotter classes: AMS, "Looking Up: Woodstock Observation Post," *Ulster County News* (Mar. 1943) (OP scrapbook). Spotter graduation: AMS, "Looking Up: Woodstock Observation Post," *Ulster County News* (Apr. 1943) (OP scrapbook). Team challenges: "Saugerties Airplane Spotters Defeat Woodstock in Contest," *Ulster County News* (Sept. 2, 1943): 4, 6; "Woodstock Spotters Win Against Saugerties," *Ulster County News* (Nov. 11, 1943): 4. Fish fries: AMS, "Looking Up: Woodstock Observation Post," *Ulster County News* (Jan. 13, 1944): 6.
20. Observation Post ordered closed: "Looking Up: Woodstock Observation Post," *Ulster County News* (Oct. 7, 1943): 4.
21. "Air Spotters Give Money to Young People," *Ulster County News* (June 15, 1944): 4.
22. "Ideals We Fight for Are Old, Said Lieut. Bob Browning," *Ulster County News* (June 4, 1942): 12.
23. Mrs. Mildred Todd: "Red Cross Unit Thanks Its Supporters," *The Overlook* 8: 35 (Jan. 3, 1941): 1. Market fair: "Market Fair Again Tomorrow," *The Overlook* 9: 7 (June 20, 1941): 3. Summary of results: "Red Cross," Woodstock Press 9: 19 (Sept. 12, 1941): 2.
24. Mrs. F. Huntington Babcock, "U.S. English Speaking Union to Cooperate in Local Aid to Woodstock England," *The Overlook* 8: 40 (Feb. 7, 1941): 5, 8; "Bundles for Britain Asks Woodstock Aid," *The Overlook* 9: 7 (June 20, 1941): 3.
25. "Red Cross," *The Overlook* 9: 15 (Aug. 15, 1941): 7.
26. "Red Cross Asks Women to Sew," *Woodstock Press* 9: 43 (Feb. 27, 1942): 1, 8; "A Word Anent a Waltz Ball," *Woodstock Press* 9: 33 (Dec. 19, 1941): 1, 8; "Large Crowd at Waltz Ball Swells War Fund to $841," *Woodstock Press* 9: 35 (Dec. 31, 1941): 3.
27. "Red Cross Tops Campaign Goal," *Woodstock Press* 9: 42 (Feb. 20, 1942): 1, 8.
28. "Harp Recital for Woodstock Red Cross," *Ulster County News* (Aug. 17, 1944): 6. Britt Sextet: "Plan Concert Here June 10," *Woodstock Press* 10: 4 (May 29, 1942): 5.
29. "Real Costumes of 70 Years Ago for 'Little Women'," *Ulster County News* (Aug. 19, 1943): 4; "'Little Women' Nets $295 for Red Cross," *Ulster County News* (Aug. 26, 1943): 6. *Junior Miss*: "Fine Performance by Woodstock Players," *Ulster County News* (Aug. 17, 1944): 4, 6.
30. "Six Truckloads of Clothing Collected," *Ulster County News* (May 31, 1945): 4.
31. War bonds, 1943: "War Bond Concert at Woodstock August 14," *Kingston Daily Freeman* 72: 244 (Aug. 5, 1943): 11; "War Bond Concert Honors Service Men," *Ulster County News* (Aug. 19, 1943): 4, 6; "Woodstock War Bond Total $27,238.25," *Ulster County News* (Sept. 9, 1943): 4. War

bonds, 1944: "Woodstock War Loan Totals $29,898, *Ulster County News* (Feb. 17, 1944): 4; "Woodstock Goes Over the Top in Bond Drive," *Ulster County News* (July 13, 1944): 4; "Woodstock Bond Sale Goes Over the Top," *Ulster County News* (Dec. 21, 1944): 4. War bonds, 1945: "Bond Quota Exceeded by $10,000," *Ulster County News* (July 12, 1945): 4; "Citations for Bond Sales," *Ulster County News* (July 19, 1945): 8; "Top Can Still Be Reached in Victory Bond Sale," *Ulster County News* (Dec. 13, 1945): 3. The total for all these comes to $186,088. A final drive tally could not be verified due to missing issues of the *Ulster County News* (Jan. 1946).

32. "Town Ranks High in Metal Collection," *The Overlook* 9: 13 (Aug. 8, 1941): 1.
33. Supporting article not found.
34. Marion Bullard, "'France Forever' Membership Increases," *Ulster County News* (Aug. 28, 1941): 12.
35. "Town Talk," *Woodstock Press* 10: 9 (July 3, 1942): 4–5.
36. "Christmas Gifts for Woodstock Soldiers, Aim of Salvage Drive," *Woodstock Press* 10: 11 (July 17, 1942): 1, 8; "Scrap Pile Mounts to 3½ Tons; More Expected as Drive Gains," *Woodstock Press* 10: 18 (Sept. 4, 1942): 1; "$636 On Hand for Xmas Gifts; Soldiers Asked to List Choices," *Woodstock Press* 10: 23 (Oct. 9, 1942): 1, 6; "Committee Spent $294 for Gifts to Soldiers; Has $340 Balance," *Woodstock Press* 10: 31 (Dec. 11, 1942): 1. In 1944: "Christmas Gifts from Salvage," *Ulster County News* (June 1, 1944): 4; "Christmas Gifts for Service Men and Women," *Ulster County News* (Oct. 12, 1944): 4.
37. "Victory Garden Project Mapped," *Woodstock Press* 9: 43 (Feb. 27, 1942): 1; "Dowd Heads Garden Work," *Woodstock Press* 9: 44 (Mar. 6, 1942): 1; "Victory Garden Program Starts; Dowd Urges All to Register," *Woodstock Press* 9: 49 (Apr. 10, 1942): 1, 5. First-year prize winners: "Victory Gardens," *Ulster County News* (June 25, 1942): 13; "Garden Notes: Victory Garden Prize Winners Announced," *Woodstock Press* 10: 14 (Aug. 7, 1942): 7. The following year: "A Bigger Potato," *Ulster County News* (Oct. 7, 1943): 4.
38. "Chinese Envoy to Speak Here," *Woodstock Press* 10: 14 (Aug. 7, 1942): 1; "China Benefit Gala Affair," *Woodstock Press* 10: 15 (Aug. 14, 1942): 1, 8; "China Benefit Nets $1,200," *Woodstock Press* 10: 16 (Aug. 21, 1942): 1, 8; "Dr. Hu Shih Is Woodstock Speaker at Relief Benefit," *Kingston Daily Freeman* 71: 256 (Aug. 18, 1942): 1, 10.
39. "France Forever Chapter to Be Organized Here," *The Overlook* 8: 51 (Apr. 25, 1941): 2.
40. France Forever accounts (AMS papers).
41. "'France Forever' Lists Program," *The Overlook* 9: 9 (July 3, 1941): 1; "French Fête Is Held at Woodstock," *Kingston Daily Freeman* 70: 227 (July 15, 1941): 3. Jane Kennedy, "Woodstock," *Kingston Daily Freeman* 70: 229 (July 17, 1941): 15. Free France program: Andrée Ruellan, File no. 8, Woodstock Artists Association archives.
42. Copy dated July 15, 1941, in AMS papers.
43. "Forty Join 'France Forever' Chapter," *Ulster County News* (July 2, 1942): 12; "French Dance Profits $500," *Woodstock Press* 10: 11 (July 17, 1942): 1.
44. "Bastille Day Celebrated in Woodstock: Noted Frenchman to Speak in Town Hall July 13," *Ulster County News* (July 5, 1945): 4; "United Nations Charter a Torch for Humanity Says Louis Dolivet," *Ulster County News* (July 19, 1945): 4, 7.
45. Fundraising amounts in AMS papers.
46. "Russia Relief Group Forms," *Woodstock Press* 10: 19 (Sept. 11, 1942): 1, 8.
47. "Woodstock's Russian War Relief Report," *Ulster County News* (May 18, 1944): 4.
48. "Basket Picnic Raises $279," *Woodstock Press* 10: 8 (June 26, 1942): 1.
49. *Tanya* benefit: "Movie to Aid Russian Relief," *Woodstock Press* 10: 14 (Aug. 7, 1942): 2; "Yakhontoff Urges 2d Front Blames Delay on 'Politics'," *Woodstock Press* 10: 22 (Oct. 2, 1942): 1, 6. "Tribute to Russia" Supper: "'Russians Suffered Too Long' Says Speaker," *Ulster County News* (June 24, 1943): 4. Kosloff benefit: "Kosloff Dance Recital for Russian Relief," *Ulster County News* (June 1, 1944): 4.
50. "Russian Christmas Party," *Ulster County News* (Dec. 6, 1945): 4.
51. "Supper Aids Small Allies," *Woodstock Press* 10: 19 (Sept. 11, 1942): 2; "Small Nations Receive $700," *Woodstock Press* 10: 22 (Oct. 2, 1942): 1. Belgium: letter dated Dec. 26, 1956, from Mrs. Drogseth to AMS. "Rendezvous in Rio": "Artists Ball Nets $600," *Woodstock Press* 10: 19 (Sept. 11, 1942): 1, 8.
52. "United Nations Festival Will Be Held at Woodstock," *Kingston Daily Freeman* 72: 262 (Aug. 26, 1943): 5; "Nations' Festival Planned at Woodstock," *Ulster County News* (Aug. 19, 1943): 4, 6; "Nine Nations Unite in Festival at Woodstock September 3 and 4," *Ulster County News* (Aug. 26, 1943): 4; "$3,300 Aid for United Nations from Woodstock Festival," *Ulster County News* (Sept. 9, 1943): 4, 6. British and Greek booths: letter postmarked Sept. 22, 1946, from Helen Shotwell to AMS. Norwegian booth: letter dated Dec. 26, 1956, from Mrs. Drogseth to AMS. Lenhard Scholl: AMS letter to the editor, *Ulster County News* (Feb. 1, 1945): 7. Supporting citation for *Catskill Mountain Star* not found.
53. Letter dated Jan. 24, 1957, from Katrina Fischer to AMS (AMS papers).
54. "Alice Henderson Appeals for Your Old Candles," *Ulster County News* (Dec. 7, 1947): 12; Mrs. William Powell, "American Friends Service Thanks Woodstock," *Ulster County News* (Dec. 28, 1947): 12.
55. "Science Church Has Part in National Relief Program," *Woodstock Press* 10: 29 (Nov. 25, 1942): 6.

CHAPTER 13
THE SOLDIERS' STORIES

1. Letter dated Aug. 17, 1946, from Anne Leaycraft to AMS; also, "Worked From Secret Jap Maps," *Ulster County News* (Dec. 6, 1945): 4.
2. "Kenneth Downer Risks Life in Ship Fire," *Ulster County News* (Sept. 28, 1944): 4.
3. Letter dated Apr. 11, 1957, from Warren Riseley to AMS.
4. Undated letter from Bob Brinkman to AMS.
5. Personal communication from Katrina Fischer to AMS; also, "Coast Guard Names A. O. Fischer 'Artist Laureate'; Wife Honored," *Woodstock Press* 10: 19 (Sept. 11, 1942): 1, 8; "The Cruise of the Campbell," *Life* 15: 1 (July 5, 1943): 57–68.
6. Account supplied by James Kinns to AMS.
7. Account supplied by Robert Carlson; whereabouts of letter unknown.
8. Letter dated Jan. 18, 1946, from Jean Barrère to AMS.
9. Paratrooper Pfc. Peter Carlson: undated letter to AMS.
10. From "The Ballad of Agincourt" by Michael Drayton; the line should actually read "Fair stood the wind for France."

11. Richard Crane: personal communication to AMS.
12. Account supplied by Ludwig Baumgarten. See World War II files at Historical Society of Woodstock.
13. Supporting citation not found.
14. Personal communication from Aubrey Milne to AMS.
15. Account based on a letter dated May 8, 1945, from Eugene J. Hagemeyer Jr. to his family (copy in AMS archives).
16. Marion Bullard, "Sparks," "Young Woodstock Scientist Worked on Atom Bomb," *Ulster County News* (Aug. 16, 1945): 4, 7.

CHAPTER 14
SOME LOCAL PERSONALITITES

1. James T. Shotwell, *The Great Decision* (New York: Macmillan, 1944): 11–13.
2. Much of the information in the section on James T. Shotwell is drawn from *Aide Mémoire: James Thomson Shotwell's Services to Peace*, 1950, Box 295, which can be found among the James T. Shotwell Papers at Columbia University—Rare Book and Manuscript Library. This document was prepared under the auspices of Columbia University for presentation to the Nobel Peace Prize Committee in 1951. For "passage of this protocol": p. 12.
3. James T. Shotwell, ed., *Economic and Social History of the World War* (Washington: Division of Economics and History, Carnegie Endowment for International Peace, 1924).
4. Theory of Clausewitz and Bismarck: *Aide Mémoire*, 14.
5. Secretary Kellogg: *Aide Mémoire*, 15.
6. Chairman of the Consultants: *Aide Mémoire*, 17, 18.
7. *Aide Mémoire*; also, *Biographical Sketch*, 1949, Box 295, James T. Shotwell Papers at Columbia University—Rare Book and Manuscript Library.
8. William K. Gregory: letter dated Apr. 23, 1958, from Mrs. Gregory to AMS (AMS papers) and personal communication from Dr. William K. Gregory to AMS.
9. Walter Weyl, background information: Maurice N. Weyl, *Walter Weyl: An Appreciation* (Philadelphia: n.p. [privately printed by Edward Stern & Co.], 1922): 10, 20, 22, 23, 27, 31.
10. Ibid., 38.
11. Ibid., 40, 52.
12. Ibid., 85–86.
13. Ibid., 90–91.
14. Le Gallienne, *Woodstock: An Essay*, 19.
15. Carl Eric Lindin, *Fallen Leaves* (booklet, n.p., n.d.; a copy can be found in the Woodstock Library).
16. Weyl, *Walter Weyl: An Appreciation*, 106.
17. Hughes Mearns, *Creative Power* (Garden City, N.Y.: Doubleday, Doran, 1929).
18. Personal communication from Hughes Mearns to AMS.
19. Background on Alexander Semmler and Hans A. Schimmerling: "Local Composers Will Sponsor Event for Artists Association," *Ulster County Townsman* (Aug. 9, 1956): 4.
20. Letter dated Mar. 14, 1946, from Dr. Frank Boudreau to AMS (AMS papers).
21. Personal communication from Manuel Komroff to AMS.
22. Will Durant: personal communication from Ira Wolfert to AMS; Dr. Will Durant, "Autobiography of Two Months," *The Overlook* 1: 11 (Aug. 22, 1931): 8–10. Sinclair Lewis: "Shadow and Substance," *Ulster County News* (May 16, 1940): 12.
23. Harold Rugg: summary of undated letter from Harold Rugg to AMS; also, personal communication from Harold Rugg to AMS; Hughes Mearns, "A Scholar With Vision," *The Overlook* 1: 3 (June 27, 1931): 8–9. Note: the projected title, *The Imagination of Man*, was published by Harper's & Row as *Imagination* in 1963.

CHAPTER 15
ARTISTS TALK ABOUT ART

1. Personal communication from Anton Refregier to AMS. Refregier background information: Jane Watson, "News and Comment," *Magazine of Art* 34: 9 (Nov. 1941): 490, 494; Rosamund Frost, "Refregier: Brave New Muralist," *Art News* 41: 4 (Apr. 1–14, 1942): 18, 30, 32. Spread on United Nations: "San Francisco Album: Anton Refregier Takes a Jaunty, Amiable View of the Second Great Bid for World Peace. History on a Sketch Pad," *Fortune* 32: 3 (Sept. 1945): 155–59.
2. "The Harvey Girls," *Life* 19: 23 (Dec. 3, 1945): 82–86; Doris Lee, "The Hollywood Gallery," *Life* 19: 16 (Oct. 15, 1945): 84–89; "An Artist in Africa," *Life* 33: 19 (Nov. 10, 1952): 109–12; American Artists Group, *Doris Lee* (New York: American Artists Group, 1946); James Thurber, *The Great Quillow*, Illustrated by Doris Lee (New York: Harcourt Brace, 1944).
3. "An Artist in Africa," *Life* 33: 19 (Nov. 10, 1952): 109.
4. The Irvington has gone through several name changes over the years. Today it is known as the Landau Grill.
5. Personal communication from Arnold Blanch to AMS.
6. Undated letter from Sigmund Menckes to AMS (AMS papers).
7. Personal communication from William Ames to AMS; "Local Composers Will Sponsor Event for Artists Association," *Ulster County Townsman* (Aug. 9, 1956): 4.
8. Personal communication from Dachine Rainer to AMS. W. H. Auden, ed., *The Criterion Book of Modern American Verse* (New York: Criterion Books, 1956). Correspondence in November 2003 with Thérese Cantine, Dachine's daughter and literary executrix, establishes *The Unbeat* as a short story. According to Ms. Cantine, her mother "did write and have published two novellas—*A Room at the Inn* (Ballantine Books, 1956) and *A Homage to Cambridge* (Contact, 1960). To my knowledge, she did not have a book called *The Unbeat*, published. Maybe it was a working title for then *The Uncomfortable Inn*."
9. Personal communication from Bruce Currie and Ethel Magafan to AMS; also (for Ethel Magafan), Archives of American Art, roll 39, frames 949–82.
10. Personal communication from Reginald Wilson to AMS.
11. Personal communication from Gwen Davies to AMS.
12. Personal communication from Hermon More to AMS.

WOODSTOCKERS IN SERVICE
MEMORIA

1. Civil War dead: Town of Woodstock Roll no. 1, Historical Record, State of New York, Bureau of Military Record, Albany, Aug. 10, 1865. Placed in Woodstock Town Clerk's Office. The Woodstock war dead plaque is now located on the flagpole at Woodstock Veterans War Memorial, Woodstock Cemetery;

this was dedicated Nov. 11, 1987, by American Legion Post 1026, Woodstock. The spellings for the names George De Freese, Charles Di Andrie and Leonhard Scholl Jr. are taken directly from the memorial. The actual spellings may be De Frees, Di Andrea and Lenhard (Scholl), according to AMS and to telephone directories of the era. The latter spellings are used in the narrative of chapter 14 and for the entries in the service records appendix.

2. World War II Project Log, p. 4 (AMS papers).
3. "Lieutenant Eno Compton, Jr. Fortress Pilot Killed in Action," *Ulster County News* (Feb. 24, 1944): 4; also, typewritten summary of his service record—probably written by a member of his family—in World War II box at Historical Society of Woodstock (copy among AMS papers).
4. World War II Project Log, p. 4 (AMS papers). In the previous edition De Frees was noted as having perished on the USS *Ingram* off Greenland. An e-mail to Jerry King, president of the USS *Ingraham* Association, establishes that De Frees was on the crew list for the USS *Ingraham*. This ship went down after a collision with an oil tanker, the USS *Chemung*, off Nova Scotia.
5. "Wounded," *Kingston Daily Freeman* 73: 298 (Oct. 5, 1944): 14; listed as killed in action in the World War II Project Log, p. 4 (AMS papers).
6. "Lt. Col Le May Missing in Action," *Ulster County News* (Oct. 12, 1944): 4; "Lt. Col. Paul Le May Awarded Legion of Merit Posthumously," *Ulster County News* (Nov. 1, 1945): 3, 4.
7. Caleb Milne, *I Dream of the Day: Letters from Caleb Milne, Africa, 1942–1943*, with an Introduction by Marjorie Kinnan Rawlings (New York: Longmans, Green, 1945).
8. "Caleb Milne Is Killed in Tunisia," *Ulster County News* (May 20, 1943): 4.
9. Enlistment: "Town Talk," *Woodstock Press* 10: 30 (Dec. 4, 1942): 9. Reported missing: "Sergeant Peacock Missing on Fortress," *Ulster County News* (Dec. 22, 1943): 6.
10. Obituary: *New York Times* (1857–Current file), ProQuest Historical Newspapers, *New York Times* (1851–2001), p. 21. Whereabouts of Major Jameson's correspondence unknown.
11. Enlistment: Grad [Charles E. Gradwell], "The Meanderer," *The Overlook* 8: 36 (Jan. 10, 1941): 4. Service: "Woodstock Tar Believed Safe," *Woodstock Press* 10: 26 (Oct. 30, 1942): 1; "One Woodstock Sailor Killed, Another Missing in War at Sea," *Woodstock Press* 10: 30 (Dec. 4, 1942): 1.
12. World War II Project Log, p. 15 (AMS papers).
13. "Leonard Scholl Dead in France," *Ulster County News* (Sept. 14, 1944): 4.
14. "One Woodstock Sailor Killed, Another Missing in War at Sea," *Woodstock Press* 10: 30 (Dec. 4, 1942): 1; details of letter in World War II service index box, Historical Society of Woodstock.

BIBLIOGRAPHY

Anjou, Gustave. *Ulster Co. N.Y. Wills*, vols. 1, 2. New York: Gustave Anjou, 1906.

Art Notes. Woodstock, N.Y. Tabloid newspaper published weekly in 1931/32.

Barnard, Daniel D. *The "Anti-rent" Movement and Outbreak in New York*. Albany: Weed & Parsons, 1846.

Beers, J. B. *History of Greene County, New York With Biographical Sketches of Its Prominent Men*. New York: J. B. Beers, 1884/Saugerties, N.Y.: Hope Farm Press, 1969.

Bond, Beverly W., Jr. *The Quit-Rent System in the American Colonies*. New Haven, Conn.: Yale University Press, 1919.

Bradbury, Anna R. *History of the City of Hudson, New York*. Hudson, N.Y.: Record Printing & Publishing, 1908.

Brink, Benjamin M. *The Early History of Saugerties 1660–1825*. Kingston, N.Y.: R. W. Anderson & Son, 1902.

Byrdcliffe Afternoons: A Series of Lectures Given at Byrdcliffe, Woodstock, New York, July 1938. Woodstock, N.Y.: Overlook Press, 1939.

Cheyney, Edward P. *The Anti-rent Agitation in the State of New York 1839–1846* no. 2. Philadelphia: Publications of the University of Pennsylvania, 1887.

Child, Hamilton. *Gazetteer and Business Directory of Ulster County, N.Y. for 1871–2*. Syracuse: Hamilton Child, 1871.

Christman, Henry. *Tin Horns and Calico*. New York: Henry Holt, 1945/Cornwallville, N.Y.: Hope Farm Press, 1975.

Clearwater, Alphonso T., ed. *The History of Ulster County, New York*. Kingston, N.Y.: W. J. van Deusen, 1907.

Commemorative Biographical Record of Ulster County, New York. Chicago: J. B. Beers, 1896.

Dangerfield, George. *Chancellor Robert R. Livingston of New York 1746–1813*. New York: Harcourt, Brace, 1960.

De Lisser, R. Lionel. *Picturesque Ulster*. Kingston, N.Y.: Styles & Bruyn, 1896.

Dellenbaugh, Frederick S. *The Hardenberghs*. Ellenville, N.Y.: Ellenville Journal Printing Co., 1935.

Democratic Journal. Kingston, N.Y. Newspaper published weekly from 1840 to 1845.

Eggleston Seelye, Elizabeth, assisted by Edward Eggleston. *Brant and Red Jacket*. New York: Dodd, Mead, 1879.

Ellis, David M. *Landlords and Farmers in the Hudson-Mohawk Region, 1790–1850*. Ithaca, N.Y.: Cornell University Press, 1946.

Fox, Dixon Ryan. *The Decline of Aristocracy in the Politics of New York*. New York: Columbia University Press, 1919.

French, J. H. *Gazetteer of the State of New York*. Syracuse: R. P. Smith, 1860.

Gallt, Frank A. *Dear Old Greene County*. Catskill, N.Y.: n.p., 1915.

Gardner, Emelyn Elizabeth. *Folklore From the Schoharie Hills, New York*. Ann Arbor: University of Michigan Press, 1937.

Gordon, Thomas F. *Gazetteer of the State of New York*. Philadelphia: n.p. (privately printed by T. K. & P. G. Collins), 1836.

Gould, Jay. *History of Delaware County and Border Wars of New York*. Roxbury, N.Y.: Keeny & Gould, 1856/New Orleans: Polyanthos, 1977.

Halsey, Francis W. *The Old New York Frontier 1614–1800*. New York: Charles Scribner's Sons, 1901.

Haring, H. A. *Our Catskill Mountains*. New York: G. P. Putnam's Sons, 1931.

History of Delaware County, N.Y. N.p.: W. W. Munsell & Co., 1880.

The Hue and Cry. Woodstock, N.Y. Newspaper published weekly during the summer of 1923; magazine published fortnightly during the summer of 1924; newspaper published weekly during the summer from 1925 to 1933; newspaper published weekly year-round in 1945.

Hunt, Charles Havens. *Life of Edward Livingston*. New York: D. Appleton & Co., 1864.

Jenkins, John S. *The Life of Silas Wright*. Auburn, N.Y.: Alden & Markham, 1947.

Johnson, Clifton, as reported by. *John Burroughs Talks: His Reminiscences and Comments*. Boston: Houghton Mifflin, 1922.

Johnston, Fred J. "Ulster County Cabinet and Glass Makers." *New York History* 17: 1 (Jan. 1936) (New York State Historical Association, Burlington, Vt.).

Kelsay, Isabel T. "The Trial of Big Thunder." *New York History* 16: 3 (July 1935) (New York State Historical Association, Burlington, Vt.).

Kingston Daily Freeman. Kingston, N.Y. Newspaper published as the *Rondout Daily Freeman* for five months in 1871; as the *Daily Freeman* from 1872 through Oct. 26, 1878; as the *Kingston Daily Freeman* from Oct. 28, 1878, through Dec. 1969; and as the *Daily Freeman* from Jan. 1970 to the present.

Le Gallienne, Richard. *Woodstock: An Essay*. Woodstock, N.Y.: Woodstock Art Association, 1923.

Livingston, John Henry. *The Minor Manors of New York* no. 12. New York: Order of Colonial Lords of Manors in America, New York Branch, 1923.

Mayham, Albert Champlin. *The Anti-rent War on Blenheim Hill*. Jefferson, N.Y.: F. L. Frazee, 1906.

McKearin, George S. and Helen. *American Glass*. New York: Crown, 1941.

Monroe, John D. *The Anti-rent War in Delaware County, New York: The Revolt Against the Rent System*. N.p. (privately printed), 1940.

Moore, N. Hudson. *Old Glass, European and American*. New York: Frederick A. Stokes Co., 1924.

Murray, Dr. David. "The Anti-rent Episode in the State of New York," in *Annual Report of the American Historical Association for the Year 1896*, vol. 1 (p. 144–45). Washington: Government Printing Office, 1897.

Olde Ulster. Kingston, N.Y. Magazine published in 10 volumes from Dec./Jan. 1905 through Dec. 1914.

The Overlook. Woodstock, N.Y. Magazine published weekly June through Sept. in 1931/32.

The Overlook. Woodstock, N.Y. Newspaper published weekly from 1933 to 1941, when the name was changed to the *Woodstock Press*.

The Phoenix. Woodstock, N.Y. Literary journal published quarterly from Mar./Apr./May 1938 through 1941 and sporadically from 1970 to 1989 (now published by Morning Star Press in Haydonville, Mass.).

The Plowshare. Woodstock, N.Y. Early Maverick literary magazine (formerly *The Wild Hawk*) published monthly from Nov. 1916 through Dec. 1920 and from Feb. 1934 through Jan. 1935.

Priest, Josiah. *A Copy of the Grants to the Van Rensselaer and Livingston Families*. Albany: J. Munsell, 1844.

Publications of the Woodstock Historical Society. Woodstock, N.Y. Series of booklets containing four or five papers each, published between July 1930 and Dec. 1955. The series was revived in 2003.

Public Papers of George Clinton: First Governor of New York, vols. 4, 5, 6. Albany: James B. Lyon, State Printer, 1900, 1901, 1902.

Rockwell, Rev. Charles. *The Catskill Mountains and the Region Around*. New York: Taintor Bros., 1867.

Schoolcraft, Henry Rowe. *Helderbergia; Or, The Apotheosis of the Heroes of the Antirent War*. Albany: J. Munsell, 1855.

Schoonmaker, Marius. *The History of Kingston, New York*. New York: Burr Printing House, 1888.

Simms, Jeptha Root. *History of Schoharie County and Border Wars of New York*. Albany: Munsell & Tanne, Printers, 1845.

Smith, Philip H. *Legends of the Shawangunk (Shon-Gum) and Its Environs*. Pawling, N.Y.: Smith & Co., 1887.

Spafford, Horatio Gates. *A Gazetteer of the State of New York*. Albany: H. C. Southwick, 1813.

Sylvester, Nathaniel Bartlett. *History of Ulster County, New York*. Philadelphia: Everts & Peck, 1880.

Tarr, Ralph S. *The Physical Geography of New York State*. New York: Macmillan, 1902.

Ulster County News. Kingston, N.Y. Launched in 1925 as a weekly supplement of the *Kingston Daily Leader* (founded in 1881); merged with the newspaper in 1948.

Ulster County Press. Stone Ridge, N.Y., and Kingston, N.Y. Newspaper published weekly from Mar. 12 through Oct. 1, 1937, and semi-weekly from Oct. 5, 1937, through July 24, 1938 (published from Kingston as of June 25, 1937, and known as the *Sunday Press* from Feb. 13 through July 24, 1938).

Ulster Republican. Kingston, N.Y. Newspaper published weekly from 1833 to 1861.

Ulster Sentinel. Kingston, N.Y. Newspaper published weekly from 1826 to 1840.

Van Buren, Augustus H. *A History of Ulster County Under the Dominion of the Dutch*. Kingston, N.Y.: n.p., 1923.

Vosburgh Rowe, Elsie. *The Story of Our Family Heritage*. Woodstock, N.Y.: privately published, 1956.

Washbon, Mrs. *Rensselaerville: Reminiscences and Rhymes*. Albany: C. Van Benthuysen & Sons, 1890.

White, Hervey. *Autobiography of Hervey White*. Unpublished manuscript, 1937; copy in Woodstock Library.

Whitehead, Ralph R. *Arrows of Dawn* no. 3. Montecito, Calif.: n.p., 1901.

Whitehead, Ralph R. *Grass of the Desert*. London: Chiswick Press, 1892.

The Wild Hawk. Woodstock, N.Y. Early Maverick literary magazine published monthly from Nov. 1911 through Oct. 1916 (later renamed *The Plowshare*).

Woodstock Bulletin. Woodstock, N.Y. Newspaper published fortnightly during spring and summer from 1928 to 1931.

Woodstock Press. Woodstock, N.Y. Newspaper (formerly *The Overlook*) published weekly in 1941/42.

Woodstock Weekly. Woodstock, N.Y. Newspaper published in 1924/25 (absorbed, in 1925 or 1926, by the *Catskill Mountain Reflector*, published in Tannersville, N.Y., by the Ahrens Publishing Co.).

Zimm, Louise Hasbrouck, Reverend Elwood Corning, Joseph Emsley and Willitt C. Jewell, eds. and comps. *Ulster County*. Vol. 1 of the series *Southeastern New York: A History of the Counties of Ulster, Dutchess, Orange, Rockland and Putnam* (3 vols.). New York: Lewis Historical Publishing Co., 1946.

LIST OF ILLUSTRATIONS

L = left; R = right; T = top; B = bottom.

INDEX

Page numbers in *italics* refer to illustrations.

C

D

E

F

I

J

K

L

M

Q

R

S

T

U

V

W

Y

Z

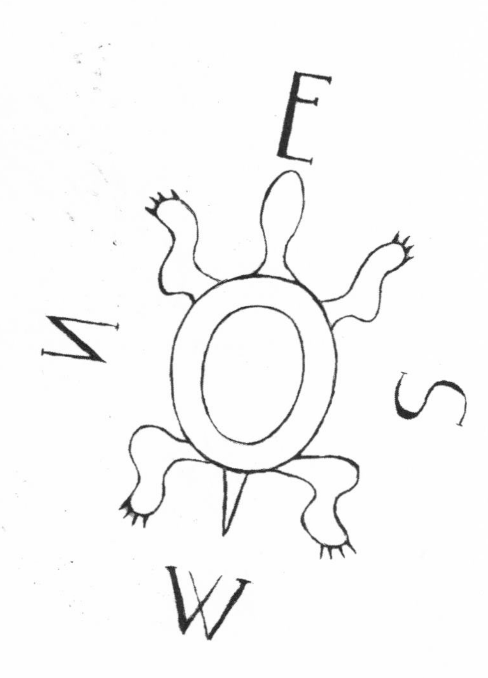

E
N
S
W